D0356464

The Editor

GEORGE JUSTICE is Dean of Humanities in the College of Liberal Arts and Sciences and Associate Vice President for Humanities and Arts in the Office of Knowledge Enterprise Development at Arizona State University. Professor of eighteenth-century British literature in ASU's Department of English, Justice is the author and editor of scholarship on the literary marketplace, authorship, and women's writing.

A NORTON CRITICAL EDITION

Jane Austen
EMMA

AN AUTHORITATIVE TEXT
CONTEXTS
CRITICISM

FOURTH EDITION

Edited by

GEORGE JUSTICE
UNIVERSITY OF MISSOURI–COLUMBIA

Previous Editions Edited by

STEPHEN M. PARRISH
LATE OF CORNELL UNIVERSITY

W · W · NORTON & COMPANY · *New York* · *London*

W. W. Norton & Company has been independent since its founding in 1923, when William Warder Norton and Mary D. Herter Norton first published lectures delivered at the People's Institute, the adult education division of New York City's Cooper Union. The firm soon expanded its program beyond the Institute, publishing books by celebrated academics from America and abroad. By mid-century, the two major pillars of Norton's publishing program—trade books and college texts—were firmly established. In the 1950s, the Norton family transferred control of the company to its employees, and today—with a staff of four hundred and a comparable number of trade, college, and professional titles published each year—W. W. Norton & Company stands as the largest and oldest publishing house owned wholly by its employees.

Manufacturing by Maple Press
Book design by Antonina Krass
Production manager: Sean Mintus

Library of Congress Cataloging-in-Publication Data

Austen, Jane, 1775–1817.
    Emma : authoritative text, backgrounds, reviews and criticism / Jane
Austen. — 4th ed. / edited by George Justice.
        p.   cm. — (A Norton critical edition)
    Includes bibliographical references.
    ISBN: 978-0-393-92764-1 (pbk.)
    1. Young women—Fiction.   2. Fathers and daughters— Fiction.
3. Female friendship—Fiction.   4. Mate selection—Fiction.   5. England—
Social life and customs—19th century—Fiction.   6. Austen, Jane,
1775–1817. Emma.   I. Justice, George.   II. Title.
    PR4034.E5   2012
    823'.7—dc23

                                                                    2011026036

W. W. Norton & Company, Inc., 500 Fifth Avenue, New York, N.Y. 10110
www.wwnorton.com
W. W. Norton & Company Ltd., Castle House, 75/76 Wells Street, London
W1T 3QT

    5   6   7   8   9   0

Contents

Criticism

Introduction

This introduction contains plot "spoilers," so if you wish to be surprised by the story, please skip ahead to the text of the novel and return to this introduction when you are done. *Emma* is a novel that not only rewards re-reading and reflection, but more or less demands to be read, re-read, discussed, and deeply considered. This introduction, therefore, might properly be used as an introduction to a re-reading of *Emma*, when the joys of experiencing the text are deepened (rather than diminished) by knowing what is about to happen. Unlike page-turners that exhaust their interest by building suspense and then producing conclusions, *Emma* provides a plot that unfolds like life, giving readers a chance to enjoy its events in the moment and then to re-experience those events through re-reading—perhaps even more intensely than we can revisit episodes in life through memory. A first reading of *Emma* relies upon the naïveté of the reader, who grasps the world of the novel largely from one character's perspective; a re-reading puts us close to the delightfully enjoyable and interesting situation of the novel's omniscient narrator.

Still, no experience of *Emma*, even multiple readings, will allow you full confidence of your interpretation. As you will be able to see from the selection of critical essays at the back of this Norton Critical Edition, literary critics writing about *Emma* have had difficulty reaching consensus on what the novel is about. Of course the novel is clearly—more so than any of Austen's other novels—about its main character, for whom it is named. But as well as we readers get to know Emma, through her own thoughts and from the outside, we do not have access to a single interpretation of her. For such a fully realized character in such a carefully rendered world, our inability to make simple judgments may reflect the complexity of lived experience. It becomes difficult to answer definitively even simple questions about the novel and its protagonist. Is Emma likable? Is she in need of reformation? Should Emma's imagination be channeled into productive domestic life? Should we condemn her for her attempts to influence the world around her, or should we admire her for her independence of intellect and spirit in a world that limits opportunities for women?

The original title page for *Emma* in 1816—the text of the novel we still depend upon today—declares it to be "by the author of 'Pride and Prejudice,' &c. &c." It was conventional in the early nineteenth century for female authors, particularly of the disreputable form of the "novel," to be so identified. It was seen as less important for readers to be able to identify an author by name. The title page served as an advertisement for the book (as well as providing this coded authorial attribution), and the publisher, John Murray, clearly felt that associating *Emma* with *Pride and Prejudice* would help spur sales. A reader picking up a new work by this unnamed author might have been led to expect the sparkling wit, comedy, romance, and even the supremely appealing heroine of *Pride and Prejudice*, which features the plucky Elizabeth Bennet (with her hopeless parents, awful younger siblings, and middling socio-economic status) triumphing in the face of long odds.

Pride and Prejudice was published in 1813. In the three years between the publication of *Pride and Prejudice* and *Emma*, Austen published *Mansfield Park* (1814), with its earnest heroine Fanny Price placed uncomfortably among her betters, awkwardly navigating a social world financially beyond—but morally beneath—her. *Mansfield Park* differs from *Pride and Prejudice* in many ways, but it shares with the earlier novel a heroine who proves her merit to a skeptical world. In their own ways, Austen's previously published novels were "Cinderella" stories, with heroines the reader could cheer to victory on the basis of merit. *Emma*, on the other hand, features a heroine whom, Austen privately admitted, "no one but myself will much like." (Each of her novels was written a few years before being published. See Jane Austen: A Chronology at the end of this volume. *Emma* was written after the publication of *Pride and Prejudice*. Complicating her audience's expectations for a heroine as appealing as Elizabeth Bennet may possibly have been on Austen's mind.)

Pride and Prejudice begins with what has become perhaps the most famous opening line in the history of the English novel: "It is a truth universally acknowledged, that a single man in possession of a good fortune, must be in want of a wife." That sentence's complex ironies set the stage for the rest of the novel. Should we accept the statement as an accurate description of the events of the novel or events in the world? Should we reject it as an amusing, if vulgar, commonplace assumption that might be held by the coarse Mrs. Bennet and others in the fictional and real worlds whose attitudes we reject? Re-reading the whole of *Pride and Prejudice* does not help: we are left with a statement that amuses us because it is both true and not true. It reduces a complex set of personal histories and particular social and historical settings to a structural norm that persists, justly or unjustly, across centuries.

At first glance, *Emma*'s opening paragraphs seem, by contrast, more direct. The novel begins, "Emma Woodhouse, handsome, clever, and rich, with a comfortable home and happy disposition, seemed to unite some of the best blessings of existence; and had lived nearly twenty-one years in the world with very little to distress or vex her." Rather than giving us the kind of ambiguous, but strongly worded moral pronouncement that opened *Pride and Prejudice* (the kind of statement the eighteenth-century moral writer, Samuel Johnson, an Austen favorite, might have written or uttered), the narrator of *Emma* delivers a crisp descriptive statement regarding her protagonist's status in the world. The word "seemed," however, provides a clue that appearances and reality might not completely coincide. We learn four paragraphs later that Emma's situation has "real evils." Her "happy disposition" is qualified by the narrator's statement that she has a "disposition to think a little too well of herself." Two uses of the word "disposition" ask us to consider what lies at the heart of Austen's characterization of Emma. Do these two uses refer to the same "disposition"? Or does the word in the first paragraph correspond to the *Oxford English Dictionary*'s definition 6 ("Natural tendency or bent of the mind, esp. in relation to moral or social qualities; mental constitution or temperament; turn of mind") while the usage in the later paragraph follows definition 7 ("7. a. . . . state of mind or feeling in respect to a thing or person; the condition of being [favourably or unfavourably] disposed towards")? If Emma's "happy disposition" is a permanent part of her character but her "disposition to think a little too well of herself" is a temporary "condition," we might garner some clues for interpretation.

In addition, how can it be possible for Emma to have lived "with very little to distress or vex her" when we learn in the following paragraph that her mother died when she was a girl? Even if her governess "had fallen little short of a mother in affection," her mother had been, we learn later from Mr. Knightley's generally reliable perspective, the "only person able to cope with her." Down to the word, the narrator's pronouncements regarding Emma's character are qualified or contradicted, sometimes within the space of a few sentences. As I mentioned at the outset, *Emma* rewards re-reading to an extent perhaps unmatched in the British novel; it is like one of the puzzles, charades, and other word games that populate the narrative, not to be unfolded without careful disentangling. But, unlike a puzzle, the novel does not offer a single "solution." Re-reading *Emma*—including re-reading it in different directions—continues to yield deeper and deeper questions and truths. The opening paragraphs should put us on guard against the kinds of delusions that our own disposition to root for an Austenian heroine might create.

Austen's Narrative Technique

Our understanding of the character of Emma, let alone our feelings toward her, are shaped by Austen's narrative technique. Some sentences, such as the novel's first sentence, seem clearly delivered in the third person, told to us by an omniscient narrator who keeps a critical distance from her main character. There is also a great deal of dialogue in the novel. The narrator reports to us directly what characters say to each other. But the narrator also uses what has been called by critics "free indirect discourse," a method in which the narrator describes in the third person what is going on in a character's mind. Rather than merely reporting the character's thoughts, however, the narrator's description of people, things, and events blends with the character's perceptions of those people, things, and events. In free indirect discourse what the character is thinking and what the narrator is describing overlap, thus providing the reader with an intense immersion into the mental world of the novel's characters. Here is an example from early on, volume I, chapter III. Note how the first of the quoted paragraphs is squarely in the third person, although it contains value judgments presumably made by the narrator, but that the subsequent paragraph (quoted in part) moves into space between the narrator and the character. The description is of Harriet Smith:

> She was a very pretty girl, and her beauty happened to be of a sort which Emma particularly admired. She was short, plump and fair, with a fine bloom, blue eyes, light hair, regular features, and a look of great sweetness; and before the end of the evening, Emma was as much pleased with her manners as her person, and quite determined to continue the acquaintance.
>
> She was not struck by any thing remarkably clever in Miss Smith's conversation, but she found her altogether very engaging—not inconveniently shy, not unwilling to talk—and yet so far from pushing, shewing so proper and becoming a deference, seeming so pleasantly grateful for being admitted to Hartfield, and so artlessly impressed by the appearance of every thing in so superior a style to what she had been used to, that she must have good sense and deserve encouragement. Encouragement should be given. Those soft blue eyes and all those natural graces should not be wasted on the inferior society of Highbury and its connections. The acquaintance she had already formed were unworthy of her. The friends from

whom she had just parted, though very good sort of people, must be doing her harm. They were a family of the name of Martin, whom Emma well knew by character, as renting a large farm of Mr. Knightley, and residing in the parish of Donwell—very creditably, she believed—she knew Mr. Knightley thought highly of them—but they must be coarse and unpolished, and very unfit to be the intimates of a girl who wanted only a little more knowledge and elegance to be quite perfect. *She* would notice her; she would improve her; she would detach her from her bad acquaintance, and introduce her into good society; she would form her opinions and manner. It would be an interesting, and certainly a very kind undertaking; highly becoming her own situation in life, her leisure, and powers.

The second paragraph begins and ends with direct acknowledgment that we are dealing with Emma's perceptions, beginning with "she was not struck" and ending with "her own situation in life, her leisure, and her powers." In between, however, Emma's judgments and perceptions are presented "as is," without any interfering narrative: "The acquaintance she had already formed were unworthy of her." The narrator is not trying to deceive us, even if this sentence, taken out of context, would seem to be an entirely ordinary judgment rendered in the third person. Throughout the novel, we are given enough clues to be able to decipher any given statement to determine whether it belongs to Emma or the narrator, but because the narrator provides access to Emma's thoughts almost exclusively, in such a graceful and seamless way, Emma's consciousness emerges with a prominence that rivals the narrator's own voice.

The combination of the narrator's intimacy with Emma and the novel's possible adverse judgment upon Emma's personality, intellect, actions, and feelings creates ambiguity for the reader. When we re-read, in light of what happens and how others perceive what happens, we can see that Emma's perceptions, usually offered without direct commentary, are woven into the texture of everything else we know about the characters, community, and events of the novel. Re-reading does not invalidate what Emma thinks, even when her thoughts are unfair. "[T]hey must be coarse and unpolished, and very unfit to be the intimates of a girl who wanted only a little more knowledge and elegance to be quite perfect." As we learn by the end of the novel, Emma's judgments of the Martins and Harriet herself are wrong—but they are not *entirely* wrong, as even the headstrong Mr. Knightley will come to confess.

The novel depicts not only Emma's reflective consciousness, but in a number of bravura passages, it demonstrates that the way we understand the "objective" world results from perceptions that are

embedded within our own particular points of view, that our perceptions are simultaneously objective and subjective. Two passages that
show this in different, and yet wonderful, ways include the short
description of the world going by as perceived by Emma while waiting
outside Ford's store for Harriet to finish her shopping (vol. 2, chapter
IX) and the compressed time passage describing the first group
expedition to pick strawberries and eat a picnic (vol. 3, chapter VI).

Here is the passage at Ford's. The details create almost a photo-
graphic slide show of small town life. By giving us these details
through Emma's perceptions of them, and by validating those perceptions with what seems like a moral judgment in the last sentence,
the novel makes a virtue of understanding the world in the way
that the novel (as a literary genre) provides. In a sense, in praising
Emma the novel praises itself and validates its own simultaneously
objective and subjective perspective on what constitutes reality.

> Harriet, tempted by every thing and swayed by half a word, was
> always very long at a purchase; and while she was still hanging
> over muslins and changing her mind, Emma went to the door
> for amusement.—Much could not be hoped from the traffic of
> even the busiest part of Highbury;—Mr. Perry walking hast-
> ily by, Mr. William Cox letting himself in at the office-door,
> Mr. Cole's carriage-horses returning from exercise, or a stray
> letter-boy on an obstinate mule, were the liveliest objects she
> could presume to expect; and when her eyes fell only on the
> butcher with his tray, a tidy old woman travelling homewards
> from shop with her full basket, two curs quarrelling over a dirty
> bone, and a string of dawdling children round the baker's little
> bow-window eyeing the gingerbread, she knew she had no rea-
> son to complain, and was amused enough; quite enough still to
> stand at the door. A mind lively and at ease, can do with seeing
> nothing, and can see nothing that does not answer.

And here is the picnic:

> She felt all the honest pride and complacency which her alli-
> ance with the present and future proprietor could fairly war-
> rant, as she viewed the respectable size and style of the
> building, its suitable, becoming, characteristic situation, low
> and sheltered—its ample gardens stretching down to meadows
> washed by a stream, of which the Abbey, with all the old
> neglect of prospect, had scarcely a sight—and its abundance of
> timber in rows and avenues, which neither fashion nor extrava-
> gance had rooted up.—The house was larger than Hartfield, and
> totally unlike it, covering a good deal of ground, rambling and
> irregular, with many comfortable, and one or two handsome

rooms.—It was just what it ought to be, and it looked what it was—and Emma felt an increasing respect for it, as the residence of a family of such true gentility, untainted in blood and understanding.—Some faults of temper John Knightley had; but Isabella had connected herself unexceptionably. She had given them neither men, nor names, nor places, that could raise a blush. These were pleasant feelings, and she walked about and indulged them till it was necessary to do as the others did, and collect round the strawberry-beds.—The whole party were assembled, excepting Frank Churchill, who was expected every moment from Richmond; and Mrs. Elton, in all her apparatus of happiness, her large bonnet and her basket, was very ready to lead the way in gathering, accepting, or talking—strawberries, and only strawberries, could now be thought or spoken of.—"The best fruit in England—every body's favourite—always wholesome.—These the finest beds and finest sorts.—Delightful to gather for one's self—the only way of really enjoying them.—Morning decidedly the best time—never tired—every sort good—hautboy infinitely superior—no comparison—the others hardly eatable—hautboys very scarce—Chili preferred—white wood finest flavour of all—price of strawberries in London—abundance about Bristol—Maple Grove—cultivation—beds when to be renewed—gardeners thinking exactly different—no general rule—gardeners never to be put out of their way—delicious fruit—only too rich to be eaten much of—inferior to cherries—currants more refreshing—only objection to gathering strawberries the stooping—glaring sun—tired to death—could bear it no longer—must go and sit in the shade."

Such, for half an hour, was the conversation—interrupted only once by Mrs. Weston, who came out, in her solicitude after her son-in-law, to inquire if he were come—and she was a little uneasy.—She had some fears of his horse.

The picnic begins with Emma's reflections on her surroundings. The "present proprietor" is, of course, Mr. Knightley, but at this moment in the novel the "future proprietor" is Emma's eldest nephew, whom she envisions as the inheritor of Donwell Abbey and all that it represents to the social order, the culture, and the nation. The solidity of the property is contrasted with the "fashion and extravagance" of more contemporary estates. The Knightleys (their name a clear indicator of their value to society), like their estate, are "just what they ought to be." This is Emma's point of view, but there is no reason to doubt its accuracy. Unlike the earlier passage, in which we moved from the narrator's third-person description to Emma's consciousness in free indirect discourse, in this passage we move from free indirect discourse almost imperceptibly to third-person narration. The description of "the whole party assembled" moves into compressed "conversation" describing the passing of the day, foreshadowing in literary history the "Time Passes" section of Virginia Woolf's great novel *To the Lighthouse*. The characters experience an inevitable fatigue caused by a long day in the hot sun. The humor of the passage stems from its realism, not from the exaggeration typical of comedy in the eighteenth century.

Psychology and Genre

The humanity with which Austen delves into the psychology of Emma and Emma's relationships with people and the world around her feels real to many readers. Emma, like other Austen characters, seems like someone we might know, and even when we find her irritating or destructive, she comes alive as a human being. Readers in the twenty-first century often have two vastly different, but both compelling and appropriate, responses to the narrative verisimilitude: some claim that the psychology and human relations depicted in the novel are universal and as accurate now as they were when the novel was written. Others become immersed in the "Regency world" through the novel, some choosing to wear clothing of the period, learn country dancing, and try to follow customs that seem pleasantly outdated.

Although the psychological and social realism of *Emma* brings us very close to the narrative and allows us to enjoy it, we need to keep in mind the distance that "Janeites"—fanatical Jane Austen admirers—acknowledge when they make attempts at holding a Regency ball or tea. *Emma* is embedded in a particular social and historical setting that informs much of the meaning of the characters' interactions and feelings. Without understanding some of this background, readers miss out on many of the finer points of the novel—missing, in some cases, when Emma is "right" and when she is "wrong." To understand these subtleties, we need to understand both the literary genre of the novel and the finely calibrated system of manners that structured social interaction during Austen's day. *Emma* fits into the broad literary category of the "novel of manners." The concept of "manners" encompasses more than behavior at the table or making sure to write thank you notes. For Austen's culture, the tightly structured aspects of life widely outnumbered the informal ones, in stark contrast to the way we often feel we live today. (Although it is worth considering that even our most "casual" of interactions today, involving articles of clothing, restaurants, etc., have their own normalized expectations for behavior and appearance.)

In effect, *Emma* has become a historical novel, capturing the manners and mores of early nineteenth-century English society. At the time, however, Austen was known for her care in depicting her society, and this skill was contrasted with the "big bow wow strain" of Sir Walter Scott, author of *Waverley* and other novels delving into prominent moments in history. Novels such as Scott's set the action in well-known places, inserting the domestic events depicted often in the genre of the novel within the context of grand history. The dedication of *Emma* to the Prince Regent (who would later become King George IV after the death of his ill father) demonstrates that Austen's reputation and identity as a writer had become known to many of the "great" in her culture. The dedication also follows the plea, in private correspondence, of the prince's domestic chaplain, J. S. Clarke, that Austen write a historical novel based on the "History of the august house of Cobourg," including Prince Leopold, whom Clarke was also serving. (See selections of this correspondence in the section on "Jane Austen: Her Art and Business" in this Norton Critical Edition.) Austen demurred, stating that her own skills lay in "pictures of domestic Life in Country Villages."

Austen and Social Class

In our own day, Austen's novels have been used as the basis of creative works by many writers and filmmakers, some attempting to capture a fidelity to costume and setting that would make a Janeite proud; and others adapting characters, plots, and situations to different time periods and cultural contexts. *Pride and Prejudice* became *Bridget Jones's Diary* (novel 1996; film 2001) and *Bride and Prejudice* (2004) as well as effective versions set in the early nineteenth century. (Please see David Monaghan's essay in this volume on televisual versions of *Emma* for a more nuanced and detailed understanding of cinematic adaptation.) In addition to movies set in the time period that attempt to bring *Emma* to life for twentieth- and twenty-first-century audiences, Amy Heckerling's movie *Clueless* (1995) translates *Emma* into contemporary American culture. The lack of a comparable focus on rigid social classes changes the character of Emma ("Cher Horowitz" in the movie) in substance as well as style.

Cher, like Emma, is rich. Otherwise, the family relationships, high school setting, interactions with friends and enemies, and expectations for personal development in *Clueless* differ a great deal from *Emma*. Emma Woodhouse's behavior might appear superficial to those who do not possess an insider's understanding of Regency customs, but instead her actions, speeches—and even her delusional matchmaking—stem from a close adherence to the norms of her status as the presiding female in a prominent household in the "gentry" in a small community in early nineteenth-century England. The narrative style provides a "depth" that Heckerling's film cannot. A high school clique differs in both style and substance from the structured hierarchies of birth and status in Jane Austen's society. Understanding the way the class system works in *Emma* becomes critical for twenty-first-century readers. Nobody in Austen's novel is "titled"—a member of the aristocracy whose wealth and mode of living would be as alien (and as fascinating) to most readers as Hollywood celebrity culture is to our world. Instead, Austen provides us with a world that would be familiar to the day-to-day lives of her first English readers—a world of gentlemen and gentlemen's daughters as well as the more well-to-do clergy and tradespeople. (Maggie Lane's essay on "Daily Life in Jane Austen's England," in "Jane Austen: Her Life and Fiction" provides additional details on the class structure of Austen's world.)

Emma and Mr. Knightley belong to the gentry, which is generally defined as the class immediately below the aristocracy. Members of the aristocracy inherited titles and great wealth; members of the gentry usually inherited wealth, too, and some also possessed titles distinguishing them for their merit or connections to the aristocracy. Distinctions within the gentry, ranging along a matrix of wealth and birth, are subtle in Jane Austen's fiction. Emma's economic status is higher than *Pride and Prejudice*'s Elizabeth Bennet—or Jane Austen herself—or most of her readers. However, they are all members of a broadly similar *social* class. Elizabeth Bennet refers to herself simply as the daughter of a gentleman, a phrase that she uses in combatting the pretensions of Lady Catherine de Bourgh that Mr. Darcy is socially above her. Similarly, Emma is the daughter of a gentleman, Mr. Woodhouse. Emma's status in Highbury depends not only upon her class and status, but her particular standing by birth and wealth in a small community. Local customs and relationships still mattered in a society with increasing, but by no means complete, geographic mobility. Emma would be a person most of the readers of the novel, as well as its characters, would have had to look up to if they lived in her community.

The relationship between Charles Bingley's sisters and Elizabeth Bennet in *Pride and Prejudice* might be said to parallel the relationship between Emma Woodhouse and Jane Fairfax, the character in *Emma* who would seem to play the role of spunky upstart. (Jane should, as Emma herself acknowledges, have been the appropriate friend for her in the community). But the Bingleys were newcomers to Netherfield; the major newcomers to Highbury are the horrid Mrs. Elton and the mysterious Frank Churchill, who is new in person but not in family. All of the social interactions—from a seemingly inessential conversation to the most profound exercise of feelings—figure into a network of relationships in the community. This network maps onto the social class system that exists nationally, but it follows its own particular customs. I use the word "network," although it is important to note that status within this network is calibrated according to an understanding of both merit and status by birth. The social system in *Emma* resembles a hierarchy (in which people are ranked on a scale), but it also involves lateral obligations that can conflict with a straightforward placement of individuals within the structure.

Everyone in the novel, and most people within early nineteenth-century culture, would judge the value of people in relationship to a number of expectations. English literary works from Geoffrey Chaucer's late fourteenth-century *Canterbury Tales* with its "worthy" Knyght to Henry Fielding's *Tom Jones* (1749), in which Tom both is and is not of the estate of "Mr. Allworthy," tackle the issue of the relationship between birth and merit. *Emma* inserts itself into the class dynamics of its culture, both overturning and confirming that a person's value should be linked simultaneously to merit and birth. Even people of great wealth, who would seem to be able to live for themselves, are judged on the basis of their contribution to the general well-being of the community.

However, much of the novel registers Emma's wish to fit everyone in her town of Highbury strictly into a hierarchy of value, sometimes misunderstanding the person's "real" status within the culture (for example, the case of Harriet Smith). By the end of the novel Emma understands better the actual structure of the social system in Highbury, which, as I state above, is as much "network" as "hierarchy." The narrator makes Emma recalibrate the relationship between birth and merit as well as better understand how others perceive reality. What makes a character "worthy" in the novel involves a combination of social standing, personal qualities, and a place in and contribution to Highbury. Mr. Woodhouse, Emma's father, quaintly uses the word "worthy" to describe the Bates women and Jane Fairfax. Although Mr. Woodhouse's valetudinarianism becomes as trying for many readers as it clearly is to his daughter, his respect for Mrs. and Miss Bates despite their poverty reveals that the more rigid, un-genteel notions Emma holds at the novel's outset are perhaps more "modern" than they are "traditional." In essence, Emma has to unlearn some of the vulgar categorizing of Mrs. Elton while preserving belief in the value of traditional social relations—and that, perhaps, is the version of progressive modernity that she gains at the novel's conclusion.

However, Emma, whether in the beginning or at the end of the novel, is clearly not the most modern person in Highbury. Certain characters whom Emma had judged to be beneath her turn out to have valuable places in the world that is developing around her. The Coles, who are "of low origin, in trade," end up at the center of a community Emma decides she would not mind gracing. (For members of the gentry, income would have been earned from their land, whether directly by farming it or renting it out, or through investments managed for them in London. To work as a merchant, whether in retail trade or in wholesale business, was a step below the "professions" of clergy and lawyer, which were the refuge of people with birth and education, but no wealth.) Emma initially disdains the notion of attending their dinner party, but then changes her mind. The novel pokes fun at her but only gently. The Coles are not the only denizens of Highbury who are seemingly tainted by the stain of having to *earn* a living in the modern economy. Mr. Weston, himself, who has married Emma's governess (a complicated relationship in social class terms that Emma is happy to overlook), made his wealth in trade. So did the family of the abhorrent Miss Augusta Hawkins, who comes to Highbury as the wife of the seemingly eligible Mr. Elton, whose own "alliances" had been but in "trade." Mr. Woodhouse, Mr. Knightley, Emma, Mrs. and Miss Bates, and the servants are all that remains of the world Emma initially understands as real. The world outside the Woodhouses in Hartfield has become modernized, that is, but not overturned. Nowhere in the novel do we see the notion that the social structure should be thoroughly reshaped according to the egalitarian theories of the French revolution. No one wishes to send Mr. Woodhouse away to convalesce and allow Mr. Cole to purchase his beloved Hartfield. Although Frank Churchill, who will inherit a significant amount of money, marries the penniless but meritorious Jane Fairfax, the appropriateness of the match is signaled by her relatives the Bateses' unimpeachable status in the community. However, the power of the old world reasserts itself in the true worthiness of Mr. Knightley and his novel-ending union with Emma. In Austen's fictional world, "worth" of merit and the "worth" of birth will mix and match in ways that, the wedded Knightleys can hope, will benefit the community and the nation, in which Highbury prospers and to which Highbury contributes prosperity. Highbury and London are separated by sixteen miles—and they depend on each other.

Gender Relations

In a similar fashion, the novel and its main character both conform to and challenge the limitations that the system of gender relationships placed on women during the period. Critics continue to argue, however, about the degree to which gender roles in Austen ought to be seen as conformist or progressive. The essays by Marilyn Butler and Claudia Johnson in the Criticism section of this Norton Critical Edition exemplify the debates among scholars in understanding the politics of women in the novel. Both Butler and Johnson ground their interpretations of the novel in the interplay between literary work and historical time period, but these scholars come up with vastly different readings. For Butler, the novel lies squarely in a conservative tradition of British novels by women in which the rebellious notions held by female characters are disciplined out of them until they accept their limited role in a world defined by traditional gender identities. The novel, according to this interpretation, plays a role in the British defense of its national values against the radical ideas of the French Revolution.

For critics like Johnson, however, the verve and intelligence with which Emma engages the world—and the very non-traditional gender role played by a sensitive male character like Mr. Knightley—suggest that the novel is upending rigidly prescriptive roles for people based on their sex. Emma is a powerful character who shapes the world around her, from managing people like her father, Mrs. Weston, and Harriet Smith, to controlling the household. Whatever is in her purview—and many things are—is subject to her intelligent management. Some feminist critics of the novel see, therefore, a celebration of female intellectual, social, and even, in some cases, economic and sexual independence for women in *Emma*; this celebration can be linked, for some critics, to a critique of society for oppressing people based on race, let alone gender. (See the short excerpt from Gabrielle White in this volume for an analysis of the novel's intervention in national debates over the slave trade.)

Before readers decide which view of the novel they will take, they should understand better both the traditional gender roles of the culture and the way in which those roles had been challenged in the fifty years preceding *Emma*. Young, marriageable women (the two terms closely overlapping, although not by any means synonymous) had been prescribed a straight-laced code of behavior, reflected and promoted by "conduct books," popular written tracts that often took the form of advice handed down from a father to a teenaged daughter. Women—that is, women of means—should be passive in their relationships with others, these conduct books lectured, but active in maintaining the household and controlling the servants. They were to be dutiful to their husbands, devoted to their children, exemplary in their religious duties, and competent in household chores. They were to learn this behavior but to act in as "artless" a manner as possible.

It may be difficult for us to understand completely the kind of "artless" behavior imposed upon women as an expectation from

their culture in the early nineteenth century. The relevant definition from the *OED* for the word "artless" is clear enough: "without
guile, sincere, ingenuous." It was widely acknowledged even during
the time period that there was a potential conflict when the reality
of sincerity could be learned effectively by self-interested individuals. Emma, Jane Fairfax, and Harriet Smith are all in their own
ways "artless," even as they try, at various times in the novel, to
appear to advantage. After dancing with her, Mr. Knightley declares
Harriet to be "[a]n unpretending, single-minded, artless girl—
infinitely to be preferred by any man of sense and taste to such a
woman as Mrs. Elton." In other words, all of these young women,
including Mrs. Elton, are the products of various forms of education that mold women to cultural expectations while also preparing them to succeed on their own terms. They have to practice a
learned skill to appear to be, in effect, without those skills! "Artlessness" represents a goal to aspire to—even Mrs. Elton, with her
vision of riding donkeys to Donwell Abbey, tries to display simplicity
just as the text reveals her simplicity to be ridiculous affectation.
The former Miss Hawkins had been educated badly, and the vulgarity she learned follows her when she becomes Mrs. Elton. Women's
education plays a critical background role in the novel, which presents us with a number of educators and a number of people in need
of education.

As a gentlewoman, Emma's formal education came primarily at
the hands of Miss Taylor (later Mrs. Weston), who was appropriately qualified to act as governess. However, Miss Taylor was perhaps not the most effective teacher, at least in delivering the
education expected from her. As we learn from the novel, the gov-
ernness was ruled by Emma's headstrong will rather than exerting
any "restraint" over Emma herself. Emma's deceased mother, we
learn, again from Mr. Knightley, was the "only person able to cope
with her. [Emma] inherits her mother's talents, and must have been
under subjection to her." Without her mother dominating an Emma
acting "in subjection," Emma's imagination was unrestrained. There
were, for Emma, other avenues toward education than her govern-
ness. She had a less formal education, albeit of mixed success itself,
at the hands of the information industry of the time period. She
read books. Mr. Knightley commends the lists of books Emma made
up for herself, rather than her actual reading. But the novel does
contain references to a shared set of home and school use textbooks
used by both the Woodhouses and the Martins. Emma possesses
Vicesimus Knox's collections of *Elegant Extracts*. First published in
1783 and reprinted often over the succeeding years, the *Elegant
Extracts* could have provided Emma with access to the best prose
and poetry of the preceding century, arranged in a format appropri-

ate for schools but also promoted for what we would call "distance education" or "home schooling."

Of course, Mr. Knightley is another kind of teacher of Emma, and some readers have been troubled by the transition he makes between older mentor and lover. For much of the novel, Emma considers Mr. Knightley as a brother, and there is a very amusing moment (on re-reading) when Emma dances with him and blithely announces that it is an acceptable partnership because he is not really too much of a "brother," as her brother-in-law and lifelong neighbor. When Emma ponders the "influence" Mr. Knightley has had on her, near the end of the novel, she focuses rather on the romantic role he has come to play in her thoughts rather than on his sometimes stern pronouncements about the need for integrity and decency. Although some critics have maintained that Mr. Knightley forcefully teaches Emma to be like him, the novel also suggests—in Mr. Knightley's words themselves—that she has taught a thing or two to him throughout the course of her life. At no point in the novel does effective education consist of a teacher filling a student with facts, skills, and interpretations that magically transform the student into a worthy person.

One could look at the novel as having twin themes: the education of Emma Woodhouse and the education of Harriet Smith. Just as Mr. Knightley mentors Emma, Emma mentors Harriet. Emma's friendship allows Harriet access into higher circles of Highbury society than she would have ordinarily had. She hopes to shape Harriet into eligible wife-material for a man of means. If Emma's intellect makes her unusual as a woman in her culture, Harriet's pliability and dimwittedness make her "artless" in a less than complimentary understanding of the word. Theirs is almost a masculine/feminine relationship (by the gender standards of the day), which has led some commentators, from Edmund Wilson earlier in the twentieth century until today, to consider seriously whether Emma is romantically (or even sexually) attracted to women. (Wilson's essay is included in this Norton Critical Edition's "Backgrounds" section.)

But Harriet undergoes a much more formal education as well. There were many schools in England, for both boys and girls, and the novel provides us with a sense of their effectiveness, or lack thereof, in Mrs. Goddard's school, where Harriet Smith lives and studies as a "parlour boarder." Mrs. Goddard's is an "old-fashioned boarding school," where, the narrator tells us, "a reasonable quantity of accomplishments were sold at a reasonable price, and where girls might be sent to be out of the way, and scramble themselves into a little education, without any danger of coming back prodigies." Does this passage attack the school or praise it as a representative of its type? The school provides "a reasonable quantity of accomplishments." What are these "accomplishments," and of what does a "reasonable quantity" consist?

Accomplishments "equipped" a young woman for her role in society. The word referred to substantial skills that help define one's contribution to the world, including the taste and elegance of manners so critical to success for a woman of Emma's class and status. At the same time, an accomplishment was something that was ornamental—that helped distinguish one woman from another as embellishments rather than the core message of education. In early nineteenth-century society, such accomplishments for women might consist of needlework, drawing, music, and other arts and skills judged appropriate for female hands and minds—"attainments" that complete a woman for society but perhaps do not make her genuinely useful either to others or to herself.

Jane Fairfax is the "really accomplished young woman" in the novel. Whereas accomplishments were generally used for women to catch a husband, Jane has been educated with frills in order that she can become an educator herself. In a world in which an unmarried woman (like her aunt, Miss Bates) had few options, the professional skills acquired by Jane through hard work were to be used to provide her with a prospect of self-support through employment as a governess rather than with pleasure in performance. Jane's employment is contrasted with the notion of independence that represents happiness for men and women alike.

> The plan was that [Jane] should be brought up for educating others; the very few hundred pounds which she inherited from her father making independence impossible. To provide for her otherwise was out of Colonel Campbell's power; for though his income, by pay and appointments, was handsome, his fortune was moderate and must be all his daughter's; but, by giving her an education, he hoped to be supplying the means of respectable subsistence hereafter.

Both Mrs. Elton and Emma put themselves down for the level of their more amateur abilities in music, drawing, etc. Mrs. Elton's self-denigration is pompous—she protests too much that she is unskilled. Emma, on the other hand, is conscious that a higher level of skill would become her as an elegant young woman—not a woman to trade those skills professionally, as Jane will have to do, but as a measure of one's taste and ability to contribute to social occasions. Of course Jane's skills really do end up catching her a husband: Frank Churchill had sung with her at Weymouth, and it is easy to imagine their falling in love over a shared skill in music. Not the ostensible purpose for her having been educated, but an appropriately happy ending for the two of them. In the context of the novel, do we look down on Emma for not having the same level of skill at the piano that Jane has? Or ought we instead to judge Emma admirable for dedicating time to charity to the downtrodden and kindness to others instead of practicing at drawing, music, or needlework?

If the latter, we need also to understand that Emma's ability to be a charitable and kind person resulted from her unique situation at Hartfield and more generally in Highbury. In a system that generally made women legally and economically dependent on husbands and fathers, Emma was able to aim for a kind of "independence" unattainable through Harriet's nor Jane's education and status. Even if men's education could destine them for independence in only a limited range of professions, it could be done. For women, independence *usually* resulted from marriage to a respectable man of means. For example, when Mr. Woodhouse bemoans Miss Taylor's transformation into Mrs. Weston, Mr. Knightley wryly says, "Poor Mr. and Miss Woodhouse, if you please; but I cannot possibly say 'poor Miss Taylor.' I have a great regard for you and Emma; but when it comes to the question of dependence or independence!—At any rate, it must be better to have only one to please than two." Mrs. Weston still has her husband to "please," but she need no longer please her employer and her pupil. The Westons' own economic fortunes and companionship seem to bode well for their happiness, especially when, near the end of the novel, Mrs. Weston is revealed to be pregnant.

Harriet's independence might have come about as a result of a marriage with Mr. Elton, as Emma blithely tells her in the midst of her matchmaking delusion. Emma contrasts the social and economic situation that Harriet would have with Mr. Elton with the prospect of marrying Mr. Martin, whose status as a tenant farmer working for Mr. Knightley would have traditionally made him "dependent" on the landowner. Emma suggests to Harriet that Mr. Martin would not be able to marry for six years, since he has "his own fortune entirely to make" rather than having been "born to an independence." Emma has, again, seen a hierarchy where there was actually a network of obligations. As it turns out, Robert Martin's strength of mind and business competence have made Mr. Knightley reliant on him. The novel suggests that for these men, as for women, a true independence involves mutual reliance rather than standing free and clear of the community. Robert Martin and Harriet Smith are both in the same network, and on the same level, and the novel emphasizes this by discussing the mutual help they will be to each other in marriage.

In the patriarchal society of early nineteenth-century England, marriage was an institution women could neither live with nor live without. Miss Bates is the primary example in the novel of an "old maid"—a woman advanced in years who never married. Her unmarried state is presented as something to be pitied—or at least treated kindly—by the rest of Highbury society. Emma, who throughout most of the novel insists that she wishes to remain single, contrasts her situation with that of Miss Bates in a speech to Harriet that will probably strike twenty-first-century readers as cruel: "It is poverty only which makes celibacy contemptible to a generous public! A single woman, with a very narrow income, must be a ridiculous, disagreeable old maid! the proper sport of boys and girls, but a single woman, of good fortune, is always respectable, and may be as sensible and pleasant as any body else." The episode at Box Hill is a natural result of Miss Bates being "contemptible," but the resulting reflection on Miss Bates and her position in society turns that contempt to pity, urging Emma on to kindness to Miss Bates. Still, there are few advantages to the life of Miss Bates, and that the novel irritates the reader with her long, frustrating speeches suggests that some of that contempt remains, regardless of the protagonist's change of heart.

Mr. Knightley, single in his late thirties, is certainly not an old maid. Emma believes his being single is tied to his independence. What Emma misses is that Mr. Knightley is in love, and the appropriate fulfillment of both his love and his independence lies in marriage with Emma, which is perfectly predictable on the basis of compatibility and income, but unusual considering the age difference. The novel *Emma* indeed presents us with mainly unconventional marriages: Mr. Woodhouse and his deceased wife with many greater abilities than he possesses; Mr. John Knightley and Isabella, who more typically reverse that combination of strong-willed and ridiculously weak and loving, but to an extent readers might find ridiculous; and Frank Churchill's parents (Mr. Weston and his first moody wife) and his aunt and uncle, among others. Marriages in *Emma* contrast with the rosy picture of progress that some historians, including Lawrence Stone, have outlined for English history. These historians of the family and social relations suggest that there is a move among members of the gentry from marriage based on the consolidation of wealth (and therefore largely arranged by parents) to marriage based on the compatibility in domestic life, and in affection (and therefore pursued by the parties themselves, with or without parental consent). "Companionate" marriage, as it has been called, relied upon a division of labor, with men working outside the home and women within it, and existed to produce happiness, social stability, and the next generation. Other historians have objected to the extent that companionate marriage held sway in England; and a literary critic might doubt the place of happy marriages in *Emma*.

In *Emma*, companionate marriages are few and far between. Prior
to the wedding of Emma and Mr. Knightley, the only marriages that
fit the general description outlined above are those of the Westons
and the Eltons, and neither of these is shown to be without flaw.
The Eltons are roundly condemned as a couple as well as individuals, even though they are a perfect, companionate match in their
own way. The former Augusta Hawkins, daughter of a Bristol merchant, comes to the marriage "possessed of an independent fortune"
of 10,000 pounds (a great deal of wealth by our standards). She and
Mr. Elton had met in the resort town of Bath, known then as a marriage market, and had quickly come to a mutual understanding.
This couple represents the novel's skeptical approach to the notion
of romantic love. Their love at first sight is a sham, and their married life repulsive. They are a nineteenth-century version of "smug
marrieds" (the phrase comes from Helen Fielding's *Bridget Jones's
Diary*)—couples who are so satisfied with themselves that they disgust all others. The Westons are more appealing, but it is clear that
their successful match results as much from the ability to ignore
each other at critical moments as they overlook each other's faults.
In general, the novel is skeptical about any societal trend, including
the contemporary fashion of marrying for love rather than for wealth
and/or status.

  Emma contains a representation of gender and relationships
not only among the youthful set translated by Heckerling's *Clueless*
but also among ages throughout the lifespan. The novel's depiction
of age—from Isabella Knightley's children on the young end to
Mr. Woodhouse and Mrs. Bates on the elder—provides a glimpse
into the way that "gender" has different meanings not only as related
to social class and marital status but also to a character's time of
life. Being a woman means something different to Emma from what
it means to Miss Bates, and the critical episode at Box Hill provides
a contrast between the two.

  It is clear that Emma is "wrong" in her behavior during the expedition to Box Hill. Our interpretive clarity results from the way
characters respond to what Emma says and how she acts, as well
as our own sense of things and the narrative description (if *not* the
narrator's explicit judgment). The weather was "fine," but it "was
downright dulness to Emma." We get a sense that things are going
emotionally wrong when the narrator describes Emma's reflection
that she and Frank had "flirted excessively" and that she had allowed
Frank to be "gallant." Our culture does not understand flirting as
a moral offense. But in the early nineteenth century, flirting as a
behavior represents a stark contrast to the solidity of, say, Donwell
Abbey: courtship was serious, and the implications of a romance
gone wrong for young women for whom there were often no

"second chances" meant that playing at love could be a serious moral offense. The words "gallant" and "gallantry" in the novel always refer to a stylized form of masculine behavior that lies in stark contrast to the plain-spoken realism of Mr. Knightley (we are told in volume III, chapter IX, that "his manners had in general so little gallantry"). Mr. Knightley is both direct and feeling; Frank Churchill is prevaricating and gallant. Both flirting and gallantry are aggressive tricks of the young that mark out their youth; flirting and gallantry are the backdrop for the crime against a fellow woman, and against humanity, that Emma commits when she mocks Miss Bates for her silliness and age.

The narrator prefaces Emma's nasty comment with "Emma could not resist," a short sentence that composes an entire paragraph. "Resist" is a transitive verb: it usually takes a direct object. What is it that Emma could not refrain from? At the very least, she could not resist uttering the sentence that first baffled and then humiliated Miss Bates. She also, apparently, could not resist unleashing her anger and aggression against Miss Bates, whether that anger is deserved or not (and see D. W. Harding's famous essay on Austen's "regulated hatred" in this Norton Critical Edition for an incisive look at this issue). Austen lets it remain unclear what, exactly, in her own mind Emma cannot resist. What else might she not have been able to resist? A penchant for cruelty? Her assertion of youthful spirits? Her frustration with the entire day? Her psychological mastery? Mr. Knightley makes it clear that whatever it is that Emma could not resist must be stamped out, or at least rechanneled, and this event has marked for many readers the moral turning point of the novel. "How could you be so unfeeling to Miss Bates? How could you be so insolent in your wit to a woman of her character, age, and situation?—Emma, I had not thought it possible." The "unfeeling" Emma is contrasted to the "feeling" Mr. Knightley—she is more stereotypically male in this scene than he ever is.

Miss Bates's "character, age, and situation" put her at a disadvantage compared to Emma. Age in particular sticks out here. Austen's culture traditionally revered age, although youths who mock characters of old age are often depicted in the literature of the time. Usually such characters are punished by their novels, the ability to be cruel to persons of advanced age representing a violation of moral and religious duties. *Emma*, instead, allows its main character to repent fully, both in consciousness and action. Her punishment comes from within, and Emma's reflections constitute her real education: "Time did not compose her. As she reflected more, she seemed but to feel it more." She is educated from "unfeeling" to a point in which she can "feel" her moral trespass, and then empathize with Miss Bates. There is little controversy regarding the fact of Emma's new self-understanding—she is initially chastened by Mr. Knightley and then, more importantly, by her own conscience. The question remains, however, whether Emma is attacked by the novel (as a butt of the narrative's satire) in order to reform herself morally and make her an appropriate spouse for Mr. Knightley and lead figure in the town of Highbury; or whether she emerges from reflection (and marriage to Mr. Knightley) still powerful as a satirist, as a woman with a formidable intellect and a powerful imagination. Does Austen punish Emma so that we may learn from her mistake? Or does she love her heroine, who emerges a better, wiser, person whom we ourselves can come to love and respect? What, ultimately, does the narrator's relationship with Emma mean for the reader's relationship with the character and the work of art?

Austen and Satire

To understand these questions, we must first understand something about eighteenth-century satire. Such satire ranged from the gentle, amused "Horatian" (after the Roman poet Horace) satire to the more scathing "Juvenalian" (after the Roman poet Juvenal) satire, which cared more for lacerating blows to the objects of its scorn than for making its audience laugh. The ostensible purpose of all satire is to reform its audience by holding up bad behavior to ridicule. The faults of a person—or a society—exposed, the readers can amend their own behavior to bring it in line with the moral norm put forward either implicitly by the work of literature or explicitly by the work's "satiric hero," a character who embodies the intelligence and behaviors meant to be promoted. The satiric butts, in contrast, absorb attacks in order to delight the audience and to provide negative examples—behaviors and traits to be avoided. Juvenalian satire relies upon "invective," a mode of direct attack upon an object to be scorned. Horatian satire, on the other hand, employs pervasive irony, in which ostensible judgments are balanced by implied, contrary judgments. In the most sophisticated uses of irony, apparent meanings and contrasting implied judgments can *both* be true—as in the example of the description of Mrs. Goddard's school, quoted above. Is Mr. Woodhouse really annoying, or do we enjoy his approach to life even if it frustrates the wishes, and the good fun, of other characters in the novel? His speeches are rendered in extensive passages that might be said to tire the reader as much or even more than they tire Mr. Woodhouse's companions (see Richard Jenkyns's amusing diatribe against Mr. Woodhouse in this volume for one such judgment). Similarly, does Miss Bates, prosing on in irritating ways, deserve scorn or sympathy—or both? Miss Bates, as illustrated in the Box Hill episode, functions as a target for satire and an object of sympathy—perhaps for the readers as well as for other characters in the novel.

Emma plays an important role in the history of satiric English novels, begun around seventy-five years earlier with the narrative attacks that Henry Fielding made upon his rival early novelist, Samuel Richardson. Fielding's *Shamela* (1741) and *Joseph Andrews* (1742) mocked Richardson's pious *Pamela* (1740–41), exposing the virtue of Richardson's servant-girl heroine as a manipulative sham. Fielding's works, including the later satiric novel *Tom Jones*, affirm a correspondence between the traditional social structure and the moral merit of some of its lead characters: Fielding's Mr. Allworthy is a predecessor of Austen's Mr. Knightley. Other satiric novels had women authors and female lead characters. In these novels, the lead characters are usually virtuous, but still run afoul of predatory men, a ridiculous social world, and family difficulties. Frances Burney was perhaps the most important woman novelist in England prior to Austen, and her novels *Evelina* (1778), *Cecilia* (1782), and *Camilla* (1796) all present women of intelligence and spirit who achieve their ends (marriage with eligible, wealthy, and virtuous men) after a set of misadventures that demonstrate the faults of the world as well as the faults of themselves. Charlotte Lennox's *The Female Quixote* (1752) provides perhaps the best example of a satiric novel by a woman that influenced *Emma*. The main character of Lennox's novel, Arabella, is a quixote (a word taken from Miguel de Cervantes' great Spanish novel, *Don Quixote*). She sees the world through the lens of her own imagination. Unlike Emma, whose imagination does not distort either the way she appears to the world or her own general understanding of moral and physical reality, Arabella looks at the world through a mind shaped by the unrealistic works of heroic romance, and her delusions make her both a figure of fun (the object of satire) and a satirist herself (her misperceptions often reveal how tawdry her contemporary world is). Arabella is ultimately reformed, largely through the intercession of a powerful figure, "the Doctor," a Johnsonian figure who reorients her toward the world of the here and now, in which she can finally marry her virtuous lover, Glanville.

Like Arabella, Emma is both a satirist and the object of satire. We see her wit play out in numerous ways, both through the thought process the narrator presents for us and through moments like the episode at Box Hill, in which her tongue lashes out, but finds only a relatively innocent satiric target in the form of Miss Bates. From Emma's social position, active work as a satirist would involve cruelty (and an abnegation of her social status, in which politeness to all is a required trait). The satire in Austen's narrative method depends on the amplification of the understated satire of Emma's dialogue combined with the explicit satire of her thoughts laid bare in free indirect discourse.

Emma's "fancy," the power of her imaginative mind, becomes critical to the satiric mission of the novel—just as Arabella's delusional view of the modern world in Lennox's novel contributed to and felt the impact of *The Female Quixote*. Matchmaking, obviously, represents the most explicit working out of Emma's imagination. Emma is a novelist who has written "novels" only in her mind. Prominent among Emma's fictionalizing are the courtship of Harriet and Mr. Elton, followed by the courtship of Harriet and Mr. Knightley. She imagines the illicit story of Jane Fairfax and Col. Dixon, and she imagines a failed romance between herself and Frank Churchill:

> Emma continued to entertain no doubt of her being in love. Her ideas only varied as to the how much. At first, she thought it was a good deal; and afterwards, but little. She had great pleasure in hearing Frank Churchill talked of; and, for his sake, greater pleasure than ever in seeing Mr. and Mrs. Weston; she was very often thinking of him, and quite impatient for a letter, that she might know how he was, how were his spirits, how was his aunt, and what was the chance of his coming to Randalls again this spring. But, on the other hand, she could not admit herself to be unhappy, nor, after the first morning, to be less disposed for employment than usual; she was still busy and cheerful; and, pleasing as he was, she could yet imagine him to have faults; and farther, though thinking of him so much, and, as she sat drawing or working, forming a thousand amusing schemes for the progress and close of their attachment, fancying interesting dialogues, and inventing elegant letters; the conclusion of every imaginary declaration on his side was that she *refused him*. Their affection was always to subside into friendship. Every thing tender and charming was to mark their parting; but still they were to part.

Emma's matchmaking, and her fantasy about a budding romance between herself and Frank Churchill, are objects of the novel's satire. We find Emma silly, at best, and destructive at worst for attempting to impose her imagination's visions upon her family and friends. Is the joke on Emma, or is the target of the novel's satire a world around her that offers women of her class and status so few outlets for their powerful minds? Mr. Knightley—and perhaps we—might blame Emma for creating brilliant reading lists that exist as theory rather than practice—and for never taking her art, or her music, seriously enough to become truly proficient. Those arts are accomplishments, as we have noted, meant to polish Emma for society. If we look into the world of Jane Austen, the novelist, one outlet for a woman of Emma's imagination might lie in composing literary works. The novel *Emma* does not allow Emma to become a novelist, just as there are no "writing" characters in Jane Austen's works.

Novel writing was most often seen as a fit occupation for women of middling status—perhaps appropriate for Jane Fairfax or even the novel-loving Harriet Smith—or for Elizabeth Bennet or Jane Austen, both financially strapped daughters of gentlemen. It is almost inconceivable, though, to see the leading lady of Highbury writing for pleasure and profit. The social system, which seems to put Emma in a position of material and social independence, constrains her energetic intellect. *Emma* does not partake of Juvenalian satire. Instead, like Alexander Pope's brilliant poem, *The Rape of the Lock* (1714), written a century earlier but similarly skewering the foibles of English society, *Emma* incorporates a Horatian form of satire that amuses its readers by pointing out the faults of characters and society without arguing for, or even offering, a plausible and cohesive alternative worldview. The end of the novel does not provide us with Emma the novelist, but it does unite Emma and Mr. Knightley, its two most worthy characters, as safeguards for the decency, rationality, pragmatism, traditionalism, and intelligence exemplified by Donwell Abbey. Mr. Knightley lives in and takes care of his community; he farms his land in a way that makes social and economic sense. The fire of Emma's imagination is neither extinguished nor burning out of control at the novel's end. Life—both silly and wonderful—will go on.

And, too, life inside and outside Highbury will move ahead. The "pilfering" of Highbury poultry yards at the conclusion of the book signals that there is either something threatening from without or rotten from within the community—the narrator withholds further details. Mr. John Knightley, after all, lives in London, where he is raising his children, who are still technically heirs of Donwell Abbey. Brunswick Square, where he and Isabella live, is a bustling suburban development catering to a professional urban class at odds with the slow pace of Highbury. Everything from transportation, with the imminence of trains in nineteenth-century England, to shifts in the food chain, developments in religion, and world affairs, including the burgeoning British Empire, await. It is unclear how much of all this Austen herself saw on the horizon, although with brothers in the Navy she was aware of Britain's expanding global interests. Even though a very modern world lies outside of the novel's narration, it certainly would have been a part of the consciousness of Austen's readers, who would purchase or borrow a book edited and printed in London and distributed by this same developing economic system throughout the land, and, indeed, overseas. *Emma* itself, as a material object in the growing field of English culture, quickly became an important part of the modern world that Highbury finds itself in the midst of.

Conclusion

Emma is a brilliant work of art. I have attempted in this introduction to provide a set of issues and a few questions that might prompt twenty-first-century students to grapple with the novel's complexities. The combination of this introduction with the supplementary materials at the close of the volume should help readers understand how the world of *Emma* is both like and unlike ours. The novel's characters—and how they think and feel—are similar to us, but they are shaped by circumstances without a precise correspondence with our own culture. Any re-reading, let alone novelistic or cinematic re-make of *Emma*, mandates reinterpretation. The novel is born anew as a work of art with every reader's experience of it, and it is reborn for each reader encountering it for a second time or more.

Emma's complexity lies in its status as a seemingly accurate picture of life. Both the objective world of things and the workings of Emma's mind are presented in a way that many readers experience as convincingly realistic. The novel provides an illusion of the workings of people in real life, such that any moral or political conclusions we draw seem to represent our own judgments of life rather than resulting from the effects of subtle and effective propaganda. "Propaganda" sounds wrong as a label, since we normally associate this word with direct and often crude attempts to push an audience's thoughts to a desired conclusion. In contrast, the art in *Emma* is so complex that, as we have seen, it has been impossible for even the most subtle literary critics to agree on the novel's moral vision and political leanings. Reading *Emma* requires interaction. We impose meaning on the text just as the text pushes its various meanings onto us. Trying to understand *Emma*, with its interplay of psychological realism and moral vision, is like trying to understand ourselves and the world; we must be both introspective and exceedingly observant of what lies around us. Complete success eludes us—we must re-read, reflect, and change our minds—and perhaps become better people for having done so.

About This Edition

About the Text

The text of this Fourth Edition of the Norton Critical *Emma* is based on the 1816 edition published by John Murray. Stephen Parrish, editor of the previous three Norton Critical Editions of the novel, accepted most emendations made by R. W. Chapman in his groundbreaking edition of Austen's novels (Oxford: Clarendon, 1932–34). I in turn have accepted some of those emendations, and some of the additional emendations made by Parrish, but I have on occasion reverted to 1816 when changes did not seem required for clear meaning. My aim has been to provide a clear text that remains faithful to the spelling, punctuation, and grammar of early nineteenth-century writing and publishing practice, even when that practice does not conform to ours.

Supplementary Materials

Following the text are supplementary materials. First, there is a section, "Contexts," which includes the subsections "Jane Austen: Her Life and Fiction" and "Jane Austen: Her Art and Business." These include writings about Austen, Austen's correspondence, and background into the customs of the period, as well as two sets of verses that are referred to in the novel. Another subsection, "The Reception of Jane Austen, 1815–1950," contains excerpts from opinions on Austen's writing from the author's own day up until the 1950s. The pieces in this section demonstrate that critics of Austen's writing could be both perceptive about the fiction and reflective of their own day's dominant literary culture.

The "Criticism" section contains scholarly and critical work on *Emma* written in the past fifty years and arranged in chronological order. These essays are meant to help readers understand the novel from literary and historical perspectives, and they might act as models, in their field of inquiry and methods, for students' own critical efforts.

Finally, this edition includes both a "Chronology" that allows readers to understand Austen's personal and professional life and a "Selected Bibliography" of works that will be helpful to budding researchers.

The Text of
EMMA

EMMA:

A NOVEL.

IN THREE VOLUMES.

—◆—

BY THE

AUTHOR OF "PRIDE AND PREJUDICE,"
&c. &c.

—◆—

VOL. I.

═══════

LONDON:

PRINTED FOR JOHN MURRAY.

—

1816.

Title and dedication pages from the 1816 edition of *Emma* are reprinted courtesy of Rare and Manuscript Collections, Cornell University Library.

TO

HIS ROYAL HIGHNESS

THE PRINCE REGENT,

THIS WORK IS,

BY HIS ROYAL HIGHNESS'S PERMISSION,

MOST RESPECTFULLY

DEDICATED,

BY HIS ROYAL HIGHNESS'S

DUTIFUL

AND OBEDIENT

HUMBLE SERVANT,

THE AUTHOR.

Volume I

Chapter I

Emma Woodhouse, handsome, clever, and rich, with a comfortable home and happy disposition, seemed to unite some of the best blessings of existence; and had lived nearly twenty-one years in the world with very little to distress or vex her.

She was the youngest of the two daughters of a most affectionate, indulgent father, and had, in consequence of her sister's marriage, been mistress of his house from a very early period. Her mother had died too long ago for her to have more than an indistinct remembrance of her caresses, and her place had been supplied by an excellent woman as governess, who had fallen little short of a mother in affection.

Sixteen years had Miss Taylor been in Mr. Woodhouse's family, less as a governess than a friend, very fond of both daughters, but particularly of Emma. Between *them* it was more the intimacy of sisters. Even before Miss Taylor had ceased to hold the nominal office of governess, the mildness of her temper had hardly allowed her to impose any restraint; and the shadow of authority being now long passed away, they had been living together as friend and friend very mutually attached, and Emma doing just what she liked; highly esteeming Miss Taylor's judgment, but directed chiefly by her own.

The real evils indeed of Emma's situation were the power of having rather too much her own way, and a disposition to think a little too well of herself; these were the disadvantages which threatened alloy to her many enjoyments. The danger, however, was at present so unperceived, that they did not by any means rank as misfortunes with her.

Sorrow came—a gentle sorrow—but not at all in the shape of any disagreeable consciousness.—Miss Taylor married. It was Miss Taylor's loss which first brought grief. It was on the wedding-day of this beloved friend that Emma first sat in mournful thought of any continuance. The wedding over and the bride-people gone, her father and herself were left to dine together, with no prospect of a third to cheer a long evening. Her father composed himself to sleep after dinner,[1] as usual, and she had then only to sit and think of what she had lost.

The event had every promise of happiness for her friend. Mr. Weston was a man of unexceptionable character, easy fortune, suitable age and pleasant manners; and there was some satisfaction in

---

1. Normally served about 4:00 P.M. (see p. 347); tea came later, and supper (if served) was close to bedtime.

5

considering with what self-denying, generous friendship she had always wished and promoted the match; but it was a black morning's work for her. The want of Miss Taylor would be felt every hour of every day. She recalled her past kindness—the kindness, the affection of sixteen years—how she had taught and how she had played with her from five years old—how she had devoted all her powers to attach and amuse her in health—and how nursed her through the various illnesses of childhood. A large debt of gratitude was owing here; but the intercourse of the last seven years, the equal footing and perfect unreserve which had soon followed Isabella's marriage on their being left to each other, was yet a dearer, tenderer recollection. It had been a friend and companion such as few possessed, intelligent, well-informed, useful, gentle, knowing all the ways of the family, interested in all its concerns, and peculiarly interested in herself, in every pleasure, every scheme of her's;—one to whom she could speak every thought as it arose, and who had such an affection for her as could never find fault.

How was she to bear the change?—It was true that her friend was going only half a mile from them; but Emma was aware that great must be the difference between a Mrs. Weston only half a mile from them, and a Miss Taylor in the house; and with all her advantages, natural and domestic, she was now in great danger of suffering from intellectual solitude. She dearly loved her father, but he was no companion for her. He could not meet her in conversation, rational or playful.

The evil of the actual disparity in their ages (and Mr. Woodhouse had not married early) was much increased by his constitution and habits; for having been a valetudinarian[2] all his life, without activity of mind or body, he was a much older man in ways than in years; and though everywhere beloved for the friendliness of his heart and his amiable temper, his talents could not have recommended him at any time.

Her sister, though comparatively but little removed by matrimony, being settled in London, only sixteen miles off, was much beyond her daily reach; and many a long October and November evening must be struggled through at Hartfield, before Christmas brought the next visit from Isabella and her husband and their little children to fill the house and give her pleasant society again.

Highbury[3], the large and populous village almost amounting to a town, to which Hartfield, in spite of its separate lawn and shrub-

2. In weak health; overly concerned with his own ailments.
3. A fictional town in the county of Surrey, located to the south and west of London. We learn later that it is sixteen miles from Brunswick Square in London, and seven miles from Box Hill, Surrey, putting it somewhere near Banstead. Surrey remains one of the most affluent counties in England, and Highbury's location puts it at the center of

beries and name, did really belong, afforded her no equals. The Woodhouses were first in consequence there. All looked up to them. She had many acquaintance in the place, for her father was universally civil, but not one among them who could be accepted in lieu of Miss Taylor for even half a day. It was a melancholy change; and Emma could not but sigh over it and wish for impossible things, till her father awoke, and made it necessary to be cheerful. His spirits required support. He was a nervous man, easily depressed; fond of every body that he was used to, and hating to part with them; hating change of every kind. Matrimony, as the origin of change, was always disagreeable; and he was by no means yet reconciled to his own daughter's marrying, nor could ever speak of her but with compassion, though it had been entirely a match of affection, when he was now obliged to part with Miss Taylor too; and from his habits of gentle selfishness and of being never able to suppose that other people could feel differently from himself, he was very much disposed to think Miss Taylor had done as sad a thing for herself as for them, and would have been a great deal happier if she had spent all the rest of her life at Hartfield. Emma smiled and chatted as cheerfully as she could, to keep him from such thoughts; but when tea came, it was impossible for him not to say exactly as he had said at dinner,

"Poor Miss Taylor!—I wish she were here again. What a pity it is that Mr. Weston ever thought of her!"

"I cannot agree with you, papa; you know I cannot. Mr. Weston is such a good-humoured, pleasant, excellent man, that he thoroughly deserves a good wife;—and you would not have had Miss Taylor live with us for ever and bear all my odd humours, when she might have a house of her own?"

"A house of her own!—but where is the advantage of a house of her own? This is three times as large.—And you have never any odd humours, my dear."

"How often we shall be going to see them and they coming to see us!—We shall be always meeting! *We* must begin, we must go and pay our wedding-visit very soon."

"My dear, how am I to get so far? Randalls[4] is such a distance. I could not walk half so far."

"No, papa, nobody thought of your walking. We must go in the carriage to be sure."

English life, traditionally rural in nature but within easy access of commercial life in London.
4. Not another village, but (like Hartfield) a house in Highbury.

"The carriage! But James will not like to put the horses to for such a little way;—and where are the poor horses to be while we are paying our visit?"

"They are to be put into Mr. Weston's stable, papa. You know we have settled all that already. We talked it all over with Mr. Weston last night. And as for James, you may be very sure he will always like going to Randalls, because of his daughter's being housemaid there. I only doubt whether he will ever take us anywhere else. That, was your doing, papa. You got Hannah that good place. Nobody thought of Hannah till you mentioned her—James is so obliged to you!"

"I am very glad I did think of her. It was very lucky, for I would not have had poor James think himself slighted upon any account; and I am sure she will make a very good servant; she is a civil, pretty-spoken girl; I have a great opinion of her. Whenever I see her, she always curtseys and asks me how I do, in a very pretty manner; and when you have had her here to do needlework, I observe she always turns the lock of the door the right way and never bangs it. I am sure she will be an excellent servant; and it will be a great comfort to poor Miss Taylor to have somebody about her that she is used to see. Whenever James goes over to see his daughter you know, she will be hearing of us. He will be able to tell her how we all are."

Emma spared no exertions to maintain this happier flow of ideas, and hoped, by the help of backgammon, to get her father tolerably through the evening, and be attacked by no regrets but her own. The backgammon-table was placed; but a visitor immediately afterwards walked in and made it unnecessary.

Mr. Knightley, a sensible man about seven or eight-and-thirty, was not only a very old and intimate friend of the family, but particularly connected with it as the elder brother of Isabella's husband. He lived about a mile from Highbury, was a frequent visitor and always welcome, and at this time more welcome than usual, as coming directly from their mutual connections in London. He had returned to a late dinner after some days absence, and now walked up to Hartfield to say that all were well in Brunswick-square. It was a happy circumstance and animated Mr. Woodhouse for some time. Mr. Knightley had a cheerful manner which always did him good; and his many inquiries after "poor Isabella" and her children were answered most satisfactorily. When this was over, Mr. Woodhouse gratefully observed,

"It is very kind of you, Mr. Knightley, to come out at this late hour to call upon us. I am afraid you must have had a shocking walk."

"Not at all, sir. It is a beautiful, moonlight night; and so mild that I must draw back from your great fire."

"But you must have found it very damp and dirty. I wish you may not catch cold."

"Dirty, sir! Look at my shoes. Not a speck on them."

"Well! that is quite surprizing, for we have had a vast deal of rain here. It rained dreadfully hard for half an hour, while we were at breakfast. I wanted them to put off the wedding."

"By the bye—I have not wished you joy. Being pretty well aware of what sort of joy you must both be feeling, I have been in no hurry with my congratulations. But I hope it all went off tolerably well. How did you all behave? Who cried most?"

"Ah! poor Miss Taylor! 'tis a sad business."

"Poor Mr. and Miss Woodhouse, if you please; but I cannot possibly say 'poor Miss Taylor.' I have a great regard for you and Emma; but when it comes to the question of dependence or independence!—At any rate, it must be better to have only one to please, than two."

"Especially when *one* of those two is such a fanciful, troublesome creature!" said Emma playfully. "That, is what you have in your head, I know—and what you would certainly say if my father were not by."

"I believe it is very true, my dear, indeed," said Mr. Woodhouse with a sigh. "I am afraid I am sometimes very fanciful and troublesome."

"My dearest papa! You do not think I could mean *you*, or suppose Mr. Knightley to mean *you*. What a horrible idea! Oh, no! I meant only myself. Mr. Knightley loves to find fault with me you know—in a joke—it is all a joke. We always say what we like to one another."

Mr. Knightley, in fact, was one of the few people who could see faults in Emma Woodhouse, and the only one who ever told her of them: and though this was not particularly agreeable to Emma herself, she knew it would be so much less so to her father, that she would not have him really suspect such a circumstance as her not being thought perfect by every body.

"Emma knows I never flatter her," said Mr. Knightley; "but I meant no reflection on any body. Miss Taylor has been used to have two persons to please; she will now have but one. The chances are that she must be a gainer."

"Well," said Emma, willing to let it pass—"you want to hear about the wedding, and I shall be happy to tell you, for we all behaved charmingly. Every body was punctual, every body in their best looks. Not a tear, and hardly a long face to be seen. Oh! no, we all felt that we were going to be only half a mile apart, and were sure of meeting every day."

"Dear Emma bears every thing so well," said her father. "But, Mr. Knightley, she is really very sorry to lose poor Miss Taylor, and I am sure she *will* miss her more than she thinks for."

Emma turned away her head, divided between tears and smiles.

"It is impossible that Emma should not miss such a companion," said Mr. Knightley. "We should not like her so well as we do, sir, if we could suppose it. But she knows how much the marriage is to Miss Taylor's advantage; she knows how very acceptable it must be at Miss Taylor's time of life to be settled in a home of her own, and how important to her to be secure of a comfortable provision, and therefore cannot allow herself to feel so much pain as pleasure. Every friend of Miss Taylor must be glad to have her so happily married."

"And you have forgotten one matter of joy to me," said Emma, "and a very considerable one—that I made the match myself. I made the match, you know, four years ago; and to have it take place, and be proved in the right, when so many people said Mr. Weston would never marry again, may comfort me for any thing."

Mr. Knightley shook his head at her. Her father fondly replied, "Ah! my dear, I wish you would not make matches and foretel things, for whatever you say always comes to pass. Pray do not make any more matches."

"I promise you to make none for myself, papa; but I must, indeed, for other people. It is the greatest amusement in the world! And after such success you know!—Every body said that Mr. Weston would never marry again. Oh, dear, no! Mr. Weston, who had been a widower so long, and who seemed so perfectly comfortable without a wife, so constantly occupied either in his business in town or among his friends here, always acceptable wherever he went, always cheerful—Mr. Weston need not spend a single evening in the year alone if he did not like it. Oh, no! Mr. Weston certainly would never marry again. Some people even talked of a promise to his wife on her death-bed, and others of the son and the uncle not letting him. All manner of solemn nonsense was talked on the subject, but I believed none of it. Ever since the day (about four years ago) that Miss Taylor and I met with him in Broadway-lane, when, because it began to mizzle,[5] he darted away with so much gallantry, and borrowed two umbrellas for us from Farmer Mitchell's, I made up my mind on the subject. I planned the match from that hour; and when such success has blessed me in this instance, dear papa, you cannot think that I shall leave off match-making."

"I do not understand what you mean by 'success;'" said Mr. Knightley. "Success supposes endeavour. Your time has been properly and delicately spent, if you have been endeavouring for the last four years to bring about this marriage. A worthy employment for a young lady's mind! But if, which I rather imagine, your making the match, as you

5. Drizzle.

call it, means only your planning it, your saying to yourself one idle day, 'I think it would be a very good thing for Miss Taylor if Mr. Weston were to marry her,' and saying it again to yourself every now and then afterwards,—why do you talk of success? where is your merit?—what are you proud of?—you made a lucky guess; and *that* is all that can be said."

"And have you never known the pleasure and triumph of a lucky guess?—I pity you.—I thought you cleverer—for depend upon it, a lucky guess is never merely luck. There is always some talent in it. And as to my poor word 'success,' which you quarrel with, I do not know that I am so entirely without any claim to it. You have drawn two pretty pictures—but I think there may be a third—a something between the do-nothing and the do-all. If I had not promoted Mr. Weston's visits here, and given many little encouragements, and smoothed many little matters, it might not have come to any thing after all. I think you must know Hartfield enough to comprehend that."

"A straight-forward, open-hearted man, like Weston, and a rational unaffected woman, like Miss Taylor, may be safely left to manage their own concerns. You are more likely to have done harm to yourself, than good to them, by interference."

"Emma never thinks of herself, if she can do good to others;" rejoined Mr. Woodhouse, understanding but in part. "But, my dear, pray do not make any more matches, they are silly things, and break up one's family circle grievously."

"Only one more, papa; only for Mr. Elton. Poor Mr. Elton! You like Mr. Elton, papa,—I must look about for a wife for him. There is nobody in Highbury who deserves him—and he has been here a whole year, and has fitted up his house so comfortably that it would be a shame to have him single any longer—and I thought when he was joining their hands to-day, he looked so very much as if he would like to have the same kind office done for him! I think very well of Mr. Elton, and this is the only way I have of doing him a service."

"Mr. Elton is a very pretty young man to be sure, and a very good young man, and I have a great regard for him. But if you want to shew him any attention, my dear, ask him to come and dine with us some day. That will be a much better thing. I dare say Mr. Knightley will be so kind as to meet him."

"With a great deal of pleasure, sir, at any time," said Mr. Knightley laughing; "and I agree with you entirely that it will be a much better thing. Invite him to dinner, Emma, and help him to the best of the fish and the chicken, but leave him to chuse his own wife. Depend upon it, a man of six or seven-and-twenty can take care of himself."

Chapter II

Mr. Weston was a native of Highbury, and born of a respectable family, which for the last two or three generations had been rising into gentility and property. He had received a good education, but on succeeding early in life to a small independence, had become indisposed for any of the more homely pursuits in which his brothers were engaged; and had satisfied an active cheerful mind and social temper by entering into the militia of his county, then embodied.[6]

Captain Weston was a general favourite; and when the chances of his military life had introduced him to Miss Churchill, of a great Yorkshire family, and Miss Churchill fell in love with him, nobody was surprized except her brother and his wife, who had never seen him, and who were full of pride and importance, which the connection would offend.

Miss Churchill, however, being of age, and with the full command of her fortune—though her fortune bore no proportion to the family-estate—was not to be dissuaded from the marriage, and it took place to the infinite mortification of Mr. and Mrs. Churchill, who threw her off with due decorum. It was an unsuitable connection, and did not produce much happiness. Mrs. Weston ought to have found more in it, for she had a husband whose warm heart and sweet temper made him think every thing due to her in return for the great goodness of being in love with him; but though she had one sort of spirit, she had not the best. She had resolution enough to pursue her own will in spite of her brother, but not enough to refrain from unreasonable regrets at that brother's unreasonable anger, nor from missing the luxuries of her former home. They lived beyond their income, but still it was nothing in comparison of Enscombe: she did not cease to love her husband, but she wanted at once to be the wife of Captain Weston, and Miss Churchill of Enscombe.

Captain Weston, who had been considered, especially by the Churchills, as making such an amazing match, was proved to have much the worst of the bargain; for when his wife died after a three years' marriage, he was rather a poorer man than at first, and with a child to maintain. From the expense of the child, however, he was soon relieved. The boy had, with the additional softening claim of a lingering illness of his mother's, been the means of a sort of reconciliation; and Mr. and Mrs. Churchill, having no children of their own, nor any other young creature of equal kindred to care for, offered to take the whole charge of the little Frank soon after her

---

6. Mobilized.

decease. Some scruples and some reluctance the widower-father may be supposed to have felt; but as they were overcome by other considerations, the child was given up to the care and the wealth of the Churchills, and he had only his own comfort to seek and his own situation to improve as he could.

A complete change of life became desirable. He quitted the militia and engaged in trade, having brothers already established in a good way in London, which afforded him a favourable opening. It was a concern which brought just employment enough. He had still a small house in Highbury, where most of his leisure days were spent; and between useful occupation and the pleasures of society, the next eighteen or twenty years of his life passed cheerfully away. He had, by that time, realized an easy competence—[7]enough to secure the purchase of a little estate adjoining Highbury, which he had always longed for—enough to marry a woman as portionless even as Miss Taylor, and to live according to the wishes of his own friendly and social disposition.

It was now some time since Miss Taylor had begun to influence his schemes; but as it was not the tyrannic influence of youth on youth, it had not shaken his determination of never settling till he could purchase Randalls, and the sale of Randalls was long looked forward to: but he had gone steadily on, with these objects in view, till they were accomplished. He had made his fortune, bought his house, and obtained his wife; and was beginning a new period of existence with every probability of greater happiness than in any yet passed through. He had never been an unhappy man; his own temper had secured him from that, even in his first marriage; but his second must shew him how delightful a well-judging and truly amiable woman could be, and must give him the pleasantest proof of its being a great deal better to chuse than to be chosen, to excite gratitude than to feel it.

He had only himself to please in his choice: his fortune was his own; for as to Frank, it was more than being tacitly brought up as his uncle's heir, it had become so avowed an adoption as to have him assume the name of Churchill on coming of age. It was most unlikely, therefore, that he should ever want his father's assistance. His father had no apprehension of it. The aunt was a capricious woman, and governed her husband entirely; but it was not in Mr. Weston's nature to imagine that any caprice could be strong enough to affect one so dear, and, as he believed, so deservedly dear. He

---

7. An adequate amount of income to live comfortably without undertaking labor (similar to the "independence" to which Mr. Weston was born). As the oldest brother, Mr. Weston initially inherited his family's wealth, while his younger brothers (like Mr. John Knightley) would have pursued professional careers. He regained his wealth and status both through marriage and through joining his brothers in business.

saw his son every year in London, and was proud of him; and his fond[8] report of him as a very fine young man had made Highbury feel a sort of pride in him too. He was looked on as sufficiently belonging to the place to make his merits and prospects a kind of common concern.

Mr. Frank Churchill was one of the boasts of Highbury, and a lively curiosity to see him prevailed, though the compliment was so little returned that he had never been there in his life. His coming to visit his father had been often talked of but never achieved.

Now, upon his father's marriage, it was very generally proposed, as a most proper attention, that the visit should take place. There was not a dissentient voice on the subject, either when Mrs. Perry drank tea with Mrs. and Miss Bates, or when Mrs. and Miss Bates returned the visit. Now was the time for Mr. Frank Churchill to come among them; and the hope strengthened when it was understood that he had written to his new mother on the occasion. For a few days every morning visit in Highbury included some mention of the handsome letter Mrs. Weston had received. "I suppose you have heard of the handsome letter Mr. Frank Churchill had written to Mrs. Weston? I understand it was a very handsome letter, indeed. Mr. Woodhouse told me of it. Mr. Woodhouse saw the letter, and he says he never saw such a handsome letter in his life."

It was, indeed, a highly-prized letter. Mrs. Weston had, of course, formed a very favourable idea of the young man; and such a pleasing attention was an irresistible proof of his great good sense, and a most welcome addition to every source and every expression of congratulation which her marriage had already secured. She felt herself a most fortunate woman; and she had lived long enough to know how fortunate she might well be thought, where the only regret was for a partial separation from friends, whose friendship for her had never cooled, and who could ill bear to part with her!

She knew that at times she must be missed; and could not think, without pain, of Emma's losing a single pleasure, or suffering an hour's ennui, from the want of her companionableness: but dear Emma was of no feeble character; she was more equal to her situation than most girls would have been, and had sense and energy and spirits that might be hoped would bear her well and happily through its little difficulties and privations. And then there was such comfort in the very easy distance of Randalls from Hartfield, so convenient for even solitary female walking, and in Mr. Weston's disposition and circumstances, which would make the approaching season no hindrance to their spending half the evenings in the week together.

---

8. Both affectionate and foolishly doating.

Her situation was altogether the subject of hours of gratitude to Mrs. Weston, and of moments only of regret; and her satisfaction—her more than satisfaction—her cheerful enjoyment was so just and so apparent, that Emma, well as she knew her father, was sometimes taken by surprize at his being still able to pity "poor Miss Taylor," when they left her at Randalls in the centre of every domestic comfort, or saw her go away in the evening attended by her pleasant husband to a carriage of her own. But never did she go without Mr. Woodhouse's giving a gentle sigh, and saying:

"Ah! poor Miss Taylor. She would be very glad to stay."

There was no recovering Miss Taylor—nor much likelihood of ceasing to pity her: but a few weeks brought some alleviation to Mr. Woodhouse. The compliments of his neighbours were over; he was no longer teased by being wished joy of so sorrowful an event; and the wedding-cake, which had been a great distress to him, was all eat up. His own stomach could bear nothing rich, and he could never believe other people to be different from himself. What was unwholesome to him, he regarded as unfit for any body; and he had, therefore, earnestly tried to dissuade them from having any wedding-cake at all, and when that proved vain, as earnestly tried to prevent any body's eating it. He had been at the pains of consulting Mr. Perry, the apothecary,[9] on the subject. Mr. Perry was an intelligent, gentlemanlike man, whose frequent visits were one of the comforts of Mr. Woodhouse's life; and, upon being applied to, he could not but acknowledge, (though it seemed rather against the bias of inclination,) that wedding-cake might certainly disagree with many—perhaps with most people, unless taken moderately. With such an opinion, in confirmation of his own, Mr. Woodhouse hoped to influence every visitor of the new-married pair; but still the cake was eaten; and there was no rest for his benevolent nerves till it was all gone.

There was a strange rumour in Highbury of all the little Perrys being seen with a slice of Mrs. Weston's wedding-cake in their hands: but Mr. Woodhouse would never believe it.

Chapter III

Mr. Woodhouse was fond of society in his own way. He liked very much to have his friends come and see him; and from various united causes, from his long residence at Hartfield, and his good nature, from his fortune, his house, and his daughter, he could command the visits of his own little circle, in a great measure as he liked. He had not much intercourse with any families beyond that

---

9. Not just a druggist, but a general medical practitioner.

circle; his horror of late hours and large dinner-parties made him unfit for any acquaintance, but such as would visit him on his own terms. Fortunately for him, Highbury, including Randalls in the same parish, and Donwell Abbey in the parish adjoining, the seat[1] of Mr. Knightley, comprehended many such. Not unfrequently, through Emma's persuasion, he had some of the chosen and the best to dine with him, but evening-parties were what he preferred, and, unless he fancied himself at any time unequal to company, there was scarcely an evening in the week in which Emma could not make up a card-table for him.

Real, long-standing regard brought the Westons and Mr. Knightley; and by Mr. Elton, a young man living alone without liking it, the privilege of exchanging any vacant evening of his own blank solitude for the elegancies and society of Mr. Woodhouse's drawing-room[2] and the smiles of his lovely daughter, was in no danger of being thrown away.

After these came a second set; among the most come-at-able of whom were Mrs. and Miss Bates and Mrs. Goddard, three ladies almost always at the service of an invitation from Hartfield, and who were fetched and carried home so often that Mr. Woodhouse thought it no hardship for either James or the horses. Had it taken place only once a year, it would have been a grievance.

Mrs. Bates, the widow of a former vicar of Highbury, was a very old lady, almost past every thing but tea and quadrille.[3] She lived with her single daughter in a very small way, and was considered with all the regard and respect which a harmless old lady, under such untoward circumstances, can excite. Her daughter enjoyed a most uncommon degree of popularity for a woman neither young, handsome, rich, nor married. Miss Bates stood in the very worst predicament in the world for having much of the public favour; and she had no intellectual superiority to make atonement to herself, or frighten those who might hate her, into outward respect. She had never boasted either beauty or cleverness. Her youth had passed without distinction, and her middle of life was devoted to the care of a failing mother, and the endeavour to make a small income go as far as possible. And yet she was a happy woman, and a woman whom no one named without good-will. It was her own universal good-will and contented temper which worked such wonders. She loved every body, was interested in every body's happiness, quick-sighted to every body's merits; thought herself a most fortunate creature, and surrounded with blessings in such an excellent

1. Estate or home.
2. An exceptionally handsome or spacious parlor (that is, living room).
3. A card game, played by four persons, related to bridge.

mother and so many good neighbours and friends, and a home that wanted for nothing. The simplicity and cheerfulness of her nature, her contented and grateful spirit, were a recommendation to every body and a mine of felicity to herself. She was a great talker upon little matters, which exactly suited Mr. Woodhouse, full of trivial communications and harmless gossip.

Mrs. Goddard was the mistress of a School—not of a seminary, or an establishment, or any thing which professed, in long sentences of refined nonsense, to combine liberal acquirements with elegant morality upon new principles and new systems—and where young ladies for enormous pay might be screwed out of health and into vanity—but a real, honest, old-fashioned Boarding-school, where a reasonable quantity of accomplishments were sold at a reasonable price, and where girls might be sent to be out of the way and scramble themselves into a little education, without any danger of coming back prodigies. Mrs. Goddard's school was in high repute—and very deservedly; for Highbury was reckoned a particularly healthy spot: she had an ample house and garden, gave the children plenty of wholesome food, let them run about a great deal in the summer, and in winter dressed their chilblains[4] with her own hands. It was no wonder that a train of twenty young couple now walked after her to church. She was a plain, motherly kind of woman, who had worked hard in her youth, and now thought herself entitled to the occasional holiday of a tea-visit; and having formerly owed much to Mr. Woodhouse's kindness, felt his particular claim on her to leave her neat parlour hung round with fancy-work[5] whenever she could, and win or lose a few sixpences by his fireside.

These were the ladies whom Emma found herself very frequently able to collect; and happy was she, for her father's sake, in the power: though, as far as she was herself concerned, it was no remedy for the absence of Mrs. Weston. She was delighted to see her father look comfortable, and very much pleased with herself for contriving things so well; but the quiet prosings[6] of three such women made her feel that every evening so spent, was indeed one of the long evenings she had fearfully anticipated.

As she sat one morning, looking forward to exactly such a close of the present day, a note was brought from Mrs. Goddard, requesting, in most respectful terms, to be allowed to bring Miss Smith with her; a most welcome request: for Miss Smith was a girl of seventeen whom Emma knew very well by sight and had long felt an interest in, on account of her beauty. A very gracious invitation was

4. Painful skin ulcers, typically on hands or feet, caused by the exposure of skin to cold and humid conditions; *dressed*: treated.
5. Ornamental needlework or embroidery.
6. Tiresome discourse.

returned, and the evening no longer dreaded by the fair mistress of the mansion.

Harriet Smith was the natural[7] daughter of somebody. Somebody had placed her, several years back, at Mrs. Goddard's school, and somebody had lately raised her from the condition of scholar to that of parlour-boarder.[8] This was all that was generally known of her history. She had no visible friends but what had been acquired at Highbury, and was now just returned from a long visit in the country to some young ladies who had been at school there with her.

She was a very pretty girl, and her beauty happened to be of a sort which Emma particularly admired. She was short, plump and fair, with a fine bloom, blue eyes, light hair, regular features, and a look of great sweetness; and before the end of the evening, Emma was as much pleased with her manners as her person, and quite determined to continue the acquaintance.

She was not struck by any thing remarkably clever in Miss Smith's conversation, but she found her altogether very engaging——not inconveniently shy, not unwilling to talk—and yet so far from pushing, shewing so proper and becoming a deference, seeming so pleasantly grateful for being admitted to Hartfield, and so artlessly[9] impressed by the appearance of every thing in so superior a style to what she had been used to, that she must have good sense and deserve encouragement. Encouragement should be given. Those soft blue eyes and all those natural graces should not be wasted on the inferior society of Highbury and its connections. The acquaintance she had already formed were unworthy of her. The friends from whom she had just parted, though very good sort of people, must be doing her harm. They were a family of the name of Martin, whom Emma well knew by character, as renting a large farm of Mr. Knightley, and residing in the parish of Donwell—very creditably she believed—she knew Mr. Knightley thought highly of them—but they must be coarse and unpolished, and very unfit to be the intimates of a girl who wanted only a little more knowledge and elegance to be quite perfect. *She* would notice her; she would improve her; she would detach her from her bad acquaintance, and introduce her into good society; she would form her opinions and her manners. It would be an interesting, and certainly a very kind undertaking; highly becoming her own situation in life, her leisure, and powers.

She was so busy in admiring those soft blue eyes, in talking and listening, and forming all these schemes in the in-betweens, that

7. Illegitimate.
8. A boarding-school student who lived with the headmaster's family.
9. Without guile; ingenuously. See Introduction for discussion.

the evening flew away at a very unusual rate; and the supper-table,[1] which always closed such parties, and for which she had been used to sit and watch the due time, was all set out and ready, and moved forwards to the fire, before she was aware. With an alacrity beyond the common impulse of a spirit which yet was never indifferent to the credit of doing every thing well and attentively, with the real good-will of a mind delighted with its own ideas, did she then do all the honours of the meal, and help and recommend the minced chicken and scalloped oysters with an urgency which she knew would be acceptable to the early hours and civil scruples of their guests.

Upon such occasions poor Mr. Woodhouse's feelings were in sad warfare. He loved to have the cloth laid, because it had been the fashion of his youth; but his conviction of suppers being very unwholesome made him rather sorry to see any thing put on it; and while his hospitality would have welcomed his visitors to every thing, his care for their health made him grieve that they would eat.

Such another small basin of thin gruel[2] as his own, was all that he could, with thorough self-approbation, recommend, though he might constrain himself, while the ladies were comfortably clearing the nicer things, to say:

"Mrs. Bates, let me propose your venturing on one of these eggs. An egg boiled very soft is not unwholesome. Serle understands boiling an egg better than any body. I would not recommend an egg boiled by any body else—but you need not be afraid—they are very small, you see—one of our small eggs will not hurt you. Miss Bates, let Emma help you to a *little* bit of tart—a *very* little bit. Ours are all apple tarts. You need not be afraid of unwholesome preserves here. I do not advise the custard. Mrs. Goddard, what say you to *half* a glass of wine? A *small* half glass—put into a tumbler of water? I do not think it could disagree with you."

Emma allowed her father to talk—but supplied her visitors in a much more satisfactory style; and on the present evening had particular pleasure in sending them away happy. The happiness of Miss Smith was quite equal to her intentions. Miss Woodhouse was so great a personage in Highbury, that the prospect of the introduction had given as much panic as pleasure—but the humble, grateful, little girl went off with highly gratified feelings, delighted with the affability with which Miss Woodhouse had treated her all the evening, and actually shaken hands with her at last!

---

1. See "Daily Life in Jane Austen's England" in this Norton Critical Edition. Mr. Woodhouse's preference for early hours and limited supper reflect his traditionalism as well as his valetudinarianism.
2. Bowl of oatmeal broth.

Chapter IV

Harriet Smith's intimacy at Hartfield was soon a settled thing. Quick and decided in her ways, Emma lost no time in inviting, encouraging, and telling her to come very often; and as their acquaintance increased, so did their satisfaction in each other. As a walking companion, Emma had very early foreseen how useful she might find her. In that respect Mrs. Weston's loss had been important. Her father never went beyond the shrubbery, where two divisions of the grounds sufficed him for his long walk, or his short, as the year varied; and since Mrs. Weston's marriage her exercise had been too much confined. She had ventured once alone to Randalls, but it was not pleasant; and a Harriet Smith, therefore, one whom she could summon at any time to a walk, would be a valuable addition to her privileges. But in every respect as she saw more of her, she approved her, and was confirmed in all her kind designs.

Harriet certainly was not clever, but she had a sweet, docile, grateful disposition; was totally free from conceit; and only desiring to be guided by any one she looked up to. Her early attachment to herself was very amiable; and her inclination for good company, and power of appreciating what was elegant and clever, shewed that there was no want of taste, though strength of understanding must not be expected. Altogether she was quite convinced of Harriet Smith's being exactly the young friend she wanted—exactly the something which her home required. Such a friend as Mrs. Weston was out of the question. Two such could never be granted. Two such she did not want. It was quite a different sort of thing—a sentiment distinct and independent. Mrs. Weston was the object of a regard, which had its basis in gratitude and esteem. Harriet would be loved as one to whom she could be useful. For Mrs. Weston there was nothing to be done; for Harriet every thing.

Her first attempts at usefulness were in an endeavour to find out who were the parents; but Harriet could not tell. She was ready to tell every thing in her power, but on this subject questions were vain. Emma was obliged to fancy what she liked—but she could never believe that in the same situation *she* should not have discovered the truth. Harriet had no penetration. She had been satisfied to hear and believe just what Mrs. Goddard chose to tell her; and looked no farther.

Mrs. Goddard, and the teachers, and the girls, and the affairs of the school in general, formed naturally a great part of her conversation—and but for her acquaintance with the Martins of Abbey-Mill-Farm, it must have been the whole. But the Martins occupied her thoughts a good deal; she had spent two very happy months with them, and now loved to talk of the pleasures of her visit, and describe the many comforts and wonders of the place. Emma encouraged her talkativeness—amused by such a picture of another set of beings, and enjoying the youthful simplicity which could speak with so much exultation of Mrs. Martin's having "*two* parlours, two very good parlours indeed; one of them quite as large as Mrs. Goddard's drawing-room; and of her having an upper maid who had lived five-and-twenty years with her; and of their having eight cows, two of them Alderneys, and one a little Welch cow, a very pretty little Welch cow, indeed; and of Mrs. Martin's saying, as she was so fond of it, it should be called *her* cow; and of their having a very handsome summer-house in their garden, where some day next year they were all to drink tea:—a very handsome summer-house, large enough to hold a dozen people."

For some time she was amused, without thinking beyond the immediate cause; but as she came to understand the family better, other feelings arose. She had taken up a wrong idea, fancying it was a mother and daughter, a son and son's wife, who all lived together; but when it appeared that the Mr. Martin, who bore a part in the narrative, and was always mentioned with approbation for his great good-nature in doing something or other, was a single man; that there was no young Mrs. Martin, no wife in the case; she did suspect danger to her poor little friend from all this hospitality and kindness—and that if she were not taken care of, she might be required to sink herself for ever.

With this inspiring notion, her questions increased in number and meaning; and she particularly led Harriet to talk more of Mr. Martin,—and there was evidently no dislike to it. Harriet was very ready to speak of the share he had had in their moonlight walks and merry evening games; and dwelt a good deal upon his being so very good-humoured and obliging. "He had gone three miles round one day, in order to bring her some walnuts, because she had said how fond she was of them—and in every thing else he was so very obliging! He had his shepherd's son into the parlour one night on purpose to sing to her. She was very fond of singing. He could sing a little himself. She believed he was very clever, and understood every thing. He had a very fine flock; and while she was with them, he had been bid more for his wool than any body in the country. She believed every body spoke well of him. His mother and sisters were very fond of him. Mrs. Martin had told her one day, (and there was a blush as she said it,) that it was impossible for any body to be a better son; and therefore she was sure whenever he married he would make a good husband. Not that she *wanted* him to marry. She was in no hurry at all."

"Well done, Mrs. Martin!" thought Emma. "You know what you are about."

"And when she had come away, Mrs. Martin was so very kind as to send Mrs. Goddard a beautiful goose: the finest goose Mrs. Goddard had ever seen. Mrs. Goddard had dressed[3] it on a Sunday, and asked all the three teachers, Miss Nash, and Miss Prince, and Miss Richardson, to sup with her."

"Mr. Martin, I suppose, is not a man of information beyond the line of his own business. He does not read?"

"Oh, yes!—that is, no—I do not know—but I believe he has read a good deal—but not what you would think any thing of. He reads the Agricultural Reports and some other books, that lay in one of the window seats—but he reads all *them* to himself. But sometimes of an evening, before we went to cards, he would read something aloud out of the Elegant Extracts—very entertaining. And I know he has read the Vicar of Wakefield. He never read the Romance of the Forest, nor the Children of the Abbey. He had never heard of such books before I mentioned them, but he is determined to get them now as soon as ever he can."[4]

The next question was:

"What sort of looking man is Mr. Martin?"

"Oh! not handsome—not at all handsome. I thought him very plain at first, but I do not think him so plain now. One does not, you know, after a time. But, did you never see him? He is in Highbury every now and then, and he is sure to ride through every week in his way to Kingston. He has passed you very often."

"That may be—and I may have seen him fifty times, but without having any idea of his name. A young farmer, whether on horseback or on foot, is the very last sort of person to raise my curiosity. The yeomanry are precisely the order of people with whom I feel I can have nothing to do. A degree or two lower, and a creditable appearance might interest me; I might hope to be useful to their families in some way or other. But a farmer can need none of my help, and is therefore in one sense as much above my notice as in every other he is below it."

"To be sure. Oh! yes, it is not likely you should ever have observed him—but he knows you very well indeed—I mean by sight."

"I have no doubt of his being a very respectable young man. I know indeed that he is so; and as such wish him well. What do you imagine his age to be?"

---

3. Prepared and cooked.
4. The *Elegant Extracts* were a series of collections of snippets of poetry, prose, and other writings edited by Vicesimus Knox and used in both schools and the home to acquaint middle-class readers with the excellencies of English literature. *The Vicar of Wakefield* was a sentimental novel by Oliver Goldsmith (1766). The *Romance of the Forest* (by Ann Radcliffe, 1791) and the *Children of the Abbey* (by Regina Maria Roche, 1796) were popular Gothic novels. In *Northanger Abbey* (published 1818) Austen affectionately mocks the terror raised by Gothic novels in young, largely female, readers.

"He was four-and-twenty the 8th of last June, and my birth-day is the 23d—just a fortnight and a day's difference! which is very odd!"

"Only four-and-twenty. That is too young to settle. His mother is perfectly right not to be in a hurry. They seem very comfortable as they are, and if she were to take any pains to marry him, she would probably repent it. Six years hence, if he could meet with a good sort of young woman in the same rank as his own, with a little money, it might be very desirable."

"Six years hence! dear Miss Woodhouse, he would be thirty years old!"

"Well, and that is as early as most men can afford to marry, who are not born to an independence. Mr. Martin, I imagine, has his fortune entirely to make—cannot be at all beforehand with the world. Whatever money he might come into when his father died, whatever his share of the family property, it is, I dare say, all afloat, all employed[5] in his stock, and so forth; and though, with diligence and good luck, he may be rich in time, it is next to impossible that he should have realised any thing yet."

"To be sure, so it is. But they live very comfortably. They have no in-doors man—else they do not want for any thing; and Mrs. Martin talks of taking a boy another year."

"I wish you may not get into a scrape, Harriet, whenever he does marry;—I mean, as to being acquainted with his wife—for though his sisters, from a superior education, are not to be altogether objected to, it does not follow that he might marry any body at all fit for you to notice. The misfortune of your birth ought to make you particularly careful as to your associates. There can be no doubt of your being a gentleman's daughter, and you must support your claim to that station by every thing within your own power, or there will be plenty of people who would take pleasure in degrading you."

"Yes, to be sure—I suppose there are. But while I visit at Hartfield, and you are so kind to me, Miss Woodhouse, I am not afraid of what any body can do."

"You understand the force of influence pretty well, Harriet; but I would have you so firmly established in good society, as to be independent even of Hartfield and Miss Woodhouse. I want to see you permanently well connected—and to that end it will be advisable to have as few odd acquaintance as may be; and, therefore, I say that if you should still be in this country when Mr. Martin marries, I wish you may not be drawn in, by your intimacy with the sisters, to be acquainted with the wife, who will probably be some mere farmer's daughter, without education."

5. Invested.

"To be sure. Yes. Not that I think Mr. Martin would ever marry any body but what had had some education—and been very well brought up. However, I do not mean to set up my opinion against your's—and I am sure I shall not wish for the acquaintance of his wife. I shall always have a great regard for the Miss Martins, especially Elizabeth, and should be very sorry to give them up, for they are quite as well educated as me. But if he marries a very ignorant, vulgar woman, certainly I had better not visit her, if I can help it."

Emma watched her through the fluctuations of this speech, and saw no alarming symptoms of love. The young man had been the first admirer, but she trusted there was no other hold, and that there would be no serious difficulty on Harriet's side to oppose any friendly arrangement of her own.

They met Mr. Martin the very next day, as they were walking on the Donwell road. He was on foot, and after looking very respectfully at her, looked with most unfeigned satisfaction at her companion. Emma was not sorry to have such an opportunity of survey; and walking a few yards forward, while they talked together, soon made her quick eye sufficiently acquainted with Mr. Robert Martin. His appearance was very neat, and he looked like a sensible young man, but his person had no other advantage; and when he came to be contrasted with gentlemen, she thought he must lose all the ground he had gained in Harriet's inclination. Harriet was not insensible of manner;[6] she had voluntarily noticed her father's gentleness with admiration as well as wonder. Mr. Martin looked as if he did not know what manner was.

They remained but a few minutes together, as Miss Woodhouse must not be kept waiting; and Harriet then came running to her with a smiling face, and in a flutter of spirits, which Miss Woodhouse hoped very soon to compose.

"Only think of our happening to meet him!—How very odd! It was quite a chance, he said, that he had not gone round by Randalls. He did not think we ever walked this road. He thought we walked towards Randalls most days. He has not been able to get the Romance of the Forest yet. He was so busy the last time he was at Kingston[7] that he quite forgot it, but he goes again to-morrow. So very odd we should happen to meet! Well, Miss Woodhouse, is he like what you expected? What do you think of him? Do you think him so very plain?"

"He is very plain, undoubtedly—remarkably plain:—but that is nothing, compared with his entire want of gentility. I had no right

6. Polite behavior.
7. Kingston-upon-Thames was an important town with what was the first bridge across the Thames west of London, around 9 miles from fictional Highbury.

to expect much, and I did not expect much; but I had no idea that he could be so very clownish,[8] so totally without air. I had imagined him, I confess, a degree or two nearer gentility."

"To be sure," said Harriet, in a mortified voice, "he is not so genteel as real gentlemen."

"I think, Harriet, since your acquaintance with us, you have been repeatedly in the company of some, such very real gentlemen, that you must yourself be struck with the difference in Mr. Martin. At Hartfield you have had very good specimens of well educated, well bred men. I should be surprized if, after seeing them, you could be in company with Mr. Martin again without perceiving him to be a very inferior creature—and rather wondering at yourself for having ever thought him at all agreeable before. Do not you begin to feel that now? Were not you struck? I am sure you must have been struck by his awkward look and abrupt manner—and the uncouthness of a voice, which I heard to be wholly unmodulated as I stood here."

"Certainly, he is not like Mr. Knightley. He has not such a fine air and way of walking as Mr. Knightley. I see the difference plain enough. But Mr. Knightley is so very fine a man!"

"Mr. Knightley's air is so remarkably good, that it is not fair to compare Mr. Martin with *him*. You might not see one in a hundred, with *gentleman* so plainly written as in Mr. Knightley. But he is not the only gentleman you have been lately used to. What say you to Mr. Weston and Mr. Elton? Compare Mr. Martin with either of *them*. Compare their manner of carrying themselves; of walking; of speaking; of being silent. You must see the difference."

"Oh, yes!—there is a great difference. But Mr. Weston is almost an old man. Mr. Weston must be between forty and fifty."

"Which makes his good manners the more valuable. The older a person grows, Harriet, the more important it is that their manners should not be bad—the more glaring and disgusting any loudness, or coarseness, or awkwardness becomes. What is passable in youth, is detestable in later age. Mr. Martin is now awkward and abrupt; what will he be at Mr. Weston's time of life?"

"There is no saying, indeed!" replied Harriet, rather solemnly.

"But there may be pretty good guessing. He will be a completely gross, vulgar farmer—totally inattentive to appearances, and thinking of nothing but profit and loss."

"Will he, indeed, that will be very bad."

"How much his business engrosses him already, is very plain from the circumstance of his forgetting to inquire for the book you recommended. He was a great deal too full of the market to think of any thing else—which is just as it should be, for a thriving man.

8. With a rural, rustic appearance—not intended to cause merriment.

What has he to do with books? And I have no doubt that he *will* thrive and be a very rich man in time—and his being illiterate and coarse need not disturb *us*."

"I wonder he did not remember the book"—was all Harriet's answer, and spoken with a degree of grave displeasure which Emma thought might be safely left to itself. She, therefore, said no more for some time. Her next beginning was,

"In one respect, perhaps, Mr. Elton's manners are superior to Mr. Knightley's or Mr. Weston's. They have more gentleness. They might be more safely held up as a pattern. There is an openness, a quickness, almost a bluntness in Mr. Weston, which every body likes in *him* because there is so much good humour with it—but that would not do to be copied. Neither would Mr. Knightley's downright, decided, commanding sort of manner—though it suits *him* very well; his figure and look, and situation in life seem to allow it; but if any young man were to set about copying him, he would not be sufferable. On the contrary, I think a young man might be very safely recommended to take Mr. Elton as a model. Mr. Elton is good humoured, cheerful, obliging, and gentle. He seems to me, to be grown particularly gentle of late. I do not know whether he has any design of ingratiating himself with either of us, Harriet, by additional softness, but it strikes me that his manners are softer than they used to be. If he means anything, it must be to please you. Did not I tell you what he said of you the other day?"

She then repeated some warm personal praise which she had drawn from Mr. Elton, and now did full justice to; and Harriet blushed and smiled, and said she had always thought Mr. Elton very agreeable.

Mr. Elton was the very person fixed on by Emma for driving the young farmer out of Harriet's head. She thought it would be an excellent match; and only too palpably desirable, natural, and probable, for her to have much merit in planning it. She feared it was what every body else must think of and predict. It was not likely, however, that any body should have equalled her in the date of the plan, as it had entered her brain during the very first evening of Harriet's coming to Hartfield. The longer she considered it, the greater was her sense of its expediency. Mr. Elton's situation was most suitable, quite the gentleman himself, and without low connections; at the same time not of any family that could fairly object to the doubtful birth of Harriet. He had a comfortable home for her, and Emma imagined a very sufficient income; for though the vicarage of Highbury was not large, he was known to have some independent property; and she thought very highly of him as a good-humoured, well-meaning, respectable young man, without any deficiency of useful understanding or knowledge of the world.

She had already satisfied herself that he thought Harriet a beautiful girl, which she trusted, with such frequent meetings at Hartfield, was foundation enough on his side; and on Harriet's, there could be little doubt that the idea of being preferred by him would have all the usual weight and efficacy. And he was really a very pleasing young man, a young man whom any woman not fastidious might like. He was reckoned very handsome; his person much admired in general, though not by her, there being a want of elegance[9] of feature which she could not dispense with:—but the girl who could be gratified by a Robert Martin's riding about the country to get walnuts for her, might very well be conquered by Mr. Elton's admiration.

Chapter V

"I do not know what your opinion may be, Mrs. Weston," said Mr. Knightley, "of this great intimacy between Emma and Harriet Smith, but I think it a bad thing."

"A bad thing! Do you really think it a bad thing?—why so?"

"I think they will neither of them do the other any good."

"You surprize me! Emma must do Harriet good: and by supplying her with a new object of interest, Harriet may be said to do Emma good. I have been seeing their intimacy with the greatest pleasure. How very differently we feel!—Not think they will do each other any good! This will certainly be the beginning of one of our quarrels about Emma, Mr. Knightley."

"Perhaps you think I am come on purpose to quarrel with you, knowing Weston to be out, and that you must still fight your own battle."

"Mr. Weston would undoubtedly support me, if he were here, for he thinks exactly as I do on the subject. We were speaking of it only yesterday, and agreeing how fortunate it was for Emma, that there should be such a girl in Highbury for her to associate with. Mr. Knightley, I shall not allow you to be a fair judge in this case. You are so much used to live alone, that you do not know the value of a companion; and perhaps no man can be a good judge of the comfort a woman feels in the society of one of her own sex, after being used to it all her life. I can imagine your objection to Harriet Smith. She is not the superior young woman which Emma's friend ought to be. But on the other hand, as Emma wants to see her better informed, it will be an inducement to her to read more herself. They will read together. She means it, I know."

---

9. The *Oxford English Dictionary*, citing this passage in *Emma*, defines "elegance" as "refined propriety." This definition captures part of the importance of the word, and the concept of elegance in the novel, but it does not convey the beauty and pleasure associated with elegance of style and substance in people and in works of culture.

"Emma has been meaning to read more ever since she was twelve years old. I have seen a great many lists of her drawing up at various times of books that she meant to read regularly through—and very good lists they were—very well chosen, and very neatly arranged— sometimes alphabetically, and sometimes by some other rule. The list she drew up when only fourteen—I remember thinking it did her judgment so much credit, that I preserved it some time; and I dare say she may have made out a very good list now. But I have done with expecting any course of steady reading from Emma. She will never submit to any thing requiring industry and patience, and a subjection of the fancy to the understanding. Where Miss Taylor failed to stimulate, I may safely affirm that Harriet Smith will do nothing.— You never could persuade her to read half so much as you wished.— You know you could not."

"I dare say," replied Mrs. Weston, smiling, "that I thought so *then*;—but since we have parted, I can never remember Emma's omitting to do any thing I wished."

"There is hardly any desiring to refresh such a memory as *that*"— said Mr. Knightley, feelingly; and for a moment or two he had done. "But I," he soon added, "who have had no such charm thrown over my senses, must still see, hear, and remember. Emma is spoiled by being the cleverest of her family. At ten years old, she had the mis- fortune of being able to answer questions which puzzled her sister at seventeen. She was always quick and assured: Isabella slow and diffident. And ever since she was twelve, Emma has been mistress of the house and of you all. In her mother she lost the only person able to cope with her. She inherits her mother's talents, and must have been under subjection to her."

"I should have been sorry, Mr. Knightley, to be dependent on *your* recommendation, had I quitted Mr. Woodhouse's family and wanted another situation; I do not think you would have spoken a good word for me to any body. I am sure you always thought me unfit for the office I held."

"Yes," said he, smiling. "You are better placed *here*; very fit for a wife, but not at all for a governess. But you were preparing yourself to be an excellent wife all the time you were at Hartfield. You might not give Emma such a complete education as your powers would seem to promise; but you were receiving a very good education from *her*, on the very material matrimonial point of submitting your own will, and doing as you were bid; and if Weston had asked me to rec- ommend him a wife, I should certainly have named Miss Taylor."

"Thank you. There will be very little merit in making a good wife to such a man as Mr. Weston."

"Why, to own the truth, I am afraid you are rather thrown away, and that with every disposition to bear, there will be nothing to be

borne. We will not despair, however. Weston may grow cross from
the wantonness of comfort, or his son may plague him."

"I hope not *that*.—It is not likely. No, Mr. Knightley, do not foretel vexation from that quarter."

"Not I, indeed. I only name possibilities. I do not pretend to
Emma's genius for foretelling and guessing. I hope, with all my
heart, the young man may be a Weston in merit, and a Churchill in
fortune.—But Harriet Smith—I have not half done about Harriet
Smith. I think her the very worst sort of companion that Emma
could possibly have. She knows nothing herself, and looks upon
Emma as knowing every thing. She is a flatterer in all her ways; and
so much the worse, because undesigned. Her ignorance is hourly
flattery. How can Emma imagine she has any thing to learn herself,
while Harriet is presenting such a delightful inferiority? And as for
Harriet, I will venture to say that *she* cannot gain by the acquaintance. Hartfield will only put her out of conceit with all the other
places she belongs to. She will grow just refined enough to be
uncomfortable with those among whom birth and circumstances
have placed her home. I am much mistaken if Emma's doctrines
give any strength of mind, or tend at all to make a girl adapt herself
rationally to the varieties of her situation in life.—They only give a
little polish."

"I either depend more upon Emma's good sense than you do, or
am more anxious for her present comfort; for I cannot lament the
acquaintance. How well she looked last night!"

"Oh! you would rather talk of her person than her mind, would
you? Very well; I shall not attempt to deny Emma's being pretty."

"Pretty! say beautiful rather. Can you imagine any thing nearer
perfect beauty than Emma altogether—face and figure?"

"I do not know what I could imagine, but I confess that I have
seldom seen a face or figure more pleasing to me than her's. But I
am a partial old friend."

"Such an eye!—the true hazel eye—and so brilliant! regular features, open countenance, with a complexion! oh! what a bloom of
full health, and such a pretty height and size; such a firm and
upright figure. There is health, not merely in her bloom, but in her
air, her head, her glance. One hears sometimes of a child being 'the
picture of health;' now Emma always gives me the idea of being the
complete picture of grown-up health. She is loveliness itself. Mr.
Knightley, is not she?"

"I have not a fault to find with her person," he replied. "I think
her all you describe. I love to look at her; and I will add this praise,
that I do not think her personally vain. Considering how very handsome she is, she appears to be little occupied with it; her vanity lies
another way. Mrs. Weston, I am not to be talked out of my dislike

of her intimacy with Harriet Smith, or my dread of its doing them both harm."

"And I, Mr. Knightley, am equally stout in my confidence of its not doing them any harm. With all dear Emma's little faults, she is an excellent creature. Where shall we see a better daughter, or a kinder sister, or a truer friend? No, no; she has qualities which may be trusted; she will never lead any one really wrong; she will make no lasting blunder; where Emma errs once, she is in the right a hundred times."

"Very well; I will not plague you any more. Emma shall be an angel, and I will keep my spleen to myself till Christmas brings John and Isabella. John loves Emma with a reasonable and therefore not a blind affection, and Isabella always thinks as he does; except when he is not quite frightened enough about the children. I am sure of having their opinions with me."

"I know that you all love her really too well to be unjust or unkind; but excuse me, Mr. Knightley, if I take the liberty (I consider myself, you know, as having somewhat of the privilege of speech that Emma's mother might have had) the liberty of hinting that I do not think any possible good can arise from Harriet Smith's intimacy being made a matter of much discussion among you. Pray excuse me; but supposing any little inconvenience may be apprehended from the intimacy, it cannot be expected that Emma, accountable to nobody but her father, who perfectly approves the acquaintance, should put an end to it, so long as it is a source of pleasure to herself. It has been so many years my province to give advice, that you cannot be surprized, Mr. Knightley, at this little remains of office."

"Not at all," cried he; "I am much obliged to you for it. It is very good advice, and it shall have a better fate than your advice has often found; for it shall be attended to."

"Mrs. John Knightley is easily alarmed, and might be made unhappy about her sister."

"Be satisfied," said he, "I will not raise any outcry. I will keep my ill-humour to myself. I have a very sincere interest in Emma. Isabella does not seem more my sister; has never excited a greater interest; perhaps hardly so great. There is an anxiety, a curiosity in what one feels for Emma. I wonder what will become of her!"

"So do I," said Mrs. Weston gently; "very much."

"She always declares she will never marry, which, of course, means just nothing at all. But I have no idea that she has yet ever seen a man she cared for. It would not be a bad thing for her to be very much in love with a proper object. I should like to see Emma in love, and in some doubt of a return; it would do her good. But there is nobody hereabouts to attach her; and she goes so seldom from home."

"There does, indeed, seem as little to tempt her to break her resolution, at present," said Mrs. Weston, "as can well be; and while she is so happy at Hartfield, I cannot wish her to be forming any attachment which would be creating such difficulties, on poor Mr. Woodhouse's account. I do not recommend matrimony at present to Emma, though I mean no slight to the state I assure you."

Part of her meaning was to conceal some favourite thoughts of her own and Mr. Weston's on the subject, as much as possible. There were wishes at Randalls respecting Emma's destiny, but it was not desirable to have them suspected; and the quiet transition which Mr. Knightley soon afterwards made to "What does Weston think of the weather; shall we have rain?" convinced her that he had nothing more to say or surmise about Hartfield.

Chapter VI

Emma could not feel a doubt of having given Harriet's fancy a proper direction and raised the gratitude of her young vanity to a very good purpose, for she found her decidedly more sensible than before of Mr. Elton's being a remarkably handsome man, with most agreeable manners; and as she had no hesitation in following up the assurance of his admiration, by agreeable hints, she was soon pretty confident of creating as much liking on Harriet's side, as there could be any occasion for. She was quite convinced of Mr. Elton's being in the fairest way of falling in love, if not in love already. She had no scruple with regard to him. He talked of Harriet, and praised her so warmly, that she could not suppose any thing wanting which a little time would not add. His perception of the striking improvement of Harriet's manner, since her introduction at Hartfield, was not one of the least agreeable proofs of his growing attachment.

"You have given Miss Smith all that she required," said he; "you have made her graceful and easy. She was a beautiful creature when she came to you, but, in my opinion, the attractions you have added are infinitely superior to what she received from nature."

"I am glad you think I have been useful to her; but Harriet only wanted drawing out, and receiving a few, very few hints. She had all the natural grace of sweetness of temper and artlessness in herself. I have done very little."

"If it were admissible to contradict a lady," said the gallant Mr. Elton—

"I have perhaps given her a little more decision of character, have taught her to think on points which had not fallen in her way before."

"Exactly so; that is what principally strikes me. So much superadded decision of character! Skilful has been the hand."

"Great has been the pleasure, I am sure. I never met with a disposition more truly amiable."

"I have no doubt of it." And it was spoken with a sort of sighing animation, which had a vast deal of the lover. She was not less pleased another day with the manner in which he seconded a sudden wish of her's, to have Harriet's picture.

"Did you ever have your likeness taken, Harriet?" said she: "Did you ever sit for your picture?"

Harriet was on the point of leaving the room, and only stopt to say, with a very interesting naïveté,

"Oh! dear, no, never."

No sooner was she out of sight, than Emma exclaimed,

"What an exquisite possession a good picture of her would be! I would give any money for it. I almost long to attempt her likeness myself. You do not know it I dare say, but two or three years ago I had a great passion for taking likenesses, and attempted several of my friends, and was thought to have a tolerable eye in general. But from one cause or another, I gave it up in disgust. But really, I could almost venture, if Harriet would sit to me. It would be such a delight to have her picture!"

"Let me entreat you," cried Mr. Elton; "it would indeed be a delight! Let me entreat you, Miss Woodhouse, to exercise so charming a talent in favour of your friend. I know what your drawings are. How could you suppose me ignorant? Is not this room rich in specimens of your landscapes and flowers; and has not Mrs. Weston some inimitable figure-pieces in her drawing-room, at Randalls?

Yes, good man!—thought Emma—but what has all that to do with taking likenesses? You know nothing of drawing. Don't pretend to be in raptures about mine. Keep your raptures for Harriet's face. "Well, if you give me such kind encouragement, Mr. Elton, I believe I shall try what I can do. Harriet's features are very delicate, which makes a likeness difficult; and yet there is a peculiarity in the shape of the eye and the lines about the mouth which one ought to catch."

"Exactly so—The shape of the eye and the lines about the mouth—I have not a doubt of your success. Pray, pray attempt it. As you will do it, it will indeed, to use your own words, be an exquisite possession."

"But I am afraid, Mr. Elton, Harriet will not like to sit. She thinks so little of her own beauty. Did not you observe her manner of answering me? How completely it meant, 'why should my picture be drawn?'"

"Oh! yes, I observed it, I assure you. It was not lost on me. But still I cannot imagine she would not be persuaded."

Harriet was soon back again, and the proposal almost immediately made; and she had no scruples which could stand many minutes against the earnest pressing of both the others. Emma wished to go to work directly, and therefore produced the portfolio containing her various attempts at portraits, for not one of them had ever been finished, that they might decide together on the best size for Harriet. Her many beginnings were displayed. Miniatures, half-lengths, whole-lengths, pencil, crayon, and water-colours had been all tried in turn. She had always wanted to do everything, and had made more progress both in drawing and music than many might have done with so little labour as she would ever submit to. She played and sang;—and drew in almost every style; but steadiness had always been wanting; and in nothing had she approached the degree of excellence which she would have been glad to command, and ought not to have failed of. She was not much deceived as to her own skill either as an artist or a musician, but she was not unwilling to have others deceived, or sorry to know her reputation for accomplishment often higher than it deserved.

There was merit in every drawing—in the least finished, perhaps the most; her style was spirited; but had there been much less, or had there been ten times more, the delight and admiration of her two companions would have been the same. They were both in extasies. A likeness pleases every body; and Miss Woodhouse's performances must be capital.

"No great variety of faces for you," said Emma. "I had only my own family to study from. There is my father—another of my father—but the idea of sitting for his picture made him so nervous, that I could only take him by stealth; neither of them very like therefore. Mrs. Weston again, and again, and again, you see. Dear Mrs. Weston! always my kindest friend on every occasion. She would sit whenever I asked her. There is my sister; and really quite her own little elegant figure!—and the face not unlike. I should have made a good likeness of her, if she would have sat longer, but she was in such a hurry to have me draw her four children that she would not be quiet. Then, here come all my attempts at three of those four children;—there they are, Henry and John and Bella, from one end of the sheet to the other, and any one of them might do for any one of the rest. She was so eager to have them drawn that I could not refuse; but there is no making children of three or four years old stand still you know; nor can it be very easy to take any likeness of them, beyond the air and complexion, unless they are coarser featured than any mama's children ever were. Here is my sketch of the fourth, who was a baby. I took him, as he was sleeping on the sofa, and it is as strong a likeness of his cockade[1] as you would wish to see. He had nestled down his head most conveniently. That's very like. I am rather proud of little George. The corner of the sofa is very good. Then here is my

1. The bows on an infant's bonnet, perhaps made of white satin ribbon.

last"—unclosing a pretty sketch of a gentleman in small size, whole-length—"my last and my best—my brother, Mr. John Knightley.—This did not want much of being finished, when I put it away in a pet,[2] and vowed I would never take another likeness. I could not help being provoked; for after all my pains, and when I had really made a very good likeness of it—(Mrs. Weston and I were quite agreed in think-ing it *very* like)—only too handsome—too flattering—but that was a fault on the right side—after all this, came poor dear Isabella's cold approbation of—"Yes, it was a little like—but to be sure it did not do him justice." We had had a great deal of trouble in persuading him to sit at all. It was made a great favour of; and altogether it was more than I could bear; and so I never would finish it, to have it apologized over as an unfavourable likeness, to every morning visitor in Brunswick-square;—and, as I said, I did then forswear ever drawing anybody again. But for Harriet's sake, or rather for my own, and as there are no husbands and wives in the case at present, I will break my resolution now."

Mr. Elton seemed very properly struck and delighted by the idea, and was repeating, "No husbands and wives in the case *at present* indeed, as you observe. Exactly so. No husbands and wives," with so interesting a consciousness, that Emma began to consider whether she had not better leave them together at once. But as she wanted to be drawing, the declaration must wait a little longer.

She had soon fixed on the size and sort of portrait. It was to be a whole-length in water-colours, like Mr. John Knightley's, and was destined, if she could please herself, to hold a very honourable sta-tion over the mantlepiece.

The sitting began; and Harriet, smiling and blushing, and afraid of not keeping her attitude and countenance, presented a very sweet mixture of youthful expression to the steady eyes of the artist. But there was no doing anything, with Mr. Elton fidgeting behind her and watching every touch. She gave him credit for stationing himself where he might gaze and gaze again without offence; but was really obliged to put an end to it, and request him to place himself else-where. It then occurred to her to employ him in reading.

"If he would be so good as to read to them, it would be a kindness indeed! It would amuse away the difficulties of her part, and lessen the irksomeness of Miss Smith's."

Mr. Elton was only too happy. Harriet listened, and Emma drew in peace. She must allow him to be still frequently coming to look; anything less would certainly have been too little in a lover; and he was ready at the smallest intermission of the pencil, to jump up and see the progress, and be charmed.—There was no being displeased

2. Fit of ill humor.

with such an encourager, for his admiration made him discern a likeness almost before it was possible. She could not respect his eye, but his love and his complaisance were unexceptionable.

The sitting was altogether very satisfactory; she was quite enough pleased with the first day's sketch to wish to go on. There was no want of likeness, she had been fortunate in the attitude, and as she meant to throw in a little improvement to the figure, to give a little more height, and considerably more elegance, she had great confidence of its being in every way a pretty drawing at last, and of its filling its destined place with credit to them both—a standing memorial of the beauty of one, the skill of the other, and the friendship of both; with as many other agreeable associations as Mr. Elton's very promising attachment was likely to add.

Harriet was to sit again the next day; and Mr. Elton, just as he ought, entreated for the permission of attending and reading to them again.

"By all means. We shall be most happy to consider you as one of the party."

The same civilities and courtesies, the same success and satisfaction, took place on the morrow, and accompanied the whole progress of the picture, which was rapid and happy. Every body who saw it was pleased, but Mr. Elton was in continual raptures, and defended it through every criticism.

"Miss Woodhouse has given her friend the only beauty she wanted,"—observed Mrs. Weston to him—not in the least suspecting that she was addressing a lover.—"The expression of the eye is most correct, but Miss Smith has not those eye-brows and eye-lashes. It is the fault of her face that she has them not."

"Do you think so?" replied he. "I cannot agree with you. It appears to me a most perfect resemblance in every feature. I never saw such a likeness in my life. We must allow for the effect of shade, you know."

"You have made her too tall, Emma," said Mr. Knightley.

Emma knew that she had, but would not own it, and Mr. Elton warmly added,

"Oh, no! certainly not too tall; not in the least too tall. Consider, she is sitting down—which naturally presents a different—which in short gives exactly the idea—and the proportions must be preserved, you know. Proportions, fore-shortening.—Oh, no! it gives one exactly the idea of such a height as Miss Smith's. Exactly so indeed!"

"It is very pretty," said Mr. Woodhouse. "So prettily done! Just as your drawings always are, my dear. I do not know any body who draws so well as you do. The only thing I do not thoroughly like is, that she seems to be sitting out of doors, with only a little shawl over her shoulders—and it makes one think she must catch cold."

"But, my dear papa, it is supposed to be summer; a warm day in summer. Look at the tree."

"But it is never safe to sit out of doors, my dear."

"You, sir, may say any thing," cried Mr. Elton; "but I must confess that I regard it as a most happy thought, the placing of Miss Smith out of doors; and the tree is touched with such inimitable spirit! Any other situation would have been much less in character. The naïveté of Miss Smith's manners—and altogether—Oh, it is most admirable! I cannot keep my eyes from it. I never saw such a likeness."

The next thing wanted was to get the picture framed; and here were a few difficulties. It must be done directly; it must be done in London; the order must go through the hands of some intelligent person whose taste could be depended on; and Isabella, the usual doer of all commissions, must not be applied to, because it was December, and Mr. Woodhouse could not bear the idea of her stirring out of her house in the fogs of December. But no sooner was the distress known to Mr. Elton, than it was removed. His gallantry[3] was always on the alert. "Might he be trusted with the commission, what infinite pleasure should he have in executing it! he could ride to London at any time. It was impossible to say how much he should be gratified by being employed on such an errand."

"He was too good!—she could not endure the thought!—she would not give him such a troublesome office for the world"—brought on the desired repetition of entreaties and assurances,—and a very few minutes settled the business.

Mr. Elton was to take the drawing to London, chuse the frame, and give the directions; and Emma thought she could so pack it as to ensure its safety without much incommoding him, while he seemed mostly fearful of not being incommoded enough.

"What a precious deposit!" said he with a tender sigh, as he received it.

"This man is almost too gallant to be in love," thought Emma. "I should say so, but that I suppose there may be a hundred different ways of being in love. He is an excellent young man, and will suit Harriet exactly; it will be an 'Exactly so,' as he says himself; but he does sigh and languish, and study for compliments rather more than I could endure as a principal. I come in for a pretty good share as a second. But it is his gratitude on Harriet's account."

Chapter VII

The very day of Mr. Elton's going to London produced a fresh occasion for Emma's services towards her friend. Harriet had been at

---

3. See Introduction. The novel distrusts gallantry as a stylized, conventional form of masculine attention to women.

Hartfield, as usual, soon after breakfast; and after a time, had gone home to return again to dinner: she returned, and sooner than had been talked of, and with an agitated, hurried look, announcing something extraordinary to have happened which she was longing to tell. Half a minute brought it all out. She had heard, as soon as she got back to Mrs. Goddard's, that Mr. Martin had been there an hour before, and finding she was not at home, nor particularly expected, had left a little parcel for her from one of his sisters, and gone away; and on opening this parcel, she had actually found, besides the two songs which she had lent Elizabeth to copy, a letter to herself; and this letter was from him, from Mr. Martin, and contained a direct proposal of marriage. "Who could have thought it! She was so surprized she did not know what to do. Yes, quite a proposal of marriage; and a very good letter, at least she thought so. And he wrote as if he really loved her very much—but she did not know—and so, she was come as fast as she could to ask Miss Woodhouse what she should do."—Emma was half ashamed of her friend for seeming so pleased and so doubtful.

"Upon my word," she cried, "the young man is determined not to lose any thing for want of asking. He will connect himself well if he can."

"Will you read the letter?" cried Harriet. "Pray do. I'd rather you would."

Emma was not sorry to be pressed. She read, and was surprised. The style of the letter was much above her expectation. There were not merely no grammatical errors, but as a composition it would not have disgraced a gentleman; the language, though plain, was strong and unaffected, and the sentiments it conveyed very much to the credit of the writer. It was short, but expressed good sense, warm attachment, liberality, propriety, even delicacy of feeling. She paused over it, while Harriet stood anxiously watching for her opinion, with a "Well, well," and was at last forced to add, "Is it a good letter? or is it too short?"

"Yes, indeed, a very good letter," replied Emma rather slowly—"so good a letter, Harriet, that every thing considered, I think one of his sisters must have helped him. I can hardly imagine the young man whom I saw talking with you the other day could express himself so well, if left quite to his own powers, and yet it is not the style of a woman; no, certainly, it is too strong and concise; not diffuse enough for a woman. No doubt he is a sensible man, and I suppose may have a natural talent for—thinks strongly and clearly—and when he takes a pen in hand, his thoughts naturally find proper words. It is so with some men. Yes, I understand the sort of mind. Vigorous, decided, with sentiments to a certain point, not coarse. A better written letter, Harriet, (returning it,) than I had expected."

"Well," said the still waiting Harriet;—"well—and—and what shall I do?"

"What shall you do! In what respect? Do you mean with regard to this letter?"

"Yes."

"But what are you in doubt of? You must answer it of course—and speedily."

"Yes. But what shall I say? Dear Miss Woodhouse, do advise me."

"Oh, no, no! the letter had much better be all your own. You will express yourself very properly, I am sure. There is no danger of your not being intelligible, which is the first thing. Your meaning must be unequivocal; no doubts or demurs: and such expressions of gratitude and concern for the pain you are inflicting as propriety requires, will present themselves unbidden to *your* mind, I am persuaded. *You* need not be prompted to write with the appearance of sorrow for his disappointment."

"You think I ought to refuse him then," said Harriet, looking down.

"Ought to refuse him! My dear Harriet, what do you mean? Are you in any doubt as to that? I thought—but I beg your pardon, perhaps I have been under a mistake. I certainly have been misunderstanding you, if you feel in doubt as to the *purport* of your answer. I had imagined you were consulting me only as to the wording of it."

Harriet was silent. With a little reserve of manner, Emma continued:

"You mean to return a favourable answer, I collect."

"No, I do not; that is, I do not mean—What shall I do? What would you advise me to do? Pray, dear Miss Woodhouse, tell me what I ought to do?"

"I shall not give you any advice, Harriet. I will have nothing to do with it. This is a point which you must settle with your own feelings."

"I had no notion that he liked me so very much," said Harriet, contemplating the letter. For a little while Emma persevered in her silence; but beginning to apprehend the bewitching flattery of that letter might be too powerful, she thought it best to say,

"I lay it down as a general rule, Harriet, that if a woman *doubts* as to whether she should accept a man or not, she certainly ought to refuse him. If she can hesitate as to 'Yes,' she ought to say 'No' directly. It is not a state to be safely entered into with doubtful feelings, with half a heart. I thought it my duty as a friend, and older than yourself, to say thus much to you. But do not imagine that I want to influence you."

"Oh! no, I am sure you are a great deal too kind to——but if you would just advise me what I had best do—No, no, I do not mean that—As you say, one's mind ought to be quite made up—One should not be hesitating—It is a very serious thing.—It will be safer to say 'No,' perhaps.—Do you think I had better say 'No?'"

"Not for the world," said Emma, smiling graciously, "would I advise you either way. You must be the best judge of your own happiness. If you prefer Mr. Martin to every other person; if you think him the most agreeable man you have ever been in company with, why should you hesitate? You blush, Harriet.—Does any body else occur to you at this moment under such a definition? Harriet, Harriet, do not deceive yourself; do not be run away with by gratitude and compassion. At this moment whom are you thinking of?"

The symptoms were favourable.—Instead of answering, Harriet turned away confused, and stood thoughtfully by the fire; and though the letter was still in her hand, it was now mechanically twisted about without regard. Emma waited the result with impatience, but not without strong hopes. At last, with some hesitation, Harriet said—

"Miss Woodhouse, as you will not give me your opinion, I must do as well as I can by myself; and I have now quite determined, and really almost made up my mind—to refuse Mr. Martin. Do you think I am right?"

"Perfectly, perfectly right, my dearest Harriet; you are doing just what you ought. While you were at all in suspense I kept my feelings to myself, but now that you are so completely decided I have no hesitation in approving. Dear Harriet, I give myself joy of this. It would have grieved me to lose your acquaintance, which must have been the consequence of your marrying Mr. Martin. While you were in the smallest degree wavering, I said nothing about it, because I would not influence; but it would have been the loss of a friend to me. I could not have visited Mrs. Robert Martin, of Abbey-Mill Farm. Now I am secure of you for ever."

Harriet had not surmised her own danger, but the idea of it struck her forcibly.

"You could not have visited me!" she cried, looking aghast. "No, to be sure you could not; but I never thought of that before. That would have been too dreadful!—What an escape—Dear Miss Woodhouse, I would not give up the pleasure and honour of being intimate with you for any thing in the world."

"Indeed, Harriet, it would have been a severe pang to lose you; but it must have been. You would have thrown yourself out of all good society. I must have given you up."

"Dear me!—How should I ever have borne it! It would have killed me never to come to Hartfield any more!"

"Dear affectionate creature!—*You* banished to Abbey-Mill Farm!—*You* confined to the society of the illiterate and vulgar all

your life! I wonder how the young man could have the assurance to
ask it. He must have a pretty good opinion of himself."

"I do not think he is conceited either, in general," said Harriet,
her conscience opposing such censure; "at least he is very good
natured, and I shall always feel much obliged to him, and have a
great regard for—but that is quite a different thing from—and you
know, though he may like me, it does not follow that I should—and
certainly I must confess that since my visiting here I have seen
people—and if one comes to compare them, person and manners,
there is no comparison at all, *one* is so very handsome and agreeable. However, I do really think Mr. Martin is a very amiable young
man, and have a great opinion of him; and his being so much
attached to me—and his writing such a letter—but as to leaving
you, it is what I would not do upon any consideration."

"Thank you, thank you, my own sweet little friend. We will not
be parted. A woman is not to marry a man merely because she is
asked, or because he is attached to her, and can write a tolerable
letter."

"Oh! no;—and it is but a short letter too."

Emma felt the bad taste of her friend, but let it pass with a "very
true; and it would be a small consolation to her, for the clownish
manner which might be offending her every hour of the day, to
know that her husband could write a good letter."

"Oh! yes, very. Nobody cares for a letter; the thing is, to be always
happy with pleasant companions. I am quite determined to refuse
him. But how shall I do? What shall I say?"

Emma assured her there would be no difficulty in the answer,
and advised its being written directly, which was agreed to, in the
hope of her assistance; and though Emma continued to protest
against any assistance being wanted, it was in fact given in the for-
mation of every sentence. The looking over his letter again, in replying to it, had such a softening tendency, that it was particularly
necessary to brace her up with a few decisive expressions; and she
was so very much concerned at the idea of making him unhappy, and
thought so much of what his mother and sisters would think and
say, and was so anxious that they should not fancy her ungrateful,
that Emma believed if the young man had come in her way at that
moment, he would have been accepted after all.

This letter, however, was written, and sealed, and sent. The business was finished, and Harriet safe. She was rather low all the evening, but Emma could allow for her amiable regrets, and sometimes
relieved them by speaking of her own affection, sometimes by
bringing forward the idea of Mr. Elton.

"I shall never be invited to Abbey-Mill again," was said in rather
a sorrowful tone.

"Nor if you were, could I ever bear to part with you, my Harriet. You are a great deal too necessary at Hartfield, to be spared to Abbey-Mill."

"And I am sure I should never want to go there; for I am never happy but at Hartfield."

Some time afterwards it was, "I think Mrs. Goddard would be very much surprized if she knew what had happened. I am sure Miss Nash would—for Miss Nash thinks her own sister very well married, and it is only a linen-draper."[4]

"One should be sorry to see greater pride or refinement in the teacher of a school, Harriet. I dare say Miss Nash would envy you such an opportunity as this of being married. Even this conquest would appear valuable in her eyes. As to anything superior for you, I suppose she is quite in the dark. The attentions of a certain person can hardly be among the tittle-tattle of Highbury yet. Hitherto I fancy you and I are the only people to whom his looks and manners have explained themselves."

Harriet blushed and smiled, and said something about wondering that people should like her so much. The idea of Mr. Elton was certainly cheering; but still, after a time, she was tender-hearted again towards the rejected Mr. Martin.

"Now he has got my letter," said she softly. "I wonder what they are all doing—whether his sisters know—if he is unhappy, they will be unhappy too. I hope he will not mind it so very much."

"Let us think of those among our absent friends who are more cheerfully employed," cried Emma. "At this moment, perhaps, Mr. Elton is shewing your picture to his mother and sisters, telling how much more beautiful is the original, and after being asked for it five or six times, allowing them to hear your name, your own dear name."

"My picture!—But he has left my picture in Bond-street."

"Has he so!—Then I know nothing of Mr. Elton. No, my dear little modest Harriet, depend upon it the picture will not be in Bond-street till just before he mounts his horse to-morrow. It is his companion all this evening, his solace, his delight. It opens his designs to his family, it introduces you among them, it diffuses through the party those pleasantest feelings of our nature, eager curiosity and warm prepossession. How cheerful, how animated, how suspicious, how busy their imaginations all are!"

Harriet smiled again, and her smiles grew stronger.

4. Retail cloth merchant.

Chapter VIII

Harriet slept at Hartfield that night. For some weeks past she had been spending more than half her time there, and gradually getting to have a bed-room appropriated to herself; and Emma judged it best in every respect, safest and kindest, to keep her with them as much as possible just at present. She was obliged to go the next morning for an hour or two to Mrs. Goddard's, but it was then to be settled that she should return to Hartfield, to make a regular visit of some days.

While she was gone, Mr. Knightley called, and sat some time with Mr. Woodhouse and Emma, till Mr. Woodhouse, who had previously made up his mind to walk out, was persuaded by his daughter not to defer it, and was induced by the entreaties of both, though against the scruples of his own civility, to leave Mr. Knightley for that purpose. Mr. Knightley, who had nothing of ceremony about him, was offering by his short, decided answers, an amusing contrast to the protracted apologies and civil hesitations of the other.

"Well, I believe, if you will excuse me, Mr. Knightley, if you will not consider me as doing a very rude thing, I shall take Emma's advice and go out for a quarter of an hour. As the sun is out, I believe I had better take my three turns while I can. I treat you without ceremony, Mr. Knightley. We invalids think we are privileged people."

"My dear sir, do not make a stranger of me."

"I leave an excellent substitute in my daughter. Emma will be happy to entertain you. And therefore I think I will beg your excuse and take my three turns—my winter walk."

"You cannot do better, sir."

"I would ask for the pleasure of your company, Mr. Knightley, but I am a very slow walker, and my pace would be tedious to you; and besides, you have another long walk before you, to Donwell Abbey."

"Thank you, sir, thank you; I am going this moment myself; and I think the sooner *you* go the better. I will fetch your great coat and open the garden door for you."

Mr. Woodhouse at last was off; but Mr. Knightley, instead of being immediately off likewise, sat down again, seemingly inclined for more chat. He began speaking of Harriet, and speaking of her with more voluntary praise than Emma had ever heard before.

"I cannot rate her beauty as you do," said he; "but she is a pretty little creature, and I am inclined to think very well of her disposition. Her character depends upon those she is with; but in good hands she will turn out a valuable woman."

"I am glad you think so; and the good hands, I hope, may not be wanting."

"Come," said he, "you are anxious for a compliment, so I will tell you that you have improved her. You have cured her of her school-girl's giggle; she really does you credit."

"Thank you. I should be mortified indeed if I did not believe I had been of some use; but it is not every body who will bestow praise where they may. *You* do not often overpower me with it."

"You are expecting her again, you say, this morning?"

"Almost every moment. She has been gone longer already than she intended."

"Something has happened to delay her; some visitors perhaps."

"Highbury gossips!—Tiresome wretches!"

"Harriet may not consider every body tiresome that you would."

Emma knew this was too true for contradiction, and therefore said nothing. He presently added, with a smile,

"I do not pretend to fix on times or places, but I must tell you that I have good reason to believe your little friend will soon hear of something to her advantage."

"Indeed! how so? of what sort?"

"A very serious sort, I assure you;" still smiling.

"Very serious! I can think of but one thing—Who is in love with her? Who makes you their confidant?"

Emma was more than half in hopes of Mr. Elton's having dropt a hint. Mr. Knightley was a sort of general friend and adviser, and she knew Mr. Elton looked up to him.

"I have some reason to think," he replied, "that Harriet Smith will soon have an offer of marriage, and from a most unexception-able[5] quarter:—Robert Martin is the man. Her visit to Abbey-Mill, this summer, seems to have done his business. He is desperately in love and means to marry her."

"He is very obliging," said Emma; "but is he sure that Harriet means to marry him?"

"Well, well, means to make her an offer then. Will that do? He came to the Abbey two evenings ago, on purpose to consult me about it. He knows I have a thorough regard for him and all his family, and, I believe, considers me as one of his best friends. He came to ask me whether I thought it would be imprudent in him to settle so early; whether I thought her too young: in short, whether I approved his choice altogether; having some apprehension per-haps of her being considered (especially since *your* making so much of her) as in a line of society above him. I was very much pleased with all that he said. I never hear better sense from any one than Robert Martin. He always speaks to the purpose; open, straight forward,

5. When referring to a person, someone to whom no exception can be taken.

and very well judging. He told me every thing; his circumstances
and plans, and what they all proposed doing in the event of his marriage. He is an excellent young man, both as son and brother. I had
no hesitation in advising him to marry. He proved to me that he
could afford it; and that being the case, I was convinced he could not
do better. I praised the fair lady too, and altogether sent him away
very happy. If he had never esteemed my opinion before, he would
have thought highly of me then; and, I dare say, left the house thinking me the best friend and counsellor man ever had. This happened
the night before last. Now, as we may fairly suppose, he would not
allow much time to pass before he spoke to the lady, and as he does
not appear to have spoken yesterday, it is not unlikely that he should
be at Mrs. Goddard's to day; and she may be detained by a visitor,
without thinking him at all a tiresome wretch."

"Pray, Mr. Knightley," said Emma, who had been smiling to herself through a great part of this speech, "how do you know that Mr.
Martin did not speak yesterday?"

"Certainly," replied he, surprised, "I do not absolutely know it;
but it may be inferred. Was not she the whole day with you?"

"Come," said she, "I will tell you something, in return for what
you have told me. He did speak yesterday—that is, he wrote, and
was refused."

This was obliged to be repeated before it could be believed; and
Mr. Knightley actually looked red with surprize and displeasure, as
he stood up, in tall indignation, and said,

"Then she is a greater simpleton than I ever believed her. What is
the foolish girl about?"

"Oh! to be sure," cried Emma, "it is always incomprehensible to a
man that a woman should ever refuse an offer of marriage. A man
always imagines a woman to be ready for anybody who asks her."

"Nonsense! a man does not imagine any such thing. But what is
the meaning of this? Harriet Smith refuse Robert Martin? madness, if it is so; but I hope you are mistaken."

"I saw her answer, nothing could be clearer."

"You saw her answer! you wrote her answer too. Emma, this is
your doing. You persuaded her to refuse him."

"And if I did, (which, however, I am far from allowing,) I should
not feel that I had done wrong. Mr. Martin is a very respectable
young man, but I cannot admit him to be Harriet's equal; and am
rather surprised indeed that he should have ventured to address
her. By your account, he does seem to have had some scruples. It is
a pity that they were ever got over."

"Not Harriet's equal!" exclaimed Mr. Knightley loudly and warmly;
and with calmer asperity, added, a few moments afterwards, "No, he
is not her equal indeed, for he is as much her superior in sense as in

situation. Emma, your infatuation about that girl blinds you. What are Harriet Smith's claims, either of birth, nature or education, to any connection higher than Robert Martin? She is the natural daughter of nobody knows whom, with probably no settled provision at all, and certainly no respectable relations. She is known only as a parlour-boarder at a common school. She is not a sensible girl, nor a girl of any information. She has been taught nothing useful, and is too young and too simple to have acquired any thing herself. At her age she can have no experience, and with her little wit, is not very likely ever to have any that can avail her. She is pretty, and she is good tempered, and that is all. My only scruple in advising the match was on his account, as being beneath his deserts, and a bad connexion for him. I felt, that as to fortune, in all probability he might do much better; and that as to a rational companion or useful helpmate, he could not do worse. But I could not reason so to a man in love, and was willing to trust to there being no harm in her, to her having that sort of disposition, which, in good hands, like his, might be easily led aright and turn out very well. The advantage of the match I felt to be all on her side; and had not the smallest doubt (nor have I now) that there would be a general cry-out upon her extreme good luck. Even *your* satisfaction I made sure of. It crossed my mind immediately that you would not regret your friend's leaving Highbury, for the sake of her being settled so well. I remember saying to myself, 'Even Emma, with all her partiality for Harriet, will think this is a good match.'"

"I cannot help wondering at your knowing so little of Emma as to say any such thing. What! think a farmer, (and with all his sense and all his merit Mr. Martin is nothing more,) a good match for my inti- mate friend! Not regret her leaving Highbury for the sake of marry- ing a man whom I could never admit as an acquaintance of my own! I wonder you should think it possible for me to have such feelings. I assure you mine are very different. I must think your statement by no means fair. You are not just to Harriet's claims. They would be estimated very differently by others as well as by myself; Mr. Martin may be the richest of the two, but he is undoubtedly her inferior as to rank in society.—The sphere in which she moves is much above his.—It would be a degradation."

"A degradation to illegitimacy and ignorance, to be married to a respectable, intelligent gentleman-farmer!"

"As to the circumstances of her birth, though in a legal sense she may be called Nobody, it will not hold in common sense. She is not to pay for the offence of others, by being held below the level of those with whom she is brought up.—There can scarcely be a doubt that her father is a gentleman—and a gentleman of fortune.—Her allow- ance is very liberal; nothing has ever been grudged for her improve- ment or comfort.—That she is a gentleman's daughter, is indubitable to me; that she associates with gentlemen's daughters, no one, I apprehend, will deny.—She is superior to Mr. Robert Martin."

"Whoever might be her parents," said Mr. Knightley, "whoever may have had the charge of her, it does not appear to have been any part of their plan to introduce her into what you would call good society. After receiving a very indifferent education she is left in Mrs. Goddard's hands to shift as she can;—to move, in short, in Mrs. Goddard's line, to have Mrs. Goddard's acquaintance. Her friends evidently thought this good enough for her; and it *was* good enough. She desired nothing better herself. Till you chose to turn her into a friend, her mind had no distaste for her own set, nor any ambition beyond it. She was as happy as possible with the Martins in the summer. She had no sense of superiority then. If she has it now, you have given it. You have been no friend to Harriet Smith, Emma. Robert Martin would never have proceeded so far, if he had not felt persuaded of her not being disinclined to him. I know him well. He has too much real feeling to address any woman on the hap-hazard of selfish passion. And as to conceit, he is the farthest from it of any man I know. Depend upon it he had encouragement."

It was most convenient to Emma not to make a direct reply to this assertion; she chose rather to take up her own line of the subject again.

"You are a very warm friend to Mr. Martin; but, as I said before, are unjust to Harriet. Harriet's claims to marry well are not so contemptible as you represent them. She is not a clever girl, but she has better sense than you are aware of, and does not deserve to have her understanding spoken of so slightingly. Waving that point, however, and supposing her to be, as you describe her, only pretty and good-natured, let me tell you, that in the degree she possesses them, they are not trivial recommendations to the world in general, for she is, in fact, a beautiful girl, and must be thought so by ninety-nine people out of an hundred; and till it appears that men are much more philosophic on the subject of beauty than they are generally supposed; till they do fall in love with well-informed minds instead of handsome faces, a girl, with such loveliness as Harriet, has a certainty of being admired and sought after, of having the power of choosing from among many, consequently a claim to be nice. Her good-nature, too, is not so very slight a claim, comprehending, as it does, real, thorough sweetness of temper and manner, a very humble opinion of herself, and a great readiness to be pleased with other people. I am very much mistaken if your sex in general would not think such beauty, and such temper, the highest claims a woman could possess."

"Upon my word, Emma, to hear you abusing the reason you have, is almost enough to make me think so too. Better be without sense, than misapply it as you do."

"To be sure!" cried she playfully, "I know *that* is the feeling of you all. I know that such a girl as Harriet is exactly what every man delights in—what at once bewitches his senses and satisfies his judgment. Oh! Harriet may pick and choose. Were you, yourself, ever to marry, she is the very woman for you. And is she, at seventeen, just entering into life, just beginning to be known, to be wondered at because she does not accept the first offer she receives? No—pray let her have time to look about her."

"I have always thought it a very foolish intimacy," said Mr. Knightley presently, "though I have kept my thoughts to myself; but I now perceive that it will be a very unfortunate one for Harriet. You will puff her up with such ideas of her own beauty, and of what she has a claim to, that, in a little while, nobody within her reach will be good enough for her. Vanity working on a weak head, produces every sort of mischief. Nothing so easy as for a young lady to raise her expectations too high. Miss Harriet Smith may not find offers of marriage flow in so fast, though she is a very pretty girl. Men of sense, whatever you may chuse to say, do not want silly wives. Men of family would not be very fond of connecting themselves with a girl of such obscurity—and most prudent men would be afraid of the inconvenience and disgrace they might be involved in, when the mystery of her parentage came to be revealed. Let her marry Robert Martin, and she is safe, respectable, and happy for ever; but if you encourage her to expect to marry greatly, and teach her to be satisfied with nothing less than a man of consequence and large fortune, she may be a parlour-boarder at Mrs. Goddard's all the rest of her life—or, at least, (for Harriet Smith is a girl who will marry somebody or other,) till she grow desperate, and is glad to catch at the old writing master's[6] son."

"We think so very differently on this point, Mr. Knightley, that there can be no use in canvassing[7] it. We shall only be making each other more angry. But as to my *letting* her marry Robert Martin, it is impossible; she has refused him, and so decidedly, I think, as must prevent any second application. She must abide by the evil of having refused him, whatever it may be; and as to the refusal itself, I will not pretend to say that I might not influence her a little; but I assure you there was very little for me or for anybody to do. His appearance is so much against him, and his manner so bad, that if she ever were disposed to favour him, she is not now. I can imagine, that before she had seen anybody superior, she might tolerate him. He was the brother of her friends, and he took pains to please her; and altogether, having seen nobody better (that must have been his

6. Penmanship teacher's.
7. Debating.

great assistant) she might not, while she was at Abbey-Mill, find him disagreeable. But the case is altered now. She knows now what gentlemen are; and nothing but a gentleman in education and manner has any chance with Harriet."

"Nonsense, errant nonsense, as ever was talked!" cried Mr. Knightley.—"Robert Martin's manners have sense, sincerity, and good-humour to recommend them; and his mind has more true gentility than Harriet Smith could understand."

Emma made no answer, and tried to look cheerfully unconcerned, but was really feeling uncomfortable and wanting him very much to be gone. She did not repent what she had done; she still thought herself a better judge of such a point of female right and refinement than he could be; but yet she had a sort of habitual respect for his judgment in general, which made her dislike having it so loudly against her; and to have him sitting just opposite her in angry state, was very disagreeable. Some minutes passed in this unpleasant silence, with only one attempt on Emma's side to talk of the weather, but he made no answer. He was thinking. The result of his thoughts appeared at last in these words.

"Robert Martin has no great loss—if he can but think so; and I hope it will not be long before he does. Your views for Harriet are best known to yourself; but as you make no secret of your love of match-making, it is fair to suppose that views, and plans, and projects you have;—and as a friend I shall just hint to you that if Elton is the man, I think it will be all labour in vain."

Emma laughed and disclaimed. He continued.

"Depend upon it, Elton will not do. Elton is a very good sort of man, and a very respectable vicar of Highbury, but not at all likely to make an imprudent match. He knows the value of a good income as well as anybody. Elton may talk sentimentally, but he will act rationally. He is as well acquainted with his own claims, as you can be with Harriet's. He knows that he is a very handsome young man, and a great favourite wherever he goes; and from his general way of talking in unreserved moments, where there are only men present, I am convinced that he does not mean to throw himself away. I have heard him speak with great animation of a large family of young ladies that his sisters are intimate with, who have all twenty thousand pounds apiece."[8]

"I am very much obliged to you," said Emma, laughing again. "If I had set my heart on Mr. Elton's marrying Harriet, it would have been very kind to open my eyes; but at present I only want to keep Harriet to myself. I have done with match-making indeed. I could

---

8. A significant sum for a wife to bring to a marriage.

never hope to equal my own doings at Randalls. I shall leave off while I am well."

"Good morning to you,"—said he, rising and walking off abruptly. He was very much vexed. He felt the disappointment of the young man, and was mortified to have been the means of promoting it, by the sanction he had given; and the part which he was persuaded Emma had taken in the affair, was provoking him exceedingly.

Emma remained in a state of vexation too; but there was more indistinctness in the causes of her's, than in his. She did not always feel so absolutely satisfied with herself, so entirely convinced that her opinions were right and her adversary's wrong, as Mr. Knightley. He walked off in more complete self-approbation than he left for her. She was not so materially cast down, however, but that a little time and the return of Harriet were very adequate restoratives. Harriet's staying away so long was beginning to make her uneasy. The possibility of the young man's coming to Mrs. Goddard's that morning, and meeting with Harriet and pleading his own cause, gave alarming ideas. The dread of such a failure after all became the prominent uneasiness; and when Harriet appeared, and in very good spirits, and without having any such reason to give for her long absence, she felt a satisfaction which settled her with her own mind, and convinced her, that let Mr. Knightley think or say what he would, she had done nothing which woman's friendship and woman's feelings would not justify.

He had frightened her a little about Mr. Elton; but when she considered that Mr. Knightley could not have observed him as she had done, neither with the interest, nor (she must be allowed to tell herself, in spite of Mr. Knightley's pretensions) with the skill of such an observer on such a question as herself, that he had spoken it hastily and in anger, she was able to believe, that he had rather said what he wished resentfully to be true, than what he knew any thing about. He certainly might have heard Mr. Elton speak with more unreserve than she had ever done, and Mr. Elton might not be of an imprudent, inconsiderate disposition as to money-matters; he might naturally be rather attentive than otherwise to them; but then, Mr. Knightley did not make due allowance for the influence of a strong passion at war with all interested motives. Mr. Knightley saw no such passion, and of course thought nothing of its effects; but she saw too much of it, to feel a doubt of its overcoming any hesitations that a reasonable prudence might originally suggest; and more than a reasonable, becoming degree of prudence, she was very sure did not belong to Mr. Elton.

Harriet's cheerful look and manner established her's: she came back, not to think of Mr. Martin, but to talk of Mr. Elton. Miss Nash had been telling her something, which she repeated immediately with great delight. Mr. Perry had been to Mrs. Goddard's to attend a sick child, and Miss Nash had seen him, and he had told Miss Nash, that as he was coming back yesterday from Clayton Park, he had met Mr. Elton, and found to his great surprize that Mr. Elton was actually on his road to London, and not meaning to return till the morrow, though it was the whist-club[9] night, which he had been never known to miss before; and Mr. Perry had remonstrated with him about it, and told him how shabby it was in him, their best player, to absent himself, and tried very much to persuade him to put off his journey only one day; but it would not do; Mr. Elton had been determined to go on, and had said in a *very particular* way indeed, that he was going on business which he would not put off for any inducement in the world; and something about a very enviable commission, and being the bearer of something exceedingly precious. Mr. Perry could not quite understand him, but he was very sure there must be a *lady* in the case, and he told him so; and Mr. Elton only looked very conscious and smiling, and rode off in great spirits. Miss Nash had told her all this, and had talked a great deal more about Mr. Elton; and said, looking so very significantly at her, "that she did not pretend to understand what his business might be, but she only knew that any woman whom Mr. Elton could prefer, she should think the luckiest woman in the world; for, beyond a doubt, Mr. Elton had not his equal for beauty or agreeableness."

Chapter IX

Mr. Knightley might quarrel with her, but Emma could not quarrel with herself. He was so much displeased, that it was longer than usual before he came to Hartfield again; and when they did meet, his grave looks shewed that she was not forgiven. She was sorry, but could not repent. On the contrary, her plans and proceedings were more and more justified, and endeared to her by the general appearances of the next few days.

The Picture, elegantly framed, came safely to hand soon after Mr. Elton's return, and being hung over the mantle-piece of the common sitting-room, he got up to look at it, and sighed out his half sentences of admiration just as he ought; and as for Harriet's feelings, they were visibly forming themselves into as strong and steady an attachment as her youth and sort of mind admitted. Emma was soon perfectly satisfied of Mr. Martin's being no otherwise remembered, than as he furnished a contrast with Mr. Elton, of the utmost advantage to the latter.

---

9. Whist was a card game much like bridge.

Her views of improving her little friend's mind, by a great deal of useful reading and conversation, had never yet led to more than a few first chapters, and the intention of going on to-morrow. It was much easier to chat than to study; much pleasanter to let her imagination range and work at Harriet's fortune, than to be labouring to enlarge her comprehension or exercise it on sober facts; and the only literary pursuit which engaged Harriet at present, the only mental provision she was making for the evening of life, was the collecting and transcribing all the riddles of every sort that she could meet with, into a thin quarto of hot-pressed paper, made up by her friend, and ornamented with cyphers and trophies.[1]

In this age of literature, such collections on a very grand scale are not uncommon. Miss Nash, head-teacher at Mrs. Goddard's, had written out at least three hundred; and Harriet, who had taken the first hint of it from her, hoped, with Miss Woodhouse's help, to get a great many more. Emma assisted with her invention, memory and taste; and as Harriet wrote a very pretty hand, it was likely to be an arrangement of the first order, in form as well as quantity.

Mr. Woodhouse was almost as much interested in the business as the girls, and tried very often to recollect something worth their putting in. "So many clever riddles as there used to be when he was young—he wondered he could not remember them! but he hoped he should in time." And it always ended in "Kitty, a fair but frozen maid."[2]

His good friend Perry too, whom he had spoken to on the subject, did not at present recollect any thing of the riddle kind; but he had desired Perry to be upon the watch, and as he went about so much, something, he thought, might come from that quarter.

It was by no means his daughter's wish that the intellects of Highbury in general should be put under requisition. Mr. Elton was the only one whose assistance she asked. He was invited to contribute any really good enigmas, charades, or conundrums that he might recollect; and she had the pleasure of seeing him most intently at work with his recollections; and at the same time, as she could perceive, most earnestly careful that nothing ungallant, nothing that did not breathe a compliment to the sex should pass his lips. They owed to him their two or three politest puzzles; and the joy and exultation with which at last he recalled, and rather sentimentally recited, that well-known charade,

---

1. Notebook of fine, glossy paper, decorated with monograms and painted figures.
2. See p. 58 for the first stanza of this popular riddle, attributed to the actor David Garrick and printed in the collection *The New Foundling Hospital for Wit* (1784), with its answer, "A Chimney Sweep." The riddle, with its risqué language, is printed in full in the supplementary materials to this Norton Critical Edition.

My first doth affliction denote,
　　Which my second is destin'd to feel
And my whole is the best antidote
　　That affliction to soften and heal.—[3]

made her quite sorry to acknowledge that they had transcribed it some pages ago already.

"Why will not you write one yourself for us, Mr. Elton?" said she; "that is the only security for its freshness; and nothing could be easier to you."

"Oh, no! he had never written, hardly ever, any thing of the kind in his life. The stupidest fellow! He was afraid not even Miss Woodhouse"—he stopt a moment—"or Miss Smith could inspire him."

The very next day however produced some proof of inspiration. He called for a few moments, just to leave a piece of paper on the table containing, as he said, a charade, which a friend of his had addressed to a young lady, the object of his admiration, but which, from his manner, Emma was immediately convinced must be his own.

"I do not offer it for Miss Smith's collection," said he. "Being my friend's, I have no right to expose it in any degree to the public eye, but perhaps you may not dislike looking at it."

The speech was more to Emma than to Harriet, which Emma could understand. There was deep consciousness about him, and he found it easier to meet her eye than her friend's. He was gone the next moment:—after another moment's pause,

"Take it," said Emma, smiling, and pushing the paper towards Harriet—"it is for you. Take your own."

But Harriet was in a tremor, and could not touch it; and Emma, never loth to be first, was obliged to examine it herself.

To Miss——.
CHARADE.

My first displays the wealth and pomp of kings,
　　Lords of the earth! their luxury and ease.
Another view of man, my second brings,
　　Behold him there, the monarch of the seas!

3. A version of this "well-known" charade (which the OED defines as "a kind of riddle, in which each syllable of the word to be guessed, and sometimes the word itself also, is enigmatically described") was published in Maria Edgeworth's *Early Lessons* (1801), with its answer, "woman." The OED defines an "enigma" as "a short composition in prose or verse, in which something is described by intentionally obscure metaphors, in order to afford an exercise for the ingenuity of the reader or hearer in guessing what is meant; a riddle," and a "conundrum" as "a riddle in the form of a question the answer to which involves a pun or play on words."

But, ah! united, what reverse we have!
　　Man's boasted power and freedom, all are flown;
Lord of the earth and sea, he bends a slave,
　　And woman, lovely woman, reigns alone.

Thy ready wit the word will soon supply,
　　May its approval beam in that soft eye!

She cast her eye over it, pondered, caught the meaning, read it through again to be quite certain, and quite mistress of the lines, and then passing it to Harriet, sat happily smiling, and saying to herself, while Harriet was puzzling over the paper in all the confusion of hope and dulness, "Very well, Mr. Elton, very well, indeed. I have read worse charades. *Courtship*—a very good hint. I give you credit for it. This is feeling your way. This is saying very plainly—'Pray, Miss Smith, give me leave to pay my addresses to you. Approve my charade and my intentions in the same glance.'

May its approval beam in that soft eye!

Harriet exactly. Soft, is the very word for her eye—of all epithets, the justest that could be given.

Thy ready wit the word will soon supply.

Humph—Harriet's ready wit! All the better. A man must be very much in love indeed, to describe her so. Ah! Mr. Knightley, I wish you had the benefit of this; I think this would convince you. For once in your life you would be obliged to own yourself mistaken. An excellent charade indeed! and very much to the purpose. Things must come to a crisis soon now."

She was obliged to break off from these very pleasant observations, which were otherwise of a sort to run into great length, by the eagerness of Harriet's wondering questions.

"What can it be, Miss Woodhouse?—what can it be? I have not an idea—I cannot guess it in the least. What can it possibly be? Do try to find it out, Miss Woodhouse. Do help me. I never saw any thing so hard. Is it kingdom? I wonder who the friend was—and who could be the young lady! Do you think it is a good one? Can it be woman?

And woman, lovely woman, reigns alone.

Can it be Neptune?

Behold him there, the monarch of the seas!

Or a trident? or a mermaid? or a shark? Oh, no! shark is only one syllable. It must be very clever, or he would not have brought it. Oh! Miss Woodhouse, do you think we shall ever find it out?"

"Mermaids and sharks! Nonsense! My dear Harriet, what are you thinking of? Where would be the use of his bringing us a charade made by a friend upon a mermaid or a shark? Give me the paper and listen.

"For Miss ——, read Miss Smith.

> My first displays the wealth and pomp of kings,
>   Lords of the earth! their luxury and ease.

That is *court*.

> Another view of man, my second brings;
>   Behold him there, the monarch of the seas!

That is *ship*;—plain as can be.—Now for the cream.

> But ah! united, (*courtship*, you know,) what reverse we have!
>   Man's boasted power and freedom, all are flown.
> Lord of the earth and sea, he bends a slave,
>   And woman, lovely woman, reigns alone.

A very proper compliment!—and then follows the application, which I think, my dear Harriet, you cannot find much difficulty in comprehending. Read it in comfort to yourself. There can be no doubt of its being written for you and to you."

Harriet could not long resist so delightful a persuasion. She read the concluding lines, and was all flutter and happiness. She could not speak. But she was not wanted to speak. It was enough for her to feel. Emma spoke for her.

"There is so pointed, and so particular a meaning in this compliment," said she, "that I cannot have a moment's doubt as to Mr. Elton's intentions. You are his object—and you will soon receive the completest proof of it. I thought it must be so. I thought I could not be so deceived; but now, it is clear; the state of his mind is as clear and decided, as my wishes on the subject have been ever since I knew you. Yes, Harriet, just so long have I been wanting the very circumstance to happen which has happened. I could never tell whether an attachment between you and Mr. Elton were most desirable or most natural. Its probability and its eligibility have really so equalled each other! I am very happy. I congratulate you, my dear Harriet, with all my heart. This is an attachment which a woman may well feel pride in creating. This is a connection which offers nothing but good. It will give you every thing that you want—consideration, independence, a proper home—it will fix you in the centre of all your real friends, close to Hartfield and to me, and confirm our intimacy for ever. This, Harriet, is an alliance which can never raise a blush in either of us."

"Dear Miss Woodhouse"—and "Dear Miss Woodhouse," was all that Harriet, with many tender embraces could articulate at first;

but when they did arrive at something more like conversation, it was sufficiently clear to her friend that she saw, felt, anticipated, and remembered just as she ought. Mr. Elton's superiority had very ample acknowledgment.

"Whatever you say is always right," cried Harriet, "and therefore I suppose, and believe, and hope it must be so; but otherwise I could not have imagined it. It is so much beyond any thing I deserve. Mr. Elton, who might marry any body! There cannot be two opinions about *him*. He is so very superior. Only think of those sweet verses— 'To Miss ——.' Dear me, how clever!—Could it really be meant for me?"

"I cannot make a question, or listen to a question about that. It is a certainty. Receive it on my judgment. It is a sort of prologue to the play, a motto to the chapter; and will be soon followed by matter-of-fact prose."

"It is a sort of thing which nobody could have expected. I am sure, a month ago, I had no more idea myself!—The strangest things do take place!"

——"When Miss Smiths and Mr. Eltons get acquainted—they do indeed—and really it is strange; it is out of the common course that what is so evidently, so palpably desirable—what courts the prearrangement of other people, should so immediately shape itself into the proper form. You and Mr. Elton are by situation called together; you belong to one another by every circumstance of your respective homes. Your marrying will be equal to the match at Randalls. There does seem to be a something in the air of Hartfield which gives love exactly the right direction, and sends it into the very channel where it ought to flow.

The course of true love never did run smooth—[4]

A Hartfield edition of Shakespeare would have a long note on that passage."

"That Mr. Elton should really be in love with me,—me, of all people, who did not know him, to speak to him, at Michaelmas![5] And he, the very handsomest man that ever was, and a man that every body looks up to, quite like Mr. Knightley! His company so sought after, that every body says he need not eat a single meal by himself if he does not chuse it; that he has more invitations than there are days in the week. And so excellent in the Church! Miss Nash has put down all the texts he has ever preached from since he came to Highbury. Dear me! When I look back to the first time I saw him! How little did I think!—The two Abbotts and I ran into the front room and peeped

4. From *A Midsummer Night's Dream* 1.1.134.
5. St. Michael's day, September 29, one of the four quarter days that mark the English business, and academic, year.

through the blind when we heard he was going by, and Miss Nash came and scolded us away, and staid to look through herself; however, she called me back presently, and let me look too, which was very good-natured. And how beautiful we thought he looked! He was arm in arm with Mr. Cole."

"This is an alliance which, whoever—whatever your friends may be, must be agreeable to them, provided at least they have common sense; and we are not to be addressing our conduct to fools. If they are anxious to see you *happily* married, here is a man whose amiable character gives every assurance of it;—if they wish to have you settled in the same country and circle which they have chosen to place you in, here it will be accomplished; and if their only object is that you should, in the common phrase, be *well* married, here is the comfortable fortune, the respectable establishment, the rise in the world which must satisfy them."

"Yes, very true. How nicely you talk; I love to hear you. You understand every thing. You and Mr. Elton are one as clever as the other. This charade!—If I had studied a twelvemonth, I could never have made any thing like it."

"I thought he meant to try his skill, by his manner of declining it yesterday."

"I do think it is, without exception, the best charade I ever read."

"I never read one more to the purpose, certainly."

"It is as long again as almost all we have had before."

"I do not consider its length as particularly in its favour. Such things in general cannot be too short."

Harriet was too intent on the lines to hear. The most satisfactory comparisons were rising in her mind.

"It is one thing," said she, presently—her cheeks in a glow—"to have very good sense in a common way, like every body else, and if there is any thing to say, to sit down and write a letter, and say just what you must, in a short way; and another, to write verses and charades like this."

Emma could not have desired a more spirited rejection of Mr. Martin's prose.

"Such sweet lines!" continued Harriet—"these two last!—But how shall I ever be able to return the paper, or say I have found it out?—Oh! Miss Woodhouse, what can we do about that?"

"Leave it to me. You do nothing. He will be here this evening, I dare say, and then I will give it him back, and some nonsense or other will pass between us, and you shall not be committed.—Your soft eyes shall chuse their own time for beaming. Trust to me."

"Oh! Miss Woodhouse, what a pity that I must not write this beautiful charade into my book! I am sure I have not got one half so good."

"Leave out the two last lines, and there is no reason why you should not write it into your book."

"Oh! but those two lines are"—— "——The best of all. Granted;— for private enjoyment; and for private enjoyment keep them. They are not at all the less written you know, because you divide them. The couplet does not cease to be, nor does its meaning change. But take it away, and all *appropriation* ceases, and a very pretty gallant charade remains, fit for any collection. Depend upon it, he would not like to have his charade slighted, much better than his passion. A poet in love must be encouraged in both capacities, or neither. Give me the book, I will write it down, and then there can be no possible reflection on you."

Harriet submitted, though her mind could hardly separate the parts, so as to feel quite sure that her friend were not writing down a declaration of love. It seemed too precious an offering for any degree of publicity.

"I shall never let that book go out of my own hands," said she.

"Very well," replied Emma, "a most natural feeling; and the longer it lasts, the better I shall be pleased. But here is my father coming: you will not object to my reading the charade to him. It will be giving him so much pleasure! He loves any thing of the sort, and especially any thing that pays woman a compliment. He has the tenderest spirit of gallantry towards us all!—You must let me read it to him."

Harriet looked grave.

"My dear Harriet, you must not refine too much upon this charade.—You will betray your feelings improperly, if you are too conscious and too quick, and appear to affix more meaning, or even quite all the meaning which may be affixed to it. Do not be over-powered by such a little tribute of admiration. If he had been anxious for secrecy, he would not have left the paper while I was by; but he rather pushed it towards me than towards you. Do not let us be too solemn on the business. He has encouragement enough to proceed, without our sighing out our souls over this charade."

"Oh! no—I hope I shall not be ridiculous about it. Do as you please."

Mr. Woodhouse came in, and very soon led to the subject again, by the recurrence of his very frequent inquiry of "Well, my dears, how does your book go on?—Have you got any thing fresh?"

"Yes, papa, we have something to read you, something quite fresh. A piece of paper was found on the table this morning—(dropt, we suppose, by a fairy)—containing a very pretty charade, and we have just copied it in."

She read it to him, just as he liked to have any thing read, slowly and distinctly, and two or three times over, with explanations of every part as she proceeded—and he was very much pleased, and, as she had foreseen, especially struck with the complimentary conclusion.

"Aye, that's very just, indeed, that's very properly said. Very true. 'Woman, lovely woman.' It is such a pretty charade, my dear, that I can easily guess what fairy brought it.—Nobody could have written so prettily, but you, Emma."

Emma only nodded, and smiled.—After a little thinking, and a very tender sigh, he added,

"Ah! it is no difficulty to see who you take after! Your dear mother was so clever at all those things! If I had but her memory! But I can remember nothing;—not even that particular riddle which you have heard me mention; I can only recollect the first stanza; and there are several.

> Kitty, a fair but frozen maid,
>   Kindled a flame I yet deplore,
> The hood-wink'd boy I called to aid,
> Though of his near approach afraid,
>   So fatal to my suit before.

And that is all that I can recollect of it—but it is very clever all the way through. But I think, my dear, you said you had got it."

"Yes, papa, it is written out in our second page. We copied it from the Elegant Extracts. It was Garrick's, you know."

"Aye, very true.—I wish I could recollect more of it.

> Kitty, a fair but frozen maid.

The name makes me think of poor Isabella; for she was very near being christened Catherine after her grandmama. I hope we shall have her here next week. Have you thought, my dear, where you shall put her—and what room there will be for the children?"

"Oh! yes—she will have her own room, of course; the room she always has;—and there is the nursery for the children,—just as usual, you know.—Why should there be any change?"

"I do not know, my dear—but it is so long since she was here!—not since last Easter, and then only for a few days.—Mr. John Knightley's being a lawyer is very inconvenient.—Poor Isabella!—She is sadly taken away from us all!—and how sorry she will be when she comes, not to see Miss Taylor here!"

"She will not be surprised, papa, at least."

"I do not know, my dear. I am sure I was very much surprised when I first heard she was going to be married."

"We must ask Mr. and Mrs. Weston to dine with us, while Isabella is here."

"Yes, my dear, if there is time.—But—(in a very depressed tone)—she is coming for only one week. There will not be time for any thing."

"It is unfortunate that they cannot stay longer—but it seems a case of necessity. Mr. John Knightley must be in town again on the 28th, and we ought to be thankful, papa, that we are to have the whole of the time they can give to the country, that two or three days are not to be taken out for the Abbey. Mr. Knightley promises to give up his claim this Christmas—though you know it is longer since they were with him, than with us."

"It would be very hard indeed, my dear, if poor Isabella were to be anywhere but at Hartfield."

Mr. Woodhouse could never allow for Mr. Knightley's claims on his brother, or any body's claims on Isabella, except his own. He sat musing a little while, and then said,

"But I do not see why poor Isabella should be obliged to go back so soon, though he does. I think, Emma, I shall try and persuade her to stay longer with us. She and the children might stay very well."

"Ah! papa—that is what you never have been able to accomplish, and I do not think you ever will. Isabella cannot bear to stay behind her husband."

This was too true for contradiction. Unwelcome as it was, Mr. Woodhouse could only give a submissive sigh; and as Emma saw his spirits affected by the idea of his daughter's attachment to her husband, she immediately led to such a branch of subject as must raise them.

"Harriet must give us as much of her company as she can while my brother and sister are here. I am sure she will be pleased with the children. We are very proud of the children, are not we, papa? I wonder which she will think the handsomest, Henry or John?"

"Aye, I wonder which she will. Poor little dears, how glad they will be to come. They are very fond of being at Hartfield, Harriet."

"I dare say they are, sir. I am sure I do not know who is not."

"Henry is a fine boy, but John is very like his mamma. Henry is the eldest, he was named after me, not after his father. John, the second, is named after his father. Some people are surprized, I believe, that the eldest was not, but Isabella would have him called Henry, which I thought very pretty of her. And he is a very clever boy, indeed. They are all remarkably clever; and they have so many pretty ways. They will come and stand by my chair, and say, 'Grandpapa, can you give me a bit of string?' and once Henry asked me for a knife, but I told him knives were only made for grandpapas. I think their father is too rough with them very often."

"He appears rough to you," said Emma, "because you are so very gentle yourself; but if you could compare him with other papas, you would not think him rough. He wishes his boys to be active and hardy; and if they misbehave, can give them a sharp word now and then; but he is an affectionate father—certainly Mr. John Knightley is an affectionate father. The children are all fond of him."

"And then their uncle comes in, and tosses them up to the ceiling in a very frightful way!"

"But they like it, papa; there is nothing they like so much. It is such enjoyment to them, that if their uncle did not lay down the rule of their taking turns, which ever began would never give way to the other."

"Well, I cannot understand it."

"That is the case with us all, papa. One half of the world cannot understand the pleasures of the other."

Later in the morning, and just as the girls were going to separate in preparation for the regular four o'clock dinner, the hero of this inimitable charade walked in again. Harriet turned away; but Emma could receive him with the usual smile, and her quick eye soon discerned in his the consciousness of having made a push—of having thrown a die; and she imagined he was come to see how it might turn up. His ostensible reason, however, was to ask whether Mr. Woodhouse's party could be made up in the evening without him, or whether he should be in the smallest degree necessary at Hartfield. If he were, every thing else must give way; but otherwise his friend Cole had been saying so much about his dining with him—had made such a point of it, that he had promised him conditionally to come.

Emma thanked him, but could not allow of his disappointing his friend on their account; her father was sure of his rubber.[6] He re-urged—she re-declined; and he seemed then about to make his bow, when taking the paper from the table, she returned it—

"Oh! here's the charade you were so obliging as to leave with us; thank you for the sight of it. We admired it so much, that I have ventured to write it into Miss Smith's collection. Your friend will not take it amiss I hope. Of course I have not transcribed beyond the eight first lines."

Mr. Elton certainly did not very well know what to say. He looked rather doubtingly—rather confused; said something about "honour;"—glanced at Emma and at Harriet, and then seeing the book open on the table, took it up, and examined it very attentively. With the view of passing off an awkward moment, Emma smilingly said,

"You must make my apologies to your friend; but so good a charade must not be confined to one or two. He may be sure of every woman's approbation while he writes with such gallantry."

"I have no hesitation in saying," replied Mr. Elton, though hesitating a good deal while he spoke, "I have no hesitation in saying—at least if my friend feels at all as I do—I have not the smallest doubt that, could he see his little effusion honoured as I see it,

6. His game of whist.

(looking at the book again, and replacing it on the table,) he would consider it as the proudest moment of his life."

After this speech he was gone as soon as possible. Emma could not think it too soon; for with all his good and agreeable qualities, there was a sort of parade in his speeches which was very apt to incline her to laugh. She ran away to indulge in the inclination, leaving the tender and the sublime of pleasure to Harriet's share.

Chapter X

Though now the middle of December, there had yet been no weather to prevent the young ladies from tolerably regular exercise; and on the morrow, Emma had a charitable visit to pay to a poor sick family, who lived a little way out of Highbury.

Their road to this detached cottage was down Vicarage-lane, a lane leading at right-angles from the broad, though irregular, main street of the place; and, as may be inferred, containing the blessed abode of Mr. Elton. A few inferior dwellings were first to be passed, and then, about a quarter of a mile down the lane rose the Vicarage; an old and not very good house, almost as close to the road as it could be. It had no advantage of situation; but had been very much smartened up by the present proprietor; and, such as it was, there could be no possibility of the two friends passing it without a slackened pace and observing eyes.—Emma's remark was—

"There it is. There go you and your riddle-book one of these days."—Harriet's was—

"Oh! what a sweet house!—How very beautiful!—There are the yellow curtains that Miss Nash admires so much."

"I do not often walk this way *now*," said Emma, as they proceeded, "but *then* there will be an inducement, and I shall gradually get intimately acquainted with all the hedges, gates, pools, and pollards[7] of this part of Highbury."

Harriet, she found, had never in her life been within side the Vicarage, and her curiosity to see it was so extreme, that, considering exteriors and probabilities, Emma could only class it, as a proof of love, with Mr. Elton's seeing ready wit in her.

"I wish we could contrive it," said she; "but I cannot think of any tolerable pretence for going in;—no servant that I want to inquire about of his housekeeper—no message from my father."

She pondered, but could think of nothing. After a mutual silence of some minutes, Harriet thus began again—

"I do so wonder, Miss Woodhouse, that you should not be married, or going to be married! so charming as you are!"—

7. Trees cut back so as to produce a thick, hedgelike growth.

Emma laughed, and replied,

"My being charming, Harriet, is not quite enough to induce me to marry; I must find other people charming—one other person at least. And I am not only, not going to be married, at present, but have very little intention of ever marrying at all."

"Ah! so you say; but I cannot believe it."

"I must see somebody very superior to any one I have seen yet, to be tempted; Mr. Elton, you know, (recollecting herself,) is out of the question: and I do *not* wish to see any such person. I would rather not be tempted. I cannot really change for the better. If I were to marry, I must expect to repent it."

"Dear me!—it is so odd to hear a woman talk so!"—

"I have none of the usual inducements of women to marry. Were I to fall in love, indeed, it would be a different thing! but I never have been in love; it is not my way, or my nature; and I do not think I ever shall. And, without love, I am sure I should be a fool to change such a situation as mine. Fortune I do not want; employment I do not want; consequence I do not want: I believe few married women are half as much mistress of their husband's house, as I am of Hartfield; and never, never could I expect to be so truly beloved and important; so always first and always right in any man's eyes as I am in my father's."

"But then, to be an old maid at last, like Miss Bates!"

"That is as formidable an image as you could present, Harriet; and if I thought I should ever be like Miss Bates! so silly—so satisfied—so smiling—so prosing—so undistinguishing and unfastidious—and so apt to tell every thing relative to every body about me, I would marry to-morrow. But between *us*, I am convinced there never can be any likeness, except in being unmarried."

"But still, you will be an old maid! and that's so dreadful!"

"Never mind, Harriet, I shall not be a poor old maid; and it is poverty only which makes celibacy contemptible to a generous public! A single woman, with a very narrow income, must be a ridiculous, disagreeable, old maid! the proper sport of boys and girls; but a single woman, of good fortune, is always respectable, and may be as sensible and pleasant as anybody else. And the distinction is not quite so much against the candour and common sense of the world as appears at first; for a very narrow income has a tendency to contract the mind, and sour the temper. Those who can barely live, and who live perforce in a very small, and generally very inferior, society, may well be illiberal and cross. This does not apply, however, to Miss Bates; she is only too good natured and too silly to suit me; but, in general, she is very much to the taste of everybody, though single and though poor. Poverty certainly has not contracted her mind: I really believe, if she had only a shilling in the world, she would be very likely to give away sixpence of it; and nobody is afraid of her: that is a great charm."

"Dear me! but what shall you do? how shall you employ yourself when you grow old?"

"If I know myself, Harriet, mine is an active, busy mind, with a great many independent resources; and I do not perceive why I should be more in want of employment at forty or fifty than one-and-twenty. Woman's usual occupations of eye and hand and mind will be open to me then, as they are now; or with no important variation. If I draw less, I shall read more; if I give up music, I shall take to carpet-work.[8] And as for objects of interest, objects for the affections, which is in truth the great point of inferiority, the want of which is really the great evil to be avoided in *not* marrying, I shall be very well off, with all the children of a sister I love so much, to care about. There will be enough of them, in all probability, to supply every sort of sensation that declining life can need. There will be enough for every hope and every fear; and though my attachment to none can equal that of a parent, it suits my ideas of comfort better than what is warmer and blinder. My nephews and nieces!—I shall often have a niece with me."

"Do you know Miss Bates's niece? That is, I know you must have seen her a hundred times—but are you acquainted?"

"Oh! yes; we are always forced to be acquainted whenever she comes to Highbury. By the bye, *that* is almost enough to put one out of conceit with a niece. Heaven forbid! at least, that I should ever bore people half so much about all the Knightleys together, as she does about Jane Fairfax. One is sick of the very name of Jane Fairfax. Every letter from her is read forty times over; her compliments to all friends go round and round again; and if she does but send her aunt the pattern of a stomacher,[9] or knit a pair of garters for her grandmother, one hears of nothing else for a month. I wish Jane Fairfax very well; but she tires me to death."

They were now approaching the cottage, and all idle topics were superseded. Emma was very compassionate; and the distresses of the poor were as sure of relief from her personal attention and kindness, her counsel and her patience, as from her purse. She understood their ways, could allow for their ignorance and their temptations, had no romantic expectations of extraordinary virtue from those, for whom education had done so little; entered into their troubles with ready sympathy, and always gave her assistance with as much intelligence as good-will. In the present instance, it was sickness and

8. Fine needlepoint work. See Introduction for a discussion of the "woman's usual occupations," often termed "accomplishments."
9. Ornamental blouse.

poverty together which she came to visit; and after remaining there as long as she could give comfort or advice, she quitted the cottage with such an impression of the scene as made her say to Harriet, as they walked away,

"These are the sights, Harriet, to do one good. How trifling they make every thing else appear!—I feel now as if I could think of nothing but these poor creatures all the rest of the day; and yet, who can say how soon it may all vanish from my mind?"

"Very true," said Harriet. "Poor creatures! one can think of nothing else."

"And really, I do not think the impression will soon be over," said Emma, as she crossed the low hedge, and tottering footstep which ended the narrow, slippery path through the cottage garden, and brought them into the lane again. "I do not think it will," stopping to look once more at all the outward wretchedness of the place, and recal the still greater within.

"Oh! dear, no," said her companion.

They walked on. The lane made a slight bend; and when that bend was passed, Mr. Elton was immediately in sight; and so near as to give Emma time only to say farther,

"Ah! Harriet, here comes a very sudden trial of our stability in good thoughts. Well, (smiling,) I hope it may be allowed that if compassion has produced exertion and relief to the sufferers, it has done all that is truly important. If we feel for the wretched, enough to do all we can for them, the rest is empty sympathy, only distressing to ourselves."

Harriet could just answer, "Oh! dear, yes," before the gentleman joined them. The wants and sufferings of the poor family, however, were the first subject on meeting. He had been going to call on them. His visit he would now defer; but they had a very interesting parley about what could be done and should be done. Mr. Elton then turned back to accompany them.

"To fall on with each other on such an errand as this," thought Emma; "to meet in a charitable scheme; this will bring a great increase of love on each side. I should not wonder if it were to bring on the declaration. It must, if I were not here. I wish I were anywhere else."

Anxious to separate herself from them as far as she could, she soon afterwards took possession of a narrow footpath, a little raised on one side of the lane, leaving them together in the main road. But she had not been there two minutes when she found that Harriet's habits of dependence and imitation were bringing her up too, and that, in short, they would both be soon after her. This would not do; she immediately stopped, under pretence of having some alteration to make in the lacing of her half-boot, and stooping down in complete occupation of the footpath, begged them to have the goodness to walk on, and she would follow in half a minute. They did as they were desired; and by the time she judged it reasonable to have done with her boot, she had the comfort of further delay in her power, being overtaken by a child from the cottage, setting out, according to orders, with her pitcher, to fetch broth from Hartfield. To walk by the side of this child, and talk to and question her, was the most natural thing in the world, or would have been the most natural, had she been acting just then without design; and by this means the others were still able to keep ahead, without any obligation of waiting for her. She gained on them, however, involuntarily; the child's pace was quick, and theirs rather slow; and she was the more concerned at it, from their being evidently in a conversation which interested them. Mr. Elton was speaking with animation, Harriet listening with a very pleased attention; and Emma having sent the child on, was beginning to think how she might draw back a little more, when they both looked around, and she was obliged to join them.

Mr. Elton was still talking, still engaged in some interesting detail; and Emma experienced some disappointment when she found that he was only giving his fair companion an account of the yesterday's party at his friend Cole's, and that she was come in herself for the Stilton cheese, the north Wiltshire,[1] the butter, the cellery, the beet-root and all the dessert.

"This would soon have led to something better of course," was her consoling reflection; "any thing interests between those who love; and any thing will serve as introduction to what is near the heart. If I could but have kept longer away!"

They now walked on together quietly, till within view of the vicar-age pales, when a sudden resolution, of at least getting Harriet into the house, made her again find something very much amiss about her boot, and fall behind to arrange it once more. She then broke the lace off short, and dexterously throwing it into a ditch, was presently obliged to entreat them to stop, and acknowledge her inability to put herself to rights so as to be able to walk home in tolerable comfort.

"Part of my lace is gone," said she, "and I do not know how I am to contrive. I really am a most troublesome companion to you both, but I hope I am not often so ill-equipped. Mr. Elton, I must beg leave to stop at your house, and ask your housekeeper for a bit of ribband or string, or any thing just to keep my boot on."

Mr. Elton looked all happiness at this proposition; and nothing could exceed his alertness and attention in conducting them into his house and endeavouring to make every thing appear to advantage.

---

1. Small, cylindrical cheeses from the county of Wiltshire, popular in the era.

The room they were taken into was the one he chiefly occupied, and looking forwards; behind it was another with which it immediately communicated; the door between them was open, and Emma passed into it with the housekeeper to receive her assistance in the most comfortable manner. She was obliged to leave the door ajar as she found it; but she fully intended that Mr. Elton should close it. It was not closed however, it still remained ajar; but by engaging the housekeeper in incessant conversation, she hoped to make it practicable for him to chuse his own subject in the adjoining room. For ten minutes she could hear nothing but herself. It could be protracted no longer. She was then obliged to be finished and make her appearance.

The lovers were standing together at one of the windows. It had a most favourable aspect; and, for half a minute, Emma felt the glory of having schemed successfully. But it would not do; he had not come to the point. He had been most agreeable, most delightful; he had told Harriet that he had seen them go by, and had purposely followed them; other little gallantries and allusions had been dropt, but nothing serious.

"Cautious, very cautious," thought Emma; "he advances inch by inch, and will hazard nothing till he believes himself secure."

Still, however, though every thing had not been accomplished by her ingenious device, she could not but flatter herself that it had been the occasion of much present enjoyment to both, and must be leading them forward to the great event.

Chapter XI

Mr. Elton must now be left to himself. It was no longer in Emma's power to superintend his happiness or quicken his measures. The coming of her sister's family was so very near at hand, that first in anticipation and then in reality, it became henceforth her prime object of interest; and during the ten days of their stay at Hartfield it was not to be expected—she did not herself expect—that any thing beyond occasional, fortuitous assistance could be afforded by her to the lovers. They might advance rapidly if they would, however; they must advance somehow or other whether they would or no. She hardly wished to have more leisure for them. There are people, who the more you do for them, the less they will do for themselves.

Mr. and Mrs. John Knightley, from having been longer than usual absent from Surry, were exciting of course rather more than the usual interest. Till this year, every long vacation since their marriage had been divided between Hartfield and Donwell Abbey; but all the holidays of this autumn had been given to sea-bathing for the children, and it was therefore many months since they had been seen in a regular way by their Surry connections, or seen at all by Mr. Woodhouse, who could not be induced to get so far as London, even for poor Isabella's sake; and who consequently was now most nervously and apprehensively happy in forestalling this too short visit.

He thought much of the evils of the journey for her, and not a little of the fatigues of his own horses and coachman who were to bring some of the party the last half of the way; but his alarms were needless; the sixteen miles being happily accomplished, and Mr. and Mrs. John Knightley, their five children, and a competent number of nursery-maids, all reaching Hartfield in safety. The bustle and joy of such an arrival, the many to be talked to, welcomed, encouraged, and variously dispersed and disposed of, produced a noise and confusion which his nerves could not have born under any other cause, nor have endured much longer even for this; but the ways of Hartfield and the feelings of her father were so respected by Mrs. John Knightley, that in spite of maternal solicitude for the immediate enjoyment of her little ones, and for their having instantly all the liberty and attendance, all the eating and drinking, and sleeping and playing, which they could possibly wish for, without the smallest delay, the children were never allowed to be long a disturbance to him, either in themselves or in any restless attendance on them.

Mrs. John Knightley was a pretty, elegant little woman, of gentle, quiet manners, and a disposition remarkably amiable and affectionate; wrapt up in her family; a devoted wife, a doating mother, and so tenderly attached to her father and sister that, but for these higher ties, a warmer love might have seemed impossible. She could never see a fault in any of them. She was not a woman of strong understanding or any quickness; and with this resemblance of her father, she inherited also much of his constitution; was delicate in her own health, over-careful of that of her children, had many fears and many nerves and was as fond of her own Mr. Wingfield in town as her father could be of Mr. Perry. They were alike too, in a general benevolence of temper, and a strong habit of regard for every old acquaintance.

Mr. John Knightley was a tall, gentleman-like, and very clever man; rising in his profession, domestic, and respectable in his private character; but with reserved manners which prevented his being generally pleasing; and capable of being sometimes out of humour. He was not an ill-tempered man, not so often unreasonably cross as to deserve such a reproach; but his temper was not his great perfection; and, indeed, with such a worshipping wife, it was hardly possible that any natural defects in it should not be increased. The extreme sweetness of her temper must hurt his. He had all the clearness and quickness of mind which she wanted, and he could sometimes act an ungracious, or say a severe thing. He was not a great favourite with his fair sister-in-law. Nothing wrong in him escaped her. She was quick in feeling the little injuries to Isabella, which Isabella never felt herself. Perhaps she might have passed over more had his manners been flattering to Isabella's sister, but they were only those of a calmly kind brother and friend, without praise and without blindness; but hardly any degree of personal compliment could have made her regardless of that greatest fault of all in her eyes which he sometimes fell into, the want of respectful forbearance towards her father. There he had not always the patience that could have been wished. Mr. Woodhouse's peculiarities and fidgettiness were sometimes provoking him to a rational remonstrance or sharp retort equally ill bestowed. It did not often happen; for Mr. John Knightley had really a great regard for his father-in-law, and generally a strong sense of what was due to him; but it was too often for Emma's charity, especially as there was all the pain of apprehension frequently to be endured, though the offence came not. The beginning, however, of every visit displayed none but the properest feelings, and this being of necessity so short might be hoped to pass away in unsullied cordiality. They had not been long seated and composed when Mr. Woodhouse, with a melancholy shake of the head and a sigh, called his daughter's attention to the sad change at Hartfield since she had been there last.

"Ah! my dear," said he, "poor Miss Taylor—It is a grievous business!"

"Oh! yes, sir," cried she with ready sympathy, "how you must miss her! And dear Emma too!—what a dreadful loss to you both!—I have been so grieved for you.—I could not imagine how you could possibly do without her.—It is a sad change indeed.—But I hope she is pretty well, sir."

"Pretty well, my dear—I hope—pretty well.—I do not know but that the place agrees with her tolerably."

Mr. John Knightley here asked Emma quietly whether there were any doubts of the air of Randalls.

"Oh! no—none in the least. I never saw Mrs. Weston better in my life—never looking so well. Papa is only speaking his own regret."

"Very much to the honour of both," was the handsome reply.

"And do you see her, sir, tolerably often?" asked Isabella in the plaintive tone which just suited her father.

Mr. Woodhouse hesitated.—"Not near so often, my dear, as I could wish."

"Oh! papa, we have missed seeing them but one entire day since they married. Either in the morning or evening of every day, excepting one, have we seen either Mr. Weston or Mrs. Weston, and generally both, either at Randalls or here—and as you may suppose, Isabella, most frequently here. They are very, very kind in their visits. Mr. Weston is really as kind as herself. Papa, if you speak in that melancholy way, you will be giving Isabella a false idea of us all. Every body must be aware that Miss Taylor must be missed, but every body ought also to be assured that Mr. and Mrs. Weston do really prevent our missing her by any means to the extent we ourselves anticipated—which is the exact truth."

"Just as it should be," said Mr. John Knightley, "and just as I hoped it was from your letters. Her wish of shewing you attention could not be doubted, and his being a disengaged and social man makes it all easy. I have been always telling you, my love, that I had no idea of the change being so very material to Hartfield as you apprehended; and now you have Emma's account, I hope you will be satisfied."

"Why to be sure," said Mr. Woodhouse—"yes, certainly—I cannot deny that Mrs. Weston, poor Mrs. Weston, does come and see us pretty often—but then—she is always obliged to go away again."

"It would be very hard upon Mr. Weston if she did not, papa.— You quite forget poor Mr. Weston."

"I think, indeed," said John Knightley pleasantly, "that Mr. Weston has some little claim. You and I, Emma, will venture to take the part of the poor husband. I, being a husband, and you not being a wife, the claims of the man may very likely strike us with equal force. As for Isabella, she has been married long enough to see the convenience of putting all the Mr. Westons aside as much as she can."

"Me, my love," cried his wife, hearing and understanding only in part.—"Are you talking about me?—I am sure nobody ought to be, or can be, a greater advocate for matrimony than I am; and if it had not been for the misery of her leaving Hartfield, I should never have thought of Miss Taylor but as the most fortunate woman in the world; and as to slighting Mr. Weston, that excellent Mr. Weston, I think there is nothing he does not deserve. I believe he is one of the very best tempered men that ever existed. Excepting yourself and your brother, I do not know his equal for temper. I shall never forget his flying Henry's kite for him that very windy day last Easter— and ever since his particular kindness last September twelvemonth in writing that note, at twelve o'clock at night, on purpose to assure me that there was no scarlet fever at Cobham, I have been convinced there could not be a more feeling heart nor a better man in existence.—If any body can deserve him, it must be Miss Taylor."

"Where is the young man?" said John Knightley. "Has he been here on this occasion—or has he not?"

"He has not been here yet," replied Emma. "There was a strong expectation of his coming soon after the marriage, but it ended in nothing; and I have not heard him mentioned lately."

"But you should tell them of the letter, my dear," said her father. "He wrote a letter to poor Mrs. Weston, to congratulate her, and a very proper, handsome letter it was. She shewed it to me. I thought it very well done indeed. Whether it was his own idea you know, one cannot tell. He is but young, and his uncle perhaps——"

"My dear papa, he is three-and-twenty.—You forget how time passes."

"Three-and-twenty!—is he indeed?—Well, I could not have thought it—and he was but two years old when he lost his poor mother! Well, time does fly indeed!—and my memory is very bad. However, it was an exceeding good, pretty letter, and gave Mr. and Mrs. Weston a great deal of pleasure. I remember it was written from Weymouth, and dated Sept. 28th—and began, 'My dear Madam,' but I forget how it went on; and it was signed 'F. C. Weston Churchill.'—I remember that perfectly."

"How very pleasing and proper of him!" cried the good-hearted Mrs. John Knightley. "I have no doubt of his being a most amiable young man. But how sad it is that he should not live at home with his father! There is something so shocking in a child's being taken away from his parents and natural home! I never can comprehend how Mr. Weston could part with him. To give up one's child! I really never could think well of any body who proposed such a thing to any body else."

"Nobody ever did think well of the Churchills, I fancy," observed Mr. John Knightley coolly. "But you need not imagine Mr. Weston to have felt what you would feel in giving up Henry or John. Mr. Weston is rather an easy, cheerful tempered man, than a man of strong feelings; he takes things as he finds them, and makes enjoyment of them somehow or other, depending, I suspect, much more upon what is called *society* for his comforts, that is, upon the power of eating and drinking, and playing whist with his neighbours five times a-week, than upon family affection, or any thing that home affords."

Emma could not like what bordered on a reflection on Mr. Weston, and had half a mind to take it up; but she struggled, and let it pass. She would keep the peace if possible; and there was something honourable and valuable in the strong domestic habits, the all-sufficiency of home to himself, whence resulted her brother's disposition to look down on the common rate of social intercourse, and those to whom it was important.—It had a high claim to forbearance.

Chapter XII

Mr. Knightley was to dine with them—rather against the inclination of Mr. Woodhouse, who did not like that any one should share with him in Isabella's first day. Emma's sense of right however had decided it; and besides the consideration of what was due to each brother, she had particular pleasure, from the circumstance of the late disagreement between Mr. Knightley and herself, in procuring him the proper invitation.

She hoped they might now become friends again. She thought it was time to make up. Making-up indeed would not do. *She* certainly had not been in the wrong, and *he* would never own that he had. Concession must be out of the question; but it was time to appear to forget that they had ever quarrelled; and she hoped it might rather assist the restoration of friendship, that when he came into the room she had one of the children with her—the youngest, a nice little girl about eight months old, who was now making her first visit to Hartfield, and very happy to be danced about in her aunt's arms. It did assist; for though he began with grave looks and short questions, he was soon led on to talk of them all in the usual way, and to take the child out of her arms with all the unceremoniousness of perfect amity. Emma felt they were friends again; and the conviction giving her at first great satisfaction, and then a little sauciness, she could not help saying, as he was admiring the baby,

"What a comfort it is, that we think alike about our nephews and nieces. As to men and women our opinions are sometimes very different; but with regard to these children, I observe we never disagree."

"If you were as much guided by nature in your estimate of men and women, and as little under the power of fancy and whim in your dealings with them, as you are where these children are concerned, we might always think alike."

"To be sure—our discordancies must always arise from my being in the wrong."

"Yes," said he, smiling—"and reason good. I was sixteen years old when you were born."

"A material difference then," she replied—"and no doubt you were much my superior in judgment at that period of our lives; but does not the lapse of one-and-twenty years bring our understandings a good deal nearer?"

"Yes—a good deal *nearer*."

"But still, not near enough to give me a chance of being right, if we think differently."

"I have still the advantage of you by sixteen years' experience, and by not being a pretty young woman and a spoiled child. Come, my dear Emma, let us be friends and say no more about it. Tell your aunt, little Emma, that she ought to set you a better example than to be renewing old grievances, and that if she were not wrong before, she is now."

"That's true," she cried—"very true. Little Emma, grow up a better woman than your aunt. Be infinitely cleverer and not half so conceited. Now, Mr. Knightley, a word or two more, and I have done. As far as good intentions went, we were *both* right, and I must say that no effects on my side of the argument have yet proved wrong. I only want to know that Mr. Martin is not very, very bitterly disappointed."

"A man cannot be more so," was his short, full answer.

"Ah!—Indeed I am very sorry.—Come, shake hands with me."

This had just taken place and with great cordiality, when John Knightley made his appearance, and "How d'ye do, George?" and "John, how are you?" succeeded in the true English style, burying under a calmness that seemed all but indifference, the real attachment which would have led either of them, if requisite, to do every thing for the good of the other.

The evening was quiet and conversible, as Mr. Woodhouse declined cards entirely for the sake of comfortable talk with his dear Isabella, and the little party made two natural divisions; on one side he and his daughter; on the other the two Mr. Knightleys; their subjects totally distinct, or very rarely mixing—and Emma only occasionally joining in one or the other.

The brothers talked of their own concerns and pursuits, but principally of those of the elder, whose temper was by much the most communicative, and who was always the greater talker. As a magistrate,[2] he had generally some point of law to consult John about, or, at least, some curious anecdote to give; and as a farmer, as keeping in hand the home-farm at Donwell, he had to tell what every field was to bear next year, and to give all such local information as could not fail of being interesting to a brother whose home it had equally been the longest part of his life, and whose attachments were strong. The plan of a drain,[3] the change of a fence, the felling of a tree, and the destination of every acre for wheat, turnips, or spring corn, was entered into with as much equality of interest by John, as his cooler manners rendered possible; and if his willing brother ever left him any thing to inquire about, his inquiries even approached a tone of eagerness.

While they were thus comfortably occupied, Mr. Woodhouse was enjoying a full flow of happy regrets and fearful affection with his daughter.

"My poor dear Isabella," said he, fondly taking her hand, and interrupting, for a few moments, her busy labours for some one of her five children—"How long it is, how terribly long since you were here! And how tired you must be after the journey! You must go to bed early, my dear—and I recommend a little gruel to you before

2. Justice of the peace.
3. Drainage ditch.

you go.—You and I will have a nice basin of gruel together. My dear Emma, suppose we all have a little gruel."

Emma could not suppose any such thing, knowing, as she did, that both the Mr. Knightleys were as unpersuadable on that article as herself;—and two basins only were ordered. After a little more discourse in praise of gruel, with some wondering as its not being taken every evening by every body, he proceeded to say, with an air of grave reflection,

"It was an awkward business, my dear, your spending the autumn at South End instead of coming here. I never had much opinion of the sea air."

"Mr. Wingfield most strenuously recommended it, sir—or we should not have gone. He recommended it for all the children, but particularly for the weakness in little Bella's throat,—both sea air and bathing."

"Ah! my dear, but Perry had many doubts about the sea doing her any good; and as to myself, I have been long perfectly convinced, though perhaps I never told you so before, that the sea is very rarely of use to any body. I am sure it almost killed me once."

"Come, come," cried Emma, feeling this to be an unsafe subject, "I must beg you not to talk of the sea. It makes me envious and miserable;—I who have never seen it! South End is prohibited, if you please. My dear Isabella, I have not heard you make one inquiry after Mr. Perry yet; and he never forgets you."

"Oh! good Mr. Perry—how is he, sir?"

"Why, pretty well; but not quite well. Poor Perry is bilious, and he has not time to take care of himself—he tells me he has not time to take care of himself—which is very sad—but he is always wanted all round the country. I suppose there is not a man in such practice any where. But then, there is not so clever a man any where."

"And Mrs. Perry and the children, how are they? do the children grow?—I have a great regard for Mr. Perry. I hope he will be calling soon. He will be so pleased to see my little ones."

"I hope he will be here to-morrow, for I have a question or two to ask him about myself of some consequence. And, my dear, whenever he comes, you had better let him look at little Bella's throat."

"Oh! my dear sir, her throat is so much better that I have hardly any uneasiness about it. Either bathing has been of the greatest service to her, or else it is to be attributed to an excellent embrocation[4] of Mr. Wingfield's, which we have been applying at times ever since August."

4. Liniment.

"It is not very likely, my dear, that bathing should have been of use to her—and if I had known you were wanting an embrocation, I would have spoken to——"

"You seem to have forgotten Mrs. and Miss Bates," said Emma, "I have not heard one inquiry after them."

"Oh! the good Bateses—I am quite ashamed of myself—but you mention them in most of your letters. I hope they are quite well. Good old Mrs. Bates—I will call upon her to-morrow, and take my children.—They are always so pleased to see my children.—And that excellent Miss Bates!—such thorough worthy people!—How are they, sir?"

"Why, pretty well, my dear, upon the whole. But poor Mrs. Bates had a bad cold about a month ago."

"How sorry I am! But colds were never so prevalent as they have been this autumn. Mr. Wingfield told me that he had never known them more general or heavy—except when it has been quite an influenza."

"That has been a good deal the case, my dear; but not to the degree you mention. Perry says that colds have been very general, but not so heavy as he has very often known them in November. Perry does not call it altogether a sickly season."

"No, I do not know that Mr. Wingfield considers it *very* sickly except—"

"Ah! my poor dear child, the truth is, that in London it is always a sickly season. Nobody is healthy in London, nobody can be. It is a dreadful thing to have you forced to live there!—so far off!—and the air so bad!"

"No, indeed—*we* are not at all in a bad air. Our part of London is so very superior to most others!—You must not confound us with London in general, my dear sir. The neighbourhood of Brunswick Square is very different from almost all the rest. We are so very airy! I should be unwilling, I own, to live in any other part of the town;—there is hardly any other that I could be satisfied to have my children in:—but *we* are so remarkably airy!—Mr. Wingfield thinks the vicinity of Brunswick Square decidedly the most favourable as to air."

"Ah! my dear, it is not like Hartfield. You make the best of it—but after you have been a week at Hartfield, you are all of you different creatures; you do not look like the same. Now I cannot say, that I think you are any of you looking well at present."

"I am sorry to hear you say so, sir; but I assure you, excepting those little nervous head-aches and palpitations which I am never entirely free from any where, I am quite well myself; and if the children were rather pale before they went to bed, it was only because they were a little more tired than usual, from their journey and the happiness of coming. I hope you will think better of their looks to-morrow; for I assure you Mr. Wingfield told me, that he did not believe he had ever sent us off altogether, in such good case. I trust, at least, that you do not think Mr. Knightley looking ill,"—turning her eyes with affectionate anxiety towards her husband.

"Middling, my dear; I cannot compliment you. I think Mr. John Knightley very far from looking well."

"What is the matter, sir?—Did you speak to me?" cried Mr. John Knightley, hearing his own name.

"I am sorry to find, my love, that my father does not think you looking well—but I hope it is only from being a little fatigued. I could have wished, however, as you know, that you had seen Mr. Wingfield before you left home."

"My dear Isabella,"—exclaimed he hastily—"pray do not concern yourself about my looks. Be satisfied with doctoring and coddling yourself and the children, and let me look as I chuse."

"I did not thoroughly understand what you were telling your brother," cried Emma, "about your friend Mr. Graham's intending to have a bailiff[5] from Scotland, to look after his new estate. But will it answer? Will not the old prejudice be too strong?"

And she talked in this way so long and successfully that, when forced to give her attention again to her father and sister, she had nothing worse to hear than Isabella's kind inquiry after Jane Fairfax;—and Jane Fairfax, though no great favourite with her in general, she was at that moment very happy to assist in praising.

"That sweet, amiable Jane Fairfax!" said Mrs. John Knightley—"It is so long since I have seen her, except now and then for a moment accidentally in town! What happiness it must be to her good old grandmother and excellent aunt, when she comes to visit them! I always regret excessively on dear Emma's account that she cannot be more at Highbury; but now their daughter is married, I suppose Colonel and Mrs. Campbell will not be able to part with her at all. She would be such a delightful companion for Emma."

Mr. Woodhouse agreed to it all, but added,

"Our little friend Harriet Smith, however, is just such another pretty kind of young person. You will like Harriet. Emma could not have a better companion than Harriet."

"I am most happy to hear it—but only Jane Fairfax one knows to be so very accomplished and superior!—and exactly Emma's age."

This topic was discussed very happily, and others succeeded of similar moment, and passed away with similar harmony; but the evening did not close without a little return of agitation. The gruel came and supplied a great deal to be said—much praise and many

5. Farm manager.

comments—undoubting decision of its wholesomeness for every constitution, and pretty severe Philippics[6] upon the many houses where it was never met with tolerable;—but, unfortunately, among the failures which the daughter had to instance, the most recent, and therefore most prominent, was in her own cook at South End, a young woman hired for the time, who never had been able to understand what she meant by a basin of nice smooth gruel, thin, but not too thin. Often as she had wished for and ordered it, she had never been able to get any thing tolerable. Here was a dangerous opening.

"Ah!" said Mr. Woodhouse, shaking his head and fixing his eyes on her with tender concern.—The ejaculation in Emma's ear expressed, "Ah! there is no end of the sad consequences of your going to South End. It does not bear talking of." And for a little while she hoped he would not talk of it, and that a silent rumination might suffice to restore him to relish of his own smooth gruel. After an interval of some minutes, however, he began with,

"I shall always be very sorry that you went to the sea this autumn, instead of coming here."

"But why should you be sorry, sir?—I assure you, it did the children a great deal of good."

"And, moreover, if you must go to the sea, it had better not have been to South End.[7] South End is an unhealthy place. Perry was surprized to hear you had fixed upon South End."

"I know there is such an idea with many people, but indeed it is quite a mistake, sir.—We all had our health perfectly well there, never found the least inconvenience from the mud; and Mr. Wingfield says it is entirely a mistake to suppose the place unhealthy; and I am sure he may be depended on, for he thoroughly understands the nature of the air, and his own brother and family have been there repeatedly."

"You should have gone to Cromer,[8] my dear, if you went any where.—Perry was a week at Cromer once, and he holds it to be the best of all the sea-bathing places. A fine open sea, he says, and very pure air. And, by what I understand, you might have had lodgings there quite away from the sea—a quarter of a mile off—very comfortable. You should have consulted Perry."

"But, my dear sir, the difference of the journey;—only consider how great it would have been.—A hundred miles, perhaps, instead of forty."

"Ah! my dear," as Perry says, "where health is at stake, nothing else should be considered; and if one is to travel, there is not much

6. Invectives.
7. Southend-on-Sea, Essex, at the mouth of the Thames Estuary, is the closest resort town to London, 40 miles to the east.
8. A resort town in Norfolk, 135 miles northeast of London.

to chuse between forty miles and an hundred.—Better not move at all, better stay in London altogether than travel forty miles to get into a worse air. This is just what Perry said. It seemed to him a very ill-judged measure."

Emma's attempts to stop her father had been vain; and when he had reached such a point at this, she could not wonder at her brother-in-law's breaking out.

"Mr. Perry," said he, in a voice of very strong displeasure, "would do as well to keep his opinion till it is asked for. Why does he make it any business of his, to wonder at what I do?—at my taking my family to one part of the coast or another?—I may be allowed, I hope, the use of my judgment as well as Mr. Perry.—I want his directions no more than his drugs." He paused—and growing cooler in a moment, added, with only sarcastic dryness, "If Mr. Perry can tell me how to convey a wife and five children a distance of an hundred and thirty miles with no greater expense or inconvenience than a distance of forty, I should be as willing to prefer Cromer to South End as he could himself."

"True, true," cried Mr. Knightley, with most ready interposition—"very true. That's a consideration indeed.—But John, as to what I was telling you of my idea of moving the path to Langham, of turning it more to the right that it may not cut through the home meadows, I cannot conceive any difficulty. I should not attempt it, if it were to be the means of inconvenience to the Highbury people, but if you call to mind exactly the present line of the path . . . . . . The only way of proving it, however, will be to turn to our maps. I shall see you at the Abbey tomorrow morning I hope, and then we will look them over, and you shall give me your opinion."

Mr. Woodhouse was rather agitated by such harsh reflections on his friend Perry, to whom he had, in fact, though unconsciously, been attributing many of his own feelings and expressions;—but the soothing attentions of his daughters gradually removed the present evil, and the immediate alertness of one brother, and better recollections of the other, prevented any renewal of it.

Chapter XIII

There could hardly be an happier creature in the world, than Mrs. John Knightley, in this short visit to Hartfield, going about every morning among her old acquaintance with her five children, and talking over what she had done every evening with her father and sister. She had nothing to wish otherwise, but that the days did not pass so swiftly. It was a delightful visit;—perfect, in being much too short.

In general their evenings were less engaged with friends than their mornings: but one complete dinner engagement, and out of

the house too, there was no avoiding, though at Christmas. Mr.
Weston would take no denial; they must all dine at Randalls one
day;—even Mr. Woodhouse was persuaded to think it a possible
thing in preference to a division of the party.

How they were all to be conveyed, he would have made a difficulty if he could, but as his son and daughter's carriage and horses
were actually at Hartfield, he was not able to make more than a
simple question on that head; it hardly amounted to a doubt; nor
did it occupy Emma long to convince him that they might in one of
the carriages find room for Harriet also.

Harriet, Mr. Elton, and Mr. Knightley, their own especial set,
were the only persons invited to meet them;—the hours were to be
early, as well as the numbers few; Mr. Woodhouse's habits and
inclination being consulted in every thing.

The evening before this great event (for it was a very great event
that Mr. Woodhouse should dine out, on the 24th of December)
had been spent by Harriet at Hartfield, and she had gone home so
much indisposed with a cold, that, but for her own earnest wish of
being nursed by Mrs. Goddard, Emma could not have allowed her
to leave the house. Emma called on her the next day, and found her
doom already signed with regard to Randalls. She was very feverish
and had a bad sore-throat: Mrs. Goddard was full of care and affection, Mr. Perry was talked of, and Harriet herself was too ill and
low to resist the authority which excluded her from this delightful
engagement, though she could not speak of her loss without many
tears.

Emma sat with her as long as she could, to attend her in Mrs.
Goddard's unavoidable absences, and raise her spirits by representing how much Mr. Elton's would be depressed when he knew her
state; and left her at last tolerably comfortable, in the sweet dependence of his having a most comfortless visit, and of their all missing
her very much. She had not advanced many yards from Mrs. Goddard's door, when she was met by Mr. Elton himself, evidently coming towards it, and as they walked on slowly together in conversation
about the invalid—of whom he, on the rumour of considerable illness, had been going to inquire, that he might carry some report of
her to Hartfield—they were overtaken by Mr. John Knightley
returning from the daily visit to Donwell, with his two eldest boys,
whose healthy, glowing faces shewed all the benefit of a country
run, and seemed to ensure a quick dispatch of the roast mutton and
rice pudding they were hastening home for. They joined company
and proceeded together. Emma was just describing the nature of
her friend's complaint;—"a throat very much inflamed, with a great
deal of heat about her, a quick low pulse, &c. and she was sorry to
find from Mrs. Goddard that Harriet was liable to very bad sore-

throats, and had often alarmed her with them."—Mr. Elton looked all alarm on the occasion, as he exclaimed,

"A sore-throat!—I hope not infectious. I hope not of a putrid infectious sort. Has Perry seen her? Indeed you should take care of yourself as well as of your friend. Let me entreat you to run no risks. Why does not Perry see her?"

Emma, who was not really at all frightened herself, tranquillized this excess of apprehension by assurances of Mrs. Goddard's experience and care; but as there must still remain a degree of uneasiness which she could not wish to reason away, which she would rather feed and assist than not, she added soon afterwards—as if quite another subject,

"It is so cold, so very cold—and looks and feels so very much like snow, that if it were to any other place or with any other party, I should really try not to go out to-day—and dissuade my father from venturing; but as he has made up his mind, and does not seem to feel the cold himself, I do not like to interfere, as I know it would be so great a disappointment to Mr. and Mrs. Weston. But, upon my word, Mr. Elton, in your case, I should certainly excuse myself. You appear to me a little hoarse already, and when you consider what demand of voice and what fatigues to-morrow will bring, I think it would be no more than common prudence to stay at home and take care of yourself to-night."

Mr. Elton looked as if he did not very well know what answer to make; which was exactly the case; for though very much gratified by the kind care of such a fair lady, and not liking to resist any advice of her's, he had not really the least inclination to give up the visit;—but Emma, too eager and busy in her own previous conceptions and views to hear him impartially, or see him with clear vision, was very well satisfied with his muttering acknowledgment of its being "very cold, certainly very cold," and walked on, rejoicing in having extricated himself from Randalls, and secured him the power of sending to inquire after Harriet every hour of the evening.

"You do quite right," said she;—"We will make your apologies to Mr. and Mrs. Weston."

But hardly had she so spoken, when she found her brother was civilly offering a seat in his carriage, if the weather were Mr. Elton's only objection, and Mr. Elton actually accepting the offer with much prompt satisfaction. It was a done thing; Mr. Elton was to go, and never had his broad handsome face expressed more pleasure than at this moment; never had his smile been stronger, nor his eyes more exulting than when he next looked at her.

"Well," said she to herself, "this is most strange!—After I had got him off so well, to chuse to go into company, and leave Harriet ill behind!—Most strange indeed!—But there is, I believe, in many men, especially single men, such an inclination—such a passion for dining out—a dinner engagement is so high in the class of their pleasures, their employments, their dignities, almost their duties, that any thing gives way to it—and this must be the case with Mr. Elton; a most valuable, amiable, pleasing young man undoubtedly, and very much in love with Harriet; but still, he cannot refuse an invitation, he must dine out wherever he is asked. What a strange thing love is! he can see ready wit in Harriet, but will not dine alone for her."

Soon afterwards Mr. Elton quitted them, and she could not but do him the justice of feeling that there was a great deal of sentiment in his manner of naming Harriet at parting; in the tone of his voice while assuring her that he should call at Mrs. Goddard's for news of her fair friend, the last thing before he prepared for the happiness of meeting her again, when he hoped to be able to give a better report; and he sighed and smiled himself off in a way that left the balance of approbation much in his favour.

After a few minutes of entire silence between them, John Knightley began with—

"I never in my life saw a man more intent on being agreeable than Mr. Elton. It is downright labour to him where ladies are concerned. With men he can be rational and unaffected, but when he has ladies to please every feature works."

"Mr. Elton's manners are not perfect," replied Emma; "but where there is a wish to please, one ought to overlook, and one does overlook a great deal. Where a man does his best with only moderate powers, he will have the advantage over negligent superiority. There is such perfect good temper and good will in Mr. Elton as one cannot but value."

"Yes," said Mr. John Knightley presently, with some slyness, "he seems to have a great deal of good-will towards *you*."

"Me!" she replied with a smile of astonishment, "are you imagining me to be Mr. Elton's object?"

"Such an imagination has crossed me, I own, Emma; and if it never occurred to you before, you may as well take it into consideration now."

"Mr. Elton in love with me!—What an idea!"

"I do not say it is so; but you will do well to consider whether it is so or not, and to regulate your behaviour accordingly. I think your manners to him encouraging. I speak as a friend, Emma. You had better look about you, and ascertain what you do, and what you mean to do."

"I thank you; but I assure you you are quite mistaken. Mr. Elton and I are very good friends, and nothing more;" and she walked on, amusing herself in the consideration of the blunders which often arise from a partial knowledge of circumstances, of the mistakes which people of high pretensions to judgment are for ever falling into; and not very well pleased with her brother for imagining her blind and ignorant, and in want of counsel. He said no more.

Mr. Woodhouse had so completely made up his mind to the visit, that in spite of the increasing coldness, he seemed to have no idea of shrinking from it, and set forward at last most punctually with his eldest daughter in his own carriage, with less apparent consciousness of the weather than either of the others; too full of the wonder of his own going, and the pleasure it was to afford at Randalls to see that it was cold, and too well wrapt up to feel it. The cold, however, was severe; and by the time the second carriage was in motion, a few flakes of snow were finding their way down, and the sky had the appearance of being so overcharged as to want only a milder air to produce a very white world in a very short time.

Emma soon saw that her companion was not in the happiest humour. The preparing and the going abroad in such weather, with the sacrifice of his children after dinner, were evils, were disagreeables at least, which Mr. John Knightley did not by any means like; he anticipated nothing in the visit that could be at all worth the purchase; and the whole of their drive to the Vicarage was spent by him in expressing his discontent.

"A man," said he, "must have a very good opinion of himself when he asks people to leave their own fireside, and encounter such a day as this, for the sake of coming to see him. He must think himself a most agreeable fellow; I could not do such a thing. It is the greatest absurdity—Actually snowing at this moment!—The folly of not allowing people to be comfortable at home—and the folly of people's not staying comfortably at home when they can! If we were obliged to go out such an evening as this, by any call of duty or business, what a hardship we should deem it;—and here are we, probably with rather thinner clothing than usual, setting forward voluntarily, without excuse, in defiance of the voice of nature, which tells man, in every thing given to his view or his feelings, to stay at home himself, and keep all under shelter that he can;—here are we setting forward to spend five dull hours in another man's house, with nothing to say or to hear that was not said and heard yesterday, and may not be said and heard again tomorrow. Going in dismal weather, to return probably in worse;—four horses and four servants taken out for nothing but to convey five idle, shivering creatures into colder rooms and worse company than they might have had at home."

Emma did not find herself equal to give the pleased assent, which no doubt he was in the habit of receiving, to emulate the "Very true, my love," which must have been usually administered by his travelling companion; but she had resolution enough to refrain from making any answer at all. She could not be complying, she dreaded being quarrelsome; her heroism reached only to silence. She allowed him to talk, and arranged the glasses, and wrapped herself up, without opening her lips.

They arrived, the carriage turned, the step was let down, and Mr. Elton, spruce, black, and smiling, was with them instantly. Emma thought with pleasure of some change of subject. Mr. Elton was all obligation and cheerfulness; he was so very cheerful in his civilities indeed, that she began to think he must have received a different account of Harriet from what had reached her. She had sent while dressing, and the answer had been, "Much the same—not better."

"My report from Mrs. Goddard's," said she presently, "was not so pleasant as I had hoped—'Not better,' was my answer."

His face lengthened immediately; and his voice was the voice of sentiment as he answered.

"Oh! no—I am grieved to find—I was on the point of telling you that when I called at Mrs. Goddard's door, which I did the very last thing before I returned to dress, I was told that Miss Smith was not better, by no means better, rather worse. Very much grieved and concerned—I had flattered myself that she must be better after such a cordial as I knew had been given in the morning."

Emma smiled and answered—"My visit was of use to the nervous part of her complaint, I hope; but not even I can charm away a sore throat; it is a most severe cold indeed. Mr. Perry has been with her, as you probably heard."

"Yes—I imagined—that is—I did not"—

"He has been used to her in these complaints, and I hope to-morrow morning will bring us both a more comfortable report. But it is impossible not to feel uneasiness. Such a sad loss to our party today!"

"Dreadful!—Exactly so, indeed.—She will be missed every moment."

This was very proper; the sigh which accompanied it was really estimable; but it should have lasted longer. Emma was rather in dismay when only half a minute afterwards he began to speak of other things, and in a voice of the greatest alacrity and enjoyment.

"What an excellent device," said he, "the use of a sheep-skin for carriages. How very comfortable they make it;—impossible to feel cold with such precautions. The contrivances of modern days indeed have rendered a gentleman's carriage perfectly complete. One is so fenced and guarded from the weather, that not a breath of air can find its way unpermitted. Weather becomes absolutely of no consequence. It is a very cold afternoon—but in this carriage we know nothing of the matter.—Ha! snows a little I see."

"Yes," said John Knightley, "and I think we shall have a good deal of it."

"Christmas weather," observed Mr. Elton. "Quite seasonable; and extremely fortunate we may think ourselves that it did not begin yesterday, and prevent this day's party, which it might very possibly have done, for Mr. Woodhouse would hardly have ventured had there been much snow on the ground; but now it is of no consequence. This is quite the season indeed for friendly meetings. At Christmas every body invites their friends about them, and people think little of even the worst weather. I was snowed up at a friend's house once for a week. Nothing could be pleasanter. I went for only one night, and could not get away till that very day se'nnight."[9]

Mr. John Knightley looked as if he did not comprehend the pleasure, but said only, coolly,

"I cannot wish to be snowed up a week at Randalls."

At another time Emma might have been amused, but she was too much astonished now at Mr. Elton's spirits for other feelings. Harriet seemed quite forgotten in the expectation of a pleasant party.

"We are sure of excellent fires," continued he, "and every thing in the greatest comfort. Charming people, Mr. and Mrs. Weston;—Mrs. Weston indeed is much beyond praise, and he is exactly what one values, so hospitable, and so fond of society;—it will be a small party, but where small parties are select, they are perhaps the most agreeable of any. Mr. Weston's dining-room does not accommodate more than ten comfortably; and for my part, I would rather, under such circumstances, fall short by two than exceed by two. I think you will agree with me, (turning with a soft air to Emma,) I think I shall certainly have your approbation, though Mr. Knightley perhaps, from being used to the large parties of London, may not quite enter into our feelings."

"I know nothing of the large parties of London, sir—I never dine with any body."

"Indeed! (in a tone of wonder and pity,) I had no idea that the law had been so great a slavery. Well, sir, the time must come when you will be paid for all this, when you will have little labour and great enjoyment."

"My first enjoyment," replied John Knightley, as they passed through the sweep-gate,[1] "will be to find myself safe at Hartfield again."

Chapter XIV

Some change of countenance was necessary for each gentleman as they walked into Mrs. Weston's drawing-room;—Mr. Elton must compose his joyous looks, and Mr. John Knightley disperse

9. One week later.
1. The sweep was a curved driveway leading up to a house.

his ill-humour. Mr. Elton must smile less, and Mr. John Knightley more, to fit them for the place.—Emma only might be as nature prompted, and shew herself just as happy as she was. To her, it was real enjoyment to be with the Westons. Mr. Weston was a great favourite, and there was not a creature in the world to whom she spoke with such unreserve, as to his wife; not any one, to whom she related with such conviction of being listened to and understood, of being always interesting and always intelligible, the little affairs, arrangements, perplexities and pleasures of her father and herself. She could tell nothing of Hartfield, in which Mrs. Weston had not a lively concern; and half an hour's interrupted communication of all those little matters on which the daily happiness of private life depends, was one of the first gratifications of each.

This was a pleasure which perhaps the whole day's visit might not afford, which certainly did not belong to the present half hour; but the very sight of Mrs. Weston, her smile, her touch, her voice was grateful to Emma, and she determined to think as little as possible of Mr. Elton's oddities, or of any thing else unpleasant, and enjoy all that was enjoyable to the utmost.

The misfortune of Harriet's cold had been pretty well gone through before her arrival. Mr. Woodhouse had been safely seated long enough to give the history of it, besides all the history of his own and Isabella's coming, and of Emma's being to follow, and had indeed just got to the end of his satisfaction that James should come and see his daughter, when the others appeared, and Mrs. Weston, who had been almost wholly engrossed by her attentions to him, was able to turn away and welcome her dear Emma.

Emma's project of forgetting Mr. Elton for a while, made her rather sorry to find, when they had all taken their places, that he was close to her. The difficulty was great of driving his strange insensibility towards Harriet, from her mind, while he not only sat at her elbow, but was continually obtruding his happy countenance on her notice, and solicitously addressing her upon every occasion. Instead of forgetting him, his behaviour was such that she could not avoid the internal suggestion of "Can it really be as my brother imagined? can it be possible for this man to be beginning to transfer his affections from Harriet to me?—Absurd and insufferable!"— Yet he would be so anxious for her being perfectly warm, would be so interested about her father, and so delighted with Mrs. Weston; and at last would begin admiring her drawings with so much zeal and so little knowledge as seemed terribly like a would-be lover, and made it some effort with her to preserve her good manners. For her own sake she could not be rude; and for Harriet's, in the hope that all would yet turn out right, she was even positively civil; but it was an effort; especially as something was going on amongst the others, in the most overpowering period of Mr. Elton's nonsense, which she particularly wished to listen to. She heard enough to know that Mr. Weston was giving some information about his son; she heard the words "my son," and "Frank," and "my son," repeated several times over; and from a few other half-syllables very much suspected that he was announcing an early visit from his son; but before she could quiet Mr. Elton, the subject was so completely past that any reviving question from her would have been awkward.

Now, it so happened that in spite of Emma's resolution of never marrying, there was something in the name, in the idea of Mr. Frank Churchill, which always interested her. She had frequently thought—especially since his father's marriage with Miss Taylor—that if she *were* to marry, he was the very person to suit her in age, character and condition. He seemed by this connection between the families quite to belong to her. She could not but suppose it to be a match that every body who knew them must think of. That Mr. and Mrs. Weston did think of it, she was very strongly persuaded; and though not meaning to be induced by him, or by any body else, to give up a situation which she believed more replete with good than any she could change it for, she had a great curiosity to see him, a decided intention of finding him pleasant, of being liked by him to a certain degree, and a sort of pleasure in the idea of their being coupled in their friends' imaginations.

With such sensations, Mr. Elton's civilities were dreadfully ill-timed; but she had the comfort of appearing very polite, while feeling very cross—and of thinking that the rest of the visit could not possibly pass without bringing forward the same information again, or the substance of it, from the open-hearted Mr. Weston.—So it proved;—for when happily released from Mr. Elton, and seated by Mr. Weston, at dinner, he made use of the very first interval in the cares of hospitality, the very first leisure from the saddle of mutton, to say to her,

"We want only two more to be just the right number. I should like to see two more here,—your pretty little friend, Miss Smith, and my son—and then I should say we were quite complete. I believe you did not hear me telling the others in the drawing-room that we are expecting Frank? I had a letter from him this morning, and he will be with us within a fortnight."

Emma spoke with a very proper degree of pleasure; and fully assented to his proposition of Mr. Frank Churchill and Miss Smith making their party quite complete.

"He has been wanting to come to us," continued Mr. Weston, "ever since September: every letter has been full of it; but he cannot command his own time. He has those to please who must be pleased, and who (between ourselves) are sometimes to be pleased only by a good many sacrifices. But now I have no doubt of seeing him here about the second week in January."

"What a very great pleasure it will be to you! and Mrs. Weston is so anxious to be acquainted with him, that she must be almost as happy as yourself."

"Yes, she would be, but that she thinks there will be another put-off. She does not depend upon his coming so much as I do: but she does not know the parties so well as I do. The case, you see, is— (but this is quite between ourselves: I did not mention a syllable of it in the other room. There are secrets in all families, you know)— The case is, that a party of friends are invited to pay a visit at Enscombe in January; and that Frank's coming depends upon their being put off. If they are not put off, he cannot stir. But I know they will, because it is a family that a certain lady, of some consequence, at Enscombe, has a particular dislike to: and though it is thought necessary to invite them once in two or three years, they always are put off when it comes to the point. I have not the smallest doubt of the issue. I am as confident of seeing Frank here before the middle of January, as I am of being here myself: but your good friend there (nodding towards the upper end of the table) has so few vagaries herself, and has been so little used to them at Hartfield, that she cannot calculate on their effects, as I have been long in the practice of doing."

"I am sorry there should be any thing like doubt in the case," replied Emma; "but am disposed to side with you, Mr. Weston. If you think he will come, I shall think so too; for you know Enscombe."

"Yes—I have some right to that knowledge; though I have never been at the place in my life.—She is an odd woman!—But I never allow myself to speak ill of her, on Frank's account; for I do believe her to be very fond of him. I used to think she was not capable of being fond of any body, except herself: but she has always been kind to him (in her way—allowing for little whims and caprices, and expecting every thing to be as she likes). And it is no small credit, in my opinion, to him, that he should excite such an affection; for, though I would not say it to any body else, she has no more heart than a stone to people in general; and the devil of a temper."

Emma liked the subject so well, that she began upon it, to Mrs. Weston, very soon after their moving into the drawing-room: wishing her joy—yet observing, that she knew the first meeting must be rather alarming.—Mrs. Weston agreed to it; but added, that she should be very glad to be secure of undergoing the anxiety of a first meeting at the time talked of: "for I cannot depend upon his coming. I cannot be so sanguine as Mr. Weston. I am very much afraid that it will all end in nothing. Mr. Weston, I dare say, has been telling you exactly how the matter stands."

"Yes—it seems to depend upon nothing but the ill-humour of Mrs. Churchill, which I imagine to be the most certain thing in the world."

"My Emma!" replied Mrs. Weston, smiling, "what is the certainty of caprice?" Then turning to Isabella, who had not been attending before—"You must know, my dear Mrs. Knightley, that we are by no means so sure of seeing Mr. Frank Churchill, in my opinion, as his father thinks. It depends entirely upon his aunt's spirits and pleasure; in short, upon her temper. To you—to my two daughters, I may venture on the truth. Mrs. Churchill rules at Enscombe, and is a very odd-tempered woman; and his coming now, depends upon her being willing to spare him."

"Oh, Mrs. Churchill; every body knows Mrs. Churchill," replied Isabella: "and I am sure I never think of that poor young man without the greatest compassion. To be constantly living with an ill-tempered person, must be dreadful. It is what we happily have never known any thing of; but it must be a life of misery. What a blessing that she never had any children! Poor little creatures, how unhappy she would have made them!"

Emma wished that she had been alone with Mrs. Weston. She should then have heard more: Mrs. Weston would speak to her, with a degree of unreserve which she would not hazard with Isabella; and, she really believed, would scarcely try to conceal any thing relative to the Churchills from her, excepting those views on the young man, of which her own imagination had already given her such instinctive knowledge. But at present there was nothing more to be said. Mr. Woodhouse very soon followed them into the drawing-room. To be sitting long after dinner, was a confinement that he could not endure. Neither wine nor conversation was any thing to him; and gladly did he move to those with whom he was always comfortable.

While he talked to Isabella, however, Emma found an opportunity of saying,

"And so you do not consider this visit from your son as by any means certain. I am sorry for it. The introduction must be unpleasant, whenever it takes place; and the sooner it could be over, the better."

"Yes; and every delay makes one more apprehensive of other delays. Even if this family, the Braithwaites, are put off, I am still afraid that some excuse may be found for disappointing us. I cannot bear to imagine any reluctance on his side; but I am sure there is a great wish on the Churchills to keep him to themselves. There is jealousy. They are jealous even of his regard for his father. In short, I can feel no dependence on his coming, and I wish Mr. Weston were less sanguine."

"He ought to come," said Emma. "If he could stay only a couple of days, he ought to come; and one can hardly conceive a young man's not having it in his power to do as much as that. A young *woman*, if she fall into bad hands, may be teazed, and kept at a distance from those she wants to be with; but one cannot comprehend a young *man's* being under such restraint, as not to be able to spend a week with his father, if he likes it."

"One ought to be at Enscombe, and know the ways of the family, before one decides upon what he can do," replied Mrs. Weston. "One ought to use the same caution, perhaps, in judging of the conduct of any one individual of any one family; but Enscombe, I believe, certainly must not be judged by general rules: *she* is so very unreasonable; and every thing gives way to her."

"But she is so fond of the nephew: he is so very great a favourite. Now, according to my idea of Mrs. Churchill, it would be most natural, that while she makes no sacrifice for the comfort of the husband, to whom she owes every thing, while she exercises incessant caprice toward *him*, she should frequently be governed by the nephew, to whom she owes nothing at all."

"My dearest Emma, do not pretend, with your sweet temper, to understand a bad one, or to lay down rules for it: you must let it go its own way. I have no doubt of his having, at times, considerable influence; but it may be perfectly impossible for him to know beforehand *when* it will be."

Emma listened, and then coolly said, "I shall not be satisfied, unless he comes."

"He may have a great deal of influence on some points," continued Mrs. Weston, "and on others, very little: and among those, on which she is beyond his reach, it is but too likely, may be this very circumstance of his coming away from them to visit us."

Chapter XV

Mr. Woodhouse was soon ready for his tea; and when he had drank his tea he was quite ready to go home; and it was as much as his three companions could do, to entertain away his notice of the lateness of the hour, before the other gentlemen appeared. Mr. Weston was chatty and convivial, and no friend to early separations of any sort; but at last the drawing-room party did receive an augmentation. Mr. Elton, in very good spirits, was one of the first to walk in. Mrs. Weston and Emma were sitting together on a sopha. He joined them immediately, and with scarcely an invitation, seated himself between them.

Emma, in good spirits too, from the amusement afforded her mind by the expectation of Mr. Frank Churchill, was willing to forget his late improprieties, and be as well satisfied with him as before, and on his making Harriet his very first subject, was ready to listen with most friendly smiles.

He professed himself extremely anxious about her fair friend—her fair, lovely, amiable friend. "Did she know?—had she heard any thing about her, since their being at Randalls?—he felt much anxiety—he must confess that the nature of her complaint alarmed him considerably." And in this style he talked on for some time very properly, not much attending to any answer, but altogether sufficiently awake to the terror of a bad sore throat; and Emma was quite in charity with him.

But at last there seemed a perverse turn; it seemed all at once as if he were more afraid of its being a bad sore throat on her account, than on Harriet's—more anxious that she should escape the infection, than that there should be no infection in the complaint. He began with great earnestness to entreat her to refrain from visiting the sick chamber again, for the present—to entreat her to *promise him* not to venture into such hazard till he had seen Mr. Perry and learnt his opinion; and though she tried to laugh it off and bring the subject back into its proper course, there was no putting an end to his extreme solicitude about her. She was vexed. It did appear—there was no concealing it—exactly like the pretence of being in love with her, instead of Harriet; an inconstancy, if real, the most contemptible and abominable! and she had difficulty in behaving with temper. He turned to Mrs. Weston to implore her assistance, "Would not she give him her support?—would not she add her persuasions to his, to induce Miss Woodhouse not to go to Mrs. Goddard's, till it were certain that Miss Smith's disorder had no infection? He could not be satisfied without a promise—would not she give him her influence in procuring it?"

"So scrupulous for others," he continued, "and yet so careless for herself! She wanted me to nurse my cold by staying at home to-day, and yet will not promise to avoid the danger of catching an ulcerated sore throat herself! Is this fair, Mrs. Weston?—Judge between us. Have not I some right to complain? I am sure of your kind support and aid."

Emma saw Mrs. Weston's surprize, and felt that it must be great, at an address which, in words and manner, was assuming to himself the right of first interest in her; and as for herself, she was too much provoked and offended to have the power of directly saying any thing to the purpose. She could only give him a look; but it was such a look as she thought must restore him to his senses; and then left the sopha, removing to a seat by her sister, and giving her all her attention.

She had not time to know how Mr. Elton took the reproof, so rapidly did another subject succeed; for Mr. John Knightley now came into the room from examining the weather, and opened on them all with the information of the ground being covered with snow, and of its still snowing fast, with a strong drifting wind; concluding with these words to Mr. Woodhouse:

"This will prove a spirited beginning of your winter engagements, sir. Something new for your coachman and horses to be making their way through a storm of snow."

Poor Mr. Woodhouse was silent from consternation; but every body else had something to say; every body was either surprized or not surprized, and had some question to ask, or some comfort to offer. Mrs. Weston and Emma tried earnestly to cheer him and turn his attention from his son-in-law, who was pursuing his triumph rather unfeelingly.

"I admired your resolution very much, sir," said he, "in venturing out in such weather, for of course you saw there would be snow very soon. Every body must have seen the snow coming on. I admired your spirit; and I dare say we shall get home very well. Another hour or two's snow can hardly make the road impassable; and we are two carriages; if *one* is blown over in the bleak part of the common field there will be the other at hand. I dare say we shall be all safe at Hartfield before midnight."

Mr. Weston, with triumph of a different sort, was confessing that he had known it to be snowing some time, but had not said a word, lest it should make Mr. Woodhouse uncomfortable, and be an excuse for his hurrying away. As to there being any quantity of snow fallen or likely to fall to impede their return, that was a mere joke; he was afraid they would find no difficulty. He wished the road might be impassable, that he might be able to keep them all at Randalls; and with the utmost good-will was sure that accommodation might be found for every body, calling on his wife to agree with him, that, with a little contrivance, every body might be lodged, which she hardly knew how to do, from the consciousness of there being but two spare rooms in the house.

"What is to be done, my dear Emma?—what is to be done?" was Mr. Woodhouse's first exclamation, and all that he could say for some time. To her he looked for comfort; and her assurances of safety, her representation of the excellence of the horses, and of James, and of their having so many friends about them, revived him a little.

His eldest daughter's alarm was equal to his own. The horror of being blocked up at Randalls, while her children were at Hartfield, was full in her imagination; and fancying the road to be now just passable for adventurous people, but in a state that admitted no delay, she was eager to have it settled, that her father and Emma should remain at Randalls, while she and her husband set forward instantly through all the possible accumulations of drifted snow that might impede them.

"You had better order the carriage directly, my love," said she; "I dare say we shall be able to get along, if we set off directly; and if we do come to any thing very bad, I can get out and walk. I am not at all afraid. I should not mind walking half the way. I could change my shoes, you know, the moment I got home; and it is not the sort of thing that gives me cold."

"Indeed!" replied he. "Then, my dear Isabella, it is the most extraordinary sort of thing in the world, for in general every thing does give you cold. Walk home!—you are prettily shod for walking home, I dare say. It will be bad enough for the horses."

Isabella turned to Mrs. Weston for her approbation of the plan. Mrs. Weston could only approve. Isabella then went to Emma; but Emma could not so entirely give up the hope of their being all able to get away; and they were still discussing the point, when Mr. Knightley, who had left the room immediately after his brother's first report of the snow, came back again, and told them that he had been out of doors to examine, and could answer for there not being the smallest difficulty in their getting home, whenever they liked it, either now or an hour hence. He had gone beyond the sweep—some way along the Highbury road—the snow was no where above half an inch deep—in many places hardly enough to whiten the ground; a very few flakes were falling at present, but the clouds were parting, and there was every appearance of its being soon over. He had seen the coachmen, and they both agreed with him in there being nothing to apprehend.

To Isabella, the relief of such tidings was very great, and they were scarcely less acceptable to Emma on her father's account, who was immediately set as much at ease on the subject as his nervous constitution allowed; but the alarm that had been raised could not be appeased so as to admit of any comfort for him while he continued at Randalls. He was satisfied of there being no present danger in returning home, but no assurances could convince him that it was safe to stay; and while the others were variously urging and recommending, Mr. Knightley and Emma settled it in a few brief sentences: thus—

"Your father will not be easy; why do not you go?"

"I am ready, if the others are."

"Shall I ring the bell?"

"Yes, do."

And the bell was rung, and the carriages spoken for. A few minutes more, and Emma hoped to see one troublesome companion deposited in his own house, to get sober and cool, and the other recover his temper and happiness when this visit of hardship were over.

The carriage came: and Mr. Woodhouse, always the first object on such occasions, was carefully attended to his own by Mr. Knightley and Mr. Weston; but not all that either could say could prevent some renewal of alarm at the sight of the snow which had actually fallen, and the discovery of a much darker night than he had been prepared for. "He was afraid they should have a very bad drive. He was afraid poor Isabella would not like it. And there would be poor Emma in the carriage behind. He did not know what they had best do. They must keep as much together as they could;" and James was talked to, and given a charge to go very slow and wait for the other carriage.

Isabella stept in after her father; John Knightley, forgetting that he did not belong to their party, stept in after his wife very naturally; so that Emma found, on being escorted and followed into the second carriage by Mr. Elton, that the door was to be lawfully shut on them, and that they were to have a tête-à-tête drive. It would not have been the awkwardness of a moment, it would have been rather a pleasure, previous to the suspicions of this very day; she could have talked to him of Harriet, and the three-quarters of a mile would have seemed but one. But now, she would rather it had not happened. She believed he had been drinking too much of Mr. Weston's good wine, and felt sure that he would want to be talking nonsense.

To restrain him as much as might be, by her own manners, she was immediately preparing to speak with exquisite calmness and gravity of the weather and the night; but scarcely had she begun, scarcely had they passed the sweep-gate and joined the other carriage, than she found her subject cut up—her hand seized—her attention demanded, and Mr. Elton actually making violent love to her: availing himself of the precious opportunity, declaring sentiments which must be already well known, hoping—fearing—adoring—ready to die if she refused him; but flattering himself that his ardent attachment and unequalled love and unexampled passion could not fail of having some effect, and in short, very much resolved on being seriously accepted as soon as possible. It really was so. Without scruple—without apology—without much apparent diffidence, Mr. Elton, the lover of Harriet, was professing himself *her* lover. She tried to stop him; but vainly; he would go on, and say it all. Angry as she was, the thought of the moment made her resolve to restrain herself when she did speak. She felt that half this folly must be drunkenness, and therefore could hope that it might belong only to the passing hour. Accordingly, with a mixture of the serious and the playful, which she hoped would best suit his half and half state, she replied,

"I am very much astonished, Mr. Elton. This to *me!* you forget yourself—you take me for my friend—any message to Miss Smith I shall be happy to deliver; but no more of this to *me*, if you please."

"Miss Smith!—Message to Miss Smith!—What could she possibly mean!"—And he repeated her words with such assurance of accent, such boastful pretence of amazement, that she could not help replying with quickness,

"Mr. Elton, this is the most extraordinary conduct! and I can account for it only in one way; you are not yourself, or you could not speak either to me, or of Harriet, in such a manner. Command yourself enough to say no more, and I will endeavour to forget it."

But Mr. Elton had only drunk wine enough to elevate his spirits, not at all to confuse his intellects. He perfectly knew his own meaning; and having warmly protested against her suspicion as most injurious, and slightly touched upon his respect for Miss Smith as her friend,—but acknowledging his wonder that Miss Smith should be mentioned at all,—he resumed the subject of his own passion, and was very urgent for a favourable answer.

As she thought less of his inebriety, she thought more of his inconstancy and presumption; and with fewer struggles for politeness, replied,

"It is impossible for me to doubt any longer. You have made yourself too clear. Mr. Elton, my astonishment is much beyond any thing I can express. After such behaviour, as I have witnessed during the last month, to Miss Smith—such attentions as I have been in the daily habit of observing—to be addressing me in this manner—this is an unsteadiness of character, indeed, which I had not supposed possible! Believe me, sir, I am far, very far, from gratified in being the object of such professions."

"Good heaven!" cried Mr. Elton, "what can be the meaning of this?—Miss Smith!—I never thought of Miss Smith in the whole course of my existence—never paid her any attentions, but as your friend: never cared whether she were dead or alive, but as your friend. If she has fancied otherwise, her own wishes have misled her, and I am very sorry—extremely sorry—But, Miss Smith, indeed!—Oh! Miss Woodhouse! who can think of Miss Smith, when Miss Woodhouse is near! No, upon my honour, there is no unsteadiness of character. I have thought only of you. I protest against having paid the smallest attention to any one else. Every thing that I have said or done, for many weeks past, has been with the sole view of marking my adoration of yourself. You cannot really, seriously, doubt it. No!—(in an accent meant to be insinuating)—I am sure you have seen and understood me."

It would be impossible to say what Emma felt, on hearing this— which of all unpleasant sensations was uppermost. She was too completely overpowered to be immediately able to reply: and two moments of silence being ample encouragement for Mr. Elton's sanguine state of mind, he tried to take her hand again, as he joyously exclaimed—

"Charming Miss Woodhouse! allow me to interpret this interesting silence. It confesses that you have long understood me."

"No, sir," cried Emma, "it confesses no such thing. So far from having long understood you, I have been in a most complete error with respect to your views, till this moment. As to myself, I am very sorry that you should have been giving way to any feelings—— Nothing could be farther from my wishes—your attachment to my friend Harriet—your pursuit of her, (pursuit, it appeared,) gave me great pleasure, and I have been very earnestly wishing you success: but had I supposed that she were not your attraction to Hartfield, I should certainly have thought you judged ill in making your visits so frequent. Am I to believe that you have never sought to recommend yourself particularly to Miss Smith?—that you never thought seriously of her?"

"Never, madam," cried he, affronted, in his turn: "never, I assure you. *I* think seriously of Miss Smith!—Miss Smith is a very good sort of girl; and I should be happy to see her respectably settled. I wish her extremely well: and, no doubt, there are men who might not object to——Every body has their level: but as for myself, I am not, I think, quite so much at a loss. I need not so totally despair of an equal alliance, as to be addressing myself to Miss Smith!—No, madam, my visits to Hartfield have been for yourself only; and the encouragement I received"——

"Encouragement!—I give you encouragement!—sir, you have been entirely mistaken in supposing it. I have seen you only as the admirer of my friend. In no other light could you have been more to me than a common acquaintance. I am exceedingly sorry: but it is well that the mistake ends where it does. Had the same behaviour continued, Miss Smith might have been led into a misconception of your views; not being aware, probably, any more than myself, of the very great inequality which you are so sensible of. But, as it is, the disappointment is single, and, I trust, will not be lasting. I have no thoughts of matrimony at present."

He was too angry to say another word; her manner too decided to invite supplication; and in this state of swelling resentment, and mutually deep mortification, they had to continue together a few minutes longer, for the fears of Mr. Woodhouse had confined them to a foot pace. If there had not been so much anger, there would have been desperate awkwardness; but their straight-forward emotions left no room for the little zigzags of embarrassment. Without knowing when the carriage turned into Vicarage-lane, or when it stopped, they found themselves, all at once, at the door of his house; and he was out before another syllable passed.—Emma then felt it indispensable to wish him a good night. The compliment was just returned, coldly and proudly; and, under indescribable irritation of spirits, she was then conveyed to Hartfield.

There she was welcomed, with the utmost delight, by her father, who had been trembling for the dangers of a solitary drive from Vicarage-lane—turning a corner which he could never bear to think of—and in strange hands—a mere common coachman—no James; and there it seemed as if her return only were wanted to make every thing go well: Mr. John Knightley, ashamed of his ill-humour, was now all kindness and attention; and so particularly solicitous for the comfort of her father, as to seem—if not quite ready to join him in a basin of gruel—perfectly sensible of its being exceedingly wholesome; and the day was concluding in peace and comfort to all their little party, except herself.—But her mind had never been in such perturbation, and it needed a very strong effort to appear attentive and cheerful till the usual hour of separating allowed her the relief of quiet reflection.

Chapter XVI

The hair was curled, and the maid sent away, and Emma sat down to think and be miserable.—It was a wretched business, indeed!—Such an overthrow of every thing she had been wishing for!—Such a development of every thing most unwelcome!—Such a blow for Harriet!—That was the worst of all. Every part of it brought pain and humiliation, of some sort or other; but, compared with the evil to Harriet, all was light; and she would gladly have submitted to feel yet more mistaken—more in error—more disgraced by mis-judgment, than she actually was, could the effects of her blunders have been confined to herself.

"If I had not persuaded Harriet into liking the man, I could have born any thing. He might have doubled his presumption to me—But poor Harriet!"

How she could have been so deceived!—He protested that he had never thought seriously of Harriet—never! She looked back as well as she could; but it was all confusion. She had taken up the idea, she supposed, and made every thing bend to it. His manners, how-ever, must have been unmarked, wavering, dubious, or she could not have been so misled.

The picture!—How eager he had been about the picture!—and the charade!—and an hundred other circumstances;—how clearly they had seemed to point at Harriet. To be sure, the charade, with its "ready wit"—but then, the "soft eyes"—in fact it suited neither; it was a jumble without taste or truth. Who could have seen through such thick-headed nonsense?

Certainly she had often, especially of late, thought his manners to herself unnecesarily gallant; but it had passed as his way, as a mere error of judgment, of knowledge, of taste, as one proof among others that he had not always lived in the best society, that with all the gentleness of his address, true elegance was sometimes wanting; but, till this very day, she had never, for an instant, suspected it to mean any thing but grateful respect to her as Harriet's friend.

To Mr. John Knightley was she indebted for her first idea on the subject, for the first start of its possibility. There was no denying that those brothers had penetration. She remembered what Mr. Knightley had once said to her about Mr. Elton, the caution he had given, the conviction he had professed that Mr. Elton would never marry indiscreetly; and blushed to think how much truer a knowledge of his character had been there shewn than any she had reached herself. It was dreadfully mortifying; but Mr. Elton was proving himself, in many respects, the very reverse of what she had meant and believed him; proud, assuming, conceited; very full of his own claims, and little concerned about the feelings of others.

Contrary to the usual course of things, Mr. Elton's wanting to pay his addresses to her had sunk him in her opinion. His professions and his proposals did him no service. She thought nothing of his attachment, and was insulted by his hopes. He wanted to marry well, and having the arrogance to raise his eyes to her, pretended to be in love; but she was perfectly easy as to his not suffering any disappointment that need be cared for. There had been no real affection either in his language or manners. Sighs and fine words had been given in abundance; but she could hardly devise any set of expressions, or fancy any tone of voice, less allied with real love. She need not trouble herself to pity him. He only wanted to aggrandize and enrich himself; and if Miss Woodhouse of Hartfield, the heiress of thirty thousand pounds, were not quite so easily obtained as he had fancied, he would soon try for Miss Somebody else with twenty, or with ten.

But—that he should talk of encouragement, should consider her as aware of his views, accepting his attentions, meaning (in short), to marry him!—should suppose himself her equal in connection or mind!—look down upon her friend, so well understanding the gradations of rank below him, and be so blind to what rose above, as to fancy himself shewing no presumption in addressing her!—It was most provoking.

Perhaps it was not fair to expect him to feel how very much he was her inferior in talent, and all the elegancies of mind. The very want of such equality might prevent his perception of it; but he must know that in fortune and consequence she was greatly his superior. He must know that the Woodhouses had been settled for several generations at Hartfield, the younger branch of a very ancient family—and that the Eltons were nobody. The landed property of Hartfield certainly was inconsiderable, being but a sort of notch in the Donwell Abbey estate, to which all the rest of Highbury belonged; but their fortune, from other sources,[2] was such as to make them scarcely secondary to Donwell Abbey itself, in every other kind of consequence; and the Woodhouses had long held a high place in the consideration of the neighbourhood which Mr. Elton had first entered not two years ago, to make his way as he could, without any alliances but in trade, or any thing to recommend him to notice but his situation and his civility.—But he had fancied her in love with him; that evidently must have been his dependence; and after raving a little about the seeming incongruity of gentle manners and a conceited head, Emma was obliged in common honesty to stop and admit that her own behaviour to him had been so complaisant and obliging, so full of courtesy and attention, as (supposing her real motive unperceived) might warrant a man of ordinary observation and delicacy, like Mr. Elton, in fancying himself a very decided favourite. If *she* had so misinterpreted his feelings, she had little right to wonder that *he*, with self-interest to blind him, should have mistaken her's.

The first error and the worst lay at her door. It was foolish, it was wrong, to take so active a part in bringing any two people together. It was adventuring too far, assuming too much, making light of what ought to be serious, a trick of what ought to be simple. She was quite concerned and ashamed, and resolved to do such things no more.

"Here have I," said she, "actually talked poor Harriet into being very much attached to this man. She might never have thought of him but for me; and certainly never would have thought of him with hope, if I had not assured her of his attachment, for she is as modest and humble as I used to think him. Oh! that I had been satisfied with persuading her not to accept young Martin. There I was quite right. That was well done of me; but there I should have stopped, and left the rest to time and chance. I was introducing her into good company, and giving her the opportunity of pleasing some one worth having; I ought not to have attempted more. But now, poor girl, her peace is cut up for some time. I have been but half a friend to her; and if she were *not* to feel this disappointment so very much, I am sure I have not an idea of any body else who would be at all desirable for her;—William Coxe—Oh! no, I could not endure William Coxe—a pert young lawyer."

2. Austen does not specify these "other sources," but they would likely have been investments—an indication that Highbury, and Hartfield in particular, were not isolated from the rest of the world. From its name, Donwell Abbey would have been a monastery converted to private property in Henry VIII's dissolution of the monasteries nearly 400 years earlier. The dissolution, like Donwell Abbey and its gentleman proprietor, marks the quintessentially English setting of the novel.

She stopt to blush and laugh at her own relapse, and then resumed a more serious, more dispiriting cogitation upon what had been, and might be, and must be. The distressing explanation she had to make to Harriet, and all that poor Harriet would be suffering, with the awkwardness of future meetings, the difficulties of continuing or discontinuing the acquaintance, of subduing feelings, concealing resentment, and avoiding eclat,[3] were enough to occupy her in most unmirthful reflections some time longer, and she went to bed at last with nothing settled but the conviction of her having blundered most dreadfully.

To youth and natural cheerfulness like Emma's, though under temporary gloom at night, the return of day will hardly fail to bring return of spirits. The youth and cheerfulness of morning are in happy analogy, and of powerful operation; and if the distress be not poignant enough to keep the eyes unclosed, they will be sure to open to sensations of softened pain and brighter hope.

Emma got up on the morrow more disposed for comfort than she had gone to bed, more ready to see alleviations of the evil before her, and to depend on getting tolerably out of it.

It was a great consolation that Mr. Elton should not be really in love with her, or so particularly amiable as to make it shocking to disappoint him—that Harriet's nature should not be of that superior sort in which the feelings are most acute and retentive—and that there could be no necessity for any body's knowing what had passed except the three principals, and especially for her father's being given a moment's uneasiness about it.

These were very cheering thoughts; and the sight of a great deal of snow on the ground did her further service, for any thing was welcome that might justify their all three being quite asunder at present.

The weather was most favourable for her; though Christmas-day, she could not go to church. Mr. Woodhouse would have been miserable had his daughter attempted it, and she was therefore safe from either exciting or receiving unpleasant and most unsuitable ideas. The ground covered with snow, and the atmosphere in that unsettled state between frost and thaw, which is of all others the most unfriendly for exercise, every morning beginning in rain or snow, and every evening setting in to freeze, she was for many days a most honourable prisoner. No intercourse with Harriet possible but by note; no church for her on Sunday any more than on Christmas-day; and no need to find excuses for Mr. Elton's absenting himself.

It was weather which might fairly confine every body at home; and though she hoped and believed him to be really taking comfort

---

3. Showy or elaborate display—perhaps also scandal.

in some society or other, it was very pleasant to have her father so well satisfied with his being all alone in his own house, too wise to stir out; and to hear him say to Mr. Knightley, whom no weather could keep entirely from them,—

"Ah! Mr. Knightley, why do not you stay at home like poor Mr. Elton?"

These days of confinement would have been, but for her private perplexities, remarkably comfortable, as such seclusion exactly suited her brother, whose feelings must always be of great importance to his companions; and he had, besides, so thoroughly cleared off his ill-humour at Randalls, that his amiableness never failed him during the rest of his stay at Hartfield. He was always agreeable and obliging, and speaking pleasantly of every body. But with all the hopes of cheerfulness, and all the present comfort of delay, there was still such an evil hanging over her in the hour of explanation with Harriet, as made it impossible for Emma to be ever perfectly at ease.

Chapter XVII

Mr. and Mrs. John Knightley were not detained long at Hartfield. The weather soon improved enough for those to move who must move; and Mr. Woodhouse having, as usual, tried to persuade his daughter to stay behind with all her children, was obliged to see the whole party set off, and return to his lamentations over the destiny of poor Isabella;—which poor Isabella, passing her life with those she doated on, full of their merits, blind to their faults, and always innocently busy, might have been a model of right feminine happiness.

The evening of the very day on which they went, brought a note from Mr. Elton to Mr. Woodhouse, a long, civil, ceremonious note, to say, with Mr. Elton's best compliments, "that he was proposing to leave Highbury the following morning in his way to Bath, where, in compliance with the pressing entreaties of some friends, he had engaged to spend a few weeks, and very much regretted the impossibility he was under, from various circumstances of weather and business, of taking a personal leave of Mr. Woodhouse, of whose friendly civilities he should ever retain a grateful sense—and had Mr. Woodhouse any commands, should be happy to attend to them."

Emma was most agreeably surprised.—Mr. Elton's absence just at this time was the very thing to be desired. She admired him for contriving it, though not able to give him much credit for the manner in which it was announced. Resentment could not have been more plainly spoken than in a civility to her father, from which she was so pointedly excluded. She had not even a share in his opening compliments.—Her name was not mentioned;—and there was so striking a change in all this, and such an ill-judged solemnity of leave-taking in his grateful acknowledgments, as she thought, at first, could not escape her father's suspicion.

It did however.—Her father was quite taken up with the surprize of so sudden a journey, and his fears that Mr. Elton might never get safely to the end of it, and saw nothing extraordinary in his language. It was a very useful note, for it supplied them with fresh matter for thought and conversation during the rest of their lonely evening. Mr. Woodhouse talked over his alarms, and Emma was in spirits to persuade them away with all her usual promptitude.

She now resolved to keep Harriet no longer in the dark. She had reason to believe her nearly recovered from her cold, and it was desirable that she should have as much time as possible for getting the better of her other complaint before the gentleman's return. She went to Mrs. Goddard's accordingly the very next day, to undergo the necessary penance of communication; and a severe one it was.— She had to destroy all the hopes which she had been so industriously feeding—to appear in the ungracious character of the one preferred—and acknowledge herself grossly mistaken and misjudging in all her ideas on one subject, all her observations, all her convictions, all her prophesies for the last six weeks.

The confession completely renewed her first shame—and the sight of Harriet's tears made her think she should never be in charity with herself again.

Harriet bore the intelligence very well—blaming nobody—and in every thing testifying such an ingenuousness of disposition and lowly opinion of herself, as must appear with particular advantage at that moment to her friend.

Emma was in the humour to value simplicity and modesty to the utmost; and all that was amiable, all that ought to be attaching, seemed on Harriet's side, not her own. Harriet did not consider herself as having any thing to complain of. The affection of such a man as Mr. Elton would have been too great a distinction.—She never could have deserved him—and nobody but so partial and kind a friend as Miss Woodhouse would have thought it possible.

Her tears fell abundantly—but her grief was so truly artless, that no dignity could have made it more respectable in Emma's eyes— and she listened to her and tried to console her with all her heart and understanding—really for the time convinced that Harriet was the superior creature of the two—and that to resemble her would be more for her own welfare and happiness than all that genius or intelligence could do.

It was rather too late in the day to set about being simple-minded and ignorant; but she left her with every previous resolution confirmed of being humble and discreet, and repressing imagination all the rest of her life. Her second duty now, inferior only to her father's claims, was to promote Harriet's comfort, and endeavour to prove her own affection in some better method than by match-making. She got her to Hartfield, and shewed her the most unvary-ing kindness, striving to occupy and amuse her, and by books and conversation, to drive Mr. Elton from her thoughts.

Time, she knew, must be allowed for this being thoroughly done; and she could suppose herself but an indifferent judge of such mat-ters in general, and very inadequate to sympathize in an attachment to Mr. Elton in particular; but it seemed to her reasonable that at Harriet's age, and with the entire extinction of all hope, such a prog-ress might be made towards a state of composure by the time of Mr. Elton's return, as to allow them all to meet again in the common routine of acquaintance, without any danger of betraying sentiments or increasing them.

Harriet did think him all perfection, and maintain the non-existence of any body equal to him in person or goodness—and did, in truth, prove herself more resolutely in love than Emma had fore-seen; but yet it appeared to her so natural, so inevitable to strive against an inclination of that sort *unrequited*, that she could not comprehend its continuing very long in equal force.

If Mr. Elton, on his return, made his own indifference as evident and indubitable as she could not doubt he would anxiously do, she could not imagine Harriet's persisting to place her happiness in the sight or the recollection of him.

Their being fixed, so absolutely fixed, in the same place, was bad for each, for all three. Not one of them had the power of removal, or of effecting any material change of society. They must encounter each other, and make the best of it.

Harriet was further unfortunate in the tone of her companions at Mrs. Goddard's; Mr. Elton being the adoration of all the teachers and great girls in the school; and it must be at Hartfield only that she could have any chance of hearing him spoken of with cooling moderation or repellant truth. Where the wound had been given, there must the cure be found if anywhere; and Emma felt that, till she saw her in the way of cure, there could be no true peace for herself.

Chapter XVIII

Mr. Frank Churchill did not come. When the time proposed drew near, Mrs. Weston's fears were justified in the arrival of a letter of excuse. For the present, he could not be spared, to his "very great mortification and regret; but still he looked forward with the hope of coming to Randalls at no distant period."

Mrs. Weston was exceedingly disappointed—much more disappointed, in fact, than her husband, though her dependence on seeing the young man had been so much more sober: but a sanguine temper, though for ever expecting more good than occurs, does not always pay for its hopes by any proportionate depression. It soon flies over the present failure, and begins to hope again. For half an hour Mr. Weston was surprized and sorry; but then he began to perceive that Frank's coming two or three months later would be a much better plan; better time of year; better weather; and that he would be able, without any doubt, to stay considerably longer with them than if he had come sooner.

These feelings rapidly restored his comfort, while Mrs. Weston, of a more apprehensive disposition, foresaw nothing but a repetition of excuses and delays; and after all her concern for what her husband was to suffer, suffered a great deal more herself.

Emma was not at this time in a state of spirits to care really about Mr. Frank Churchill's not coming, except as a disappointment at Randalls. The acquaintance at present had no charm for her. She wanted, rather, to be quiet, and out of temptation; but still, as it was desirable that she should appear, in general, like her usual self, she took care to express as much interest in the circumstance, and enter as warmly into Mr. and Mrs. Weston's disappointment, as might naturally belong to their friendship.

She was the first to announce it to Mr. Knightley; and exclaimed quite as much as was necessary, (or, being acting a part, perhaps rather more,) at the conduct of the Churchills, in keeping him away. She then proceeded to say a good deal more than she felt, of the advantage of such an addition to their confined society in Surry; the pleasure of looking at some body new; the gala-day to Highbury entire, which the sight of him would have made; and ending with reflections on the Churchills again, found herself directly involved in a disagreement with Mr. Knightley; and, to her great amusement, perceived that she was taking the other side of the question from her real opinion, and making use of Mrs. Weston's arguments against herself.

"The Churchills are very likely in fault," said Mr. Knightley, coolly; "but I dare say he might come if he would."

"I do not know why you should say so. He wishes exceedingly to come; but his uncle and aunt will not spare him."

"I cannot believe that he has not the power of coming, if he made a point of it. It is too unlikely, for me to believe it without proof."

"How odd you are! What has Mr. Frank Churchill done, to make you suppose him such an unnatural creature?"

"I am not supposing him at all an unnatural creature, in suspecting that he may have learnt to be above his connections, and to care very little for any thing but his own pleasure, from living with those who have always set him the example of it. It is a great deal more natural than one could wish, that a young man, brought up by those who are proud, luxurious, and selfish, should be proud, luxurious, and selfish too. If Frank Churchill had wanted to see his father, he would have contrived it between September and January. A man at his age—what is he?—three or four-and-twenty—cannot be without the means of doing as much as that. It is impossible."

"That's easily said, and easily felt by you, who have always been your own master. You are the worst judge in the world, Mr. Knightley, of the difficulties of dependence. You do not know what it is to have tempers to manage."

"It is not to be conceived that a man of three or four-and-twenty should not have liberty of mind or limb to that amount. He cannot want money—he cannot want leisure. We know, on the contrary, that he has so much of both, that he is glad to get rid of them at the idlest haunts in the kingdom. We hear of him for ever at some watering-place or other. A little while ago, he was at Weymouth.[4] This proves that he can leave the Churchills."

"Yes, sometimes he can."

"And those times are, whenever he thinks it worth his while; whenever there is any temptation of pleasure."

"It is very unfair to judge of any body's conduct, without an intimate knowledge of their situation. Nobody, who has not been in the interior of a family, can say what the difficulties of any individual of that family may be. We ought to be acquainted with Enscombe, and with Mrs. Churchill's temper, before we pretend to decide upon what her nephew can do. He may, at times, be able to do a great deal more than he can at others."

"There is one thing, Emma, which a man can always do, if he chuses, and that is, his duty; not by manœuvring and finessing, but by vigour and resolution. It is Frank Churchill's duty to pay this attention to his father. He knows it to be so, by his promises and messages; but if he wished to do it, it might be done. A man who felt rightly would say at once, simply and resolutely, to Mrs. Churchill— 'Every sacrifice of mere pleasure you will always find me ready to make to your convenience; but I must go and see my father immediately. I know he would be hurt by my failing in such a mark of respect to him on the present occasion. I shall, therefore, set off tomorrow.'—If he would say so to her at once, in the tone of decision becoming a man, there would be no opposition made to his going."

"No," said Emma, laughing; "but perhaps there might be some made to his coming back again. Such language for a young man

---

4. In Dorset, in the southwest of England; *watering-place*: a seaside resort.

entirely dependent, to use!—Nobody but you, Mr. Knightley, would imagine it possible. But you have not an idea of what is requisite in situations directly opposite to your own. Mr. Frank Churchill to be making such a speech as that to the uncle and aunt, who have brought him up, and are to provide for him!—Standing up in the middle of the room, I suppose, and speaking as loud as he could!—How can you imagine such conduct practicable?"

"Depend upon it, Emma, a sensible man would find no difficulty in it. He would feel himself in the right; and the declaration—made, of course, as a man of sense would make it, in a proper manner—would do him more good, raise him higher, fix his interest stronger with the people he depended on, than all that a line of shifts and expedients can ever do. Respect would be added to affection. They would feel that they could trust him; that the nephew, who had done rightly by his father, would do rightly by them; for they know, as well as he does, as well as all the world must know, that he ought to pay this visit to his father; and while meanly exerting their power to delay it, are in their hearts not thinking the better of him for submitting to their whims. Respect for right conduct is felt by every body. If he would act in this sort of manner, on principle, consistently, regularly, their little minds would bend to his."

"I rather doubt that. You are very fond of bending little minds; but where little minds belong to rich people in authority, I think they have a knack of swelling out, till they are quite as unmanageable as great ones. I can imagine, that if you, as you are, Mr. Knightley, were to be transported and placed all at once in Mr. Frank Churchill's situation, you would be able to say and do just what you have been recommending for him; and it might have a very good effect. The Churchills might not have a word to say in return; but then, you would have no habits of early obedience and long observance to break through. To him who has, it might not be so easy to burst forth at once into perfect independence, and set all their claims on his gratitude and regard at nought. He may have as strong a sense of what would be right, as you can have, without being so equal under particular circumstances to act up to it."

"Then, it would not be so strong a sense. If it failed to produce equal exertion, it could not be an equal conviction."

"Oh! the difference of situation and habit! I wish you would try to understand what an amiable young man may be likely to feel in directly opposing those, whom as child and boy he has been looking up to all his life."

"Your amiable young man is a very weak young man, if this be the first occasion of his carrying through a resolution to do right against the will of others. It ought to have been an habit with him by this time, of following his duty, instead of consulting expediency. I can allow for the fears of the child, but not of the man. As he became rational, he ought to have roused himself and shaken off all that was unworthy in their authority. He ought to have opposed the first attempt on their side to make him slight his father. Had he begun as he ought, there would have been no difficulty now."

"We shall never agree about him," cried Emma; "but that is nothing extraordinary. I have not the least idea of his being a weak young man: I feel sure that he is not. Mr. Weston would not be blind to folly, though in his own son; but he is very likely to have a more yielding, complying, mild disposition than would suit your notions of man's perfection. I dare say he has; and though it may cut him off from some advantages, it will secure him many others."

"Yes; all the advantages of sitting still when he ought to move, and of leading a life of mere idle pleasure, and fancying himself extremely expert in finding excuses for it. He can sit down and write a fine flourishing letter, full of professions and falsehoods, and persuade himself that he has hit upon the very best method in the world of preserving peace at home and preventing his father's having any right to complain. His letters disgust me."

"Your feelings are singular. They seem to satisfy every body else."

"I suspect they do not satisfy Mrs. Weston. They hardly can satisfy a woman of her good sense and quick feelings: standing in a mother's place, but without a mother's affection to blind her. It is on her account that attention to Randalls is doubly due, and she must doubly feel the omission. Had she been a person of consequence herself, he would have come I dare say; and it would not have signified whether he did or no. Can you think your friend behind-hand in these sort of considerations? Do you suppose she does not often say all this to herself? No, Emma, your amiable young man can be amiable only in French, not in English. He may be very 'aimable,' have very good manners, and be very agreeable; but he can have no English delicacy towards the feelings of other people: nothing really amiable about him."

"You seem determined to think ill of him."

"Me!—not at all," replied Mr. Knightley, rather displeased; "I do not want to think ill of him. I should be as ready to acknowledge his merits as any other man; but I hear of none, except what are merely personal; that he is well grown and good-looking, with smooth, plausible manners."

"Well, if he have nothing else to recommend him, he will be a treasure at Highbury. We do not often look upon fine young men, well-bred and agreeable. We must not be nice and ask for all the virtues into the bargain. Cannot you imagine, Mr. Knightley, what a *sensation*[5] his coming will produce? There will be but one subject throughout the parishes of Donwell and Highbury; but one interest—one object of curiosity; it will be all Mr. Frank Churchill; we shall think and speak of nobody else."

"You will excuse my being so much overpowered. If I find him conversible, I shall be glad of his acquaintance; but if he is only a chattering coxcomb, he will not occupy much of my time or thoughts."

"My idea of him is, that he can adapt his conversation to the taste of every body, and has the power as well as the wish of being universally agreeable. To you, he will talk of farming; to me, of drawing or music; and so on to every body, having that general information on all subjects which will enable him to follow the lead, or take the lead, just as propriety may require, and to speak extremely well on each; that is my idea of him."

"And mine," said Mr. Knightley warmly, "is, that if he turn out any thing like it, he will be the most insufferable fellow breathing! What! at three-and-twenty to be the king of his company—the great man—the practised politician, who is to read every body's character, and make every body's talents conduce to the display of his own superiority; to be dispensing his flatteries around, that he may make all appear like fools compared with himself! My dear Emma, your own good sense could not endure such a puppy when it came to the point."

"I will say no more about him," cried Emma, "you turn every thing to evil. We are both prejudiced; you against, I for him; and we have no chance of agreeing till he is really here."

"Prejudiced! I am not prejudiced."

"But I am very much, and without being at all ashamed of it. My love for Mr. and Mrs. Weston gives me a decided prejudice in his favour."

"He is a person I never think of from one month's end to another," said Mr. Knightley, with a degree of vexation, which made Emma immediately talk of something else, though she could not comprehend why he should be angry.

To take a dislike to a young man, only because he appeared to be of a different disposition from himself, was unworthy the real liberality of mind which she was always used to acknowledge in him; for with all the high opinion of himself, which she had often laid to his charge, she had never before for a moment supposed it could make him unjust to the merit of another.

---

5. Austen's italics indicate the novelty of the word, which was particularly used to describe excited or violent feelings raised by celebrities and in works of art like the Gothic novels enjoyed by Harriet Smith.

Volume II

Chapter I

Emma and Harriet had been walking together one morning, and, in Emma's opinion, been talking enough of Mr. Elton for that day. She could not think that Harriet's solace or her own sins required more; and she was therefore industriously getting rid of the subject as they returned;—but it burst out again when she thought she had succeeded, and after speaking some time of what the poor must suffer in winter, and receiving no other answer than a very plaintive—"Mr. Elton is so good to the poor!" she found something else must be done.

They were just approaching the house where lived Mrs. and Miss Bates. She determined to call upon them and seek safety in numbers. There was always sufficient reason for such an attention; Mrs. and Miss Bates loved to be called on, and she knew she was considered by the very few who presumed ever to see imperfection in her, as rather negligent in that respect, and as not contributing what she ought to the stock of their scanty comforts.

She had had many a hint from Mr. Knightley and some from her own heart, as to her deficiency—but none were equal to counteract the persuasion of its being very disagreeable,—a waste of time—tiresome women—and all the horror of being in danger of falling in with the second rate and third rate of Highbury, who were calling on them for ever, and therefore she seldom went near them. But now she made the sudden resolution of not passing their door without going in—observing, as she proposed it to Harriet, that, as well as she could calculate, they were just now quite safe from any letter from Jane Fairfax.

The house belonged to people in business. Mrs. and Miss Bates occupied the drawing-room floor; and there, in the very moderate sized apartment, which was every thing to them, the visitors were most cordially and even gratefully welcomed; the quiet neat old lady, who with her knitting was seated in the warmest corner, wanting even to give up her place to Miss Woodhouse, and her more active, talking daughter, almost ready to overpower them with care and kindness, thanks for their visit, solicitude for their shoes, anxious inquiries after Mr. Woodhouse's health, cheerful communications about her mother's, and sweet-cake from the beaufet[1]—"Mrs. Cole had just been there, just called in for ten minutes, and had been so good as to sit an hour with them, and *she* had taken a piece of cake and been so kind as to say she liked it very much; and

1. Buffet.

therefore she hoped Miss Woodhouse and Miss Smith would do them the favour to eat a piece too."

The mention of the Coles was sure to be followed by that of Mr. Elton. There was intimacy between them, and Mr. Cole had heard from Mr. Elton since his going away. Emma knew what was coming; they must have the letter over again, and settle how long he had been gone, and how much he was engaged in company, and what a favourite he was wherever he went, and how full the Master of the Ceremonies' ball had been; and she went through it very well, with all the interest and all the commendation that could be requisite, and always putting forward to prevent Harriet's being obliged to say a word.

This she had been prepared for when she entered the house; but meant, having once talked him handsomely over, to be no farther incommoded by any troublesome topic, and to wander at large amongst all the Mistresses and Misses of Highbury and their card-parties. She had not been prepared to have Jane Fairfax succeed Mr. Elton; but he was actually hurried off by Miss Bates, she jumped away from him at last abruptly to the Coles, to usher in a letter from her niece.

"Oh! yes—Mr. Elton, I understood—certainly as to dancing—Mrs. Cole was telling me that dancing at the rooms at Bath was—Mrs. Cole was so kind as to sit some time with us, talking of Jane; for as soon as she came in, she began inquiring after her, Jane is so very great a favourite there. Whenever she is with us, Mrs. Cole does not know how to shew her kindness enough; and I must say that Jane deserves it as much as anybody can. And so she began inquiring after her directly, saying, 'I know you cannot have heard from Jane lately, because it is not her time for writing;' and when I immediately said, 'But indeed we have, we had a letter this very morning,' I do not know that I ever saw anybody more surprised. 'Have you, upon your honour!' said she; 'well, that is quite unexpected. Do let me hear what she says.'"

Emma's politeness was at hand directly, to say, with smiling interest—

"Have you heard from Miss Fairfax so lately? I am extremely happy. I hope she is well?"

"Thank you. You are so kind!" replied the happily deceived aunt, while eagerly hunting for the letter.—"Oh! here it is. I was sure it could not be far off; but I had put my huswife[2] upon it, you see, without being aware, and so it was quite hid, but I had it in my hand so very lately that I was almost sure it must be on the table. I was reading it to Mrs. Cole, and since she went away, I was reading it again to my mother, for it is such a pleasure to her—a letter from Jane—that

2. Pocket sewing-case.

she can never hear it often enough; so I knew it could not be far off, and here it is, only just under my huswife—and since you are so kind as to wish to hear what she says;—but, first of all, I really must, in justice to Jane, apologise for her writing so short a letter—only two pages you see—hardly two—and in general she fills the whole paper and crosses half.[3] My mother often wonders that I can make it out so well. She often says, when the letter is first opened, 'Well, Hetty, now I think you will be put to it to make out all that chequer-work'—don't you, ma'am?—And then I tell her, I am sure she would contrive to make it out herself, if she had nobody to do it for her—every word of it—I am sure she would pore over it till she had made out every word. And, indeed, though my mother's eyes are not so good as they were, she can see amazingly well still, thank God! with the help of spectacles. It is such a blessing! My mother's are really very good indeed. Jane often says, when she is here, 'I am sure, grandmama, you must have had very strong eyes to see as you do—and so much fine work as you have done too!—I only wish my eyes may last me as well.'"

All this spoken extremely fast obliged Miss Bates to stop for breath; and Emma said something very civil about the excellence of Miss Fairfax's handwriting.

"You are extremely kind," replied Miss Bates highly gratified; "you who are such a judge, and write so beautifully yourself. I am sure there is nobody's praise that could give us so much pleasure as Miss Woodhouse's. My mother does not hear; she is a little deaf you know. Ma'am," addressing her, "do you hear what Miss Woodhouse is so obliging to say about Jane's handwriting?"

And Emma had the advantage of hearing her own silly compliment repeated twice over before the good old lady could comprehend it. She was pondering, in the mean while, upon the possibility, without seeming very rude, of making her escape from Jane Fairfax's letter, and had almost resolved on hurrying away directly under some slight excuse, when Miss Bates turned to her again and seized her attention.

"My mother's deafness is very trifling you see—just nothing at all. By only raising my voice, and saying anything two or three times over, she is sure to hear; but then she is used to my voice. But it is very remarkable that she should always hear Jane better than she does me. Jane speaks so distinct! However, she will not find her grandmama at all deafer than she was two years ago; which is saying a great deal at my mother's time of life—and it really is full two years, you know, since she was here. We never were so long without

---

3. To save paper, which was expensive, correspondents would fill the page, and then turn the paper 90 degrees and continue writing across the page.

seeing her before, and as I was telling Mrs. Cole, we shall hardly know how to make enough of her now."

"Are you expecting Miss Fairfax here soon?"

"Oh, yes; next week."

"Indeed!—That must be a very great pleasure."

"Thank you. You are very kind. Yes, next week. Every body is so surprized; and every body says the same obliging things. I am sure she will be as happy to see her friends at Highbury, as they can be to see her. Yes, Friday or Saturday; she cannot say which, because Colonel Campbell will be wanting the carriage himself one of those days. So very good of them to send her the whole way! But they always do, you know. Oh, yes, Friday or Saturday next. That is what she writes about. That is the reason of her writing out of rule, as we call it; for, in the common course, we should not have heard from her before next Tuesday or Wednesday."

"Yes, so I imagined. I was afraid there could be little chance of my hearing any thing of Miss Fairfax to-day."

"So obliging of you! No, we should not have heard, if it had not been for this particular circumstance, of her being to come here so soon. My mother is so delighted!—for she is to be three months with us at least. Three months, she says so, positively, as I am going to have the pleasure of reading to you. The case is, you see, that the Campbells are going to Ireland. Mrs. Dixon has persuaded her father and mother to come over and see her directly. They had not intended to go over till the summer, but she is so impatient to see them again—for till she married, last October, she was never away from them so much as a week, which must make it very strange to be in different kingdoms, I was going to say, but however different countries,[4] and so she wrote a very urgent letter to her mother—or her father, I declare I do not know which it was, but we shall see presently in Jane's letter—wrote in Mr. Dixon's name as well as her own, to press their coming over directly, and they would give them the meeting in Dublin, and take them back to their country-seat, Baly-craig, a beautiful place, I fancy. Jane has heard a great deal of its beauty; from Mr. Dixon I mean—I do not know that she ever heard about it from any body else; but it was very natural, you know, that he should like to speak of his own place while he was paying his addresses—and as Jane used to be very often walking out with them—for Colonel and Mrs. Campbell were very particular about their daughter's not walking out often with only Mr. Dixon, for which I do not at all blame them; of course she heard everything he might be telling Miss Campbell about his own home in Ireland. And I think

4. Miss Bates refers to the creation of the United Kingdom in 1801 by the Acts of Union bringing together the formerly separate kingdoms of Great Britain and Ireland.

she wrote us word that he had shewn them some drawings of the place, views that he had taken himself. He is a most amiable, charming young man, I believe. Jane was quite longing to go to Ireland, from his account of things."

At this moment, an ingenious and animating suspicion entering Emma's brain with regard to Jane Fairfax, this charming Mr. Dixon, and the not going to Ireland, she said, with the insidious design of further discovery,

"You must feel it very fortunate that Miss Fairfax should be allowed to come to you at such a time. Considering the very particular friendship between her and Mrs. Dixon, you could hardly have expected her to be excused from accompanying Colonel and Mrs. Campbell."

"Very true, very true, indeed. The very thing that we have always been rather afraid of; for we should not have liked to have her at such a distance from us, for months together—not able to come if anything was to happen. But you see, every thing turns out for the best. They want her (Mr. and Mrs. Dixon) excessively to come over with Colonel and Mrs. Campbell; quite depend upon it; nothing can be more kind or pressing than their *joint* invitation, Jane says, as you will hear presently; Mr. Dixon does not seem in the least backward in any attention. He is a most charming young man. Ever since the service he rendered Jane at Weymouth, when they were out in that party on the water, and she, by the sudden whirling round of something or other among the sails, would have been dashed into the sea at once, and actually was all but gone, if he had not, with the greatest presence of mind, caught hold of her habit—(I can never think of it without trembling!)—But ever since we had the history of that day, I have been so fond of Mr. Dixon!"

"But, in spite of all her friend's urgency, and her own wish of seeing Ireland, Miss Fairfax prefers devoting the time to you and Mrs. Bates?"

"Yes—entirely her own doing, entirely her own choice; and Colonel and Mrs. Campbell think she does quite right, just what they should recommend; and indeed they particularly *wish* her to try her native air, as she has not been quite so well as usual lately."

"I am concerned to hear of it. I think they judge wisely. But Mrs. Dixon must be very much disappointed. Mrs. Dixon, I understand, has no remarkable degree of personal beauty; is not, by any means, to be compared with Miss Fairfax."

"Oh! no. You are very obliging to say such things—but certainly not. There is no comparison between them. Miss Campbell always was absolutely plain—but extremely elegant and amiable."

"Yes, that of course."

"Jane caught a bad cold, poor thing! so long ago as the 7th of November, (as I am going to read to you,) and has never been well since. A long time, is not it, for a cold to hang upon her? She never mentioned it before, because she would not alarm us. Just like her! so considerate!—But however, she is so far from well, that her kind friends the Campbells think she had better come home, and try an air that always agrees with her; and they have no doubt that three or four months at Highbury will entirely cure her—and it is certainly a great deal better that she should come here, than go to Ireland, if she is unwell. Nobody could nurse her, as we should do."

"It appears to me the most desirable arrangement in the world."

"And so she is to come to us next Friday or Saturday, and the Campbells leave town in their way to Holyhead the Monday following—as you will find from Jane's letter. So sudden!—You may guess, dear Miss Woodhouse, what a flurry it has thrown me in! If it was not for the drawback of her illness—but I am afraid we must expect to see her grown thin, and looking very poorly. I must tell you what an unlucky thing happened to me, as to that. I always make a point of reading Jane's letters through to myself first, before I read them aloud to my mother, you know, for fear of there being any thing in them to distress her. Jane desired me to do it, so I always do: and so I began to-day with my usual caution; but no sooner did I come to the mention of her being unwell, than I burst out quite frightened with, 'Bless me! poor Jane is ill!'—which my mother, being on the watch, heard distinctly, and was sadly alarmed at. However, when I read on, I found it was not near so bad as I fancied at first; and I make so light of it now to her, that she does not think much about it. But I cannot imagine how I could be so off my guard! If Jane does not get well soon, we will call in Mr. Perry. The expense shall not be thought of; and though he is so liberal, and so fond of Jane that I dare say he would not mean to charge anything for attendance, we could not suffer it to be so, you know. He has a wife and family to maintain, and is not to be giving away his time. Well, now I have just given you a hint of what Jane writes about, we will turn to her letter, and I am sure she tells her own story a great deal better than I can tell it for her."

"I am afraid we must be running away," said Emma, glancing at Harriet, and beginning to rise—"My father will be expecting us. I had no intention, I thought I had no power of staying more than five minutes, when I first entered the house. I merely called, because I would not pass the door without inquiring after Mrs. Bates; but I have been so pleasantly detained! Now, however, we must wish you and Mrs. Bates good morning."

And not all that could be urged to detain her succeeded. She regained the street—happy in this, that though much had been forced on her against her will, though she had in fact heard the whole substance of Jane Fairfax's letter, she had been able to escape the letter itself.

Chapter II

Jane Fairfax was an orphan, the only child of Mrs. Bates's youngest daughter.

The marriage of Lieut. Fairfax, of the —— regiment of infantry, and Miss Jane Bates, had had its day of fame and pleasure, hope and interest; but nothing now remained of it, save the melancholy remembrance of him dying in action abroad—of his widow sinking under consumption and grief soon afterwards—and this girl.

By birth she belonged to Highbury: and when at three years old, on losing her mother, she became the property, the charge, the consolation, the fondling of her grandmother and aunt, there had seemed every probability of her being permanently fixed there; of her being taught only what very limited means could command, and growing up with no advantages of connection or improvement to be engrafted on what nature had given her in a pleasing person, good understanding, and warm-hearted, well meaning relations.

But the compassionate feelings of a friend of her father gave a change to her destiny. This was Colonel Campbell, who had very highly regarded Fairfax, as an excellent officer and most deserving young man; and farther; had been indebted to him for such attentions, during a severe camp-fever, as he believed had saved his life. These were claims which he did not learn to overlook, though some years passed away from the death of poor Fairfax, before his own return to England put anything in his power. When he did return, he sought out the child and took notice of her. He was a married man, with only one living child, a girl, about Jane's age: and Jane became their guest, paying them long visits and growing a favourite with all; and, before she was nine years old, his daughter's great fondness for her, and his own wish of being a real friend, united to produce an offer from Colonel Campbell of undertaking the whole charge of her education. It was accepted; and from that period Jane had belonged to Colonel Campbell's family, and had lived with them entirely, only visiting her grandmother from time to time.

The plan was that she should be brought up for educating others; the very few hundred pounds which she inherited from her father making independence impossible. To provide for her otherwise was out of Colonel Campbell's power; for though his income, by pay and appointments, was handsome, his fortune was moderate and must be all his daughter's; but, by giving her an education, he hoped to be supplying the means of respectable subsistance hereafter.

Such was Jane Fairfax's history. She had fallen into good hands, known nothing but kindness from the Campbells, and been given an excellent education. Living constantly with right-minded and well-informed people, her heart and understanding had received every advantage of discipline and culture; and Col. Campbell's residence being in London, every lighter talent had been done full justice to, by the attendance of first-rate masters. Her disposition and abilities were equally worthy of all that friendship could do; and at eighteen or nineteen she was, as far as such an early age can be qualified for the care of children, fully competent to the office of instruction herself; but she was too much beloved to be parted with. Neither father nor mother could promote, and the daughter could not endure it. The evil day was put off. It was easy to decide that she was still too young; and Jane remained with them, sharing, as another daughter, in all the rational pleasures of an elegant society, and a judicious mixture of home and amusement, with only the drawback of the future, the sobering suggestions of her own good understanding to remind her that all this might soon be over.

The affection of the whole family, the warm attachment of Miss Campbell in particular, was the more honourable to each party from the circumstance of Jane's decided superiority both in beauty and acquirement. That nature had given it in feature could not be unseen by the young woman, nor could her higher powers of mind be unfelt by the parents. They continued together with unabated regard however, till the marriage of Miss Campbell, who by that chance, that luck which so often defies anticipation in matrimonial affairs, giving attraction to what is moderate rather than to what is superior, engaged the affections of Mr. Dixon, a young man, rich and agreeable, almost as soon as they were acquainted; and was eligibly and happily settled, while Jane Fairfax had yet her bread to earn.

This event had very lately taken place; too lately for any thing to be yet attempted by her less fortunate friend towards entering on her path of duty; though she had now reached the age which her own judgment had fixed on for beginning. She had long resolved that one-and-twenty should be the period. With the fortitude of a devoted noviciate, she had resolved at one-and-twenty to complete the sacrifice, and retire from all the pleasure of life, of rational intercourse, equal society, peace and hope, to penance and mortification for ever.

The good sense of Colonel and Mrs. Campbell could not oppose such a resolution, though their feelings did. As long as they lived, no exertions would be necessary, their home might be her's for ever; and for their own comfort they would have retained her wholly; but this would be selfishness:—what must be at last, had better be soon. Perhaps they began to feel it might have been kinder and wiser to have resisted the temptation of any delay, and spared her from a taste of such enjoyments of ease and leisure as must now be relinquished. Still, however, affection was glad to catch at any reasonable excuse for not hurrying on the wretched moment. She had never been quite well since the time of their daughter's marriage; and till she should have completely recovered her usual strength, they must forbid her engaging in duties, which, so far from being compatible with a weakened frame and varying spirits, seemed, under the most favourable circumstances, to require something more than human perfection of body and mind to be discharged with tolerable comfort.

With regard to her not accompanying them to Ireland, her account to her aunt contained nothing but truth, though there might be some truths not told. It was her own choice to give the time of their absence to Highbury; to spend, perhaps, her last months of perfect liberty with those kind relations to whom she was so very dear: and the Campbells, whatever might be their motive or motives, whether single, or double, or treble, gave the arrangement their ready sanction, and said, that they depended more on a few months spent in her native air, for the recovery of her health, than on any thing else. Certain it was that she was to come; and that Highbury, instead of welcoming that perfect novelty which had been so long promised it— Mr. Frank Churchill—must put up for the present with Jane Fairfax, who could bring only the freshness of a two years absence.

Emma was sorry;—to have to pay civilities to a person she did not like through three long months!—to be always doing more than she wished, and less than she ought! Why she did not like Jane Fairfax might be a difficult question to answer; Mr. Knightley had once told her it was because she saw in her the really accomplished young woman, which she wanted to be thought herself; and though the accusation had been eagerly refuted at the time, there were moments of self-examination in which her conscience could not quite acquit her. But "she could never get acquainted with her: she did not know how it was, but there was such coldness and reserve— such apparent indifference whether she pleased or not—and then, her aunt was such an eternal talker!—and she was made such a fuss with by every body!—and it had been always imagined that they were to be so intimate—because their ages were the same, every body had supposed they must be so fond of each other." These were her reasons—she had no better.

It was a dislike so little just—every imputed fault was so magnified by fancy, that she never saw Jane Fairfax the first time after any considerable absence, without feeling that she had injured her; and now, when the due visit was paid, on her arrival, after a two years' interval, she was particularly struck with the very appearance and manners, which for those two whole years she had been depreciating. Jane Fairfax was very elegant, remarkably elegant; and she had herself the highest value for elegance. Her height was pretty, just such as almost everybody would think tall, and nobody could think very tall; her figure particularly graceful; her size a most becoming medium, between fat and thin, though a slight appearance of ill-health seemed to point out the likeliest evil of the two. Emma could not but feel all this; and then, her face—her features—there was more beauty in them all together than she had remembered; it was not regular, but it was very pleasing beauty. Her eyes, a deep grey, with dark eye-lashes and eye-brows, had never been denied their praise; but the skin, which she had been used to cavil at, as wanting colour, had a clearness and delicacy which really needed no fuller bloom. It was a style of beauty, of which elegance was the reigning character, and as such, she must, in honour, by all her principles, admire it:—elegance, which, whether of person or of mind, she saw so little in Highbury. There, not to be vulgar, was distinction, and merit.

In short, she sat, during the first visit, looking at Jane Fairfax with twofold complacency; the sense of pleasure and the sense of rendering justice, and was determining that she would dislike her no longer. When she took in her history, indeed, her situation, as well as her beauty; when she considered what all this elegance was destined to, what she was going to sink from, how she was going to live, it seemed impossible to feel any thing but compassion and respect; especially, if to every well-known particular entitling her to interest, were added the highly probable circumstance of an attach-ment to Mr. Dixon, which she had so naturally started to herself. In that case, nothing could be more pitiable or more honourable than the sacrifices she had resolved on. Emma was very willing now to acquit her of having seduced Mr. Dixon's affections from his wife, or of any thing mischievous which her imagination had suggested at first. If it were love, it might be simple, single, successless love on her side alone. She might have been unconsciously sucking in the sad poison, while a sharer of his conversation with her friend; and from the best, the purest of motives, might now be denying herself this visit to Ireland, and resolving to divide herself effectually from him and his connections by soon beginning her career of laborious duty.

Upon the whole, Emma left her with such softened, charitable feelings, as made her look around in walking home, and lament that Highbury afforded no young man worthy of giving her inde-pendence; nobody that she could wish to scheme about for her.

These were charming feelings—but not lasting. Before she had committed herself by any public profession of eternal friendship for Jane Fairfax, or done more towards a recantation of past preju-dices and errors, than saying to Mr. Knightley, "She certainly is handsome; she is better than handsome!" Jane had spent an evening at Hartfield with her grandmother and aunt, and every thing was relapsing much into its usual state. Former provocations re-appeared. The aunt was as tiresome as ever; more tiresome, because anxiety for her health was now added to admiration of her powers; and they had to listen to the description of exactly how little bread and butter she ate for breakfast, and how small a slice of mutton for dinner, as well as to see exhibitions of new caps and new work-bags[5] for her mother and herself; and Jane's offences rose again. They had music; Emma was obliged to play; and the thanks and praise which necessarily followed appeared to her an affectation of candour, an air of greatness, meaning only to shew off in higher style her own very superior performance. She was, besides, which was the worst of all, so cold, so cautious! There was no getting at her real opinion. Wrapt up in a cloak of politeness, she seemed determined to hazard nothing. She was disgustingly, was suspiciously reserved.

If any thing could be more, where all was most, she was more reserved on the subject of Weymouth and the Dixons than any thing. She seemed bent on giving no real insight into Mr. Dixon's character, or her own value for his company, or opinion of the suitableness of the match. It was all general approbation and smoothness; nothing delineated or distinguished. It did her no service however. Her caution was thrown away. Emma saw its artifice, and returned to her first surmises. There probably *was* something more to conceal than her own preference; Mr. Dixon, perhaps, had been very near changing one friend for the other, or been fixed only to Miss Campbell, for the sake of the future twelve thousand pounds.

The like reserve prevailed on other topics. She and Mr. Frank Churchill had been at Weymouth at the same time. It was known that they were a little acquainted; but not a syllable of real information could Emma procure as to what he truly was. "Was he handsome?"—"She believed he was reckoned a very fine young man." "Was he agreeable?"—"He was generally thought so." "Did he appear a sensible young man; a young man of information?"—"At a watering-place, or in a common London acquaintance, it was difficult to decide on such points. Manners were all that could be safely judged of, under a much longer knowledge than they had yet had of Mr. Churchill. She believed every body found his manners pleasing." Emma could not forgive her.

Chapter III

Emma could not forgive her;—but as neither provocation nor resentment were discerned by Mr. Knightley, who had been of the party, and had seen only proper attention and pleasing behaviour

5. For needlework.

on each side, he was expressing the next morning, being at Hart-field again on business with Mr. Woodhouse, his approbation of the whole; not so openly as he might have done had her father been out of the room, but speaking plain enough to be very intelligible to Emma. He had been used to think her unjust to Jane, and had now great pleasure in marking an improvement.

"A very pleasant evening," he began, as soon as Mr. Woodhouse had been talked into what was necessary, told that he understood, and the papers swept away;—"particularly pleasant. You and Miss Fairfax gave us some very good music. I do not know a more luxuri-ous state, sir, than sitting at one's ease to be entertained a whole evening by two such young women; sometimes with music and some-times with conversation. I am sure Miss Fairfax must have found the evening pleasant, Emma. You left nothing undone. I was glad you made her play so much, for having no instrument at her grandmoth-er's, it must have been a real indulgence."

"I am happy you approved," said Emma, smiling, "but I hope I am not often deficient in what is due to guests at Hartfield."

"No, my dear," said her father instantly, "*that* I am sure you are not. There is nobody half so attentive and civil as you are. If any thing, you are too attentive. The muffin last night—if it had been handed round once, I think it would have been enough."

"No," said Mr. Knightley, nearly at the same time, "you are not often deficient; not often deficient either in manner or comprehen-sion. I think you understand me, therefore."

An arch look expressed—"I understand you well enough;" but she said only, "Miss Fairfax is reserved."

"I always told you she was—a little; but you will soon overcome all that part of her reserve which ought to be overcome, all that has its foundation in diffidence. What arises from discretion must be honoured."

"You think her diffident. I do not see it."

"My dear Emma," said he, moving from his chair into one close by her, "you are not going to tell me, I hope, that you had not a pleasant evening."

"Oh! no; I was pleased with my own perseverance in asking ques-tions, and amused to think how little information I obtained."

"I am disappointed," was his only answer.

"I hope every body had a pleasant evening," said Mr. Woodhouse, in his quiet way. "I had. Once, I felt the fire rather too much; but then I moved back my chair a little, a very little, and it did not dis-turb me. Miss Bates was very chatty and good-humoured, as she always is, though she speaks rather too quick. However, she is very agreeable, and Mrs. Bates too, in a different way. I like old friends; and Miss Jane Fairfax is a very pretty sort of young lady, a very pretty and a very well-behaved young lady indeed. She must have found the evening agreeable, Mr. Knightley, because she had Emma."

"True, sir; and Emma, because she had Miss Fairfax."

Emma saw his anxiety, and wishing to appease it, at least for the present, said, and with a sincerity which no one could question—

"She is a sort of elegant creature that one cannot keep one's eyes from. I am always watching her to admire; and I do pity her from my heart."

Mr. Knightley looked as if he were more gratified than he cared to express; and before he could make any reply, Mr. Woodhouse, whose thoughts were on the Bates's, said—

"It is a great pity that their circumstances should be so confined! a great pity indeed! and I have often wished—but it is so little one can venture to do—small, trifling presents, of any thing uncommon—Now we have killed a porker, and Emma thinks of sending them a loin or a leg; it is very small and delicate—Hartfield pork is not like any other pork—but still it is pork—and, my dear Emma, unless one could be sure of their making it into steaks, nicely fried, as our's are fried, without the smallest grease, and not roast it, for no stomach can bear roast pork—I think we had better send the leg—do not you think so, my dear?"

"My dear papa, I sent the whole hind-quarter. I knew you would wish it. There will be the leg to be salted, you know, which is so very nice, and the loin to be dressed directly in any manner they like."

"That's right, my dear, very right. I had not thought of it before, but that was the best way. They must not over-salt the leg; and then, if it is not over-salted, and if it is very thoroughly boiled, just as Serle boils our's, and eaten very moderately of, with a boiled turnip, and a little carrot or parsnip, I do not consider it unwholesome."

"Emma," said Mr. Knightley presently, "I have a piece of news for you. You like news—and I heard an article in my way hither that I think will interest you."

"News! Oh! yes, I always like news. What is it?—why do you smile so?—where did you hear it?—at Randalls?"

He had time only to say,

"No, not at Randalls; I have not been near Randalls,"

When the door was thrown open, and Miss Bates and Miss Fairfax walked into the room. Full of thanks, and full of news, Miss Bates knew not which to give quickest. Mr. Knightley soon saw that he had lost his moment, and that not another syllable of communication could rest with him.

"Oh! my dear sir, how are you this morning? My dear Miss Woodhouse—I come quite overpowered. Such a beautiful hind-quarter of pork! You are too bountiful! Have you heard the news? Mr. Elton is going to be married."

Emma had not had time even to think of Mr. Elton, and she was so completely surprised that she could not avoid a little start, and a little blush, at the sound.

"There is my news:—I thought it would interest you," said Mr. Knightley, with a smile which implied a conviction of some part of what had passed between them.

"But where could *you* hear it!" cried Miss Bates. "Where could you possibly hear it, Mr. Knightley? For it is not five minutes since I received Mrs. Cole's note—no, it cannot be more than five—or at least ten—for I had got my bonnet and spencer[6] on, just ready to come out—I was only gone down to speak to Patty again about the pork—Jane was standing in the passage—were not you, Jane?—for my mother was so afraid that we had not any salting-pan large enough. So I said I would go down and see, and Jane said, 'Shall I go down instead? for I think you have a little cold, and Patty has been washing the kitchen.' "Oh! my dear, said I—well, and just then came the note. A Miss Hawkins—that's all I know. A Miss Hawkins of Bath. But, Mr. Knightley, how could you possibly have heard it? for the very moment Mr. Cole told Mrs. Cole of it, she sat down and wrote to me. A Miss Hawkins"—

"I was with Mr. Cole on business an hour and half ago. He had just read Elton's letter as I was shewn in, and handed it to me directly."

"Well! that is quite—I suppose there never was a piece of news more generally interesting. My dear sir, you really are too bountiful. My mother desires her very best compliments and regards, and a thousand thanks, and says you really quite oppress her."

"We consider our Hartfield pork," replied Mr. Woodhouse— "indeed it certainly is, so very superior to all other pork, that Emma and I cannot have a greater pleasure than"—

"Oh! my dear sir, as my mother says, our friends are only too good to us. If ever there were people who, without having great wealth themselves, had every thing they could wish for, I am sure it is us. We may well say that 'our lot is cast in a goodly heritage.'[7] Well, Mr. Knightley, and so you actually saw the letter; well"—

"It was short, merely to announce—but cheerful, exulting, of course."—Here was a sly glance at Emma. "He had been so fortunate as to—I forget the precise words—one has no business to remember them. The information was, as you state, that he was going to be married to a Miss Hawkins. By his style, I should imagine it just settled."

---

6. Close-fitting jacket or bodice.
7. Chapman notes the echo of Psalms 16.7.

"Mr. Elton going to be married!" said Emma, as soon as she could speak. "He will have everybody's wishes for his happiness."

"He is very young to settle," was Mr. Woodhouse's observation. "He had better not be in a hurry. He seemed to me very well off as he was. We were always glad to see him at Hartfield."

"A new neighbour for us all, Miss Woodhouse!" said Miss Bates, joyfully; "my mother is so pleased!—she says she cannot bear to have the poor old Vicarage without a mistress. This is great news, indeed. Jane, you have never seen Mr. Elton!—no wonder that you have such a curiosity to see him."

Jane's curiosity did not appear of that absorbing nature as wholly to occupy her.

"No—I have never seen Mr. Elton," she replied, starting on this appeal; "is he—is he a tall man?"

"Who shall answer that question?" cried Emma. "My father would say 'yes,' Mr. Knightley, 'no;' and Miss Bates and I that he is just the happy medium. When you have been here a little longer, Miss Fairfax, you will understand that Mr. Elton is the standard of perfection in Highbury, both in person and mind."

"Very true, Miss Woodhouse, so she will. He is the very best young man—But, my dear Jane, if you remember, I told you yesterday he was precisely the height of Mr. Perry. Miss Hawkins,—I dare say, an excellent young woman. His extreme attention to my mother—wanting her to sit in the vicarage-pew, that she might hear the better, for my mother is a little deaf, you know—it is not much, but she does not hear quite quick. Jane says that Colonel Campbell is a little deaf. He fancied bathing might be good for it—the warm bath—but she says it did him no lasting benefit. Colonel Campbell, you know, is quite our angel. And Mr. Dixon seems a very charming young man, quite worthy of him. It is such a happiness when good people get together—and they always do. Now, here will be Mr. Elton and Miss Hawkins; and there are the Coles, such very good people; and the Perrys—I suppose there never was a happier or a better couple than Mr. and Mrs. Perry. I say, sir," turning to Mr. Woodhouse, "I think there are few places with such society as Highbury. I always say, we are quite blessed in our neighbours.—My dear sir, if there is one thing my mother loves better than another, it is pork—a roast loin of pork"—

"As to who, or what Miss Hawkins is, or how long he has been acquainted with her," said Emma, "nothing I suppose can be known. One feels that it cannot be a very long acquaintance. He has been gone only four weeks."

Nobody had any information to give; and, after a few more wonderings, Emma said,

"You are silent, Miss Fairfax—but I hope you mean to take an interest in this news. You, who have been hearing and seeing so much of late on these subjects, who must have been so deep in the business on Miss Campbell's account—we shall not excuse your being indifferent about Mr. Elton and Miss Hawkins."

"When I have seen Mr. Elton," replied Jane, "I dare say I shall be interested—but I believe it requires *that* with me. And as it is some months since Miss Campbell married, the impression may be a little worn off."

"Yes, he has been gone just four weeks, as you observe, Miss Woodhouse," said Miss Bates, "four weeks yesterday.—A Miss Hawkins.—Well, I had always rather fancied it would be some young lady hereabouts; not that I ever——Mrs. Cole once whispered to me—but I immediately said, 'No, Mr. Elton is a most worthy young man—but'——In short, I do not think I am particularly quick at those sort of discoveries. I do not pretend to it. What is before me, I see. At the same time, nobody could wonder if Mr. Elton should have aspired——Miss Woodhouse lets me chatter on, so good-humouredly. She knows I would not offend for the world. How does Miss Smith do? She seems quite recovered now. Have you heard from Mrs. John Knightley lately? Oh! those dear little children. Jane, do you know I always fancy Mr. Dixon like Mr. John Knightley? I mean in person—tall, and with that sort of look—and not very talkative."

"Quite wrong, my dear aunt; there is no likeness at all."

"Very odd! but one never does form a just idea of any body beforehand. One takes up a notion, and runs away with it. Mr. Dixon, you say, is not, strictly speaking, handsome."

"Handsome! Oh! no—far from it—certainly plain. I told you he was plain."

"My dear, you said that Miss Campbell would not allow him to be plain, and that you yourself—"

"Oh! as for me, my judgment is worth nothing. Where I have a regard, I always think a person well-looking. But I gave what I believed the general opinion, when I called him plain."

"Well, my dear Jane, I believe we must be running away. The weather does not look well, and grandmamma will be uneasy. You are too obliging, my dear Miss Woodhouse; but we really must take leave. This has been a most agreeable piece of news indeed. I shall just go round by Mrs. Cole's; but I shall not stop three minutes: and, Jane, you had better go home directly—I would not have you out in a shower!—We think she is the better for Highbury already. Thank you, we do indeed. I shall not attempt calling on Mrs. Goddard, for I really do not think she cares for any thing but *boiled* pork: when we dress the leg it will be another thing. Good morning to you, my dear sir. Oh! Mr. Knightley is coming too. Well, that is so very!—I am sure if Jane is tired, you will be so kind as to give her your arm.—Mr. Elton, and Miss Hawkins.—Good morning to you."

Emma, alone with her father, had half her attention wanted by him, while he lamented that young people would be in such a hurry to marry—and to marry strangers too—and the other half she could give to her own view of the subject. It was to herself an amusing and a very welcome piece of news, as proving that Mr. Elton could not have suffered long; but she was sorry for Harriet: Harriet must feel it—and all that she could hope was, by giving the first information herself, to save her from hearing it abruptly from others. It was now about the time that she was likely to call. If she were to meet Miss Bates in her way!—and upon its beginning to rain, Emma was obliged to expect that the weather would be detaining her at Mrs. Goddard's, and that the intelligence would undoubtedly rush upon her without preparation.

The shower was heavy, but short; and it had not been over five minutes, when in came Harriet, with just the heated, agitated look which hurrying thither with a full heart was likely to give; and the "Oh! Miss Woodhouse, what do you think has happened!" which instantly burst forth, had all the evidence of corresponding perturbation. As the blow was given, Emma felt that she could not now shew greater kindness than in listening; and Harriet, unchecked, ran eagerly through what she had to tell. "She had set out from Mrs. Goddard's half an hour ago—she had been afraid it would rain—she had been afraid it would pour down every moment—but she thought she might get to Hartfield first—she had hurried on as fast as possible; but then, as she was passing by the house where a young woman was making up a gown for her, she thought she would just step in and see how it went on; and though she did not seem to stay half a moment there, soon after she came out it began to rain, and she did not know what to do; so she ran on directly, as fast as she could, and took shelter at Ford's."—Ford's was the principal woollen-draper, linen-draper, and haberdasher's shop united; the shop first in size and fashion in the place.—"And so, there she had set, without an idea of any thing in the world, full ten minutes, perhaps—where, all of a sudden, who should come in—to be sure it was so very odd!—but they always dealt at Ford's—who should come in, but Elizabeth Martin and her brother!—Dear Miss Woodhouse! only think. I thought I should have fainted. I did not know what to do. I was sitting near the door—Elizabeth saw me directly; but he did not; he was busy with the umbrella. I am sure she saw me, but she looked away directly, and took no notice; and they both went to quite the farther end of the shop; and I kept sitting near the door!—Oh! dear; I was so miserable! I am sure I must have been as white as my gown. I could not go away you know, because of the rain; but I did so wish myself any where in the world but there.—Oh! dear, Miss Woodhouse—well, at least, I fancy, he looked round and saw me; for instead of going on with their buyings, they began whispering to one another. I am sure they were talking of me; and I could not help thinking that he was persuading her to speak to me—(do you think he was, Miss Woodhouse?)—for presently she came forward—came quite up to me, and asked how I did, and seemed ready to shake hands, if I would. She did not do any of it in the same way that she used; I could see she was altered; but, however, she seemed to *try* to be very friendly, and we shook hands, and stood talking some time; but I know no more what I said—I was in such a tremble!—I remember she said she was sorry we never met now; which I thought almost too kind! Dear, Miss Woodhouse, I was absolutely miserable! By that time, it was beginning to hold up, and I was determined that nothing should stop me from getting away—and then—only think!—I found he was coming up towards me too—slowly you know, and as if he did not quite know what to do; and so he came and spoke, and I answered—and I stood for a minute, feeling dreadfully, you know, one can't tell how; and then I took courage, and said it did not rain, and I must go: and so off I set; and I had not got three yards from the door, when he came after me, only to say, if I was going to Hartfield, he thought I had much better go round by Mr. Cole's stables, for I should find the near way quite floated[8] by this rain. Oh! dear, I thought it would have been the death of me! So I said, I was very much obliged to him: you know I could not do less; and then he went back to Elizabeth, and I came round by the stables—I believe I did—but I hardly knew where I was, or any thing about it. Oh! Miss Woodhouse, I would rather done any thing than have had it happen: and yet, you know, there was a sort of satisfaction in seeing him behave so pleasantly and so kindly. And Elizabeth, too. Oh! Miss Woodhouse, do talk to me and make me comfortable again."

Very sincerely did Emma wish to do so; but it was not immediately in her power. She was obliged to stop and think. She was not thoroughly comfortable herself. The young man's conduct, and his sister's, seemed the result of real feeling, and she could not but pity them. As Harriet described it, there had been an interesting mixture of wounded affection and genuine delicacy in their behaviour. But she had believed them to be well meaning, worthy people before; and what difference did this make in the evils of the connection? It was folly to be disturbed by it. Of course, he must be sorry to lose her—they must be all sorry. Ambition, as well as love,

8. I.e., flooded.

had probably been mortified. They might all have hoped to rise by Harriet's acquaintance: and besides, what was the value of Harriet's description?—so easily pleased—so little discerning;—what signified her praise?

She exerted herself; and did try to make her comfortable, by considering all that had passed as a mere trifle, and quite unworthy of being dwelt on.

"It might be distressing, for the moment," said she; "but you seem to have behaved extremely well; and it is over—and may never—can never, as a first meeting, occur again, and therefore you need not think about it."

Harriet said, "very true;" and she "would not think about it;" but still she talked of it—still she could talk of nothing else; and Emma, at last, in order to put the Martins out of her head, was obliged to hurry on the news, which she had meant to give with so much tender caution; hardly knowing herself whether to rejoice or be angry, ashamed or only amused, at such a state of mind in poor Harriet—such a conclusion of Mr. Elton's importance with her!

Mr. Elton's rights, however, gradually revived. Though she did not feel the first intelligence as she might have done the day before, or an hour before, its interest soon increased; and before their first conversation was over, she had talked herself into all the sensations of curiosity, wonder and regret, pain and pleasure, as to this fortunate Miss Hawkins, which could conduce to place the Martins under proper subordination in her fancy.

Emma learned to be rather glad that there had been such a meeting. It had been serviceable in deadening the first shock, without retaining any influence to alarm. As Harriet now lived, the Martins could not get at her, without seeking her, where hitherto they had wanted either the courage or the condescension to seek her; for since her refusal of the brother, the sisters had never been at Mrs. Goddard's; and a twelve-month might pass without their being thrown together again, with any necessity, or even any power of speech.

Chapter IV

Human nature is so well disposed towards those who are in interesting situations, that a young person, who either marries or dies, is sure of being kindly spoken of.

A week had not passed since Miss Hawkins's name was first mentioned in Highbury, before she was, by some means or other, discovered to have every recommendation of person and mind; to be handsome, elegant, highly accomplished, and perfectly amiable: and when Mr. Elton himself arrived to triumph in his happy prospects, and circulate the fame of her merits, there was very little more for him to do, than to tell her Christian name, and say whose music she principally played.

Mr. Elton returned, a very happy man. He had gone away rejected and mortified—disappointed in a very sanguine hope, after a series of what had appeared to him strong encouragement; and not only losing the right lady, but finding himself debased to the level of a very wrong one. He had gone away deeply offended—he came back engaged to another—and to another as superior, of course, to the first, as under such circumstances what is gained always is to what is lost. He came back gay and self-satisfied, eager and busy, caring nothing for Miss Woodhouse, and defying Miss Smith.

The charming Augusta Hawkins, in addition to all the usual advantages of perfect beauty and merit, was in possession of an independent fortune, of so many thousands as would always be called ten; a point of some dignity, as well as some convenience: the story told well; he had not thrown himself away—he had gained a woman of 10,000*l*. or thereabouts; and he had gained her with such delightful rapidity—the first hour of introduction had been so very soon followed by distinguishing notice; the history which he had to give Mrs. Cole of the rise and progress of the affair was so glorious—the steps so quick, from the accidental rencontre,[9] to the dinner at Mr. Green's, and the party at Mrs. Brown's—smiles and blushes rising in importance—with consciousness and agitation richly scattered— the lady had been so easily impressed—so sweetly disposed—had in short, to use a most intelligible phrase, been so very ready to have him, that vanity and prudence were equally contented.

He had caught both substance and shadow—both fortune and affection, and was just the happy man he ought to be; talking only of himself and his own concerns—expecting to be congratulated— ready to be laughed at—and, with cordial, fearless smiles, now addressing all the young ladies of the place, to whom, a few weeks ago, he would have been more cautiously gallant.

The wedding was no distant event, as the parties had only themselves to please, and nothing but the necessary preparations to wait for; and when he set out for Bath again, there was a general expectation, which a certain glance of Mrs. Cole's did not seem to contradict, that when he next entered Highbury he would bring his bride.

During his present short stay, Emma had barely seen him; but just enough to feel that the first meeting was over, and to give her the impression of his not being improved by the mixture of pique and pretension, now spread over his air. She was, in fact, beginning very much to wonder that she had ever thought him pleasing at all;

9. Chance meeting.

and his sight was so inseparably connected with some very disagreeable feelings, that except in a moral light, as a penance, a lesson, a source of profitable humiliation to her own mind, she would
have been thankful to be assured of never seeing him again. She
wished him very well; but he gave her pain, and his welfare twenty
miles off would administer most satisfaction.

The pain of his continued residence in Highbury, however, must
certainly be lessened by his marriage. Many vain solicitudes would
be prevented—many awkwardnesses smoothed by it. A *Mrs. Elton*
would be an excuse for any change of intercourse; former intimacy
might sink without remark. It would be almost beginning their life
of civility again.

Of the lady, individually, Emma thought very little. She was
good enough for Mr. Elton, no doubt; accomplished enough for
Highbury—handsome enough—to look plain, probably, by Harriet's
side. As to connection, there Emma was perfectly easy; persuaded,
that after all his own vaunted claims and disdain of Harriet, he had
done nothing. On that article, truth seemed attainable. *What* she
was, must be uncertain; but *who* she was, might be found out; and
setting aside the 10,000*l.* it did not appear that she was at all Harriet's superior. She brought no name, no blood, no alliance. Miss
Hawkins was the youngest of the two daughters of a Bristol—
merchant, of course, he must be called; but, as the whole of the
profits of his mercantile life appeared so very moderate, it was not
unfair to guess the dignity of his line of trade had been very moderate also. Part of every winter she had been used to spend in Bath; but
Bristol was her home, the very heart of Bristol; for though the father
and mother had died some years ago, an uncle remained—in the law
line—nothing more distinctly honourable was hazarded of him, than
that he was in the law line; and with him the daughter had lived.
Emma guessed him to be the drudge of some attorney, and too stupid
to rise. And all the grandeur of the connection seemed dependent on
the elder sister, who was *very well married*, to a gentleman in a *great
way*, near Bristol, who kept two carriages! That was the wind-up of
the history; that was the glory of Miss Hawkins.

Could she but have given Harriet her feelings about it all! She
had talked her into love; but alas! she was not so easily to be talked
out of it. The charm of an object to occupy the many vacancies of
Harriet's mind was not to be talked away. He might be superseded
by another; he certainly would indeed; nothing could be clearer;
even a Robert Martin would have been sufficient; but nothing else,
she feared, would cure her. Harriet was one of those, who, having
once begun, would be always in love. And now, poor girl! she was
considerably worse from this re-appearance of Mr. Elton. She was
always having a glimpse of him somewhere or other. Emma saw

him only once; but two or three times every day Harriet was sure *just* to meet with him, or *just* to miss him, *just* to hear his voice, or see his shoulder, *just* to have something occur to preserve him in her fancy, in all the favouring warmth of surprize and conjecture. She was, moreover, perpetually hearing about him; for, excepting when at Hartfield, she was always among those who saw no fault in Mr. Elton, and found nothing so interesting as the discussion of his concerns; and every report, therefore, every guess—all that had already occurred, all that might occur in the arrangement of his affairs, comprehending income, servants, and furniture, was continually in agitation around her. Her regard was receiving strength by invariable praise of him, and her regrets kept alive, and feelings irritated by ceaseless repetitions of Miss Hawkins's happiness, and continual observation of, how much he seemed attached!—his air as he walked by the house—the very sitting of his hat, being all in proof of how much he was in love!

Had it been allowable entertainment, had there been no pain to her friend, or reproach to herself, in the waverings of Harriet's mind, Emma would have been amused by its variations. Sometimes Mr. Elton predominated, sometimes the Martins; and each was occasionally useful as a check to the other. Mr. Elton's engagement had been the cure of the agitation of meeting Mr. Martin. The unhappiness produced by the knowledge of that engagement had been a little put aside by Elizabeth Martin's calling at Mrs. Goddard's a few days afterwards. Harriet had not been at home; but a note had been prepared and left for her, written in the very style to touch; a small mixture of reproach, with a great deal of kindness; and till Mr. Elton himself appeared, she had been much occupied by it, continually pondering over what could be done in return, and wishing to do more than she dared to confess. But Mr. Elton, in person, had driven away all such cares. While he staid, the Martins were forgotten; and on the very morning of his setting off for Bath again, Emma, to dissipate some of the distress it occasioned, judged it best for her to return Elizabeth Martin's visit.

How that visit was to be acknowledged—what would be necessary—and what might be safest, had been a point of some doubtful consideration. Absolute neglect of the mother and sisters, when invited to come, would be ingratitude. It must not be: and yet the danger of a renewal of the acquaintance!—

After much thinking, she could determine on nothing better, than Harriet's returning the visit; but in a way that, if they had understanding, should convince them that it was to be only a formal acquaintance. She meant to take her in the carriage, leave her at the Abbey Mill, while she drove a little farther, and call for her again so soon, as to allow no time for insidious applications or dangerous recurrences to the past, and give the most decided proof of what degree of intimacy was chosen for the future.

She could think of nothing better: and though there was something in it which her own heart could not approve—something of ingratitude, merely glossed over—it must be done, or what would become of Harriet?

Chapter V

Small heart had Harriet for visiting. Only half an hour before her friend called for her at Mrs. Goddard's, her evil stars had led her to the very spot where, at that moment, a trunk, directed to *The Rev. Philip Elton, White-Hart, Bath*, was to be seen under the operation of being lifted into the butcher's cart, which was to convey it to where the coaches past; and every thing in this world, excepting that trunk and the direction, was consequently a blank.

She went, however; and when they reached the farm, and she was to be put down, at the end of the broad, neat gravel-walk, which led between espalier apple-trees[1] to the front door, the sight of every thing which had given her so much pleasure the autumn before, was beginning to revive a little local agitation; and when they parted, Emma observed her to be looking around with a sort of fearful curiosity, which determined her not to allow the visit to exceed the proposed quarter of an hour. She went on herself, to give that portion of time to an old servant who was married, and settled in Donwell.

The quarter of an hour brought her punctually to the white gate again; and Miss Smith receiving her summons, was with her without delay, and unattended by any alarming young man. She came solitarily down the gravel walk—a Miss Martin just appearing at the door, and parting with her seemingly with ceremonious civility.

Harriet could not very soon give an intelligible account. She was feeling too much; but at last Emma collected from her enough to understand the sort of meeting, and the sort of pain it was creating. She had seen only Mrs. Martin and the two girls. They had received her doubtingly, if not coolly; and nothing beyond the merest commonplace had been talked almost all the time—till just at last, when Mrs. Martin's saying, all of a sudden, that she thought Miss Smith was grown, had brought on a more interesting subject, and a warmer manner. In that very room she had been measured last September, with her two friends. There were the pencilled marks and memorandums on the wainscot by the window. *He* had done it. They all seemed to remember the day, the hour, the party, the occasion—to feel the same consciousness, the same regrets—to be ready to return

---

1. Trees pruned and trained to grow on a lattice.

to the same good understanding; and they were just growing again like themselves, (Harriet, as Emma must suspect, as ready as the best of them to be cordial and happy,) when the carriage re-appeared, and all was over. The style of the visit, and the shortness of it, were then felt to be decisive. Fourteen minutes to be given to those with whom she had thankfully passed six weeks not six months ago!—Emma could not but picture it all, and feel how justly they might resent, how naturally Harriet must suffer. It was a bad business. She would have given a great deal, or endured a great deal, to have had the Martins in a higher rank of life. They were so deserving, that a *little* higher should have been enough: but as it was, how could she have done otherwise?—Impossible!—She could not repent. They must be separated; but there was a great deal of pain in the process—so much to herself at this time, that she soon felt the necessity of a little consolation, and resolved on going home by way of Randalls to procure it. Her mind was quite sick of Mr. Elton and the Martins. The refreshment of Randalls was absolutely necessary.

It was a good scheme; but on driving to the door they heard that neither "master nor mistress was at home;" they had both been out some time; the man believed they were gone to Hartfield.

"This is too bad," cried Emma, as they turned away. "And now we shall just miss them; too provoking!—I do not know when I have been so disappointed." And she leaned back in the corner, to indulge her murmurs, or to reason them away; probably a little of both—such being the commonest process of a not ill-disposed mind. Presently the carriage stopt; she looked up; it was stopt by Mr. and Mrs. Weston, who were standing to speak to her. There was instant pleasure in the sight of them, and still greater pleasure was conveyed in sound—for Mr. Weston immediately accosted her with,

"How d'ye do?—how d'ye do?—We have been sitting with your father—glad to see him so well. Frank comes to-morrow—I had a letter this morning—we see him to-morrow by dinner time to a certainty—he is at Oxford to-day, and he comes for a whole fortnight; I knew it would be so. If he had come at Christmas he could not have staid three days; I was always glad he did not come at Christmas; now we are going to have just the right weather for him, fine, dry, settled weather. We shall enjoy him completely; every thing has turned out exactly as we could wish."

There was no resisting such news, no possibility of avoiding the influence of such a happy face as Mr. Weston's, confirmed as it all was by the words and the countenance of his wife, fewer and quieter, but not less to the purpose. To know that *she* thought his coming certain was enough to make Emma consider it so, and sincerely did she rejoice in their joy. It was a most delightful reanimation of exhausted spirits. The worn-out past was sunk in the freshness of what was coming; and in the rapidity of half a moment's thought, she hoped Mr. Elton would now be talked of no more.

Mr. Weston gave her the history of the engagements at Enscombe, which allowed his son to answer for having an entire fortnight at his command, as well as the route and the method of his journey; and she listened, and smiled, and congratulated.

"I shall soon bring him over to Hartfield," said he, at the conclusion.

Emma could imagine she saw a touch of the arm at this speech, from his wife.

"We had better move on, Mr. Weston," said she, "we are detaining the girls."

"Well, well, I am ready;"—and turning again to Emma, "but you must not be expecting such a *very* fine young man; you have only had *my* account you know; I dare say he is really nothing extraordinary:"—though his own sparkling eyes at the moment were speaking a very different conviction.

Emma could look perfectly unconscious and innocent, and answer in a manner that appropriated nothing.

"Think of me to-morrow, my dear Emma, about four o'clock," was Mrs. Weston's parting injunction; spoken with some anxiety, and meant only for her.

"Four o'clock!—depend upon it he will be here by three," was Mr. Weston's quick amendment; and so ended a most satisfactory meeting. Emma's spirits were mounted quite up to happiness; every thing wore a different air; James and his horses seemed not half so sluggish as before. When she looked at the hedges, she thought the elder at least must soon be coming out; and when she turned round to Harriet, she saw something like a look of spring, a tender smile even there.

"Will Mr. Frank Churchill pass through Bath as well as Oxford?"—was a question, however, which did not augur much.[2]

But neither geography nor tranquillity could come all at once, and Emma was now in a humour to resolve that they should both come in time.

The morning of the interesting day arrived, and Mrs. Weston's faithful pupil did not forget either at ten, or eleven, or twelve o'clock, that she was to think of her at four.

"My dear, dear, anxious friend,"—said she, in mental soliloquy, while walking down stairs from her own room, "always over-careful for every body's comfort but your own; I see you now in all your little fidgets, going again and again into his room, to be sure that all is right." The clock struck twelve as she passed through the hall.

---

2. Highly implausible route from Yorkshire to Surrey.

"'Tis twelve, I shall not forget to think of you four hours hence; and by this time to-morrow, perhaps, or a little later, I may be thinking of the possibility of their all calling here. I am sure they will bring him soon."

She opened the parlour door, and saw two gentlemen sitting with her father—Mr. Weston and his son. They had been arrived only a few minutes, and Mr. Weston had scarcely finished his explanation of Frank's being a day before his time, and her father was yet in the midst of his very civil welcome and congratulations, when she appeared, to have her share of surprize, introduction, and pleasure.

The Frank Churchill so long talked of, so high in interest, was actually before her—he was presented to her, and she did not think too much had been said in his praise; he was a *very* good looking young man; height, air, address, all were unexceptionable, and his countenance had a great deal of the spirit and liveliness of his father's; he looked quick and sensible. She felt immediately that she should like him; and there was a well-bred ease of manner, and a readiness to talk, which convinced her that he came intending to be acquainted with her, and that acquainted they soon must be.

He had reached Randalls the evening before. She was pleased with the eagerness to arrive which had made him alter his plan, and travel earlier, later, and quicker, that he might gain half a day.

"I told you yesterday," cried Mr. Weston with exultation, "I told you all that he would be here before the time named. I remembered what I used to do myself. One cannot creep upon a journey; one cannot help getting on faster than one has planned; and the pleasure of coming in upon one's friends before the look-out begins, is worth a great deal more than any little exertion it needs."

"It is a great pleasure where one can indulge in it," said the young man, "though there are not many houses that I should presume on so far; but in coming *home* I felt I might do any thing."

The word *home* made his father look on him with fresh complacency. Emma was directly sure that he knew how to make himself agreeable; the conviction was strengthened by what followed. He was very much pleased with Randalls, thought it a most admirably arranged house, would hardly allow it even to be very small, admired the situation, the walk to Highbury, Highbury itself, Hartfield still more, and professed himself to have always felt the sort of interest in the country which none but one's *own* country gives, and the greatest curiosity to visit it. That he should never have been able to indulge so amiable a feeling before, passed suspiciously through Emma's brain; but still if it were a falsehood, it was a pleasant one, and pleasantly handled. His manner had no air of study or exaggeration. He did really look and speak as if in a state of no common enjoyment.

Their subjects in general were such as belong to an opening acquaintance. On his side were the inquiries,—"Was she a horse-woman?—Pleasant rides?—Pleasant walks?—Had they a large neighbourhood?—Highbury, perhaps, afforded society enough?— There were several very pretty houses in and about it.—Balls—had they balls?—Was it a musical society?"

But when satisfied on all these points, and their acquaintance proportionably advanced, he contrived to find an opportunity, while their two fathers were engaged with each other, of introducing his mother-in-law, and speaking of her with so much handsome praise, so much warm admiration, so much gratitude for the happiness she secured to his father, and her very kind reception of himself, as was an additional proof of his knowing how to please—and of his certainly thinking it worth while to try to please her. He did not advance a word of praise beyond what she knew to be thoroughly deserved by Mrs. Weston; but undoubtedly he could know very lit-tle of the matter. He understood what would be welcome; he could be sure of little else. "His father's marriage," he said, "had been the wisest measure, every friend must rejoice in it; and the family from whom he had received such a blessing must be ever considered as having conferred the highest obligation on him."

He got as near as he could to thanking her for Miss Taylor's mer-its, without seeming quite to forget that in the common course of things it was to be rather supposed that Miss Taylor had formed Miss Woodhouse's character, than Miss Woodhouse Miss Taylor's. And at last, as if resolved to qualify his opinion completely for trav-elling round to its object, he wound it all up with astonishment at the youth and beauty of her person.

"Elegant, agreeable manners, I was prepared for," said he; "but I confess that, considering every thing, I had not expected more than a very tolerably well-looking woman of a certain age; I did not know that I was to find a pretty young woman in Mrs. Weston."

"You cannot see too much perfection in Mrs. Weston for my feel-ings," said Emma; "were you to guess her to be *eighteen*, I should listen with pleasure; but *she* would be ready to quarrel with you for using such words. Don't let her imagine that you have spoken of her as a pretty young woman."

"I hope I should know better," he replied; "no, depend upon it, (with a gallant bow,) that in addressing Mrs. Weston I should under-stand whom I might praise without any danger of being thought extravagant in my terms."

Emma wondered whether the same suspicion of what might be expected from their knowing each other, which had taken strong possession of her mind, had ever crossed his; and whether his com-pliments were to be considered as marks of acquiescence, or proofs of defiance. She must see more of them to understand his ways; at present she only felt they were agreeable.

She had no doubt of what Mr. Weston was often thinking about. His quick eye she detected again and again glancing towards them with a happy expression; and even, when he might have determined not to look, she was confident that he was often listening.

Her own father's perfect exemption from any thought of the kind, the entire deficiency in him of all such sort of penetration or suspicion, was a most comfortable circumstance. Happily he was not farther from approving matrimony than from foreseeing it.—Though always objecting to every marriage that was arranged, he never suffered beforehand from the apprehension of any; it seemed as if he could not think so ill of any two persons' understanding as to suppose they meant to marry till it were proved against them. She blessed the favouring blindness. He could now, without the drawback of a single unpleasant surmise, without a glance forward at any possible treachery in his guest, give way to all his natural kind-hearted civility in solicitous inquiries after Mr. Frank Churchill's accommodation on his journey, through the sad evils of sleeping two nights on the road, and express very genuine unmixed anxiety to know that he had certainly escaped catching cold—which, however, he could not allow him to feel quite assured of himself till after another night.

A reasonable visit paid, Mr. Weston began to move.—"He must be going. He had business at the Crown about his hay, and a great many errands for Mrs. Weston at Ford's; but he need not hurry any body else." His son, too well bred to hear the hint, rose immediately also, saying,

"As you are going farther on business, sir, I will take the opportunity of paying a visit, which must be paid some day or other, and therefore may as well be paid now. I have the honour of being acquainted with a neighbour of yours, (turning to Emma,) a lady residing in or near Highbury; a family of the name of Fairfax. I shall have no difficulty, I suppose, in finding the house; though Fairfax, I believe, is not the proper name—I should rather say Barnes, or Bates. Do you know any family of that name?"

"To be sure we do," cried his father; "Mrs. Bates—we passed her house—I saw Miss Bates at the window. True, true, you are acquainted with Miss Fairfax; I remember you knew her at Weymouth, and a fine girl she is. Call upon her, by all means."

"There is no necessity for my calling this morning," said the young man; "another day would do as well; but there was that degree of acquaintance at Weymouth which"—

"Oh! go to-day, go to-day. Do not defer it. What is right to be done cannot be done too soon. And, besides, I must give you a hint, Frank;

any want of attention to her *here* should be carefully avoided. You saw her with the Campbells when she was the equal of everybody she mixed with, but here she is with a poor old grandmother, who has barely enough to live on. If you do not call early it will be a slight."

The son looked convinced.

"I have heard her speak of the acquaintance," said Emma, "she is a very elegant young woman."

He agreed to it, but with so quiet a "Yes," as inclined her almost to doubt his real concurrence; and yet there must be a very distinct sort of elegance for the fashionable world, if Jane Fairfax could be thought only ordinarily gifted with it.

"If you were never particularly struck by her manners before," said she, "I think you will to-day. You will see her to advantage; see her and hear her—no, I am afraid you will not hear her at all, for she has an aunt who never holds her tongue."

"You are acquainted with Miss Jane Fairfax, sir, are you?" said Mr. Woodhouse, always the last to make his way in conversation; "then give me leave to assure you that you will find her a very agreeable young lady. She is staying here on a visit to her grandmamma and aunt, very worthy people; I have known them all my life. They will be extremely glad to see you, I am sure, and one of my servants shall go with you to shew you the way."

"My dear sir, upon no account in the world; my father can direct me."

"But your father is not going so far; he is only going to the Crown, quite on the other side of the street, and there are a great many houses; you might be very much at a loss, and it is a very dirty walk, unless you keep on the foot-path; but my coachman can tell you where you had best cross the street."

Mr. Frank Churchill still declined it, looking as serious as he could, and his father gave his hearty support by calling out, "My good friend, this is quite unnecessary; Frank knows a puddle of water when he sees it, and as to Mrs. Bates's, he may get there from the Crown in a hop, step, and jump."

They were permitted to go alone; and with a cordial nod from one, and a graceful bow from the other, the two gentlemen took leave. Emma remained very well pleased with this beginning of the acquaintance, and could now engage to think of them all at Randalls any hour of the day with full confidence in their comfort.

Chapter VI

The next morning brought Mr. Frank Churchill again. He came with Mrs. Weston, to whom and to Highbury he seemed to take very cordially. He had been sitting with her, it appeared, most companionably at home, till her usual hour of exercise; and on being desired to chuse their walk, immediately fixed on Highbury.—"He did not doubt there being very pleasant walks in every direction, but if left to him, he should always chuse the same. Highbury, that airy, cheerful, happy-looking Highbury, would be his constant attraction."—Highbury, with Mrs. Weston, stood for Hartfield; and she trusted to its bearing the same construction with him. They walked thither directly.

Emma had hardly expected them: for Mr. Weston, who had called in for half a minute, in order to hear that his son was very handsome, knew nothing of their plans; and it was an agreeable surprize to her, therefore, to perceive them walking up to the house together, arm in arm. She was wanting to see him again, and especially to see him in company with Mrs. Weston, upon his behaviour to whom her opinion of him was to depend. If he were deficient there, nothing should make amends for it. But on seeing them together, she became perfectly satisfied. It was not merely in fine words or hyperbolical compliment that he paid his duty; nothing could be more proper or pleasing than his whole manner to her—nothing could more agreeably denote his wish of considering her as a friend and securing her affection. And there was time enough for Emma to form a reasonable judgment, as their visit included all the rest of the morning. They were all three walking about together for an hour or two—first round the shrubberies of Hartfield, and afterwards in Highbury. He was delighted with every thing; admired Hartfield sufficiently for Mr. Woodhouse's ear; and when their going farther was resolved on, confessed his wish to be made acquainted with the whole village, and found matter of commendation and interest much oftener than Emma could have supposed.

Some of the objects of his curiosity spoke very amiable feelings. He begged to be shewn the house which his father had lived in so long, and which had been the home of his father's father; and on recollecting that an old woman who had nursed him was still living, walked in quest of her cottage from one end of the street to the other; and though in some points of pursuit or observation there was no positive merit, they shewed, altogether, a good-will towards Highbury in general, which must be very like a merit to those he was with.

Emma watched and decided, that with such feelings as were now shewn, it could not be fairly supposed that he had been ever voluntarily absenting himself; that he had not been acting a part, or making a parade of insincere professions; and that Mr. Knightley certainly had not done him justice.

Their first pause was at the Crown inn, an inconsiderable house, though the principal one of the sort, where a couple of pair of post-horses were kept,[3] more for the convenience of the neighbourhood than from any run on the road; and his companions had not expected to be detained by any interest excited there; but in passing it they gave the history of the large room visibly added; it had been built many years ago for a ball-room, and while the neighbourhood had been in a particularly populous, dancing state, had been occasionally used as such;—but such brilliant days had long passed away, and now the highest purpose for which it was ever wanted was to accommodate a whist club established among the gentlemen and half-gentlemen of the place. He was immediately interested. Its character as a ball-room caught him; and instead of passing on, he stopt for several minutes at the two superior sashed windows which were open, to look in and contemplate its capabilities, and lament that its original purpose should have ceased. He saw no fault in the room, he would acknowledge none which they suggested. No, it was long enough, broad enough, handsome enough. It would hold the very number for comfort. They ought to have balls there at least every fortnight through the winter. Why had not Miss Woodhouse revived the former good old days of the room?—She who could do any thing in Highbury! The want of proper families in the place, and the conviction that none beyond the place and its immediate environs could be tempted to attend, were mentioned; but he was not satisfied. He could not be persuaded that so many good-looking houses as he saw around him, could not furnish numbers enough for such a meeting; and even when particulars were given and families described, he was still unwilling to admit that the inconvenience of such a mixture would be any thing, or that there would be the smallest difficulty in every body's returning into their proper place the next morning. He argued like a young man very much bent on dancing; and Emma was rather surprized to see the constitution of the Weston prevail so decidedly against the habits of the Churchills. He seemed to have all the life and spirit, cheerful feelings, and social inclinations of his father, and nothing of the pride or reserve of Enscombe. Of pride, indeed, there was, perhaps, scarcely enough; his indifference to a confusion of rank, bordered too much on inelegance of mind. He could be no judge, however, of the evil he was holding cheap. It was but an effusion of lively spirits.

At last he was persuaded to move on from the front of the Crown; and being now almost facing the house where the Bateses lodged,

3. Horses kept at an inn for the use of "post-riders" or for hire. Horses could travel only so far without rest, and travelers without their own horses could employ riders or hire horses from post to post for a rapid journey.

Emma recollected his intended visit the day before, and asked him if he had paid it.

"Yes, oh! yes—he replied; I was just going to mention it. A very successful visit:—I saw all the three ladies; and felt very much obliged to you for your preparatory hint. If the talking aunt had taken me quite by surprize, it must have been the death of me. As it was, I was only betrayed into paying a most unreasonable visit. Ten minutes would have been all that was necessary, perhaps all that was proper; and I had told my father I should certainly be at home before him—but there was no getting away, no pause; and, to my utter astonishment, I found, when he (finding me no where else) joined me there at last, that I had been actually sitting with them very nearly three quarters of an hour. The good lady had not given me the possibility of escape before."

"And how did you think Miss Fairfax looking?"

"Ill, very ill—that is, if a young lady can ever be allowed to look ill. But the expression is hardly admissible, Mrs. Weston, is it? Ladies can never look ill. And, seriously, Miss Fairfax is naturally so pale, as almost always to give the appearance of ill health.—A most deplorable want of complexion."

Emma would not agree to this, and began a warm defence of Miss Fairfax's complexion. "It was certainly never brilliant, but she would not allow it to have a sickly hue in general; and there was a softness and delicacy in her skin which gave peculiar elegance to the character of her face." He listened with all due deference; acknowledged that he had heard many people say the same—but yet he must confess, that to him nothing could make amends for the want of the fine glow of health. Where features were indifferent, a fine complexion gave beauty to them all; and where they were good, the effect was—fortunately he need not attempt to describe what the effect was.

"Well," said Emma, "there is no disputing about taste.—At least you admire her except her complexion."

He shook his head and laughed.—"I cannot separate Miss Fairfax and her complexion."

"Did you see her often at Weymouth? Were you often in the same society?"

At this moment they were approaching Ford's, and he hastily exclaimed, "Ha! this must be the very shop that every body attends every day of their lives, as my father informs me. He comes to Highbury himself, he says, six days out of the seven, and has always business at Ford's. If it be not inconvenient to you, pray let us go in, that I may prove myself to belong to the place, to be a true citizen of Highbury. I must buy something at Ford's. It will be taking out my freedom.—I dare say they sell gloves."

"Oh! yes, gloves and every thing. I do admire your patriotism. You will be adored in Highbury. You were very popular before you came, because you were Mr. Weston's son—but lay out half-a-guinea at Ford's, and your popularity will stand upon your own virtues."

They went in; and while the sleek, well-tied parcels of "Men's Beavers" and "York Tan" were bringing down and displaying on the counter, he said—"But I beg your pardon, Miss Woodhouse, you were speaking to me, you were saying something at the very moment of this burst of my *amor patriæ*.[4] Do not let me lose it. I assure you the utmost stretch of public fame would not make me amends for the loss of any happiness in private life."

"I merely asked, whether you had known much of Miss Fairfax and her party at Weymouth."

"And now that I understand your question, I must pronounce it to be a very unfair one. It is always the lady's right to decide on the degree of acquaintance. Miss Fairfax must already have given her account.—I shall not commit myself by claiming more than she may chuse to allow."

"Upon my word! you answer as discreetly as she could do herself. But her account of every thing leaves so much to be guessed, she is so very reserved, so very unwilling to give the least information about any body, that I really think you may say what you like of your acquaintance with her."

"May I indeed?—Then I will speak the truth, and nothing suits me so well. I met her frequently at Weymouth. I had known the Campbells a little in town; and at Weymouth we were very much in the same set. Col. Campbell is a very agreeable man, and Mrs. Campbell a friendly, warm-hearted woman. I like them all."

"You know Miss Fairfax's situation in life, I conclude; what she is destined to be."

"Yes—(rather hesitatingly)—believe I do."

"You get upon delicate subjects, Emma," said Mrs. Weston smiling, "remember that I am here.—Mr. Frank Churchill hardly knows what to say when you speak of Miss Fairfax's situation in life. I will move a little farther off."

"I certainly do forget to think of *her*," said Emma, "as having ever been any thing but my friend and my dearest friend."

He looked as if he fully understood and honoured such a sentiment.

When the gloves were bought and they had quitted the shop again, "Did you ever hear the young lady we were speaking of, play?" said Frank Churchill.

4. Patriotism.

"Ever hear her!" repeated Emma. "You forget how much she belongs to Highbury. I have heard her every year of our lives since we both began. She plays charmingly."

"You think so, do you?—I wanted the opinion of some one who could really judge. She appeared to me to play well, that is, with considerable taste, but I know nothing of the matter myself.—I am excessively fond of music, but without the smallest skill or right of judging of any body's performance.—I have been used to hear her's admired; and I remember one proof of her being thought to play well:—a man, a very musical man, and in love with another woman— engaged to her—on the point of marriage—would yet never ask that other woman to sit down to the instrument, if the lady in question could sit down instead—never seemed to like to hear one if he could hear the other. That I thought, in a man of known musical talent, was some proof."

"Proof, indeed!" said Emma, highly amused.—"Mr. Dixon is very musical, is he? We shall know more about them all, in half an hour, from you, than Miss Fairfax would have vouchsafed in half a year."

"Yes, Mr. Dixon and Miss Campbell were the persons; and I thought it a very strong proof."

"Certainly—very strong it was; to own the truth, a great deal stronger than, if I had been Miss Campbell, would have been at all agreeable to me. I could not excuse a man's having more music than love—more ear than eye—a more acute sensibility to fine sounds than to my feelings. How did Miss Campbell appear to like it?"

"It was her very particular friend, you know."

"Poor comfort!" said Emma, laughing. "One would rather have a stranger preferred than one's very particular friend—with a stranger it might not recur again—but the misery of having a very particular friend always at hand, to do every thing better than one does oneself!—Poor Mrs. Dixon! Well, I am glad she is gone to settle in Ireland."

"You are right. It was not very flattering to Miss Campbell; but she really did not seem to feel it."

"So much the better—or so much the worse:—I do not know which. But, be it sweetness or be it stupidity in her—quickness of friendship, or dulness of feeling—there was one person, I think, who must have felt it: Miss Fairfax herself. *She* must have felt the improper and dangerous distinction."

"As to that—I do not—"

"Oh! do not imagine that I expect an account of Miss Fairfax's sensations from you or from any body else. They are known to no human being, I guess, but herself. But if she continued to play whenever she was asked by Mr. Dixon, one may guess what one chuses."

"There appeared such a perfectly good understanding among them all—" he began rather quickly, but checking himself, added, "however, it is impossible for me to say on what terms they really were—how it might all be behind the scenes. I can only say that there was smoothness outwardly. But you, who have known Miss Fairfax from a child, must be a better judge of her character, and of how she is likely to conduct herself in critical situations, than I can be."

"I have known her from a child, undoubtedly; we have been children and women together; and it is natural to suppose that we should be intimate,—that we should have taken to each other whenever she visited her friends. But we never did. I hardly know how it has happened; a little, perhaps, from the wickedness on my side which was prone to take disgust towards a girl so idolized and so cried up as she always was; by her aunt and grandmother, and all their set. And then, her reserve—I never could attach myself to any one so completely reserved."

"It is a most repulsive quality, indeed," said he. "Oftentimes very convenient, no doubt, but never pleasing. There is safety in reserve, but no attraction. One cannot love a reserved person."

"Not till the reserve ceases towards oneself; and then the attraction may be the greater. But I must be more in want of a friend, or an agreeable companion, than I have yet been, to take the trouble of conquering any body's reserve to procure one. Intimacy between Miss Fairfax and me is quite out of the question. I have no reason to think ill of her—not the least—except that such extreme and perpetual cautiousness of word and manner, such a dread of giving a distinct idea about any body, is apt to suggest suspicions of there being something to conceal."

He perfectly agreed with her: and after walking together so long, and thinking so much alike, Emma felt herself so well acquainted with him, that she could hardly believe it to be only their second meeting. He was not exactly what she had expected; less of the man of the world in some of his notions, less of the spoiled child of fortune, therefore better than she had expected. His ideas seemed more moderate—his feelings warmer. She was particularly, struck by his manner of considering Mr. Elton's house, which, as well as the church, he would go and look at, and would not join them in finding much fault with. No, he could not believe it a bad house; not such a house as a man was to be pitied for having. If it were to be shared with the woman he loved, he could not think any man to be pitied for having that house. There must be ample room in it for every real comfort. The man must be a blockhead who wanted more.

Mrs. Weston laughed, and said he did not know what he was talking about. Used only to a large house himself, and without ever thinking how many advantages and accommodations were attached to its size, he could be no judge of the privations inevitably belonging to a small one. But Emma, in her own mind, determined that he *did* know what he was talking about, and that he shewed a very amiable inclination to settle early in life, and to marry, from worthy motives. He might not be aware of the inroads on domestic peace to be occasioned by no housekeeper's room, or a bad butler's pantry, but no doubt he did perfectly feel that Enscombe could not make him happy, and that whenever he were attached, he would willingly give up much of wealth to be allowed an early establishment.

Chapter VII

Emma's very good opinion of Frank Churchill was a little shaken the following day, by hearing that he was gone off to London, merely to have his hair cut. A sudden freak seemed to have seized him at breakfast, and he had sent for a chaise[5] and set off, intending to return to dinner, but with no more important view that appeared than having his hair cut. There was certainly no harm in his travelling sixteen miles twice over on such an errand; but there was an air of foppery and nonsense in it which she could not approve. It did not accord with the rationality of plan, the moderation in expense, or even the unselfish warmth of heart which she had believed herself to discern in him yesterday. Vanity, extravagance, love of change, restlessness of temper, which must be doing something, good or bad; heedlessness as to the pleasure of his father and Mrs. Weston, indifferent as to how his conduct might appear in general; he became liable to all these changes.[6] His father only called him a coxcomb, and thought it a very good story; but that Mrs. Weston did not like it, was clear enough, by her passing it over as quickly as possible, and making no other comment than that "all young people would have their little whims."

With the exception of this little blot, Emma found that his visit hitherto had given her friend only good ideas of him. Mrs. Weston was very ready to say how attentive and pleasant a companion he made himself—how much she saw to like in his disposition altogether. He appeared to have a very open temper—certainly a very cheerful and lively one; she could observe nothing wrong in his notions, a great deal decidedly right; he spoke of his uncle with warm regard, was fond of talking of him—said he would be the best man in the world if he were left to himself; and though there was no being attached to the aunt, he acknowledged her kindness with gratitude, and seemed to mean always to speak of her with respect.

5. A light, open carriage; *sudden freak*: capricious whim.
6. Chapman and others emend "changes" from 1816 to "charges."

This was all very promising; and, but for such an unfortunate fancy for having his hair cut, there was nothing to denote him unworthy of the distinguished honour which her imagination had given him; the honour, if not of being really in love with her, of being at least very near it, and saved only by her own indifference—(for still her resolution held of never marrying)—the honour, in short, of being marked out for her by all their joint acquaintance.

Mr. Weston, on his side, added a virtue to the account which must have some weight. He gave her to understand that Frank admired her extremely—thought her very beautiful and very charming; and with so much to be said for him altogether, she found she must not judge him harshly. As Mrs. Weston observed, "all young people would have their little whims."

There was one person among his new acquaintance in Surry, not so leniently disposed. In general he was judged, throughout the parishes of Donwell and Highbury, with great candour; liberal allowances were made for the little excesses of such a handsome young man—one who smiled so often and bowed so well; but there was one spirit among them not to be softened, from its power of censure, by bows or smiles—Mr. Knightley. The circumstance was told him at Hartfield; for the moment, he was silent; but Emma heard him almost immediately afterwards say to himself, over a newspaper he held in his hand, "Hum! just the trifling, silly fellow I took him for." She had half a mind to resent; but an instant's observation convinced her that it was really said only to relieve his own feelings, and not meant to provoke; and therefore she let it pass.

Although in one instance the bearers of not good tidings, Mr. and Mrs. Weston's visit this morning was in another respect particularly opportune. Something occurred while they were at Hartfield, to make Emma want their advice; and, which was still more lucky, she wanted exactly the advice they gave.

This was the occurrence:—The Coles had been settled some years in Highbury, and were very good sort of people—friendly, liberal, and unpretending; but, on the other hand, they were of low origin, in trade, and only moderately genteel. On their first corning into the country, they had lived in proportion to their income, quietly, keeping little company, and that little unexpensively; but the last year or two had brought them a considerable increase of means—the house in town had yielded greater profits, and fortune in general had smiled on them. With their wealth, their views increased; their want of a larger house, their inclination for more company. They added to their house, to their number of servants, to their expenses of every sort; and by this time were, in fortune and style of living, second only to the family at Hartfield. Their love of society and their new dining-room, prepared every body for their keeping dinner-company; and a few parties, chiefly among the single men, had already taken place. The regular and best families Emma could hardly suppose they would presume to invite—neither Donwell, nor Hartfield, nor Randalls. Nothing should tempt *her* to go, if they did; and she regretted that her father's known habits would be giving her refusal less meaning than she could wish. The Coles were very respectable in their way, but they ought to be taught that it was not for them to arrange the terms on which the superior families would visit them. This lesson, she very much feared, they would receive only from herself; she had little hope of Mr. Knightley, none of Mr. Weston.

But she had made up her mind how to meet this presumption so many weeks before it appeared, that when the insult came at last, it found her very differently affected. Donwell and Randalls had received their invitation, and none had come for her father and herself; and Mrs. Weston's accounting for it with "I suppose they will not take the liberty with you; they know you do not dine out," was not quite sufficient. She felt that she should like to have had the power of refusal; and afterwards, as the idea of the party to be assembled there, consisting precisely of those whose society was dearest to her, occurred again and again, she did not know that she might not have been tempted to accept. Harriet was to be there in the evening, and the Bateses. They had been speaking of it as they walked about Highbury the day before, and Frank Churchill had most earnestly lamented her absence. Might not the evening end in a dance? had been a question of his. The bare possibility of it acted as a further irritation on her spirits; and her being left in solitary grandeur, even supposing the omission to be intended as a compliment, was but poor comfort.

It was the arrival of this very invitation while the Westons were at Hartfield, which made their presence so acceptable; for though her first remark, on reading it, was that "of course it must be declined," she so very soon proceeded to ask them what they advised her to do, that their advice for her going was most prompt and successful.

She owned that, considering every thing, she was not absolutely without inclination for the party. The Coles expressed themselves so properly—there was so much real attention in the manner of it—so much consideration for her father. "They would have solicited the honour earlier, but had been waiting the arrival of a folding-screen from London, which they hoped might keep Mr. Woodhouse from any draught of air, and therefore induce him the more readily to give them the honour of his company." Upon the whole, she was very persuadable; and it being briefly settled among themselves how it might be done without neglecting his comfort—how certainly Mrs. Goddard, if not Mrs. Bates, might be depended on for bearing him company—Mr. Woodhouse was to be talked into an acquiescence of his daughter's going out to dinner on a day now near at hand, and spending the whole evening away from him. As for *his* going, Emma did not wish him to think it possible; the hours would be too late, and the party too numerous. He was soon pretty well resigned.

"I am not fond of dinner-visiting," said he—"I never was. No more is Emma. Late hours do not agree with us. I am sorry Mr. and Mrs. Cole should have done it. I think it would be much better if they would come in one afternoon next summer, and take their tea with us—take us in their afternoon walk; which they might do, as our hours are so reasonable, and yet get home without being out in the damp of the evening. The dews of a summer evening are what I would not expose any body to. However, as they are so very desirous to have dear Emma dine with them, and as you will both be there, and Mr. Knightley too, to take care of her, I cannot wish to prevent it, provided the weather be what it ought, neither damp, nor cold, nor windy." Then turning to Mrs. Weston, with a look of gentle reproach—"Ah! Miss Taylor, if you had not married, you would have staid at home with me."

"Well, sir," cried Mr. Weston, "as I took Miss Taylor away, it is incumbent on me to supply her place, if I can; and I will step to Mrs. Goddard in a moment, if you wish it."

But the idea of any thing to be done in a *moment*, was increasing, not lessening Mr. Woodhouse's agitation. The ladies knew better how to allay it. Mr. Weston must be quiet, and every thing deliberately arranged.

With this treatment, Mr. Woodhouse was soon composed enough for talking as usual. "He should be happy to see Mrs. Goddard. He had a great regard for Mrs. Goddard; and Emma should write a line, and invite her. James could take the note. But first of all, there must be an answer written to Mrs. Cole."

"You will make my excuses, my dear, as civilly as possible. You will say that I am quite an invalid, and go no where, and therefore must decline their obliging invitation; beginning with my *compliments*, of course. But you will do every thing right. I need not tell you what is to be done. We must remember to let James know that the carriage will be wanted on Tuesday. I shall have no fears for you with him. We have never been there above once since the new approach was made; but still I have no doubt that James will take you very safely. And when you get there, you must tell him at what time you would have him come for you again; and you had better name an early hour. You will not like staying late. You will get very tired when tea is over."

"But you would not wish me to come away before I am tired, papa?"

"Oh! no, my love; but you will soon be tired. There will be a great many people talking at once. You will not like the noise."

"But, my dear sir," cried Mr. Weston, "if Emma comes away early, it will be breaking up the party."

"And no great harm if it does," said Mr. Woodhouse. "The sooner every party breaks up, the better."

"But you do not consider how it may appear to the Coles. Emma's going away directly after tea might be giving offence. They are good-natured people, and think little of their own claims; but still they must feel that any body's hurrying away is no great compliment; and Miss Woodhouse's doing it would be more thought of than any other person's in the room. You would not wish to disappoint and mortify the Coles, I am sure, sir; friendly, good sort of people as ever lived, and who have been your neighbours these *ten* years."

"No, upon no account in the world. Mr. Weston, I am much obliged to you for reminding me. I should be extremely sorry to be giving them any pain. I know what worthy people they are. Perry tells me that Mr. Cole never touches malt liquor. You would not think it to look at him, but he is bilious—Mr. Cole is very bilious. No, I would not be the means of giving them any pain. My dear Emma, we must consider this. I am sure, rather than run the risk of hurting Mr. and Mrs. Cole, you would stay a little longer than you might wish. You will not regard being tired. You will be perfectly safe, you know, among your friends."

"Oh, yes, papa. I have no fears at all for myself; and I should have no scruples of staying as late as Mrs. Weston, but on your account. I am only afraid of your sitting up for me. I am not afraid of your not being exceedingly comfortable with Mrs. Goddard. She loves piquet,[7] you know; but when she is gone home, I am afraid you will be sitting up by yourself, instead of going to bed at your usual time—and the idea of that would entirely destroy my comfort. You must promise me not to sit up."

He did, on the condition of some promises on her side: such as that, if she came home cold, she would be sure to warm herself thoroughly; if hungry, that she would take something to eat; that her own maid should sit up for her; and that Serle and the butler should see that every thing were safe in the house, as usual.

Chapter VIII

Frank Churchill came back again; and if he kept his father's dinner waiting, it was not known at Hartfield; for Mrs. Weston was too anxious for his being a favourite with Mr. Woodhouse, to betray any imperfection which could be concealed.

7. Card game for two players.

He came back, had had his hair cut, and laughed at himself with a very good grace, but without seeming really at all ashamed of what he had done. He had no reason to wish his hair longer, to conceal any confusion of face; no reason to wish the money unspent, to improve his spirits. He was quite as undaunted and as lively as ever; and after seeing him, Emma thus moralized to herself:—

"I do not know whether it ought to be so, but certainly silly things do cease to be silly if they are done by sensible people in an impudent way. Wickedness is always wickedness, but folly is not always folly.—It depends upon the character of those who handle it. Mr. Knightley, he is *not* a trifling, silly young man. If he were, he would have done this differently. He would either have gloried in the achievement, or been ashamed of it. There would have been either the ostentation of a coxcomb, or the evasions of a mind too weak to defend its own vanities.—No, I am perfectly sure that he is not trifling or silly."

With Tuesday came the agreeable prospect of seeing him again, and for a longer time than hitherto; of judging of his general manners, and by inference, of the meaning of his manners towards herself; of guessing how soon it might be necessary for her to throw coldness into her air; and of fancying what the observations of all those might be, who were now seeing them together for the first time.

She meant to be very happy, in spite of the scene being laid at Mr. Cole's; and without being able to forget that among the failings of Mr. Elton, even in the days of his favour, none had disturbed her more than his propensity to dine with Mr. Cole.

Her father's comfort was amply secured, Mrs. Bates as well as Mrs. Goddard being able to come; and her last pleasing duty, before she left the house, was to pay her respects to them as they sat together after dinner; and while her father was fondly noticing the beauty of her dress, to make the two ladies all the amends in her power, by helping them to large slices of cake and full glasses of wine, for whatever unwilling self-denial his care of their constitution might have obliged them to practise during the meal.—She had provided a plentiful dinner for them; she wished she could know that they had been allowed to eat it.

She followed another carriage to Mr. Cole's door; and was pleased to see that it was Mr. Knightley's; for Mr. Knightley keeping no horses, having little spare money and a great deal of health, activity, and independence, was too apt, in Emma's opinion, to get about as he could, and not use his carriage so often as became the owner of Donwell Abbey. She had an opportunity now of speaking her approbation while warm from her heart, for he stopped to hand her out.

"This is coming as you should do," said she, "like a gentleman.—I am quite glad to see you."

He thanked her, observing, "How lucky that we should arrive at the same moment! for if we had met first in the drawing-room, I doubt whether you would have discerned me to be more of a gentleman than usual.—You might not have distinguished how I came, by my look or manner."

"Yes I should, I am sure I should. There is always a look of consciousness or bustle when people come in a way which they know to be beneath them. You think you carry it off very well, I dare say, but with you it is a sort of bravado, an air of affected unconcern; I always observe it whenever I meet you under those circumstances. *Now* you have nothing to try for. You are not afraid of being supposed ashamed. You are not striving to look taller than any body else. *Now* I shall really be very happy to walk into the same room with you."

"Nonsensical girl!" was his reply, but not at all in anger.

Emma had as much reason to be satisfied with the rest of the party as with Mr. Knightley. She was received with a cordial respect which could not but please, and given all the consequence she could wish for. When the Westons arrived, the kindest looks of love, the strongest of admiration were for her, from both husband and wife; the son approached her with a cheerful eagerness which marked her as his peculiar object, and at dinner she found him seated by her—and, as she firmly believed, not without some dexterity on his side.

The party was rather large, as it included one other family, a proper unobjectionable country family, whom the Coles had the advantage of naming among their acquaintance, and the male part of Mr. Cox's family, the lawyer of Highbury. The less worthy females were to come in the evening, with Miss Bates, Miss Fairfax, and Miss Smith; but already, at dinner, they were too numerous for any subject of conversation to be general; and while politics and Mr. Elton were talked over, Emma could fairly surrender all her attention to the pleasantness of her neighbour. The first remote sound to which she felt herself obliged to attend, was the name of Jane Fairfax. Mrs. Cole seemed to be relating something of her that was expected to be very interesting. She listened, and found it well worth listening to. That very dear[8] part of Emma, her fancy, received an amusing supply. Mrs. Cole was telling that she had been calling on Miss Bates, and as soon as she entered the room had been struck by the sight of a pianoforté—a very elegant looking instrument—not a grand, but a large-sized square pianoforté, and the substance of the story, the end of all the dialogue which ensured of surprize, and inquiry, and congratulations on her side, and explanations on Miss Bates's, was, that this pianoforté had arrived from Broadwood's the

---

8. Precious, but also in English usage, costly or expensive.

day before, to the great astonishment of both aunt and niece—entirely unexpected; that at first, by Miss Bates's account, Jane herself was quite at a loss, quite bewildered to think who could possibly have ordered it—but now, they were both perfectly satisfied that it could be from only one quarter;—of course it must be from Col. Campbell.

"One can suppose nothing else," added Mrs. Cole, "and I was only surprized that there could ever have been a doubt. But Jane, it seems, had a letter from them very lately, and not a word was said about it. She knows their ways best; but I should not consider their silence as any reason for their not meaning to make the present. They might chuse to surprize her."

Mrs. Cole had many to agree with her; every body who spoke on the subject was equally convinced that it must come from Col. Campbell, and equally rejoiced that such a present had been made; and there were enough ready to speak to allow Emma to think her own way, and still listen to Mrs. Cole.

"I declare, I do not know when I have heard any thing that has given me more satisfaction!—It always has quite hurt me that Jane Fairfax, who plays so delightfully, should not have an instrument. It seemed quite a shame, especially considering how many houses there are where fine instruments are absolutely thrown away. This is like giving ourselves a slap, to be sure! and it was but yesterday I was telling Mr. Cole, I really was ashamed to look at our new grand pianoforté in the drawing-room, while I do not know one note from another, and our little girls, who are but just beginning, perhaps may never make any thing of it; and there is poor Jane Fairfax, who is mistress of music, has not any thing of the nature of an instrument, not even the pitifullest old spinnet in the world, to amuse herself with.—I was saying this to Mr. Cole but yesterday, and he quite agreed with me; only he is so particularly fond of music that he could not help indulging himself in the purchase, hoping that some of our good neighbours might be so obliging occasionally to put it at a better use than we can; and that really is the reason why the instrument was bought—or else I am sure we ought to be ashamed of it.—We are in great hopes that Miss Woodhouse may be prevailed with to try it this evening."

Miss. Woodhouse made the proper acquiescence; and finding that nothing more was to be entrapped from any communication of Mrs. Cole's, turned to Frank Churchill.

"Why do you smile?" said she.

"Nay, why do you?"

"Me!—I suppose I smile for pleasure at Col. Campbell's being so rich and so liberal.—It is a handsome present."

"Very."

"I rather wonder that it was never made before."

"Perhaps Miss Fairfax has never been staying here so long before."

"Or that he did not give her the use of their own instrument—which must now be shut up in London, untouched by any body."

"That is a grand pianoforté, and he might think it too large for Mrs. Bates's house."

"You may *say* what you chuse—but your countenance testifies that your *thoughts* on this subject are very much like mine."

"I do not know. I rather believe you are giving me more credit for acuteness than I deserve. I smile because you smile, and shall probably suspect whatever I find you suspect; but at present I do not see what there is to question. If Col. Campbell is not the person, who can be?"

"What do you say to Mrs. Dixon?"

"Mrs. Dixon! very true indeed. I had not thought of Mrs. Dixon. She must know as well as her father, how acceptable an instrument would be; and perhaps the mode of it, the mystery, the surprize, is more like a young woman's scheme than an elderly man's. It is Mrs. Dixon I dare say. I told you that your suspicions would guide mine."

"If so, you must extend your suspicions and comprehend *Mr.* Dixon in them."

"Mr. Dixon.—Very well. Yes, I immediately perceive that it must be the joint present of Mr. and Mrs. Dixon. We were speaking the other day, you know, of his being so warm an admirer of her performance."

"Yes, and what you told me on that head, confirmed an idea which I had entertained before.—I do not mean to reflect upon the good intentions of either Mr. Dixon or Miss Fairfax, but I cannot help suspecting either that, after making his proposals to her friend, he had the misfortune to fall in love with *her*, or that he became conscious of a little attachment on her side. One might guess twenty things without guessing exactly the right; but I am sure there must be a particular cause for her chusing to come to Highbury instead of going with the Campbells to Ireland. Here, she must be leading a life of privation and penance; there it would have been all enjoyment. As to the pretence of trying her native air, I look upon that as a mere excuse.—In the summer it might have passed; but what can any body's native air do for them in the months of January, February, and March? Good fires and carriages would be much more to the purpose in most cases of delicate health, and I dare say in her's. I do not require you to adopt all my suspicions, though you make so noble a profession of doing it, but I honestly tell you what they are."

"And, upon my word, they have an air of great probability. Mr. Dixon's preference of her music to her friend's, I can answer for being very decided."

"And then, he saved her life. Did you ever hear of that?—A water-party; and by some accident she was falling overboard. He caught her."

"He did. I was there—one of the party."

"Were you really?—Well!—But you observed nothing of course, for it seems to be a new idea to you.—If I had been there, I think I should have made some discoveries."

"I dare say you would; but I, simple I, saw nothing but the fact, that Miss Fairfax was nearly dashed from the vessel and that Mr. Dixon caught her.—It was the work of a moment. And though the consequent shock and alarm was very great and much more durable—indeed I believe it was half an hour before any of us were comfortable again—yet that was too general a sensation for any thing of peculiar anxiety to be observable. I do not mean to say, however, that you might not have made discoveries."

The conversation was here interrupted. They were called on to share in the awkwardness of a rather long interval between the courses, and obliged to be as formal and as orderly as the others; but when the table was again safely covered, when every corner dish was placed exactly right, and occupation and ease were generally restored, Emma said,

"The arrival of this pianoforté is decisive with me. I wanted to know a little more, and this tells me quite enough. Depend upon it, we shall soon hear that it is a present from Mr. and Mrs. Dixon."

"And if the Dixons should absolutely deny all knowledge of it we must conclude it to come from the Campbells."

"No, I am sure it is not from the Campbells. Miss Fairfax knows it is not from the Campbells, or they would have been guessed at first. She would not have been puzzled, had she dared fix on them. I may not have convinced you perhaps, but I am perfectly convinced myself that Mr. Dixon is a principal in the business."

"Indeed you injure me if you suppose me unconvinced. Your reasonings carry my judgment along with them entirely. At first, while I supposed you satisfied that Col. Campbell was the giver, I saw it only as paternal kindness, and thought it the most natural thing in the world. But when you mentioned Mrs. Dixon, I felt how much more probably that it should be the tribute of warm female friendship. And now I can see it in no other light than as an offering of love."

There was no occasion to press the matter farther. The conviction seemed real; he looked as if he felt it. She said no more, other subjects took their turn; and the rest of the dinner passed away; the dessert succeeded, the children came in, and were talked to and admired amid the usual rate of conversation; a few clever things said, a few downright silly, but by much the larger proportion neither the one

nor the other—nothing worse than every day remarks, dull repetitions, old news, and heavy jokes.

The ladies had not been long in the drawing-room, before the
other ladies, in their different divisions, arrived. Emma watched
the entrée of her own particular little friend; and if she could not
exult in her dignity and grace, she could not only love the blooming
sweetness and the artless manner, but could most heartily rejoice
in that light, cheerful, unsentimental disposition which allowed
her so many alleviations of pleasure, in the midst of the pangs of
disappointed affection. There she sat—and who would have guessed
how many tears she had been lately shedding? To be in company,
nicely dressed herself and seeing others nicely dressed, to sit and
smile and look pretty, and say nothing, was enough for the happiness
of the present hour. Jane Fairfax did look and move superior; but
Emma suspected she might have been glad to change feelings with
Harriet, very glad to have purchased the mortification of having
loved—yes, of having loved even Mr. Elton in vain—by the surrender of all the dangerous pleasure of knowing herself beloved by the
husband of her friend.

In so large a party it was not necessary that Emma should
approach her. She did not wish to speak of the pianoforté, she felt
too much in the secret herself, to think the appearance of curiosity
or interest fair, and therefore purposely kept at a distance; but by
the others, the subject was almost immediately introduced, and she
saw the blush of consciousness with which congratulations were
received, the blush of guilt which accompanied the name of "my
excellent friend Col. Campbell."

Mrs. Weston, kind-hearted and musical, was particularly interested by the circumstance, and Emma could not help being amused
at her perseverance in dwelling on the subject; and having so much
to ask and to say as to tone, touch, and pedal, totally unsuspicious
of that wish of saying as little about it as possible, which she plainly
read in the fair heroine's countenance.

They were soon joined by some of the gentlemen; and the very first
of the early was Frank Churchill. In he walked, the first and the
handsomest; and after paying his compliments en passant to Miss
Bates and her niece, made his way directly to the opposite side of the
circle, where sat Miss Woodhouse; and till he could find a seat by
her, would not sit at all. Emma divined what every body present must
be thinking. She was his object, and every body must perceive it. She
introduced him to her friend, Miss Smith, and, at convenient
moments afterwards, heard what each thought of the other. "He had
never seen so lovely a face, and was delighted with her naïveté." And
she,—"Only to be sure it was paying him too great a compliment, but

she did think there were some looks a little like Mr. Elton." Emma restrained her indignation, and only turned from her in silence.

Smiles of intelligence passed between her and the gentleman on first glancing towards Miss Fairfax; but it was most prudent to avoid speech. He told her that he had been impatient to leave the dining-room—hated sitting long—was always the first to move when he could—that his father, Mr. Knightley, Mr. Cox, and Mr. Cole, were left very busy over parish business—that as long as he had staid, however, it had been pleasant enough, as he found them in general a set of gentlemen-like, sensible men; and spoke so handsomely of Highbury altogether—thought it so abundant in agreeable families—that Emma began to feel she had been used to despise the place rather too much. She questioned him as to the society in Yorkshire—the extent of the neighbourhood about Enscombe, and the sort; and could make out from his answers that, as far as Enscombe was concerned, there was very little going on; that their visitings were among a range of great families, none very near; and that even when days were fixed, and invitations accepted, it was an even chance that Mrs. Churchill were not in health or spirits for going; that they made a point of visiting no fresh person; and that, though he had his separate engagements, it was not without difficulty, without considerable address *at times*, that he could get away, or introduce an acquaintance for a night.

She saw that Enscombe could not satisfy, and that Highbury, taken in its best, might reasonably please a young man who had more retirement at home than he liked. His importance at Enscombe was very evident. He did not boast, but it naturally betrayed itself, that he had persuaded his aunt where his uncle could do nothing, and on her laughing and noticing it, he owned that he believed (excepting one or two points) he could *with time* persuade her to any thing. One of those points on which his influence failed, he then mentioned. He had wanted very much to go abroad—had been very eager indeed to be allowed to travel—but she would not hear of it. This had happened the year before. *Now*, he said, he was beginning to have no longer the same wish.

The unpersuadable point, which he did not mention, Emma guessed to be good behaviour to his father.

"I have made a most wretched discovery," said he, after a short pause.—"I have been here a week to-morrow—half my time. I never knew days fly so fast. A week to-morrow!—And I have hardly begun to enjoy myself. But just got acquainted with Mrs. Weston, and others!—I hate the recollection."

"Perhaps you may now begin to regret that you spent one whole day, out of so few, in having your hair cut."

"No," said he, smiling, "that is no subject of regret at all. I have no pleasure in seeing my friends, unless I can believe myself fit to be seen."

The rest of the gentlemen being now in the room, Emma found herself obliged to turn from him for a few minutes, and listen to Mr. Cole. When Mr. Cole had moved away, and her attention could be restored as before, she saw Frank Churchill looking intently across the room at Miss Fairfax, who was sitting exactly opposite.

"What is the matter?" said she.

He started. "Thank you for rousing me," he replied. "I believe I have been very rude; but really Miss Fairfax has done her hair in so odd a way—so very odd a way—that I cannot keep my eyes from her. I never saw any thing so outrée!—Those curls!—This must be a fancy of her own. I see nobody else looking like her!—I must go and ask her whether it is an Irish fashion. Shall I?—Yes, I will—I declare I will—and you shall see how she takes it;—whether she colours."

He was gone immediately; and Emma soon saw him standing before Miss Fairfax, and talking to her; but as to its effect on the young lady, as he had improvidently placed himself exactly between them, exactly in front of Miss Fairfax, she could absolutely distinguish nothing.

Before he could return to his chair, it was taken by Mrs. Weston.

"This is the luxury of a large party," said she:—"one can get near every body, and say every thing. My dear Emma, I am longing to talk to you. I have been making discoveries and forming plans, just like yourself, and I must tell them while the idea is fresh. Do you know how Miss Bates and her niece came here?"

"How!—They were invited, were not they?"

"Oh! yes—but how they were conveyed hither?—the manner of their coming?"

"They walked, I conclude. How else could they come?"

"Very true.—Well, a little while ago it occurred to me how very sad it would be to have Jane Fairfax walking home again, late at night, and cold as the nights are now. And as I looked at her, though I never saw her appear to more advantage, it struck me that she was heated, and would therefore be particularly liable to take cold. Poor girl! I could not bear the idea of it; so, as soon as Mr. Weston came into the room, and I could get at him, I spoke to him about the carriage. You may guess how readily he came into my wishes; and having his approbation, I made my way directly to Miss Bates, to assure her that the carriage would be at her service before it took us home; for I thought it would be making her comfortable at once. Good soul! she was as grateful as possible, you may be sure. 'Nobody was ever so fortunate as herself!'—but with many, many thanks,—there was no occasion to trouble us, for Mr. Knightley's carriage had brought, and was to take them home again.' I was quite surprized;—very glad, I am sure; but really quite surprized. Such a very kind attention—and so thoughtful an attention!—the sort of thing that so few men would think of. And, in short, from knowing his usual ways, I am very much inclined to think that it was for their accommodation the carriage was used at all. I do suspect he would not have had a pair of horses for himself, and that it was only as an excuse for assisting them."

"Very likely," said Emma—"nothing more likely. I know no man more likely than Mr. Knightley to do the sort of thing—to do any thing really good-natured, useful, considerate, or benevolent. He is not a gallant man, but he is a very humane one; and this, considering Jane Fairfax's ill health, would appear a case of humanity to him;—and for an act of un-ostentatious kindness, there is nobody whom I would fix on more than on Mr. Knightley. I know he had horses to-day—for we arrived together; and I laughed at him about it, but he said not a word that could betray."

"Well," said Mrs. Weston, smiling, "you give him credit for more simple, disinterested benevolence in this instance than I do; for while Miss Bates was speaking, a suspicion darted into my head, and I have never been able to get it out again. The more I think of it, the more probable it appears. In short, I have made a match between Mr. Knightley and Jane Fairfax. See the consequence of keeping you company!—What do you say to it?"

"Mr. Knightley and Jane Fairfax!" exclaimed Emma. "Dear Mrs. Weston, how could you think of such a thing?—Mr. Knightley!—Mr. Knightley must not marry!—You would not have little Henry cut out from Donwell?—Oh! no, no, Henry must have Donwell. I cannot at all consent to Mr. Knightley's marrying; and I am sure it is not at all likely. I am amazed that you should think of such a thing."

"My dear Emma, I have told you what led me to think of it. I do not want the match—I do not want to injure dear little Henry—but the idea has been given me by circumstances; and if Mr. Knightley really wished to marry, you would not have him refrain on Henry's account, a boy of six years old, who knows nothing of the matter?"

"Yes, I would. I could not bear to have Henry supplanted.—Mr. Knightley marry!—No, I have never had such an idea, and I cannot adopt it now. And Jane Fairfax, too, of all women!"

"Nay, she has always been a first favourite with him, as you very well know."

"But the imprudence of such a match!"

"I am not speaking of its prudence; merely its probability."

"I see no probability in it, unless you have any better foundation than what you mention. His good-nature, his humanity, as I tell you, would be quite enough to account for the horses. He has a great regard for the Bateses, you know, independent of Jane Fairfax—and is always glad to shew them attention. My dear Mrs. Weston, do not take to match-making. You do it very ill. Jane Fairfax mistress of the Abbey!—Oh! no, no;—very feeling revolts. For his own sake, I would not have him do so mad a thing."

"Imprudent, if you please—but not mad. Excepting inequality of fortune, and perhaps a little disparity of age, I can see nothing unsuitable."

"But Mr. Knightley does not want to marry. I am sure he has not the least idea of it. Do not put it into his head. Why should he marry?—He is as happy as possible by himself; with his farm, and his sheep, and his library, and all the parish to manage; and he is extremely fond of his brother's children. He has no occasion to marry, either to fill up his time or his heart."

"My dear Emma, as long as he thinks so, it is so; but if he really loves Jane Fairfax——"

"Nonsense! He does not care about Jane Fairfax. In the way of love, I am sure he does not. He would do any good to her, or her family; but——"

"Well," said Mrs. Weston, laughing, "perhaps the greatest good he could do them, would be to give Jane such a respectable home."

"If it would be good to her, I am sure it would be evil to himself; a very shameful and degrading connection. How would he bear to have Miss Bates belonging to him?—To have her haunting the Abbey, and thanking him all day long for his great kindness in marrying Jane?—'So very kind and obliging!—But he always had been such a very kind neighbour!' And then fly off, through half a sentence, to her mother's old petticoat. 'Not that it was such a very old petticoat either—for still it would last a great while—and, indeed, she must thankfully say that their petticoats were all very strong.'"

"For shame, Emma! Do not mimic her. You divert me against my conscience. And, upon my word, I do not think Mr. Knightley would be much disturbed by Miss Bates. Little things do not irritate him. She might talk on; and if he wanted to say any thing himself, he would only talk louder, and drown her voice. But the question is not, whether it would be a bad connexion for him, but whether he wishes it; and I think he does. I have heard him speak, and so must you, so very highly of Jane Fairfax! The interest he takes in her—his anxiety about her health—his concern that she should have no happier prospect! I have heard him express himself so warmly on those points!—Such an admirer of her performance on the pianoforté, and of her voice! I have heard him say that he could listen to her for ever. Oh! and I had almost forgotten one idea that occurred to me—this pianoforté that has been sent her by somebody—though we have all been so well satisfied to consider it a present from the Campbells, may it not be from Mr. Knightley? I cannot help suspecting him. I think he is just the person to do it, even without being in love."

"Then it can be no argument to prove that he is in love. But I do not think it is at all a likely thing for him to do. Mr. Knightley does nothing mysteriously."

"I have heard him lamenting her having no instrument repeat-edly; oftener than I should suppose such a circumstance would, in the common course of things, occur to him."

"Very well; and if he had intended to give her one, he would have told her so."

"There might be scruples of delicacy, my dear Emma. I have a very strong notion that it comes from him. I am sure he was par-ticularly silent when Mrs. Cole told us of it at dinner."

"You take up an idea, Mrs. Weston, and run away with it; as you have many a time reproached me with doing. I see no sign of attachment—I believe nothing of the pianoforté—and proof only shall convince me that Mr. Knightley has any thought of marrying Jane Fairfax."

They combated the point some time longer in the same way; Emma rather gaining ground over the mind of her friend; for Mrs. Weston was the most used of the two to yield; till a little bustle in the room shewed them that tea was over, and the instrument in preparation;—and at the same moment Mr. Cole approaching to entreat Miss Woodhouse would do them the honour of trying it. Frank Churchill, of whom, in the eagerness of her conversation with Mrs. Weston, she had been seeing nothing, except that he had found a seat by Miss Fairfax, followed Mr. Cole, to add his very pressing entreaties; and as, in every respect, it suited Emma best to lead, she gave a very proper compliance.

She knew the limitations of her own powers too well to attempt more than she could perform with credit; she wanted neither taste nor spirit in the little things which are generally acceptable, and could accompany her own voice well. One accompaniment to her song took her agreeably by surprize—a second, slightly but correctly taken by Frank Churchill. Her pardon was duly begged at the close of the song, and every thing usual followed. He was accused of hav-ing a delightful voice, and a perfect knowledge of music; which was properly denied; and that he knew nothing of the matter, and had no voice at all, roundly asserted. They sang together once more; and Emma would then resign her place to Miss Fairfax, whose perfor-mance, both vocal and instrumental, she never could attempt to conceal from herself, was infinitely superior to her own.

With mixed feelings, she seated herself at a little distance from the numbers round the instrument, to listen. Frank Churchill sang again. They had sung together once or twice, it appeared, at Weymouth. But the sight of Mr. Knightley among the most attentive, soon drew away half Emma's mind; and she fell into a train of thinking on the subject of Mrs. Weston's suspicions, to which the sweet sounds of the united voices gave only momentary interruptions. Her objections to Mr. Knightley's marrying did not in the least subside. She could see nothing but evil in it. It would be a great disappointment to Mr. John Knightley; consequently to Isabella. A real injury to the children—a most mortifying change, and material loss to them all;—a very great deduction from her father's daily comfort—and, as to herself, she could not at all endure the idea of Jane Fairfax at Donwell Abbey. A Mrs. Knightley for them all to give way to!—No—Mr. Knightley must never marry. Little Henry must remain the heir of Donwell.

Presently Mr. Knightley looked back, and came and sat down by her. They talked at first only of the performance. His admiration was certainly very warm; yet she thought, but for Mrs. Weston, it would not have struck her. As a sort of touchstone, however, she began to speak of his kindness in conveying the aunt and niece; and though his answer was in the spirit of cutting the matter short, she believed it to indicate only his disinclination to dwell on any kindness of his own.

"I often feel concerned," said she, "that I dare not make *our* carriage more useful on such occasions. It is not that I am without the wish; but you know how impossible my father would deem it that James should put-to for such a purpose."

"Quite out of the question, quite out of the question," he replied;—"but you must often wish it, I am sure." And he smiled with such seeming pleasure at the conviction, that she must proceed another step.

"This present from the Campbells," said she—"This pianoforté is very kindly given."

"Yes," he replied, and without the smallest apparent embarrassment.—"But they would have done better had they given her notice of it. Surprizes are foolish things. The pleasure is not enhanced, and the inconvenience is often considerable. I should have expected better judgment in Colonel Campbell."

From that moment, Emma could have taken her oath that Mr. Knightley had had no concern in giving the instrument. But whether he were entirely free from peculiar attachment—whether there were no actual preference—remained a little longer doubtful. Towards the end of Jane's second song, her voice grew thick.

"That will do," said he, when it was finished, thinking aloud— "You have sung quite enough for one evening—now, be quiet."

Another song, however, was soon begged for. "One more;—they would not fatigue Miss Fairfax on any account, and would only ask for one more." And Frank Churchill was heard to say, "I think you could manage this without effort; the first part is so very trifling. The strength of the song falls on the second."

Mr. Knightley grew angry.

"That fellow," said he, indignantly, "thinks of nothing but shewing off his own voice. This must not be." And touching Miss Bates, who at that moment passed near—"Miss Bates, are you mad, to let your niece sing herself hoarse in this manner? Go, and interfere. They have no mercy on her."

Miss Bates, in her real anxiety for Jane, could hardly stay even to be grateful, before she stept forward and put an end to all further singing. Here ceased the concert part of the evening, for Miss Woodhouse and Miss Fairfax were the only young-lady-performers; but soon (within five minutes) the proposal of dancing—originating nobody exactly knew where—was so effectually promoted by Mr. and Mrs. Cole, that every thing was rapidly clearing away to give proper space. Mrs. Weston, capital in her country-dances, was seated, and beginning an irresistible waltz; and Frank Churchill, coming up with most becoming gallantry to Emma, had secured her hand, and led her up to the top.

While waiting till the other young people could pair themselves off, Emma found time, in spite of the compliments she was receiving on her voice and her taste, to look about, and see what became of Mr. Knightley. This would be a trial. He was no dancer in general. If he were to be very alert in engaging Jane Fairfax now, it might augur something. There was no immediate appearance. No; he was talking to Mrs. Cole—he was looking on unconcerned; Jane was asked by somebody else, and he was still talking to Mrs. Cole.

Emma had no longer an alarm for Henry; his interest was yet safe; and she led off the dance with genuine spirit and enjoyment. Not more than five couple could be mustered; but the rarity and the suddenness of it made it very delightful, and she found herself well matched in a partner. They were a couple worth looking at.

Two dances, unfortunately, were all that could be allowed. It was growing late, and Miss Bates became anxious to get home, on her mother's account. After some attempts, therefore, to be permitted to begin again, they were obliged to thank Mrs. Weston, look sorrowful, and have done.

"Perhaps it is as well," said Frank Churchill, as he attended Emma to her carriage. "I must have asked Miss Fairfax, and her languid dancing would not have agreed with me, after your's."

Chapter IX

Emma did not repent her condescension in going to the Coles. The visit afforded her many pleasant recollections the next day; and all that she might be supposed to have lost on the side of dignified seclusion, must be amply repaid in the splendour of popularity. She must have delighted the Coles—worthy people, who deserved to be made happy!—And left a name behind her that would not soon die away.

Perfect happiness, even in memory, is not common; and there were two points on which she was not quite easy. She doubted whether she had not transgressed the duty of woman by woman, in betraying her suspicions of Jane Fairfax's feelings to Frank Churchill. It was hardly right; but it had been so strong an idea, that it would escape her, and his submission to all that she told, was a compliment to her penetration which made it difficult for her to be quite certain that she ought to have held her tongue.

The other circumstance of regret related also to Jane Fairfax; and there she had no doubt. She did unfeignedly and unequivocally regret the inferiority of her own playing and singing. She did most heartily grieve over the idleness of her childhood—and sat down and practised vigorously an hour and a half.

She was then interrupted by Harriet's coming in; and if Harriet's praise could have satisfied her, she might soon have been comforted.

"Oh! if I could but play as well as you and Miss Fairfax!"

"Don't class us together, Harriet. My playing is no more like her's, than a lamp is like sunshine."

"Oh! dear—I think you play the best of the two. I think you play quite as well as she does. I am sure I had much rather hear you. Every body last night said how well you played."

"Those who knew any thing about it, must have felt the difference. The truth is, Harriet, that my playing is just good enough to be praised, but Jane Fairfax's is much beyond it."

"Well, I always shall think that you play quite as well as she does, or that if there is any difference nobody would ever find it out. Mr. Cole said how much taste you had; and Mr. Frank Churchill talked a great deal about your taste, and that he valued taste much more than execution."

"Ah! but Jane Fairfax has them both, Harriet."

"Are you sure? I saw she had execution, but I did not know she had any taste. Nobody talked about it. And I hate Italian singing.—There is no understanding a word of it. Besides, if she does play so very well, you know, it is no more than she is obliged to do, because she will have to teach. The Coxes were wondering last night whether she would get into any great family. How did you think the Coxes looked?"

"Just as they always do—very vulgar."

"They told me something," said Harriet rather hesitatingly, "but it is nothing of any consequence."

Emma was obliged to ask what they had told her, though fearful of its producing Mr. Elton.

"They told me—that Mr. Martin dined with them last Saturday."

"Oh!"

"He came to their father upon some business, and he asked him to stay dinner."

"Oh!"

"They talked a great deal about him, especially Anne Cox. I do not know what she meant, but she asked me if I thought I should go and stay there again next summer."

"She meant to be impertinently curious, just as such an Anne Cox should be."

"She said he was very agreeable the day he dined there. He sat by her at dinner. Miss Nash thinks either of the Coxes would be very glad to marry him."

"Very likely.—I think they are, without exception, the most vulgar girls in Highbury."

Harriet had business at Ford's.—Emma thought it most prudent to go with her. Another accidental meeting with the Martins was possible, and, in her present state, would be dangerous.

Harriet, tempted by every thing and swayed by half a word, was always very long at a purchase; and while she was still hanging over muslins and changing her mind, Emma went to the door for amusement.—Much could not be hoped from the traffic of even the busiest part of Highbury;—Mr. Perry walking hastily by, Mr. William Cox letting himself in at the office door, Mr. Cole's carriage horses returning from exercise, or a stray letter-boy on an obstinate mule, were the liveliest objects she could presume to expect; and when her eyes fell only on the butcher with his tray, a tidy old woman travelling homewards from shop with her full basket, two curs quarrelling over a dirty bone, and a string of dawdling children round the baker's little bow-window eyeing the gingerbread, she knew she had no reason to complain, and was amused enough; quite enough still to stand at the door. A mind lively and at ease, can do with seeing nothing, and can see nothing that does not answer.

She looked down the Randalls road. The scene enlarged; two persons appeared; Mrs. Weston and her son-in-law; they were walking into Highbury;—to Hartfield of course. They were stopping, however, in the first place at Mrs. Bates's; whose house was a little nearer Randalls than Ford's; and had all but knocked, when Emma caught their eye.—Immediately they crossed the road and came forward to her; and the agreeableness of yesterday's engagement seemed to give fresh pleasure to the present meeting. Mrs. Weston informed her that she was going to call on the Bateses, in order to hear the new instrument.

"For my companion tells me," said she, "that I absolutely promised Miss Bates last night, that I would come this morning. I was not aware of it myself. I did not know that I had fixed a day, but as he says I did, I am going now."

"And while Mrs. Weston pays her visit, I may be allowed, I hope," said Frank Churchill, "to join your party and wait for her at Hartfield—if you are going home?"

Mrs. Weston was disappointed.

"I thought you meant to go with me. They would be very much pleased."

"Me! I should be quite in the way. But, perhaps—I may be equally in the way here. Miss Woodhouse looks as if she did not want me. My aunt always sends me off when she is shopping. She says I fidget her to death; and Miss Woodhouse looks as if she could almost say the same. What am I to do?"

"I am here on no business of my own," said Emma, "I am only waiting for my friend. She will probably have soon done, and then we shall go home. But you had better go with Mrs. Weston and hear the instrument."

"Well, if you advise it.—But (with a smile) if Col. Campbell should have employed a careless friend, and if it should prove to have an indifferent tone—what shall I say? I shall be no support to Mrs. Weston. She might do very well by herself. A disagreeable truth would be palateable through her lips, but I am the wretchedest being in the world at a civil falsehood."

"I do not believe any such thing," replied Emma.—"I am persuaded that you can be as insincere as your neighbours, when it is necessary; but there is no reason to suppose the instrument is indifferent. Quite otherwise indeed, if I understood Miss Fairfax's opinion last night."

"Do come with me," said Mrs. Weston, "if it be not very disagreeable to you. It need not detain us long. We will go to Hartfield afterwards. We will follow them to Hartfield. I really wish you to call with me. It will be felt so great an attention! and I always thought you meant it."

He could say no more; and with the hope of Hartfield to reward him, returned with Mrs. Weston to Mrs. Bates's door. Emma watched them in, and then joined Harriet at the interesting counter,—trying, with all the force of her own mind, to convince her that if she wanted plain muslin it was of no use to look at figured; and that a blue ribbon, be it ever so beautiful, would still never match her yellow pattern. At last it was all settled, even to the destination of the parcel.

"Should I send it to Mrs. Goddard's, ma'am?" asked Mrs. Ford. "Yes—no—yes, to Mrs. Goddard's. Only my pattern gown is at Hartfield. No you shall send it to Hartfield, if you please. But then, Mrs.

Goddard will want to see it.—And I could take the pattern gown home any day. But I shall want the ribbon directly—so it had better go to Hartfield—at least the ribbon. You could make it into two parcels, Mrs. Ford, could not you?"

"It is not worth while, Harriet, to give Mrs. Ford the trouble of two parcels."

"No more it is."

"No trouble in the world, ma'am," said the obliging Mrs. Ford.

"Oh! but indeed I would much rather have it only in one. Then, if you please, you shall send it all to Mrs. Goddard's—I do not know—No, I think, Miss Woodhouse, I may just as well have it sent to Hartfield, and take it home with me at night. What do you advise?"

"That you do not give another half-second to the subject. To Hartfield, if you please, Mrs. Ford."

"Aye, that will be much best," said Harriet, quite satisfied, "I should not at all like to have it sent to Mrs. Goddard's."

Voices approached the shop—or rather one voice and two ladies; Mrs. Weston and Miss Bates met them at the door.

"My dear Miss Woodhouse," said the latter, "I am just run across to entreat the favour of you to come and sit down with us a little while, and give us your opinion of our new instrument; you and Miss Smith. How do you do, Miss Smith?—Very well I thank you.— And I begged Mrs. Weston to come with me, that I might be sure of succeeding."

"I hope Mrs. Bates and Miss Fairfax are"——

"Very well, I am much obliged to you. My mother is delightfully well; and Jane caught no cold last night. How is Mr. Woodhouse?—I am so glad to hear such a good account. Mrs. Weston told me you were here.—Oh! then, said I, I must run across, I am sure Miss Woodhouse will allow me just to run across and entreat her to come in; my mother will be so very happy to see her—and now we are such a nice party, she cannot refuse. 'Aye, pray do,' said Mr. Frank Churchill, 'Miss Woodhouse's opinion of the instrument will be worth having.'—But, said I, I shall be more sure of succeeding if one of you will go with me.—'Oh!' said he, 'wait half-a-minute till I have finished my job.'—For, would you believe it, Miss Woodhouse, there he is, in the most obliging manner in the world, fastening in the rivet of my mother's spectacles.—The rivet came out, you know, this morning.—So very obliging!—For my mother had no use of her spectacles—could not put them on. And, by the bye, every body ought to have two pair of spectacles; they should indeed. Jane said so. I meant to take them over to John Saunders the first thing I did, but something or other hindered me all the morning; first one thing, then another, there is no saying what, you know. At one time Patty came to say she thought the kitchen chimney wanted sweeping. Oh!

said I, Patty do not come with your bad news to me. Here is the rivet of your mistress's spectacles out. Then the baked apples came home, Mrs. Wallis sent them by her boy; they are extremely civil and obliging to us, the Wallises, always—I have heard some people say that Mrs. Wallis can be uncivil and give a very rude answer, but we have never known any thing but the greatest attention from them. And it cannot be for the value of our custom now, for what is our consumption of bread, you know? Only three of us—besides dear Jane at present—and she really eats nothing—makes such a shocking breakfast, you would be quite frightened if you saw it. I dare not let my mother know how little she eats—so I say one thing and then I say another, and it passes off. But about the middle of the day she gets hungry, and there is nothing she likes so well as these baked apples, and they are extremely wholesome, for I took the opportunity the other day of asking Mr. Perry; I happened to meet him in the street. Not that I had any doubt before—I have so often heard Mr. Woodhouse recommend a baked apple. I believe it is the only way that Mr. Woodhouse thinks the fruit thoroughly wholesome. We have apple dumplings, however, very often. Patty makes an excellent apple-dumpling. Well, Mrs. Weston, you have prevailed, I hope, and these ladies will oblige us."

Emma would be "very happy to wait on Mrs. Bates, &c." and they did at last move out of the shop, with no further delay from Miss Bates than,

"How do you do, Mrs. Ford? I beg your pardon. I did not see you before. I hear you have a charming collection of new ribbons from town. Jane came back delighted yesterday. Thank ye, the gloves do very well—only a little too large about the wrist; but Jane is taking them in."

"What was I talking of?" said she, beginning again when they were all in the street.

Emma wondered on what, of all the medley, she would fix.

"I declare I cannot recollect what I was talking of.—Oh! my mother's spectacles. So very obliging of Mr. Frank Churchill! 'Oh!' said he, 'I do think I can fasten the rivet; I like a job of this kind excessively.'—Which you know shewed him to be so very . . . . . Indeed I must say that, much as I had heard of him before and much as I had expected, he very far exceeds any thing . . . . . I do congratulate you, Mrs. Weston, most warmly. He seems every thing the fondest parent could . . . . . 'Oh!' said he, 'I can fasten the rivet. I like a job of that sort excessively.' I never shall forget his manner. And when I brought out the baked apples from the closet, and hoped our friends would be so very obliging as to take some, 'Oh!' said he directly, 'there is nothing in the way of fruit half so good, and these are the finest looking home-baked apples I ever saw in

my life.' That, you know, was so very . . . . . . And I am sure, by
his manner, it was no compliment. Indeed they are very delightful
apples, and Mrs. Wallis does them full justice—only we do not
have them baked more than twice, and Mr. Woodhouse made us
promise to have them done three times—but Miss Woodhouse will
be so good as not to mention it. The apples themselves are the very
finest sort for baking, beyond a doubt; all from Donwell—some of
Mr. Knightley's most liberal supply. He sends us a sack every year;
and certainly there never was such a keeping apple any where as
one of his trees—I believe there is two of them. My mother says the
orchard was always famous in her younger days. But I was really
quite shocked the other day—for Mr. Knightley called one morning, and Jane was eating these apples, and we talked about them
and said how much she enjoyed them, and he asked whether we
were not got to the end of our stock. 'I am sure you must be,' said
he, 'and I will send you another supply; for I have a great many
more than I can ever use. William Larkins let me keep a larger
quantity than usual this year. I will send you some more, before
they get good for nothing.' So I begged he would not—for really as
to ours being gone, I could not absolutely say that we had a great
many left—it was but half a dozen indeed; but they should be all
kept for Jane; and I could not at all bear that he should be sending
us more, so liberal as he had been already; and Jane said the same.
And when he was gone, she almost quarrelled with me—No, I
should not say quarrelled, for we never had a quarrel in our lives;
but she was quite distressed that I had owned the apples were so
nearly gone; she wished I had made him believe we had a great
many left. Oh! said I, my dear, I did say as much as I could. However, the very same evening William Larkins came over with a large
basket of apples, the same sort of apples, a bushel at least, and
I was very much obliged, and went down and spoke to William Larkins and said every thing, as you may suppose. William Larkins is
such an old acquaintance! I am always glad to see him. But, however, I found afterwards from Patty, that William said it was all the
apples of *that* sort his master had; he had brought them all—and
now his master had not one left to bake or boil. William did not
seem to mind it himself, he was so pleased to think his master had
sold so many; for William, you know, thinks more of his master's
profit than any thing; but Mrs. Hodges, he said, was quite displeased at their being all sent away. She could not bear that her
master should not be able to have another apple-tart this spring. He
told Patty this, but bid her not mind it, and be sure not to say any
thing to us about it, for Mrs. Hodges *would* be cross sometimes,
and as long as so many sacks were sold, it did not signify who ate
the remainder. And so Patty told me, and I was excessively shocked

indeed! I would not have Mr. Knightley know any thing about it for the world! He would be so very . . . . I wanted to keep it from Jane's knowledge; but unluckily, I had mentioned it before I was aware."

Miss Bates had just done as Patty opened the door; and her visitors walked up stairs without having any regular narration to attend to, pursued only by the sounds of her desultory good-will.

"Pray take care, Mrs. Weston, there is a step at the turning. Pray take care, Miss Woodhouse, ours is rather a dark staircase—rather darker and narrower than one could wish. Miss Smith, pray take care. Miss Woodhouse, I am quite concerned, I am sure you hit your foot. Miss Smith, the step at the turning."

Chapter X

The appearance of the little sitting-room as they entered, was tranquillity itself; Mrs. Bates, deprived of her usual employment, slumbering on one side of the fire, Frank Churchill, at a table near her, most deedily[9] occupied about her spectacles, and Jane Fairfax, standing with her back to them, intent on her pianoforté.

Busy as he was, however, the young man was yet able to shew a most happy countenance on seeing Emma again.

"This is a pleasure," said he, in rather a low voice, "coming at least ten minutes earlier than I had calculated. You find me trying to be useful; tell me if you think I shall succeed."

"What!" said Mrs. Weston, "have not you finished it yet? you would not earn a very good livelihood as a working-silversmith at this rate."

"I have not been working uninterruptedly," he replied, "I have been assisting Miss Fairfax in trying to make her instrument stand steadily, it was not quite firm; an unevenness in the floor, I believe. You see we have been wedging one leg with paper. This was very kind of you to be persuaded to come. I was almost afraid you would be hurrying home."

He contrived that she should be seated by him; and was sufficiently employed in looking out the best baked apple for her, and trying to make her help or advise him in his work, till Jane Fairfax was quite ready to sit down to the pianoforté again. That she was not immediately ready, Emma did suspect to arise from the state of her nerves; she had not yet possessed the instrument long enough to touch it without emotion; she must reason herself into the power of performance; and Emma could not but pity such feelings, whatever their origin, and could not but resolve never to expose them to her neighbour again.

9. Busily.

At last Jane began, and though the first bars were feebly given, the powers of the instrument were gradually done full justice to. Mrs. Weston had been delighted before, and was delighted again; Emma joined her in all her praise; and the pianoforté, with every proper discrimination, was pronounced to be altogether of the highest promise.

"Whoever Col. Campbell might employ," said Frank Churchill, with a smile at Emma, "the person has not chosen ill. I heard a good deal of Col. Campbell's taste at Weymouth; and the softness of the upper notes I am sure is exactly what he and *all that party* would particularly prize. I dare say, Miss Fairfax, that he either gave his friend very minute directions, or wrote to Broadwood himself. Do not you think so?"

Jane did not look around. She was not obliged to hear. Mrs. Weston had been speaking to her at the same moment.

"It is not fair," said Emma in a whisper, "mine was a random guess. Do not distress her."

He shook his head with a smile, and looked as if he had very little doubt and very little mercy. Soon afterwards he began again,

"How much your friends in Ireland must be enjoying your pleasure on this occasion, Miss Fairfax. I dare say they often think of you, and wonder which will be the day, the precise day of the instrument's coming to hand. Do you imagine Col. Campbell knows the business to be going forward just at this time?—Do you imagine it to be the consequence of an immediate commission from him, or that he may have sent only a general direction, an order indefinite as to time, to depend upon contingencies and conveniencies?"

He paused. She could not but hear; she could not avoid answering,

"Till I have a letter from Col. Campbell," said she, in a voice of forced calmness, "I can imagine nothing with any confidence. It must be all conjecture."

"Conjecture—aye, sometimes one conjectures right, and sometimes one conjectures wrong. I wish I could conjecture how soon I shall make this rivet quite firm. What nonsense one talks, Miss Woodhouse, when hard at work, if one talks at all;—your real workmen, I suppose, hold their tongues; but we gentlemen labourers if we get hold of a word—Miss Fairfax said something about conjecturing. There, it is done. I have the pleasure, madam, (to Mrs. Bates,) of restoring your spectacles, healed for the present."

He was very warmly thanked both by mother and daughter; to escape a little from the latter, he went to the pianoforté, and begged Miss Fairfax, who was still sitting at it, to play something more.

"If you are very kind," said he, "it will be one of the waltzes we danced last night;—let me live them over again. You did not enjoy them as I did; you appeared tired the whole time. I believe you were glad we danced no longer; but I would have given worlds—all the worlds one ever has to give—for another half hour."

She played.

"What felicity it is to hear a tune again which *has* made one happy!—If I mistake not that was danced at Weymouth."

She looked up at him for a moment, coloured deeply, and played something else. He took some music from a chair near the pianoforté, and turning to Emma, said,

"Here is something quite new to me. Do you know it?—Cramer.[1]—And here are a new set of Irish melodies. That, from such a quarter, one might expect. This was all sent with the instrument. Very thoughtful of Col. Campbell, was not it?—He knew Miss Fairfax could have no music here. I honour that part of the attention particularly; it shews it to have been so thoroughly from the heart. Nothing hastily done; nothing incomplete. True affection only could have prompted it."

Emma wished he would be less pointed, yet could not help being amused; and when on glancing her eye towards Jane Fairfax she caught the remains of a smile, when she saw that with all the deep blush of consciousness, there had been a smile of secret delight, she had less scruple in the amusement, and much less compunction with respect to her.—This amiable, upright, perfect Jane Fairfax was apparently cherishing very reprehensible feelings.

He brought all the music to her, and they looked it over together.—Emma took the opportunity of whispering,

"You speak too plain. She must understand you."

"I hope she does. I would have her understand me. I am not in the least ashamed of my meaning."

"But really, I am half ashamed, and wish I had never taken up the idea."

"I am very glad you did, and that you communicated it to me. I have now a key to all her odd looks and ways. Leave shame to her. If she does wrong, she ought to feel it."

"She is not entirely without it, I think."

"I do not see much sign of it. She is playing *Robin Adair* at this moment—*his* favourite."[2]

Shortly afterwards Miss Bates, passing near the window, descried Mr. Knightley on horseback not far off.

"Mr. Knightley I declare!—I must speak to him if possible, just to thank him. I will not open the window here; it would give you all

1. Probably Johann Baptist Cramer (1771–1858), the foremost pianist of the day, whose *Studies* are still widely played.
2. Song from the perspective of a woman reminiscing about a man who had loved her but toyed with her emotions. See p. 361 for full text.

cold; but I can go into my mother's room you know. I dare say he will come in when he knows who is here. Quite delightful to have you all meet so!—Our little room so honoured!"

She was in the adjoining chamber while she still spoke, and opening the casement there, immediately called Mr. Knightley's attention, and every syllable of their conversation was as distinctly heard by the others, as if it had passed within the same apartment.

"How d'ye do?—how d'ye do?—Very well, I thank you. So obliged to you for the carriage last night. We were just in time; my mother just ready for us. Pray come in; do come in. You will find some friends here."

So began Miss Bates; and Mr. Knightley seemed determined to be heard in his turn, for most resolutely and commandingly did he say,

"How is your niece, Miss Bates?—I want to inquire after you all, but particularly your niece. How is Miss Fairfax?—I hope she caught no cold last night. How is she to-day? Tell me how Miss Fairfax is."

And Miss Bates was obliged to give a direct answer before he would hear her in any thing else. The listeners were amused; and Mrs. Weston gave Emma a look of particular meaning. But Emma still shook her head in steady scepticism.

"So obliged to you!—so very much obliged to you for the carriage," resumed Miss Bates.

He cut her short with,

"I am going to Kingston. Can I do any thing for you?"

"Oh! dear, Kingston—are you?—Mrs. Cole was saying the other day she wanted something from Kingston."

"Mrs. Cole has servants to send. Can I do any thing for *you*?"

"No, I thank you. But do come in. Who do you think is here?—Miss Woodhouse and Miss Smith; so kind as to call to hear the new pianoforté. Do put up your horse at the Crown, and come in."

"Well," said he in a deliberating manner, "for five minutes, perhaps."

"And here is Mrs. Weston and Mr. Frank Churchill too!—Quite delightful; so many friends!"

"No, not now, I thank you. I could not stay two minutes. I must get on to Kingston as fast as I can."

"Oh! do come in. They will be so very happy to see you."

"No, no, your room is full enough. I will call another day, and hear the pianoforte."

"Well, I am so sorry!—Oh! Mr. Knightley, what a delightful party last night; how extremely pleasant.—Did you ever see such dancing?—Was not it delightful?—Miss Woodhouse and Mr. Frank Churchill; I never saw any thing equal to it."

"Oh! very delightful indeed; I can say nothing less, for I suppose Miss Woodhouse and Mr. Frank Churchill are hearing every thing

that passes. And (raising his voice still more) I do not see why Miss
Fairfax should not be mentioned too. I think Miss Fairfax dances
very well; and Mrs. Weston is the very best country-dance player,
without exception, in England. Now, if your friends have any gratitude, they will say something pretty loud about you and me in return;
but I cannot stay to hear it."

"Oh! Mr. Knightley, one moment more; something of consequence—so shocked!—Jane and I are both so shocked about the
apples!"

"What is the matter now?"

"To think of your sending us all your store apples. You said you
had a great many, and now you have not one left. We really are so
shocked! Mrs. Hodges may well be angry. William Larkins mentioned it here. You should not have done it, indeed you should not.
Ah! he is off. He never can bear to be thanked. But I thought he
would have staid now, and it would have been a pity not to have
mentioned . . . . Well, (returning into the room,) I have not been
able to succeed. Mr. Knightley cannot stop. He is going to Kingston. He asked me if he could do any thing" . . . .

"Yes," said Jane, "we heard his kind offers, we heard every thing."

"Oh! yes, my dear, I dare say you might, because you know the
door was open, and the window was open, and Mr. Knightley spoke
loud. You must have heard everything to be sure. 'Can I do any
thing for you at Kingston?' said he; so I just mentioned . . . . Oh!
Miss Woodhouse, must you be going?—You seem but just come—so
very obliging of you."

Emma found it really time to be at home; the visit had already
lasted long; and on examining watches, so much of the morning
was perceived to be gone, that Mrs. Weston and her companion
taking leave also, could allow themselves only to walk with the two
young ladies to Hartfield gates, before they set off for Randalls.

Chapter XI[3]

It may be possible to do without dancing entirely. Instances have
been known of young people passing many, many months succes-
sively, without being at any ball of any description, and no material
injury accrue either to body or mind;—but when a beginning is
made—when the felicities of rapid motion have once been, though
slightly, felt—it must be a very heavy set that does not ask for more.

Frank Churchill had danced once at Highbury, and longed to
dance again; and the last half hour of an evening which Mr. Woodhouse was persuaded to spend with his daughter at Randalls, was

---

3. Misnumbered XIII in 1816.

passed by the two young people in schemes on the subject. Frank's was the first idea; and his the greatest zeal in pursuing it; for the lady was the best judge of the difficulties, and the most solicitous for accommodation and appearance. But still she had inclination enough for shewing people again how delightfully Mr. Frank Churchill and Miss Woodhouse danced—for doing that in which she need not blush to compare herself with Jane Fairfax—and even for simple dancing itself, without any of the wicked aids of vanity—to assist him first in pacing out the room they were in to see what it could be made to hold—and then in taking the dimensions of the other parlour, in the hope of discovering, in spite of all that Mr. Weston could say of their exactly equal size, that it was a little the largest.

His first proposition and request, that the dance begun at Mr. Cole's should be finished there—that the same party should be collected, and the same musician engaged, met with the readiest acquiescence. Mr. Weston entered into the idea with thorough enjoyment, and Mrs. Weston most willingly undertook to play as long as they could wish to dance; and the interesting employment had followed, of reckoning up exactly who there would be, and portioning out the indispensable division of space to every couple.

"You and Miss Smith, and Miss Fairfax, will be three, and the two Miss Coxes five," had been repeated many times over. "And there will be the two Gilberts, young Cox, my father, and myself, besides Mr. Knightley. Yes, that will be quite enough for pleasure. You and Miss Smith, and Miss Fairfax, will be three, and the two Miss Coxes five; and for five couple there will be plenty of room."

But soon it came to be on one side,

"But will there be good room for five couple?—I really do not think there will."

On another,

"And after all, five couple are not enough to make it worth while to stand up. Five couple are nothing, when one thinks seriously about it. It will not do to *invite* five couple. It can be allowable only as the thought of the moment."

Somebody said that *Miss* Gilbert was expected at her brother's, and must be invited with the rest. Somebody else believed *Mrs.* Gilbert would have danced the other evening, if she had been asked. A word was put in for a second young Cox; and at last, Mr. Weston naming one family of cousins who must be included, and another of very old acquaintance who could not be left out, it became a certainty that the five couple would be at least ten, and a very interesting speculation in what possible manner they could be disposed of.

The doors of the two rooms were just opposite each other. "Might not they use both rooms, and dance across the passage?" It seemed the best scheme; and yet it was not so good but that many of them wanted a better. Emma said it would be awkward; Mrs. Weston was in distress about the supper; and Mr. Woodhouse opposed it earnestly, on the score of health. It made him so very unhappy, indeed, that it could not be persevered in.

"Oh! no," said he; "it would be the extreme of imprudence. I could not bear it for Emma!—Emma is not strong. She would catch a dreadful cold. So would poor little Harriet. So you would all. Mrs. Weston, you would be quite laid up; do not let them talk of such a wild thing. Pray do not let them talk of it. That young man (speaking lower) is very thoughtless. Do not tell his father, but that young man is not quite the thing. He has been opening the doors very often this evening, and keeping them open very inconsiderately. He does not think of the draught. I do not mean to set you against him, but indeed he is not quite the thing!"

Mrs. Weston was sorry for such a charge. She knew the importance of it, and said every thing in her power to do it away. Every door was now closed, the passage plan given up, and the first scheme of dancing only in the room they were in resorted to again; and with such goodwill on Frank Churchill's part, that the space which a quarter of an hour before he had deemed barely sufficient for five couple, was now endeavoured to be made out quite enough for ten.

"We were too magnificent," said he. "We allowed unnecessary room. Ten couple may stand here very well."

Emma demurred. "It would be a crowd—a sad crowd; and what could be worse than dancing without space to turn in?"

"Very true," he gravely replied; "it was very bad." But still he went on measuring, and still he ended with,

"I think there will be very tolerable room for ten couple."

"No, no," said she, "you are quite unreasonable. It would be dreadful to be standing so close! Nothing can be farther from pleasure than to be dancing in a crowd—and a crowd in a little room!"

"There is no denying it," he replied. "I agree with you exactly. A crowd in a little room—Miss Woodhouse, you have the art of giving pictures in a few words. Exquisite, quite exquisite!—Still, however, having proceeded so far, one is unwilling to give the matter up. It would be a disappointment to my father—and altogether—I do not know that—I am rather of opinion that ten couple might stand here very well."

Emma perceived that the nature of his gallantry was a little self-willed, and that he would rather oppose than lose the pleasure of dancing with her; but she took the compliment, and forgave the rest. Had she intended ever to *marry* him, it might have been worth while to pause and consider, and try to understand the value of his preference, and the character of his temper; but for all the purposes of their acquaintance, he was quite amiable enough.

Before the middle of the next day, he was at Hartfield; and he entered the room with such an agreeable smile as certified the continuance of the scheme. It soon appeared that he came to announce an improvement.

"Well, Miss Woodhouse," he almost immediately began, "your inclination for dancing has not been quite frightened away, I hope, by the terrors of my father's little rooms. I bring a new proposal on the subject:—a thought of my father's, which waits only your approbation to be acted upon. May I hope for the honour of your hand for the two first dances of this little projected ball, to be given, not as Randalls, but at the Crown Inn?"

"The Crown!"

"Yes; if you and Mr. Woodhouse see no objection, and I trust you cannot, my father hopes his friends will be so kind as to visit him there. Better accommodations, he can promise them, and not a less grateful welcome than at Randalls. It is his own idea. Mrs. Weston sees no objection to it, provided you are satisfied. This is what we all feel. Oh! you were perfectly right! Ten couple, in either of the Randalls rooms, would have been insufferable!—Dreadful!—I felt how right you were the whole time, but was too anxious for securing *any thing* to like to yield. Is not it a good exchange?—You consent—I hope you consent?"

"It appears to me a plan that nobody can object to, if Mr. and Mrs. Weston do not. I think it admirable; and, as far as I can answer for myself, shall be most happy —— It seems the only improvement that could be. Papa, do you not think it an excellent improvement?"

She was obliged to repeat and explain it, before it was fully comprehended; and then, being quite new, further representations were necessary to make it acceptable.

"No; he thought it very far from an improvement—a very bad plan—much worse than the other. A room at an inn was always damp and dangerous; never properly aired, or fit to be inhabited. If they must dance, they had better dance at Randalls. He had never been in the room at the Crown in his life—did not know the people who kept it by sight.—Oh! no—a very bad plan. They would catch worse colds at the Crown than any where."

"I was going to observe, sir," said Frank Churchill, "that one of the great recommendations of this change would be the very little danger of any body's catching cold—so much less danger at the Crown than at Randalls! Mr. Perry might have reason to regret the alteration, but nobody else could."

"Sir," said Mr. Woodhouse, rather warmly, "you are very much mistaken if you suppose Mr. Perry to be that sort of character.

Mr. Perry is extremely concerned when any of us are ill. But I do not understand how the room at the Crown can be safer for you than your father's house."

"From the very circumstance of its being larger, sir. We shall have no occasion to open the windows at all—not once the whole evening; and it is that dreadful habit of opening the windows, letting in cold air upon heated bodies, which (as you well know, sir) does the mischief."

"Open the windows!—but surely, Mr. Churchill, nobody would think of opening the windows at Randalls. Nobody could be so imprudent! I never heard of such a thing. Dancing with open windows!—I am sure, neither your father nor Mrs. Weston (poor Miss Taylor that was) would suffer it."

"Ah! sir—but a thoughtless young person will sometimes step behind a window-curtain, and throw up a sash, without its being suspected. I have often known it done myself."

"Have you indeed, sir?—Bless me! I never could have supposed it. But I live out of the world, and am often astonished at what I hear. However, this does make a difference; and, perhaps, when we come to talk it over—but these sort of things require a good deal of consideration. One cannot resolve upon them in a hurry. If Mr. and Mrs. Weston will be so obliging as to call here one morning, we may talk it over, and see what can be done."

"But, unfortunately, sir, my time is so limited——"

"Oh!" interrupted Emma, "there will be plenty of time for talking every thing over. There is no hurry at all. If it can be contrived to be at the Crown, papa, it will be very convenient for the horses. They will be so near their own stable."

"So they will, my dear. That is a great thing. Not that James ever complains; but it is right to spare our horses when we can. If I could be sure of the rooms being thoroughly aired—but is Mrs. Stokes to be trusted? I doubt it. I do not know her, even by sight."

"I can answer for every thing of that nature, sir, because it will be under Mrs. Weston's care. Mrs. Weston undertakes to direct the whole."

"There, papa!—Now you must be satisfied—Our own dear Mrs. Weston, who is carefulness itself. Do not you remember what Mr. Perry said, so many years ago, when I had the measles? 'If *Miss Taylor* undertakes to wrap Miss Emma up, you need not have any fears, sir.' How often have I heard you speak of it as such a compliment to her!"

"Aye, very true. Mr. Perry did say so. I shall never forget it. Poor little Emma! You were very bad with the measles; that is, you would have been very bad, but for Perry's great attention. He came four times a day for a week. He said, from the first, it was a very good sort—which was out great comfort; but the measles are a dreadful complaint. I hope whenever poor Isabella's little ones have the measles, she will send for Perry."

"My father and Mrs. Weston are at the Crown at this moment," said Frank Churchill, "examining the capabilities of the house. I left them there and came on to Hartfield, impatient for your opinion, and hoping you might be persuaded to join them and give your advice on the spot. I was desired to say so from both. It would be the greatest pleasure to them, if you could allow me to attend you there. They can do nothing satisfactorily without you."

Emma was most happy to be called to such a council; and her father, engaging to think it all over while she was gone, the two young people set off together without delay for the Crown. There were Mr. and Mrs. Weston; delighted to see her and receive her approbation, very busy and very happy in their different way; she, in some little distress; and he, finding every thing perfect.

"Emma," said she, "this paper is worse than I expected. Look! in places you see it is dreadfully dirty; and the wainscot is more yellow and forlorn than any thing I[4] could have imagined."

"My dear, you are too particular," said her husband. "What does all that signify? You will see nothing of it by candle-light. It will be as clean as Randalls by candle-light. We never see any thing of it on our club-nights."

The ladies here probably exchanged looks which meant, "Men never know when things are dirty or not;" and the gentlemen perhaps thought each to himself, "Women will have their little nonsenses and needless cares."

One perplexity, however, arose, which the gentlemen did not disdain. It regarded a supper-room. At the time of the ball-room's being built, suppers had not been in question; and a small card-room adjoining, was the only addition. What was to be done? This card-room would be wanted as a card-room now; or, if cards were conveniently voted unnecessary by their four selves, still was not it too small for any comfortable supper? Another room of much better size might be secured for the purpose; but it was at the other end of the house, and a long awkward passage must be gone through to get at it. This made a difficulty. Mrs. Weston was afraid of draughts for the young people in that passage; and neither Emma nor the gentlemen could tolerate the prospect of being miserably crowded at supper.

Mrs. Weston proposed having no regular supper; merely sandwiches, &c. set out in the little room; but that was scouted as a wretched suggestion. A private dance, without sitting down to supper, was pronounced an infamous fraud upon the rights of men and

4. The "I" was omitted in error from 1816.

women; and Mrs. Weston must not speak of it again. She then took another line of expediency, and looking into the doubtful room, observed,

"I do not think it *is* so very small. We shall not be many, you know."

And Mr. Weston at the same time, walking briskly with long steps through the passage, was calling out,

"You talk a great deal of the length of this passage, my dear. It is a mere nothing after all; and not the least draught from the stairs."

"I wish," said Mrs. Weston, "one could know which arrangement our guests in general would like best. To do what would be most generally pleasing must be our object—if one could but tell what that would be."

"Yes, very true," cried Frank, "very true. You want your neighbours' opinions. I do not wonder at you. If one could ascertain what the chief of them—the Coles, for instance. They are not far off. Shall I call upon them? Or Miss Bates? She is still nearer.—And I do not know whether Miss Bates is not as likely to understand the inclinations of the rest of the people as any body. I think we do want a larger council. Suppose I go and invite Miss Bates to join us?"

"Well—if you please," said Mrs. Weston rather hesitating, "if you think she will be of any use."

"You will get nothing to the purpose from Miss Bates," said Emma. "She will be all delight and gratitude, but she will tell you nothing. She will not even listen to your questions. I see no advantage in consulting Miss Bates."

"But she is so amusing, so extremely amusing! I am very fond of hearing Miss Bates talk. And I need not bring the whole family, you know."

Here Mr. Weston joined them, and on hearing what was proposed, gave it his decided approbation.

"Aye, do, Frank.—Go and fetch Miss Bates, and let us end the matter at once. She will enjoy the scheme, I am sure; and I do not know a properer person for shewing us how to do away difficulties. Fetch Miss Bates. We are growing a little too nice.[5] She is a standing lesson of how to be happy. But fetch them both. Invite them both."

"Both sir! Can the old lady?" . . .

"The old lady! No, the young lady, to be sure. I shall think you a great blockhead, Frank, if you bring the aunt without the niece."

"Oh! I beg your pardon, sir. I did not immediately recollect. Undoubtedly if you wish it, I will endeavour to persuade them both." And away he ran.

Long before he re-appeared, attending the short, neat, brisk-moving aunt, and her elegant niece,—Mrs. Weston, like a sweet-tempered woman and a good wife, had examined the passage again,

5. Difficult to please.

and found the evils of it much less than she had supposed before—
indeed very trifling; and here ended the difficulties of decision. All
the rest, in speculation at least, was perfectly smooth. All the minor
arrangements of table and chair, lights and music, tea and supper,
made themselves; or were left as mere trifles to be settled at any time
between Mrs. Weston and Mrs. Stokes.—Every body invited, was
certainly to come; Frank had already written to Enscombe to propose staying a few days beyond his fortnight, which could not possibly be refused. And a delightful dance it was to be.

Most cordially, when Miss Bates arrived, did she agree that it
must. As a counsellor she was not wanted; but as an approver, (a
much safer character,) she was truly welcome. Her approbation, at
once general and minute, warm and incessant, could not but please;
and for another half-hour they were all walking to and fro, between
the different rooms, some suggesting, some attending, and all in
happy enjoyment of the future. The party did not break up without
Emma's being positively secured for the two first dances by the hero
of the evening, nor without her overhearing Mr. Weston whisper to
his wife, "He has asked her, my dear. That's right. I knew he would!"

Chapter XII

One thing only was wanting to make the prospect of the ball completely satisfactory to Emma—its being fixed for a day within the
granted term of Frank Churchill's stay in Surry; for, in spite of Mr.
Weston's confidence, she could not think it so very impossible that
the Churchills might not allow their nephew to remain a day
beyond his fortnight. But this was not judged feasible. The preparations must take their time, nothing could be properly ready till the
third week were entered on, and for a few days they must be planning, proceeding and hoping in uncertainty—at the risk—in her
opinion, the great risk, of its being all in vain.

Enscombe however was gracious, gracious in fact, if not in word.
His wish of staying longer evidently did not please; but it was not
opposed. All was safe and prosperous; and as the removal of one
solicitude generally makes way for another, Emma, being now certain of her ball, began to adopt as the next vexation Mr. Knightley's
provoking indifference about it. Either because he did not dance
himself, or because the plan had been formed without his being consulted, he seemed resolved that it should not interest him, determined against its exciting any present curiosity, or affording him any
future amusement. To her voluntary communications Emma could
get no more approving reply, than,

"Very well. If the Westons think it worth while to be at all this
trouble for a few hours of noisy entertainment, I have nothing to
say against it, but that they shall not choose pleasures for me.—Oh!

yes, I must be there, I could not refuse; and I will keep as much awake as I can; but I would rather be at home, looking over William Larkins's week's account; much rather, I confess.—Pleasure in seeing dancing!—not I, indeed—I never look at it—I do not know who does.—Fine dancing, I believe, like virtue, must be its own reward. Those who are standing by are usually thinking of something very different."

This Emma felt was aimed at her; and it made her quite angry. It was not in compliment to Jane Fairfax however that he was so indifferent, or so indignant: he was not guided by *her* feelings in reprobating the ball, for *she* enjoyed the thought of it to an extraordinary degree. It made her animated—open hearted—she voluntarily said;—

"Oh! Miss Woodhouse, I hope nothing may happen to prevent the ball. What a disappointment it would be! I do look forward to it, I own, with *very* great pleasure."

It was not to oblige Jane Fairfax therefore that he would have preferred the society of William Larkins. No!—she was more and more convinced that Mrs. Weston was quite mistaken in that surmise. There was a great deal of friendly and of compassionate attachment on his side—but no love.

Alas! there was soon no leisure for quarrelling with Mr. Knightley. Two days of joyful security were immediately followed by the overthrow of everything. A letter arrived from Mr. Churchill to urge his nephew's instant return. Mrs. Churchill was unwell—far too unwell to do without him; she had been in a very suffering state (so said her husband) when writing to her nephew two days before, though from her usual unwillingness to give pain, and constant habit of never thinking of herself, she had not mentioned it; but now she was too ill to trifle, and must entreat him to set off for Enscombe without delay.

The substance of this letter was forwarded to Emma, in a note from Mrs. Weston, instantly. As to his going, it was inevitable. He must be gone within a few hours, though without feeling any real alarm for his aunt, to lessen his repugnance. He knew her illnesses; they never occurred but for her own convenience.

Mrs. Weston added, "that he could only allow himself time to hurry to Highbury, after breakfast, and take leave of the few friends there whom he could suppose to feel any interest in him; and that he might be expected at Hartfield very soon."

This wretched note was the finalé of Emma's breakfast. When once it had been read, there was no doing any thing, but lament and exclaim. The loss of the ball—the loss of the young man—and all that the young man might be feeling!—It was too wretched!—Such a delightful evening as it would have been!—Every body so happy! and she and her partner the happiest!—"I said it would be so," was the only consolation.

Her father's feelings were quite distinct. He thought principally of Mrs. Churchill's illness, and wanted to know how she was treated; and as for the ball, it was shocking to have dear Emma disappointed; but they would all be safer at home.

Emma was ready for her visitor some time before he appeared; but if this reflected at all upon his impatience, his sorrowful look and total want of spirits when he did come might redeem him. He felt the going away almost too much to speak of it. His dejection was most evident. He sat really lost in thought for the first few minutes; and when rousing himself, it was only to say,

"Of all horrid things, leave-taking is the worst."

"But you will come again," said Emma. "This will not be your only visit to Randalls."

"Ah!—(shaking his head)—the uncertainty of when I may be able to return!—I shall try for it with a zeal!—It will be the object of all my thoughts and cares!—and if my uncle and aunt go to town this spring—but I am afraid—they did not stir last spring—I am afraid it is a custom gone for ever."

"Our poor ball must be quite given up."

"Ah! that ball!—why did we wait for any thing?—why not seize the pleasure at once?—How often is happiness destroyed by preparation, foolish preparation!—You told us it would be so.—Oh! Miss Woodhouse, why are you always so right?"

"Indeed, I am very sorry to be right in this instance. I would much rather have been merry than wise."

"If I can come again, we are still to have our ball. My father depends on it. Do not forget your engagement."

Emma looked graciously.

"Such a fortnight as it has been!" he continued; "every day more precious and more delightful than the day before!—every day making me less fit to bear any other place. Happy those, who can remain at Highbury!"

"As you do us such ample justice now," said Emma, laughing, "I will venture to ask, whether you did not come a little doubtingly at first? Do not we rather surpass your expectations? I am sure we do. I am sure you did not much expect to like us. You would not have been so long in coming, if you had had a pleasant idea of Highbury."

He laughed rather consciously; and though denying the sentiment, Emma was convinced that it had been so.

"And you must be off this very morning?"

"Yes; my father is to join me here: we shall walk back together, and I must be off immediately. I am almost afraid that every moment will bring him."

"Not five minutes to spare even for your friends Miss Fairfax and Miss Bates? How unlucky! Miss Bates's powerful, argumentative mind might have strengthened yours."

"Yes—I *have* called there; passing the door, I thought it better. It was a right thing to do. I went in for three minutes, and was detained by Miss Bates's being absent. She was out; and I felt it impossible not to wait till she came in. She is a woman that one may, that one *must* laugh at; but that one would not wish to slight. It was better to pay my visit, then"—

He hesitated, got up, walked to a window.

"In short," said he, "perhaps, Miss Woodhouse——I think you can hardly be quite without suspicion"—

He looked at her, as if wanting to read her thoughts. She hardly knew what to say. It seemed like the fore-runner of something absolutely serious, which she did not wish. Forcing herself to speak, therefore, in the hope of putting it by, she calmly said,

"You were quite in the right; it was most natural to pay your visit, then"—

He was silent. She believed he was looking at her; probably reflecting on what she had said, and trying to understand the manner. She heard him sigh. It was natural for him to feel that he had *cause* to sigh. He could not believe her to be encouraging him. A few awkward moments passed, and he sat down again; and in a more determined manner said,

"It was something to feel that all the rest of my time might be given to Hartfield. My regard for Hartfield is most warm"—

He stopt again, rose again, and seemed quite embarrassed.—He was more in love with her than Emma had supposed; and who can say how it might have ended, if his father had not made his appearance? Mr. Woodhouse soon followed; and the necessity of exertion made him composed.

A very few minutes more, however, completed the presented trial. Mr. Weston, always alert when business was to be done, and as incapable of procrastinating any evil that was inevitable, as of foreseeing any that was doubtful, said, "It was time to go;" and the young man, though he might and did sigh, could not but agree, and rise to take leave.

"I shall hear about you all," said he; "that is my chief consolation. I shall hear of every thing that is going on among you. I have engaged Mrs. Weston to correspond with me. She has been so kind as to promise it. Oh! the blessing of a female correspondent, when one is really interested in the absent!—she will tell me every thing. In her letters I shall be at dear Highbury again."

A very friendly shake of the hand, a very earnest "Good bye," closed the speech, and the door had soon shut out Frank Churchill.

Short had been the notice—short their meeting; he was gone; and Emma felt so sorry to part, and foresaw so great a loss to their little society from his absence as to begin to be afraid of being too sorry, and feeling it too much.

It was a sad change. They had been meeting almost every day since his arrival. Certainly his being at Randalls had given great spirit to the last two weeks—indescribable spirit; the idea, the expectation of seeing him which every morning had brought, the assurance of his attentions, his liveliness, his manners! It had been a very happy fortnight, and forlorn must be the sinking from it into the common course of Hartfield days. To complete every other recommendation, he had *almost* told her that he loved her. What strength, or what constancy of affection he might be subject to, was another point; but at present she could not doubt his having a decidedly warm admiration, a conscious preference of herself; and this persuasion, joined to all the rest, made her think that she *must* be a little in love with him, in spite of every previous determination against it.

"I certainly must," said she. "This sensation of listlessness, weariness, stupidity, this disinclination to sit down and employ myself, this feeling of every thing's being dull and insipid about the house!—I must be in love; I should be the oddest creature in the world if I were not—for a few weeks at least. Well! evil to some is always good to others. I shall have many fellow-mourners for the ball, if not for Frank Churchill; but Mr. Knightley will be happy. He may spend the evening with his dear William Larkins now if he likes."

Mr. Knightley, however, shewed no triumphant happiness. He could not say that he was sorry on his own account; his very cheerful look would have contradicted him if he had; but he said, and very steadily, that he was sorry for the disappointment of the others, and with considerable kindness added,

"You, Emma, who have so few opportunities of dancing, you are really out of luck; you are very much out of luck!"

It was some days before she saw Jane Fairfax, to judge of her honest regret in this woeful change; but when they did meet, her composure was odious. She had been particularly unwell, however, suffering from head-ache to a degree, which made her aunt declare, that had the ball taken place, she did not think Jane could have attended it; and it was charity to impute some of her unbecoming indifference to the languor of ill-health.

Chapter XIII

Emma continued to entertain no doubt of her being in love. Her ideas only varied as to the how much. At first, she thought it was a good deal; and afterwards, but little. She had great pleasure in

hearing Frank Churchill talked of; and, for his sake, greater pleasure than ever in seeing Mr. and Mrs. Weston; she was very often
thinking of him, and quite impatient for a letter, that she might
know how he was, how were his spirits, how was his aunt, and what
was the chance of his coming to Randalls again this spring. But, on
the other hand, she could not admit herself to be unhappy, nor, after
the first morning, to be less disposed for employment than usual; she
was still busy and cheerful; and, pleasing as he was, she could yet
imagine him to have faults; and farther, though thinking of him so
much, and, as she sat drawing or working, forming a thousand amusing schemes for the progress and close of their attachment, fancying
interesting dialogues, and inventing elegant letters; the conclusion of
every imaginary declaration on his side was that she *refused him*.
Their affection was always to subside into friendship. Every thing
tender and charming was to mark their parting: but still they were to
part. When she became sensible of this, it struck her that she could
not be very much in love; for in spite of her previous and fixed determination never to quit her father, never to marry, a strong attachment certainly must produce more of a struggle than she could
foresee in her own feelings.

"I do not find myself making any use of the word *sacrifice*," said
she.—"In not one of all my clever replies, my delicate negatives, is
there any allusion to making a sacrifice. I do suspect that he is not
really necessary to my happiness. So much the better. I certainly will
not persuade myself to feel more than I do. I am quite enough in
love. I should be sorry to be more."

Upon the whole, she was equally contented with her view of his
feelings.

"*He* is undoubtedly very much in love—every thing denotes it—
very much in love indeed!—and when he comes again, if his affection
continue, I must be on my guard not to encourage it.—It would be
most inexcusable to do otherwise, as my own mind is quite made up.
Not that I imagine he can think I have been encouraging him hitherto. No, if he had believed me at all to share his feelings, he would
not have been so wretched. Could he have thought himself encouraged, his looks and language at parting would have been different.—
Still, however, I must be on my guard. This is in the supposition of his
attachment continuing what it now is; but I do not know that I expect
it will; I do not look upon him to be quite the sort of man—I do not
altogether build upon his steadiness or constancy.—His feelings are
warm, but I can imagine them rather changeable.—Every consideration of the subject, in short, makes me thankful that my happiness is
not more deeply involved.—I shall do very well again after a little
while—and then, it will be a good thing over; for they say every body
is in love once in their lives, and I shall have been let off easily."

When his letter to Mrs. Weston arrived, Emma had the perusal of it; and she read it with a degree of pleasure and admiration which made her at first shake her head over her own sensations, and think she had undervalued their strength. It was a long, well-written letter, giving the particulars of his journey and of his feelings, expressing all the affection, gratitude, and respect which was natural and honourable, and describing every thing exterior and local that could be supposed attractive, with spirit and precision. No suspicious flourishes now of apology or concern; it was the language of real feeling towards Mrs. Weston; and the transition from Highbury to Enscombe, the contrast between the places in some of the first blessings of social life was just enough touched on to shew how keenly it was felt, and how much more might have been said but for the restraints of propriety.— The charm of her own name was not wanting. *Miss Woodhouse* appeared more than once, and never without a something of pleasing connection, either a compliment to her taste, or a remembrance of what she had said; and in the very last time of its meeting her eye, unadorned as it was by any such broad wreath of gallantry, she yet could discern the effect of her influence and acknowledge the greatest compliment perhaps of all conveyed. Compressed into the very lowest vacant corner were these words—"I had not a spare moment on Tuesday, as you know, for Miss Woodhouse's beautiful little friend. Pray make my excuses and adieus to her." This, Emma could not doubt, was all for herself. Harriet was remembered only from being *her* friend. His information and prospects as to Enscombe were neither worse nor better than had been anticipated; Mrs. Churchill was recovering, and he dared not yet, even in his own imagination, fix a time for coming to Randalls again.

Gratifying, however, and stimulative as was the letter in the material part, its sentiments, she yet found, when it was folded up and returned to Mrs. Weston, that it had not added any lasting warmth, that she could still do without the writer, and that he must learn to do without her. Her intentions were unchanged. Her resolution of refusal only grew more interesting by the addition of a scheme for his subsequent consolation and happiness. His recollection of Harriet, and the words which clothed it, the "beautiful little friend," suggested to her the idea of Harriet's succeeding her in his affections. Was it impossible?—No.—Harriet undoubtedly was greatly his inferior in understanding; but he had been very much struck with the loveliness of her face and the warm simplicity of her manner; and all the probabilities of circumstance and connection were in her favour.—For Harriet, it would be advantageous and delightful indeed.

"I must not dwell upon it," said she.—"I must not think of it. I know the danger of indulging such speculations. But stranger things have happened; and when we cease to care for each other as we do now, it will be the means of confirming us in that sort of true disinterested friendship which I can already look forward to with pleasure."

It was well to have a comfort in store on Harriet's behalf, though it might be wise to let the fancy touch it seldom; for evil in that quarter was at hand. As Frank Churchill's arrival had succeeded Mr. Elton's engagement in the conversation of Highbury, as the latest interest had entirely born down the first, so now upon Frank Churchill's disappearance, Mr. Elton's concerns were assuming the most irresistible form.—His wedding-day was named. He would soon be among them again; Mr. Elton and his bride. There was hardly time to talk over the first letter from Enscombe before "Mr. Elton and his bride" was in every body's mouth, and Frank Churchill was forgotten. Emma grew sick at the sound. She had had three weeks of happy exemption from Mr. Elton; and Harriet's mind, she had been willing to hope, had been lately gaining strength. With Mr. Weston's ball in view at least, there had been a great deal of insensibility to other things; but it was now too evident that she had not attained such a state of composure as could stand against the actual approach—new carriage, bell ringing and all.

Poor Harriet was in a flutter of spirits which required all the reasonings and soothings and attentions of every kind that Emma could give. Emma felt that she could not do too much for her, that Harriet had a right to all her ingenuity and all her patience; but it was heavy work to be for ever convincing without producing any effect, for ever agreed to, without being able to make their opinions the same. Harriet listened submissively, and said "it was very true—it was just as Miss Woodhouse described—it was not worth while to think about them—and she would not think about them any longer"—but no change of subject could avail, and the next half hour saw her as anxious and restless about the Eltons as before.—At last Emma attacked her on another ground.

"Your allowing yourself to be so occupied and so unhappy about Mr. Elton's marrying, Harriet, is the strongest reproach you can make *me*. You could not give me a greater reproof for the mistake I fell into. It was all my doing, I know. I have not forgotten it, I assure you.—Deceived myself, I did very miserably deceive you—and it will be a painful reflection to me for ever. Do not imagine me in danger of forgetting it."

Harriet felt this too much to utter more than a few words of eager exclamation. Emma continued,

"I have not said, exert yourself Harriet for my sake; think less, talk less of Mr. Elton for my sake; because for your own sake rather, I would wish it to be done, for the sake of what is more important than my comfort, a habit of self-command in you, a consideration of what is your duty, an attention to propriety, an endeavour to avoid the suspicions of others, to save your health and credit, and restore your tranquillity. These are the motives which I have been pressing on you. They are very important—and sorry I am that you cannot feel them sufficiently to act upon them. My being saved from pain is a very secondary consideration. I want you to save yourself from greater pain. Perhaps I may sometimes have felt that Harriet would not forget what was due—or rather what would be kind by me."

This appeal to her affections did more than all the rest. The idea of wanting gratitude and consideration for Miss Woodhouse, whom she really loved extremely, made her wretched for a while, and when the violence of grief was comforted away, still remained powerful enough to prompt to what was right and support her in it very tolerably.

"You, who have been the best friend I ever had in my life—Want gratitude to you!—Nobody is equal to you!—I care for nobody as I do for you!—Oh! Miss Woodhouse, how ungrateful I have been!"

Such expressions, assisted as they were by every thing that look and manner could do, made Emma feel that she had never loved Harriet so well, nor valued her affection so highly before.

"There is no charm equal to tenderness of heart," said she afterwards to herself. "There is nothing to be compared to it. Warmth and tenderness of heart, with an affectionate, open manner, will beat all the clearness of head in the world, for attraction. I am sure it will. It is tenderness of heart which makes my dear father so generally beloved—which gives Isabella all her popularity.—I have it not—but I know how to prize and respect it.—Harriet is my superior in all the charm and all the felicity it gives. Dear Harriet!—I would not change you for the clearest-headed, longest-sighted, best-judging female breathing. Oh! the coldness of a Jane Fairfax!—Harriet is worth a hundred such.—And for a wife—a sensible man's wife—it is invaluable. I mention no names; but happy the man who changes Emma for Harriet!"

Chapter XIV

Mrs. Elton was first seen at church: but though devotion might be interrupted, curiosity could not be satisfied by a bride in a pew, and it must be left for the visits in form which were then to be paid, to settle whether she were very pretty indeed, or only rather pretty, or not pretty at all.

Emma had feelings, less of curiosity than of pride or propriety, to make her resolve on not being the last to pay her respects; and she made a point of Harriet's going with her, that the worst of the business might be gone through as soon as possible.

She could not enter the house again, could not be in the same room to which she had with such vain artifice retreated three months ago, to lace up her boot, without *recollecting*. A thousand vexatious thoughts would recur. Compliments, charades, and horrible blunders; and it was not to be supposed that poor Harriet should not be recollecting too; but she behaved very well, and was only rather pale and silent. The visit was of course short; and there was so much embarrassment and occupation of mind to shorten it, that Emma would not allow herself entirely to form an opinion of the lady, and on no account to give one, beyond the nothing-meaning terms of being "elegantly dressed, and very pleasing."

She did not really like her. She would not be in a hurry to find fault, but she suspected that there was no elegance;—ease but not elegance.—She was almost sure that for a young woman, a stranger, a bride, there was too much ease. Her person was rather good; her face not unpretty; but neither feature, nor air, nor voice, nor manner, were elegant. Emma thought at least it would turn out so.

As for Mr. Elton, his manners did not appear—but no, she would not permit a hasty or a witty word from herself about his manners. It was an awkward ceremony at any time to be receiving wedding-visits, and a man had need be all grace to acquit himself well through it. The woman was better off; she might have the assistance of fine clothes, and the privilege of bashfulness, but the man had only his own good sense to depend on; and when she considered how peculiarly unlucky poor Mr. Elton was in being in the same room at once with the woman he had just married, the woman he had wanted to marry, and the woman whom he had been expected to marry, she must allow him to have the right to look as little wise, and to be as much affectedly, and as little really easy as could be.

"Well, Miss Woodhouse," said Harriet, when they had quitted the house, and after waiting in vain for her friend to begin; "Well, Miss Woodhouse, (with a gentle sigh,) what do you think of her?—Is not she very charming?"

There was a little hesitation in Emma's answer.

"Oh! yes—very—a very pleasing young woman."

"I think her beautiful, quite beautiful."

"Very nicely dressed, indeed; a remarkably elegant gown."

"I am not at all surprized that he should have fallen in love."

"Oh! no—there is nothing to surprize one at all.—A pretty fortune; and she came in his way."

"I dare say," returned Harriet, sighing again, "I dare say she was very much attached to him."

"Perhaps she might; but it is not every man's fate to marry the woman who loves him best. Miss Hawkins perhaps wanted a home, and thought this the best offer she was likely to have."

"Yes," said Harriet earnestly, "and well she might, nobody could ever have a better. Well, I wish them happy with all my heart. And now, Miss Woodhouse, I do not think I shall mind seeing them again. He is just as superior as ever;—but being married, you know, it is quite a different thing. No, indeed, Miss Woodhouse, you need not be afraid; I can sit and admire him now without any great misery. To know that he has not thrown himself away, is such a comfort!— She does seem a charming young woman, just what he deserves. Happy creature! He called her 'Augusta.' How delightful!"

When the visit was returned, Emma made up her mind. She could then see more and judge better. From Harriet's happening not to be at Hartfield, and her father's being present to engage Mr. Elton, she had a quarter of an hour of the lady's conversation to herself, and could composedly attend to her; and the quarter of an hour quite convinced her that Mrs. Elton was a vain woman, extremely well satisfied with herself, and thinking much of her own importance; that she meant to shine and be very superior, but with manners which had been formed in a bad school, pert and familiar; that all her notions were drawn from one set of people, and one style of living; that if not foolish she was ignorant, and that her society would certainly do Mr. Elton no good.

Harriet would have been a better match. If not wise or refined herself, she would have connected him with those who were; but Miss Hawkins, it might be fairly supposed from her easy conceit, had been the best of her own set. The rich brother-in-law near Bristol was the pride of the alliance, and his place and his carriages were the pride of him.

The very first subject after being seated was Maple Grove, "My brother Mr. Suckling's seat"—a comparison of Hartfield to Maple Grove. The grounds of Hartfield were small, but neat and pretty; and the house was modern and well-built. Mrs. Elton seemed most favourably impressed by the size of the room, the entrance, and all that she could see or imagine. "Very like Maple Grove indeed!—She was quite struck by the likeness!—That room was the very shape and size of the morning-room at Maple Grove; her sister's favourite room."—Mr. Elton was appealed to.—"Was not it astonishingly like?—She could really almost fancy herself at Maple Grove."

"And the staircase—You know, as I came in, I observed how very like the staircase was; placed exactly in the same part of the house. I really could not help exclaiming! I assure you, Miss Woodhouse, it is very delightful to me, to be reminded of a place I am so extremely partial to as Maple Grove. I have spent so many happy months there! (with a little sigh[6] of sentiment). A charming place, undoubtedly.

6. 1816 has "sign," which is probably a printer's error.

Every body who sees it is struck by its beauty; but to me, it has been quite a home. Whenever you are transplanted, like me, Miss Wood-house, you will understand how very delightful it is to meet with any thing at all like what one has left behind. I always say this is quite one of the evils of matrimony."

Emma made as slight a reply as she could; but it was fully suffi-cient for Mrs. Elton, who only wanted to be talking herself.

"So extremely like Maple Grove! And it is not merely the house—the grounds, I assure you, as far as I could observe, are strik-ingly like. The laurels at Maple Grove are in the same profusion as here, and stand very much in the same way—just across the lawn; and I had a glimpse of a fine large tree, with a bench round it, which put me so exactly in mind! My brother and sister will be enchanted with this place. People who have extensive grounds themselves are always pleased with any thing in the same style."

Emma doubted the truth of this sentiment. She had a great idea that people who had extensive grounds themselves cared very little for the extensive grounds of any body else; but it was not worth while to attack an error so double-dyed,[7] and therefore only said in reply,

"When you have seen more of this country, I am afraid you will think you have over-rated Hartfield. Surry is full of beauties."

"Oh! yes, I am quite aware of that. It is the garden of England, you know. Surry is the garden of England."

"Yes; but we must not rest our claims on this distinction. Many counties, I believe, are called the garden of England, as well as Surry."

"No, I fancy not," replied Mrs. Elton, with a most satisfied smile. "I never heard any county but Surry called so."[8]

Emma was silenced.

"My brother and sister have promised us a visit in the spring, or summer at farthest," continued Mrs. Elton; "and that will be our time for exploring. While they are with us, we shall explore a great deal, I dare say. They will have their barouche-landau, of course, which holds four perfectly; and therefore, without saying any thing of *our* carriage, we should be able to explore the different beauties extremely well. They would hardly come in their chaise, I think, at that season of the year. Indeed, when the time draws on, I shall decidedly recommend their bringing the barouche-landau; it will be so very much preferable. When people come into a beautiful country of this sort, you know, Miss Woodhouse, one naturally wishes them to see as much as possible; and Mr. Suckling is extremely fond of

7. Stained deeply.
8. Emma was right. The phrase was applied to various counties.

exploring. We explored to King's-Weston twice last summer, in that way, most delightfully, just after their first having the barouche-landau. You have many parties of that kind here, I suppose, Miss Woodhouse, every summer?"

"No; not immediately here. We are rather out of distance of the very striking beauties which attract the sort of parties you speak of; and we are a very quiet set of people, I believe; more disposed to stay at home than engage in schemes of pleasure."

"Ah! there is nothing like staying at home, for real comfort. Nobody can be more devoted to home than I am. I was quite a proverb for it at Maple Grove. Many a time has Selina said, when she has been going to Bristol, 'I really cannot get this girl to move from the house. I absolutely must go in by myself, though I hate being stuck up in the barouche-landau without a companion; but Augusta, I believe, with her own good will, would never stir beyond the park paling.' Many a time has she said so; and yet I am no advocate for entire seclusion. I think, on the contrary, when people shut themselves up entirely from society, it is a very bad thing; and that it is much more advisable to mix in the world in a proper degree, without living in it either too much or too little. I perfectly understand your situation, however, Miss Woodhouse—(looking towards Mr. Woodhouse)—Your father's state of health must be a great drawback. Why does not he try Bath?—Indeed he should. Let me recommend Bath to you. I assure you I have no doubt of its doing Mr. Woodhouse good."

"My father tried it more than once, formerly; but without receiving any benefit; and Mr. Perry, whose name, I dare say, is not unknown to you, does not conceive it would be at all more likely to be useful now."

"Ah! that's a great pity; for I assure you, Miss Woodhouse, where the waters do agree, it is quite wonderful the relief they give. In my Bath life, I have seen such instances of it! And it is so cheerful a place, that it could not fail of being of use to Mr. Woodhouse's spirits, which, I understand, are sometimes much depressed. And as to its recommendations to *you*, I fancy I need not take much pains to dwell on them. The advantages of Bath to the young are pretty generally understood. It would be a charming introduction for you, who have lived so secluded a life; and I could immediately secure you some of the best society in the place. A line from me would bring you a little host of acquaintance; and my particular friend, Mrs. Partridge, the lady I have always resided with when in Bath, would be most happy to shew you any attentions, and would be the very person for you to go into public with."

It was as much as Emma could bear, without being impolite. The idea of her being indebted to Mrs. Elton for what was called an

introduction—of her going into public under the auspices of a
friend of Mrs. Elton's, probably some vulgar, dashing widow, who,
with the help of a boarder, just made a shift to live!—The dignity of
Miss Woodhouse, of Hartfield, was sunk indeed!

She restrained herself, however, from any of the reproofs she could
have given, and only thanked Mrs. Elton coolly; "but their going to
Bath was quite out of the question; and she was not perfectly convinced that the place might suit her better than her father." And
then, to prevent further outrage and indignation, changed the subject directly:

"I do not ask whether you are musical, Mrs. Elton. Upon these
occasions, a lady's character generally precedes her; and Highbury
has long known that you are a superior performer."

"Oh! no, indeed; I must protest against any such idea. A superior
performer!—very far from it, I assure you. Consider from how partial
a quarter your information came. I am doatingly fond of music—
passionately fond;—and my friends say I am not entirely devoid of
taste; but as to any thing else, upon my honour my performance is
mediocre to the last degree. You, Miss Woodhouse, I well know, play
delightfully. I assure you it has been the greatest satisfaction, comfort, and delight to me, to hear what a musical society I am got into.
I absolutely cannot do without music. It is a necessary of life to me;
and having always been used to a very musical society, both at Maple
Grove and in Bath, it would have been a most serious sacrifice. I
honestly said as much to Mr. E. when he was speaking of my future
home, and expressing his fears lest the retirement of it should be
disagreeable; and the inferiority of the house too—knowing what
I had been accustomed to—of course he was not wholly without
apprehension. When he was speaking of it in that way, I honestly said
that *the world* I could give up—parties, balls, plays—for I had no fear
of retirement. Blessed with so many resources within myself, the
world was not necessary to *me*. I could do very well without it. To
those who had no resources it was a different thing; but my resources
made me quite independent. And as to smaller-sized rooms than I
had been used to, I really could not give it a thought. I hoped I was
perfectly equal to any sacrifice of that description. Certainly I had
been accustomed to every luxury at Maple Grove; but I did assure
him that two carriages were not necessary to my happiness, nor were
spacious apartments. 'But,' said I, 'to be quite honest, I do not think
I can live without something of a musical society. I condition for
nothing else; but without music, life would be a blank to me.'"

"We cannot suppose," said Emma, smiling, "that Mr. Elton would
hesitate to assure you of there being a *very* musical society in Highbury; and I hope you will not find he has outstepped the truth more
than may be pardoned, in consideration of the motive."

"No, indeed, I have no doubts at all on that head. I am delighted to find myself in such a circle. I hope we shall have many sweet little concerts together. I think, Miss Woodhouse, you and I must establish a musical club, and have regular weekly meetings at your house, or ours. Will not it be a good plan? If *we* exert ourselves, I think we shall not be long in want of allies. Something of that nature would be desirable for *me*, as an inducement to keep me in practice; for married women, you know—there is a sad story against them, in general. They are but too apt to give up music."

"But you, who are so extremely fond of it—there can be no danger, surely."

"I should hope not; but really when I look round among my acquaintance, I tremble. Selina has entirely given up music—never touches the instrument—though she played sweetly. And the same may be said of Mrs. Jeffreys—Clara Partridge, that was—and of the two Milmans, now Mrs. Bird and Mrs. James Cooper; and of more than I can enumerate. Upon my word it is enough to put one in a fright. I used to be quite angry with Selina; but really I begin now to comprehend that a married woman has many things to call her attention. I believe I was half an hour this morning shut up with my housekeeper."

"But every thing of that kind," said Emma, "will soon be in so regular a train——"

"Well," said Mrs. Elton, laughing, "we shall see."

Emma, finding her so determined upon neglecting her music, had nothing more to say; and, after a moment's pause, Mrs. Elton chose another subject.

"We have been calling at Randalls," said she, "and found them both at home; and very pleasant people they seem to be. I like them extremely. Mr. Weston seems an excellent creature—quite a first-rate favourite with me already, I assure you. And *she* appears so truly good—there is something so motherly and kind-hearted about her, that it wins upon one directly. She was your governess, I think?"

Emma was almost too much astonished to answer; but Mrs. Elton hardly waited for the affirmative before she went on.

"Having understood as much, I was rather astonished to find her so very lady-like! But she is really quite the gentlewoman."

"Mrs. Weston's manners," said Emma, "were always particularly good. Their propriety, simplicity, and elegance, would make them the safest model for any young woman."

"And who do you think came in while we were there?"

Emma was quite at a loss. The tone implied some old acquaintance—and how could she possibly guess?

"Knightley!" continued Mrs. Elton;—"Knightley himself!—Was not it lucky?—for, not being within when he called the other day,

I had never seen him before; and of course, as so particular a friend of Mr. E.'s, I had a great curiosity. 'My friend Knightley' had been so often mentioned, that I was really impatient to see him; and I must do my cara sposo[9] the justice to say that he need not be ashamed of his friend. Knightley is quite the gentleman. I like him very much. Decidedly, I think, a very gentleman-like man."

Happily it was now time to be gone. They were off; and Emma could breathe.

"Insufferable woman!" was her immediate exclamation. "Worse than I had supposed. Absolutely insufferable! Knightley!—I could not have believed it. Knightley!—never seen him in her life before, and call him Knightley!—and discover that he is a gentleman! A little upstart, vulgar being, with her Mr. E., and her cara sposo, and her resources, and all her airs of pert pretension and under-bred finery. Actually to discover that Mr. Knightley is a gentleman! I doubt whether he will return the compliment, and discover her to be a lady. I could not have believed it! And to propose that she and I should unite to form a musical club! One would fancy we were bosom friends! And Mrs. Weston!—Astonished that the person who had brought me up should be a gentlewoman! Worse and worse. I never met with her equal. Much beyond my hopes. Harriet is disgraced by any comparison. Oh! what would Frank Churchill say to her, if he were here? How angry and how diverted he would be! Ah! there I am—thinking of him directly. Always the first person to be thought of! How I catch myself out! Frank Churchill comes as regularly into my mind!"——

All this ran so glibly through her thoughts, that by the time her father had arranged himself, after the bustle of the Eltons' departure, and was ready to speak, she was very tolerably capable of attending.

"Well, my dear," he deliberately began, "considering we never saw her before, she seems a very pretty sort of young lady; and I dare say she was very much pleased with you. She speaks a little too quick. A little quickness of voice there is which rather hurts the ear. But I believe I am nice;[1] I do not like strange voices; and nobody speaks like you and poor Miss Taylor. However, she seems a very obliging, pretty-behaved young lady, and no doubt will make him a very good wife. Though I think he had better not have married. I made the best excuses I could for not having been able to wait on[2] him and Mrs. Elton on this happy occasion; I said that I hoped I *should* in the

---

9. (Mangled) Italian for "dear husband."
1. Extremely particular.
2. Pay a visit to.

course of the summer. But I ought to have gone before. Not to wait upon a bride is very remiss. Ah! it shews what a sad invalid I am! But I do not like the corner into Vicarage-lane."

"I dare say your apologies were accepted, sir. Mr. Elton knows you."

"Yes: but a young lady—a bride—I ought to have paid my respects to her if possible. It was being very deficient."

"But, my dear papa, you are no friend to matrimony; and there-fore why should you be so anxious to pay your respects to a *bride*? It ought to be no recommendation to *you*. It is encouraging people to marry if you make so much of them."

"No, my dear, I never encouraged any body to marry, but I would always wish to pay every proper attention to a lady—and a bride, especially, is never to be neglected. More is avowedly due to *her*. A bride, you know, my dear, is always the first in company, let the oth-ers be who they may."

"Well, papa, if this is not encouragement to marry, I do not know what is. And I should never have expected you to be lending your sanction to such vanity-baits for poor young ladies."

"My dear, you do not understand me. This is a matter of mere common politeness and good-breeding, and has nothing to do with any encouragement to people to marry."

Emma had done. Her father was growing nervous, and could not understand *her*. Her mind returned to Mrs. Elton's offences, and long, very long, did they occupy her.

Chapter XV

Emma was not required, by any subsequent discovery, to retract her ill opinion of Mrs. Elton. Her observation had been pretty correct. Such as Mrs. Elton appeared to her on this second interview, such she appeared whenever they met again,—self-important, presuming, familiar, ignorant, and ill-bred. She had a little beauty and a little accomplishment, but so little judgment that she thought herself coming with superior knowledge of the world, to enliven and improve a country neighbourhood; and conceived Miss Hawkins to have held such a place in society as Mrs. Elton's consequence only could surpass.

There was no reason to suppose Mr. Elton thought at all differ-ently from his wife. He seemed not merely happy with her, but proud. He had the air of congratulating himself on having brought such a woman to Highbury, as not even Miss Woodhouse could equal; and the greater part of her new acquaintance, disposed to com-mend, or not in the habit of judging, following the lead of Miss

Bates's good-will or taking it for granted that the bride must be as clever and as agreeable as she professed herself, were very well satisfied; so that Mrs. Elton's praise passed from one mouth to another as it ought to do, unimpeded by Miss Woodhouse, who readily continued her first contribution and talked with a good grace of her being "very pleasant and very elegantly dressed."

In one respect Mrs. Elton grew even worse than she had appeared at first. Her feelings altered towards Emma.—Offended, probably, by the little encouragement which her proposals of intimacy met with, she drew back in her turn and gradually became much more cold and distant; and though the effect was agreeable, the ill-will which produced it was necessarily increasing Emma's dislike. Her manners too—and Mr. Elton's, were unpleasant towards Harriet. They were sneering and negligent. Emma hoped it must rapidly work Harriet's cure; but the sensations which could prompt such behaviour sunk them both very much.—It was not to be doubted that poor Harriet's attachment had been an offering to conjugal unreserve, and her own share in the story, under a colouring the least favourable to her and the most soothing to him, had in all likelihood been given also. She was, of course, the object of their joint dislike.—When they had nothing else to say, it must be always easy to begin abusing Miss Woodhouse; and the enmity which they dared not shew in open disrespect to her, found a broader vent in contemptuous treatment of Harriet.

Mrs. Elton took a great fancy to Jane Fairfax; and from the first. Not merely when a state of warfare with one young lady might be supposed to recommend the other, but from the very first; and she was not satisfied with expressing a natural and reasonable admiration—but without solicitation, or plea, or privilege, she must be wanting to assist and befriend her.—Before Emma had forfeited her confidence, and about the third time of their meeting, she heard all Mrs. Elton's knight-errantry on the subject.—

"Jane Fairfax is absolutely charming, Miss Woodhouse.—I quite rave about Jane Fairfax.—A sweet, interesting creature. So mild and lady-like—and with such talents!—I assure you I think she has very extraordinary talents. I do not scruple to say that she plays extremely well. I know enough of music to speak decidedly on that point. Oh! she is absolutely charming! You will laugh at my warmth—but upon my word, I talk of nothing but Jane Fairfax.—And her situation is so calculated to affect one!—Miss Woodhouse, we must exert ourselves and endeavour to do something for her. We must bring her forward. Such talents as her's must not be suffered to remain unknown.—I dare say you have heard those charming lines of the poet,

'Full many a flower is born to blush unseen,
    'And waste its fragrance on the desert air.'[3]

We must not allow them to be verified in sweet Jane Fairfax."

"I cannot think there is any danger of it," was Emma's calm answer—"and when you are better acquainted with Miss Fairfax's situation and understand what her home has been, with Col. and Mrs. Campbell, I have no idea that you will suppose her talents can be unknown."

"Oh! but dear Miss Woodhouse, she is now in such retirement, such obscurity, so thrown away.—Whatever advantages she may have enjoyed with the Campbells are so palpably at an end! And I think she feels it. I am sure she does. She is very timid and silent. One can see that she feels the want of encouragement. I like her the better for it. I must confess it is a recommendation to me. I am a great advocate for timidity—and I am sure one does not often meet with it.—But in those who are at all inferior, it is extremely prepossessing. Oh! I assure you, Jane Fairfax is a very delightful character, and interests me more than I can express."

"You appear to feel a great deal—but I am not aware how you or any of Miss Fairfax's acquaintance here, any of those who have known her longer than yourself, can shew her any other attention than"——

"My dear Miss Woodhouse, a vast deal may be done by those who dare to act. You and I need not be afraid. If *we* set the example, many will follow it as far as they can; though all have not our situations. *We* have carriages to fetch and convey her home, and *we* live in a style which could not make the addition of Jane Fairfax, at any time, the least inconvenient.—I should be extremely displeased if Wright were to send us up such a dinner, as could make me regret having asked *more* than Jane Fairfax to partake of it. I have no idea of that sort of thing. It is not likely that I *should*, considering what I have been used to. My greatest danger, perhaps, in housekeeping, may be quite the other way, in doing too much, and being too careless of expense. Maple Grove will probably be my model more than it ought to be—for we do not at all affect to equal my brother, Mr. Suckling,[4] in income.—However, my resolution is taken as to noticing Jane Fairfax.—I shall certainly have her very often at my house, shall introduce her wherever I can, shall have musical parties to draw out her talents, and shall be constantly on the watch for an eligible situation. My acquaintance is so very extensive, that I have

3. From Thomas Gray's "Elegy Written in a Country Church-yard," which has "sweetness" for "fragrance." The misquotation may have been a lapse on Jane Austen's part, as it occurs again in *Northanger Abbey* in the author's voice.
4. I.e., brother-in-law.

little doubt of hearing of something to suit her shortly.—I shall introduce her, of course, very particularly to my brother and sister when they come to us. I am sure they will like her extremely; and when she gets a little acquainted with them, her fears will completely wear off, for there really is nothing in the manners of either but what is highly conciliating.—I shall have her very often indeed while they are with me, and I dare say we shall sometimes find a seat for her in the barouche-landau in some of our exploring parties."

"Poor Jane Fairfax!"—thought Emma.—"You have not deserved this. You may have done wrong with regard to Mr. Dixon, but this is a punishment beyond what you can have merited!—The kindness and protection of Mrs. Elton!—'Jane Fairfax and Jane Fairfax.' Heavens! Let me not suppose that she dares go about, Emma Woodhouse-ing me!—But upon my honour, there seem no limits to the licentiousness of that woman's tongue!"

Emma had not to listen to such paradings again—to any so exclusively addressed to herself—so disgustingly decorated with a "dear Miss Woodhouse." The change on Mrs. Elton's side soon afterwards appeared, and she was left in peace—neither forced to be the very particular friend of Mrs. Elton, nor, under Mrs. Elton's guidance, the very active patroness of Jane Fairfax, and only sharing with others in a general way, in knowing what was felt, what was meditated, what was done.

She looked on with some amusement.—Miss Bates's gratitude for Mrs. Elton's attentions to Jane was in the first style of guileless simplicity and warmth. She was quite one of her worthies—the most amiable, affable, delightful woman—just as accomplished and condescending as Mrs. Elton meant to be considered. Emma's only surprize was that Jane Fairfax should accept those attentions and tolerate Mrs. Elton as she seemed to do. She heard of her walking with the Eltons, sitting with the Eltons, spending a day with the Eltons! This was astonishing!—She could not have believed it possible that the taste or the pride of Miss Fairfax could endure such society and friendship as the Vicarage had to offer.

"She is a riddle, quite a riddle!" said she.—"To chuse to remain here month after month, under privations of every sort! And now to chuse the mortification of Mrs. Elton's notice and the penury of her conversation, rather than return to the superior companions who have always loved her with such real, generous affection."

Jane had come to Highbury professedly for three months; the Campbells were gone to Ireland for three months; but now the Campbells had promised their daughter to stay at least till Midsummer,[5] and fresh invitations had arrived for her to join them there. Accord-

5. About June 21.

ing to Miss Bates—it all came from her—Mrs. Dixon had written most pressingly. Would Jane but go, means were to be found, servants sent, friends contrived—no travelling difficulty allowed to exist; but still she had declined it!

"She must have some motive, more powerful than appears, for refusing this invitation," was Emma's conclusion. "She must be under some sort of penance, inflicted either by the Campbells or herself. There is great fear, great caution, great resolution somewhere.— She is *not* to be with the *Dixons*. The decree is issued by somebody. But why must she consent to be with the Eltons?—Here is quite a separate puzzle."

Upon her speaking her wonder aloud on that part of the subject, before the few who knew her opinion of Mrs. Elton, Mrs. Weston ventured this apology for Jane.

"We cannot suppose that she has any great enjoyment at the Vicarage, my dear Emma—but it is better than being always at home. Her aunt is a good creature, but, as a constant companion, must be very tiresome. We must consider what Miss Fairfax quits, before we condemn her taste for what she goes to."

"You are right, Mrs. Weston," said Mr. Knightley warmly, "Miss Fairfax is as capable as any of us of forming a just opinion of Mrs. Elton. Could she have chosen with whom to associate, she would not have chosen her. But (with a reproachful smile at Emma) she receives attentions from Mrs. Elton, which nobody else pays her."

Emma felt that Mrs. Weston was giving her a momentary glance; and she was herself struck by his warmth. With a faint blush, she presently replied,

"Such attentions as Mrs. Elton's, I should have imagined, would rather disgust than gratify Miss Fairfax. Mrs. Elton's invitations I should have imagined any thing but inviting."

"I should not wonder," said Mrs. Weston, "if Miss Fairfax were to have been drawn on beyond her own inclination, by her aunt's eagerness in accepting Mrs. Elton's civilities for her. Poor Miss Bates may very likely have committed her niece and hurried her into a greater appearance of intimacy than her own good sense would have dictated, in spite of the very natural wish of a little change."

Both felt rather anxious to hear him speak again; and after a few minutes silence, he said,

"Another thing must be taken into consideration too—Mrs. Elton does not talk *to* Miss Fairfax as she speaks *of* her. We all know the difference between the pronouns he or she and thou, the plainest-spoken amongst us; we all feel the influence of a something beyond common civility in our personal intercourse with each other—a something more early implanted. We cannot give any body the disagreeable hints that we may have been very full of the hour before.

We feel things differently. And besides the operation of this, as a general principle, you may be sure that Miss Fairfax awes Mrs. Elton by her superiority both of mind and manner; and that face to face Mrs. Elton treats her with all the respect which she has a claim to. Such a woman as Jane Fairfax probably never fell in Mrs. Elton's way before—and no degree of vanity can prevent her acknowledging her own comparative littleness in action, if not in consciousness."

"I know how highly you think of Jane Fairfax," said Emma. Little Henry was in her thoughts, and a mixture of alarm and delicacy made her irresolute what else to say.

"Yes," he replied, "any body may know how highly I think of her."

"And yet," said Emma, beginning hastily and with an arch look, but soon stopping—it was better, however, to know the worst at once—she hurried on—"And yet, perhaps, you may hardly be aware yourself how highly it is. The extent of your admiration may take you by surprize some day or other."

Mr. Knightley was hard at work upon the lower buttons of his thick leather gaiters, and either the exertion of getting them together, or some other cause, brought the colour into his face as he answered,

"Oh! are you there?—But you are miserably behind-hand. Mr. Cole gave me a hint of it six weeks ago."

He stopped.—Emma felt her foot pressed by Mrs. Weston, and did not herself know what to think. In a moment he went on—

"That will never be, however, I can assure you. Miss Fairfax, I dare say, would not have me if I were to ask her—and I am very sure I shall never ask her."

Emma returned her friend's pressure with interest; and was pleased enough to exclaim,

"You are not vain, Mr. Knightley. I will say that for you."

He seemed hardly to hear her; he was thoughtful—and in a manner which shewed him not pleased, soon afterwards said,

"So you have been settling that I should marry Jane Fairfax."

"No indeed I have not. You have scolded me too much for match-making, for me to presume to take such a liberty with you. What I said just now, meant nothing. One says those sort of things, of course, without any idea of a serious meaning. Oh! no, upon my word I have not the smallest wish for your marrying Jane Fairfax or Jane any body. You would not come in and sit with us in this comfortable way, if you were married."

Mr. Knightley was thoughtful again. The result of his reverie was, "No, Emma, I do not think the extent of my admiration for her will ever take me by surprize.—I never had a thought of her in that way, I assure you." And soon afterwards, "Jane Fairfax is a very charming young woman—but not even Jane Fairfax is perfect. She has a fault. She has not the open temper which a man would wish for in a wife."

Emma could not but rejoice to hear that she had a fault. "Well," said she, "and you soon silenced Mr. Cole, I suppose?"[6]

"Yes, very soon. He gave me a quiet hint; I told him he was mistaken; he asked my pardon and said no more. Cole does not want to be wiser or wittier than his neighbours."

"In that respect how unlike dear Mrs. Elton, who wants to be wiser and wittier than all the world! I wonder how she speaks of the Coles—what she calls them! How can she find any appellation for them, deep enough in familiar vulgarity? She calls you, Knightley—what can she do for Mr. Cole? And so I am not to be surprised that Jane Fairfax accepts her civilities and consents to be with her. Mrs. Weston, your argument weighs most with me. I can much more readily enter into the temptation of getting away from Miss Bates, than I can believe in the triumph of Miss Fairfax's mind over Mrs. Elton. I have no faith in Mrs. Elton's acknowledging herself the inferior in thought, word, or deed; or in her being under any restraint beyond her own scanty rule of good-breeding. I cannot imagine that she will not be continually insulting her visitor with praise, encouragement, and offers of service; that she will not be continually detailing her magnificent intentions, from the procuring her a permanent situation to the including her in those delightful exploring parties which are to take place in the barouche-landau."

"Jane Fairfax has feeling," said Mr. Knightley—"I do not accuse her of want of feeling. Her sensibilities, I suspect, are strong—and her temper excellent in its power of forbearance, patience, self-controul; but it wants openness. She is reserved, more reserved, I think, than she used to be—And I love an open temper. No—till Cole alluded to my supposed attachment, it had never entered my head. I saw Jane Fairfax and conversed with her, with admiration and pleasure always—but with no thought beyond."

"Well, Mrs. Weston," said Emma triumphantly when he left them, "what do you say now to Mr. Knightley's marrying Jane Fairfax?"

"Why really, dear Emma, I say that he is so very much occupied by the idea of *not* being in love with her, that I should not wonder if it were to end in his being so at last. Do not beat me."

Chapter XVI

Every body in and about Highbury who had ever visited Mr. Elton, was disposed to pay him attention on his marriage. Dinner-parties and evening-parties were made for him and his lady; and invitations

---

6. 1816 has "supposed," obviously an error.

flowed in so fast that she had soon the pleasure of apprehending they were never to have a disengaged day.

"I see how it is," said she. "I see what a life I am to lead among you. Upon my word we shall be absolutely dissipated. We really seem quite the fashion. If this is living in the country, it is nothing very formidable. From Monday next to Saturday, I assure you we have not a disengaged day!—A woman with fewer resources than I have, need not have been at a loss."

No invitation came amiss to her. Her Bath habits made evening-parties perfectly natural to her, and Maple Grove had given her a taste for dinners. She was a little shocked at the want of two drawing rooms, at the poor attempt at rout-cakes,[7] and there being no ice in the Highbury card parties. Mrs. Bates, Mrs. Perry, Mrs. Goddard and others, were a good deal behind hand in knowledge of the world, but *she* would soon shew them how every thing ought to be arranged. In the course of the spring she must return their civilities by one very superior party—in which her card tables should be set out with their separate candles and unbroken packs in the true style—and more waiters engaged for the evening than their own establishment could furnish, to carry round the refreshments at exactly the proper hour, and in the proper order.

Emma, in the meanwhile, could not be satisfied without a dinner at Hartfield for the Eltons. They must not do less than others, or she should be exposed to odious suspicions, and imagined capable of pitiful resentment. A dinner there must be. After Emma had talked about it for ten minutes, Mr. Woodhouse felt no unwillingness, and only made the usual stipulation of not sitting at the bottom of the table himself, with the usual regular difficulty of deciding who should do it for him.

The persons to be invited, required little thought. Besides the Eltons, it must be the Westons and Mr. Knightley; so far it was all of course—and it was hardly less inevitable that poor little Harriet must be asked to make the eighth:—but this invitation was not given with equal satisfaction, and on many accounts Emma was particularly pleased by Harriet's begging to be allowed to decline it. "She would rather not be in *his* company more than she could help. She was not yet quite able to see him and his charming happy wife together, without feeling uncomfortable. If Miss Woodhouse would not be displeased, she would rather stay at home." It was precisely what Emma would have wished, had she deemed it possible enough for wishing. She was delighted with the fortitude of her little friend—for fortitude she knew it was in her to give up being in company and stay at home; and she could now invite the very person

7. Rich little cakes for entertaining.

whom she really wanted to make the eighth, Jane Fairfax.—Since her last conversation with Mrs. Weston and Mr. Knightley, she was more conscience-stricken about Jane Fairfax than she had often been.—Mr. Knightley's words dwelt with her. He had said that Jane Fairfax received attentions from Mrs. Elton which nobody else paid her.

"This is very true," said she, "at least as far as relates to me, which was all that was meant—and it is very shameful.—Of the same age—and always knowing her—I ought to have been more her friend.—She will never like me now. I have neglected her too long. But I will shew her greater attention than I have done."

Every invitation was successful. They were all disengaged and all happy.—The preparatory interest of this dinner, however, was not yet over. A circumstance rather unlucky occurred. The two eldest little Knightleys were engaged to pay their grandpapa and aunt a visit of some weeks in the spring, and their papa now proposed bringing them, and staying one whole day at Hartfield—which one day would be the very day of this party.—His professional engagements did not allow of his being put off, but both father and daughter were disturbed by its happening so. Mr. Woodhouse considered eight persons at dinner together as the utmost that his nerves could bear—and here would be a ninth—and Emma apprehended that it would be a ninth very much out of humour at not being able to come even to Hartfield for forty-eight hours without falling in with a dinner-party.

She comforted her father better than she could comfort herself, by representing that though he certainly would make them nine, yet he always said so little, that the increase of noise would be very immaterial. She thought it in reality a sad exchange for herself, to have him with his grave looks and reluctant conversation opposed to her instead of his brother.

The event was more favourable to Mr. Woodhouse than to Emma. John Knightley came; but Mr. Weston was unexpectedly summoned to town and must be absent on the very day. He might be able to join them in the evening, but certainly not to dinner. Mr. Woodhouse was quite at ease; and the seeing him so, with the arrival of the little boys and the philosophic composure of her brother on hearing his fate, removed the chief of even Emma's vexation.

The day came, the party were punctually assembled, and Mr. John Knightley seemed early to devote himself to the business of being agreeable. Instead of drawing his brother off to a window while they waited for dinner, he was talking to Miss Fairfax. Mrs. Elton, as elegant as lace and pearls could make her, he looked at in silence—wanting only to observe enough for Isabella's information—but Miss Fairfax was an old acquaintance and a quiet girl, and he could talk to her. He had met her before breakfast as he was returning from a walk with his little boys, when it had been just beginning to rain. It was natural to have some civil hopes on the subject, and he said,

"I hope you did not venture far, Miss Fairfax, this morning, or I am sure you must have been wet.—*We* scarcely got home in time. I hope you turned directly."

"I went only to the post-office," said she, "and reached home before the rain was much. It is my daily errand. I always fetch the letters when I am here. It saves trouble, and is a something to get me out. A walk before breakfast does me good."

"Not a walk in the rain, I should imagine."

"No, but it did not absolutely rain when I set out."

Mr. John Knightley smiled, and replied,

"That is to say, you chose to have your walk, for you were not six yards from your own door when I had the pleasure of meeting you; and Henry and John had seen more drops than they could count long before. The post-office has a great charm at one period of our lives. When you have lived to my age, you will begin to think letters are never worth going through the rain for."

There was a little blush, and then this answer,

"I must not hope to be ever situated as you are, in the midst of every dearest connection, and therefore I cannot expect that simply growing older should make me indifferent about letters."

"Indifferent! Oh! no—I never conceived you could become indifferent. Letters are no matter of indifference; they are generally a very positive curse."

"You are speaking of letters of business; mine are letters of friendship."

"I have often thought them the worst of the two," replied he coolly. "Business, you know, may bring money, but friendship hardly ever does."

"Ah! you are not serious now. I know Mr. John Knightley too well—I am very sure he understands the value of friendship as well as any body. I can easily believe that letters are very little to you, much less than to me, but it is not your being ten years older than myself which makes the difference, it is not age, but situation. You have every body dearest to you always at hand, I, probably, never shall again; and therefore till I have outlived all my affections, a post-office, I think, must always have power to draw me out, in worse weather than to-day."

"When I talked of your being altered by time, by the progress of years," said John Knightley, "I meant to imply the change of situation which time usually brings. I consider one as including the other. Time will generally lessen the interest of every attachment not within the daily circle—but that is not the change I had in view for you. As an old friend, you will allow me to hope, Miss Fairfax, that ten years hence you may have as many concentrated objects as I have."

It was kindly said, and very far from giving offence. A pleasant "thank you" seemed meant to laugh it off, but a blush, a quivering lip, a tear in the eye, shewed that it was felt beyond a laugh. Her attention was now claimed by Mr. Woodhouse, who being, according to his custom on such occasions, making the circle of his guests, and paying his particular compliments to the ladies, was ending with her—and with all his mildest urbanity, said,

"I am very sorry to hear, Miss Fairfax, of your being out this morning in the rain. Young ladies should take care of themselves.—Young ladies are delicate plants. They should take care of their health and their complexion. My dear, did you change your stockings?"

"Yes, sir, I did indeed; and I am very much obliged by your kind solicitude about me."

"My dear Miss Fairfax, young ladies are very sure to be cared for.—I hope your good grandmamma and aunt are well. They are some of my very old friends. I wish my health allowed me to be a better neighbour. You do us a great deal of honour to-day, I am sure. My daughter and I are both highly sensible of your goodness, and have the greatest satisfaction in seeing you at Hartfield."

The kind-hearted, polite old man might then sit down and feel that he had done his duty, and made every fair lady welcome and easy.

By this time, the walk in the rain had reached Mrs. Elton, and her remonstrances now opened upon Jane.

"My dear Jane, what is this I hear?—Going to the post-office in the rain!—This must not be, I assure you.—You sad girl, how could you do such a thing?—It is a sign I was not there to take care of you."

Jane very patiently assured her that she had not caught any cold.

"Oh! do not tell *me*. You really are a very sad girl, and do not know how to take care of yourself.—To the post-office indeed! Mrs. Weston, did you ever hear the like? You and I must positively exert our authority."

"My advice," said Mrs. Weston kindly and persuasively, "I certainly do feel tempted to give. Miss Fairfax, you must not run such risks.—Liable as you have been to severe colds, indeed you ought to be particularly careful, especially at this time of year. The spring I always think requires more than common care. Better wait an hour or two, or even half a day for your letters, than run the risk of bringing on your cough again. Now do not you feel that you had? Yes, I am sure you are much too reasonable. You look as if you would not do such a thing again."

"Oh! she *shall not* do such a thing again," eagerly rejoined Mrs. Elton. "We will not allow her to do such a thing again:"—and nodding significantly—"there must be some arrangement made, there must indeed. I shall speak to Mr. E. The man who fetches our letters every morning (one of our men, I forget his name) shall inquire for your's too and bring them to you. That will obviate all difficulties you know; and from *us* I really think, my dear Jane, you can have no scruple to accept such an accommodation."

"You are extremely kind," said Jane; "but I cannot give up my early walk. I am advised to be out of doors as much as I can, I must walk somewhere, and the post-office is an object; and upon my word, I have scarcely ever had a bad morning before."

"My dear Jane, say no more about it. The thing is determined, that is (laughing affectedly) as far as I can presume to determine any thing without the concurrence of my lord and master. You know, Mrs. Weston, you and I must be cautious how we express ourselves. But I do flatter myself, my dear Jane, that my influence is not entirely worn out. If I meet with no insuperable difficulties therefore, consider that point as settled."

"Excuse me," said Jane earnestly, "I cannot by any means consent to such an arrangement, so needlessly troublesome to your servant. If the errand were not a pleasure to me, it could be done, as it always is when I am not here, by my grandmamma's."

"Oh! my dear; but so much as Patty has to do!—And it is a kindness to employ our men."

Jane looked as if she did not mean to be conquered; but instead of answering, she began speaking again to Mr. John Knightley.

"The post-office is a wonderful establishment!" said she.—"The regularity and dispatch of it! If one thinks of all that it has to do, and all that it does so well, it is really astonishing!"

"It is certainly very well regulated."

"So seldom that any negligence or blunder appears! So seldom that a letter, among the thousands that are constantly passing about the kingdom, is even carried wrong—and not one in a million, I suppose, actually lost! And when one considers the variety of hands, and of bad hands too, that are to be deciphered, it increases the wonder!"

"The clerks grow expert from habit.—They must begin with some quickness of sight and hand, and exercise improves them. If you want any further explanation," continued he, smiling, "they are paid for it. That is the key to a great deal of capacity. The public pays and must be served well."

The varieties of hand-writing were farther talked of, and the usual observations made.

"I have heard it asserted," said John Knightley, "that the same sort of hand-writing often prevails in a family; and where the same master teaches, it is natural enough. But for that reason, I should imagine the likeness must be chiefly confined to the females, for boys have very little teaching after an early age, and scramble into any hand they can get. Isabella and Emma, I think, do write very much alike. I have not always known their writing apart."

"Yes," said his brother hesitatingly, "there is a likeness. I know what you mean—but Emma's hand is the strongest."

"Isabella and Emma both write beautifully," said Mr. Woodhouse; "and always did. And so does poor Mrs. Weston"—with half a sigh and half a smile at her.

"I never saw any gentleman's handwriting"—Emma began, looking also at Mrs. Weston; but stopped, on perceiving that Mrs. Weston was attending to some one else—and the pause gave her time to reflect, "Now, how am I going to introduce him?—Am I unequal to speaking his name at once before all these people? Is it necessary for me to use any roundabout phrase?—Your Yorkshire friend—your correspondent in Yorkshire;—that would be the way, I suppose, if I were very bad.—No, I can pronounce his name without the smallest distress. I certainly get better and better.—Now for it."

Mrs. Weston was disengaged and Emma began again—"Mr. Frank Churchill writes one of the best gentlemen's hands I ever saw."

"I do not admire it," said Mr. Knightley. "It is too small—wants strength. It is like a woman's writing."

This was not submitted to by either lady. They vindicated him against the base aspersion. "No, it by no means wanted strength—it was not a large hand, but very clear and certainly strong. Had not Mrs. Weston any letter about her to produce?" No, she had heard from him very lately, but having answered the letter, had put it away.

"If we were in the other room," said Emma, "if I had my writing-desk, I am sure I could produce a specimen. I have a note of his.—Do not you remember, Mrs. Weston, employing him to write for you one day?"

"He chose to say he was employed"——

"Well, well, I have that note; and can shew it after dinner to convince Mr. Knightley."

"Oh! when a gallant young man, like Mr. Frank Churchill," said Mr. Knightley drily, "writes to a fair lady like Miss Woodhouse, he will, of course, put forth his best."

Dinner was on table.—Mrs. Elton, before she could be spoken to, was ready; and before Mr. Woodhouse had reached her with his request to be allowed to hand her into the dining-parlour, was saying—

"Must I go first? I really am ashamed of always leading the way."

Jane's solicitude about fetching her own letters had not escaped Emma. She had heard and seen it all; and felt some curiosity to know whether the wet walk of this morning had produced any. She suspected that it *had*; that it would not have been so resolutely encountered but in full expectation of hearing from some one very dear, and that it had not been in vain. She thought there was an air of greater happiness than usual—a glow both of complexion and spirits.

She could have made an inquiry or two, as to the expedition and the expense of the Irish mails;—it was at her tongue's end—but she abstained. She was quite determined not to utter a word that should hurt Jane Fairfax's feelings; and they followed the other ladies out of the room, arm in arm, with an appearance of good-will highly becoming to the beauty and grace of each.

Chapter XVII

When the ladies returned to the drawing-room after dinner, Emma found it hardly possible to prevent their making two distinct parties;—with so much perseverance in judging and behaving ill did Mrs. Elton engross Jane Fairfax and slight herself. She and Mrs. Weston were obliged to be almost always either talking together or silent together. Mrs. Elton left them no choice. If Jane repressed her for a little time, she soon began again; and though much that passed between them was in a half-whisper, especially on Mrs. Elton's side, there was no avoiding a knowledge of their principal subjects:—The post-office—catching cold—fetching letters—and friendship, were long under discussion; and to them succeeded one, which must be at least equally unpleasant to Jane—inquiries whether she had yet heard of any situation likely to suit her, and professions of Mrs. Elton's meditated activity.

"Here is April come!" said she, "I get quite anxious about you. June will soon be here."

"But I have never fixed on June or any other month—merely looked forward to the summer in general."

"But have you really heard of nothing?"

"I have not even made an inquiry; I do not wish to make any yet."

"Oh! my dear, we cannot begin too early; you are not aware of the difficulty of procuring exactly the desirable thing."

"I not aware!" said Jane, shaking her head; "dear Mrs. Elton, who can have thought of it as I have done?"

"But you have not seen so much of the world as I have. You do not know how many candidates there always are for the *first* situations. I saw a vast deal of that in the neighbourhood round Maple Grove. A cousin of Mr. Suckling, Mrs. Bragge, had such an infinity of applications; every body was anxious to be in her family, for she moves in the first circle. Wax-candles in the school-room![8] You may imagine how

---

8. Wax candles were more expensive—and had a less offensive odor—than the more common tallow candles.

desirable! Of all houses in the kingdom, Mrs. Bragge's is the one I would most wish to see you in."

"Col. and Mrs. Campbell are to be in town again by midsummer," said Jane. "I must spend some time with them; I am sure they will want it;—afterwards I may probably be glad to dispose of myself. But I would not wish you to take the trouble of making any inquiries at present."

"Trouble! aye, I know your scruples. You are afraid of giving me trouble; but I assure you, my dear Jane, the Campbells can hardly be more interested about you than I am. I shall write to Mrs. Partridge in a day or two, and shall give her a strict charge to be on the look-out for any thing eligible."

"Thank you, but I would rather you did not mention the subject to her; till the time draws nearer, I do not wish to be giving any body trouble."

"But, my dear child, the time *is* drawing near; here is April, and June, or say even July, is very near, with such business to accomplish before us. Your inexperience really amuses me! A situation such as you deserve, and your friends would require for you, is no every day occurrence, is not obtained at a moment's notice; indeed, indeed, we must begin inquiring directly."

"Excuse me, ma'am, but this is by no means my intention; I make no inquiry myself, and should be sorry to have any made by my friends. When I am quite determined as to the time, I am not at all afraid of being long unemployed. There are places in town, offices, where inquiry would soon produce something—Offices for the sale—not quite of human flesh—but of human intellect."

"Oh! my dear, human flesh! You quite shock me; if you mean a fling at the slave-trade, I assure you Mr. Suckling was always rather a friend to the abolition."

"I did not mean, I was not thinking of the slave-trade," replied Jane; "governess-trade, I assure you, was all that I had in view; widely different certainly as to the guilt of those who carry it on; but as to the greater misery of the victims, I do not know where it lies. But I only mean to say that there are advertising offices, and that by applying to them I should have no doubt of very soon meeting with something that would do."

"Something that would do!" repeated Mrs. Elton. "Aye, *that* may suit your humble ideas of yourself;—I know what a modest creature you are; but it will not satisfy your friends to have you taking up with any thing that may offer, any inferior, commonplace situation, in a family not moving in a certain circle, or able to command the elegancies of life."

"You are very obliging; but as to all that, I am very indifferent; it would be no object to me to be with the rich; my mortifications, I think, would only be the greater; I should suffer more from comparison. A gentleman's family is all that I should condition for."

"I know you, I know you; you would take up with any thing; but I shall be a little more nice, and I am sure the good Campbells will be quite on my side; with your superior talents, you have a right to move in the first circle. Your musical knowledge alone would entitle you to name your own terms, have as many rooms as you like, and mix in the family as much as you chose;—that is—I do not know—if you knew the harp, you might do all that, I am very sure; but you sing as well as play;—yes, I really believe you might, even without the harp, stipulate for what you chose;—and you must and shall be delightfully, honourably and comfortably settled before the Campbells or I have any rest."

"You may well class the delight, the honour, and the comfort of such a situation together," said Jane, "they are pretty sure to be equal; however, I am very serious in not wishing any thing to be attempted at present for me. I am exceedingly obliged to you, Mrs. Elton, I am obliged to any body who feels for me, but I am quite serious in wishing nothing to be done till the summer. For two or three months longer I shall remain where I am, and as I am."

"And I am quite serious too, I assure you," replied Mrs. Elton gaily, "in resolving to be always on the watch, and employing my friends to watch also, that nothing really unexceptionable may pass us."

In this style she ran on; never thoroughly stopped by any thing till Mr. Woodhouse came into the room; her vanity had then a change of object, and Emma heard her saying in the same half-whisper to Jane,

"Here comes this dear old beau of mine, I protest!—Only think of his gallantry in coming away before the other men!—what a dear creature he is;—I assure you I like him excessively. I admire all that quaint, old-fashioned politeness; it is much more to my taste than modern ease; modern ease often disgusts me. But this good old Mr. Woodhouse, I wish you had heard his gallant speeches to me at dinner. Oh! I assure you I began to think my cara sposa[9] would be absolutely jealous. I fancy I am rather a favourite; he took notice of my gown. How do you like it?—Selina's choice—handsome, I think, but I do not know whether it is not over-trimmed; I have the greatest dislike to the idea of being over-trimmed—quite a horror of finery. I must put on a few ornaments *now*, because it is expected of me. A bride, you know, must appear like a bride, but my natural taste is all for simplicity; a simple style of dress is so infinitely preferable to finery. But I am quite in the minority, I believe; few people seem to value simplicity of dress,—shew and finery are every thing.

9. See p. 192, n. 9.

I have some notion of putting such a trimming as this to my white and silver poplin. Do you think it will look well?"

The whole party were but just reassembled in the drawing-room when Mr. Weston made his appearance among them. He had returned to a late dinner, and walked to Hartfield as soon as it was over. He had been too much expected by the best judges, for surprize—but there was great joy. Mr. Woodhouse was almost as glad to see him now, as he would have been sorry to see him before. John Knightley only was in mute astonishment.—That a man who might have spent his evening quietly at home after a day of business in London, should set off again, and walk half-a-mile to another man's house, for the sake of being in mixed company till bed-time, of finishing his day in the efforts of civility and the noise of numbers, was a circumstance to strike him deeply. A man who had been in motion since eight o'clock in the morning, and might now have been still, who had been long talking, and might have been silent, who had been in more than one crowd, and might have been alone!—Such a man, to quit the tranquillity and independence of his own fire-side, and on the evening of a cold sleety April day rush out again into the world!—Could he by a touch of his finger have instantly taken back his wife, there would have been a motive; but his coming would probably prolong rather than break up the party. John Knightley looked at him with amazement, then shrugged his shoulders, and said, "I could not have believed it even of *him*."

Mr. Weston meanwhile, perfectly unsuspicious of the indignation he was exciting, happy and cheerful as usual, and with all the right of being principal talker, which a day spent any where from home confers, was making himself agreeable among the rest; and having satisfied the inquiries of his wife as to his dinner, convincing her that none of all her careful directions to the servants had been forgotten, and spread abroad what public news he had heard, was proceeding to a family communication, which, though principally addressed to Mrs. Weston, he had not the smallest doubt of being highly interesting to every body in the room. He gave her a letter, it was from Frank, and to herself; he had met with it in his way, and had taken the liberty of opening it.

"Read it, read it," said he, "it will give you pleasure; only a few lines—will not take you long; read it to Emma."

The two ladies looked over it together; and he sat smiling and talking to them the whole time, in a voice a little subdued, but very audible to every body.

"Well, he is coming, you see; good news, I think. Well, what do you say to it?—I always told you he would be here again soon, did not I?—Anne, my dear, did not I always tell you so, and you would not believe me?—In town next week, you see—at the latest, I dare

say; for *she* is as impatient as the black gentleman[1] when any thing
is to be done; most likely they will be there to-morrow or Saturday.
As to her illness, all nothing of course. But it is an excellent thing
to have Frank among us again, so near as town. They will stay a
good while when they do come, and he will be half his time with us.
This is precisely what I wanted. Well, pretty good news, is not it?
Have you finished it? Has Emma read it all? Put it up, put it up; we
will have a good talk about it some other time, but it will not do
now. I shall only just mention the circumstance to the others in a
common way."

Mrs. Weston was most comfortably pleased on the occasion. Her
looks and words had nothing to restrain them. She was happy, she
knew she was happy, and knew she ought to be happy. Her congratulations were warm and open; but Emma could not speak so
fluently. *She* was a little occupied in weighing her own feelings, and
trying to understand the degree of her agitation, which she rather
thought was considerable.

Mr. Weston, however, too eager to be very observant, too communicative to want others to talk, was very well satisfied with what
she did say, and soon moved away to make the rest of his friends
happy by a partial communication of what the whole room must
have overheard already.

It was well that he took every body's joy for granted, or he might
not have thought either Mr. Woodhouse or Mr. Knightley particularly delighted. They were the first entitled, after Mrs. Weston and
Emma, to be made happy;—from them he would have proceeded to
Miss Fairfax, but she was so deep in conversation with John Knightley, that it would have been too positive an interruption; and finding himself close to Mrs. Elton, and her attention disengaged, he
necessarily began on the subject with her.

Chapter XVIII

"I hope I shall soon have the pleasure of introducing my son to
you," said Mr. Weston.

Mrs. Elton, very willing to suppose a particular compliment intended her by such a hope, smiled most graciously.

"You have heard of a certain Frank Churchill, I presume," he
continued—"and know him to be my son, though he does not bear
my name."

"Oh! yes, and I shall be very happy in his acquaintance. I am sure
Mr. Elton will lose no time in calling on him; and we shall both
have great pleasure in seeing him at the Vicarage."

---

1. His delicate way of saying "impatient as the devil."

"You are very obliging.—Frank will be extremely happy, I am sure.—He is to be in town next week, if not sooner. We have notice of it in a letter to-day. I met the letters in my way this morning, and seeing my son's hand, presumed to open it—though it was not directed to me—it was to Mrs. Weston. She is his principal correspondent, I assure you. I hardly ever get a letter."

"And so you absolutely opened what was directed to her! oh! Mr. Weston—(laughing affectedly) I must protest against that.—A most dangerous precedent indeed!—I beg you will not let your neighbours follow your example.—Upon my word, if this is what I am to expect, we married women must begin to exert ourselves!—Oh! Mr. Weston, I could not have believed it of you!"

"Aye, we men are sad fellows. You must take care of yourself, Mrs. Elton.—This letter tells—it is a short letter—written in a hurry, merely to give us notice—it tells us that they are all coming up to town directly, on Mrs. Churchill's account—she has not been well the whole winter, and thinks Enscombe too cold for her—so they are all to move southward without loss of time."

"Indeed!—from Yorkshire, I think. Enscombe is in Yorkshire?"

"Yes, they are about 190 miles from London. A considerable journey."

"Yes, upon my word, very considerable. Sixty-five miles farther than from Maple Grove to London. But what is distance, Mr. Weston, to people of large fortune?—You would be amazed to hear how my brother, Mr. Suckling, sometimes flies about. You will hardly believe me—but twice in one week he and Mr. Bragge went to London and back again with four horses."

"The evil of the distance from Enscombe," said Mr. Weston, "is, that Mrs. Churchill, *as we understand*, has not been able to leave the sopha for a week together. In Frank's last letter she complained, he said, of being too weak to get into her conservatory[2] without having both his arm and his uncle's! This, you know, speaks a great degree of weakness—but now she is so impatient to be in town, that she means to sleep only two nights on the road.—So Frank writes word. Certainly, delicate ladies have very extraordinary constitutions, Mrs. Elton. You must grant me that."

"No, indeed, I shall grant you nothing. I always take the part of my own sex. I do indeed. I give you notice—You will find me a formidable antagonist on that point. I always stand up for women—and I assure you, if you knew how Selina feels with respect to sleeping at an inn, you would not wonder at Mrs. Churchill's making incredible exertions to avoid it. Selina says it is quite horror to her—and I believe I have caught a little of her nicety. She always

---

2. Probably a greenhouse attached to the house.

travels with her own sheets; an excellent precaution. Does Mrs. Churchill do the same?"

"Depend upon it, Mrs. Churchill does every thing that any other fine lady ever did. Mrs. Churchill will not be second to any lady in the land for"—

Mrs. Elton eagerly interposed with,

"Oh! Mr. Weston, do not mistake me. Selina is no fine lady, I assure you. Do not run away with such an idea."

"Is not she? Then she is no rule for Mrs. Churchill, who is as thorough a fine lady as any body ever beheld."

Mrs. Elton began to think she had been wrong in disclaiming so warmly. It was by no means her object to have it believed that her sister was *not* a fine lady; perhaps there was want of spirit in the pretence of it;—and she was considering in what way she had best retract, when Mr. Weston went on.

"Mrs. Churchill is not much in my good graces, as you may suspect—but this is quite between ourselves. She is very fond of Frank, and therefore I would not speak ill of her. Besides, she is out of health now; but *that* indeed, by her own account, she has always been. I would not say so to every body, Mrs. Elton, but I have not much faith in Mrs. Churchill's illness."

"If she is really ill, why not go to Bath, Mr. Weston?—To Bath, or to Clifton?"

"She has taken it into her head that Enscombe is too cold for her. The fact is, I suppose, that she is tired of Enscombe. She has now been a longer time stationary there, than she ever was before, and she begins to want change. It is a retired place. A fine place, but very retired."

"Aye—like Maple Grove, I dare say. Nothing can stand more retired from the road than Maple Grove. Such an immense plantation all round it! You seem shut out from every thing—in the most complete retirement.—And Mrs. Churchill probably has not health of spirits like Selina to enjoy that sort of seclusion. Or, perhaps she may not have resources enough in herself to be qualified for a country life. I always say a woman cannot have too many resources—and I feel very thankful that I have so many myself as to be quite independent of society."

"Frank was here in February for a fortnight."

"So I remember to have heard. He will find an *addition* to the society of Highbury when he comes again; that is, if I may presume to call myself an addition. But perhaps he may never have heard of there being such a creature in the world."

This was too loud a call for a compliment to be passed by, and Mr. Weston, with a very good grace, immediately exclaimed,

"My dear madam! Nobody but yourself could imagine such a thing possible. Not heard of you!—I believe Mrs. Weston's letters lately have been full of very little else than Mrs. Elton."

He had done his duty and could return to his son.

"When Frank left us," continued he, "it was quite uncertain when we might see him again, which makes this day's news doubly welcome. It has been completely unexpected. That is, I always had a strong persuasion he would be here again soon, I was sure something favourable would turn up—but nobody believed me. He and Mrs. Weston were both dreadfully desponding. 'How could he contrive to come? And how could it be supposed that his uncle and aunt would spare him again?' and so forth—I always felt that something would happen in our favour; and so it has, you see. I have observed, Mrs. Elton, in the course of my life, that if things are going untowardly one month, they are sure to mend the next."

"Very true, Mr. Weston, perfectly true. It is just what I used to say to a certain gentleman in company in the days of courtship, when, because things did not go quite right, did not proceed with all the rapidity which suited his feelings, he was apt to be in despair, and exclaim that he was sure at this rate it would be *May* before Hymen's saffron robe would be put on[3] for us! Oh! the pains I have been at to dispel those gloomy ideas and give him cheerfuller views! The carriage—we had disappointments about the carriage;—one morning, I remember, he came to me quite in despair."

She was stopped by a slight fit of coughing, and Mr. Weston instantly seized the opportunity of going on.

"You were mentioning May. May is the very month which Mrs. Churchill is ordered, or has ordered herself, to spend in some warmer place than Enscombe—in short, to spend in London; so that we have the agreeable prospect of frequent visits from Frank the whole spring—precisely the season of the year which one should have chosen for it: days almost at the longest; weather genial and pleasant, always inviting one out, and never too hot for exercise. When he was here before, we made the best of it; but there was a good deal of wet, damp, cheerless weather; there always is in February, you know, and we could not do half that we intended. Now will be the time. This will be complete enjoyment; and I do not know, Mrs. Elton, whether the uncertainty of our meetings, the sort of constant expectation there will be of his coming in to-day or to-morrow, and at any hour, may not be more friendly to happiness than having him actually in the house. I think it is so. I think it is the state of mind which gives most spirit and delight. I hope you will be pleased with

3. A pretentious way of alluding to a wedding, by quoting Milton's "L'Allegro."

my son; but you must not expect a prodigy. He is generally thought a fine young man, but do not expect a prodigy. Mrs. Weston's partiality for him is very great, and, as you may suppose, most gratifying to me. She thinks nobody equal to him."

"And I assure you, Mr. Weston, I have very little doubt that my opinion will be decidedly in his favour. I have heard too much in praise of Mr. Frank Churchill.—At the same time it is fair to observe, that I am one of those who always judge for themselves, and are by no means implicitly guided by others. I give you notice that as I find your son, so I shall judge of him.—I am no flatterer."

Mr. Weston was musing.

"I hope," said he presently, "I have not been severe upon poor Mrs. Churchill. If she is ill I should be sorry to do her injustice; but there are some traits in her character which make it difficult for me to speak of her with the forbearance I could wish. You cannot be ignorant, Mrs. Elton, of my connection with the family, nor of the treatment I have met with; and, between ourselves, the whole blame of it is to be laid to her. She was the instigator. Frank's mother would never have been slighted as she was but for her. Mr. Churchill has pride; but his pride is nothing to his wife's: his is a quiet, indolent, gentlemanlike sort of pride that would harm nobody, and only make himself a little helpless and tiresome; but her pride is arrogance and insolence! And what inclines one less to bear, she has no fair pretence of family or blood. She was nobody when he married her, barely the daughter of a gentleman; but ever since her being turned into a Churchill she has out-Churchill'd them all in high and mighty claims: but in herself, I assure you, she is an upstart."

"Only think! well, that must be infinitely provoking! I have quite a horror of upstarts. Maple Grove has given me a thorough disgust to people of that sort; for there is a family in that neighbourhood who are such an annoyance to my brother and sister from the airs they give themselves! Your description of Mrs. Churchill made me think of them directly. People of the name of Tupman, very lately settled there, and encumbered with many low connections, but giving themselves immense airs, and expecting to be on a footing with the old established families. A year and a half is the very utmost that they can have lived at West Hall; and how they got their fortune nobody knows. They came from Birmingham, which is not a place to promise much, you know, Mr. Weston. One has not great hopes from Birmingham. I always say there is something direful in the sound: but nothing more is positively known of the Tupmans, though a good many things I assure you are suspected; and yet by their manners they evidently think themselves equal even to my brother, Mr. Suckling, who happens to be one of their nearest neighbours.

It is infinitely too bad. Mr. Suckling, who has been eleven years a resident at Maple Grove, and whose father had it before him—I believe, at least—I am almost sure that old Mr. Suckling had completed the purchase before his death."

They were interrupted. Tea was carrying round, and Mr. Weston, having said all that he wanted, soon took the opportunity of walking away.[4]

After tea, Mr. and Mrs. Weston, and Mr. Elton sat down with Mr. Woodhouse to cards. The remaining five were left to their own powers, and Emma doubted their getting on very well; for Mr. Knightley seemed little disposed for conversation; Mrs. Elton was wanting notice, which nobody had inclination to pay, and she was herself in a worry of spirits which would have made her prefer being silent.

Mr. John Knightley proved more talkative than his brother. He was to leave them early the next day; and he soon began with—

"Well, Emma, I do not believe I have any thing more to say about the boys; but you have your sister's letter, and every thing is down at full length there we may be sure. My charge would be much more concise than her's, and probably not much in the same spirit; all that I have to recommend being comprised in, do not spoil them, and do not physic[5] them."

"I rather hope to satisfy you both," said Emma, "for I shall do all in my power to make them happy, which will be enough for Isabella; and happiness must preclude false indulgence and physic."

"And if you find them troublesome, you must send them home again."

"That is very likely. You think so, do not you?"

"I hope I am aware that they may be too noisy for your father—or even may be some incumbrance to you, if your visiting-engagements continue to increase as much as they have done lately."

"Increase!"

"Certainly; you must be sensible that the last half year has made a great difference in your way of life."

"Difference! No indeed I am not."

"There can be no doubt of your being much more engaged with company than you used to be. Witness this very time. Here am I come down for only one day, and you are engaged with a dinner-party!—When did it happen before, or any thing like it? Your neighbourhood is increasing, and you mix more with it. A little while ago, every letter to Isabella brought an account of fresh gaieties; dinners

---

4. 1816 has "way," obviously a printer's error.
5. Dose them with medicine.

at Mr. Cole's, or balls at the Crown. The difference which Randalls, Randalls alone makes in your goings-on, is very great."

"Yes," said his brother quickly, "it is Randalls that does it all."

"Very well—and as Randalls, I suppose, is not likely to have less influence than heretofore, it strikes me as a possible thing, Emma, that Henry and John may be sometimes in the way. And if they are, I only beg you to send them home."

"No," cried Mr. Knightley, "that need not be the consequence. Let them be sent to Donwell. I shall certainly be at leisure."

"Upon my word," exclaimed Emma, "you amuse me! I should like to know how many of all my numerous engagements take place without your being of the party; and why I am to be supposed in danger of wanting leisure to attend to the little boys. These amazing engagements of mine—what have they been? Dining once with the Coles—and having a ball talked of, which never took place. I can understand you—(nodding at Mr. John Knightley)—your good fortune in meeting with so many of your friends at once here, delights you too much to pass unnoticed. But you, (turning to Mr. Knightley,) who know how very, very seldom I am ever two hours from Hartfield, why you should foresee such a series of dissipation for me, I cannot imagine. And as to my dear little boys, I must say, that if aunt Emma has not time for them, I do not think they would fare much better with uncle Knightley, who is absent from home about five hours where she is absent one—and who, when he is at home, is either reading to himself or settling his accounts."

Mr. Knightley seemed to be trying not to smile; and succeeded without difficulty, upon Mrs. Elton's beginning to talk to him.

Volume III

Chapter I

A very little quiet reflection was enough to satisfy Emma as to the nature of her agitation on hearing this news of Frank Churchill. She was soon convinced that it was not for herself she was feeling at all apprehensive or embarrassed; it was for him. Her own attachment had really subsided into a mere nothing; it was not worth thinking of;—but if he, who had undoubtedly been always so much the most in love of the two, were to be returning with the same warmth of sentiment which he had taken away, it would be very distressing. If a separation of two months should not have cooled him, there were dangers and evils before her:—caution for him and for herself would be necessary. She did not mean to have her own affections entangled again, and it would be incumbent on her to avoid any encouragement of his.

She wished she might be able to keep him from an absolute declaration. That would be so very painful a conclusion of their present acquaintance!—and yet, she could not help rather anticipating
something decisive. She felt as if the spring would not pass without
bringing a crisis, an event, a something to alter her present composed and tranquil state.

It was not very long, though rather longer than Mr. Weston had
foreseen, before she had the power of forming some opinion of
Frank Churchill's feelings. The Enscombe family were not in town
quite so soon as had been imagined, but he was at Highbury very
soon afterwards. He rode down for a couple of hours; he could not
yet do more; but as he came from Randall's immediately to Hartfield, she could then exercise all her quick observation, and speedily determine how he was influenced, and how she must act. They
met with the utmost friendliness. There could be no doubt of his
great pleasure in seeing her. But she had an almost instant doubt of
his caring for her as he had done, of his feeling the same tenderness in the same degree. She watched him well. It was a clear thing
he was less in love than he had been. Absence, with the conviction
probably of her indifference, had produced this very natural and
very desirable effect.

He was in high spirits; as ready to talk and laugh as ever, and
seemed delighted to speak of his former visit, and recur to old stories: and he was not without agitation. It was not in his calmness
that she read his comparative indifference. He was not calm; his
spirits were evidently fluttered; there was restlessness about him.
Lively as he was, it seemed a liveliness that did not satisfy himself:
but what decided her belief on the subject, was his staying only a
quarter of an hour, and hurrying away to make other calls in Highbury. "He had seen a group of old acquaintance in the street as he
passed—he had not stopped, he would not stop for more than a
word—but he had the vanity to think they would be disappointed if
he did not call, and much as he wished to stay longer at Hartfield,
he must hurry off."

She had no doubt as to his being less in love—but neither his agitated spirits, nor his hurrying away, seemed like a perfect cure; and
she was rather inclined to think it implied a dread of her returning
power, and a discreet resolution of not trusting himself with her
long.

This was the only visit from Frank Churchill in the course of ten
days. He was often hoping, intending to come—but was always
prevented. His aunt could not bear to have him leave her. Such was
his own account at Randall's. If he were quite sincere, if he really
tried to come, it was to be inferred that Mrs. Churchill's removal to
London had been of no service to the wilful or nervous part of her
disorder. That she was really ill was very certain; he had declared

himself convinced of it, at Randall's. Though much might be fancy, he could not doubt, when he looked back, that she was in a weaker state of health than she had been a half a year ago. He did not believe it to proceed from any thing that care and medicine might not remove, or at least that she might not have many years of existence before her; but he could not be prevailed on by all his father's doubts, to say that her complaints were merely imaginary, or that she was as strong as ever.

It soon appeared that London was not the place for her. She could not endure its noise. Her nerves were under continual irritation and suffering; and by the ten days' end, her nephew's letter to Randall's communicated a change of plan. They were going to remove immediately to Richmond. Mrs. Churchill had been recommended to the medical skill of an eminent person there, and had otherwise a fancy for the place. A ready-furnished house in a favourite spot was engaged, and much benefit expected from the change.

Emma heard that Frank wrote in the highest spirits of this arrangement, and seemed most fully to appreciate the blessing of having two months before him of such near neighbourhood to many dear friends—for the house was taken for May and June. She was told that now he wrote with the greatest confidence of being often with them, almost as often as he could even wish.

Emma saw how Mr. Weston understood these joyous prospects. He was considering her as the source of all the happiness they offered. She hoped it was not so. Two months must bring it to the proof.

Mr. Weston's own happiness was indisputable. He was quite delighted. It was the very circumstance he could have wished for. Now, it would be really having Frank in their neighbourhood. What were nine miles to a young man?—An hour's ride. He would be always coming over. The difference in that respect of Richmond and London was enough to make the whole difference of seeing him always and seeing him never. Sixteen miles—nay, eighteen—it must be full eighteen to Manchester-street—was a serious obstacle. Were he ever able to get away, the day would be spent in coming and returning. There was no comfort in having him in London; he might as well be at Enscombe; but Richmond was the very distance for easy intercourse. Better than nearer!

One good thing was immediately brought to a certainty by this removal,—the ball at the Crown. It had not been forgotten before, but it had been soon acknowledged vain to attempt to fix a day. Now, however, it was absolutely to be; every preparation was resumed, and very soon after the Churchills had removed to Richmond, a few lines from Frank, to say that his aunt felt already much better for the change, and that he had no doubt of being able to join them for twenty-four hours at any given time, induced them to name as early a day as possible.

Mr. Weston's ball was to be a real thing. A very few to-morrows stood between the young people of Highbury and happiness.

Mr. Woodhouse was resigned. The time of year lightened the evil to him. May was better for every thing than February. Mrs. Bates was engaged to spend the evening at Hartfield, James had due notice, and he sanguinely hoped that neither dear little Henry nor dear little John would have any thing the matter with them, while dear Emma were gone.

Chapter II

No misfortune occurred, again to prevent the ball. The day approached, the day arrived; and, after a morning of some anxious watching, Frank Churchill, in all the certainty of his own self, reached Randall's before dinner, and every thing was safe.

No second meeting had there yet been between him and Emma. The room at the Crown was to witness it;—but it would be better than a common meeting in a crowd. Mr. Weston had been so very earnest in his entreaties for her early attendance, for her arriving there as soon as possible after themselves, for the purpose of taking her opinion as to the propriety and comfort of the rooms before any other persons came, that she could not refuse him, and must therefore spend some quiet interval in the young man's company. She was to convey Harriet, and they drove to the Crown in good time, the Randalls' party just sufficiently before them.

Frank Churchill seemed to have been on the watch; and though he did not say much, his eyes declared that he meant to have a delightful evening. They all walked about together, to see that every thing was as it should be; and within a few minutes were joined by the contents of another carriage, which Emma could not hear the sound of at first, without great surprise. "So unreasonably early!" she was going to exclaim; but she presently found that it was a family of old friends, who were coming, like herself, by particular desire, to help Mr. Weston's judgement; and they were so very closely followed by another carriage of cousins, who had been entreated to come early with the same distinguishing earnestness, on the same errand, that it seemed as if half the company might soon be collected together for the purpose of preparatory inspection.

Emma perceived that her taste was not the only taste on which Mr. Weston depended, and felt, that to be the favourite and inti- mate of a man who had so many intimates and confidantes, was not the very first distinction in the scale of vanity. She liked his open manners, but a little less of open-heartedness would have made him a higher character.—General benevolence, but not general friendship, made a man what he ought to be.—She could fancy such a man.

The whole party walked about, and looked, and praised again; and then, having nothing else to do, formed a sort of half circle round the fire, to observe in their various modes, till other subjects were started, that, though *May*, a fire in the evening was still very pleasant.

Emma found that it was not Mr. Weston's fault that the number of privy counsellors was not yet larger. They had stopped at Mrs. Bates's door to offer the use of their carriage, but the aunt and niece were to be brought by the Eltons.

Frank was standing by her, but not steadily; there was a restlessness, which showed a mind not at ease. He was looking about, he was going to the door, he was watching for the sound of other carriages,—impatient to begin, or afraid of being always near her.

Mrs. Elton was spoken of. "I think she must be here soon," said he. "I have a great curiosity to see Mrs. Elton, I have heard so much of her. It cannot be long, I think, before she comes."

A carriage was heard. He was on the move immediately; but coming back, said,

"I am forgetting that I am not acquainted with her. I have never seen either Mr. or Mrs. Elton. I have no business to put myself forward."

Mr. and Mrs. Elton appeared; and all the smiles and the proprieties passed.

"But Miss Bates and Miss Fairfax!" said Mr. Weston, looking about. "We thought you were to bring them."

The mistake had been slight. The carriage was sent for them now. Emma longed to know what Frank's first opinion of Mrs. Elton might be; how he was affected by the studied elegance of her dress, and her smiles of graciousness. He was immediately qualifying himself to form an opinion, by giving her very proper attention, after the introduction had passed.

In a few minutes the carriage returned.—Somebody talked of rain.—"I will see that there are umbrellas, sir," said Frank to his father: "Miss Bates must not be forgotten:" and away he went. Mr. Weston was following; but Mrs. Elton detained him, to gratify him by her opinion of his son; and so briskly did she begin, that the young man himself, though by no means moving slowly, could hardly be out of hearing.

"A very fine young man indeed, Mr. Weston. You know I candidly told you I should form my own opinion; and I am happy to say that I am extremely pleased with him.—You may believe me. I never compliment. I think him a very handsome young man, and his manners are precisely what I like and approve—so truly the gentleman, without the least conceit or puppyism. You must know I have a vast dislike to puppies—quite a horror of them. They were never tolerated at Maple Grove. Neither Mr. Suckling nor me had ever any patience with them; and we used sometimes to say very cutting things! Selina, who is mild almost to a fault, bore with them much better."

While she talked of his son, Mr. Weston's attention was chained; but when she got to Maple Grove, he could recollect that there were ladies just arriving to be attended to, and with happy smiles must hurry away.

Mrs. Elton turned to Mrs. Weston. "I have no doubt of its being our carriage with Miss Bates and Jane. Our coachman and horses are so extremely expeditious!—I believe we drive faster than anybody.—What a pleasure it is to send one's carriage for a friend!—I understand you were so kind as to offer, but another time it will be quite unnecessary. You may be very sure I shall always take care of *them*."

Miss Bates and Miss Fairfax, escorted by the two gentlemen, walked into the room; and Mrs. Elton seemed to think it as much her duty as Mrs. Weston's to receive them. Her gestures and move-ments might be understood by any one who looked on like Emma, but her words, every body's words, were soon lost under the inces-sant flow of Miss Bates, who came in talking, and had not finished her speech under many minutes after her being admitted into the circle at the fire. As the door opened she was heard,

"So very obliging of you!—No rain at all. Nothing to signify. I do not care for myself. Quite thick shoes. And Jane declares—Well!— (as soon as she was within the door) Well! This is brilliant indeed!— This is admirable!—Excellently contrived, upon my word. Nothing wanting. Could not have imagined it.—So well lighted up.—Jane, Jane, look—did you ever see any thing? Oh! Mr. Weston, you must really have had Aladdin's lamp. Good Mrs. Stokes would not know her own room again. I saw her as I came in; she was standing in the entrance. 'Oh! Mrs. Stokes,' said I—but I had not time for more."— She was now met by Mrs. Weston.—"Very well, I thank you, ma'am. I hope you are quite well. Very happy to hear it. So afraid you might have a headach!—seeing you pass by so often, and knowing how much trouble you must have. Delighted to hear it indeed. Ah! dear Mrs. Elton, so obliged to you for the carriage!—excellent time.— Jane and I quite ready. Did not keep the horses a moment. Most comfortable carriage.—Oh! and I am sure our thanks are due to you, Mrs. Weston, on that score—Mrs. Elton had most kindly sent Jane a note, or we should have been.—But two such offers in one day!— Never were such neighbours. I said to my mother, 'Upon my word, ma'am——.' Thank you, my mother is remarkably well. Gone to

Mr. Woodhouse's. I made her take her shawl—for the evenings are
not warm—her large new shawl—Mrs. Dixon's wedding present.—So
kind of her to think of my mother! Bought at Weymouth, you
know—Mr. Dixon's choice. There were three others, Jane says,
which they hesitated about some time. Colonel Campbell rather preferred an olive. My dear Jane, are you sure you did not wet your
feet?—It was but a drop or two, but I am so afraid:—but Mr. Frank
Churchill was so extremely—and there was a mat to step upon—I
shall never forget his extreme politeness.—Oh! Mr. Frank Churchill,
I must tell you my mother's spectacles have never been in fault since;
the rivet never came out again. My mother often talks of your good-
nature. Does not she, Jane?—Do not we often talk of Mr. Frank
Churchill?—Ah! here's Miss Woodhouse.—Dear Miss Woodhouse,
how do you do?—Very well I thank you, quite well. This is meeting
quite in fairy-land!—Such a transformation!—Must not compliment,
I know—(eyeing Emma most complacently)—that would be rude—
but upon my word, Miss Woodhouse, you do look—how do you like
Jane's hair!—You are a judge.—She did it all herself. Quite wonderful how she does her hair!—No hairdresser from London I think
could.—Ah! Dr. Hughes I declare—and Mrs. Hughes. Must go and
speak to Dr. and Mrs. Hughes for a moment.—How do you do? How
do you do?—Very well, I thank you. This is delightful, is not it?—
Where's dear Mr. Richard?—Oh! there he is. Don't disturb him.
Much better employed talking to the young ladies. How do you do,
Mr. Richard?—I saw you the other day as you rode through the
town——Mrs. Otway, I protest!—and good Mr. Otway, and Miss
Otway and Miss Caroline.—Such a host of friends!—and Mr. George
and Mr. Arthur!—How do you do? How do you all do?—Quite well,
I am much obliged to you. Never better.—Don't I hear another
carriage?—Who can this be?—very likely the worthy Coles.—Upon
my word, this is charming to be standing about among such friends!
And such a noble fire!—I am quite roasted. No coffee, I thank you,
for me—never take coffee.—A little tea if you please, sir, by and
bye,—no hurry—Oh! here it comes. Every thing so good!"

Frank Churchill returned to his station by Emma; and as soon as
Miss Bates was quiet, she found herself necessarily overhearing the
discourse of Mrs. Elton and Miss Fairfax, who were standing a little
way behind her.—He was thoughtful. Whether he were overhearing
too, she could not determine. After a good many compliments to
Jane on her dress and look, compliments very quietly and properly
taken, Mrs. Elton was evidently wanting to be complimented
herself—and it was, "How do you like my gown?—How do you like
my trimming?—How has Wright done my hair?"—with many other
relative questions, all answered with patient politeness. Mrs. Elton
then said,

"Nobody can think less of dress in general than I do—but upon such an occasion as this, when everybody's eyes are so much upon me, and in compliment to the Westons—who I have no doubt are giving this ball chiefly to do me honour—I would not wish to be inferior to others. And I see very few pearls in the room except mine.—So Frank Churchill is a capital dancer, I understand.—We shall see if our styles suit.—A fine young man certainly is Frank Churchill. I like him very well."

At this moment Frank began talking so vigorously, that Emma could not but imagine he had overheard his own praises, and did not want to hear more;—and the voices of the ladies were drowned for awhile, till another suspension brought Mrs. Elton's tones again distinctly forward.—Mr. Elton had just joined them, and his wife was exclaiming,

"Oh! you have found us out at last, have you, in our seclusion?—I was this moment telling Jane, I thought you would begin to be impatient for tidings of us."

"Jane!"—repeated Frank Churchill, with a look of surprise and displeasure.—"That is easy—but Miss Fairfax does not disapprove it, I suppose."

"How do you like Mrs. Elton?" said Emma in a whisper.

"Not at all."

"You are ungrateful."

"Ungrateful!—What do you mean?" Then changing from a frown to a smile—"No, do not tell me—I do not want to know what you mean.—Where is my father?—When are we to begin dancing?"

Emma could hardly understand him; he seemed in an odd humour. He walked off to find his father, but was quickly back again with both Mr. and Mrs. Weston. He had met with them in a little perplexity, which must be laid before Emma. It had just occurred to Mrs. Weston that Mrs. Elton must be asked to begin the ball; that she would expect it; which interfered with all their wishes of giving Emma that distinction.—Emma heard the sad truth with fortitude.

"And what are we to do for a proper partner for her?" said Mr. Weston. "She will think Frank ought to ask her."

Frank turned instantly to Emma, to claim her former promise; and boasted himself an engaged man, which his father looked his most perfect approbation of—and it then appeared that Mrs. Weston was wanting *him* to dance with Mrs. Elton himself, and that their business was to help to persuade him into it, which was done pretty soon.—Mr. Weston and Mrs. Elton led the way, Mr. Frank Churchill and Miss Woodhouse followed. Emma must submit to stand second to Mrs. Elton, though she had always considered the ball as peculiarly for her. It was almost enough to make her think of marrying.

Mrs. Elton had undoubtedly the advantage, at this time, in vanity completely gratified; for though she had intended to begin with Frank Churchill, she could not lose by the change. Mr. Weston might be his son's superior.—In spite of this little rub, however, Emma was smiling with enjoyment, delighted to see the respectable length of the set as it was forming, and to feel that she had so many hours of unusual festivity before her.—She was more disturbed by Mr. Knightley's not dancing, than by any thing else.—There he was, among the standers-by, where he ought not to be; he ought to be dancing,—not classing himself with the husbands, and fathers, and whist-players, who were pretending to feel an interest in the dance till their rubbers were made up,[1]—so young as he looked!—He could not have appeared to greater advantage perhaps any where, than where he had placed himself. His tall, firm, upright figure, among the bulky forms and stooping shoulders of the elderly men, was such as Emma felt must draw every body's eyes; and, excepting her own partner, there was not one among the whole row of young men who could be compared with him.—He moved a few steps nearer, and those few steps were enough to prove in how gentle-manlike a manner, with what natural grace, he must have danced, would he but take the trouble.—Whenever she caught his eye, she forced him to smile; but in general he was looking grave. She wished he could love a ball-room better, and could like Frank Churchill better.—He seemed often observing her. She must not flatter herself that he thought of her dancing, but if he were criti-cising her behaviour, she did not feel afraid. There was nothing like flirtation between her and her partner. They seemed more like cheerful, easy friends, than lovers. That Frank Churchill thought less of her than he had done, was indubitable.

The ball proceeded pleasantly. The anxious cares, the incessant attentions of Mrs. Weston, were not thrown away. Every body seemed happy; and the praise of being a delightful ball, which is seldom bestowed till after a ball has ceased to be, was repeatedly given in the very beginning of the existence of this. Of very impor-tant, very recordable events, it was not more productive than such meetings usually are. There was one, however, which Emma thought something of.—The two last dances before supper were begun, and Harriet had no partner;—the only young lady sitting down;—and so equal had been hitherto the number of dancers, that how there could be any one disengaged was the wonder!—But Emma's wonder less-ened soon afterwards, on seeing Mr. Elton sauntering about. He would not ask Harriet to dance if it were possible to be avoided: she

---

1. Until they had the appropriate players and situation for a best-of-three match in the fashionable card game.

was sure he would not—and she was expecting him every moment to escape into the card-room.

Escape, however, was not his plan. He came to the part of the room where the sitters-by were collected, spoke to some, and walked about in front of them, as if to show his liberty, and his resolution of maintaining it. He did not omit being sometimes directly before Miss Smith, or speaking to those who were close to her.—Emma saw it. She was not yet dancing; she was working her way up from the bottom, and had therefore leisure to look around, and by only turning her head a little she saw it all. When she was half way up the set,[2] the whole group were exactly behind her, and she would no longer allow her eyes to watch; but Mr. Elton was so near, that she heard every syllable of a dialogue which just then took place between him and Mrs. Weston; and she perceived that his wife, who was standing immediately above her, was not only listening also, but even encouraging him by significant glances.—The kind-hearted, gentle Mrs. Weston had left her seat to join him and say, "Do not you dance, Mr. Elton?" to which his prompt reply was, "Most readily, Mrs. Weston, if you will dance with me."

"Me!—oh! no—I would get you a better partner than myself. I am no dancer."

"If Mrs. Gilbert wishes to dance," said he, "I shall have great pleasure, I am sure—for, though beginning to feel myself rather an old married man, and that my dancing days are over, it would give me very great pleasure at any time to stand up with an old friend like Mrs. Gilbert."

"Mrs. Gilbert does not mean to dance, but there is a young lady disengaged whom I should be very glad to see dancing—Miss Smith." "Miss Smith!—oh!—I had not observed.—You are extremely obliging—and if I were not an old married man.—But my dancing days are over, Mrs. Weston. You will excuse me. Any thing else I should be most happy to do, at your command—but my dancing days are over."

Mrs. Weston said no more; and Emma could imagine with what surprise and mortification she must be returning to her seat. This was Mr. Elton! the amiable, obliging, gentle Mr. Elton.—She looked round for a moment; he had joined Mr. Knightley at a little distance, and was arranging himself for settled conversation, while smiles of high glee passed between him and his wife.

She would not look again. Her heart was in a glow, and she feared her face might be as hot.

In another moment a happier sight caught her;—Mr. Knightley leading Harriet to the set!—Never had she been more surprised,

---

2. "Number of couples required to perform a country dance or a square dance" (*OED*).

seldom more delighted, than at that instant. She was all pleasure and gratitude, both for Harriet and herself, and longed to be thanking him; and though too distant for speech, her countenance said much, as soon as she could catch his eye again.

His dancing proved to be just what she had believed it, extremely good; and Harriet would have seemed almost too lucky, if it had not been for the cruel state of things before, and for the very complete enjoyment and very high sense of the distinction which her happy features announced. It was not thrown away on her, she bounded higher than ever, flew farther down the middle, and was in a continual course of smiles.

Mr. Elton had retreated into the card-room, looking (Emma trusted) very foolish. She did not think he was quite so hardened as his wife, though growing very like her;—*she* spoke some of her feelings, by observing audibly to her partner,

"Knightley has taken pity on poor little Miss Smith!—Very good-natured, I declare."

Supper was announced. The move began; and Miss Bates might be heard from that moment, without interruption, till her being seated at table and taking up her spoon.

"Jane, Jane, my dear Jane, where are you?—Here is your tippet.[3] Mrs. Weston begs you to put on your tippet. She says she is afraid there will be draughts in the passage, though every thing has been done—One door nailed up—Quantities of matting—My dear Jane, indeed you must. Mr. Churchill, oh! you are too obliging!—How well you put it on!—so gratified!—Excellent dancing indeed!—Yes, my dear, I ran home, as I said I should, to help grandmamma to bed, and got back again, and nobody missed me.—I set off without saying a word, just as I told you. Grandmamma was quite well, had a charming evening with Mr. Woodhouse, a vast deal of chat, and backgammon.—Tea was made down stairs, biscuits and baked apples and wine before she came away: amazing luck in some of her throws:[4] and she inquired a great deal about you, how you were amused, and who were your partners. "Oh!" said I, "I shall not forestall Jane; I left her dancing with Mr. George Otway; she will love to tell you all about it herself to-morrow: her first partner was Mr. Elton, I do not know who will ask her next, perhaps Mr. William Cox." My dear sir, you are too obliging.—Is there nobody you would not rather?—I am not helpless. Sir, you are most kind. Upon my word, Jane on one arm, and me on the other!—Stop, stop, let us stand a little back, Mrs. Elton is going; dear Mrs. Elton, how elegant she looks!—Beautiful lace!—Now we all follow in her train. Quite the queen of

3. Loose scarf or cape.
4. That is, of the dice, in backgammon.

the evening!—Well, here we are at the passage. Two steps, Jane, take care of the two steps. Oh! no, there is but one. Well, I was persuaded there were two. How very odd! I was convinced there were two, and there is but one. I never saw any thing equal to the comfort and style—Candles every where.—I was telling you of your grand-mamma, Jane,—There was a little disappointment.—The baked apples and biscuits, excellent in their way, you know; but there was a delicate fricassee of sweetbread and some asparagus brought in at first, and good Mr. Woodhouse, not thinking the asparagus quite boiled enough, sent it all out again. Now there is nothing grand-mamma loves better than sweetbread and asparagus—so she was rather disappointed, but we agreed we would not speak of it to any body, for fear of its getting round to dear Miss Woodhouse, who would be so very much concerned!—Well, this is brilliant! I am all amazement! could not have supposed any thing!—Such elegance and profusion!—I have seen nothing like it since—Well, where shall we sit? where shall we sit? Any where, so that Jane is not in a draught. Where *I* sit is of no consequence. Oh! do you recommend this side?— Well, I am sure, Mr. Churchill—only it seems too good—but just as you please. What you direct in this house cannot be wrong. Dear Jane, how shall we ever recollect half the dishes for grandmamma? Soup too! Bless me! I should not be helped so soon, but it smells most excellent, and I cannot help beginning."

Emma had no opportunity of speaking to Mr. Knightley till after supper; but, when they were all in the ball-room again, her eyes invited him irresistibly to come to her and be thanked. He was warm in his reprobation of Mr. Elton's conduct; it had been unpardonable rudeness; and Mrs. Elton's looks also received the due share of censure.

"They aimed at wounding more than Harriet," said he. "Emma, why is it that they are your enemies?"

He looked with smiling penetration; and, on receiving no answer, added, "*She* ought not to be angry with you, I suspect, whatever he may be.—To that surmise, you say nothing, of course; but confess, Emma, that you did want him to marry Harriet."

"I did," replied Emma, "and they cannot forgive me."

He shook his head; but there was a smile of indulgence with it, and he only said,

"I shall not scold you. I leave you to your own reflections."

"Can you trust me with such flatterers?—Does my vain spirit ever tell me I am wrong?"

"Not your vain spirit, but your serious spirit.—If one leads you wrong, I am sure the other tells you of it."

"I do own myself to have been completely mistaken in Mr. Elton. There is a littleness about him which you discovered, and which

I did not: and I was fully convinced of his being in love with Harriet. It was through a series of strange blunders!"

"And, in return for your acknowledging so much, I will do you the justice to say, that you would have chosen for him better than he has chosen for himself.—Harriet Smith has some first-rate qualities, which Mrs. Elton is totally without. An unpretending, single-minded, artless girl—infinitely to be preferred by any man of sense and taste to such a woman as Mrs. Elton. I found Harriet more conversable than I expected."

Emma was extremely gratified.—They were interrupted by the bustle of Mr. Weston calling on every body to begin dancing again.

"Come Miss Woodhouse, Miss Otway, Miss Fairfax, what are you all doing?—Come Emma, set your companions the example. Every body is lazy! Every body is asleep!"

"I am ready," said Emma, "whenever I am wanted."

"Whom are you going to dance with?" asked Mr. Knightley.

She hesitated a moment, and then replied, "With you, if you will ask me."

"Will you?" said he, offering his hand.

"Indeed I will. You have shown that you can dance, and you know we are not really so much brother and sister as to make it at all improper."

"Brother and sister! no, indeed."

Chapter III

This little explanation with Mr. Knightley gave Emma considerable pleasure. It was one of the agreeable recollections of the ball, which she walked about the lawn the next morning to enjoy.—She was extremely glad that they had come to so good an understanding respecting the Eltons, and that their opinions of both husband and wife were so much alike; and his praise of Harriet, his concession in her favour, was peculiarly gratifying. The impertinence of the Eltons, which for a few minutes had threatened to ruin the rest of her evening, had been the occasion of some of its highest satisfactions; and she looked forward to another happy result—the cure of Harriet's infatuation.—From Harriet's manner of speaking of the circumstances before they quitted the ball-room, she had strong hopes. It seemed as if her eyes were suddenly opened, and she were enabled to see that Mr. Elton was not the superior creature she had believed him. The fever was over, and Emma could harbour little fear of the pulse being quickened again by injurious courtesy. She depended on the evil feelings of the Eltons for supplying all the discipline of pointed neglect that could be further requisite.— Harriet rational, Frank Churchill not too much in love, and Mr.

Knightley not wanting to quarrel with her, how very happy a summer must be before her!

She was not to see Frank Churchill this morning. He had told her that he could not allow himself the pleasure of stopping at Hartfield, as he was to be at home by the middle of the day. She did not regret it.

Having arranged all these matters, looked them through, and put them all to rights, she was just turning to the house with spirits freshened up for the demands of the two little boys, as well as of their grandpapa, when the great iron sweep-gate opened, and two persons entered whom she had never less expected to see together—Frank Churchill, with Harriet leaning on his arm—actually Harriet!—A moment sufficed to convince her that something extraordinary had happened. Harriet looked white and frightened, and he was trying to cheer her.—The iron gates and the front door were not twenty yards asunder;—they were all three soon in the hall, and Harriet immediately sinking into a chair fainted away.

A young lady who faints, must be recovered; questions must be answered, and surprises be explained. Such events are very interesting, but the suspense of them cannot last long. A few minutes made Emma acquainted with the whole.

Miss Smith, and Miss Bickerton, another parlour boarder at Mrs. Goddard's, who had been also at the ball, had walked out together, and taken a road, the Richmond road, which, though apparently public enough for safety, had led them into alarm.—About half a mile beyond Highbury, making a sudden turn, and deeply shaded by elms on each side, it became for a considerable stretch very retired; and when the young ladies had advanced some way into it, they had suddenly perceived at a small distance before them, on a broader patch of greensward by the side, a party of gipsies. A child on the watch, came towards them to beg; and Miss Bickerton, excessively frightened, gave a great scream, and calling on Harriet to follow her, ran up a steep bank, cleared a slight hedge at the top, and made the best of her way by a short cut back to Highbury. But poor Harriet could not follow. She had suffered very much from cramp after dancing, and her first attempt to mount the bank brought on such a return of it as made her absolutely powerless—and in this state, and exceedingly terrified, she had been obliged to remain.

How the trampers might have behaved, had the young ladies been more courageous, must be doubtful; but such an invitation for attack could not be resisted; and Harriet was soon assailed by half a dozen children, headed by a stout woman and a great boy, all clamorous, and impertinent in look, though not absolutely in word.—More and more frightened, she immediately promised them money, and taking out her purse, gave them a shilling, and begged them not to want

more, or to use her ill.—She was then able to walk, though but
slowly, and was moving away—but her terror and her purse were too
tempting, and she was followed, or rather surrounded, by the whole
gang, demanding more.

In this state Frank Churchill had found her, she trembling and
conditioning, they loud and insolent. By a most fortunate chance
his leaving Highbury had been delayed so as to bring him to her
assistance at this critical moment. The pleasantness of the morning
had induced him to walk forward, and leave his horses to meet him
by another road, a mile or two beyond Highbury—and happening
to have borrowed a pair of scissars the night before of Miss Bates,
and to have forgotten to restore them, he had been obliged to stop
at her door, and go in for a few minutes: he was therefore later than
he had intended; and being on foot, was unseen by the whole party
till almost close to them. The terror which the woman and boy had
been creating in Harriet was then their own portion. He had left
them completely frightened; and Harriet eagerly clinging to him,
and hardly able to speak, had just strength enough to reach Hartfield, before her spirits were quite overcome. It was his idea to bring
her to Hartfield: he had thought of no other place.

This was the amount of the whole story,—of his communication
and of Harriet's as soon as she had recovered her senses and
speech.—He dared not stay longer than to see her well; these several delays left him not another minute to lose; and Emma engaging to give assurance of her safety to Mrs. Goddard, and notice of
there being such a set of people in the neighbourhood to Mr. Knightley, he set off, with all the grateful blessings that she could utter for
her friend and herself.

Such an adventure as this,—a fine young man and a lovely young
woman thrown together in such a way, could hardly fail of suggesting certain ideas to the coldest heart and the steadiest brain. So
Emma thought, at least. Could a linguist, could a grammarian,
could even a mathematician have seen what she did, have witnessed their appearance together, and heard their history of it,
without feeling that circumstances had been at work to make them
peculiarly interesting to each other?—How much more must an
imaginist,[5] like herself, be on fire with speculation and foresight!—
especially with such a ground-work of anticipation as her mind had
already made.

It was a very extraordinary thing! Nothing of the sort had ever
occurred before to any young ladies in the place, within her memory;
no rencontre, no alarm of the kind;—and now it had happened to
the very person, and at the very hour, when the other very person

5. "A person with great imaginative powers" (OED).

was chancing to pass by to rescue her!—It certainly was very extraordinary!—And knowing, as she did, the favourable state of mind of each at this period, it struck her the more. He was wishing to get the better of his attachment to herself, she just recovering from her mania for Mr. Elton. It seemed as if every thing united to promise the most interesting consequences. It was not possible that the occurrence should not be strongly recommending each to the other.

In the few minutes' conversation which she had yet had with him, while Harriet had been partially insensible, he had spoken of her terror, her naïveté, her fervor as she seized and clung to his arm, with a sensibility amused and delighted; and just at last, after Harriet's own account had been given, he had expressed his indignation at the abominable folly of Miss Bickerton in the warmest terms. Every thing was to take its natural course, however, neither impelled nor assisted. She would not stir a step, nor drop a hint. No, she had had enough of interference. There could be no harm in a scheme, a mere passive scheme. It was no more than a wish. Beyond it she would on no account proceed.

Emma's first resolution was to keep her father from the knowledge of what had passed,—aware of the anxiety and alarm it would occasion: but she soon felt that concealment must be impossible. Within half an hour it was known all over Highbury. It was the very event to engage those who must talk most, the young and the low; and all the youth and servants in the place were soon in the happiness of frightful news. The last night's ball seemed lost in the gipsies. Poor Mr. Woodhouse trembled as he sat, and, as Emma had foreseen, would scarcely be satisfied without their promising never to go beyond the shrubbery again. It was some comfort to him that many inquiries after himself and Miss Woodhouse (for his neighbours knew that he loved to be inquired after), as well as Miss Smith, were coming in during the rest of the day; and he had the pleasure of returning for answer, that they were all very indifferent—which, though not exactly true, for she was perfectly well, and Harriet not much otherwise, Emma would not interfere with. She had an unhappy state of health in general for the child of such a man, for she hardly knew what indisposition was; and if he did not invent illnesses for her, she could make no figure in a message.

The gipsies did not wait for the operations of justice; they took themselves off in a hurry. The young ladies of Highbury might have walked again in safety before their panic began, and the whole history dwindled soon into a matter of little importance but to Emma and her nephews:—in her imagination it maintained its ground, and Henry and John were still asking every day for the story of Harriet and the gipsies, and still tenaciously setting her right if she varied in the slightest particular from the original recital.

Chapter IV

A very few days had passed after this adventure, when Harriet came one morning to Emma with a small parcel in her hand, and after sitting down and hesitating, thus began:

"Miss Woodhouse—if you are at leisure—I have something that I should like to tell you—a sort of confession to make—and then, you know, it will be over."

Emma was a good deal surprised; but begged her to speak. There was a seriousness in Harriet's manner which prepared her, quite as much as her words, for something more than ordinary.

"It is my duty, and I am sure it is my wish," she continued, "to have no reserves with you on this subject. As I am happily quite an altered creature in *one respect*, it is very fit that you should have the satisfaction of knowing it. I do not want to say more than is necessary—I am too much ashamed of having given way as I have done, and I dare say you understand me."

"Yes," said Emma, "I hope I do."

"How could I so long a time be fancying myself! . . . ." cried Harriet, warmly. "It seems like madness! I can see nothing at all extraordinary in him now.—I do not care whether I meet him or not—except that of the two I had rather not see him—and indeed I would go any distance round to avoid him—but I do not envy his wife in the least; I neither admire nor envy her, as I have done: she is very charming, I dare say, and all that, but I think her very ill-tempered and disagreeable—I shall never forget her look the other night!—However, I assure you, Miss Woodhouse, I wish her no evil.—No, let them be ever so happy together, it will not give me another moment's pang: and to convince you that I have been speaking truth, I am now going to destroy—what I ought to have destroyed long ago—what I ought never to have kept—I know that very well (blushing as she spoke).— However, now I will destroy it all—and it is my particular wish to do it in your presence, that you may see how rational I am grown. Cannot you guess what this parcel holds?" said she, with a conscious look.

"Not the least in the world.—Did he ever give you anything?"

"No—I cannot call them gifts; but they are things that I have valued very much."

She held the parcel towards her, and Emma read the words *Most precious treasures* on the top. Her curiosity was greatly excited. Harriet unfolded the parcel, and she looked on with impatience. Within abundance of silver paper was a pretty little Tunbridge-ware box,[6] which Harriet opened: it was well lined with the softest cotton; but,

6. Box decorated with wood mosaic.

excepting the cotton, Emma saw only a small piece of court plaister.[7]

"Now," said Harriet, "you *must* recollect."

"No, indeed I do not."

"Dear me! I should not have thought it possible you could forget what passed in this very room about court plaister, one of the very last times we ever met in it!—It was but a very few days before I had my sore throat—just before Mr. and Mrs. John Knightley came—I think the very evening.—Do not you remember his cutting his finger with your new penknife, and your recommending court plaister?—But as you had none about you, and knew I had, you desired me to supply him; and so I took mine out and cut him a piece; but it was a great deal too large, and he cut it smaller, and kept playing some time with what was left, before he gave it back to me. And so then, in my nonsense, I could not help making a treasure of it—so I put it by never to be used, and looked at it now and then as a great treat."

"My dearest Harriet!" cried Emma, putting her hand before her face, and jumping up, "you make me more ashamed of myself than I can bear. Remember it? Ay, I remember it all now; all, except your saving this relick—I knew nothing of that till this moment—but the cutting the finger, and my recommending court plaister, and saying I had none about me!—Oh! my sins, my sins!—And I had plenty all the while in my pocket!—One of my senseless tricks!—I deserve to be under a continual blush all the rest of my life.— Well—(sitting down again) go on—what else?"

"And had you really some at hand yourself?—I am sure I never suspected it, you did it so naturally."

"And so you actually put this piece of court plaister by for his sake!" said Emma, recovering from her state of shame and feeling divided between wonder and amusement. And secretly she added to herself, "Lord bless me! when should I ever have thought of putting by in cotton a piece of court plaister that Frank Churchill had been pulling about!—I never was equal to this."

"Here," resumed Harriet, turning to her box again, "here is something still more valuable, I mean that *has been* more valuable, because this is what did really once belong to him, which the court plaister never did."

Emma was quite eager to see this superior treasure. It was the end of an old pencil,—the part without any lead.

"This was really his," said Harriet.—"Do not you remember one morning?—no, I dare say you do not. But one morning—I forget exactly the day—but perhaps it was the Tuesday or Wednesday before

7. Adhesive tape used to cover superficial wounds.

that evening, he wanted to make a memorandum in his pocket-book; it was about spruce beer.[8] Mr. Knightley had been telling him something about brewing spruce beer, and he wanted to put it down; but when he took out his pencil, there was so little lead that he soon cut it all away, and it would not do, so you lent him another, and this was left upon the table as good for nothing. But I kept my eye on it; and, as soon as I dared, caught it up, and never parted with it again from that moment."

"I do remember it," cried Emma; "I perfectly remember it.— Talking about spruce beer.—Oh! yes—Mr. Knightley and I both saying we liked it, and Mr. Elton's seeming resolved to learn to like it too. I perfectly remember it.—Stop; Mr. Knightley was standing just here, was not he?—I have an idea he was standing just here."

"Ah! I do not know. I cannot recollect.—It is very odd, but I cannot recollect.—Mr. Elton was sitting here, I remember, much about where I am now."—

"Well go on."

"Oh! that's all. I have nothing more to show you, or to say—except that I am now going to throw them both behind[9] the fire, and I wish you to see me do it."

"My poor dear Harriet! and have you actually found happiness in treasuring up these things?"

"Yes, simpleton as I was!—but I am quite ashamed of it now, and wish I could forget as easily as I can burn them. It was very wrong of me, you know, to keep any remembrances, after he was married. I knew it was—but had not resolution enough to part with them."

"But, Harriet, is it necessary to burn the court plaister?—I have not a word to say for the bit of old pencil, but the court plaister might be useful."

"I shall be happier to burn it," replied Harriet. "It has a disagreeable look to me. I must get rid of every thing.—There it goes, and there is an end, thank Heaven! of Mr. Elton."

"And when," thought Emma, "will there be a beginning of Mr. Churchill?"

She had soon afterwards reason to believe that the beginning was already made, and could not but hope that the gipsy, though she had *told* no fortune, might be proved to have made Harriet's.— About a fortnight after the alarm, they came to a sufficient explanation, and quite undesignedly. Emma was not thinking of it at the moment, which made the information she received more valuable. She merely said, in the course of some trivial chat, "Well, Harriet,

8. "A fermented beverage made with an extract from the leaves and branches of the spruce fir" (*OED*).
9. That is, on the back of.

whenever you marry I would advise you to do so and so"—and thought no more of it, till after a minute's silence she heard Harriet say in a very serious tone, "I shall never marry."

Emma then looked up, and immediately saw how it was; and after a moment's debate, as to whether it should pass unnoticed or not, replied,

"Never marry!—This is a new resolution."

"It is one that I shall never change, however."

After another short hesitation, "I hope it does not proceed from——I hope it is not in compliment to Mr. Elton?"

"Mr. Elton indeed!" cried Harriet indignantly.—Oh! no"—and Emma could just catch the words, "so superior to Mr. Elton!"[1]

She then took a longer time for consideration. Should she proceed no farther?—should she let it pass, and seem to suspect nothing?—Perhaps Harriet might think her cold or angry if she did; or perhaps if she were totally silent, it might only drive Harriet into asking her to hear too much; and against any thing like such an unreserve as had been, such an open and frequent discussion of hopes and chances, she was perfectly resolved.—She believed it would be wiser for her to say and know at once, all that she meant to say and know. Plain dealing was always best. She had previously determined how far she would proceed, on any application of the sort; and it would be safer for both, to have the judicious law of her own brain laid down with speed.—She was decided, and thus spoke—

"Harriet, I will not affect to be in doubt of your meaning. Your resolution, or rather your expectation of never marrying, results from an idea that the person whom you might prefer, would be too greatly your superior in situation to think of you. Is not it so?"

"Oh! Miss Woodhouse, believe me I have not the presumption to suppose—Indeed I am not so mad.—But it is a pleasure to me to admire him at a distance—and to think of his infinite superiority to all the rest of the world, with the gratitude, wonder, and veneration, which are so proper, in me especially."

"I am not at all surprised at you, Harriet. The service he rendered you was enough to warm your heart."

"Service! oh! it was such an inexpressible obligation!—The very recollection of it, and all that I felt at the time—when I saw him coming—his noble look—and my wretchedness before. Such a change! In one moment such a change! From perfect misery to perfect happiness."

"It is very natural. It is natural, and it is honourable.—Yes, honourable, I think, to choose so well and so gratefully.—But that it

---

1. Our usage would dictate an opening quotation mark before "Oh!" The breathless quality of Harriet's speech is conveyed by the omission in the 1816 edition.

will be a fortunate preference is more than I can promise. I do not advise you to give way to it, Harriet. I do not by any means engage for its being returned. Consider what you are about. Perhaps it will be wisest in you to check your feelings while you can: at any rate do not let them carry you far, unless you are persuaded of his liking you. Be observant of him. Let his behaviour be the guide of your sensations. I give you this caution now, because I shall never speak to you again on the subject. I am determined against all interference. Henceforward I know nothing of the matter. Let no name ever pass our lips. We were very wrong before; we will be cautious now.—He is your superior, no doubt, and there do seem objections and obstacles of a very serious nature; but yet, Harriet, more wonderful things have taken place, there have been matches of greater disparity. But take care of yourself. I would not have you too sanguine;[2] though, however it may end, be assured that your raising your thoughts to *him*, is a mark of good taste which I shall always know how to value."

Harriet kissed her hand in silent and submissive gratitude. Emma was very decided in thinking such an attachment no bad thing for her friend. Its tendency would be to raise and refine her mind—and it must be saving her from the danger of degradation.

Chapter V

In this state of schemes, and hopes, and connivance, June opened upon Hartfield. To Highbury in general it brought no material change. The Eltons were still talking of a visit from the Sucklings, and of the use to be made of their barouche-landau; and Jane Fairfax was still at her grandmother's; and as the return of the Campbells from Ireland was again delayed, and August, instead of Midsummer, fixed for it, she was likely to remain there full two months longer, provided at least she were able to defeat Mrs. Elton's activity in her service, and save herself from being hurried into a delightful situation against her will.

Mr. Knightley, who, for some reason best known to himself, had certainly taken an early dislike to Frank Churchill, was only growing to dislike him more. He began to suspect him of some double dealing in his pursuit of Emma. That Emma was his object appeared indisputable. Every thing declared it; his own attentions, his father's hints, his mother-in-law's guarded silence; it was all in unison; words, conduct, discretion, and indiscretion, told the same story. But while so many were devoting him to Emma, and Emma herself making him over to Harriet, Mr. Knightley began to suspect him of some inclination to trifle with Jane Fairfax. He could not understand it;

2. Hopeful.

but there were symptoms of intelligence between them—he thought so at least—symptoms of admiration on his side, which, having once observed, he could not persuade himself to think entirely void of meaning, however he might wish to escape any of Emma's errors of imagination. *She* was not present when the suspicion first arose. He was dining with the Randalls' family, and Jane at the Eltons'; and he had seen a look, more than a single look, at Miss Fairfax, which, from the admirer of Miss Woodhouse, seemed somewhat out of place. When he was again in their company, he could not help remembering what he had seen; nor could he avoid observations which, unless it were like Cowper and his fire at twilight,

"Myself creating what I saw,"[3]

brought him yet stronger suspicion of there being something of private liking, of private understanding even, between Frank Churchill and Jane.

He had walked up one day after dinner, as he very often did, to spend his evening at Hartfield. Emma and Harriet were going to walk; he joined them; and, on returning, they fell in with a larger party, who, like themselves, judged it wisest to take their exercise early, as the weather threatened rain; Mr. and Mrs. Weston and their son, Miss Bates and her niece, who had accidentally met. They all united; and, on reaching Hartfield gates, Emma, who knew it was exactly the sort of visiting that would be welcome to her father, pressed them all to go in and drink tea with him. The Randalls' party agreed to it immediately; and after a pretty long speech from Miss Bates, which few persons listened to, she also found it possible to accept dear Miss Woodhouse's most obliging invitation.

As they were turning into the grounds, Mr. Perry passed by on horseback. The gentlemen spoke of his horse.

"By the bye," said Frank Churchill to Mrs. Weston presently, "what became of Mr. Perry's plan of setting up his carriage?"

Mrs. Weston looked surprised, and said, "I did not know that he ever had any such plan."

"Nay, I had it from you. You wrote me word of it three months ago."

"Me! impossible!"

---

3. From *The Task*, Book IV, "The Winter Evening":

> Me oft has fancy, ludicrous and wild,
> Sooth'd with a waking dream of houses, tow'rs,
> Trees, churches, and strange visages, express'd
> In the red cinders, while with poring eye
> I gaz'd, myself creating what I saw.

"Indeed you did. I remember it perfectly. You mentioned it as what was certainly to be very soon. Mrs. Perry had told somebody, and was extremely happy about it. It was owing to *her* persuasion, as she thought his being out in bad weather did him a great deal of harm. You must remember it now?"

"Upon my word I never heard of it till this moment."

"Never! really, never!—Bless me! how could it be?—Then I must have dreamt it—but I was completely persuaded—Miss Smith, you walk as if you were tired. You will not be sorry to find yourself at home."

"What is this?—What is this?" cried Mr. Weston, "about Perry and a carriage? Is Perry going to set up his carriage, Frank? I am glad he can afford it. You had it from himself, had you?"

"No, sir," replied his son, laughing, "I seem to have had it from nobody.—Very odd!—I really was persuaded of Mrs. Weston's having mentioned it in one of her letters to Enscombe, many weeks ago, with all these particulars—but as she declares she never heard a syllable of it before, of course it must have been a dream. I am a great dreamer. I dream of every body at Highbury when I am away—and when I have gone through my particular friends, then I begin dreaming of Mr. and Mrs. Perry."

"It is odd though," observed his father, "that you should have had such a regular connected dream about people whom it was not very likely you should be thinking of at Enscombe. Perry's setting up his carriage! and his wife's persuading him to it, out of care for his health—just what will happen, I have no doubt, some time or other; only a little premature. What an air of probability sometimes runs through a dream! And at others, what a heap of absurdities it is! Well, Frank, your dream certainly shows that Highbury is in your thoughts when you are absent. Emma, you are a great dreamer, I think?"

Emma was out of hearing. She had hurried on before her guests to prepare her father for their appearance, and was beyond the reach of Mr. Weston's hint.

"Why, to own the truth," cried Miss Bates, who had been trying in vain to be heard the last two minutes, "if I must speak on this subject, there is no denying that Mr. Frank Churchill might have—I do not mean to say that he did not dream it—I am sure I have sometimes the oddest dreams in the world—but if I am questioned about it, I must acknowledge that there was such an idea last spring; for Mrs. Perry herself mentioned it to my mother, and the Coles knew of it as well as ourselves—but it was quite a secret, known to nobody else, and only thought of about three days. Mrs. Perry was very anxious that he should have a carriage, and came to my mother in great spirits one morning because she thought she had prevailed. Jane, don't you remember grandmamma's telling us of it when we got home?—I forgot where we had been walking to—very likely to Randall's; yes, I think it was to Randall's. Mrs. Perry was always particularly fond of my mother—indeed I do not know who is not—and she had mentioned it to her in confidence; she had no objection to her telling us, of course, but it was not to go beyond: and, from that day to this, I never mentioned it to a soul that I know of. At the same time, I will not positively answer for my having never dropt a hint, because I know I do sometimes pop out a thing before I am aware. I am a talker, you know; I am rather a talker; and now and then I have let a thing escape me which I should not. I am not like Jane; I wish I were. I will answer for it *she* never betrayed the least thing in the world. Where is she?—Oh! just behind. Perfectly remember Mrs. Perry's coming.—Extraordinary dream indeed!"

They were entering the hall. Mr. Knightley's eyes had preceded Miss Bates's in a glance at Jane. From Frank Churchill's face, where he thought he saw confusion suppressed or laughed away, he had involuntarily turned to her's; but she was indeed behind, and too busy with her shawl. Mr. Weston had walked in. The two other gentlemen waited at the door to let her pass. Mr. Knightley suspected in Frank Churchill the determination of catching her eye—he seemed watching her intently—in vain, however, if it were so—Jane passed between them into the hall, and looked at neither.

There was no time for farther remark or explanation. The dream must be borne with, and Mr. Knightley must take his seat with the rest round the large modern circular table which Emma had introduced at Hartfield, and which none but Emma could have had power to place there and persuade her father to use, instead of the small-sized Pembroke,[4] on which two of his daily meals had, for forty years, been crowded. Tea passed pleasantly, and nobody seemed in a hurry to move.

"Miss Woodhouse," said Frank Churchill, after examining a table behind him, which he could reach as he sat, "have your nephews taken away their alphabets—their box of letters? It used to stand here. Where is it? This is a sort of dull-looking evening, that ought to be treated rather as winter than summer. We had great amusement with those letters one morning. I want to puzzle you again."

Emma was pleased with the thought; and producing the box, the table was quickly scattered over with alphabets, which no one seemed so much disposed to employ as their two selves. They were rapidly forming words for each other, or for any body else who would be puzzled. The quietness of the game made it particularly eligible for Mr. Woodhouse, who had often been distressed by the more

4. Drop-leaf table.

animated sort, which Mr. Weston had occasionally introduced, and who now sat happily occupied in lamenting, with tender melancholy, over the departure of the "poor little boys" or in fondly pointing out, as he took up any stray letter near him, how beautifully Emma had written it.

Frank Churchill placed a word before Miss Fairfax. She gave a slight glance round the table, and applied herself to it. Frank was next to Emma, Jane opposite them—and Mr. Knightley so placed as to see them all; and it was his object to see as much as he could, with as little apparent observation. The word was discovered; and with a faint smile pushed away. If meant to be immediately mixed with the others, and buried from sight, she should have looked on the table instead of looking just across, for it was not mixed; and Harriet, eager after every fresh word, and finding out none, directly took it up, and fell to work. She was sitting by Mr. Knightley, and turned to him for help. The word was *blunder* and as Harriet exultingly proclaimed it, there was a blush on Jane's cheek which gave it a meaning not otherwise ostensible. Mr. Knightley connected it with the dream; but how it could all be, was beyond his comprehension. How the delicacy, the discretion of his favourite could have been so lain asleep! He feared there must be some decided involvement. Disingenuousness and double-dealing seemed to meet him at every turn. These letters were but the vehicle for gallantry and trick. It was a child's play, chosen to conceal a deeper game on Frank Churchill's part.

With great indignation did he continue to observe him; with great alarm and distrust, to observe also his two blinded companions. He saw a short word prepared for Emma, and given to her with a look sly and demure. He saw that Emma had soon made it out, and found it highly entertaining, though it was something which she judged it proper to appear to censure; for she said, "Nonsense! for shame!" He heard Frank Churchill next say, with a glance towards Jane, "I will give it to her—shall I?"—and as clearly heard Emma opposing it with eager laughing warmth. "No, no, you must not; you shall not, indeed."

It was done however. This gallant young man, who seemed to love without feeling, and to recommend himself without complaisance, directly handed over the word to Miss Fairfax, and with a particular degree of sedate civility entreated her to study it. Mr. Knightley's excessive curiosity to know what this word might be, made him seize every possible moment for darting his eye towards it, and it was not long before he saw it to be *Dixon*. Jane Fairfax's perception seemed to accompany his; her comprehension was certainly more equal to the covert meaning, the superior intelligence, of those five letters so arranged. She was evidently displeased; looked up, and seeing herself watched, blushed more deeply than he had ever perceived her, and saying only, "I did not know that proper names were allowed," pushed away the letters with even an angry spirit, and looked resolved to be engaged by no other word that could be offered. Her face was averted from those who had made the attack, and turned towards her aunt.

"Ay, very true, my dear," cried the latter, though Jane had not spoken a word—"I was just going to say the same thing. It is time for us to be going indeed. The evening is closing in, and grandmamma will be looking for us. My dear sir, you are too obliging. We really must wish you good night."

Jane's alertness in moving, proved her as ready as her aunt had preconceived. She was immediately up, and wanting to quit the table; but so many were also moving, that she could not get away; and Mr. Knightley thought he saw another collection of letters anxiously pushed towards her, and resolutely swept away by her unexamined. She was afterwards looking for her shawl—Frank Churchill was looking also—it was growing dusk, and the room was in confusion; and how they parted, Mr. Knightley could not tell.

He remained at Hartfield after all the rest, his thoughts full of what he had seen; so full, that when the candles came to assist his observations, he must—yes, he certainly must, as a friend—an anxious friend—give Emma some hint, ask her some question. He could not see her in a situation of such danger, without trying to preserve her. It was his duty.

"Pray, Emma," said he, "may I ask in what lay the great amusement, the poignant sting of the last word given to you and Miss Fairfax? I saw the word, and am curious to know how it could be so very entertaining to the one, and so very distressing to the other."

Emma was extremely confused. She could not endure to give him the true explanation; for though her suspicions were by no means removed, she was really ashamed of having ever imparted them.

"Oh!" she cried in evident embarrassment, "it all meant nothing; a mere joke among ourselves."

"The joke," he replied gravely, "seemed confined to you and Mr. Churchill."

He had hoped she would speak again, but she did not. She would rather busy herself about any thing than speak. He sat a little while in doubt. A variety of evils crossed his mind. Interference—fruitless interference. Emma's confusion, and the acknowledged intimacy, seemed to declare her affection engaged. Yet he would speak. He owed it to her, to risk any thing that might be involved in an unwelcome interference, rather than her welfare; to encounter any thing, rather than the remembrance of neglect in such a cause.

"My dear Emma," said he at last, with earnest kindness, "do you think you perfectly understand the degree of acquaintance between the gentleman and lady we have been speaking of?"

"Between Mr. Frank Churchill and Miss Fairfax? Oh! yes, perfectly.—Why do you make a doubt of it?"

"Have you never at any time had reason to think that he admired her, or that she admired him?"

"Never, never!"—she cried with a most open eagerness—"Never, for the twentieth part of a moment, did such an idea occur to me. And how could it possibly come into your head?"

"I have lately imagined that I saw symptoms of attachment between them—certain expressive looks, which I did not believe meant to be public."

"Oh! you amuse me excessively. I am delighted to find that you can vouchsafe to let your imagination wander—but it will not do—very sorry to check you in your first essay—but indeed it will not do. There is no admiration between them, I do assure you; and the appearances which have caught you, have arisen from some peculiar circumstances—feelings rather of a totally different nature:—it is impossible exactly to explain:—there is a good deal of nonsense in it—but the part which is capable of being communicated, which is sense, is, that they are as far from any attachment or admiration for one another, as any two beings in the world can be. That is, I *presume* it so be so on her side, and can *answer* for its being so on his. I will answer for the gentleman's indifference."

She spoke with a confidence which staggered, with a satisfaction which silenced, Mr. Knightley. She was in gay spirits, and would have prolonged the conversation, wanting to hear the particulars of his suspicions, every look described, and all the wheres and hows of a circumstance which highly entertained her: but his gaiety did not meet her's. He found he could not be useful, and his feelings were too much irritated for talking. That he might not be irritated into an absolute fever, by the fire which Mr. Woodhouse's tender habits required almost every evening throughout the year, he soon afterwards took a hasty leave, and walked home to the coolness and solitude of Donwell Abbey.

Chapter VI

After being long fed with hopes of a speedy visit from Mr. and Mrs. Suckling, the Highbury world were obliged to endure the mortification of hearing that they could not possibly come till the autumn. No such importation of novelties could enrich their intellectual stores at present. In the daily interchange of news, they must be again restricted to the other topics with which for a while the Sucklings' coming had been united, such as the last accounts of Mrs. Churchill, whose health seemed every day to supply a different report, and the situation of Mrs. Weston, whose happiness it was to be hoped might eventually be as much increased by the arrival of a child, as that of all her neighbours was by the approach of it.

Mrs. Elton was very much disappointed. It was the delay of a great deal of pleasure and parade. Her introductions and recommendations must all wait, and every projected party be still only talked of. So she thought at first;—but a little consideration convinced her that every thing need not be put off. Why should not they explore to Box Hill[5] though the Sucklings did not come? They could go there again with them in the autumn. It was settled that they should go to Box Hill. That there was to be such a party had been long generally known: it had even given the idea of another. Emma had never been to Box Hill; she wished to see what every body found so well worth seeing, and she and Mr. Weston had agreed to choose some fine morning and drive thither. Two or three more of the chosen only were to be admitted to join them, and it was to be done in a quiet, unpretending, elegant way, infinitely superior to the bustle and preparations, the regular eating and drinking, and pic-nic parade of the Eltons and the Sucklings.

This was so very well understood between them, that Emma could not but feel some surprise, and a little displeasure, on hearing from Mr. Weston that he had been proposing to Mrs. Elton, as her brother and sister had failed her, that the two parties should unite, and go together; and that as Mrs. Elton had very readily acceded to it, so it was to be, if she had no objection. Now, as her objection was nothing but her very great dislike of Mrs. Elton, of which Mr. Weston must already be perfectly aware, it was not worth bringing forward again:—it could not be done without a reproof to him, which would be giving pain to his wife; and she found herself therefore obliged to consent to an arrangement which she would have done a great deal to avoid; an arrangement which would probably expose her even to the degradation of being said to be of Mrs. Elton's party! Every feeling was offended; and the forbearance of her outward submission left a heavy arrear due of secret severity in her reflections on the unmanageable good-will of Mr. Weston's temper.

"I am glad you approve of what I have done," said he very comfortably. "But I thought you would. Such schemes as these are nothing without numbers. One cannot have too large a party. A large party secures its own amusement. And she is a good-natured woman after all. One could not leave her out."

5. A well-known pleasure spot in Surrey. "[F]rom this hill, in clear weather, the view stretches quite over the Weald of Sussex to the South Downs; and by the help of glasses the town of Horsham, Ashdown Forest, the Earl of Egremont's seat at Petworth and the South Downs, as they range between Brighthelmstone and Arundel, may be plainly seen, besides an unbounded prospect into Kent" (*The Curiosities, Natural and Artificial, of the Island of Great Britain* [London, 1775, p. 62]).

Emma denied none of it aloud, and agreed to none of it in private.

It was now the middle of June, and the weather fine; and Mrs. Elton was growing impatient to name the day, and settle with Mr. Weston as to pigeon-pies and cold lamb, when a lame carriage-horse threw every thing into sad uncertainty. It might be weeks, it might be only a few days, before the horse were useable, but no preparations could be ventured on, and it was all melancholy stagnation. Mrs. Elton's resources were inadequate to such an attack.

"Is not this most vexatious, Knightley?" she cried.—And such weather for exploring!—These delays and disappointments are quite odious. What are we to do?—The year will wear away at this rate, and nothing done. Before this time last year I assure you we had had a delightful exploring party from Maple Grove to Kings Weston."

"You had better explore to Donwell," replied Mr. Knightley. "That may be done without horses. Come, and eat my strawberries. They are ripening fast."

If Mr. Knightley did not begin seriously, he was obliged to proceed so, for his proposal was caught at with delight; and the "Oh! I should like it of all things," was not plainer in words than manner. Donwell was famous for its strawberry-beds, which seemed a plea for the invitation: but no plea was necessary; cabbage-beds would have been enough to tempt the lady, who only wanted to be going somewhere. She promised him again and again to come—much oftener than he doubted—and was extremely gratified by such a proof of intimacy, such a distinguishing compliment as she chose to consider it.

"You may depend upon me," said she. "I certainly will come. Name your day, and I will come. You will allow me to bring Jane Fairfax?"

"I cannot name a day," said he, "till I have spoken to some others whom I would wish to meet you."

"Oh! leave all that to me. Only give me a carte-blanche.—I am Lady Patroness, you know. It is my party. I will bring friends with me."

"I hope you will bring Elton," said he:—but I will not trouble you to give any other invitations."

"Oh! now you are looking very sly. But consider;—you need not be afraid of delegating power to *me*. I am no young lady on her preferment.[6] Married women, you know, may be safely authorized. It is my party. Leave it all to me. I will invite your guests."

"No,"—he calmly replied,—"there is but one married woman in the world whom I can ever allow to invite what guests she pleases to Donwell, and that one is——"

---

6. Seeking marriage.

"—Mrs. Weston, I suppose," interrupted Mrs. Elton, rather mortified.

"No—Mrs. Knightley;—and, till she is in being, I will manage such matters myself."

"Ah! you are an odd creature!" she cried, satisfied to have no one preferred to herself.—"You are a humourist,[7] and may say what you like. Quite a humourist. Well, I shall bring Jane with me—Jane and her aunt.—The rest I leave to you. I have no objections at all to meeting the Hartfield family. Don't scruple. I know you are attached to them."

"You certainly will meet them if I can prevail; and I shall call on Miss Bates in my way home."

"That's quite unnecessary; I see Jane every day:—but as you like. It is to be a morning scheme, you know, Knightley; quite a simple thing. I shall wear a large bonnet, and bring one of my little baskets hanging on my arm. Here,—probably this basket with pink ribbon. Nothing can be more simple, you see. And Jane will have such another. There is to be no form or parade—a sort of gipsy party.—We are to walk about your gardens, and gather the strawberries ourselves, and sit under trees;—and whatever else you may like to provide, it is to be all out of doors—a table spread in the shade, you know. Everything as natural and simple as possible. Is not that your idea?"

"Not quite. My idea of the simple and the natural will be to have the table spread in the dining-room. The nature and the simplicity of gentlemen and ladies, with their servants and furniture, I think is best observed by meals within doors. When you are tired of eating strawberries in the garden, there shall be cold meat in the house."

"Well—as you please; only don't have a great set out. And, by the bye, can I or my housekeeper be of any use to you with our opinion?—Pray be sincere, Knightley. If you wish me to talk to Mrs. Hodges, or to inspect anything——."

"I have not the least wish for it, I thank you."

"Well—but if any difficulties should arise, my housekeeper is extremely clever."

"I will answer for it, that mine thinks herself full as clever, and would spurn anybody's assistance."

"I wish we had a donkey. The thing would be for us all to come on donkies, Jane, Miss Bates, and me—and my caro sposo walking by. I really must talk to him about purchasing a donkey. In a country life I perceive it to be a sort of necessary; for, let a woman have ever so many resources, it is not possible for her to be always shut

7. A whimsical person. Mrs. Elton, of course, misinterprets Mr. Knightley completely.

up at home;—and very long walks, you know——in summer there is dust, and in winter there is dirt."

"You will not find either, between Donwell and Highbury. Donwell-lane is never dusty, and now it is perfectly dry. Come on a donkey, however, if you prefer it. You can borrow Mrs. Cole's. I would wish every thing to be as much to your taste as possible."

"That I am sure you would. Indeed I do you justice, my good friend. Under that peculiar sort of dry, blunt manner, I know you have the warmest heart. As I tell Mr. E., you are a thorough humourist.—Yes, believe me, Knightley, I am fully sensible of your attention to me in the whole of this scheme. You have hit upon the very thing to please me."

Mr. Knightley had another reason for avoiding a table in the shade. He wished to persuade Mr. Woodhouse, as well as Emma, to join the party; and he knew that to have any of them sitting down out of doors to eat would inevitably make him ill. Mr. Woodhouse must not, under the specious pretence of a morning drive, and an hour or two spent at Donwell, be tempted away to his misery.

He was invited on good faith. No lurking horrors were to upbraid him for his easy credulity. He did consent. He had not been at Donwell for two years. "Some very fine morning, he, and Emma, and Harriet, could go very well; and he could sit still with Mrs. Weston, while the dear girls walked about the gardens. He did not suppose they could be damp now, in the middle of the day. He should like to see the old house again exceedingly, and should be very happy to meet Mr. and Mrs. Elton, and any other of his neighbours.—He could not see any objection at all to his, and Emma's, and Harriet's, going there some very fine morning. He thought it very well done of Mr. Knightley to invite them—very kind and sensible—much cleverer than dining out.—He was not fond of dining out."

Mr. Knightley was fortunate in every body's most ready concurrence. The invitation was every where so well received, that it seemed as if, like Mrs. Elton, they were all taking the scheme as a particular compliment to themselves.—Emma and Harriet professed very high expectations of pleasure from it; and Mr. Weston, unasked, promised to get Frank over to join them, if possible; a proof of approbation and gratitude which could have been dispensed with.—Mr. Knightley was then obliged to say that he should be glad to see him; and Mr. Weston engaged to lose no time in writing, and spare no arguments to induce him to come.

In the meanwhile the lame horse recovered so fast, that the party to Box Hill was again under happy consideration; and at last Donwell was settled for one day, and Box Hill for the next,—the weather appearing exactly right.

Under a bright mid-day sun, at almost Midsummer, Mr. Woodhouse was safely conveyed in his carriage, with one window down, to partake of this al-fresco party; and in one of the most comfortable rooms in the Abbey, especially prepared for him by a fire all the morning, he was happily placed, quite at his ease, ready to talk with pleasure of what had been atchieved, and advise every body to come and sit down, and not to heat themselves.—Mrs. Weston, who seemed to have walked there on purpose to be tired, and sit all the time with him, remained, when all the others were invited or persuaded out, his patient listener and sympathizer.

It was so long since Emma had been at the Abbey, that as soon as she was satisfied of her father's comfort, she was glad to leave him, and look around her; eager to refresh and correct her memory with more particular observation, more exact understanding of a house and grounds which must ever be so interesting to her and all her family.

She felt all the honest pride and complacency which her alliance with the present and future proprietor could fairly warrant, as she viewed the respectable size and style of the building, its suitable, becoming, characteristic situation, low and sheltered—its ample gardens stretching down to meadows washed by a stream, of which the Abbey, with all the old neglect of prospect, had scarcely a sight—and its abundance of timber in rows and avenues, which neither fashion nor extravagance had rooted up.—The house was larger than Hartfield, and totally unlike it, covering a good deal of ground, rambling and irregular, with many comfortable and one or two handsome rooms.—It was just what it ought to be, and it looked what it was—and Emma felt an increasing respect for it, as the residence of a family of such true gentility, untainted in blood and understanding.—Some faults of temper John Knightley had; but Isabella had connected herself unexceptionably. She had given them neither men, nor names, nor places, that could raise a blush. These were pleasant feelings, and she walked about and indulged them till it was necessary to do as the others did, and collect round the strawberry beds.—The whole party were assembled, excepting Frank Churchill, who was expected every moment from Richmond; and Mrs. Elton, in all her apparatus of happiness, her large bonnet and her basket, was very ready to lead the way in gathering, accepting, or talking—strawberries, and only strawberries, could now be thought or spoken of.—"The best fruit in England—every body's favourite—always wholesome.—These the finest beds and finest sorts.—Delightful to gather for one's self—the only way of really enjoying them.—Morning decidedly the best time—never tired—every sort good—hautboy infinitely superior—no comparison—the others hardly eatable—hautboys very scarcer—Chili preferred—white wood finest flavour of all—price of strawberries in London—abundance about Bristol—Maple Grove—cultivation—beds when to be renewed—gardeners thinking exactly different—no general rule—gardeners never to be put out of their way—delicious fruit—only too rich to be eaten much of—inferior to cherries—currants more refreshing—only objection to gathering strawberries the stooping—glaring sun—tired to death—could bear it no longer—must go and sit in the shade."

Such, for half an hour, was the conversation—interrupted only once by Mrs. Weston, who came out, in her solicitude after her son-in-law, to inquire if he were come—and she was a little uneasy.—She had some fears of his horse.

Seats tolerably in the shade were found; and now Emma was obliged to overhear what Mrs. Elton and Jane Fairfax were talking of.—A situation, a most desirable situation, was in question. Mrs. Elton had received notice of it that morning, and was in raptures. It was not with Mrs. Suckling, it was not with Mrs. Bragge, but in felicity and splendour it fell short only of them: it was with a cousin of Mrs. Bragge, an acquaintance of Mrs. Suckling, a lady known at Maple Grove. Delightful, charming, superior, first circles, spheres, lines, ranks, every thing—and Mrs. Elton was wild to have the offer closed with immediately.—On her side, all was warmth, energy, and triumph—and she positively refused to take her friend's negative, though Miss Fairfax continued to assure her that she would not at present engage in any thing, repeating the same motives which she had been heard to urge before.—Still Mrs. Elton insisted on being authorized to write an acquiescence by the morrow's post.—How Jane could bear it at all, was astonishing to Emma.—She did look vexed, she did speak pointedly—and at last, with a decision of action unusual to her, proposed a removal.—"Should not they walk?—Would not Mr. Knightley show them the gardens—all the gardens?—She wished to see the whole extent."—The pertinacity of her friend seemed more than she could bear.

It was hot; and after walking some time over the gardens in a scattered, dispersed way, scarcely any three together, they insensibly followed one another to the delicious shade of a broad short avenue of limes, which stretching beyond the garden at an equal distance from the river, seemed the finish of the pleasure grounds.—It led to nothing; nothing but a view at the end over a low stone wall with high pillars, which seemed intended, in their erection, to give the appearance of an approach to the house, which never had been there. Disputable, however, as might be the taste of such a termination, it was in itself a charming walk, and the view which closed it extremely pretty.—The considerable slope, at nearly the foot of which the Abbey stood, gradually acquired a steeper form beyond its grounds; and at half a mile distant was a bank of considerable abruptness and grandeur, well clothed with wood;—and at the bottom of this bank, favourably placed and sheltered, rose the

Abbey-Mill Farm, with meadows in front, and the river making a close and handsome curve around it.

It was a sweet view—sweet to the eye and the mind. English verdure, English culture, English comfort, seen under a sun bright, without being oppressive.

In this walk Emma and Mr. Weston found all the others assembled; and towards this view she immediately perceived Mr. Knightley and Harriet distinct from the rest, quietly leading the way. Mr. Knightley and Harriet!—It was an odd tête-à-tête; but she was glad to see it.—There had been a time when he would have scorned her as a companion, and turned from her with little ceremony. Now they seemed in pleasant conversation. There had been a time also when Emma would have been sorry to see Harriet in a spot so favourable for the Abbey-Mill Farm; but now she feared it not. It might be safely viewed with all its appendages of prosperity and beauty, its rich pastures, spreading flocks, orchard in blossom, and light column of smoke ascending.—She joined them at the wall, and found them more engaged in talking than in looking around. He was giving Harriet information as to modes of agriculture, &c. and Emma received a smile which seemed to say, "There are my own concerns. I have a right to talk on such subjects, without being suspected of introducing Robert Martin."—She did not suspect him. It was too old a story.—Robert Martin had probably ceased to think of Harriet.—They took a few turns together along the walk.—The shade was most refreshing, and Emma found it the pleasantest part of the day.

The next remove was to the house; they must all go in and eat;—and they were all seated and busy, and still Frank Churchill did not come. Mrs. Weston looked, and looked in vain. His father would not own himself uneasy, and laughed at her fears; but she could not be cured of wishing that he would part with his black mare. He had expressed himself as to coming, with more than common certainty. "His aunt was so much better, that he had not a doubt of getting over to them."—Mrs. Churchill's state, however, as many were ready to remind her, was liable to such sudden variation as might disappoint her nephew in the most reasonable dependence—and Mrs. Weston was at last persuaded to believe, or to say, that it must be by some attack of Mrs. Churchill that he was prevented coming.—Emma looked at Harriet while the point was under consideration; she behaved very well, and betrayed no emotion.

The cold repast was over, and the party were to go out once more to see what had not yet been seen, the old Abbey fish-ponds; perhaps get as far as the clover, which was to be begun cutting on the morrow, or, at any rate, have the pleasure of being hot, and growing cool again.—Mr. Woodhouse, who had already taken his little round in the highest part of the gardens, where no damps from the river were imagined even by him, stirred no more; and his daughter resolved to remain with him, that Mrs. Weston might be persuaded away by her husband to the exercise and variety which her spirits seemed to need.

Mr. Knightley had done all in his power for Mr. Woodhouse's entertainment. Books of engravings, drawers of medals, cameos, corals, shells, and every other family collection within his cabinets, had been prepared for his old friend, to while away the morning; and the kindness had perfectly answered. Mr. Woodhouse had been exceedingly well amused. Mrs. Weston had been showing them all to him, and now he would show them all to Emma;—fortunate in having no other resemblance to a child, than in a total want of taste for what he saw, for he was slow, constant, and methodical.—Before this second looking over was begun, however, Emma walked into the hall for the sake of a few moments' free observation of the entrance and ground-plot of the house—and was hardly there, when Jane Fairfax appeared, coming quickly in from the garden, and with a look of escape.— Little expecting to meet Miss Woodhouse so soon, there was a start at first; but Miss Woodhouse was the very person she was in quest of.

"Will you be so kind," said she, "when I am missed, as to say that I am gone home?—I am going this moment.—My aunt is not aware how late it is, nor how long we have been absent—but I am sure we shall be wanted, and I am determined to go directly.—I have said nothing about it to any body. It would only be giving trouble and distress. Some are gone to the ponds, and some to the lime walk. Till they all come in I shall not be missed; and when they do, will you have the goodness to say that I am gone?"

"Certainly, if you wish it;—but you are not going to walk to Highbury alone?"

"Yes—what should hurt me?—I walk fast. I shall be at home in twenty minutes."

"But it is too far, indeed it is, to be walking quite alone. Let my father's servant go with you.—Let me order the carriage. It can be round in five minutes."

"Thank you, thank you—but on no account.—I would rather walk.—And for *me* to be afraid of walking alone!—I, who may so soon have to guard others!"

She spoke with great agitation; and Emma very feelingly replied, "That can be no reason for your being exposed to danger now. I must order the carriage. The heat even would be danger.—You are fatigued already."

"I am"—she answered—"I am fatigued; but it is not the sort of fatigue—quick walking will refresh me.—Miss Woodhouse, we all know at times what it is to be wearied in spirits. Mine, I confess, are exhausted. The greatest kindness you can show me, will be to let me have my own way, and only say that I am gone when it is necessary."

Emma had not another word to oppose. She saw it all; and entering into her feelings, promoted her quitting the house immediately,
and watched her safely off with the zeal of a friend. Her parting look
was grateful—and her parting words, "Oh! Miss Woodhouse, the
comfort of being sometimes alone!"—seemed to burst from an overcharged heart, and to describe somewhat of the continual endurance
to be practised by her, even towards some of those who loved her best.

"Such a home, indeed! such an aunt!" said Emma, as she turned
back into the hall again. "I do pity you. And the more sensibility you
betray of their just horrors, the more I shall like you."

Jane had not been gone a quarter of an hour, and they had only
accomplished some views of St. Mark's Place, Venice, when Frank
Churchill entered the room. Emma had not been thinking of him,
she had forgotten to think of him—but she was very glad to see
him. Mrs. Weston would be at ease. The black mare was blameless;
they were right who had named Mrs. Churchill as the cause. He
had been detained by a temporary increase of illness in her; a nervous seizure, which had lasted some hours—and he had quite given
up every thought of coming, till very late;—and had he known how
hot a ride he should have, and how late, with all his hurry, he must
be, he believed he should not have come at all. The heat was excessive; he had never suffered any thing like it—almost wished he had
staid at home—nothing killed him like heat—he could bear any
degree of cold, &c. but heat was intolerable—and he sat down, at
the greatest possible distance from the slight remains of Mr. Woodhouse's fire, looking very deplorable.

"You will soon be cooler, if you sit still," said Emma.

"As soon as I am cooler I shall go back again. I could very ill be
spared—but such a point had been made of my coming! You will all
be going soon I suppose; the whole party breaking up. I met *one* as
I came—Madness in such weather!—absolute madness!"

Emma listened, and looked, and soon perceived that Frank
Churchill's state might be best defined by the expressive phrase of
being out of humour. Some people were always cross when they were
hot. Such might be his constitution; and as she knew that eating and
drinking were often the cure of such incidental complaints, she recommended his taking some refreshment; he would find abundance
of every thing in the dining-room—and she humanely pointed out
the door.

"No—he should not eat. He was not hungry; it would only make
him hotter." In two minutes, however, he relented in his own favour;
and muttering something about spruce beer, walked off. Emma
returned her attention to her father, saying in secret—

"I am glad I have done being in love with him. I should not like a
man who is so soon discomposed by a hot morning. Harriet's sweet
easy temper will not mind it."

He was gone long enough to have had a very comfortable meal, and came back all the betters—grown quite cool—and, with good manners, like himself—able to draw a chair close to them, take an interest in their employment; and regret, in a reasonable way, that he should be so late. He was not in his best spirits, but seemed trying to improve them; and, at last, made himself talk nonsense very agreeably. They were looking over views in Swisserland.

"As soon as my aunt gets well, I shall go abroad," said he. "I shall never be easy till I have seen some of these places. You will have my sketches, some time or other, to look at—or my tour to read—or my poem. I shall do something to expose myself."

"That may be—but not by sketches in Swisserland. You will never go to Swisserland. Your uncle and aunt will never allow you to leave England."

"They may be induced to go too. A warm climate may be prescribed for her. I have more than half an expectation of our all going abroad. I assure you I have. I feel a strong persuasion, this morning, that I shall soon be abroad. I ought to travel. I am tired of doing nothing. I want a change. I am serious, Miss Woodhouse, whatever your penetrating eyes may fancy—I am sick of England—and would leave it to-morrow, if I could."

"You are sick of prosperity and indulgence. Cannot you invent a few hardships for yourself, and be contented to stay?"

"*I* sick of prosperity and indulgence!—You are quite mistaken. I do not look upon myself as either prosperous or indulged. I am thwarted in every thing material. I do not consider myself at all a fortunate person."

"You are not quite so miserable, though, as when you first came. Go and eat and drink a little more, and you will do very well. Another slice of cold meat, another draught of Madeira and water, will make you nearly on a par with the rest of us."

"No—I shall not stir. I shall sit by you. You are my best cure."

"We are going to Box Hill to-morrow;—you will join us. It is not Swisserland, but it will be something for a young man so much in want of a change. You will stay, and go with us?"

"No, certainly not; I shall go home in the cool of the evening."

"But you may come again in the cool of to-morrow morning."

"No—It will not be worth while. If I come, I shall be cross."

"Then pray stay at Richmond."

"But if I do, I shall be crosser still. I can never bear to think of you all there without me."

"These are difficulties which you must settle for yourself. Choose your own degree of crossness. I shall press you no more."

The rest of the party were now returning, and all were soon collected. With some there was great joy at the sight of Frank Churchill;

others took it very composedly; but there was a very general distress and disturbance on Miss Fairfax's disappearance being explained. That it was time for every body to go, concluded the subject; and with a short final arrangement for the next day's scheme, they parted. Frank Churchill's little inclination to exclude himself increased so much, that his last words to Emma were,

"Well;—if *you* wish me to stay, and join the party, I will."

She smiled her acceptance; and nothing less than a summons from Richmond was to take him back before the following evening.

Chapter VII

They had a very fine day for Box Hill; and all the other outward circumstances of arrangement, accommodation, and punctuality, were in favour of a pleasant party. Mr. Weston directed the whole, officiating safely between Hartfield and the vicarage, and every body was in good time. Emma and Harriet went together; Miss Bates and her niece, with the Eltons; the gentlemen on horseback. Mrs. Weston remained with Mr. Woodhouse. Nothing was wanting but to be happy when they got there. Seven miles were travelled in expectation of enjoyment, and every body had a burst of admiration on first arriving; but in the general amount of the day there was deficiency. There was a languor, a want of spirits, a want of union, which could not be got over. They separated too much into parties. The Eltons walked together; Mr. Knightley took charge of Miss Bates and Jane; and Emma and Harriet belonged to Frank Churchill. And Mr. Weston tried, in vain, to make them harmonize better. It seemed at first an accidental division, but it never materially varied. Mr. and Mrs. Elton, indeed, showed no unwillingness to mix, and be as agreeable as they could: but during the two whole hours that were spent on the hill, there seemed a principle of separation, between the other parties, too strong for any fine prospects, or any cold collation,[8] or any cheerful Mr. Weston, to remove.

At first it was downright dulness to Emma. She had never seen Frank Churchill so silent and stupid. He said nothing worth hearing—looked without seeing—admired without intelligence—listened without knowing what she said. While he was so dull, it was no wonder that Harriet should be dull likewise, and they were both insufferable.

When they all sat down it was better; to her taste a great deal better, for Frank Churchill grew talkative and gay, making her his first object. Every distinguishing attention that could be paid, was paid to her. To amuse her, and be agreeable in her eyes, seemed all that he

8. Light meal.

cared for—and Emma, glad to be enlivened, not sorry to be flattered, was gay and easy too, and gave him all the friendly encouragement, the admission to be gallant, which she had ever given in the first and most animating period of their acquaintance; but which now, in her own estimation, meant nothing, though in the judgment of most people looking on it must have had such an appearance as no English word but flirtation could very well describe. "Mr. Frank Churchill and Miss Woodhouse flirted together excessively." They were laying themselves open to that very phrase—and to having it sent off in a letter to Maple Grove by one lady, to Ireland by another. Not that Emma was gay and thoughtless from any real felicity; it was rather because she felt less happy than she had expected. She laughed because she was disappointed; and though she liked him for his attentions, and thought them all, whether in friendship, admiration, or playfulness, extremely judicious, they were not winning back her heart. She still intended him for her friend.

"How much I am obliged to you," said he, "for telling me to come today!—If it had not been for you, I should certainly have lost all the happiness of this party. I had quite determined to go away again."

"Yes, you were very cross; and I do not know what about, except that you were too late for the best strawberries. I was a kinder friend than you deserved. But you were humble. You begged hard to be commanded to come."

"Don't say I was cross. I was fatigued. The heat overcame me."

"It is hotter to-day."

"Not to my feelings. I am perfectly comfortable to-day."

"You are comfortable because you are under command."

"Your command?—Yes."

"Perhaps I intended you to say so, but I meant self-command. You had, somehow or other, broken bounds yesterday, and run away from your own management; but to-day you are got back again—and as I cannot be always with you, it is best to believe your temper under your own command rather than mine."

"It comes to the same thing. I can have no self-command without a motive. You order me, whether you speak or not. And you can be always with me. You are always with me."

"Dating from three o'clock yesterday. My perpetual influence could not begin earlier, or you would not have been so much out of humour before."

"Three o'clock yesterday! That is your date. I thought I had seen you first in February."

"Your gallantry is really unanswerable. But (lowering her voice)—nobody speaks except ourselves, and it is rather too much to be talking nonsense for the entertainment of seven silent people."

"I say nothing of which I am ashamed," replied he, with lively impudence. "I saw you first in February. Let every body on the Hill hear me if they can. Let my accents swell to Mickleham on one side, and Dorking on the other. I saw you first in February." And then whispering—"Our companions are excessively stupid. What shall we do to rouse them? Any nonsense will serve. They *shall* talk. Ladies and gentlemen, I am ordered by Miss Woodhouse (who, wherever she is, presides,) to say, that she desires to know what you are all thinking of."

Some laughed, and answered good-humouredly. Miss Bates said a great deal; Mrs. Elton swelled[9] at the idea of Miss Woodhouse's presiding; Mr. Knightley's answer was the most distinct.

"Is Miss Woodhouse sure that she would like to hear what we are all thinking of?"

"Oh! no, no"—cried Emma, laughing as carelessly as she could—"Upon no account in the world. It is the very last thing I would stand the brunt of just now. Let me hear any thing rather than what you are all thinking of. I will not say quite all. There are one or two, perhaps, (glancing at Mr. Weston and Harriet,) whose thoughts I might not be afraid of knowing."

"It is a sort of thing," cried Mrs. Elton emphatically, "which *I* should not have thought myself privileged to inquire into. Though, perhaps, as the *Chaperon* of the party—*I* never was in any circle—exploring parties—young ladies—married women—"

Her mutterings were chiefly to her husband; and he murmured, in reply,

"Very true, my love, very true. Exactly so, indeed—quite unheard of—but some ladies say any thing. Better pass it off as a joke. Every body knows what is due to *you*."

"It will not do," whispered Frank to Emma, "they are most of them affronted. I will attack them with more address. Ladies and gentle-men—I am ordered by Miss Woodhouse to say, that she waves her right of knowing exactly what you may all be thinking of, and only requires something very entertaining from each of you, in a general way. Here are seven of you, besides myself, (who, she is pleased to say, am very entertaining already,) and she only demands from each of you either one thing very clever, be it prose or verse, original or repeated—or two things moderately clever—or three things very dull indeed, and she engages to laugh heartily at them all."

"Oh! very well," exclaimed Miss Bates, "then I need not be uneasy. 'Three things very dull indeed.' That will just do for me, you know. I shall be sure to say three dull things as soon as ever I open my

9. Similar to "puffed up." The figurative meaning blends with our knowledge of Mr. Elton's "broad handsome face."

mouth, shan't I?—(looking round with the most good-humoured dependence on every body's assent)—Do not you all think I shall?"

Emma could not resist.

"Ah! ma'am, but there may be a difficulty. Pardon me—but you will be limited as to number—only three at once."

Miss Bates, deceived by the mock ceremony of her manner, did not immediately catch her meaning; but, when it burst on her, it could not anger, though a slight blush showed that it could pain her.

"Ah!—well—to be sure. Yes, I see what she means, (turning to Mr. Knightley,) and I will try to hold my tongue. I must make myself very disagreeable, or she would not have said such a thing to an old friend."

"I like your plan," cried Mr. Weston. "Agreed, agreed. I will do my best. I am making a conundrum. How will a conundrum reckon?"

"Low, I am afraid, sir, very low," answered his son;—"but we shall be indulgent—especially to any one who leads the way."

"No, no," said Emma, "it will not reckon low. A conundrum of Mr. Weston's shall clear him and his next neighbour. Come, sir, pray let me hear it."

"I doubt it's being very clever myself," said Mr. Weston. "It is too much a matter of fact, but here it is.—What two letters of the alphabet are there, that express perfection?"

"What two letters!—express perfection! I am sure I do not know."

"Ah! you will never guess. You, (to Emma), I am certain, will never guess.—I will tell you.—M. and A.—Em—ma.—Do you understand?"

Understanding and gratification came together. It might be a very indifferent piece of wit; but Emma found a great deal to laugh at and enjoy in it—and so did Frank and Harriet.—It did not seem to touch the rest of the party equally; some looked very stupid about it, and Mr. Knightley gravely said,

"This explains the sort of clever thing that is wanted, and Mr. Weston has done very well for himself; but he must have knocked up[1] every body else. *Perfection* should not have come quite so soon."

"Oh! for myself, I protest I must be excused," said Mrs. Elton; "*I* really cannot attempt—I am not at all fond of the sort of thing. I had an acrostic once sent to me upon my own name, which I was not at all pleased with. I knew who it came from. An abominable puppy!—You know who I mean—(nodding to her husband). These kind of things are very well at Christmas, when one is sitting round the fire; but quite out of place, in my opinion, when one is exploring about the country in summer. Miss Woodhouse must excuse me. I am not one of those who have witty things at every body's service. I do not pre-

1. Exhausted.

tend to be a wit. I have a great deal of vivacity in my own way, but I really must be allowed to judge when to speak and when to hold my tongue. Pass us, if you please, Mr. Churchill. Pass Mr. E., Knightley, Jane, and myself. We have nothing clever to say—not one of us."

"Yes, yes, pray pass *me*," added her husband, with a sort of sneering consciousness; "*I* have nothing to say that can entertain Miss Woodhouse, or any other young lady. An old married man—quite good for nothing. Shall we walk, Augusta?"

"With all my heart. I am really tired of exploring so long on one spot. Come, Jane, take my other arm."

Jane declined it, however, and the husband and wife walked off. "Happy couple!" said Frank Churchill, as soon as they were out of hearing:—"How well they suit one another!—Very lucky—marrying as they did, upon an acquaintance formed only in a public place!— They only knew each other, I think, a few weeks in Bath! Peculiarly lucky!—for as to any real knowledge of a person's disposition that Bath, or any public place, can give—it is all nothing; there can be no knowledge. It is only by seeing women in their own homes, among their own set, just as they always are, that you can form any just judgment. Short of that, it is all guess and luck—and will generally be ill-luck. How many a man has committed himself on a short acquaintance, and rued it all the rest of his life!"

Miss Fairfax, who had seldom spoken before, except among her own confederates, spoke now.

"Such things do occur, undoubtedly."—She was stopped by a cough. Frank Churchill turned towards her to listen.

"You were speaking," said he, gravely. She recovered her voice.

"I was only going to observe, that though such unfortunate circumstances do sometimes occur both to men and women, I cannot imagine them to be very frequent. A hasty and imprudent attachment may arise—but there is generally time to recover from it afterwards; I would be understood to mean, that it can be only weak, irresolute characters, (whose happiness must be always at the mercy of chance,) who will suffer an unfortunate acquaintance to be an inconvenience, an oppression for ever."

He made no answer; merely looked, and bowed in submission; and soon afterwards said, in a lively tone,

"Well, I have so little confidence in my own judgment, that whenever I marry, I hope somebody will choose my wife for me. Will you? (turning to Emma.) Will you choose a wife for me?—I am sure I should like any body fixed on by you. You provide for the family, you know, (with a smile at his father). Find somebody for me. I am in no hurry. Adopt her, educate her."

"And make her like myself."

"By all means, if you can."

"Very well. I undertake the commission. You shall have a charming wife."

"She must be very lively, and have hazle eyes. I care for nothing else. I shall go abroad for a couple of years—and when I return, I shall come to you for my wife. Remember."

Emma was in no danger of forgetting. It was a commission to touch every favourite feeling. Would not Harriet be the very creature described?—Hazle eyes excepted, two years more might make her all that he wished. He might even have Harriet in his thoughts at the moment; who could say? Referring the education to her seemed to imply it.

"Now, ma'am," said Jane to her aunt, "shall we join Mrs. Elton?"

"If you please, my dear. With all my heart. I am quite ready. I was ready to have gone with her, but this will do just as well. We shall soon overtake her. There she is—no, that's somebody else. That's one of the ladies in the Irish car party, not at all like her.—Well, I declare—"

They walked off, followed in half a minute by Mr. Knightley. Mr. Weston, his son, Emma, and Harriet, only remained; and the young man's spirits now rose to a pitch almost unpleasant. Even Emma grew tired at last of flattery and merriment, and wished herself rather walking quietly about with any of the others, or sitting almost alone, and quite unattended to, in tranquil observation of the beautiful views beneath her. The appearance of the servants looking out for them to give notice of the carriages was a joyful sight; and even the bustle of collecting and preparing to depart, and the solicitude of Mrs. Elton to have *her* carriage first, were gladly endured, in the prospect of the quiet drive home which was to close the very questionable enjoyments of this day of pleasure. Such another scheme, composed of so many ill-assorted people, she hoped never to be betrayed into again.

While waiting for the carriage, she found Mr. Knightley by her side. He looked around, as if to see that no one were near, and then said,

"Emma, I must once more speak to you as I have been used to do: a privilege rather endured than allowed, perhaps, but I must still use it. I cannot see you acting wrong, without a remonstrance. How could you be *so* unfeeling to Miss Bates? How could you be so insolent in your wit to a woman of her character, age, and situation?—Emma, I had not thought it possible."

Emma recollected, blushed, was sorry, but tried to laugh it off.

"Nay, how could I help saying what I did?—Nobody could have helped it. It was not so very bad. I dare say she did not understand me."

"I assure you she did. She felt your full meaning. She has talked of it since. I wish you could have heard how she talked of it—with

what candour and generosity. I wish you could have heard her hon-
ouring your forbearance in being able to pay her such attentions, as
she was for ever receiving from yourself and your father, when her
society must be so irksome."

"Oh!" cried Emma, "I know there is not a better creature in the
world: but you must allow, that what is good and what is ridiculous
are most unfortunately blended in her."

"They are blended," said he, "I acknowledge; and, were she prosperous, I could allow much for the occasional prevalence of the
ridiculous over the good. Were she a woman of fortune, I would leave
every harmless absurdity to take its chance, I would not quarrel with
you for any liberties of manner. Were she your equal in situation—
but, Emma, consider how far this is from being the case. She is poor;
she has sunk from the comforts she was born to; and, if she live to
old age, must probably sink more. Her situation should secure your
compassion. It was badly done indeed!—You, whom she had known
from an infant, whom she had seen grow up from a period when her
notice was an honour, to have you now, in thoughtless spirits, and
the pride of the moment, laugh at her, humble her—and before her
niece, too—and before others, many of whom (certainly *some*,)
would be entirely guided by *your* treatment of her.—This is not pleasant to me; but I must, I will,—I will tell you truths while I can, satisfied with proving myself your friend by very faithful counsel, and
trusting that you will some time or other do me greater justice than
you can do now."

While they talked, they were advancing towards the carriage; it
was ready; and, before she could speak again, he had handed her in.
He had misinterpreted the feelings which kept her face averted, and
her tongue motionless. They were combined only of anger against
herself, mortification, and deep concern. She had not been able
to speak; and, on entering the carriage, sunk back for a moment
overcome—then reproaching herself for having taken no leave,
making no acknowledgement, parting in apparent sullenness, she
looked out with voice and hand eager to show a difference; but it was
just too late. He had turned away, and the horses were in motion.
She continued to look back, but in vain; and soon, with what
appeared unusual speed, they were half way down the hill, and every
thing left far behind. She was vexed beyond what could have been
expressed—almost beyond what she could conceal. Never had she
felt so agitated, mortified, grieved, at any circumstance in her life.
She was most forcibly struck. The truth of his representation there
was no denying. She felt it at her heart. How could she have been so
brutal, so cruel to Miss Bates!—How could she have exposed herself
to such ill opinion in any one she valued! And how suffer him to leave
her without saying one word of gratitude, of concurrence, of common kindness!

Time did not compose her. As she reflected more, she seemed but to feel it more. She never had been so depressed. Happily it was not necessary to speak. There was only Harriet, who seemed not in spirits herself, fagged,[2] and very willing to be silent; and Emma felt the tears running down her cheeks almost all the way home, without being at any trouble to check them, extraordinary as they were.

Chapter VIII

The wretchedness of a scheme to Box Hill was in Emma's thoughts all the evening. How it might be considered by the rest of the party, she could not tell. They, in their different homes, and their different ways, might be looking back on it with pleasure; but in her view it was a morning more completely misspent, more totally bare of rational satisfaction at the time, and more to be abhorred in recollection, than any she had ever passed. A whole evening of backgammon with her father, was felicity to it. *There* indeed, lay real pleasure, for there she was giving up the sweetest hours of the twenty-four to his comfort; and feeling that, unmerited as might be the degree of his fond affection and confiding esteem, she could not, in her general conduct, be open to any severe reproach. As a daughter, she hoped she was not without a heart. She hoped no one could have said to her, "How could you be so unfeeling to your father?—I must, I will tell you truths while I can." Miss Bates should never again—no, never! If attention, in future, could do away the past, she might hope to be forgiven. She had been often remiss, her conscience told her so; remiss, perhaps, more in thought than fact; scornful, ungracious. But it should be so no more. In the warmth of true contrition, she would call upon her the very next morning, and it should be the beginning, on her side, of a regular, equal, kindly intercourse.

She was just as determined when the morrow came, and went early, that nothing might prevent her. It was not unlikely, she thought, that she might see Mr. Knightley in her way; or, perhaps, he might come in while she were paying her visit. She had no objection. She would not be ashamed of the appearance of the penitence, so justly and truly hers. Her eyes were towards Donwell as she walked, but she saw him not.

"The ladies were all at home." She had never rejoiced at the sound before, nor ever before entered the passage, nor walked up the stairs, with any wish of giving pleasure, but in conferring obligation, or of deriving it, except in subsequent ridicule.

2. Fatigued.

There was a bustle on her approach; a good deal of moving and talking. She heard Miss Bates's voice, something was to be done in a hurry; the maid looked frightened and awkward; hoped she would be pleased to wait a moment, and then ushered her in too soon. The aunt and niece seemed both escaping to the adjoining room. Jane she had a distinct glimpse of, looking extremely ill; and, before the door had shut them out, she heard Miss Bates saying, "Well, my dear, I shall *say* you are laid down upon the bed, and I am sure you are ill enough."

Poor old Mrs. Bates, civil and humble as usual, looked as if she did not quite understand what was going on.

"I am afraid Jane is not very well," said she, "but I do not know; they *tell* me she is well. I dare say my daughter will be here presently, Miss Woodhouse. I hope you find a chair. I wish Hetty had not gone. I am very little able—Have you a chair, ma'am? Do you sit where you like? I am sure she will be here presently."

Emma seriously hoped she would. She had a moment's fear of Miss Bates keeping away from her. But Miss Bates soon came— "Very happy and obliged"—but Emma's conscience told her that there was not the same cheerful volubility as before—less ease of look and manner. A very friendly inquiry after Miss Fairfax, she hoped, might lead the way to a return of old feelings. The touch seemed immediate.

"Ah! Miss Woodhouse, how kind you are!—I suppose you have heard—and are come to give us joy. This does not seem much like joy, indeed, in me—(twinkling away a tear or two)—but it will be very trying for us to part with her, after having had her so long, and she has a dreadful headach just now, writing all the morning:—such long letters, you know, to be written to Colonel Campbell, and Mrs. Dixon. 'My dear,' said I, 'you will blind yourself'—for tears were in her eyes perpetually. One cannot wonder, one cannot wonder. It is a great change; and though she is amazingly fortunate—such a situation, I suppose, as no young woman before ever met with on first going out—do not think us ungrateful, Miss Woodhouse, for such surprising good fortune—(again dispersing her tears)—but, poor dear soul! if you were to see what a headach she has. When one is in great pain, you know one cannot feel any blessing quite as it may deserve. She is as low as possible. To look at her, nobody would think how delighted and happy she is to have secured such a situation. You will excuse her not coming to you—she is not able—she is gone into her own room—I want her to lie down upon the bed. 'My dear,' said I, 'I shall say you are laid down upon the bed:' but, however, she is not; she is walking about the room. But, now that she has written her letters, she says she shall soon be well. She will be extremely sorry to miss seeing you, Miss Woodhouse, but your kindness will excuse her.

You were kept waiting at the door—I was quite ashamed—but somehow there was a little bustle—for it so happened that we had not heard the knock, and till you were on the stairs, we did not know any body was coming. 'It is only Mrs. Cole,' said I, 'depend upon it. Nobody else would come so early.' 'Well,' said she, 'it must be borne some time or other, and it may as well be now.' But then Patty came in, and said it was you. 'Oh!' said I, 'it is Miss Woodhouse: I am sure you will like to see her.'—'I can see nobody,' said she; and up she got, and would go away; and that was what made us keep you waiting— and extremely sorry and ashamed we were. 'If you must go, my dear, said I, 'you must, and I will say you are laid down upon the bed.'"

Emma was most sincerely interested. Her heart had been long growing kinder towards Jane; and this picture of her present sufferings acted as a cure of every former ungenerous suspicion, and left her nothing but pity; and the remembrance of the less just and less gentle sensations of the past, obliged her to admit that Jane might very naturally resolve on seeing Mrs. Cole or any other steady friend, when she might not bear to see herself. She spoke as she felt, with earnest regret and solicitude—sincerely wishing that the circumstances which she collected from Miss Bates to be now actually determined on, might be as much for Miss Fairfax's advantage and comfort as possible. "It must be a severe trial to them all. She had understood it was to be delayed till Colonel Campbell's return."

"So very kind!" replied Miss Bates. "But you are always kind."

There was no bearing such an 'always;' and to break through her dreadful gratitude, Emma made the direct inquiry of—

"Where—may I ask?—is Miss Fairfax going?"

"To a Mrs. Smallridge—charming woman—most superior—to have the charge of her three little girls—delightful children. Impossible that any situation could be more replete with comfort; if we except, perhaps, Mrs. Suckling's own family, and Mrs. Bragge's; but Mrs. Smallridge is intimate with both, and in the very same neighbourhood:—lives only four miles from Maple Grove. Jane will be only four miles from Maple Grove."

"Mrs. Elton, I suppose, has been the person to whom Miss Fairfax owes——"

"Yes, our good Mrs. Elton. The most indefatigable, true friend. She would not take a denial. She would not let Jane say 'No;' for when Jane first heard of it, (it was the day before yesterday, the very morning we were at Donwell,) when Jane first heard of it, she was quite decided against accepting the offer, and for the reasons you mention; exactly as you say, she had made up her mind to close with nothing till Colonel Campbell's return, and nothing should induce her to enter into any engagement at present—and so she told Mrs. Elton over and over again—and I am sure I had no more idea that she would change her mind!—but that good Mrs. Elton, whose judgement never fails her, saw farther than I did. It is not every body that would have stood out in such a kind way as she did, and refuse to take Jane's answer; but she positively declared she would *not* write any such denial yesterday, as Jane wished her; she would wait—and, sure enough, yesterday evening it was all settled that Jane should go. Quite a surprise to me! I had not the least idea!—Jane took Mrs. Elton aside, and told her at once, that upon thinking over the advantages of Mrs. Suckling's situation, she had come to the resolution of accepting it.—I did not know a word of it till it was all settled."

"You spent the evening with Mrs. Elton?"

"Yes, all of us; Mrs. Elton would have us come. It was settled so, upon the hill, while we were walking about with Mr. Knightley. 'You *must all* spend your evening with us,' said she—I positively must have you *all* come.'"

"Mr. Knightley was there too, was he?"

"No, not Mr. Knightley; he declined it from the first; and though I thought he would come, because Mrs. Elton declared she would not let him off, he did not;—but my mother, and Jane, and I, were all there, and a very agreeable evening we had. Such kind friends, you know, Miss Woodhouse, one must always find agreeable, though every body seemed rather fagged after the morning's party. Even pleasure, you know, is fatiguing—and I cannot say that any of them seemed very much to have enjoyed it. However, *I* shall always think it a very pleasant party, and feel extremely obliged to the kind friends who included me in it."

"Miss Fairfax, I suppose, though you were not aware of it, had been making up her mind the whole day."

"I dare say she had."

"Whenever the time may come, it must be unwelcome to her and all her friends—but I hope her engagement will have every alleviation that is possible—I mean, as to the character and manners of the family."

"Thank you, dear Miss Woodhouse. Yes, indeed, there is every thing in the world that can make her happy in it. Except the Sucklings and Bragges, there is not such another nursery establishment, so liberal and elegant, in all Mrs. Elton's acquaintance. Mrs. Smallridge, a most delightful woman!—A style of living almost equal to Maple Grove—and as to the children, except the little Sucklings and little Bragges, there are not such elegant sweet children any where. Jane will be treated with such regard and kindness!—It will be nothing but pleasure, a life of pleasure.—And her salary!—I really cannot venture to name her salary to you, Miss Woodhouse. Even you, used as you are to great sums, would hardly believe that so much could be given to a young person like Jane."

"Ah! madam," cried Emma, "if other children are at all like what I remember to have been myself, I should think five times the amount of what I have ever yet heard named as a salary on such occasions, dearly earned."

"You are so noble in your ideas!"

"And when is Miss Fairfax to leave you?"

"Very soon, very soon indeed; that's the worst of it. Within a fortnight. Mrs. Smallridge is in a great hurry. My poor mother does not know how to bear it. So then, I try to put it out of her thoughts, and say, Come ma'am, do not let us think about it any more."

"Her friends must all be sorry to lose her; and will not Colonel and Mrs. Campbell be sorry to find that she has engaged herself before their return?"

"Yes; Jane says she is sure they will; but yet, this is such a situation as she cannot feel herself justified in declining. I was so astonished when she first told me what she had been saying to Mrs. Elton, and when Mrs. Elton at the same moment came congratulating me upon it! It was before tea—stay—no, it could not be before tea, because we were just going to cards—and yet it was before tea, because I remember thinking—Oh! no, now I recollect, now I have it; something happened before tea, but not that. Mr. Elton was called out of the room before tea, old John Abdy's son wanted to speak with him. Poor old John, I have a great regard for him; he was clerk to my poor father twenty-seven years; and now, poor old man, he is bed-ridden, and very poorly with the rheumatic gout in his joints—I must go and see him to-day; and so will Jane, I am sure, if she gets out at all. And poor John's son came to talk to Mr. Elton about relief from the parish: he is very well to do himself, you know, being head man at the Crown, ostler,[3] and every thing of that sort, but still he cannot keep his father without some help; and so, when Mr. Elton came back, he told us what John ostler had been telling him, and then it came out about the chaise having been sent to Randall's to take Mr. Frank Churchill to Richmond. That was what happened before tea. It was after tea that Jane spoke to Mrs. Elton."

Miss Bates would hardly give Emma time to say how perfectly new this circumstance was to her; but as without supposing it possible that she could be ignorant of any of the particulars of Mr. Frank Churchill's going, she proceeded to give them all, it was of no consequence.

What Mr. Elton had learnt from the ostler on the subject, being the accumulation of the ostler's own knowledge, and the knowledge of the servants at Randall's, was, that a messenger had come over from Richmond soon after the return of the party from Box Hill—

3. Stableman.

which messenger, however, had been no more than was expected; and that Mr. Churchill had sent his nephew a few lines, containing, upon the whole, a tolerable account of Mrs. Churchill, and only wishing him not to delay coming back beyond the next morning early; but that Mr. Frank Churchill having resolved to go home directly, without waiting at all, and his horse seeming to have got a cold, Tom had been sent off immediately for the Crown chaise, and the ostler had stood out and seen it pass by, the boy going a good pace, and driving very steady.

There was nothing in all this either to astonish or interest, and it caught Emma's attention only as it united with the subject which already engaged her mind. The contrast between Mrs. Churchill's importance in the world, and Jane Fairfax's, struck her; one was every thing, the other nothing—and she sat musing on the difference of woman's destiny, and quite unconscious on what her eyes were fixed, till roused by Miss Bates's saying,

"Ay, I see what you are thinking of, the piano forté. What is to become of that?—Very true. Poor dear Jane was talking of it just now.—You must go,' said she. 'You and I must part. You will have no business here.—Let it stay, however,' said she; 'give it house-room till Colonel Campbell comes back. I shall talk about it to him; he will settle for me; he will help me out of all my difficulties.'—And to this day, I do believe, she knows not whether it was his present or his daughter's."

Now Emma was obliged to think of the piano forté; and the remembrance of all her former fanciful and unfair conjectures was so little pleasing, that she soon allowed herself to believe her visit had been long enough; and, with a repetition of every thing that she could venture to say of the good wishes which she really felt, took leave.

Chapter IX

Emma's pensive meditations, as she walked home, were not interrupted; but in entering the parlour, she found those who must rouse her. Mr. Knightley and Harriet had arrived during her absence, and were sitting with her father.—Mr. Knightley immediately got up, and in a manner decidedly graver than usual, said,

"I would not go away without seeing you, but I have no time to spare, and therefore must now be gone directly. I am going to London, to spend a few days with John and Isabella. Have you any thing to send or say, besides the 'love,' which nobody carries?"

"Nothing at all. But is not this a sudden scheme?"

"Yes—rather—I have been thinking of it some little time."

Emma was sure he had not forgiven her; he looked unlike himself. Time, however, she thought, would tell him that they ought to be

friends again. While he stood, as if meaning to go, but not going—
her father began his inquiries.

"Well, my dear, and did you get there safely?—And how did you
find my worthy old friend and her daughter?—I dare say they must
have been very much obliged to you for coming. Dear Emma has
been to call on Mrs. and Miss Bates, Mr. Knightley, as I told you
before. She is always so attentive to them!"

Emma's colour was heightened by this unjust praise; and with
a smile, and shake of the head, which spoke much, she looked at
Mr. Knightley.—It seemed as if there were an instantaneous impression in her favour, as if his eyes received the truth from her's, and all
that had passed of good in her feelings were at once caught and
honoured.—He looked at her with a glow of regard. She was warmly
gratified—and in another moment still more so, by a little movement
of more than common friendliness on his part.—He took her hand;—
whether she had not herself made the first motion, she could not
say—she might, perhaps, have rather offered it—but he took her
hand, pressed it, and certainly was on the point of carrying it to his
lips—when, from some fancy or other, he suddenly let it go.—Why
he should feel such a scruple, why he should change his mind when
it was all but done, she could not perceive.—He would have judged
better, she thought, if he had not stopped.—The intention, however,
was indubitable; and whether it was that his manners had in general
so little gallantry, or however else it happened, but she thought nothing became him more.—It was with him, of so simple, yet so dignified a nature.—She could not but recall the attempt with great
satisfaction. It spoke such perfect amity.—He left them immediately
afterwards—gone in a moment. He always moved with the alertness
of a mind which could neither be undecided nor dilatory, but now he
seemed more sudden than usual in his disappearance.

Emma could not regret her having gone to Miss Bates, but she
wished she had left her ten minutes earlier;—it would have been
a great pleasure to talk over Jane Fairfax's situation with Mr.
Knightley.—Neither would she regret that he should be going to
Brunswick Square, for she knew how much his visit would be
enjoyed—but it might have happened at a better time—and to have
had longer notice of it, would have been pleasanter.—They parted
thorough friends, however; she could not be deceived as to the meaning of his countenance, and his unfinished gallantry;—it was all
done to assure her that she had fully recovered his good opinion.—He
had been sitting with them half an hour, she found. It was a pity that
she had not come back earlier!

In the hope of diverting her father's thoughts from the disagree-
ableness of Mr. Knightley's going to London; and going so suddenly;
and going on horseback, which she knew would be all very bad;

Emma communicated her news of Jane Fairfax, and her dependence on the effect was justified; it supplied a very useful check,—
interested, without disturbing him. He had long made up his mind to
Jane Fairfax's going out as governess, and could talk of if cheerfully,
but Mr. Knightley's going to London had been an unexpected blow.

"I am very glad indeed, my dear, to hear she is to be so comfortably
settled. Mrs. Elton is very good-natured and agreeable, and I dare say
her acquaintance are just what they ought to be. I hope it is a dry
situation, and that her health will be taken good care of. It ought to
be a first object, as I am sure poor Miss Taylor's always was with me.
You know, my dear, she is going to be to this new lady what Miss
Taylor was to us. And I hope she will be better off in one respect, and
not be induced to go away after it has been her home so long."

The following day brought news from Richmond to throw every
thing else into the back-ground. An express arrived at Randall's to
announce the death of Mrs. Churchill! Though her nephew had had
no particular reason to hasten back on her account, she had not lived
above six-and-thirty hours after his return. A sudden seizure of a different nature from any thing foreboded by her general state, had carried her off after a short struggle. The great Mrs. Churchill was no
more.

It was felt as such things must be felt. Every body had a degree of
gravity and sorrow; tenderness towards the departed, solicitude for
the surviving friends; and, in a reasonable time, curiosity to know
where she would be buried. Goldsmith tells us, that when lovely
woman stoops to folly, she has nothing to do but to die;[4] and when
she stoops to be disagreeable, it is equally to be recommended as
a clearer of ill-fame. Mrs. Churchill, after being disliked at least
twenty-five years, was now spoken of with compassionate allowances. In one point she was fully justified. She had never been admitted before to be seriously ill. The event acquitted her of all the
fancifulness, and all the selfishness of imaginary complaints.

"Poor Mrs. Churchill! no doubt she had been suffering a great
deal: more than any body had ever supposed—and continual pain
would try the temper. It was a sad event—a great shock—with all her
faults, what would Mr. Churchill do without her? Mr. Churchill's
loss would be dreadful indeed. Mr. Churchill would never get over
it."—Even Mr. Weston shook his head, and looked solemn, and said,
"Ah! poor woman, who would have thought it!" and resolved, that his
mourning should be as handsome as possible; and his wife sat sighing and moralizing over her broad hems with a commiseration and
good sense, true and steady. How it would affect Frank was among

---

4. "When lovely woman stoops to folly" is the first line of a song in Oliver Goldsmith's
Vicar of Wakefield.

the earliest thoughts of both. It was also a very early speculation with Emma. The character of Mrs. Churchill, the grief of her husband—her mind glanced over them both with awe and compassion—and then rested with lightened feelings on how Frank might be affected by the event, how benefited, how freed. She saw in a moment all the possible good. Now, an attachment to Harriet Smith would have nothing to encounter. Mr. Churchill, independent of his wife, was feared by nobody; an easy, guidable man, to be persuaded into any thing by his nephew. All that remained to be wished was, that the nephew should form the attachment, as, with all her good will in the cause, Emma could feel no certainty of its being already formed.

Harriet behaved extremely well on the occasion, with great self-command. Whatever she might feel of brighter hope, she betrayed nothing. Emma was gratified, to observe such a proof in her of strengthened character, and refrained from any allusion that might endanger its maintenance. They spoke, therefore, of Mrs. Churchill's death with mutual forbearance.

Short letters from Frank were received at Randall's, communicating all that was immediately important of their state and plans. Mr. Churchill was better than could be expected; and their first removal, on the departure of the funeral for Yorkshire, was to be to the house of a very old friend in Windsor, to whom Mr. Churchill had been promising a visit the last ten years. At present, there was nothing to be done for Harriet; good wishes for the future were all that could yet be possible on Emma's side.

It was a more pressing concern to show attention to Jane Fairfax, whose prospects were closing, while Harriet's opened, and whose engagements now allowed of no delay in any one at Highbury, who wished to show her kindness—and with Emma it was grown into a first wish. She had scarcely a stronger regret than for her past coldness; and the person, whom she had been so many months neglecting, was now the very one on whom she would have lavished every distinction of regard or sympathy. She wanted to be of use to her; wanted to show a value for her society, and testify respect and consideration. She resolved to prevail on her to spend a day at Hartfield. A note was written to urge it. The invitation was refused, and by a verbal message. "Miss Fairfax was not well enough to write;" and when Mr. Perry called at Hartfield, the same morning, it appeared that she was so much indisposed as to have been visited, though against her own consent, by himself, and that she was suffering under severe headachs, and a nervous fever to a degree, which made him doubt the possibility of her going to Mrs. Smallridge's at the time proposed. Her health seemed for the moment completely deranged—appetite quite gone—and though there were no absolutely alarming symptoms, nothing touching the pulmonary complaint, which was the standing apprehension of the family, Mr. Perry was uneasy about her. He thought she had undertaken more than she was equal to, and that she felt it so herself, though she would not own it. Her spirits seemed overcome. Her present home, he could not but observe, was unfavourable to a nervous disorder:—confined always to one room;—he could have wished it otherwise—and her good aunt, though his very old friend, he must acknowledge to be not the very best companion for an invalid of that description. Her care and attention could not be questioned; they were, in fact, only too great. He very much feared that Miss Fairfax derived more evil than good from them. Emma listened with the warmest concern; grieved for her more and more, and looked around eager to discover some way of being useful. To take her—be it only an hour or two—from her aunt, to give her change of air and scene, and quiet rational conversation, even for an hour or two, might do her good; and the following morning she wrote again to say, in the most feeling language she could command, that she would call for her in the carriage at any hour that Jane would name—mentioning that she had Mr. Perry's decided opinion, in favour of such exercise for his patient. The answer was only in this short note:

"Miss Fairfax's compliments and thanks, but is quite unequal to any exercise."

Emma felt that her own note had deserved something better; but it was impossible to quarrel with words, whose tremulous inequality showed indisposition so plainly, and she thought only of how she might best counteract this unwillingness to be seen or assisted. In spite of the answer, therefore, she ordered the carriage, and drove to Mrs. Bates's, in the hope that Jane would be induced to join her—but it would not do;—Miss Bates came to the carriage door, all gratitude, and agreeing with her most earnestly in thinking an airing might be the greatest service—and every thing that message could do was tried—but all in vain. Miss Bates was obliged to return without success; Jane was quite unpersuadable; the mere proposal of going out seemed to make her worse.—Emma wished she could have seen her, and tried her own powers; but, almost before she could hint the wish, Miss Bates made it appear that she had promised her niece on no account to let Miss Woodhouse in. "Indeed, the truth was, that poor dear Jane could not bear to see anybody—anybody at all—Mrs. Elton, indeed, could not be denied—and Mrs. Cole had made such a point—and Mrs. Perry had said so much—but, except them, Jane would really see nobody."

Emma did not want to be classed with the Mrs. Eltons, the Mrs. Perrys, and the Mrs. Coles, who would force themselves anywhere; neither could she feel any right of preference herself—she submitted, therefore, and only questioned Miss Bates farther as to her niece's appetite and diet, which she longed to be able to assist. On that subject poor Miss Bates was very unhappy, and very communicative; Jane would hardly eat any thing:—Mr. Perry recommended nourishing food; but every thing they could command (and never had anybody such good neighbours) was distasteful.

Emma, on reaching home, called the housekeeper directly, to an examination of her stores; and some arrow-root[5] of very superior quality was speedily despatched to Miss Bates with a most friendly note. In half an hour the arrow-root was returned, with a thousand thanks from Miss Bates, but "dear Jane would not be satisfied without its being sent back; it was a thing she could not take—and, moreover, she insisted on her saying, that she was not at all in want of any thing."

When Emma afterwards heard that Jane Fairfax had been seen wandering about the meadows, at some distance from Highbury, on the afternoon of the very day on which she had, under the plea of being unequal to any exercise, so peremptorily refused to go out with her in the carriage, she could have no doubt—putting every thing together—that Jane was resolved to receive no kindness from *her*. She was sorry, very sorry. Her heart was grieved for a state which seemed but the more pitiable from this sort of irritation of spirits, inconsistency of action, and inequality of powers; and it mortified her that she was given so little credit for proper feeling, or esteemed so little worthy as a friend: but she had the consolation of knowing that her intentions were good, and of being able to say to herself, that could Mr. Knightley have been privy to all her attempts of assisting Jane Fairfax, could he even have seen into her heart, he would not, on this occasion, have found any thing to reprove.

Chapter X

One morning, about ten days after Mrs. Churchill's decease, Emma was called down stairs to Mr. Weston, who "could not stay five minutes, and wanted particularly to speak with her."—He met her at the parlour door, and hardly asking her how she did, in the natural key of his voice, sunk it immediately, to say, unheard by her father,

"Can you come to Randall's at any time this morning?—Do, if it be possible. Mrs. Weston wants to see you. She must see you."

"Is she unwell?"

"No, no, not at all—only a little agitated. She would have ordered the carriage, and come to you, but she must see you *alone*,—and that you know—(nodding towards her father)—Humph!—Can you come?"

---

5. A nutritious vegetable starch.

"Certainly. This moment, if you please. It is impossible to refuse what you ask in such a way. But what can be the matter?—Is she really not ill?"

"Depend upon me—but ask no more questions. You will know it all in time. The most unaccountable business! But hush, hush!"

To guess what all this meant, was impossible even for Emma. Something really important seemed announced by his looks; but, as her friend was well, she endeavoured not to be uneasy, and settling it with her father, that she would take her walk now, she and Mr. Weston were soon out of the house together, and on their way at a quick pace for Randall's.

"Now,"—said Emma, when they were fairly beyond the sweep gates,—"now, Mr. Weston, do let me know what has happened."

"No, no,"—he gravely replied.—"Don't ask me. I promised my wife to leave it all to her. She will break it to you better than I can. Do not be impatient, Emma; it will all come out too soon."

"Break it to me," cried Emma, standing still with terror.—"Good God!—Mr. Weston, tell me at once.—Something has happened in Brunswick Square. I know it has. Tell me, I charge you tell me this moment what it is."

"No, indeed you are mistaken."—

"Mr. Weston do not trifle with me.—Consider how many of my dearest friends are now in Brunswick Square. Which of them is it?—I charge you by all that is sacred, not to attempt concealment."

"Upon my word, Emma."—

"Your word!—why not your honour!—why not say upon your honour, that it has nothing to do with any of them? Good Heavens!—What can be to be *broke* to me, that does not[6] relate to one of that family?"

"Upon my honour," said he very seriously, "it does not. It is not in the smallest degree connected with any human being of the name of Knightley."

Emma's courage returned, and she walked on.

"I was wrong," he continued, "in talking of its being *broke* to you. I should not have used the expression. In fact, it does not concern you—it concerns only myself,—that is, we hope.—Humph!—In short, my dear Emma, there is no occasion to be so uneasy about it. I don't say that it is not a disagreeable business—but things might be much worse.—If we walk fast, we shall soon be at Randall's."

Emma found that she must wait; and now it required little effort. She asked no more questions therefore, merely employed her own fancy, and that soon pointed out to her the probability of its being some money concern—something just come to light, of a disagreeable

6. 1816 omits "not," probably in error, as Chapman suggests.

nature in the circumstances of the family,—something which the late event at Richmond had brought forward. Her fancy was very active. Half a dozen natural children, perhaps—and poor Frank cut off!—This, though very undesirable, would be no matter of agony to her. It inspired little more than an animating curiosity.

"Who is that gentleman on horseback?" said she, as they proceeded—speaking more to assist Mr. Weston in keeping his secret, than with any other view.

"I do not know.—One of the Otways.—Not Frank;—it is not Frank, I assure you. You will not see him. He is half way to Windsor by this time."

"Has your son been with you, then?"

"Oh! yes—did not you know?—Well, well, never mind."

For a moment he was silent; and then added, in a tone much more guarded and demure,

"Yes, Frank came over this morning, just to ask us how we did."

They hurried on, and were speedily at Randall's.—"Well, my dear," said he, as they entered the room—"I have brought her, and now I hope you will soon be better. I shall leave you together. There is no use in delay. I shall not be far off, if you want me."—And Emma distinctly heard him add, in a lower tone, before he quitted the room,— "I have been as good as my word. She has not the least idea."

Mrs. Weston was looking so ill, and had an air of so much perturbation that Emma's uneasiness increased; and the moment they were alone, she eagerly said,

"What is it my dear friend? Something of a very unpleasant nature, I find, has occurred;—do let me know directly what it is. I have been walking all this way in complete suspense. We both abhor suspense. Do not let mine continue longer. It will do you good to speak of your distress, whatever it may be."

"Have you indeed no idea?" said Mrs. Weston in a trembling voice. "Cannot you, my dear Emma—cannot you form a guess as to what you are to hear?"

"So far as that it relates to Mr. Frank Churchill, I do guess."

"You are right. It does relate to him, and I will tell you directly;" (resuming her work, and seeming resolved against looking up.) "He has been here this very morning, on a most extraordinary errand. It is impossible to express our surprise. He came to speak to his father on a subject,—to announce an attachment—"

She stopped to breathe. Emma thought first of herself, and then of Harriet.

"More than an attachment, indeed," resumed Mrs. Weston; "an engagement—a positive engagement.—What will you say, Emma— what will anybody say, when it is known that Frank Churchill and Miss Fairfax are engaged;—nay, that they have been long engaged!"

Emma even jumped with surprise;—and, horror-struck, exclaimed,

"Jane Fairfax!—Good God! You are not serious? You do not mean it?"

"You may well be amazed," returned Mrs. Weston, still averting her eyes, and talking on with eagerness, that Emma might have time to recover—"You may well be amazed. But it is even so. There has been a solemn engagement between them ever since October— formed at Weymouth, and kept a secret from everybody. Not a creature knowing it but themselves—neither the Campbells, nor her family, nor his.—It is so wonderful, that though perfectly con- vinced of the fact, it is yet almost incredible to myself. I can hardly believe it.—I thought I knew him."

Emma scarcely heard what was said.—Her mind was divided between two ideas—her own former conversations with him about Miss Fairfax; and poor Harriet;—and for some time she could only exclaim, and require confirmation, repeated confirmation.

"Well," said she at last, trying to recover herself; "this is a cir- cumstance which I must think of at least half a day, before I can at all comprehend it. What!—engaged to her all the winter—before either of them came to Highbury?"

"Engaged since October,—secretly engaged.—It has hurt me, Emma, very much. It has hurt his father equally. *Some part* of his conduct we cannot excuse."

Emma pondered a moment, and then replied, "I will not pretend *not* to understand you; and to give you all the relief in my power, be assured that no such effect has followed his attentions to me, as you are apprehensive of."

Mrs. Weston looked up, afraid to believe; but Emma's counte- nance was as steady as her words.

"That you may have less difficulty in believing this boast, of my present perfect indifference," she continued, "I will farther tell you, that there was a period in the early part of our acquaintance, when I did like him, when I was very much disposed to be attached to him—nay, was attached—and how it came to cease, is perhaps the wonder. Fortunately, however, it did cease. I have really for some time past, for at least these three months, cared nothing about him. You may believe me, Mrs. Weston. This is the simple truth."

Mrs. Weston kissed her with tears of joy; and when she could find utterance, assured her, that this protestation had done her more good than any thing else in the world could do.

"Mr. Weston will be almost as much relieved as myself," said she. "On this point we have been wretched. It was our darling wish that you might be attached to each other—and we were persuaded that it was so.—Imagine what we have been feeling on your account."

"I have escaped; and that I should escape, may be a matter of grateful wonder to you and myself. But this does not acquit *him*, Mrs. Weston; and I must say, that I think him greatly to blame.

What right had he to come among us with affection and faith engaged, and with manners so *very* disengaged? What right had he to endeavour to please, as he certainly did—to distinguish any one young woman with persevering attention, as he certainly did—while he really belonged to another?—How could he tell what mischief he might be doing?—How could he tell that he might not be making me in love with him?—very wrong, very wrong indeed."

"From something that he said, my dear Emma, I rather imagine—"

"And how could *she* bear such behaviour! Composure with a witness! to look on, while repeated attentions were offering to another woman, before her face, and not resent it.—That is a degree of placidity, which I can neither comprehend nor respect."

"There were misunderstandings between them, Emma; he said so expressly. He had not time to enter into much explanation. He was here only a quarter of an hour, and in a state of agitation which did not allow the full use even of the time he could stay—but that there had been misunderstandings he decidedly said. The present crisis, indeed, seemed to be brought on by them; and those misunderstandings might very possibly arise from the impropriety of his conduct."

"Impropriety! Oh! Mrs. Weston—it is too calm a censure. Much, much beyond impropriety!—It has sunk him, I cannot say how it has sunk him in my opinion. So unlike what a man should be!—None of that upright integrity, that strict adherence to truth and principle, that disdain of trick and littleness, which a man should display in every transaction of his life."

"Nay, dear Emma, now I must take his part; for though he has been wrong in this instance, I have known him long enough to answer for his having many, very many good qualities; and—"

"Good God!" cried Emma, not attending to her.—"Mrs. Smallridge, too! Jane actually on the point of going as governess! What could he mean by such horrible indelicacy? To suffer her to engage herself—to suffer her even to think of such a measure!"

"He knew nothing about it, Emma. On this article I can fully acquit him. It was a private resolution of her's not communicated to him—or at least not communicated in a way to carry conviction.—Till yesterday, I know he said he was in the dark as to her plans. They burst on him, I do not know how, but by some letter or message—and it was the discovery of what she was doing, of this very project of her's which determined him to come forward at once, own it all to his uncle, throw himself on his kindness, and, in short, put an end to the miserable state of concealment that had been carrying on so long."

Emma began to listen better.

"I am to hear from him soon," continued Mrs. Weston. "He told me at parting, that he should soon write; and he spoke in a manner which seemed to promise me many particulars that could not be given now. Let us wait, therefore, for this letter. It may bring many extenuations. It may make many things intelligible and excusable which now are not to be understood. Don't let us be severe, don't let us be in a hurry to condemn him. Let us have patience. I must love him; and now that I am satisfied on one point, the one material point, I am sincerely anxious for its all turning out well, and ready to hope that it may. They must both have suffered a great deal under such a system of secrecy and concealment."

"*His* sufferings," replied Emma drily, "do not appear to have done him much harm. Well, and how did Mr. Churchill take it?"

"Most favourable for his nephew—gave his consent with scarcely a difficulty. Conceive what the events of a week have done in that family! While poor Mrs. Churchill lived, I suppose there could not have been a hope, a chance, a possibility;—but scarcely are her remains at rest in the family vault, than her husband is persuaded to act exactly opposite to what she would have required. What a blessing it is, when undue influence does not survive the grave!—He gave his consent with very little persuasion."

"Ah!" thought Emma, "he would have done as much for Harriet."

"This was settled last night, and Frank was off with the light this morning. He stopped at Highbury, at the Bates's, I fancy, some time—and then came on hither; but was in such a hurry to get back to his uncle, to whom he is just now more necessary than ever, that, as I tell you, he could stay with us but a quarter of an hour.—He was very much agitated—very much, indeed—to a degree that made him appear quite a different creature from any thing I had ever seen him before.—In addition to all the rest, there had been the shock of finding her so very unwell, which he had had no previous suspicion of— and there was every appearance of his having been feeling a great deal."

"And do you really believe the affair to have been carrying on with such perfect secrecy?—The Campbells, the Dixons, did none of them know of the engagement?"

Emma could not speak the name of Dixon without a little blush.

"None; not one. He positively said that it had been known to no being in the world but their two selves."

"Well," said Emma, "I suppose we shall gradually grow reconciled to the idea, and I wish them very happy. But I shall always think it a very abominable sort of proceeding. What has it been but a system of hypocrisy and deceit,—espionage, and treachery?—To come among us with professions of openness and simplicity; and such a league in secret to judge us all!—Here have we been, the whole winter and spring, completely duped, fancying ourselves all on an equal footing of truth and honour, with two people in the midst of us who may have been carrying round, comparing and sitting in judgment on sentiments and words that were never meant for both to hear.—They must take the consequence, if they have heard each other spoken of in a way not perfectly agreeable!"

"I am quite easy on that head," replied Mrs. Weston. "I am very sure that I never said any thing of either to the other, which both might not have heard."

"You are in luck.—Your only blunder was confined to my ear, when you imagined a certain friend of our's in love with the lady."

"True. But as I have always had a thoroughly good opinion of Miss Fairfax, I never could, under any blunder, have spoken ill of her; and as to speaking ill of him, there I must have been safe."

At this moment Mr. Weston appeared at a little distance from the window, evidently on the watch. His wife gave him a look which invited him in; and, while he was coming round, added, "Now, dearest Emma, let me intreat you to say and look every thing that may set his heart at ease, and incline him to be satisfied with the match. Let us make the best of it—and, indeed, almost every thing may be fairly said in her favour. It is not a connexion to gratify; but if Mr. Churchill does not feel that, why should we? and it may be a very fortunate circumstance for him, for Frank, I mean, that he should have attached himself to a girl of such steadiness of character and good judgment as I have always given her credit for—and still am disposed to give her credit for, in spite of this one great deviation from the strict rule of right. And how much may be said in her situation for even that error!"

"Much indeed!" cried Emma, feelingly. "If a woman can ever be excused for thinking only of herself, it is in a situation like Jane Fairfax's.—Of such, one may almost say, that 'the world is not their's, nor the world's law.'"[7]

She met Mr. Weston on his entrance, with a smiling countenance, exclaiming,

"A very pretty trick you have been playing me, upon my word! This was a device, I suppose, to sport with my curiosity and exercise my talent of guessing. But you really frightened me. I thought you had lost half your property, at least. And here, instead of its being a matter of condolence, it turns out to be one of congratulation.—I congratulate you, Mr. Weston, with all my heart, on the prospect of having one of the most lovely and accomplished young women in England for your daughter."

7. An echo of *Romeo and Juliet* 5.1.72. In 1751, Samuel Johnson had used the phrase in *The Rambler*, No. 107, which discusses innocent women betrayed by libertines and led into prostitution.

A glance or two between him and his wife, convinced him that all was as right as this speech proclaimed; and its happy effect on his spirits was immediate. His air and voice recovered their usual briskness: he shook her heartily and gratefully by the hand, and entered on the subject in a manner to prove, that he now only wanted time and persuasion to think the engagement no very bad thing. His companions suggested only what could palliate imprudence, or smooth objections; and by the time they had talked it all over together, and he had talked it all over again with Emma, in their walk back to Hartfield, he was become perfectly reconciled, and not far from thinking it the very best thing that Frank could possibly have done.

Chapter XI

"Harriet, poor Harriet!"—Those were the words; in them lay the tormenting ideas which Emma could not get rid of, and which constituted the real misery of the business to her. Frank Churchill had behaved very ill by herself—very ill in many ways,—but it was not so much *his* behaviour as her *own*, which made her so angry with him. It was the scrape which he had drawn her into on Harriet's account, that gave the deepest hue to his offence.—Poor Harriet! to be a second time the dupe of her misconceptions and flattery. Mr. Knightley had spoken prophetically, when he once said, "Emma, you have been no friend to Harriet Smith."—She was afraid she had done her nothing but disservice.—It was true that she had not to charge herself, in this instance as in the former, with being the sole and original author of the mischief; with having suggested such feelings as might otherwise never have entered Harriet's imagination; for Harriet had acknowledged her admiration and preference of Frank Churchill before she had ever given her a hint on the subject; but she felt completely guilty of having encouraged what she might have repressed. She might have prevented the indulgence and increase of such sentiments. Her influence would have been enough. And now she was very conscious that she ought to have prevented them.—She felt that she had been risking her friend's happiness on most insufficient grounds. Common sense would have directed her to tell Harriet, that she must not allow herself to think of him, and that there were five hundred chances to one against his ever caring for her.—"But, with common sense," she added, "I am afraid I have had little to do."

She was extremely angry with herself. If she could not have been angry with Frank Churchill too, it would have been dreadful.—As for Jane Fairfax, she might at least relieve her feelings from any present solicitude on her account. Harriet would be anxiety enough; she need no longer be unhappy about Jane, whose troubles and whose ill health having, of course, the same origin, must be equally under cure.—Her days of insignificance and evil were over.—She would soon be well, and happy, and prosperous.—Emma could now imagine why her own attentions had been slighted. This discovery laid many smaller matters open. No doubt it had been from jealousy.—In Jane's eyes she had been a rival; and well might any thing she could offer of assistance or regard be repulsed. An airing in the Hartfield carriage would have been the rack, and arrow-root from the Hartfield store-room must have been poison. She understood it all; and as far as her mind could disengage itself from the injustice and selfishness of angry feelings, she acknowledged that Jane Fairfax would have neither elevation nor happiness beyond her desert. But poor Harriet was such an engrossing charge! There was little sympathy to be spared for any body else. Emma was sadly fearful that this second disappointment would be more severe than the first. Considering the very superior claims of the object, it ought; and judging by its apparently stronger effect on Harriet's mind, producing reserve and self-command, it would.—She must communicate the painful truth, however, and as soon as possible. An injunction of secresy had been among Mr. Weston's parting words. "For the present, the whole affair was to be completely a secret. Mr. Churchill had made a point of it, as a token of respect to the wife he had so very recently lost; and everybody admitted it to be no more than due decorum."—Emma had promised; but still Harriet must be excepted. It was her superior duty.

In spite of her vexation, she could not help feeling it almost ridiculous, that she should have the very same distressing and delicate office to perform by Harriet, which Mrs. Weston had just gone through by herself. The intelligence, which had been so anxiously announced to her, she was now to be anxiously announcing to another. Her heart beat quick on hearing Harriet's footstep and voice; so, she supposed, had poor Mrs. Weston felt when *she* was approaching Randall's. Could the event of the disclosure bear an equal resemblance!—But of that, unfortunately, there could be no chance.

"Well, Miss Woodhouse!" cried Harriet, coming eagerly into the room—"is not this the oddest news that ever was?"

"What news do you mean?" replied Emma, unable to guess, by look or voice, whether Harriet could indeed have received any hint.

"About Jane Fairfax. Did you ever hear any thing so strange? Oh!—you need not be afraid of owning it to me, for Mr. Weston has told me himself. I met him just now. He told me it was to be a great secret; and, therefore, I should not think of mentioning it to any body but you, but he said you knew it."

"What did Mr. Weston tell you?"—said Emma, still perplexed.

"Oh! he told me all about it; that Jane Fairfax and Mr. Frank Churchill are to be married, and that they have been privately engaged to one another this long while. How very odd!"

It was, indeed, so odd; Harriet's behaviour was so extremely odd, that Emma did not know how to understand it. Her character appeared absolutely changed. She seemed to propose showing no agitation, or disappointment, or peculiar concern in the discovery. Emma looked at her, quite unable to speak.

"Had you any idea," cried Harriet, "of his being in love with her?—You, perhaps, might.—You (blushing as she spoke) who can see into everybody's heart; but nobody else——"

"Upon my word," said Emma, "I begin to doubt my having any such talent. Can you seriously ask me, Harriet, whether I imagined him attached to another woman at the very time that I was—tacitly, if not openly—encouraging you to give way to your own feelings?—I never had the slightest suspicion, till within the last hour, of Mr. Frank Churchill's having the least regard for Jane Fairfax. You may be very sure that if I had, I should have cautioned you accordingly."

"Me!" cried Harriet, colouring, and astonished. "Why should you caution me?—You do not think I care about Mr. Frank Churchill."

"I am delighted to hear you speak so stoutly on the subject," replied Emma, smiling; "but you do not mean to deny that there was a time—and not very distant either—when you gave me reason to understand that you did care about him?"

"Him!—never, never. Dear Miss Woodhouse, how could you so mistake me?" turning away distressed.

"Harriet!" cried Emma, after a moment's pause—"What do you mean?—Good Heaven! what do you mean?—Mistake you!—Am I to suppose then?——"

She could not speak another word.—Her voice was lost; and she sat down, waiting in great terror till Harriet should answer.

Harriet, who was standing at some distance, and with face turned from her, did not immediately say any thing; and when she did speak, it was in a voice nearly as agitated as Emma's.

"I should not have thought it possible," she began, "that you could have misunderstood me! I know we agreed never to name him—but considering how infinitely superior he is to every body else, I should not have thought it possible that I could be supposed to mean any other person. Mr. Frank Churchill, indeed! I do not know who would ever look at him in the company of the other. I hope I have a better taste than to think of Mr. Frank Churchill, who is like nobody by his side. And that you should have been so mistaken, is amazing!—I am sure, but for believing that you entirely approved and meant to encourage me in my attachment, I should have considered it at first too great a presumption almost, to dare to think of him. At first, if you had not told me that more wonderful things had happened; that there had been matches of greater disparity (those were your very words);—I should not have dared to give way to—I should not have thought it possible—But if *you*, who had been always acquainted with him——"

"Harriet!" cried Emma, collecting herself resolutely—"Let us understand each other now, without the possibility of farther mistake. Are you speaking of—Mr. Knightley?"

"To be sure I am. I never could have an idea of anybody else—and so I thought you knew. When we talked about him, it was clear as possible."

"Not quite," returned Emma, with forced calmness, "for all that you then said, appeared to me to relate to a different person. I could almost assert that you had *named* Mr. Frank Churchill. I am sure the service Mr. Frank Churchill had rendered you, in protecting you from the gipsies, was spoken of."

"Oh! Miss Woodhouse, how you do forget!"

"My dear Harriet, I perfectly remember the substance of what I said on the occasion. I told you that I did not wonder at your attachment; that considering the service he had rendered you, it was extremely natural:—and you agreed to it, expressing yourself very warmly as to your sense of that service, and mentioning even what your sensations had been in seeing him come forward to your rescue.—The impression of it is strong on my memory."

"Oh, dear," cried Harriet, "now I recollect what you mean; but I was thinking of something very different at the time. It was not the gipsies—it was not Mr. Frank Churchill that I meant. No! (with some elevation) I was thinking of a much more precious circumstance—of Mr. Knightley's coming and asking me to dance, when Mr. Elton would not stand up with me; and when there was no other partner in the room. That was the kind action; that was the noble benevolence and generosity; that was the service which made me begin to feel how superior he was to every other being upon earth."

"Good God!" cried Emma, "this has been a most unfortunate—most deplorable mistake!—What is to be done?"

"You would not have encouraged me, then, if you had understood me. At least, however, I cannot be worse off than I should have been, if the other had been the person; and now—it *is* possible——."

She paused a few moments. Emma could not speak.

"I do not wonder, Miss Woodhouse," she resumed, "that you should feel a great difference between the two, as to me or as to anybody. You must think one five hundred million times more above me than the other. But I hope, Miss Woodhouse, that supposing—that if—strange as it may appear—. But you know they were your own words, that *more* wonderful things had happened, matches of *greater* disparity had taken place than between Mr. Frank Churchill and me; and, therefore, it seems as if such a thing even as this, may have occurred before—and if I should be so fortunate, beyond expression, as to—if Mr. Knightley should really—if *he* does not mind the disparity, I hope, dear Miss Woodhouse, you will not set yourself against it, and try to put difficulties in the way. But you are too good for that, I am sure."

Harriet was standing at one of the windows. Emma turned round to look at her in consternation, and hastily said,

"Have you any idea of Mr. Knightley's returning your affection?"

"Yes," replied Harriet modestly, but not fearfully—"I must say that I have."

Emma's eyes were instantly withdrawn; and she sat silently meditating, in a fixed attitude, for a few minutes. A few minutes were sufficient for making her acquainted with her own heart. A mind like her's, once opening to suspicion, made rapid progress. She touched—she admitted—she acknowledged the whole truth. Why was it so much worse that Harriet should be in love with Mr. Knightley, than with Frank Churchill? Why was the evil so dreadfully increased by Harriet's having some hope of a return? It darted through her, with the speed of an arrow, that Mr. Knightley must marry no one but herself!

Her own conduct, as well as her own heart, was before her in the same few minutes. She saw it all with a clearness which had never blessed her before. How improperly had she been acting by Harriet! How inconsiderate, how indelicate, how irrational, how unfeeling had been her conduct! What blindness, what madness, had led her on! It struck her with dreadful force, and she was ready to give it every bad name in the world. Some portion of respect for herself, however, in spite of all these demerits—some concern for her own appearance, and a strong sense of justice by Harriet—(there would be no need of *compassion* to the girl who believed herself loved by Mr. Knightley—but justice required that she should not be made unhappy by any coldness now,) gave Emma the resolution to sit and endure farther with calmness, with even apparent kindness.—For her own advantage indeed, it was fit that the utmost extent of Harriet's hopes should be enquired into; and Harriet had done nothing to forfeit the regard and interest which had been so voluntarily formed and maintained—or to deserve to be slighted by the person, whose counsels had never led her right.—Rousing from reflection, therefore, and subduing her emotion, she turned to Harriet again, and, in a more inviting accent, renewed the conversation; for as to the subject which had first introduced it, the wonderful story of Jane Fairfax, that was quite sunk and lost.—Neither of them thought but of Mr. Knightley and themselves.

Harriet, who had been standing in no unhappy reverie, was yet very glad to be called from it, by the now encouraging manner of such a judge, and such a friend as Miss Woodhouse, and only wanted invitation, to give the history of her hopes with great, though trembling delight.—Emma's tremblings as she asked, and as she listened, were better concealed than Harriet's, but they were not less. Her voice was not unsteady; but her mind was in all the perturbation that such a developement of self, such a burst of threatening evil, such a confusion of sudden and perplexing emotions, must create.— She listened with much inward suffering, but with great outward patience, to Harriet's detail.—Methodical, or well arranged, or very well delivered, it could not be expected to be; but it contained, when separated from all the feebleness and tautology of the narration, a substance to sink her spirit—especially with the corroborating circumstances, which her own memory brought in favour of Mr. Knightley's most improved opinion of Harriet.

Harriet had been conscious of a difference in his behaviour ever since those two decisive dances.—Emma knew that he had, on that occasion, found her much superior to his expectation. From that evening, or at least from the time of Miss Woodhouse's encouraging her to think of him, Harriet had begun to be sensible of his talking to her much more than she had been used to do, and of his having indeed quite a different manner towards her; a manner of kindness and sweetness!—Latterly she had been more and more aware of it. When they had been all walking together, he had so often come and walked by her, and talked so very delightfully!—He seemed to want to be acquainted with her. Emma knew it to have been very much the case. She had often observed the change, to almost the same extent.— Harriet repeated expressions of approbation and praise from him— and Emma felt them to be in the closest agreement with what she had known of his opinion of Harriet. He praised her for being without art or affectation, for having simple, honest, generous, feelings.— She knew that he saw such recommendations in Harriet; he had dwelt on them to her more than once.—Much that lived in Harriet's memory, many little particulars of the notice she had received from him, a look, a speech, a removal from one chair to another, a compliment implied, a preference inferred, had been unnoticed, because unsuspected by Emma. Circumstances that might swell to half an hour's relation, and contained multiplied proofs to her who had seen them, had passed undiscerned by her who now heard them; but the two latest occurrences to be mentioned, the two of strongest promise to Harriet, were not without some degree of witness from Emma herself.—The first, was his walking with her apart from the others, in the lime walk at Donwell, where they had been walking some time before Emma came, and he had taken pains (as she was convinced) to draw her from the rest to himself—and at first, he had talked to her in a more particular way than he had ever done before, in a very particular way indeed!—(Harriet could not recall it without a blush.) He seemed to be almost asking her, whether her affections were engaged.—But as soon as she (Miss Woodhouse) appeared likely to join them, he changed the subject, and began talking about farming:—The second, was having sat talking with her nearly half an hour before Emma came back from her visit, the very last morning of his being at Hartfield—though, when he first came in, he had said that he could not stay five minutes—and his having told her, during their conversation, that though he must go to London, it was very much against his inclination that he left home at all, which was much more (as Emma felt) than he had acknowledged to *her*. The superior degree of confidence towards Harriet, which this one article marked, gave her severe pain.

On the subject of the first of the two circumstances, she did, after a little reflection, venture the following question. "Might he not?—Is not it possible, that when enquiring, as you thought, into the state of your affections, he might be alluding to Mr. Martin—he might have Mr. Martin's interest in view?"—But Harriet rejected the suspicion with spirit.

"Mr. Martin! No indeed!—There was not a hint of Mr. Martin. I hope I know better now, than to care for Mr. Martin, or to be suspected of it."

When Harriet had closed her evidence, she appealed to her dear Miss Woodhouse, to say whether she had not good ground for hope.

"I never should have presumed to think of it at first," said she, "but for you. You told me to observe him carefully, and let his behaviour be the rule of mine—and so I have. But now I seem to feel that I may deserve him; and that if he does choose me, it will not be any thing so very wonderful."

The bitter feelings occasioned by this speech, the many bitter feelings, made the utmost exertion necessary on Emma's side to enable her to say in reply,

"Harriet, I will only venture to declare, that Mr. Knightley is the last man in the world, who would intentionally give any woman the idea of his feeling for her more than he really does."

Harriet seemed ready to worship her friend for a sentence so satisfactory; and Emma was only saved from raptures and fondness, which at the moment would have been dreadful penance, by the sound of her father's footsteps. He was coming through the hall. Harriet was too much agitated to encounter him. "She could not compose herself—Mr. Woodhouse would be alarmed—she had better go;"—with most ready encouragement from her friend, therefore, she passed off through another door—and the moment she was gone, this was the spontaneous burst of Emma's feelings: "Oh God! that I had never seen her!"

The rest of the day, the following night, were hardly enough for her thoughts.—She was bewildered amidst the confusion of all that had rushed on her within the last few hours. Every moment had brought a fresh surprise; and every surprise must be matter of humiliation to her.—How to understand it all! How to understand the deceptions she had been thus practising on herself, and living under!—The blunders, the blindness of her own head and heart!— she sat still, she walked about, she tried her own room, she tried the shrubbery—in every place, every posture, she perceived that she had acted most weakly; that she had been imposed on by others in a most mortifying degree; that she had been imposing on herself in a degree yet more mortifying; that she was wretched, and should probably find this day but the beginning of wretchedness.

To understand, thoroughly understand her own heart, was the first endeavour. To that point went every leisure moment which her father's claims on her allowed, and every moment of involuntary absence of mind.

How long had Mr. Knightley been so dear to her, as every feeling declared him now to be? When had his influence, such influence begun?—When had he succeeded to that place in her affection, which Frank Churchill had once, for a short period, occupied?— She looked back; she compared the two—compared them, as they had always stood in her estimation, from the time of the latter's becoming known to her—and as they must at any time have been compared by her, had it—oh! had it, by any blessed felicity, occurred to her, to institute the comparison.—She saw that there never had been a time when she did not consider Mr. Knightley as infinitely the superior, or when his regard for her had not been infinitely the most dear. She saw, that in persuading herself, in fancying, in acting to the contrary, she had been entirely under a delusion, totally ignorant of her own heart—and, in short, that she had never really cared for Frank Churchill at all!

This was the conclusion of the first series of reflection. This was the knowledge of herself, on the first question of inquiry, which she reached; and without being long in reaching it.—She was most sorrowfully indignant; ashamed of every sensation but the one revealed to her—her affection for Mr. Knightley.—Every other part of her mind was disgusting.

With insufferable vanity had she believed herself in the secret of everybody's feelings; with unpardonable arrogance proposed to arrange everybody's destiny. She was proved to have been universally mistaken; and she had not quite done nothing—for she had done mischief. She had brought evil on Harriet, on herself, and she too much feared, on Mr. Knightley.—Were this most unequal of all connexions to take place, on her must rest all the reproach of having given it a beginning; for his attachment, she must believe to be produced only by a consciousness of Harriet's;—and even were this not the case, he would never have known Harriet at all but for her folly.

Mr. Knightley and Harriet Smith!—It was an union to distance every wonder of the kind.—The attachment of Frank Churchill and Jane Fairfax became common-place, threadbare, stale in the comparison, exciting no surprise, presenting no disparity, affording nothing to be said or thought.—Mr. Knightley and Harriet Smith!—Such an elevation on her side! Such a debasement on his!—It was horrible to Emma to think how it must sink him in the general opinion, to foresee the smiles, the sneers, the merriment it would prompt at his expense; the mortification and disdain of his brother, the thousand inconveniences to himself.—Could it be?—No; it was impossible. And yet it was far, very far, from impossible.—Was it a new circumstance for a man of first-rate abilities to be captivated by very inferior powers? Was it new for one, perhaps too busy to seek, to be the prize of a girl who would seek him?—Was it new for any thing in this world to be unequal, inconsistent, incongruous—or for chance and circumstance (as second causes) to direct the human fate?

Oh! had she never brought Harriet forward! Had she left her where she ought, and where he had told her she ought!—Had she not, with a folly which no tongue could express, prevented her marrying the unexceptionable young man who would have made her happy and respectable in the line of life to which she ought to belong—all would have been safe; none of this dreadful sequel would have been.

How Harriet could ever have had the presumption to raise her thoughts to Mr. Knightley!—How she could dare to fancy herself the chosen of such a man till actually assured of it!—But Harriet was less humble, had fewer scruples than formerly.—Her inferiority, whether of mind or situation, seemed little felt.—She had seemed more sensible of Mr. Elton's being to stoop in marrying her, than she now seemed of Mr. Knightley's.—Alas! was that her own doing too? Who had been at pains to give Harriet notions of self-consequence but herself?—Who but herself had taught her, that she was to elevate herself if possible, and that her claims were great to a high worldly establishment?—If Harriet, from being humble, were grown vain, it was her doing too.

Chapter XII

Till now that she was threatened with its loss, Emma had never known how much of her happiness depended on being *first* with Mr. Knightley, first in interest and affection.—Satisfied that it was so, and feeling it her due, she had enjoyed it without reflection; and only in the dread of being supplanted, found how inexpressibly important it had been.—Long, very long, she felt she had been first; for, having no female connexions of his own, there had been only Isabella whose claims could be compared with hers, and she had always known exactly how far he loved and esteemed Isabella. She had herself been first with him for many years past. She had not deserved it; she had often been negligent or perverse, slighting his advice, or even wilfully opposing him, insensible of half his merits, and quarrelling with him because he would not acknowledge her false and insolent estimate of her own—but still, from family attachment and habit, and thorough excellence of mind, he had loved her, and watched over her from a girl, with an endeavour to improve her, and an anxiety for her doing right, which no other creature had at all shared. In spite of all her faults, she knew she was dear to him; might she not say, very dear?—When the suggestions of hope, however, which must follow here, presented themselves, she could not presume to indulge them. Harriet Smith might think herself not unworthy of being peculiarly, exclusively, passionately loved by Mr. Knightley. *She* could not. She could not flatter herself with any idea of blindness in his attachment to *her.* She had received a very recent proof of its impartiality.—How shocked had he been by her behaviour to Miss Bates! How directly, how strongly had he expressed himself to her on the subject!—Not too strongly for the offence—but far, far too strongly to issue from any feeling softer than upright justice and clear-sighted good will.— She had no hope, nothing to deserve the name of hope, that he could have that sort of affection for herself which was now in question; but there was a hope (at times a slight one, at times much stronger,) that Harriet might have deceived herself, and be overrating his regard for *her.*—Wish it she must, for his sake—be the consequence nothing to herself, but his remaining single all his life. Could she be secure of that, indeed, of his never marrying at all, she believed she should be perfectly satisfied.—Let him but continue the same Mr. Knightley to her and her father, the same Mr. Knightley to all the world; let Donwell and Hartfield lose none of their precious intercourse of friendship and confidence, and her peace would be fully secured.—Marriage, in fact, would not do for her. It would be incompatible with what she owed to her father, and with what she felt for him. Nothing should separate her from her father. She would not marry, even if she were asked by Mr. Knightley.

It must be her ardent wish that Harriet might be disappointed; and she hoped, that when able to see them together again, she might at least be able to ascertain what the chances for it were.—She should see them henceforward with the closest observance; and wretchedly as she had hitherto misunderstood even those she was watching, she did not know how to admit that she could be blinded here.—He was expected back every day. The power of observation would be soon given—frightfully soon it appeared when her thoughts were in one course. In the meanwhile, she resolved against seeing Harriet.—It would do neither of them good, it would do the subject no good, to be talking of it farther.—She was resolved not to be convinced, as long as she could doubt, and yet had no authority for opposing Harriet's confidence. To talk would be only to irritate.— She wrote to her, therefore, kindly, but decisively, to beg that she would not, at present, come to Hartfield; acknowledging it to be her conviction, that all farther confidential discussion of *one* topic had better be avoided; and hoping, that if a few days were allowed to pass before they met again, except in the company of others—she objected only to a tête-à-tête—they might be able to act as if they had forgotten the conversation of yesterday.—Harriet submitted, and approved, and was grateful.

This point was just arranged, when a visitor arrived to tear Emma's thoughts a little from the one subject which had engrossed them, sleeping or waking, the last twenty-four hours—Mrs. Weston, who had been calling on her daughter-in-law elect, and took Hartfield in her way home, almost as much in duty to Emma as in pleasure to herself, to relate all the particulars of so interesting an interview.

Mr. Weston had accompanied her to Mrs. Bates's, and gone through his share of this essential attention most handsomely; but she having then induced Miss Fairfax to join her in an airing, was now returned with much more to say, and much more to say with satisfaction, than a quarter of an hour spent in Mrs. Bates's parlour, with all the incumbrance of awkward feelings, could have afforded.

A little curiosity Emma had; and she made the most of it while her friend related. Mrs. Weston had set off to pay the visit in a good deal of agitation herself; and in the first place had wished not to go at all at present, to be allowed merely to write to Miss Fairfax instead, and to defer this ceremonious call till a little time had passed, and Mr. Churchill could be reconciled to the engagement's becoming known; as, considering every thing, she thought such a visit could not be paid without leading to reports:—but Mr. Weston had thought differently; he was extremely anxious to shew his approbation to Miss Fairfax and her family, and did not conceive that any suspicion could be excited by it; or if it were, that it would be of any consequence; for "such things," he observed, "always got about." Emma smiled, and felt that Mr. Weston had very good reason for saying so. They had gone, in short—and very great had been the evident distress and confusion of *the* lady. She had hardly been able to speak a word, and every look and action had shown how deeply she was suffering from consciousness. The quiet, heartfelt satisfaction of the old lady, and the rapturous delight of her daughter—who proved even too joyous to talk as usual, had been a gratifying, yet almost an affecting, scene. They were both so truly respectable in their happiness, so disinterested in every sensation; thought so much of Jane; so much of everybody, and so little of themselves, that every kindly feeling was at work for them. Miss Fairfax's recent illness had offered a fair plea for Mrs. Weston to invite her to an airing; she had drawn back and declined at first, but on being pressed had yielded; and in the course of their drive, Mrs. Weston had, by gentle encouragement, overcome so much of her embarrassment, as to bring her to converse on the important subject. Apologies for her seemingly ungracious silence in their first reception, and the warmest expressions of the gratitude she was always feeling towards herself and Mr. Weston, must necessarily open the cause; but when these effusions were put by, they had talked a good deal of the present and of the future state of the engagement. Mrs. Weston was convinced that such conversation must be the greatest relief to her companion, pent up within her own mind as every thing had so long been, and was very much pleased with all that she had said on the subject.

"On the misery of what she had suffered, during the concealment of so many months," continued Mrs. Weston, "she was energetic. This was one of her expressions. 'I will not say, that since I entered into the engagement I have not had some happy moments; but I can say, that I have never known the blessing of one tranquil hour:'—and the quivering lip, Emma, which uttered it, was an attestation that I felt at my heart."

"Poor girl!" said Emma. "She thinks herself wrong, then, for having consented to a private engagement?"

"Wrong!—No one, I believe, can blame her more than she is disposed to blame herself. 'The consequence,' said she, 'has been a state of perpetual suffering to me; and so it ought. But after all the punishment that misconduct can bring, it is still not less misconduct. Pain is no expiation. I never can be blameless. I have been acting contrary to all my sense of right; and the fortunate turn that every thing has taken, and the kindness I am now receiving, is what my conscience tells me ought not to be. Do not imagine, madam,' she continued, 'that I was taught wrong. Do not let any reflection fall on the principles or the care of the friends who brought me up. The error has been all my own; and I do assure you that, with all the excuse that present circumstances may appear to give, I shall yet dread making the story known to Colonel Campbell.'"

"Poor girl!" said Emma again. "She loves him then excessively, I suppose. It must have been from attachment only, that she could be led to form the engagement. Her affection must have overpowered her judgment."

"Yes, I have no doubt of her being extremely attached to him."

"I am afraid," returned Emma, sighing, "that I must often have contributed to make her unhappy."

"On your side, my love, it was very innocently done. But she probably had something of that in her thoughts, when alluding to the misunderstandings which he had given us hints of before. One natural consequence of the evil she had involved herself in," she said, "was that of making her *unreasonable*. The consciousness of having done amiss, had exposed her to a thousand inquietudes, and made her captious and irritable to a degree that must have been— that had been—hard for him to bear. 'I did not make the allowances,' said she, 'which I ought to have done, for his temper and spirits—his delightful spirits, and that gaiety, that playfulness of disposition, which under any other circumstances, would, I am sure, have been as constantly bewitching to me, as they were at first.' She then began to speak of you, and of the great kindness you had shown her during her illness; and with a blush which showed me how it was all connected, desired me, whenever I had an opportunity, to thank you—I could not thank you too much—for every wish and every endeavour to do her good. She was sensible that you had never received any proper acknowledgment from herself."

"If I did not know her to be happy now," said Emma, seriously, "which, in spite of every little drawback from her scrupulous conscience, she must be, I could not bear these thanks;—for, oh! Mrs. Weston, if there were an account drawn up of the evil and the good I have done Miss Fairfax!—Well, (checking herself, and trying to be more lively), this is all to be forgotten. You are very kind to bring me these interesting particulars. They show her to the greatest advantage. I am sure she is very good—I hope she will be very happy. It is fit that the fortune should be on his side, for I think the merit will be all on her's."

Such a conclusion could not pass unanswered by Mrs. Weston. She thought well of Frank in almost every respect; and, what was more, she loved him very much, and her defence was, therefore, earnest. She talked with a great deal of reason, and at least equal affection—but she had too much to urge for Emma's attention; it was soon gone to Brunswick Square or to Donwell; she forgot to attempt to listen; and when Mrs. Weston ended with "We have not yet had the letter we are so anxious for, you know, but I hope it will soon come," she was obliged to pause before she answered, and at last obliged to answer at random, before she could at all recollect what letter it was which they were so anxious for.

"Are you well, my Emma?" was Mrs. Weston's parting question.

"Oh! perfectly. I am always well, you know. Be sure to give me intelligence of the letter as soon as possible."

Mrs. Weston's communications furnished Emma with more food for unpleasant reflection, by increasing her esteem and compassion, and her sense of past injustice towards Miss Fairfax. She bitterly regretted not having sought a closer acquaintance with her, and blushed for the envious feelings which had certainly been, in some measure, the cause. Had she followed Mr. Knightley's known wishes, in paying that attention to Miss Fairfax, which was every way her due; had she tried to know her better; had she done her part towards intimacy; had she endeavoured to find a friend there instead of in Harriet Smith; she must, in all probability, have been spared from every pain which pressed on her now.—Birth, abilities, and education, had been equally marking one as an associate for her, to be received with gratitude; and the other—what was she?— Supposing even that they had never become intimate friends; that she had never been admitted into Miss Fairfax's confidence on this important matter—which was most probable—still, in knowing her as she ought, and as she might, she must have been preserved from the abominable suspicions of an improper attachment to Mr. Dixon, which she had not only so foolishly fashioned and harboured herself, but had so unpardonably imparted; an idea which she greatly feared had been made a subject of material distress to the delicacy of Jane's feelings, by the levity or carelessness of Frank Churchill's. Of all the sources of evil surrounding the former, since her coming to Highbury, she was persuaded that she must herself have been the worst. She must have been a perpetual enemy. They never could have been all three together, without her having stabbed Jane Fairfax's peace in a thousand instances; and on Box Hill, perhaps, it had been the agony of a mind that would bear no more.

The evening of this day was very long, and melancholy, at Hartfield. The weather added what it could of gloom. A cold stormy rain set in, and nothing of July appeared but in the trees and shrubs, which the wind was despoiling, and the length of the day, which only made such cruel sights the longer visible.

The weather affected Mr. Woodhouse, and he could only be kept tolerably comfortable by almost ceaseless attention on his daughter's side, and by exertions which had never cost her half so much before. It reminded her of their first forlorn tête-à-tête, on the evening of Mrs. Weston's wedding-day; but Mr. Knightley had walked in then, soon after tea, and dissipated every melancholy fancy. Alas! such delightful proofs of Hartfield's attraction, as those sort of visits conveyed, might shortly be over. The picture which she had then drawn of the privations of the approaching winter, had proved erroneous; no friends had deserted them, no pleasures had been lost.—But her present forebodings she feared would experience no similar contradiction. The prospect before her now, was threatening to a degree that could not be entirely dispelled—that might not be even partially brightened. If all took place that might take place among the circle of her friends, Hartfield must be comparatively deserted; and she left to cheer her father with the spirits only of ruined happiness.

The child to be born at Randall's must be a tie there even dearer than herself; and Mrs. Weston's heart and time would be occupied by it. They should lose her; and, probably, in great measure, her husband also.—Frank Churchill would return among them no more; and Miss Fairfax, it was reasonable to suppose, would soon cease to belong to Highbury. They would be married, and settled either at or near Enscombe. All that were good would be withdrawn; and if to these losses, the loss of Donwell were to be added, what would remain of cheerful or of rational society within their reach? Mr. Knightley to be no longer coming there for his evening comfort!—No longer walking in at all hours, as if ever willing to change his own home for their's!—How was it to be endured? And if he were to be lost to them for Harriet's sake; if he were to be thought of hereafter, as finding in Harriet's society all that he wanted; if Harriet were to be the chosen, the first, the dearest, the friend, the wife to whom he looked for all the best blessings of existence; what could be increasing Emma's wretchedness but the reflection never far distant from her mind, that it had been all her own work?

When it came to such a pitch as this, she was not able to refrain from a start, or a heavy sigh, or even from walking about the room for a few seconds—and the only source whence any thing like consolation or composure could be drawn, was in the resolution of her own better conduct, and the hope that, however inferior in spirit and gaiety might be the following and every future winter of her life to the past, it would yet find her more rational, more acquainted with herself, and leave her less to regret when it were gone.

Chapter XIII

The weather continued much the same all the following morning; and the same loneliness, and the same melancholy, seemed to reign at Hartfield—but in the afternoon it cleared; the wind changed into a softer quarter; the clouds were carried off; the sun appeared; it was summer again. With all the eagerness which such a transition gives, Emma resolved to be out of doors as soon as possible. Never had the exquisite sight, smell, sensation of nature, tranquil, warm, and brilliant after a storm, been more attractive to her. She longed for the serenity they might gradually introduce; and on Mr. Perry's coming in soon after dinner, with a disengaged hour to give her father, she lost no time in hurrying into the shrubbery.—There, with spirits freshened, and thoughts a little relieved, she had taken a few turns, when she saw Mr. Knightley passing through the garden door, and coming towards her.—It was the first intimation of his being returned from London. She had been thinking of him the moment before, as unquestionably sixteen miles distant.—There was time only for the quickest arrangement of mind. She must be collected and calm. In half a minute they were together. The "How d'ye do's," were quiet and constrained on each side. She asked after their mutual friends; they were all well.—When had he left them?— Only that morning. He must have had a wet ride.—Yes.—He meant to walk with her, she found. "He had just looked into the dining-room, and as he was not wanted there, preferred being out of doors."—She thought he neither looked nor spoke cheerfully; and the first possible cause for it, suggested by her fears, was, that he had perhaps been communicating his plans to his brother, and was pained by the manner in which they had been received.

They walked together. He was silent. She thought he was often looking at her, and trying for a fuller view of her face than it suited her to give. And this belief produced another dread. Perhaps he wanted to speak to her, of his attachment to Harriet; he might be watching for encouragement to begin.—She did not, could not, feel equal to lead the way to any such subject. He must do it all himself. Yet she could not bear this silence. With him it was most unnatural. She considered—resolved—and, trying to smile, began—

"You have some news to hear, now you are come back, that will rather surprise you."

"Have I?" said he quietly, and looking at her; "of what nature?"

"Oh! the best nature in the world—a wedding."

After waiting a moment, as if to be sure she intended to say no more, he replied,

"If you mean Miss Fairfax and Frank Churchill, I have heard that already."

"How is it possible?" cried Emma, turning her glowing cheeks towards him; for while she spoke, it occurred to her that he might have called at Mrs. Goddard's in his way.

"I had a few lines on parish business from Mr. Weston this morning, and at the end of them he gave me a brief account of what had happened."

Emma was quite relieved, and could presently say, with a little more composure,

"*You* probably have been less surprised than any of us, for you have had your suspicions.—I have not forgotten that you once tried to give me a caution.—I wish I had attended to it—but—(with a sinking voice and a heavy sigh) I seem to have been doomed to blindness."

For a moment or two nothing was said, and she was unsuspicious of having excited any particular interest, till she found her arm drawn within his, and pressed against his heart, and heard him thus saying, in a tone of great sensibility, speaking low,

"Time, my dearest Emma, time will heal the wound.—Your own excellent sense—your exertions for your father's sake—I know you will not allow yourself—." Her arm was pressed again, as he added, in a more broken and subdued accent, "The feelings of the warmest friendship—Indignation—Abominable scoundrel!"—And in a louder, steadier tone, he concluded with, "He will soon be gone. They will soon be in Yorkshire. I am sorry for *her*. She deserves a better fate."

Emma understood him; and as soon as she could recover from the flutter of pleasure, excited by such tender consideration, replied,

"You are very kind—but you are mistaken—and I must set you right.—I am not in want of that sort of compassion. My blindness to what was going on, led me to act by them in a way that I must always be ashamed of, and I was very foolishly tempted to say and do many things which may well lay me open to unpleasant conjectures, but I have no other reason to regret that I was not in the secret earlier."

"Emma!" cried he, looking eagerly at her, "are you, indeed?"—but checking himself—"No, no, I understand you—forgive me—I am pleased that you can say even so much.—He is no object of regret, indeed! and it will not be very long, I hope, before that becomes the acknowledgment of more than your reason.—Fortunate that your affections were not farther entangled!—I could never, I confess, from your manners, assure myself as to the degree of what you felt—I could only be certain that there was a preference—and a preference which I never believed him to deserve.—He is a disgrace to the name of man.—And is he to be rewarded with that sweet young woman?—Jane, Jane, you will be a miserable creature."

"Mr. Knightley," said Emma, trying to be lively, but really confused—"I am in a very extraordinary situation. I cannot let you continue in your error; and yet, perhaps, since my manners gave such an impression, I have as much reason to be ashamed of confessing that I never have been at all attached to the person we are speaking of, as it might be natural for a woman to feel in confessing exactly the reverse.—But I never have."

He listened in perfect silence. She wished him to speak, but he would not. She supposed she must say more before she were entitled to his clemency; but it was a hard case to be obliged still to lower herself in his opinion. She went on, however.

"I have very little to say for my own conduct.—I was tempted by his attentions, and allowed myself to appear pleased.—An old story, probably—a common case—and no more than has happened to hundreds of my sex before; and yet it may not be the more excusable in one who sets up as I do for Understanding. Many circumstances assisted the temptation. He was the son of Mr. Weston—he was continually here—I always found him very pleasant—and, in short, for (with a sigh) let me swell out the causes ever so ingeniously, they all centre in this at last—my vanity was flattered, and I allowed his attentions. Latterly, however—for some time indeed—I have had no idea of their meaning any thing.—I thought them a habit, a trick, nothing that called for seriousness on my side. He has imposed on me, but he has not injured me. I have never been attached to him. And now I can tolerably comprehend his behaviour. He never wished to attach me. It was merely a blind to conceal his real situation with another.—It was his object to blind all about him; and no one, I am sure, could be more effectually blinded than myself—except that I was *not* blinded—that it was my good fortune—that, in short, I was somehow or other safe from him."

She had hoped for an answer here—for a few words to say that her conduct was at least intelligible; but he was silent; and, as far as she could judge, deep in thought. At last, and tolerably in his usual tone, he said,

"I have never had a high opinion of Frank Churchill.—I can suppose, however, that I may have under-rated him. My acquaintance with him has been but trifling.—And even if I have not under-rated him hitherto, he may yet turn out well.—With such a woman he has a chance.—I have no motive for wishing him ill—and for her sake, whose happiness will be involved in his good character and conduct, I shall certainly wish him well."

"I have no doubt of their being happy together," said Emma; "I believe them to be very mutually and very sincerely attached."

"He is a most fortunate man!" returned Mr. Knightley, with energy. "So early in life—at three and twenty—a period when, if a man chooses a wife, he generally chooses ill. At three and twenty to have drawn such a prize!—What years of felicity that man, in all human calculation, has before him!—Assured of the love of such a woman—the disinterested love, for Jane Fairfax's character vouches for her disinterestedness; every thing in his favour,—equality of situation—I mean, as far as regards society, and all the habits and manners that are important; equality in every point but one—and that one, since the purity of her heart is not to be doubted, such as must increase his felicity, for it will be his to bestow the only advantages she wants.—A man would always wish to give a woman a better home than the one he takes her from; and he who can do it, where there is no doubt of *her* regard, must, I think, be the happiest of mortals.—Frank Churchill is, indeed, the favourite of fortune. Every thing turns out for his good.—He meets with a young woman at a watering-place, gains her affection, cannot even weary her by negligent treatment—and had he and all his family sought round the world for a perfect wife for him, they could not have found her superior.—His aunt is in the way.—His aunt dies.—He has only to speak.—His friends are eager to promote his happiness.—He has used every body ill—and they are all delighted to forgive him.—He is a fortunate man indeed!"

"You speak as if you envied him."

"And I do envy him, Emma. In one respect he is the object of my envy."

Emma could say no more. They seemed to be within half a sentence of Harriet, and her immediate feeling was to avert the subject, if possible. She made her plan; she would speak of something totally different—the children in Brunswick Square; and she only waited for breath to begin, when Mr. Knightley startled her, by saying,

"You will not ask me what is the point of envy.—You are determined, I see, to have no curiosity.—You are wise—but *I* cannot be wise. Emma, I must tell what you will not ask, though I may wish it unsaid the next moment."

"Oh! then, don't speak it, don't speak it," she eagerly cried. "Take a little time, consider, do not commit yourself."

"Thank you," said he, in an accent of deep mortification, and not another syllable followed.

Emma could not bear to give him pain. He was wishing to confide in her—perhaps to consult her;—cost her what it would, she would listen. She might assist his resolution, or reconcile him to it; she might give just praise to Harriet, or, by representing to him his own independence, relieve him from that state of indecision, which must be more intolerable than any alternative to such a mind as his.—They had reached the house.

"You are going in, I suppose," said he.

"No"—replied Emma—quite confirmed by the depressed manner in which he still spoke—"I should like to take another turn. Mr. Perry is not gone." And, after proceeding a few steps, she added—"I stopped you ungraciously, just now, Mr. Knightley, and, I am afraid, gave you pain.—But if you have any wish to speak openly to me as a friend, or to ask my opinion of any thing that you may have in contemplation—as a friend, indeed, you may command me.—I will hear whatever you like. I will tell you exactly what I think."

"As a friend!"—repeated Mr. Knightley.—"Emma, that I fear is a word—No, I have no wish—Stay, yes, why should I hesitate?—I have gone too far already for concealment.—Emma, I accept your offer—Extraordinary as it may seem, I accept it, and refer myself to you as a friend.—Tell me, then, have I no chance of ever succeeding?"

He stopped in his earnestness to look the question, and the expression of his eyes overpowered her.

"My dearest Emma," said he, "for dearest you will always be, whatever the event of this hour's conversation, my dearest, most beloved Emma—tell me at once. Say 'No,' if it is to be said."—She could really say nothing.—"You are silent," he cried, with great animation; "absolutely silent! at present I ask no more."

Emma was almost ready to sink under the agitation of this moment. The dread of being awakened from the happiest dream, was perhaps the most prominent feeling.

"I cannot make speeches, Emma:"—he soon resumed; and in a tone of such sincere, decided, intelligible tenderness as was tolerably convincing.—"If I loved you less, I might be able to talk about it more. But you know what I am.—You hear nothing but truth from me.—I have blamed you, and lectured you, and you have borne it as no other woman in England would have borne it.—Bear with the truths I would tell you now, dearest Emma, as well as you have borne with them. The manner, perhaps, may have as little to recommend them. God knows, I have been a very indifferent lover.—But you understand me.—Yes, you see, you understand my feelings—and will return them if you can. At present, I ask only to hear, once to hear your voice."

While he spoke, Emma's mind was most busy, and, with all the wonderful velocity of thought, had been able—and yet without losing a word—to catch and comprehend the exact truth of the whole; to see that Harriet's hopes had been entirely groundless, a mistake, a delusion, as complete a delusion as any of her own—that Harriet was nothing; that she was every thing herself; that what she had been saying relative to Harriet had been all taken as the language of her own feelings; and that her agitation, her doubts, her reluctance, her discouragement, had been all received as discouragement from herself.—And not only was there time for these convictions, with all their glow of attendant happiness; there was time also to rejoice that Harriet's secret had not escaped her, and to resolve that it need not and should not.—It was all the service she could now render her poor friend; for as to any of that heroism of sentiment which might have prompted her to entreat him to transfer his affection from herself to Harriet, as infinitely the most worthy of the two—or even the more simple sublimity of resolving to refuse him at once and for ever, with-out vouchsafing any motive, because he could not marry them both, Emma had it not. She felt for Harriet, with pain and with contrition; but no flight of generosity run mad, opposing all that could be prob-able or reasonable, entered her brain. She had led her friend astray, and it would be a reproach to her for ever; but her judgment was as strong as her feelings, and as strong as it had ever been before, in reprobating any such alliance for him, as most unequal and degrad-ing. Her way was clear, though not quite smooth.—She spoke then, on being so entreated.—What did she say?—Just what she ought, of course. A lady always does.—She said enough to show there need not be despair—and to invite him to say more himself. He *had* despaired at one period; he had received such an injunction to caution and silence, as for the time crushed every hope;—she had begun by refusing to hear him.—The change had perhaps been somewhat sudden;—her proposal of taking another turn, her renewing the conversation which she had just put an end to, might be a little extraordinary!—She felt its inconsistency; but Mr. Knightley was so obliging as to put up with it, and seek no farther explanation.

Seldom, very seldom, does complete truth belong to any human disclosure; seldom can it happen that something is not a little disguised, or a little mistaken; but where, as in this case, though the conduct is mistaken, the feelings are not, it may not be very material.—Mr. Knightley could not impute to Emma a more relenting heart than she possessed, or a heart more disposed to accept of his.

He had, in fact, been wholly unsuspicious of his own influence. He had followed her into the shrubbery with no idea of trying it. He had come, in his anxiety to see how she bore Frank Churchill's engagement, with no selfish view, no view at all, but of endeavour-ing, if she allowed him an opening, to soothe or to counsel her.—The rest had been the work of the moment, the immediate effect of what he heard, on his feelings. The delightful assurance of her total indifference towards Frank Churchill, of her having a heart completely disengaged from him, had given birth to the hope, that, in time, he might gain her affection himself;—but it had been no present hope—he had only, in the momentary conquest of eager-ness over judgment, aspired to be told that she did not forbid his attempt to attach her.—The superior hopes which gradually opened were so much the more enchanting.—The affection, which he had been asking to be allowed to create if he could, was already his!—Within half an hour, he had passed from a thoroughly distressed state of mind, to something so like perfect happiness, that it could bear no other name.

Her change was equal.—This one half hour had given to each the same precious certainty of being beloved, had cleared from each the same degree of ignorance, jealousy, or distrust.—On his side, there had been a long-standing jealousy, old as the arrival, or even the expectation, of Frank Churchill.—He had been in love with Emma, and jealous of Frank Churchill, from about the same period, one sentiment having probably enlightened him as to the other. It was his jealousy of Frank Churchill that had taken him from the country.—The Box-Hill party had decided him on going away. He would save himself from witnessing again such permitted, encouraged attentions.—He had gone to learn to be indifferent.— But he had gone to a wrong place. There was too much domestic happiness in his brother's house; woman wore too amiable a form in it; Isabella was too much like Emma—differing only in those striking inferiorities, which always brought the other brilliancy before him, for much to have been done, even had his time been longer.—He had staid on, however, vigorously, day after day—till this very morning's post had conveyed the history of Jane Fairfax.— Then, with the gladness which must be felt, nay, which he did not scruple to feel, having never believed Frank Churchill to be at all deserving Emma, was there so much fond solicitude, so much keen anxiety for her, that he could stay no longer.[8] He had ridden home through the rain; and had walked up directly after dinner, to see how this sweetest and best of all creatures, faultless in spite of all her faults, bore the discovery.

He had found her agitated and low.—Frank Churchill was a villain.—He heard her declare that she had never loved him. Frank Churchill's character was not desperate.—She was his own Emma, by hand and word, when they returned into the house; and if he could have thought of Frank Churchill then, he might have deemed him a very good sort of fellow.

Chapter XIV

What totally different feelings did Emma take back into the house from what she had brought out!—she had then been only daring to hope for a little respite of suffering;—she was now in an exquisite flutter of happiness, and such happiness moreover as she believed must still be greater when the flutter should have passed away.

They sat down to tea—the same party round the same table— how often it had been collected!—and how often had her eyes fallen on the same shrubs in the lawn, and observed the same beautiful effect of the western sun!—But never in such a state of spirits, never in anything like it; and it was with difficulty that she could

8. As Chapman suggests, the question mark here in 1816 must be an error.

summon enough of her usual self to be the attentive lady of the house, or even the attentive daughter.

Poor Mr. Woodhouse little suspected what was plotting against him in the breast of that man whom he was so cordially welcoming, and so anxiously hoping might not have taken cold from his ride.—Could he have seen the heart, he would have cared very little for the lungs; but without the most distant imagination of the impending evil, without the slightest perception of anything extraordinary in the looks or ways of either, he repeated to them very comfortably all the articles of news he had received from Mr. Perry, and talked on with much self-contentment, totally unsuspicious of what they could have told him in return.

As long as Mr. Knightley remained with them, Emma's fever continued; but when he was gone, she began to be a little tranquillized and subdued—and in the course of the sleepless night, which was the tax for such an evening, she found one or two such very serious points to consider, as made her feel, that even her happiness must have some alloy. Her father—and Harriet. She could not be alone without feeling the full weight of their separate claims; and how to guard the comfort of both to the utmost, was the question. With respect to her father, it was a question soon answered. She hardly knew yet what Mr. Knightley would ask; but a very short parley with her own heart produced the most solemn resolution of never quitting her father.—She even wept over the idea of it, as a sin of thought. While he lived, it must be only an engagement; but she flattered herself, that if divested of the danger of drawing her away, it might become an increase of comfort to him.—How to do her best by Harriet, was of more difficult decision;—how to spare her from any unnecessary pain; how to make her any possible atonement; how to appear least her enemy?—On these subjects, her perplexity and distress were very great—and her mind had to pass again and again through every bitter reproach and sorrowful regret that had ever surrounded it.—She could only resolve at last, that she would still avoid a meeting with her, and communicate all that need be told by letter; that it would be inexpressibly desirable to have her removed just now for a time from Highbury, and—indulging in one scheme more—nearly resolve, that it might be practicable to get an invitation for her to Brunswick Square.—Isabella had been pleased with Harriet; and a few weeks spent in London must give her some amusement.—She did not think it in Harriet's nature to escape being benefited by novelty and variety, by the streets, the shops, and the children.—At any rate, it would be a proof of attention and kindness in herself, from whom every thing was due; a separation for the present; an averting of the evil day, when they must all be together again.

She rose early, and wrote her letter to Harriet; an employment which left her so very serious, so nearly sad, that Mr. Knightley, in walking up to Hartfield to breakfast, did not arrive at all too soon; and half an hour stolen afterwards to go over the same ground again with him, literally and figuratively, was quite necessary to reinstate her in a proper share of the happiness of the evening before.

He had not left her long, by no means long enough for her to have the slightest inclination for thinking of anybody else, when a letter was brought her from Randall's—a very thick letter;—she guessed what it must contain, and deprecated the necessity of reading it.— She was now in perfect charity with Frank Churchill; she wanted no explanations, she wanted only to have her thoughts to herself— and as for understanding any thing he wrote, she was sure she was incapable of it.—It must be waded through, however. She opened the packet; it was too surely so;—a note from Mrs. Weston to herself, ushered in the letter from Frank to Mrs. Weston.

"I have the greatest pleasure, my dear Emma, in forwarding to you the enclosed. I know what thorough justice you will do it, and have scarcely a doubt of its happy effect.—I think we shall never materially disagree about the writer again; but I will not delay you by a long preface.—We are quite well.—This letter has been the cure of all the little nervousness I have been feeling lately.—I did not quite like your looks on Tuesday, but it was an ungenial morning; and though you will never own being affected by weather, I think every body feels a northeast wind.—I felt for your dear father very much in the storm of Tuesday afternoon and yesterday morning, but had the comfort of hearing last night, by Mr. Perry, that it had not made him ill.

"Your's ever,
"A. W."

[*To Mrs. Weston.*]

Windsor—July.

MY DEAR MADAM,

"If I made myself intelligible yesterday, this letter will be expected; but expected or not, I know it will be read with candour and indulgence.—You are all goodness, and I believe there will be need of even all your goodness to allow for some parts of my past conduct.— But I have been forgiven by one who had still more to resent. My courage rises while I write. It is very difficult for the prosperous to be humble. I have already met with such success in two applications for pardon, that I may be in danger of thinking myself too sure of your's, and of those among your friends who have had any ground of offence.—You must all endeavour to comprehend the exact nature of my situation when I first arrived at Randall's; you must consider me as having a secret which was to be kept at all hazards. This was the fact. My right to place myself in a situation requiring such concealment, is another question. I shall not discuss it here. For my temptation to *think* it a right, I refer every caviller to a brick house, sashed windows below, and casements above, in Highbury. I dared not address her openly; my difficulties in the then state of Enscombe must be too well known to require definition; and I was fortunate enough to prevail, before we parted at Weymouth, and to induce the most upright female mind in the creation to stoop in charity to a secret engagement.—Had she refused, I should have gone mad.— But you will be ready to say, what was your hope in doing this?— What did you look forward to?—To any thing, every thing—to time, chance, circumstance, slow effects, sudden bursts, perseverance and weariness, health and sickness. Every possibility of good was before me, and the first of blessings secured, in obtaining her promises of faith and correspondence. If you need farther explanation, I have the honour, my dear madam, of being your husband's son, and the advantage of inheriting a disposition to hope for good, which no inheritance of houses or lands can ever equal the value of.—See me, then, under these circumstances, arriving on my first visit to Randall's;— and here I am conscious of wrong, for that visit might have been sooner paid. You will look back and see that I did not come till Miss Fairfax was in Highbury; and as *you* were the person slighted, you will forgive me instantly; but I must work on my father's compassion, by reminding him, that so long as I absented myself from his house, so long I lost the blessing of knowing you. My behaviour, during the very happy fortnight which I spent with you, did not, I hope, lay me open to reprehension, excepting on one point. And now I come to the principal, the only important part of my conduct while belonging to you, which excites my own anxiety, or requires very solicitous explanation. With the greatest respect, and the warmest friendship, do I mention Miss Woodhouse; my father perhaps will think I ought to add, with the deepest humiliation.—A few words which dropped from him yesterday spoke his opinion, and some censure I acknowledge myself liable to.—My behaviour to Miss Woodhouse indicated, I believe, more than it ought.—In order to assist a concealment so essential to me, I was led on to make more than an allowable use of the sort of intimacy into which we were immediately thrown.—I cannot deny that Miss Woodhouse was my ostensible object—but I am sure you will believe the declaration, that had I not been convinced of her indifference, I would not have been induced by any selfish views to go on.—Amiable and delightful as Miss Woodhouse is, she never gave me the idea of a young woman likely to be attached; and that she was perfectly free from any tendency to being attached to me, was as much my conviction as my wish.—She received my attentions with an easy, friendly, goodhumoured play-fulness, which exactly suited me. We seemed to understand each other. From our relative situation, those attentions were her due, and were felt to be so.—Whether Miss Woodhouse began really to under-stand me before the expiration of that fortnight, I cannot say;—when I called to take leave of her, I remember that I was within a moment of confessing the truth, and I then fancied she was not without sus-picion; but I have no doubt of her having since detected me, at least in some degree.—She may not have surmised the whole, but her quickness must have penetrated a part. I cannot doubt it. You will find, whenever the subject becomes freed from its present restraints, that it did not take her wholly by surprise. She frequently gave me hints of it. I remember her telling me at the ball, that I owed Mrs. Elton gratitude for her attentions to Miss Fairfax.—I hope this his-tory of my conduct towards her will be admitted by you and my father as great extenuation of what you saw amiss. While you considered me as having sinned against Emma Woodhouse, I could deserve nothing from either. Acquit me here, and procure for me, when it is allowable, the acquittal and good wishes of that said Emma Wood-house, whom I regard with so much brotherly affection, as to long to have her as deeply and as happily in love as myself.—Whatever strange things I said or did during that fortnight, you have now a key to. My heart was in Highbury, and my business was to get my body thither as often as might be, and with the least suspicion. If you remember any queernesses, set them all to the right account.—Of the piano-forté so much talked of, I feel it only necessary to say, that its being ordered was absolutely unknown to Miss F—, who would never have allowed me to send it, had any choice been given her.— The delicacy of her mind throughout the whole engagement, my dear madam, is much beyond my power of doing justice to. You will soon, I earnestly hope, know her thoroughly yourself.—No description can describe her. She must tell you herself what she is—yet not by word, for never was there a human creature who would so designedly sup-press her own merit.—Since I began this letter, which will be longer than I foresaw, I have heard from her.—She gives a good account of her own health; but as she never complains, I dare not depend. I want to have your opinion of her looks. I know you will soon call on her; she is living in dread of the visit. Perhaps it is paid already. Let me hear from you without delay; I am impatient for a thousand par-ticulars. Remember how few minutes I was at Randall's, and in how bewildered, how mad a state: and I am not much better yet; still insane either from happiness or misery. When I think of the kind-ness and favour I have met with, of her excellence and patience, and my uncle's generosity, I am mad with joy: but when I recollect all the uneasiness I occasioned her, and how little I deserve to be forgiven, I am mad with anger. If I could but see her again!—But I must not propose it yet. My uncle has been too good for me to encroach.—I must still add to this long letter. You have not heard all that you ought to hear. I could not give any connected detail yesterday; but the suddenness, and, in one light, the unseasonableness, with which the affair burst out, needs explanation; for though the event of the 26th ult.,[9] as you will conclude, immediately opened to me the happiest prospects, I should not have presumed on such early measures, but from the very particular circumstances, which left me not an hour to lose. I should myself have shrunk from any thing so hasty, and she would have felt every scruple of mine with multiplied strength and refinement.—But I had no choice. The hasty engagement she had entered into with that woman——Here, my dear madam, I was obliged to leave off abruptly, to recollect and compose myself.—I have been walking over the country, and am now, I hope, rational enough to make the rest of my letter what it ought to be.—It is, in fact, a most mortifying retrospect for me. I behaved shamefully. And here I can admit, that my manners to Miss W., in being unpleasant to Miss F., were highly blamable. *She* disapproved them, which ought to have been enough.—My plea of concealing the truth she did not think sufficient.—She was displeased; I thought unreasonably so: I thought her, on a thousand occasions, unnecessarily scrupulous and cautious: I thought her even cold. But she was always right. If I had followed her judgment, and subdued my spirits to the level of what she deemed proper, I should have escaped the greatest unhappiness I have ever known.—We quarrelled.—Do you remember the morning spent at Donwell?—*There* every little dissatisfaction that had occurred before came to a crisis. I was late; I met her walking home by herself, and wanted to walk with her, but she would not suffer it. She absolutely refused to allow me, which I then thought most unreasonable. Now, however, I see nothing in it but a very natural and consistent degree of discretion. While I, to blind the world to our engagement, was behaving one hour with objectionable particularity to another woman, was she to be consenting the next to a proposal which might have made every previous caution useless?—Had we been met walking together between Donwell and Highbury, the truth must have been suspected.—I was mad enough, however, to resent.—I doubted her affection. I doubted it more the next day on Box-Hill; when, provoked by such conduct on my side, such shameful, insolent neglect of her, and such apparent devotion to Miss W., as it would have been impossible for any woman of sense to endure, she spoke her resentment in a form of words perfectly intelligible to me.—In short, my dear madam, it was a quarrel blameless on her side, abominable on mine; and I returned the same evening to Richmond, though I might have staid with you till the next morning, merely because I would be as angry with her as possible. Even then, I was not such a fool as not to mean to be reconciled in time; but I

9. The twenty-sixth of last month.

was the injured person, injured by her coldness, and I went away determined that she should make the first advances.—I shall always congratulate myself that you were not of the Box-Hill party. Had you witnessed my behaviour there, I can hardly suppose you would ever have thought well of me again. Its effect upon her appears in the immediate resolution it produced: as soon as she found I was really gone from Randall's, she closed with the offer of that officious Mrs. Elton; the whole system of whose treatment of her, by the bye, has ever filled me with indignation and hatred. I must not quarrel with a spirit of forbearance which has been so richly extended towards myself; but, otherwise, I should loudly protest against the share of it which that woman has known.—"Jane," indeed!—You will observe that I have not yet indulged myself in calling her by that name, even to you. Think, then, what I must have endured in hearing it bandied between the Eltons with all the vulgarity of needless repetition, and all the insolence of imaginary superiority. Have patience with me, I shall soon have done.—She closed with this offer, resolving to break with me entirely, and wrote the next day to tell me that we never were to meet again.—*She felt the engagement to be a source of repentance and misery to each: she dissolved it.*—This letter reached me on the very morning of my poor aunt's death. I answered it within an hour; but from the confusion of my mind, and the multiplicity of business falling on me at once, my answer, instead of being sent with all the many other letters of that day, was locked up in my writing-desk; and I, trusting that I had written enough, though but a few lines, to satisfy her, remained without any uneasiness.—I was rather disappointed that I did not hear from her again speedily; but I made excuses for her, and was too busy, and—may I add?—too cheerful in my views to be captious.—We removed to Windsor; and two days afterwards I received a parcel from her, my own letters all returned!—and a few lines at the same time by the post, stating her extreme surprise at not having had the smallest reply to her last; and adding, that as silence on such a point could not be misconstrued, and as it must be equally desirable to both to have every subordinate arrangement concluded as soon as possible, she now sent me, by a safe conveyance, all my letters, and requested, that if I could not directly command her's, so as to send them to Highbury within a week, I would forward them after that period to her at——: in short, the full direction to Mr. Smallridge's, near Bristol, stared me in the face. I knew the name, the place, I knew all about it, and instantly saw what she had been doing. It was perfectly accordant with that resolution of character which I knew her to possess; and the secrecy she had maintained, as to any such design in her former letter, was equally descriptive of its anxious delicacy. For the world would not she have seemed to threaten me.—Imagine the shock; imagine how, till I had actually detected my own blunder, I raved at the blunders of the post.—What was to be done?—One thing only.—I must speak to my uncle. Without his sanction I could not hope to be listened to again.—I spoke; circumstances were in my favour; the late event had softened away his pride, and he was, earlier than I could have anticipated, wholly reconciled and complying; and could say at last, poor man! with a deep sigh, that he wished I might find as much happiness in the marriage state as he had done.—I felt that it would be of a different sort.—Are you disposed to pity me for what I must have suffered in opening the cause to him, for my suspense while all was at stake?—No; do not pity me till I reached Highbury, and saw how ill I had made her. Do not pity me till I saw her wan, sick looks.—I reached Highbury at the time of day when, from my knowledge of their late breakfast hour, I was certain of a good chance of finding her alone.—I was not disappointed; and at last I was not disappointed either in the object of my journey. A great deal of very reasonable, very just displeasure I had to persuade away. But it is done; we are reconciled, dearer, much dearer, than ever, and no moment's uneasiness can ever occur between us again. Now, my dear madam, I will release you; but I could not conclude before. A thousand and a thousand thanks for all the kindness you have ever shown me, and ten thousand for the attentions your heart will dictate towards her.—If you think me in a way to be happier than I deserve, I am quite of your opinion.—Miss W. calls me the child of good fortune. I hope she is right.—In one respect, my good fortune is undoubted, that of being able to subscribe myself,

Your obliged and affectionate Son,

F. C. WESTON CHURCHILL.

Chapter XV

This letter must make its way to Emma's feelings. She was obliged, in spite of her previous determination to the contrary, to do it all the justice that Mrs. Weston foretold. As soon as she came to her own name, it was irresistible; every line relating to herself was interesting, and almost every line agreeable; and when this charm ceased, the subject could still maintain itself, by the natural return of her former regard for the writer, and the very strong attraction which any picture of love must have for her at that moment. She never stopt till she had gone through the whole; and though it was impossible not to feel that he had been wrong, yet he had been less wrong than she had supposed—and he had suffered, and was very sorry—and he was so grateful to Mrs. Weston, and so much in love with Miss Fairfax, and she was so happy herself, that there was no being severe; and could he have entered the room, she must have shaken hands with him as heartily as ever.

She thought so well of the letter, that when Mr. Knightley came again, she desired him to read it. She was sure of Mrs. Weston's wishing it to be communicated; especially to one, who, like Mr. Knightley, had seen so much to blame in his conduct.

"I shall be very glad to look it over," said he, "but it seems long. I will take it home with me at night."

But that would not do. Mr. Weston was to call in the evening, and she must return it by him.

"I would rather be talking to you," he replied; "but as it seems a matter of justice, it shall be done."

He began—stopping, however, almost directly to say, "Had I been offered the sight of one of this gentleman's letters to his mother-in-law a few months ago, Emma, it would not have been taken with such indifference."

He proceeded a little farther, reading to himself; and then, with a smile, observed, "Humph!—a fine complimentary opening:—But it is his way. One man's style must not be the rule of another's. We will not be severe."

"It will be natural for me," he added shortly afterwards, "to speak my opinion aloud as I read. By doing it, I shall feel that I am near you. It will not be so great a loss of time: but if you dislike it——"

"Not at all. I should wish it."

Mr. Knightley returned to his reading with greater alacrity.

"He trifles here," said he, "as to the temptation. He knows he is wrong, and has nothing rational to urge.—Bad.—He ought not to have formed the engagement.—'His father's disposition:'—he is unjust, however, to his father. Mr. Weston's sanguine temper[1] was a blessing on all his upright and honourable exertions; but Mr. Weston earned every present comfort before he endeavoured to gain it.— Very true; he did not come till Miss Fairfax was here."

"And I have not forgotten," said Emma, "how sure you were that he might have come sooner if he would. You pass it over very handsomely—but you were perfectly right."

"I was not quite impartial in my judgment, Emma:—but yet, I think—had *you* not been in the case—I should still have distrusted him."

When he came to Miss Woodhouse, he was obliged to read the whole of it aloud—all that related to her, with a smile; a look; a shake of the head; a word or two of assent, or disapprobation; or merely of love, as the subject required; concluding, however, seriously, and, after steady reflection, thus—

"Very bad—though it might have been worse.—Playing a most dangerous game. Too much indebted to the event for his acquittal.— No judge of his own manners by you.—Always deceived in fact by his own wishes, and regardless of little besides his own convenience.—

1. Optimism, cheerfulness.

Fancying you to have fathomed his secret. Natural enough!—his own mind full of intrigue, that he should suspect it in others.— Mystery; Finesse—how they pervert the understanding! My Emma, does not every thing serve to prove more and more the beauty of truth and sincerity in all our dealings with each other?"

Emma agreed to it, and with a blush of sensibility on Harriet's account, which she could not give any sincere explanation of.

"You had better go on," said she.

He did so, but very soon stopt again to say, "the piano-forte! Ah! That was the act of a very, very young man, one too young to consider whether the inconvenience of it might not very much exceed the pleasure. A boyish scheme, indeed!—I cannot comprehend a man's wishing to give a woman any proof of affection which he knows she would rather dispense with; and he did know that she would have prevented the instrument's coming if she could."

After this, he made some progress without any pause. Frank Churchill's confession of having behaved shamefully was the first thing to call for more than a word in passing.

"I perfectly agree with you, sir,"—was then his remark. "You did behave very shamefully. You never wrote a truer line." And having gone through what immediately followed of the basis of their disagreement, and his persisting to act in direct opposition to Jane Fairfax's sense of right, he made a fuller pause to say, "This is very bad.—He had induced her to place herself, for his sake, in a situation of extreme difficulty and uneasiness, and it should have been his first object to prevent her from suffering unnecessarily.—She must have had much more to contend with, in carrying on the correspondence, than he could. He should have respected even unreasonable scruples, had there been such; but her's were all reasonable. We must look to her one fault, and remember that she had done a wrong thing in consenting to the engagement, to bear that she should have been in such a state of punishment."

Emma knew that he was now getting to the Box-Hill party, and grew uncomfortable. Her own behaviour had been so very improper! She was deeply ashamed, and a little afraid of his next look. It was all read, however, steadily, attentively, and without the smallest remark; and, excepting one momentary glance at her, instantly withdrawn, in the fear of giving pain—no remembrance of Box-Hill seemed to exist.

"There is no saying much for the delicacy of our good friends, the Eltons," was his next observation.—"His feelings are natural.— What! actually resolve to break with him entirely!—She felt the engagement to be a source of repentance and misery to each—she dissolved it.—What a view this gives of her sense of his behaviour!— Well, he must be a most extraordinary——"

"Nay, nay, read on.—You will find how very much he suffers."

"I hope he does," replied Mr. Knightley coolly, and resuming the letter.—"'Smallridge!'—What does this mean? What is all this?"

"She had engaged to go as governess to Mrs. Smallridge's children—a dear friend of Mrs. Elton's—a neighbour of Maple Grove; and, by the bye, I wonder how Mrs. Elton bears the disappointment."

"Say nothing, my dear Emma, while you oblige me to read—not even of Mrs. Elton. Only one page more. I shall soon have done. What a letter the man writes!"

"I wish you would read it with a kinder spirit towards him."

"Well, there *is* feeling here.—He does seem to have suffered in finding her ill.—Certainly, I can have no doubt of his being fond of her. 'Dearer, much dearer than ever.' I hope he may long continue to feel all the value of such a reconciliation.—He is a very liberal thanker, with his thousands and tens of thousands.—'Happier than I deserve.' Come, he knows himself there. 'Miss Woodhouse calls me the child of good fortune.'—Those were Miss Woodhouse's words, were they?—And a fine ending—and there is the letter. The child of good fortune! That was your name for him, was it?"

"You do not appear so well satisfied with his letter as I am; but still you must, at least I hope you must, think the better of him for it. I hope it does him some service with you."

"Yes, certainly it does. He has had great faults, faults of inconsideration and thoughtlessness; and I am very much of his opinion in thinking him likely to be happier than he deserves: but still as he is, beyond a doubt, really attached to Miss Fairfax, and will soon, it may be hoped, have the advantage of being constantly with her, I am very ready to believe his character will improve, and acquire from her's the steadiness and delicacy of principle that it wants. And now, let me talk to you of something else. I have another person's interest at present so much at heart, that I cannot think any longer about Frank Churchill. Ever since I left you this morning, Emma, my mind was been hard at work on one subject."

The subject followed; it was in plain, unaffected, gentleman-like English, such as Mr. Knightley used even to the woman he was in love with, how to be able to ask her to marry him, without attacking the happiness of her father. Emma's answer was ready at the first word. "While her dear father lived, any change of condition must be impossible for her. She could never quit him." Part only of this answer, however, was admitted. The impossibility of her quitting her father, Mr. Knightley felt as strongly as herself; but the inadmissibility of any other change, he could not agree to. He had been thinking it over most deeply, most intently; he had at first hoped to induce Mr. Woodhouse to remove with her to Donwell; he had wanted to believe it feasible, but his knowledge of Mr. Woodhouse would not suffer him to deceive himself long; and now he confessed his persuasion, that such a transplantation would be a risk of her father's comfort, perhaps even of his life, which must not be hazarded. Mr. Woodhouse taken from Hartfield!—No, he felt that it ought not to be attempted. But the plan which had arisen on the sacrifice of this, he trusted his dearest Emma would not find in any respect objectionable; it was, that he should be received at Hartfield; that so long as her father's happiness—in other words his life—required Hartfield to continue her home, it should be his likewise.

Of their all removing to Donwell, Emma had already had her own passing thoughts. Like him, she had tried the scheme and rejected it; but such an alternative as this had not occurred to her. She was sensible of all the affection it evinced. She felt that, in quitting Donwell, he must be sacrificing a great deal of independence of hours and habits; that in living constantly with her father, and in no house of his own, there would be much, very much, to be borne with. She promised to think of it, and advised him to think of it more; but he was fully convinced, that no reflection could alter his wishes or his opinion on the subject. He had given it, he could assure her, very long and calm consideration; he had been walking away from William Larkins the whole morning, to have his thoughts to himself.

"Ah! there is one difficulty unprovided for," cried Emma. "I am sure William Larkins will not like it. You must get his consent before you ask mine."

She promised, however, to think of it; and pretty nearly promised, moreover, to think of it with the intention of finding it a very good scheme.

It is remarkable, that Emma, in the many, very many, points of view in which she was now beginning to consider Donwell Abbey, was never struck with any sense of injury to her nephew Henry, whose rights as heir expectant had formerly been so tenaciously regarded. Think she must of the possible difference to the poor little boy; and yet she only gave herself a saucy conscious smile about it, and found amusement in detecting the real cause of that violent dislike of Mr. Knightley's marrying Jane Fairfax, or any body else, which at the time she had wholly imputed to the amiable solicitude of the sister and the aunt.

This proposal of his, this plan of marrying and continuing at Hartfield—the more she contemplated it, the more pleasing it became. His evils seemed to lessen, her own advantages to increase, their mutual good to outweigh every drawback. Such a companion for herself in the periods of anxiety and cheerlessness before her!— Such a partner in all those duties and cares to which time must be giving increase of melancholy!

She would have been too happy but for poor Harriet; but every blessing of her own seemed to involve and advance the sufferings of her friend, who must now be even excluded from Hartfield. The delightful family-party which Emma was securing for herself, poor Harriet must, in mere charitable caution, be kept at a distance from. She would be a loser in every way. Emma could not deplore her future absence as any deduction from her own enjoyment. In such a party, Harriet would be rather a dead weight than otherwise; but for the poor girl herself, it seemed a peculiarly cruel necessity that was to be placing her in such a state of unmerited punishment.

In time, of course, Mr. Knightley would be forgotten, that is, supplanted; but this could not be expected to happen very early. Mr. Knightley himself would be doing nothing to assist the cure;—not like Mr. Elton. Mr. Knightley, always so kind, so feeling, so truly considerate for every body, would never deserve to be less worshipped than now; and it really was too much to hope even of Harriet, that she could be in love with more than *three* men in one year.

Chapter XVI

It was a very great relief to Emma to find Harriet as desirous as herself to avoid a meeting. Their intercourse was painful enough by letter. How much worse, had they been obliged to meet!

Harriet expressed herself very much as might be supposed, with-out reproaches, or apparent sense of ill usage; and yet Emma fan-cied there was a something of resentment, a something bordering on it in her style, which increased the desirableness of their being separate.—It might be only her own consciousness; but it seemed as if an angel only could have been quite without resentment under such a stroke.

She had no difficulty in procuring Isabella's invitation; and she was fortunate in having a sufficient reason for asking it, without resorting to invention.—There was a tooth amiss. Harriet really wished, and had wished some time, to consult a dentist. Mrs. John Knightley was delighted to be of use; any thing of ill-health was a recommendation to her—and though not so fond of a dentist as of a Mr. Wingfield, she was quite eager to have Harriet under her care.—When it was thus settled on her sister's side, Emma proposed it to her friend, and found her very persuadable.—Harriet was to go; she was invited for at least a fortnight; she was to be conveyed in Mr. Wood-house's carriage.—It was all arranged, it was all completed, and Har-riet was safe in Brunswick Square.

Now Emma could, indeed, enjoy Mr. Knightley's visits; now she could talk, and she could listen with true happiness, unchecked by that sense of injustice, of guilt, of something most painful, which had haunted her when remembering how disappointed a heart was near her, how much might at that moment, and at a little distance, be enduring by the feelings which she had led astray herself.

The difference of Harriet at Mrs. Goddard's, or in London, made perhaps an unreasonable difference in Emma's sensations; but she could not think of her in London without objects of curiosity and employment, which must be averting the past, and carrying her out of herself.

She would not allow any other anxiety to succeed directly to the place in her mind which Harriet had occupied. There was a communication before her, one which *she* only could be competent to make—the confession of her engagement to her father; but she would have nothing to do with it at present.—She had resolved to defer the disclosure till Mrs. Weston were safe and well. No additional agitation should be thrown at this period among those she loved—and the evil should not act on herself by anticipation before the appointed time.—A fortnight, at least, of leisure and peace of mind, to crown every warmer, but more agitating, delight, should be her's.

She soon resolved, equally as a duty and a pleasure, to employ half an hour of this holiday of spirits in calling on Miss Fairfax.— She ought to go—and she was longing to see her; the resemblance of their present situations increasing every other motive of good will. It would be a *secret* satisfaction; but the consciousness of a similarity of prospect would certainly add to the interest with which she should attend to any thing Jane might communicate.

She went—she had driven once unsuccessfully to the door, but had not been into the house since the morning after Box-Hill, when poor Jane had been in such distress as had filled her with compassion, though all the worst of her sufferings had been unsuspected.— The fear of being still unwelcome, determined her, though assured of their being at home, to wait in the passage, and send up her name.—She heard Patty announcing it; but no such bustle succeeded as poor Miss Bates had before made so happily intelligible.—No; she heard nothing but the instant reply of, "Beg her to walk up;"—and a moment afterwards she was met on the stairs by Jane herself, coming eagerly forward, as if no other reception of her were felt sufficient.— Emma had never seen her look so well, so lovely, so engaging. There was consciousness, animation, and warmth; there was every thing which her countenance or manner could ever have wanted.—She came forward with an offered hand; and said, in a low, but very feeling tone,

"This is most kind, indeed!—Miss Woodhouse, it is impossible for me to express——I hope you will believe——Excuse me for being so entirely without words."

Emma was gratified, and would soon have shown no want of words, if the sound of Mrs. Elton's voice from the sitting-room had not checked her, and made it expedient to compress all her friendly and all her congratulatory sensations into a very, very earnest shake of the hand.

Mrs. Bates and Mrs. Elton were together. Miss Bates was out, which accounted for the previous tranquillity. Emma could have wished Mrs. Elton elsewhere; but she was in a humour to have patience with every body; and as Mrs. Elton met her with unusual graciousness, she hoped the rencontre would do them no harm.

She soon believed herself to penetrate Mrs. Elton's thoughts, and understand why she was, like herself, in happy spirits; it was being in Miss Fairfax's confidence, and fancying herself acquainted with what was still a secret to other people. Emma saw symptoms of it immediately in the expression of her face; and while paying her own compliments to Mrs. Bates, and appearing to attend to the good old lady's replies, she saw her with a sort of anxious parade of mystery fold up a letter which she had apparently been reading aloud to Miss Fairfax, and return it into the purple and gold ridicule[2] by her side, saying, with significant nods,

"We can finish this some other time, you know. You and I shall not want opportunities. And, in fact, you have heard all the essential already. I only wanted to prove to you that Mrs. S. admits our apology, and is not offended. You see how delightfully she writes. Oh! she is a sweet creature! You would have doated on her, had you gone.—But not a word more. Let us be discreet—quite on our good behaviour.—Hush!—You remember those lines—I forget the poem at this moment:

"For when a lady's in the case,
"You know all other things give place."[3]

Now I say, my dear, in *our* case, for *lady*, read——mum! a word to the wise.—I am in a fine flow of spirits, an't I? But I want to set your heart at ease as to Mrs. S.—*My* representation, you see, has quite appeased her."

And again, on Emma's merely turning her head to look at Mrs. Bates's knitting, she added, in a half whisper,

"I mentioned no *names*, you will observe.—Oh! no; cautious as a minister of state. I managed it extremely well."

Emma could not doubt. It was a palpable display, repeated on every possible occasion. When they had all talked a little while in

2. Reticule, or small purse.
3. The quotation is from "The Hare and Many Friends," a fable by John Gay (1685–1732). In the poem, a "stately bull" is speaking of a "fav'rite cow."

harmony of the weather and Mrs. Weston, she found herself abruptly addressed with,

"Do not you think, Miss Woodhouse, our saucy little friend here is charmingly recovered?—Do not you think her cure does Perry the highest credit?—(here was a side-glance of great meaning at Jane.) Upon my word, Perry has restored her in a wonderful short time!—Oh! if you had seen her, as I did, when she was at the worst!"—And when Mrs. Bates was saying something to Emma, whispered farther, "We do not say a word of any *assistance* that Perry might have; not a word of a certain young physician from Windsor.—Oh! no; Perry shall have all the credit."

"I have scarce had the pleasure of seeing you, Miss Woodhouse," she shortly afterwards began, "since the party to Box-Hill. Very pleasant party. But yet I think there was something wanting. Things did not seem—that is, there seemed a little cloud upon the spirits of some.—So it appeared to me at least, but I might be mistaken. However, I think it answered so far as to tempt one to go again. What say you both to our collecting the same party, and exploring to Box-Hill again, while the fine weather lasts?—It must be the same party, you know, quite the same party, not *one* exception."

Soon after this Miss Bates came in, and Emma could not help being diverted by the perplexity of her first answer to herself, resulting, she supposed, from doubt of what might be said, and impatience to say every thing.

"Thank you, dear Miss Woodhouse, you are all kindness.—It is impossible to say—Yes, indeed, I quite understand—dearest Jane's prospects—that is, I do not mean.—But she is charmingly recovered.—How is Mr. Woodhouse?—I am so glad.—Quite out of my power.—Such a happy little circle as you find us here.—Yes, indeed.—Charming young man!—that is—so very friendly; I mean good Mr. Perry!—such attention to Jane!"—And from her great, her more than commonly thankful delight towards Mrs. Elton for being there, Emma guessed that there had been a little show of resentment towards Jane, from the vicarage quarter, which was now graciously overcome.—After a few whispers, indeed, which placed it beyond a guess, Mrs. Elton, speaking louder, said,

"Yes, here I am, my good friend; and here I have been so long, that anywhere else I should think it necessary to apologize: but the truth is, that I am waiting for my lord and master. He promised to join me here, and pay his respects to you."

"What! are we to have the pleasure of a call from Mr. Elton?—That will be a favour indeed! for I know gentlemen do not like morning visits, and Mr. Elton's time is so engaged."

"Upon my word it is, Miss Bates.—He really is engaged from morning to night.—There is no end of people's coming to him, on some pretence or other.—The magistrates, and overseers, and churchwardens, are always wanting his opinion. They seem not able to do any thing without him.—Upon my word, Mr. E., I often say, rather you than I.—I do not know what would become of my crayons and my instrument, if I had half so many applicants.'—Bad enough as it is, for I absolutely neglect them both to an unpardonable degree.—I believe I have not played a bar this fortnight.—However, he is coming, I assure you: yes, indeed, on purpose to wait on you all."—And putting up her hand to screen her words from Emma—"A congratulatory visit, you know.—Oh! yes, quite indispensable."

Miss Bates looked about her, so happily!—

"He promised to come to me as soon as he could disengage himself from Knightley; but he and Knightley are shut up together in deep consultation.—Mr. E. is Knightley's right hand."

Emma would not have smiled for the world, and only said, "Is Mr. Elton gone on foot to Donwell?—He will have a hot walk."

"Oh! no, it is a meeting at the Crown, a regular meeting. Weston and Cole will be there too; but one is apt to speak only of those who lead.—I fancy Mr. E. and Knightley have every thing their own way."

"Have not you mistaken the day?" said Emma. "I am almost certain that the meeting at the Crown is not till to-morrow.—Mr. Knightley was at Hartfield yesterday, and spoke of it as for Saturday."

"Oh! no; the meeting is certainly to-day," was the abrupt answer, which denoted the impossibility of any blunder on Mrs. Elton's side.—"I do believe," she continued, "this is the most troublesome parish that ever was. We never heard of such things at Maple Grove."

"Your parish there was small," said Jane.

"Upon my word, my dear, I do not know, for I never heard the subject talked of."

"But it is proved by the smallness of the school, which I have heard you speak of, as under the patronage of your sister and Mrs. Bragge; the only school, and not more than five-and-twenty children."

"Ah! you clever creature, that's very true. What a thinking brain you have! I say, Jane, what a perfect character you and I should make, if we could be shaken together. My liveliness and your solidity would produce perfection.—Not that I presume to insinuate, however, that *some* people may not think *you* perfection already.— But hush!—not a word, if you please."

It seemed an unnecessary caution; Jane was wanting to give her words, not to Mrs. Elton, but to Miss Woodhouse, as the latter plainly saw. The wish of distinguishing her, as far as civility permitted, was very evident, though it could not often proceed beyond a look.

Mr. Elton made his appearance. His lady greeted him with some of her sparkling vivacity.

"Very pretty, sir, upon my word; to send me on here, to be an encumbrance to my friends, so long before you vouchsafe to come!—But you knew what a dutiful creature you had to deal with. You knew I should not stir till my lord and master appeared.—Here have I been sitting this hour, giving these young ladies a sample of true conjugal obedience—for who can say, you know, how soon it may be wanted?"

Mr. Elton was so hot and tired, that all this wit seemed thrown away. His civilities to the other ladies must be paid; but his subsequent object was to lament over himself for the heat he was suffering, and the walk he had had for nothing.

"When I got to Donwell," said he, "Knightley could not be found. Very odd! very unaccountable! after the note I sent him this morning, and the message he returned, that he should certainly be at home till one."

"Donwell!" cried his wife—"My dear Mr. E., you have not been to Donwell!—You mean the Crown; you come from the meeting at the Crown."

"No, no, that's to-morrow; and I particularly wanted to see Knightley to-day on that very account.—Such a dreadful broiling morning!—I went over the fields too—(speaking in a tone of great ill usage,) which made it so much the worse. And then not to find him at home! I assure you I am not at all pleased. And no apology left, no message for me. The housekeeper declared she knew nothing of my being expected.—Very extraordinary!—And nobody knew at all which way he was gone. Perhaps to Hartfield, perhaps to the Abbey Mill, perhaps into his woods.—Miss Woodhouse, this is not like our friend Knightley.—Can you explain it?"

Emma amused herself by protesting that it was very extraordinary indeed, and that she had not a syllable to say for him.

"I cannot imagine," cried Mrs. Elton, (feeling the indignity as a wife ought to do,) "I cannot imagine how he could do such a thing by you, of all people in the world! The very last person whom one should expect to be forgotten!—My dear Mr. E., he must have left a message for you, I am sure he must.—Not even Knightley could be so very eccentric;—and his servants forgot it. Depend upon it, that was the case: and very likely to happen with the Donwell servants, who are all, I have often observed, extremely awkward and remiss.—I am sure I would not have such a creature as his Harry stand at our sideboard for any consideration. And as for Mrs. Hodges, Wright holds her very cheap indeed.—She promised Wright a receipt, and never sent it."

"I met William Larkins," continued Mr. Elton, "as I got near the house, and he told me I should not find his master at home, but I did not believe him.—William seemed rather out of humour. He did not know what was come to his master lately, he said, but he could hardly ever get the speech of him. I have nothing to do with William's wants, but it really is of very great importance that *I* should see Knightley to day; and it becomes a matter, therefore, of very serious inconvenience that I should have had this hot walk to no purpose."

Emma felt that she could not do better than go home directly. In all probability she was at this very time waited for there; and Mr. Knightley might be preserved from sinking deeper in aggression towards Mr. Elton, if not towards William Larkins.

She was pleased, on taking leave, to find Miss Fairfax determined to attend her out of the room, to go with her even down stairs; it gave her an opportunity which she immediately made use of, to say,

"It is as well, perhaps, that I have not had the possibility. Had you not been surrounded by other friends, I might have been tempted to introduce a subject, to ask questions, to speak more openly than might have been strictly correct.—I feel that I should certainly have been impertinent."

"Oh!" cried Jane, with a blush and an hesitation which Emma thought infinitely more becoming to her than all the elegance of all her usual composure—"there would have been no danger. The danger would have been of my wearying you. You could not have gratified me more than by expressing an interest——. Indeed, Miss Woodhouse, (speaking more collectedly,) with the consciousness which I have of misconduct, very great misconduct, it is particularly consoling to me to know that those of my friends, whose good opinion is most worth preserving, are not disgusted to such a degree as to—I have not time for half that I could wish to say. I long to make apologies, excuses, to urge something for myself. I feel it so very due. But, unfortunately—in short, if your compassion does not stand my friend——"

"Oh! you are too scrupulous, indeed you are," cried Emma, warmly, and taking her hand. "You owe me no apologies; and every body to whom you might be supposed to owe them, is so perfectly satisfied, so delighted even—"

"You are very kind, but I know what my manners were to you.—So cold and artificial!—I had always a part to act.—It was a life of deceit!—I know that I must have disgusted you."

"Pray say no more. I feel that all the apologies should be on my side. Let us forgive each other at once. We must do whatever is to be done quickest, and I think our feelings will lose no time there. I hope you have pleasant accounts from Windsor?"

"Very."

"And the next news, I suppose, will be, that we are to lose you— just as I begin to know you."

"Oh! as to all that, of course nothing can be thought of yet. I am here till claimed by Colonel and Mrs. Campbell."

"Nothing can be actually settled yet, perhaps," replied Emma, smiling—"but, excuse me, it must be thought of."

The smile was returned as Jane answered,

"You are very right; it has been thought of. And I will own to you, (I am sure it will be safe), that so far as our living with Mr. Churchill at Enscombe, it is settled. There must be three months, at least, of deep mourning; but when they are over, I imagine there will be nothing more to wait for."

"Thank you, thank you.—This is just what I wanted to be assured of.—Oh! if you knew how much I love every thing that is decided and open!—Good bye, good bye."

Chapter XVII

Mrs. Weston's friends were all made happy by her safety;[4] and if the satisfaction of her well-doing could be increased to Emma, it was by knowing her to be the mother of a little girl. She had been decided in wishing for a Miss Weston. She would not acknowledge that it was with any view of making a match for her, hereafter, with either of Isabella's sons; but she was convinced that a daughter would suit both father and mother best. It would be a great comfort to Mr. Weston as he grew older—and even Mr. Weston might be growing older ten years hence—to have his fireside enlivened by the sports and the nonsense, the freaks and the fancies of a child never banished from home;[5] and Mrs. Weston—no one could doubt that a daughter would be most to her; and it would be quite a pity that any one who so well knew how to teach, should not have their powers in exercise again.

"She has had the advantage, you know, of practising on me," she continued—"like La Baronne d'Almane on La Comtesse d'Ostalis, in Madame de Genlis' Adelaide and Theodore,[6] and we shall now see her own little Adelaide educated on a more perfect plan."

"That is," replied Mr. Knightley, "she will indulge her even more than she did you, and believe that she does not indulge her at all. It will be the only difference."

"Poor child!" cried Emma; "at that rate, what will become of her?"

"Nothing very bad.—The fate of thousands. She will be disagreeable in infancy, and correct herself as she grows older. I am losing all my bitterness against spoilt children, my dearest Emma. I, who am owing all my happiness to *you*, would not it be horrible ingratitude in me to be severe on them?"

---

4. A delicate way of indicating that Mrs. Weston has safely delivered her child, not an entirely assured outcome considering the state of obstetrics at the time.

5. Sent away to school.

6. The title of the English translation (1783) of this novel.

Emma laughed, and replied: "But I had the assistance of all your endeavours to counteract the indulgence of other people. I doubt whether my own sense would have corrected me without it."

"Do you?—I have no doubt. Nature gave you understanding:—Miss Taylor gave you principles. You must have done well. My interference was quite as likely to do harm as good. It was very natural for you to say, what right has he to lecture me?—and I am afraid very natural for you to feel that it was done in a disagreeable manner. I do not believe I did you any good. The good was all to myself, by making you an object of the tenderest affection to me. I could not think about you so much without doating on you, faults and all; and by dint of fancying so many errors, have been in love with you ever since you were thirteen at least."

"I am sure you were of use to me," cried Emma. "I was very often influenced rightly by you—oftener than I would own at the time. I am very sure you did me good. And if poor little Anna Weston is to be spoiled, it will be the greatest humanity in you to do as much for her as you have done for me, except falling in love with her when she is thirteen."

"How often, when you were a girl, have you said to me, with one of your saucy looks—'Mr. Knightley, I am going to do so and so; papa says I may, or, I have Miss Taylor's leave'—something which, you knew, I did not approve. In such cases my interference was giving you two bad feelings instead of one."

"What an amiable creature I was!—No wonder you should hold my speeches in such affectionate remembrance."

"'Mr. Knightley.'—You always called me, 'Mr. Knightley;' and, from habit, it has not so very formal a sound.—And yet it is formal. I want you to call me something else, but I do not know what."

"I remember once calling you 'George,' in one of my amiable fits, about ten years ago. I did it because I thought it would offend you; but, as you made no objection, I never did it again."

"And cannot you call me 'George' now?"

"Impossible!—I never can call you any thing but 'Mr. Knightley.' I will not promise even to equal the elegant terseness of Mrs. Elton, by calling you Mr. K.—But I will promise," she added presently, laughing and blushing—"I will promise to call you once by your Christian name. I do not say when, but perhaps you may guess where;—in the building in which N. takes M. for better, for worse."[7]

Emma grieved that she could not be more openly just to one important service which his better sense would have rendered her, to the advice which would have saved her from the worst of all her

---

7. The building is the church, and the N and M are found in the standard English marriage service as alphabetic markers to the various readings and responses.

womanly follies—her wilful intimacy with Harriet Smith; but it was too tender a subject.—She could not enter on it.—Harriet was very seldom mentioned between them. This, on his side, might merely proceed from her not being thought of; but Emma was rather inclined to attribute it to delicacy, and a suspicion, from some appearances, that their friendship were declining. She was aware herself, that, parting under any other circumstances, they certainly should have corresponded more, and that her intelligence would not have rested, as it now almost wholly did, on Isabella's letters. He might observe that it was so. The pain of being obliged to practise concealment towards him, was very little inferior to the pain of having made Harriet unhappy.

Isabella sent quite as good an account of her visitor as could be expected; on her first arrival she had thought her out of spirits, which appeared perfectly natural, as there was a dentist to be consulted; but, since that business had been over, she did not appear to find Harriet different from what she had known her before.—Isabella, to be sure, was no very quick observer; yet if Harriet had not been equal to playing with the children, it would not have escaped her. Emma's comforts and hopes were most agreeably carried on, by Harriet's being to stay longer; her fortnight was likely to be a month at least. Mr. and Mrs. John Knightley were to come down in August, and she was invited to remain till they could bring her back.

"John does not even mention your friend," said Mr. Knightley. "Here is his answer, if you like to see it."

It was the answer to the communication of his intended marriage. Emma accepted it with a very eager hand, with an impatience all alive to know what he would say about it, and not at all checked by hearing that her friend was unmentioned.

"John enters like a brother into my happiness," continued Mr. Knightley, "but he is no complimenter; and though I well know him to have, likewise, a most brotherly affection for you, he is so far from making flourishes, that any other young woman might think him rather cool in her praise. But I am not afraid of your seeing what he writes."

"He writes like a sensible man," replied Emma, when she had read the letter. "I honour his sincerity. It is very plain that he considers the good fortune of the engagement as all on my side, but that he is not without hope of my growing, in time, as worthy of your affection, as you think me already. Had he said any thing to bear a different construction, I should not have believed him."

"My Emma, he means no such thing. He only means——"

"He and I should differ very little in our estimation of the two,"—interrupted she, with a sort of serious smile—"much less, perhaps, than he is aware of, if we could enter without ceremony or reserve on the subject."

"Emma, my dear Emma—"

"Oh!" she cried with more thorough gaiety, "if you fancy your brother does not do me justice, only wait till my dear father is in the secret, and hear his opinion. Depend upon it, he will be much farther from doing *you* justice. He will think all the happiness, all the advantage, on your side of the question; all the merit on mine. I wish I may not sink into 'poor Emma' with him at once.—His tender compassion towards oppressed worth can go no farther."

"Ah!" he cried, "I wish your father might be half as easily convinced as John will be, of our having every right that equal worth can give, to be happy together. I am amused by one part of John's letter—did you notice it?—where he says, that my information did not take him wholly by surprise, that he was rather in expectation of hearing something of the kind."

"If I understood your brother, he only means so far as your having some thoughts of marrying. He had no idea of me. He seems perfectly unprepared for that."

"Yes, yes—but I am amused that he should have seen so far into my feelings. What has he been judging by?—I am not conscious of any difference in my spirits or conversation that could prepare him at this time for my marrying any more than at another.—But it was so, I suppose. I dare say there was a difference when I was staying with them the other day. I believe I did not play with the children quite so much as usual. I remember one evening the poor boys saying, 'Uncle seems always tired now.'"

The time was coming when the news must spread farther, and other persons' reception of it tried. As soon as Mrs. Weston was sufficiently recovered to admit Mr. Woodhouse's visits, Emma having it in view that her gentle reasonings should be employed in the cause, resolved first to announce it at home, and then at Randall's.—But how to break it to her father at last!—She had bound herself to do it, in such an hour of Mr. Knightley's absence, or when it came to the point her heart would have failed her, and she must have put it off; but Mr. Knightley was to come at such a time, and follow up the beginning she was to make.—She was forced to speak, and to speak cheerfully too. She must not make it a more decided subject of misery to him, by a melancholy tone herself. She must not appear to think it a misfortune.—With all the spirits she could command, she prepared him first for something strange, and then, in a few words, said, that if his consent and approbation could be obtained—which she trusted, would be attended with no difficulty, since it was meant to promote the happiness of all—she and Mr. Knightley meant to marry; by which means Hartfield would receive the constant addition of that person's company whom she knew he loved, next to his daughters and Mrs. Weston, best in the world.

Poor man!—it was at first a considerable shock to him, and he tried earnestly to dissuade her from it. She was reminded, more than once, of her having always said she would never marry, and assured that it would be a great deal better for her to remain single; and told of poor Isabella, and poor Miss Taylor.—But it would not do. Emma hung about him affectionately, and smiled, and said it must be so; and that he must not class her with Isabella and Mrs. Weston, whose marriages taking them from Hartfield, had, indeed, made a melancholy change: but she was not going from Hartfield; she should be always there; she was introducing no change in their numbers or their comforts but for the better; and she was very sure that he would be a great deal the happier for having Mr. Knightley always at hand, when he were once got used to the idea.—Did not he love Mr. Knightley very much?—He would not deny that he did, she was sure.—Whom did he ever want to consult on business but Mr. Knightley?—Who was so useful to him, who so ready to write his letters, who so glad to assist him?—Who so cheerful, so attentive, so attached to him?—Would not he like to have him always on the spot?—Yes. That was all very true. Mr. Knightley could not be there too often; he should be glad to see him every day;—but they did see him every day as it was.—Why could not they go on as they had done?

Mr. Woodhouse could not be soon reconciled; but the worst was overcome, the idea was given; time and continual repetition must do the rest.—To Emma's entreaties and assurances succeeded Mr. Knightley's, whose fond praise of her gave the subject even a kind of welcome; and he was soon used to be talked to by each, on every fair occasion.—They had all the assistance which Isabella could give, by letters of the strongest approbation; and Mrs. Weston was ready, on the first meeting, to consider the subject in the most serviceable light—first, as a settled, and secondly, as a good one—well aware of the nearly equal importance of the two recommendations to Mr. Woodhouse's mind.—It was agreed upon, as what was to be; and every body by whom he was used to be guided assuring him that it would be for his happiness; and having some feelings himself which almost admitted it, he began to think that some time or other—in another year or two, perhaps—it might not be so very bad if the marriage did take place.

Mrs. Weston was acting no part, feigning no feelings in all that she said to him in favour of the event.—She had been extremely surprised, never more so, than when Emma first opened the affair to her; but she saw in it only increase of happiness to all, and had no scruple in urging him to the utmost.—She had such a regard for Mr. Knightley, as to think he deserved even her dearest Emma; and it was in every respect so proper, suitable, and unexceptionable a connexion, and in one respect, one point of the highest importance, so peculiarly eligible, so singularly fortunate, that now it seemed as if Emma could not safely have attached herself to any other creature, and that she had herself been the stupidest of beings in not having thought of it, and wished it long ago.—How very few of those men in a rank of life to address Emma would have renounced their own home for Hartfield! And who but Mr. Knightley could know and bear with Mr. Woodhouse, so as to make such an arrangement desirable!—The difficulty of disposing of poor Mr. Woodhouse has been always felt in her husband's plans and her own, for a marriage between Frank and Emma. How to settle the claims of Enscombe and Hartfield had been a continual impediment—less acknowledged by Mr. Weston than by herself—but even he had never been able to finish the subject better than by saying—"Those matters will take care of themselves; the young people will find a way."—But here there was nothing to be shifted off in a wild speculation on the future. It was all right, all open, all equal. No sacrifice on any side worth the name. It was a union of the highest promise of felicity in itself, and without one real, rational difficulty to oppose or delay it.

Mrs. Weston, with her baby on her knee, indulging in such reflections as these, was one of the happiest women in the world. If any thing could increase her delight, it was perceiving that the baby would soon have outgrown its first set of caps.

The news was universally a surprise wherever it spread; and Mr. Weston had his five minutes share of it; but five minutes were enough to familiarize the idea to his quickness of mind.—He saw the advantages of the match, and rejoiced in them with all the constancy of his wife; but the wonder of it was very soon nothing; and by the end of an hour he was not far from believing that he had always foreseen it.

"It is to be a secret, I conclude," said he. "These matters are always a secret, till it is found out that every body knows them. Only let me be told when I may speak out.—I wonder whether Jane has any suspicion."

He went to Highbury the next morning, and satisfied himself on that point. He told her the news. Was not she like a daughter, his eldest daughter?—he must tell her; and Miss Bates being present, it passed, of course, to Mrs. Cole, Mrs. Perry, and Mrs. Elton, immediately afterwards. It was no more than the principals were prepared for; they had calculated from the time of its being known at Randall's, how soon it would be over Highbury; and were thinking of themselves, as the evening wonder in many a family circle, with great sagacity.

In general, it was a very well approved match. Some might think him, and others might think her, the most in luck. One set might recommend their all removing to Donwell, and leaving Hartfield for the John Knightleys; and another might predict disagreements among their servants; but yet, upon the whole, there was no serious objection raised, except in one habitation, the vicarage.—There, the surprise was not softened by any satisfaction. Mr. Elton cared little about it, compared with his wife; he only hoped "the young lady's pride would now be contented;" and supposed "she had always meant to catch Knightley if she could;" and, on the point of living at Hartfield, could daringly exclaim, "Rather he than I!"—But Mrs. Elton was very much discomposed indeed.—"Poor Knightley! poor fellow!—sad business for him.—She was extremely concerned; for, though very eccentric, he had a thousand good qualities.—How could he be so taken in?—Did not think him at all in love—not in the least.—Poor Knightley!—There would be an end of all pleasant intercourse with him.—How happy he had been to come and dine with them whenever they asked him! But that would be all over now.—Poor fellow!—No more exploring parties to Donwell made for *her*. Oh! no; there would be a Mrs. Knightley to throw cold water on every thing.—Extremely disagreeable! But she was not at all sorry that she had abused the housekeeper the other day.—Shocking plan, living together. It would never do. She knew a family near Maple Grove who had tried it, and been obliged to separate before the end of the first quarter.

Chapter XVIII

Time passed on. A few more to-morrows, and the party from London would be arriving. It was an alarming change; and Emma was thinking of it one morning as what must bring a great deal to agitate and grieve her, when Mr. Knightley came in, and distressing thoughts were put by. After the first chat of pleasure he was silent; and then, in a graver tone, began with,

"I have something to tell you, Emma; some news."

"Good or bad?" said she, quickly, looking up in his face.

"I do not know which it ought to be called."

"Oh! good I am sure.—I see it in your countenance. You are trying not to smile."

"I am afraid," said he, composing his features, "I am very much afraid, my dear Emma, that you will not smile when you hear it."

"Indeed! but why so?—I can hardly imagine that any thing which pleases or amuses you, should not please and amuse me too."

"There is one subject," he replied, "I hope but one, on which we do not think alike." He paused a moment, again smiling, with his eyes fixed on her face. "Does nothing occur to you?—Do not you recollect?—Harriet Smith."

Her cheeks flushed at the name, and she felt afraid of something, though she knew not what.

"Have you heard from her yourself this morning?" cried he. "You have, I believe, and know the whole."

"No, I have not; I know nothing; pray tell me."

"You are prepared for the worst, I see—and very bad it is. Harriet Smith marries Robert Martin."

Emma gave a start, which did not seem like being prepared—and her eyes, in eager gaze, said, "No, this is impossible!" but her lips were closed.

"It is so, indeed," continued Mr. Knightley; "I have it from Robert Martin himself. He left me not half an hour ago."

She was still looking at him with the most speaking amazement.

"You like it, my Emma, as little as I feared.—I wish our opinions were the same. But in time they will. Time, you may be very sure, will make one or the other of us think differently; and, in the meanwhile, we need not talk much on the subject."

"You mistake me, you quite mistake me," she replied, exerting herself. "It is not that such a circumstance would now make me unhappy, but I cannot believe it. It seems an impossibility!—You cannot mean to say, that Harriet Smith has accepted Robert Martin. You cannot mean that he has even proposed to her again—yet. You only mean, that he intends it."

"I mean that he has done it," answered Mr. Knightley, with smiling but determined decision, "and been accepted."

"Good God!" she cried.—"Well!"—Then having recourse to her workbasket, in excuse for leaning down her face, and concealing all the exquisite feelings of delight and entertainment which she knew she must be expressing, she added, "Well, now tell me every thing; make this intelligible to me. How, where, when?—Let me know it all. I never was more surprised—but it does not make me unhappy, I assure you.—How—how has it been possible?"

"It is a very simple story. He went to town on business three days ago, and I got him to take charge of some papers which I was wanting to send to John.—He delivered these papers to John, at his chambers, and was asked by him to join their party the same evening to Astley's.[8] They were going to take the two eldest boys to Astley's. The party was to be our brother and sister, Henry, John——and Miss

---

8. Philip Astley (1742–1814) was an equestrian performer and producer of popular entertainment. This party would have visited his third amphitheater, the Olympic Pavilion, built in 1806 and sold in 1813 to a great financial loss.

Smith. My friend Robert could not resist. They called for him in their way; were all extremely amused; and my brother asked him to dine with them the next day—which he did—and in the course of that visit (as I understand) he found an opportunity of speaking to Harriet; and certainly did not speak in vain.—She made him, by her acceptance, as happy even as he is deserving. He came down by yesterday's coach, and was with me this morning immediately after breakfast, to report his proceedings, first on my affairs, and then on his own. This is all that I can relate of the how, where, and when. Your friend Harriet will make a much longer history when you see her.—She will give you all the minute particulars, which only woman's language can make interesting.—In our communications we deal only in the great.—However, I must say that Robert Martin's heart seemed for *him* and to *me*, very overflowing; and that he did mention, without its being much to the purpose, that on quitting their box at Astley's, my brother took charge of Mrs. John Knightley and little John, and he followed with Miss Smith and Henry; and that at one time they were in such a crowd, as to make Miss Smith rather uneasy."

He stopped.—Emma dared not attempt any immediate reply. To speak, she was sure would be to betray a most unreasonable degree of happiness. She must wait a moment, or he would think her mad. Her silence disturbed him; and after observing her a little while, he added,

"Emma, my love, you said that this circumstance would not now make you unhappy; but I am afraid it gives you more pain than you expected. His situation is an evil—but you must consider it as what satisfies your friend; and I will answer for your thinking better and better of him as you know him more. His good sense and good principles would delight you.—As far as the man is concerned, you could not wish your friend in better hands. His rank in society I would alter if I could; which is saying a great deal I assure you, Emma.—You laugh at me about William Larkins; but I could quite as ill spare Robert Martin."

He wanted her to look up and smile; and having now brought herself not to smile too broadly—she did—cheerfully answering,

"You need not be at any pains to reconcile me to the match. I think Harriet is doing extremely well. *Her* connexions may be worse than *his*. In respectability of character, there can be no doubt that they are. I have been silent from surprise merely, excessive surprise. You cannot imagine how suddenly it has come on me! how peculiarly unprepared I was!—for I had reason to believe her very lately more determined against him, much more, than she was before."

"You ought to know your friend best," replied Mr. Knightley; "but I should say she was a good-tempered, soft-hearted girl, not likely to be very, very determined against any young man who told her he loved her."

Emma could not help laughing as she answered, "Upon my word, I believe you know her quite as well as I do.—But, Mr. Knightley, are you perfectly sure that she has absolutely and downright *accepted* him.—I could suppose she might in time—but can she already?— Did not you misunderstand him?—You were both talking of other things; of business, shows of cattle, or new drills[9]—and might not you, in the confusion of so many subjects, mistake him?—It was not Harriet's hand that he was certain of—it was the dimensions of some famous ox."

The contrast between the countenance and air of Mr. Knightley and Robert Martin was, at this moment, so strong to Emma's feelings, and so strong was the recollection of all that had so recently passed on Harriet's side, so fresh the sound of those words, spoken with such emphasis, "No, I hope I know better than to think of Robert Martin," that she was really expecting the intelligence to prove, in some measure, premature. It could not be otherwise.

"Do you dare say this?" cried Mr. Knightley. "Do you dare to suppose me so great a blockhead, as not to know what a man is talking of?—What do you deserve?"

"Oh! I always deserve the best treatment, because I never put up with any other; and, therefore, you must give me a plain, direct answer. Are you quite sure that you understand the terms on which Mr. Martin and Harriet now are?"

"I am quite sure," he replied, speaking very distinctly, "that he told me she had accepted him; and that there was no obscurity, nothing doubtful, in the words he used; and I think I can give you a proof that it must be so. He asked my opinion as to what he was now to do. He knew of no one but Mrs. Goddard to whom he could apply for information of her relations or friends. Could I mention any thing more fit to be done, than to go to Mrs. Goddard? I assured him that I could not. Then, he said, he would endeavor to see her in the course of this day."

"I am perfectly satisfied," replied Emma, with the brightest smiles, "and most sincerely wish them happy."

"You are materially changed since we talked on this subject before."

"I hope so—for at that time I was a fool."

"And I am changed also; for I am now very willing to grant you all Harriet's good qualities. I have taken some pains for your sake, and for Robert Martin's sake, (whom I have always had reason to believe as much in love with her as ever,) to get acquainted with her. I have

---

9. Seed-sowing machines.

often talked to her a good deal. You must have seen that I did. Sometimes, indeed, I have thought you were half suspecting me of pleading poor Martin's cause, which was never the case: but, from all my observations, I am convinced of her being an artless, amiable girl, with very good notions, very seriously good principles, and placing her happiness in the affections and utility of domestic life.—Much of this, I have no doubt, she may thank you for."

"Me!" cried Emma, shaking her head.—"Ah! poor Harriet!"

She checked herself, however, and submitted quietly to a little more praise than she deserved.

Their conversation was soon afterwards closed by the entrance of her father. She was not sorry. She wanted to be alone. Her mind was in a state of flutter and wonder, which made it impossible for her to be collected. She was in dancing, singing, exclaiming spirits; and till she had moved about, and talked to herself, and laughed and reflected, she could be fit for nothing rational.

Her father's business was to announce James's being gone out to put the horses to, preparatory to their now daily drive to Randall's; and she had, therefore, an immediate excuse for disappearing.

The joy, the gratitude, the exquisite delight of her sensations may be imagined. The sole grievance and alloy thus removed in the prospect of Harriet's welfare, she was really in danger of becoming too happy for security.—What had she to wish for? Nothing, but to grow more worthy of him, whose intentions and judgment had been ever so superior to her own. Nothing, but that the lessons of her past folly might teach her humility and circumspection in future.

Serious she was, very serious in her thankfulness, and in her resolutions; and yet there was no preventing a laugh, sometimes in the very midst of them. She must laugh at such a close! Such an end of the doleful disappointment of five weeks back! Such a heart—such a Harriet!

Now there would be pleasure in her returning.—Every thing would be a pleasure. It would be a great pleasure to know Robert Martin.

High in the rank of her most serious and heartfelt felicities, was the reflection that all necessity of concealment from Mr. Knightley would soon be over. The disguise, equivocation, mystery, so hateful to her to practise, might soon be over. She could now look forward to giving him that full and perfect confidence which her disposition was most ready to welcome as a duty.

In the gayest and happiest spirits she set forward with her father; not always listening, but always agreeing to what he said; and, whether in speech or silence, conniving at the comfortable persuasion of his being obliged to go to Randall's every day, or poor Mrs. Weston would be disappointed.

They arrived.—Mrs. Weston was alone in the drawing-room:—but hardly had they been told of the baby, and Mr. Woodhouse received the thanks for coming, which he asked for, when a glimpse was caught through the blind, of two figures passing near the window.

"It is Frank and Miss Fairfax," said Mrs. Weston. "I was just going to tell you of our agreeable surpise in seeing him arrive this morning. He stays till to-morrow, and Miss Fairfax has been persuaded to spend the day with us.—They are coming in, I hope."

In half a minute they were in the room. Emma was extremely glad to see him—but there was a degree of confusion—a number of embarrassing recollections on each side. They met readily and smiling, but with a consciousness which at first allowed little to be said; and having all sat down again, there was for some time such a blank in the circle, that Emma began to doubt whether the wish now indulged, which she had long felt, of seeing Frank Churchill once more, and of seeing him with Jane, would yield its propor-tion of pleasure. When Mr. Weston joined the party, however, and when the baby was fetched, there was no longer a want of subject or animation—or of courage and opportunity for Frank Churchill to draw near her and say,

"I have to thank you, Miss Woodhouse, for a very kind forgiving message in one of Mrs. Weston's letters. I hope time has not made you less willing to pardon. I hope you do not retract what you then said."

"No, indeed," cried Emma, most happy to begin, "not in the least. I am particularly glad to see and shake hands with you—and to give you joy in person."

He thanked her with all his heart, and continued some time to speak with serious feeling of his gratitude and happiness.

"Is not she looking well?" said he, turning his eyes towards Jane. "Better than she ever used to do?—You see how my father and Mrs. Weston doat upon her."

But his spirits were soon rising again; and with laughing eyes, after mentioning the expected return of the Campbells, he named the name of Dixon.—Emma blushed, and forbad its being pro-nounced in her hearing.

"I can never think of it," she cried, "without extreme shame."

"The shame," he answered, "is all mine, or ought to be. But is it possible that you had no suspicion?—I mean of late. Early, I know you had none."

"I never had the smallest, I assure you."

"That appears quite wonderful. I was once very near—and I wish I had—it would have been better. But though I was always doing wrong things, they were very *bad* wrong things, and such as did me no service.—It would have been a much better transgression had I broken the bond of secrecy and told you every thing."

"It is not now worth a regret," said Emma.

"I have some hope," resumed he, "of my uncle's being persuaded to pay a visit at Randall's; he wants to be introduced to her. When the Campbells are returned, we shall meet them in London, and continue there, I trust, till we may carry her northward.—But now, I am at such a distance from her—is not it hard, Miss Woodhouse?—Till this morning, we have not once met since the day of reconciliation. Do not you pity me?"

Emma spoke her pity so very kindly, that, with a sudden accession of gay thought, he cried,

"Ah! by the bye,"—then sinking his voice, and looking demure for the moment—"I hope Mr. Knightley is well?" He paused.—She coloured and laughed.—"I know you saw my letter, and think you may remember my wish in your favour. Let me return your congratulations.—I assure you that I have heard the news with the warmest interest and satisfaction.—He is a man whom I cannot presume to praise."

Emma was delighted, and only wanted him to go on in the same style; but his mind was the next moment in his own concerns and with his own Jane, and his next words were,

"Did you ever see such a skin?—such smoothness! such delicacy!—and yet without being actually fair.—One cannot call her fair. It is a most uncommon complexion, with her dark eyelashes and hair—a most distinguishing complexion!—So peculiarly the lady in it.—Just colour enough for beauty."

"I have always admired her complexion," replied Emma, archly; "but do not I remember the time when you found fault with her for being so pale?—When we first began to talk of her.—Have you quite forgotten?"

"Oh! no—what an impudent dog I was!—How could I dare—"

But he laughed so heartily at the recollection, that Emma could not help saying,

"I do suspect that in the midst of your perplexities at that time, you had very great amusement in tricking us all.—I am sure you had.—I am sure it was a consolation to you."

"Oh! no, no, no—how can you suspect me of such a thing?—I was the most miserable wretch!"

"Not quite so miserable as to be insensible to mirth. I am sure it was a source of high entertainment to you, to feel that you were taking us all in.—Perhaps I am the readier to suspect, because, to tell you the truth, I think it might have been some amusement to myself in the same situation. I think there is a little likeness between us."

He bowed.

"If not in our dispositions," she presently added, with a look of true sensibility, "there is a likeness in our destiny; the destiny which bids fair to connect us with two characters so much superior to our own."

"True, true," he answered, warmly. "No, not true on your side. You can have no superior, but most true on mine.—She is a complete angel. Look at her. Is not she an angel in every gesture? Observe the turn of her throat. Observe her eyes, as she is looking up at my father.—You will be glad to hear (inclining his head, and whispering seriously) that my uncle means to give her all my aunt's jewels. They are to be new set. I am resolved to have some in an ornament for the head. Will not it be beautiful in her dark hair?"

"Very beautiful, indeed," replied Emma: and she spoke so kindly, that he gratefully burst out,

"How delighted I am to see you again! and to see you in such excellent looks!—I would not have missed this meeting for the world. I should certainly have called at Hartfield, had you failed to come."

The others had been talking of the child, Mrs. Weston giving an account of a little alarm she had been under, the evening before, from the infant's appearing not quite well. She believed she had been foolish, but it had alarmed her, and she had been within half a minute of sending for Mr. Perry. Perhaps she ought to be ashamed, but Mr. Weston had been almost as uneasy as herself.—In ten minutes, however, the child had been perfectly well again. This was her history; and particularly interesting it was to Mr. Woodhouse, who commended her very much for thinking of sending for Perry, and only regretted that she had not done it. "She should always send for Perry, if the child appeared in the slightest degree disordered, were it only for a moment. She could not be too soon alarmed, nor send for Perry too often. It was a pity, perhaps, that he had not come last night; for, though the child seemed well now, very well considering, it would probably have been better if Perry had seen it."

Frank Churchill caught the name.

"Perry!" said he to Emma, and trying, as he spoke, to catch Miss Fairfax's eye. "My friend Mr. Perry! What are they saying about Mr. Perry?—Has he been here this morning?—And how does he travel now?—Has he set up his carriage?"

Emma soon recollected, and understood him; and while she joined in the laugh, it was evident from Jane's countenance that she too was really hearing him, though trying to seem deaf.

"Such an extraordinary dream of mine!" he cried. "I can never think of it without laughing.—She hears us, she hear us, Miss Woodhouse. I see it in her cheek, her smile, her vain attempt to frown. Look at her. Do not you see that, at this instant, the very passage of her own letter, which sent me the report, is passing under her eye—that the whole blunder is spread before her—that she can attend to nothing else, though pretending to listen to the others?"

Jane was forced to smile completely, for a moment; and the smile partly remained as she turned towards him, and said in a conscious, low, yet steady voice,

"How you can bear such recollections, is astonishing to me!—
They *will* sometimes obtrude—but how you can *court* them!"

He had a great deal to say in return, and very entertainingly; but
Emma's feelings were chiefly with Jane, in the argument; and on
leaving Randall's, and falling naturally into a comparison of the two
men, she felt, that pleased as she had been to see Frank Churchill,
and really regarding him as she did with friendship, she had never
been more sensible of Mr. Knightley's high superiority of character.
The happiness of this most happy day, received its completion, in
the animated contemplation of his worth which this comparison
produced.

Chapter XIX

If Emma had still, at intervals, an anxious feeling for Harriet, a
momentary doubt of its being possible for her to be really cured of
her attachment to Mr. Knightley, and really able to accept another
man from unbiassed inclination, it was not long that she had to suffer from the recurrence of any such uncertainty. A very few days
brought the party from London, and she had no sooner an opportunity of being one hour alone with Harriet, than she became perfectly satisfied—unaccountable as it was!—that Robert Martin had
thoroughly supplanted Mr. Knightley, and was now forming all her
views of happiness.

Harriet was a little distressed—did look a little foolish at first; but
having once owned that she had been presumptuous and silly, and
self-deceived, before, her pain and confusion seemed to die away
with the words, and leave her without a care for the past, and with
the fullest exultation in the present and future; for, as to her friend's
approbation, Emma had instantly removed every fear of that nature,
by meeting her with the most unqualified congratulations.—Harriet
was most happy to give every particular of the evening at Astley's,
and the dinner the next day; she could dwell on it all with the utmost
delight. But what did such particulars explain?—The fact was, as
Emma could now acknowledge, that Harriet had always liked Robert
Martin; and that his continuing to love her had been irresistible.—
Beyond this, it must ever be unintelligible to Emma.

The event, however, was most joyful, and every day was giving her
fresh reason for thinking so.—Harriet's parentage became known.
She proved to be the daughter of a tradesman, rich enough to afford
her the comfortable maintenance which had ever been her's, and
decent enough to have always wished for concealment.—Such was
the blood of gentility which Emma had formerly been so ready to
vouch for!—It was likely to be as untainted, perhaps, as the blood of
many a gentleman: but what a connexion had she been preparing for
Mr. Knightley—or for the Churchills—or even for Mr. Elton!—The

stain of illegitimacy, unbleached by nobility or wealth, would have been a stain indeed.

No objection was raised on the father's side; the young man was treated liberally; it was all as it should be: and as Emma became acquainted with Robert Martin, who was now introduced at Hartfield, she fully acknowledged in him all the appearance of sense and worth which could bid fairest for her little friend. She had no doubt of Harriet's happiness with any good tempered man; but with him, and in the home he offered, there would be the hope of more, of security, stability, and improvement. She would be placed in the midst of those who loved her, and who had better sense than herself; retired enough for safety, and occupied enough for cheerfulness. She would be never led into temptation, nor left for it to find her out. She would be respectable and happy; and Emma admitted her to be the luckiest creature in the world, to have created so steady and persevering an affection in such a man;—or, if not quite the luckiest, to yield only to herself.

Harriet, necessarily drawn away by her engagements with the Martins, was less and less at Hartfield; which was not to be regretted.—The intimacy between her and Emma must sink; their friendship must change into a calmer sort of goodwill; and, fortunately, what ought to be, and must be, seemed already beginning, and in the most gradual, natural manner.

Before the end of September, Emma attended Harriet to church, and saw her hand bestowed on Robert Martin with so complete a satisfaction, as no remembrances, even connected with Mr. Elton as he stood before them, could impair.—Perhaps, indeed, at that time she scarcely saw Mr. Elton, but as the clergyman whose blessing at the altar might next fall on herself.—Robert Martin and Harriet Smith, the latest couple engaged of the three, were the first to be married.

Jane Fairfax had already quitted Highbury, and was restored to the comforts of her beloved home with the Campbells.—The Mr. Churchills were also in town; and they were only waiting for November.

The intermediate month was the one fixed on, as far as they dared, by Emma and Mr. Knightley.—They had determined that their marriage ought to be concluded while John and Isabella were still at Hartfield, to allow them the fortnight's absence in a tour to the sea-side, which was the plan.—John and Isabella, and every other friend, were agreed in approving it. But Mr. Woodhouse—how was Mr. Woodhouse to be induced to consent?—he, who had never yet alluded to their marriage but as a distant event.

When first sounded on the subject, he was so miserable, that they were almost hopeless.—A second allusion, indeed, gave less

pain.—He began to think it was to be, and that he could not prevent it—a very promising step of the mind on its way to resignation.
Still, however, he was not happy. Nay, he appeared so much otherwise, that his daughter's courage failed. She could not bear to see
him suffering, to know him fancying himself neglected; and though
her understanding almost acquiesced in the assurance of both the
Mr. Knightleys, that when once the event were over, his distress
would be soon over too, she hesitated—she could not proceed.

In this state of suspense they were befriended, not by any sudden
illumination of Mr. Woodhouse's mind, or any wonderful change of
his nervous system, but by the operation of the same system in
another way.—Mrs. Weston's poultry-house was robbed one night
of all her turkies—evidently by the ingenuity of man. Other poultry-
yards in the neighbourhood also suffered.—Pilfering was *house-
breaking* to Mr. Woodhouse's fears.—He was very uneasy; and but
for the sense of his son-in-law's protection, would have been under
wretched alarm every night of his life. The strength, resolution,
and presence of mind of the Mr. Knightleys, commanded his fullest
dependance. While either of them protected him and his, Hartfield
was safe.—But Mr. John Knightley must be in London again by the
end of the first week in November.

The result of this distress was, that, with a much more voluntary,
cheerful consent than his daughter had ever presumed to hope for at
the moment, she was able to fix her wedding-day—and Mr. Elton was
called on, within a month from the marriage of Mr. and Mrs. Robert
Martin, to join the hands of Mr. Knightley and Miss Woodhouse.

The wedding was very much like other weddings, where the parties have no taste for finery or parade; and Mrs. Elton, from the particulars detailed by her husband, thought it all extremely shabby, and
very inferior to her own.—"Very little white satin, very few lace veils;
a most pitiful business!—Selina would stare when she heard of it."—
But, in spite of these deficiencies, the wishes, the hopes, the confidence, the predictions of the small band of true friends who
witnessed the ceremony, were fully answered in the perfect happiness of the union.[1]

---

1. In the *Memoir* of his aunt, James Austen-Leigh reported that Jane Austen "took a kind
of parental interest in the beings whom she had created, and did not dismiss them from
her thoughts when she had finished her last chapter," and that "she would if asked, tell
us many little particulars about the subsequent career of some of her people." In this
way he learned "that Mr. Woodhouse survived his daughter's marriage, and kept her
and Mr. Knightley from settling at Donwell, about two years; and that the letters
placed by Frank Churchill before Jane Fairfax, which she swept away unread [see
p. 241], contained the word 'pardon.'"

CONTEXTS

JANE AUSTEN.

This image, from Austen-Leigh's *Memoir* (1870), depicts an idealized woman writer, in keeping with the hagiographic impulse not only of Austen family members but also of the Victorian culture that "rediscovered" Austen in the second half of the nineteenth century.

Jane Austen
Her Life and Fiction

The "family memoir" was a distinct genre in the early nineteenth century, and it was particularly used to depict women writers as correct in their morals, religion, and private life. The excerpts by Henry Thomas Austen and James E. Austen-Leigh presented here helped shape a long-dominant understanding of Jane Austen as a spinster author who wrote in private for largely private purposes. Austen's correspondence, on the other hand, demonstrates that Austen may have shared as much with the wicked "Lady Susan" of her juvenilia as with the more prim Fanny Price in *Mansfield Park*. And recent analysis of her interactions with the book world in London would suggest that Austen was an author keenly aware of her own authorship and proud to be known for her writing—and to be compensated for her authorial labor.

HENRY THOMAS AUSTEN
Biographical Notice[†]

* * *

Jane Austen was born on the 16th of December, 1775, at Steventon, in the county of Hants.[1] Her father was Rector of that parish upwards of forty years. There he resided, in the conscientious and unassisted discharge of his ministerial duties, until he was turned of seventy years. Then he retired with his wife, our authoress, and her sister, to Bath, for the remainder of his life, a period of about four years. Being not only a profound scholar, but possessing a most exquisite taste in every species of literature, it is not wonderful that his daughter Jane should, at a very early age, have become sensible to the charms of style, and enthusiastic in the cultivation of her own language. On the death of her father she removed, with her mother and sister, for a

---

† From Henry Thomas Austen, "Biographical Notice of the Author," prefixed to the first edition of *Northanger Abbey and Persuasion* (London, 1818) v–xvi.
1. Hampshire [*Editor*].

short time, to Southampton, and finally, in 1809, to the pleasant village of Chawton, in the same county. From this place she sent into the world those novels, which by many have been placed on the same shelf as the works of a D'Arblay and an Edgeworth.[2] Some of these novels had been the gradual performances of her previous life. For though in composition she was equally rapid and correct, yet an invincible distrust of her own judgement induced her to withhold her works from the public, till time and many perusals had satisfied her that the charm of recent composition was dissolved. * * *

Of personal attractions she possessed a considerable share. Her stature was that of true elegance. It could not have been increased without exceeding the middle height. Her carriage and deportment were quiet, yet graceful. Her features were separately good. Their assemblage produced an unrivalled expression of that cheerfulness, sensibility, and benevolence, which were her real characteristics. Her complexion was of the finest texture. It might with truth be said, that her eloquent blood spoke through her modest cheek. Her voice was extremely sweet. She delivered herself with fluency and precision. Indeed she was formed for elegant and rational society, excelling in conversation as much as in composition. In the present age it is hazardous to mention accomplishments. Our authoress would, probably, have been inferior to few in such acquirements, had she not been so superior to most in higher things. She had not only an excellent taste for drawing, but, in her earlier days, evinced great power of hand in the management of the pencil. Her own musical attainments she held very cheap. Twenty years ago they would have been thought more of, and twenty years hence many a parent will expect their daughters to be applauded for meaner performances. She was fond of dancing, and excelled in it. It remains now to add a few observations on that which her friends deemed more important, on those endowments which sweetened every hour of their lives.

If there be an opinion current in the world, that perfect placidity of temper is not reconcileable to the most lively imagination, and the keenest relish for wit, such an opinion will be rejected for ever by those who have had the happiness of knowing the authoress of the following works. Though the frailties, foibles, and follies of others could not escape her immediate detection, yet even on their vices did she never trust herself to comment with unkindness. The affectation of candour is not uncommon; but she had no affectation. Faultless herself, as nearly as human nature can be, she always sought, in the faults of others, something to excuse, to forgive, or forget. Where extenuation was impossible, she had a sure refuge in silence. She never uttered either a hasty, a silly, or a severe expres-

---

2. Madame D'Arblay was Frances Burney; she and Maria Edgeworth were England's two most celebrated women novelists before Jane Austen [*Editor*].

sion. In short, her temper was as polished as her wit. Nor were her manners inferior to her temper. They were of the happiest kind. No one could be often in her company without feeling a strong desire of obtaining her friendship, and cherishing a hope of having obtained it. She was tranquil without reserve or stiffness; and communicative without intrusion or self-sufficiency. She became an authoress entirely from taste and inclination. Neither the hope of fame nor profit mixed with her early motives. Most of her works, as before observed, were composed many years previous to their publication. It was with extreme difficulty that her friends, whose partiality she suspected whilst she honoured their judgement, could prevail on her to publish her first work. * * * So much did she shrink from notoriety, that no accumulation of fame would have induced her, had she lived, to affix her name to any productions of her pen. In the bosom of her own family she talked of them freely, thankful for praise, open to remark, and submissive to criticism. But in public she turned away from any allusion to the character of an authoress. She read aloud with very great taste and effect. Her own works, probably, were never heard to so much advantage as from her own mouth; for she partook largely in all the best gifts of the comic muse. She was a warm and judicious admirer of landscape, both in nature and on canvass. * * *

Her reading was very extensive in history and belles lettres; and her memory extremely tenacious. Her favourite moral writers were Johnson in prose, and Cowper in verse. It is difficult to say at what age she was not intimately acquainted with the merits and defects of the best essays and novels in the English language. Richardson's power of creating, and preserving the consistency of his characters, as particularly exemplified in "Sir Charles Grandison," gratified the natural discrimination of her mind, whilst her taste secured her from the errors of his prolix style and tedious narrative. She did not rank any work of Fielding quite so high. Without the slightest affectation she recoiled from every thing gross. Neither nature, wit nor humour, could make her amends for so very low a scale of morals.

JAMES E. AUSTEN-LEIGH

Memoir of Jane Austen[†]

[N]ow, in my old age, I am asked whether my memory will serve to rescue from oblivion any events of her life or any traits of her character to satisfy the enquiries of a generation of readers who have been born since she died. Of events her life was singularly barren: few

---

† From *A Memoir of Jane Austen*, by her Nephew James E. Austen-Leigh, 2nd ed. Transcription by George Justice. (London: Richard Bentley and Son, 1871)

changes and no great crisis ever broke the smooth current of its course. Even her fame may be said to have been posthumous: it did not attain to any vigorous life till she had ceased to exist. Her talents did not introduce her to the notice of other writers, or connect her with the literary world, or in any degree pierce through the obscurity of her domestic retirement. * * * Many may care to know whether the moral rectitude, the correct taste, and the warm affection with which she invested her ideal characters, were really existing in the native source whence those ideas flowed, and were actually exhibited by her in the various relations of life. I can indeed bear witness that there was scarcely a charm in her most delightful characters that was not a true reflection of her own sweet temper and loving heart.

*   *   *

Her own family were so much, and the rest of the world so little, to Jane Austen, that some brief mention of her brothers and sister is necessary in order to give any idea of the objects which principally occupied her thoughts and filled her heart, especially as some of them, from their characters or professions in life, may be supposed to have had more or less influence on her writings: though I feel some reluctance in bringing before public notice persons and circumstances essentially private.

*   *   *

These two brothers have been dwelt on longer than the others because their honourable career accounts for Jane Austen's partiality for the Navy, as well as for the readiness and accuracy with which she wrote about it. She was always very careful not to meddle with matters which she did not thoroughly understand. She never touched upon politics, law, or medicine, subjects which some novel writers have ventured on rather too boldly, and have treated, perhaps, with more brilliancy than accuracy.

*   *   *

This was the small circle * * * within which Jane Austen found her wholesome pleasures, duties, and interests, and beyond which she went very little into society in the last ten years of her life. There was so much that was agreeable and attractive in this family party that its members may be excused if they were inclined to live somewhat too exclusively within it. They might see in each other much to love and esteem, and something to admire. The family talk had abundance of spirit and vivacity, and was never troubled by disagreements even in little matters, for it was not their habit to dispute or argue with each other: above all, there was strong family affection and firm union, never to be broken but by death. It cannot be doubted that all this had its influence on the author in the construction of her stories, in which a family party usually supplies the narrow stage, while the interest is made to revolve around a few actors. * * * Her acquaintance, in fact, constituted the very class from which she took her imaginary characters, ranging from the member of parliament, or large landed proprietor, to the young curate or younger midshipman of equally good family; and I think that the influence of these early associations may be traced in her writings, especially in two particulars. First, that she is entirely free from the vulgarity, which is so offensive in some novels, of dwelling on the outward appendages of wealth or rank, as if they were things to which the writer was unaccustomed; and, secondly, that she deals as little with very low as with very high stations in life.

* * *

In person she was very attractive; her figure was rather tall and slender, her step light and firm, and her whole appearance expressive of health and animation. In complexion she was a clear brunette with a rich colour; she had full round cheeks, with mouth and nose small and well formed, bright hazel eyes, and brown hair forming natural curls close round her face. If not so regularly handsome as her sister, yet her countenance had a peculiar charm of its own to the eyes of most beholders. At the time of which I am now writing, she never was seen, either morning or evening, without a cap; I believe that she and her sister were generally thought to have taken to the garb of middle age earlier than their years or their looks required; and that, though remarkably neat in their dress as in all their ways, they were scarcely sufficiently regardful of the fashionable, or the becoming.

She was not highly accomplished according to the present standard. * * * Jane herself was fond of music, and had a sweet voice, both in singing and in conversation; in her youth she had received some instruction on the pianoforte; and * * * she practiced daily, chiefly before breakfast. I believe she did so partly that she might not disturb the rest of the party who were less fond of music. In the evening she would sometimes sing, to her own accompaniment, some simple old songs, the words and airs of which, now never heard, still linger in my memory.

She read French with facility, and knew something of Italian. * * * It was not, however, what she *knew*, but what she *was*, that distinguished her from others. * * * Her unusually quick sense of the ridiculous led her to play with all the commonplaces of everyday life, whether as regarded persons or things; but she never played with its serious duties or responsibilities, nor did she ever turn individuals into ridicule. * * * She was as far as possible from being censorious or satirical. * * * The laugh which she occasionally raised was by imagining for her neighbors, as she was equally ready to imagine for her friends or herself, impossible contingencies, or by relating in prose or verse some trifling anecdote coloured to her own fancy, or in writing a fictitious history of what they were supposed to have said or done, which could deceive nobody.

* * *

[S]he had no separate study to retire to, and most of the work must have been done in the general sitting-room, subject to all kinds of casual interruptions. She was careful that her occupation should not be suspected by servants, or visitors, or any persons beyond her own family party. She wrote upon small sheets of paper which could easily be put away, or covered with a piece of blotting paper. There was, between the front door and the offices, a swing door which creaked when it was opened; but she objected to having this little inconvenience remedied, because it gave her notice when anyone was coming.

* * *

Jane Austen lived in entire seclusion from the literary world: neither by correspondence, nor by personal intercourse was she known to any contemporary authors. It is probable that she was never in company with any person whose talents or whose celebrity equalled her own; so that her powers never could have been sharpened by collision with superior intellects, nor her imagination aided by their casual suggestions. Whatever she produced was a genuine home-made article. Even during the last two or three years of her life, when her works were rising in the estimation of the public, they did not enlarge her circle of acquaintance. Few of her readers knew even her name, and none knew more of her than her name. I doubt whether it would be possible to mention any other author of note, whose personal obscurity was so complete.

JANE AUSTEN

Letters to Her Sister, Cassandra[†]

[An Account of a Ball, 1800]

Steventon Thursday Novr 20th [1800]

My dear Cassandra

* * * Your desiring to hear from me on Sunday will perhaps bring on you a more particular account of the Ball than you may care for,

† From *Jane Austen's Letters*, ed. Deirdre Le Faye, 3rd ed. (New York: Oxford UP, 1995) letters 27, 44, 96. Reprinted by permission of Oxford University Press.

because one is prone to think much more of such things the morning after they happen, than when time has entirely driven them out of one's recollection.—It was a pleasant Evening, Charles[1] found it remarkably so, but I cannot tell why, unless the absence of Miss Terry—towards whom his conscience reproaches him with now being perfect indifferent—was a releif to him.—There were only twelve dances, of which I danced nine, & was merely prevented from dancing the rest by the want of a partner.—We began at 10, supped at 1, & were at Deane before 5.—There were but 50 people in the room; very few families indeed from our side of the Country, & not many more from the other.—My partners were the two St. Johns, Hooper Holder—and very prodigious—Mr. Mathew, with whom I called the last, & whom I liked the best of my little stock.—There were very few Beauties, & such as there were, were not very handsome. Miss Iremonger did not look well, & Mrs. Blount was the only one much admired. She appeared exactly as she did in September, with the same broad face, diamond bandeau, white shoes, pink husband, & fat neck.—The two Miss Coxes were there; I traced in one the remains of the vulgar, broad featured girl who danced at Enham eight years ago;—the other is refined into a nice, composed looking girl like Catherine Bigg.—I looked at Sir Thomas Champneys & thought of poor Rosalie; I looked at his daughter & thought her a queer animal with a white neck.—Mrs. Warren, I was constrained to think a very fine young woman, which I much regret. She has got rid of some part of her child, & danced away with great activity, looking by no means very large.—Her husband is ugly enough; uglier even than his cousin John; but he does not look so *very* old.—The Miss Maitlands are both prettyish; very like Anne; with brown skins, large dark eyes, & a good deal of nose.—The General has got the Gout, and Mrs. Maitland the Jaundice.—Miss Debary, Susan & Sally all in black, but without any Statues, made their appearance, & I was as civil to them as their bad breath would allow me. They told me nothing new of Martha.—I mean to go to her on Thursday, unless Charles should determine on coming over again with his friend Shipley for the Basingstoke ball, in which case I shall not go till friday.—I shall write to you again however before I set off, & I shall hope to hear from you in the mean time. If I do not stay for the Ball, I would not on any account do so uncivil a thing by the Neighbourhood as to set off at that very time for another place, & shall therefore make a point of not being later than Thursday *morning.*—Mary said that I looked very well last night; I wore my aunt's gown & handkercheif, & my hair was at least tidy, which was all my ambition.—I will now have done with the Ball; & I moreover go and dress for dinner.

---

1. Jane's brother Charles Austen, then twenty-one years old [*Editor*].

[*The Events of a Day, 1805*]

Gay S^t—Sunday Evening, April 21st [1805]

My dear Cassandra

* * * Yesterday was a busy day with me, or at least with my feet & my stockings; I was walking almost all day long; I went to Sydney Gardens soon after one, & did not return till four, & after dinner I walked to Weston.—My morning engagement was with the Cookes, & our party consisted of George & Mary, a M^r & Miss Bendish who had been with us at the Concert, & the youngest Miss Whitby;—not Julia, we have done with her, she is very ill, but Mary; Mary Whitby's turn is actually come to be grown up & have a fine complexion & wear great square muslin shawls, I have not expressly enumerated myself among the party, but there I was, & my cousin George was very kind & talked sense to me every now & then in the intervals of his more animated fooleries with Miss Bendish, who is very young & rather handsome, & whose gracious manners, ready wit, & solid remarks put me somewhat in mind of my old acquaintance Lucy Lefroy.—There was a monstrous deal of stupid quizzing, & common-place nonsense talked, but scarcely any Wit;—all that border'd on it, or on Sense came from my Cousin George, whom altogether I like very well.—Mr Bendish seems nothing more than a tall young Man.—I met Mr F. Bonham the other day, & almost his first salutation was 'So Miss Austen your cousin is come'.—My Evening Engagement & walk was with Miss Armstrong, who had called on me the day before, & gently upbraided me in her turn with change of manners to her since she had been in Bath, or at least of late. Unlucky me! that my notice should be of such consequence & my Manners so bad!—She was so well-disposed, & so reasonable that I soon forgave her, & made this engagement with her in proof of it.—She is really an agreable girl, so I think I may like her, & her great want of a companion at home, which may well make any tolerable acquaintance important to her, gives her another claim on my attention. I shall endeavour as much as possible to keep my Intimacies in their proper place, & prevent their clashing. * * *

[*The Events of Two Days, 1813*]

Saturday Novr 6—Godmersham Park [1813]

My dearest Cassandra

Having half an hour before breakfast—(very snug, in my own room, lovely morn^g, excellent fire, fancy me) I will give you some account of the last two days. And yet, what is there to be told?—I shall get foolishly minute unless I cut the matter short.—We met only the Brittons at Chilham Castle, besides a Mr. & Mrs. Osborne &

a Miss Lee staying in the House, & were only 14 altogether. My B^r & Fanny[2] thought it the pleasantest party they had ever known there & I was very well entertained by bits & scraps.—I had long wanted to see Dr. Britton, & his wife amuses me very much with her affected refinement & elegance.—Miss Lee I found very conversible; she admires Crabbe[3] as she ought.—She is at an age of reason, ten years older than myself at least. She was at the famous Ball at Chilham Castle, so of course you remember her.—By the bye, as I must leave off being young, I find many Douceurs[4] in being a sort of Chaperon for I am put on the Sofa near the Fire & can drink as much wine as I like. We had Music in the Even^g, Fanny & Miss Wildman played, & Mr. James Wildman sat close by & listened, or pretended to listen.— Yesterday was a day of dissipation all through, first came Sir Brook to dissipate us before breakfast—then there was a call from Mr. Sherer, then a regular morn^g visit from Lady Honeywood in her way home from Eastwell—then Sir Brook & Edward set off—then we dined (5 in number) at ½ past 4—then we had coffee, & at 6 Miss Clewes, Fanny & I draved away. We had a beautiful night for our frisks.—We were earlier than we need have been, but after a time Lady B. & her two companions appeared, we had kept places for them & there we sat, all six in a row, under a side wall, I between Lucy Foote & Miss Clewes.—Lady B. was much what I expected, I could not determine whether she was rather handsome or very plain.—I liked her, for being in a hurry to have the Concert over & get away, & for getting away at last with a great deal of decision & promtness, not waiting to compliment & dawdle & fuss about seeing *dear Fanny*, who was half the even^g in another part of the room with her friends the Plumptres. I am growing too minute, so I will go to Breakfast.

When the Concert was over, Mrs. Harrison & I found each other out & had a very comfortable little complimentary friendly chat. She is a sweet Woman, still quite a sweet Woman in herself, & so like her Sister!—I could almost have thought I was speaking to Mrs. Lefroy.— She introduced me to her Daughter, whom I think pretty, but most dutifully inferior to la Mere Beauté.[5] The Faggs & the Hammonds were there, Wm Hammond the only young Man of renown. *Miss* looked very handsome, but I prefer her little, smiling, flirting Sister Julia.—I was just introduced at last to Mary Plumptre, but should hardly know her again. She was delighted with *me* however, good enthusiastic Soul!—And Lady B. found me handsomer than she expected, so you see I am not so very bad as you might think for.—It was 12 before we reached home. We were all dog-tired, but pretty

---

2. Jane's niece, daughter of her brother Edward [*Editor*].
3. George Crabbe (1754–1832), author of *The Village* and other poems both realistic and satirical [*Editor*].
4. Pleasures [*Editor*].
5. Literally, the mother beauty [*Editor*].

well today, Miss Clewes says she has not caught cold, & Fanny's does not seem worse. I was so tired that I began to wonder how I should get through the Ball next Thursday, but there will be so much more variety then in walking about, & probably so much less heat that perhaps I may not feel it more. My China Crape is still kept for the Ball. Enough of the Concert. * * *

Since I wrote last, my 2^d Edit.[6] has stared me in the face.—Mary tells me that Eliza means to buy it. I wish she may. It can hardly depend upon any more Fyfield Estates.—I cannot help hoping that *many* will feel themselves obliged to buy it. I shall not mind imagining it a disagreeable Duty to them, so as they do it. Mary heard before she left home, that it was very much admired at Cheltenham, & that it was given to Miss Hamilton.[7] It is pleasant to have such a respectable Writer named. I cannot tire *you* I am sure on this subject, or I would apologise. * * *

MAGGIE LANE

Daily Life in Jane Austen's England[†]

Meals and Manners

BREAKFAST

The breakfast of Jane Austen's day was eaten late, between nine and ten, often after some shopping, walking or letter-writing had been accomplished. Even something as simple as breakfast reflected the spirit of the age. Consisting of toast and tea, eaten and drunk from fine china, Regency breakfast was as different from the hunks of bread, cheese and ale of former times, taken from wooden platters and pewter mugs, as from the hot dishes of kedgeree, devilled kidneys, bacon and eggs and so forth under which Victorian sideboards groaned. Toast, which was made by the family themselves on toasting forks at the fire, was thought to have been invented by the English to enable the butter to spread more easily in their cold rooms. On the same fire the kettle would be boiled for the tea or, less usually, coffee. These drinks were still a novelty in English life, tea having been introduced from China, and coffee from Ethiopia, in the middle of the preceding century. Precious commodities, they were kept under lock and key, the responsibility not of the servants, but of the mistress. Their expense meant that hot drinks were not

---

6. Of *Sense and Sensibility*, first published in 1811 [*Editor*].
7. Elizabeth Hamilton (1756?–1816), novelist and essayist.
† From *Jane Austen's World* (London: Carlton Books Ltd., 1996) 40–41, 68–69. Reprinted by permission of Carlton Books.

consumed throughout the day, as we are used to, but made their appearance only at breakfast and again in the evening. In grand houses a greater variety of fare was provided, but still not what we think of as the traditional English breakfast. Mrs Austen, staying at Stoneleigh Abbey, admiringly lists "Chocolate Coffee and Tea, Plumb Cake, Pound Cake, Hot Rolls, Cold Rolls, Bread and Butter, and dry toast for me".

THE MIDDAY MEAL

Jane Austen uses the word "luncheon" once and "nuncheon" once, but both refer to midday meals taken at an inn. Refreshment taken by the family in their own homes in the middle of the day was a casual, stop-gap affair that had not yet acquired the dignity of a name. Nor were social invitations ever issued for this meal, though if visitors were present, food would be offered—as Elizabeth Bennet experiences at Pemberley, where there is cold meat, cake and hot-house fruit; and Edmund Bertram at Mansfield Parsonage, where Dr Grant himself carries round the sandwich tray. This nameless mid-day snack of cold food and drink had arisen to fill the gap caused by the increasing lateness of the dinner hour.

DINNER

For centuries the English had eaten their dinner in the middle of the day, when it could be cooked and consumed in natural light. But in the eighteenth century, as leisure and prosperity increased, there was a gradual but constant shift in the dinner hour, with the most fashionable people always dining later than their social inferiors. That is, the dinner hour for all classes grew later as the century progressed; but at any one moment in time, the social status of a family could be gauged by when they dined. The Austens provide a striking example of the shift taking place within individual households. In 1798, writing from Steventon to Godmersham, Jane remarked, "We dine now at half after Three, and have done dinner I suppose before you begin . . . I am afraid you will despise us." But by 1808 she could write, "We never dine now till five".

Dinner was the event of the day. The meal was as elaborate as the resources of the family would allow—that is, as the skill and number of their servants could produce. Multiple dishes of fish, meat and game would be placed on the table, together with a few side dishes of vegetables and two or three puddings. This was known as a "course", and everybody helped their neighbours to what they wanted. In grander households, the remains would be cleared away and a second similar "course" of savoury and sweet dishes would follow, with the emphasis this time less on great joints of meat and more on "made" dishes. Next the cloth would be removed and an assortment of nuts, sweetmeats, etc. would be placed on the table with wine; this was known as "dessert", and at this point the servants would withdraw. Finally the hostess would rise, at which signal all the other women followed her to the drawing room, leaving the men a further hour or so of drinking and uninhibited conversation in the dining room.

A typical course at dinner would include a wide variety of dishes as seen in this contemporary menu plan.

TEA

When Jane Austen mentions characters taking tea together, she is not referring to our "afternoon tea", which did not exist then, but to the serving of the beverage about an hour after the end of dinner, when the men would eventually rejoin the ladies in the drawing room. Sometimes invitations were issued just for this "tea" (sometimes coffee was also served), especially to social inferiors. Thus Harriet Smith, Jane Fairfax and Miss Bates are invited to the Coles "to drink tea", while Emma, Mr Knightley and the Westons arrive earlier to dine. Nobody seems to have taken offence at what seems a very offensive custom!

SUPPER

As dinner became later, supper dwindled to a negligible snack, usually something on a tray. The exception was on the evening of a ball. Then, late hours, great expenditure of energy and the prospect of a cold drive home called for real sustenance, which always included soup, and to drink negus—a mixture of boiling water, wine, lemon, spices and calves-foot jelly.

* * *

Rich and Poor

The society of the eighteenth century was rigid and hierarchical, maintained by deference from below and paternalism from above. There was a greater degree of social mobility in Britain than in other European countries, but by and large it was influence, rather than merit that enabled a man to advance.

During Jane Austen's lifetime this rigidity was beginning to break down, as the middle classes became more numerous, more prosperous and more aspirational. The novels of her maturity demonstrate an awareness—somewhat uneasy—of these pressures from below. The assumptions of natural superiority entertained by her class were being challenged. But despite her generally conservative stance, in the young Prices, the Martins of Abbey Mill Farm, and the naval characters of *Persuasion*, she acknowledges the validity of the challenge.

THE ARISTOCRACY

After the monarchy, at the top of the social pyramid came the 200 or so families whose head was a peer of the realm (Duke, Marquess, Earl, Viscount). By 1780 some had incomes touching £50,000 p.a., derived mainly from rents but often also from government office.

Their country seats—of which some had more than one—were on a magnificent scale and were administered not so much as homes but as local power bases and centres of impressive hospitality. Here, and in their grand town houses, which they occupied during the parliamentary season, from January until July, they entertained, conspired, arranged dynastic marriages, dispensed political influence, and ran the country. Having no experience of life in such households—except for attending the occasional ball—Jane Austen never writes about them.

THE GENTRY

Like the aristocracy but in a smaller way, the landed gentry also derived their incomes from rents. About a thousand of them, in Jane Austen's day, were titled, but the great majority were not. The two titled ranks were baronet, whose title passed to his eldest son, and knight, whose title died with him. Sir Thomas Bertram and Sir Walter Elliot are both baronets; Sir William Lucas and Sir Henry Russell are knights. The wives of both ranks took the title of Lady, along with their husband's surname: Lady Bertram, Lady Russell, etc. When a character in Jane Austen is known by her Christian name together with the title Lady—such as Lady Catherine de Bourgh and Lady Anne Darcy—it means her father was a peer and she retains her birthright title, whomever she marries. Lady Anne Darcy, for example, marries a commoner, albeit a rich one; her husband and son are plain Mr Darcy.

The House of Commons in Jane Austen's day was made up of the landed gentry, titled or untitled, together with the sons or other close relations of peers, and members of the Irish peerage. In the novels, both Sir Thomas Bertram and Mr Palmer (of *Sense and Sensibility*) are Members of Parliament. Others of this class were public figures locally, becoming Sheriffs of their county, Justices of the Peace and magistrates. Lady Catherine is a JP and Mr Knightley a magistrate, as was Jane's land-owning brother Edward Knight. Many others, of course, simply lived quiet private lives, without much exertion of any kind; even so, they would be looked up to as the squires of their local communities. Sharing tastes and outlook with the landed gentry, and almost certainly intimately related to them, the minor gentry were younger sons and their families whose incomes derived chiefly from the fruits of their professions. The three professions open to gentlemen were the Church of England, the armed services and the law, in all of which Jane Austen places a number of her male characters. Together, the lesser landed gentry and the professional minor gentry constituted the world she knew and was at home in describing.

THE NEW MIDDLE CLASSES

Just as Jane Austen barely mentions the aristocracy, so she only glances at the existence of the members of the minor professions, whose status was at best that of "half-gentlemen"—the term is her own—used in *Emma*, that most class-conscious of novels. Surgeons and apothecaries, teachers and musicians, merchants and attorneys held a dubious place in society; they were educated men, but without "breeding" or "good connections". Beneath them were the tenant-farmers, tradesmen and clerks who constituted the lower middle class. The term middle classes, incidentally, was first used in 1797, and the term working classes in 1813. Before that the usual words for the levels of society were ranks and orders; the phrase "the lower orders" persisted into the twentieth century.

LABOURERS, SERVANTS AND THE POOR

Of course the vast majority of the population lived out the whole of their miserable lives labouring or serving others. The Industrial Revolution had already begun to create the horrific living conditions of the great manufacturing towns in the Midlands and North, but this was unknown to the people of Jane Austen's world; it took the Victorians to discover what had happened in their own country. To Jane Austen, the lower orders would have meant servants, labourers on the land, and paupers, their existence accepted as part of the natural order of things. Armies of servants were employed in the great houses, while anybody with any pretensions to gentility employed at least one servant. Servants in Jane Austen's world seem well-treated and at least enjoy shelter and sufficient food. The average wage of an agricultural labourer in the period was seven or eight shillings (35–40p).

Only in *Emma* are there glimpses of the teeming poor outside the world of the great house. Emma visits a sick cottager; the ostler John Abdy cannot maintain his father who can no longer work; gypsies obtain money with menaces, and Mrs Weston's poultry houses are pilfered. Just as every other class is capable of divisions and subdivisions, so the poor could be divided into the deserving and the undeserving. The social spectrum of Highbury, already wider than in any other Austen novel, includes both.

Jane Austen
Her Art and Business

Jane Austen's Correspondence with J. S. Clarke[†]

J. S. Clarke[1] to Jane Austen
[asking her to write a novel about a clergyman]

Carlton House Nov[r]: 16[r]: 1815.

Dear Madam.

* * * Accept my sincere thanks for the pleasure your Volumes have given me: in the perusal of them I felt a great inclination to write & say so. And I also dear Madam wished to be allowed to ask you, to delineate in some future Work the Habits of Life and Character and enthusiasm of a Clergyman—who should pass his time between the metropolis & the Country—who should be something like Beatties Minstrel[2]

> Silent when glad, affectionate tho' shy
> And now his look was most demurely sad
> & now he laughd aloud yet none knew why—

Neither Goldsmith[3]—nor La Fontaine in his Tableau de Famille— have in my mind quite delineated an English Clergyman, at least of the present day—Fond of, & entirely engaged in Literature—no man's Enemy but his own. Pray dear Madam think of these things.

> Believe me at all times
> With sincerity & respect
> Your faithful & obliged Servant
> J. S. Clarke
> Librarian. * * *

---

† From *Jane Austen's Letters*, ed. Deirdre Le Faye, 3rd ed. (New York: Oxford UP, 1995) letters 124(D), 125(A), 126, 130, 132(D), 132(A), 138(A), 138(D), 139. Reprinted by permission of Oxford University Press.
1. Clarke was domestic chaplain to the Prince Regent, Prince of Wales. Jane Austen had written him to inquire whether, and how, she might dedicate some future work to the prince. In this letter, his reply, Clarke gives her an answer, observes that "The Regent has read & admired all your publications," and goes on to express a wish of his own [*Editor*].
2. *The Minstrel*, by James Beattie, was a long, descriptive poem on the progress of genius, published 1771–74 [*Editor*].
3. He probably alludes to Goldsmith's *Vicar of Wakefield* [*Editor*].

Jane Austen to J. S. Clarke
[explaining why she cannot]

Dec. 11. [1815]

Dear Sir

* * * I am quite honoured by your thinking me capable of drawing such a Clergyman as you gave the sketch of in your note of Nov.
16th. But I assure you I am *not*. The comic part of the Character I
might be equal to, but not the Good, the Enthusiastic, the Literary.
Such a man's conversation must at times be on subjects of science
and philosophy, of which I know nothing; or at least be occasionally
abundant in quotations and allusions which a woman who, like me,
knows only her own mother tongue, and has read very little in that,
would be totally without the power of giving. A classical education,
or at any rate a very extensive acquaintance with English literature,
ancient and modern, appears to me quite indispensable for the person who would do any justice to your clergyman; and I think I may
boast myself to be, with all possible vanity, the most unlearned and
uninformed female who ever dared to be an authoress.

Believe me, dear Sir,
Your obliged and faithful humb^bl Ser^t.
Jane Austen

J. S. Clarke to Jane Austen
[asking again]

Carlton House Thursday [? Dec. 21], 1815

My dear Madam

* * * Pray continue to write, & make all your friends send Sketches
to help you—and Memoires pour servir[4]—as the French term it.
Do let us have an English Clergyman after *your* fancy—much novelty may be introduced—shew dear Madam what good would be
done if Tythes[5] were taken away entirely, and describe him burying
his own mother—as I did—because the High Priest of the Parish
in which she died—did not pay her remains the respect he ought to
do. I have never recovered the Shock. Carry your Clergyman to Sea
as the Friend of some distinguished Naval Character about a
Court—you can then bring foreward like Le Sage[6] many interesting Scenes of Character & Interest.

4. He evidently means "reminders" [*Editor*].
5. Agricultural taxes [*Editor*].
6. French dramatist and novelist, now looked upon as a forerunner of Fielding and Smol-
lett [*Editor*].

But forgive me, I cannot write to you without wishing to elicit your Genius;—& I fear I cannot do that, without trespassing on your Patience and Good Nature. * * *

Yours dear Madam, very sincerely
J. S. Clarke.

J. S. Clarke to Jane Austen
[*proposing a historical romance*]

Pavilion: March 27, 1816.

Dear Miss Austen,

* * * Perhaps when you again appear in print you may chuse to dedicate your volumes to Prince Leopold:[7] any Historical Romance, illustrative of the History of the august house of Cobourg, would just now be very interesting.

Believe me at all times,
Dear Miss Austen,
Your obliged friend,
J. S. Clarke.

Jane Austen to J. S. Clarke
[*decisively refusing*]

[April 1, 1816]

My dear Sir

* * * You are very very kind in your hints as to the sort of composition which might recommend me at present, and I am fully sensible that an Historical Romance, founded on the House of Saxe Cobourg, might be much more to the purpose of Profit or Popularity than such pictures of domestic Life in Country Villages as I deal in—but I could no more write a Romance than an Epic Poem.—I could not sit seriously down to write a serious Romance under any other motive than to save my Life; & if it were indispensable for me to keep it up & never relax into laughing at myself or other people, I am sure I should be hung before I had finished the first Chapter.— No—I must keep to my own style & go on in my own Way; and though I may never succeed again in that, I am convinced that I should totally fail in any other.

I remain, my dear Sir,
Your very much obliged, and very sincere friend,
J. Austen

Chawton, near Alton, April 1, 1816.

7. In whose household Clarke was then serving [*Editor*].

Jane Austen's Correspondence with John Murray†

Jane Austen to John Murray
[inquiring about status of manuscript of Emma]

Friday 3 November 1815

Sir

My Brother's severe Illness has prevented his replying to Yours of Oct: 15, on the subject of the MS of *Emma* now in your hands[1]—and as he is, though recovering, still in a state which we are fearful of harrassing by Business & I am at the same time desirous of coming to some decision on the affair in question, I must request the favour of you to call on me here, on any day after the present that may suit you best * * *.—A short conversation may perhaps do more than much Writing. * * *

I am Sir,
Your Ob. Hum: Serv[t],
Jane Austen

Jane Austen to John Murray
[impatient regarding printers' delays]

Thursday 23 November 1815

Sir

My Brother's note last Monday has been so fruitless, that I am afraid there can be little chance of my writing to any good effect; but yet I am so very much disappointed & vexed by the delays of the Printers, that I cannot help begging to know whether there is no hope of their being quickened.—Instead of the Work being ready by the end of the present month, it will hardly, at the rate we now proceed, be finished by the end of the next, and as I expect to leave London early in Dec[r], it is of consequence that no more time should be lost.—Is it likely that the Printers will be influenced to greater Dispatch & Punctuality by knowing that the Work is to be dedicated, by Permission, to the Prince Regent?—If you can make that circumstance operate, I shall be very glad. * * *

I remain, Sir,
Y[r] ob. HumServ[t]
J. Austen

---

† John Samuel Murray (1778–1843) followed his father in the "bookselling" business, becoming one of the most well known and influential publishers of his time. He was Byron's publisher, and he founded the important *Quarterly Review*. For Austen, he published *Emma* and the second edition of *Mansfield Park*, which was published "for the author" (meaning, at the author's risk), charging Austen his customary 10 percent commission. Reprinted by permission of Oxford University Press.

1. Henry Austen served in the role of his sister's literary agent. Here we can see that in his absence, Austen asserts her own role in corresponding with the publisher.

Jane Austen to John Murray
[*eager for the novel to sell as rapidly as possible*]

Monday 11 December 1815

Dear Sir

As I find that *Emma* is advertized for publication as early as Saturday next, I think it best to lose no time in settling all that remains to be settled on the subject, & adopt this method of doing so, as involving the smallest tax on your time.—

In the first place, I beg you to understand that I leave the terms on which the Trade[2] should be supplied with the work, entirely to your Judgement, entreating you to be guided in every such arrangement by your own experience of what is most likely to clear off the Edition rapidly. I shall be satisfied with whatever you feel to be best. * * *

I remain dear Sir,
Y[r] faithful HumServ[t],
J. Austen

Jane Austen to John Murray
[*returning positive review by Scott in* Quarterly Review]

Monday 1 April 1816

Dear Sir

I return you the Quarterly Reveiw [*sic*] with many Thanks. The Authoress of *Emma* has no reason I think to complain of her treatment in it—except in the total omission of Mansfield Park.—I cannot but be sorry that so clever a Man as the Reviewer of *Emma*, should consider it as unworthy of being noticed.—You will be pleased to hear that I have received the Prince's Thanks for the *handsome* Copy I sent him of *Emma*. Whatever he may think of *my* share of the Work, *Yours* seems to have been quite right.—

* * *

I remain, dear Sir,
Yours very faithfully
J. Austen

_____
2. Retail booksellers.

JANE AUSTEN

Plan of a Novel, According to Hints from Various Quarters[†]

Scene to be in the Country, Heroine the Daughter of a Clergyman, one who after having lived much in the World had retired from it, & settled in a Curacy, with a very small fortune of his own.—He, the most excellent Man that can be imagined, perfect in Character, Temper & Manners—without the smallest drawback or peculiarity to prevent his being the most delightful companion to his Daughter from one year's end to the other.—Heroine a faultless Character herself—, perfectly good, with much tenderness & sentiment, & not the least Wit—very highly accomplished, understanding modern Languages & (generally speaking) everything that the most accomplished young Women learn, but particularly excelling in Music—her favourite pursuit—& playing equally well on the Piano Forte & Harp—& singing in the first stile. Her Person, quite beautiful—dark eyes & plump cheeks.—Book to open with the description of Father & Daughter—who are to converse in long speeches, elegant Language—& a tone of high, serious sentiment.—The Father to be induced, at his Daughter's earnest request, to relate to her the past events of his Life. This Narrative will reach through the greatest part of the 1st vol.—as besides all the circumstances of his attachment to her Mother & their Marriage, it will comprehend his going to sea as Chaplain to a distinguished Naval Character about the Court, his going afterwards to Court himself, which introduced him to a great variety of Characters & involved him in many interesting situations, concluding with his opinion of the Benefits to result from Tythes[1] being done away, & his having buried his own Mother (Heroine's lamented Grandmother) in consequence of the High Priest of the Parish in which she died, refusing to pay her Remains the respect due to them. The Father to be of a very literary turn, an Enthusiast in Literature, nobody's Enemy but his own—at the same time most zealous in the discharge of his Pastoral Duties, the model of an exemplary Parish Priest.—The heroine's friendship to be sought after by a young Woman in the same Neighbourhood, of Talents & Shrewdness, with light eyes & a fair skin, but having a considerable degree of Wit, Heroine shall shrink from the acquaintance.—From

[†] From *The Works of Jane Austen*, collected and edited from the manuscripts by R. W. Chapman, vol. 6, *Minor Works* (London: Oxford UP, 1954) 428–30. Reprinted by permission of Oxford University Press. The marginal notes, in which Jane Austen identified the friends who suggested various elements of this satiric design, are omitted.
1. See Clarke's letter to Jane Austen, December 21, 1815 (354–55) [*Editor*].

this outset, the Story will proceed, & contain a striking variety of adventures. Heroine & her Father never above a fortnight together in one place, *he* being driven from his Curacy by the vile arts of some totally unprincipled & heart-less young Man, desperately in love with the Heroine, & pursuing her with unrelenting passion—no sooner settled in one Country of Europe than they are necessitated to quit it & retire to another—always making new acquaintance, & always obliged to leave them.—This will of course exhibit a wide variety of Characters—but there will be no mixture; the scene will be for ever shifting from one Set of People to another—but all the Good will be unexceptionable in every respect—and there will be no foibles or weaknesses but with the Wicked, who will be completely depraved & infamous, hardly a resemblance of Humanity left in them.—Early in her career, in the progress of her first removals, Heroine must meet with the Hero—all perfection of course—& only prevented from paying his addresses to her, by some excess of refinement.—Wherever she goes, somebody falls in love with her, & she receives repeated offers of Marriage—which she always refers wholly to her Father, exceedingly angry that *he* sh^d not be first applied to.—Often carried away by the anti-hero, but rescued either by her Father or the Hero—often reduced to support herself & her Father by her Talents & work for her Bread;—continually cheated & defrauded of her hire, worn down to a Skeleton, & now & then starved to death—. At last, hunted out of civilized Society, denied the poor Shelter of the humblest Cottage, they are compelled to retreat into Kamschatka[2] where the poor Father, quite worn down, finding his end approaching, throws himself on the Ground, & after 4 or 5 hours of tender advice & parental Admonition to his miserable Child, expires in a fine burst of Literary Enthusiasm, intermingled with Invectives again(st) Holder's of Tythes.—Heroine inconsolable for some time—but afterwards crawls back towards her former Country—having at least 20 narrow escapes of falling into the hands of Anti-hero—& at last in the very nick of time, turning a corner to avoid him, runs into the arms of the Hero himself, who having just shaken off the scruples which fetter'd him before, was at the very moment setting off in pursuit of her.—The Tenderest & completest Eclaircissement[3] takes place & they are happily united.—Throughout the whole work, Heroine to be in the most elegant Society & living in high style. The name of the work *not* to be *Emma*—but of the same sort as S & S. and P & P.[4]

---

2. Presumably the peninsula off Siberia [*Editor*].
3. Elucidation, or resolution [*Editor*].
4. *Sense and Sensibility* and *Pride and Prejudice* [*Editor*].

A Riddle [Kitty, a fair, but frozen maid][†]

By the Same. [David Garrick]

Kitty, a fair, but frozen maid,
　Kindled a flame I still deplore;
The hood-wink'd boy I call'd in aid,
Much of his near approach afraid,
　So fatal to my suit before.

At length, proptious to my pray'r,
　The little urchin came;
At once he sought the midway air,
And soon he clear'd, with dextrous care,
　The bitter relicks of my flame.

To Kitty, Fanny now succeeds,
　She kindles slow, but lasting fires:
With care my appetite she feeds;
Each day some willing victim bleeds,
　To satisfy my strange desires.

Say, by what title[*], or what name,
　Must I this youth address?
Cupid and he are not the same,
Tho' both can raise, or quench a flame—
　I'll kiss you, if you guess.

---

† From *The new foundling hospital for wit. Being a collection of fugitive pieces, in prose and verse, not in any other collection. With several pieces never before published.* London: printed for J. Debrett, 1784. Vol. 2, 182–83. Garrick's riddle and the folk song "Robin Adair" provide important context to key scenes in *Emma*. Austen's audience would have been familiar with both pieces. The riddle offers a glimpse into the sometimes bawdy world of literary culture, knowledge of which might seem surprising for the valetudinarian Mr. Woodhouse. The situation of the speaker in "Robin Adair" resembles that of Jane Fairfax.

* The chimney-sweeper.

Robin Adair[†]

What's this dull town to me?
　　Robin's not near.
What was't I wish'd to see?
　　What wish'd to hear?
Where's all the joy and mirth
Made this town heaven on earth?
　　Oh! they are all fled with thee,
　　　Robin Adair.

What made the assembly shine?—
　　Robin Adair.
What the ball look so fine,
　　Robin was there:
What, when the play was o'er,
What made my heart so sore?—
　　Oh! it was parting with
　　　Robin Adair.

But thou art cold to me,
　　Robin Adair.
But now thou'rt cold to me,
　　Robin Adair.
Yet he I lov'd so well
Still in my heart shall dwell:
　　Oh! I can ne'er forget
　　　Robin Adair.

[†]　From *A Garland of New Songs* (Newcastle upon Tyne: J. Marshall, 1800).

The Reception of Jane Austen, 1815–1950

This section includes brief excerpts from Sir Walter Scott, the best-known living author of Jane Austen's era, whose poetry, fiction, and nonfiction dominated literary culture, up to Edmund Wilson. Wilson's Freudian analysis has led contemporary critics to examine the character of Emma through a lens that combines the psychological with the sexual.

JANE AUSTEN

Opinions of *Emma*[†]

Captn Austen.—liked it extremely, observing that though there might be more Wit in P&P—& an higher Morality in MP—yet altogether, on account of it's peculiar air of Nature throughout, he preferred it to either.

Miss Sharp—better than MP.—but not so well as P. & P.—pleased with the Heroine for her Originality, delighted with Mr K—& called Mrs Elton beyond praise.—dissatisfied with Jane Fairfax.

Fanny K.—not so well as either P. & P. or MP.—could not bear *Emma* herself.—Mr Knightley delightful.—Should like J. F.—if she knew more of her.—

Mr Shean—did not think it equal to either M P—(which he liked the best of all) or P & P.—Displeased with my pictures of Clergymen.—

Miss Bigg—on reading it a second time, liked Miss Bates much better than at first, & expressed herself as liking all the people of Highbury in general, except Harriet Smith—but c^d not help still thinking *her* too silly in her Loves.

Mrs Digweed—did not like it so well as the others, in fact if she had not known the Author, could hardly have got through it.

Henry Sanford—very much pleased with it—delighted with Miss Bates, but thought Mrs Elton the best-drawn Character in the Book.—Mansfield Park however, still his favourite.

[†] Austen compiled and recorded her family and acquaintances' responses to the novel. This selection of the "Opinions" is taken from a facsimile of the manuscript.

Miss Isabella Herries—did not like it—objected to my exposing the sex in the character of the Heroine—convinced that I had meant M^rs and Miss Bates for some acquaintance of theirs—People whom I never heard of before.—

Mrs Dickson—did not much like it—thought it *very* inferior to P. & P.—Liked it the less, from there being a M^r & Mrs Dixon in it.—

Mr B. Lefroy—thought that if there had been more Incident, it would be equal to any of the others.—The Characters quite as well drawn & supported as in any, & from being more Everyday ones, the more entertaining.—Did not like the Heroine so well as any of the others. Miss Bates excellent, but rather too much of her. M^r and Mrs Elton admirable & John Knightley a sensible Man.—

Mr Fowle—read only the first & last Chapters, because he had heard it was not interesting.—

Mrs C. Cage wrote thus to Fanny—"A great many thanks for the loan of *Emma*, which I am delighted with. I like it better than any. Every character is thoroughly kept up. I must enjoy reading it again with Charles. Miss Bates is incomparable, but I was nearly killed with those precious treasures! They are Unique, & really with more fun than I can express. I am at Highbury all day, & I can't help feeling I have just got into a new set of acquaintance. No one writes such good sense. & so very comfortable.

Mrs Wroughton—did not like it so well as P. & P.—Thought the Authoress wrong, in such times as these, to draw such Clergymen as Mr Collins & Mr Elton.

Mr Jeffery (of the Edinburgh Review) was kept up by it three nights.

SIR WALTER SCOTT

Review of *Emma*†

* * *

[I]t becomes doubly the duty of the critic to treat with kindness as well as candour works which, like this one before us, proclaim a knowledge of the human heart, with the power and resolution to bring that knowledge to the service of honour and virtue. The author is already known to the public by the two novels announced in her title-page,[1] and both, the last especially, attracted, with justice, an attention from the public far superior to what is granted to the ephemeral productions which supply the regular demand of watering-places and circulating libraries. * * *

---

† From the *Quarterly Review* 14 (1815): 188–201.
1. *Sense and Sensibility* and *Pride and Prejudice* [*Editor*].

We * * * bestow no mean compliment upon the author of Emma, when we say that, keeping close to common incidents, and to such characters as occupy the ordinary walks of life, she has produced sketches of such spirit and originality, that we never miss the excitation which depends upon a narrative of uncommon events, arising from the consideration of minds, manners, and sentiments, greatly above our own. In this class she stands almost alone * * *. [H]er most distinguished characters do not rise greatly above well-bred country gentlemen and ladies; and those which are sketched with most originality and precision, belong to a class rather below that standard. The narrative of all her novels is composed of such common occurrences as may have fallen under the observation of most folks; and her dramatis personae conduct themselves upon the motives and principles which the readers may recognize as ruling their own and that of most of their acquaintances. The kind of moral, also, which these novels inculcate, applies equally to the paths of common life. * * *

The author's knowledge of the world, and the peculiar tact with which she presents characters that the reader cannot fail to recognize, reminds us something of the merits of the Flemish school of painting. The subjects are not often elegant, and certainly never grand; but they are finished up to nature, and with a precision which delights the reader. This is a merit which it is very difficult to illustrate by extracts, because it pervades the whole work, and is not to be comprehended from a single passage. * * *[2]

Perhaps the reader may collect from the preceding specimen both the merits and faults of the author. The former consists much in the force of a narrative conducted with much neatness and point, and a quiet yet comic dialogue, in which the characters of the speakers evolve themselves with dramatic effect. The faults, on the contrary, arise from the minute detail which the author's plan comprehends. Characters of folly or simplicity, such as those of old Woodhouse and Miss Bates, are ridiculous when first presented, but if too often brought forward or too long dwelt upon, their prosing is apt to become as tiresome in fiction as in real society. * * *

2. Scott quotes a long passage from vol. I, chap. XII.

THOMAS BABINGTON MACAULAY

Review of Madame D'Arblay's *Diaries and Journals*[†]

* * *

Shakespeare has had neither equal nor second. But among the writers who, in the point which we have noticed, have approached nearest to the manner of the grand master, we have no hesitation in placing Jane Austen, a woman of whom England is justly proud. She has given us a multitude of characters, all, in a certain sense, common-place, all such as we meet every day. Yet they are all as perfectly discriminated from each other as if they were the most eccentric of human beings. * * *

CHARLOTTE BRONTË

Letter to W. S. Williams, April 12, 1850[‡]

* * *

I have likewise read one of Miss Austen's works "Emma"—read it with interest and with just the degree of admiration which Miss Austen herself would have thought sensible and suitable—anything like warmth or enthusiasm; anything energetic, poignant, heartfelt, is utterly out of place in commending these works: all such demonstration the authoress would have met with a well-bred sneer, would have calmly scorned as outré and extravagant. She does her business of delineating the surface of the lives of genteel English people curiously well; there is a Chinese fidelity, a miniature delicacy in the painting: she ruffles her reader by nothing vehement, disturbs him by nothing profound: the Passions are perfectly unknown to her; she rejects even a speaking acquaintance with that stormy Sisterhood; even to the Feelings she vouchsafes no more than an occasional graceful but distant recognition; too frequent converse with them would ruffle the smooth elegance of her progress. Her business is not half so much with the human heart as with the human eyes, mouth, hands and feet; what sees keenly, speaks aptly, moves

[†] Thomas Babington Macaulay (1800–1859) was a preeminent literary figure of the Victorian era. A historian, essayist, and poet, he contributed frequently to periodicals of the day, including the *Edinburgh Review*, for which he wrote this review of Madame D'Arblay's (Frances Burney's) *Diaries and Journals*, which had been recently published (*Edinburgh Review*, LXXVI [January 1843]).

[‡] From *The Brontës: Their Lives, Friendships, Correspondence*, vol. III. Thomas James Wise and J. Alexander Symington, eds. (Boston: Houghton Mifflin, 1933).

flexibly, it suits her to study, but what throbs fast and full, though hidden, what the blood rushes through, what is the unseen seat of Life and the sentient target of death—*this* Miss Austen ignores; she no more, with her mind's eye, beholds the heart of her race than each man, with bodily vision sees the heart in his heaving breast. Jane Austen was a complete and most sensible lady, but a very incomplete, and rather insensible (*not senseless*) woman, if this is heresy—I cannot help it. If I said it to some people (Lewes for instance) they would directly accuse me of advocating exaggerated heroics, but I am not afraid of your falling into any such vulgar error. * * *

GEORGE HENRY LEWES

The Novels of Jane Austen[†]

[T]he real secret of Miss Austen's success lies in her having the exquisite and rare gift of dramatic creation of character. Scott says of her, "She had a talent for describing the involvements, and feelings, and characters of ordinary life, which is to me the most wonderful I ever met with. The big bow-wow strain I can do myself like any now going; but the exquisite touch, which renders ordinary commonplace things and characters interesting, from the truth of the description and the sentiment, is denied me. What a pity such a gifted creature died so early!"[1] Generously said; but high as the praise is, it is as much below the real excellence of Miss Austen, as the "big bow-wow strain" is below the incomparable power of the Waverley Novels. Scott felt, but did not define, the excellence of Miss Austen. The very word "describing" is altogether misplaced and misleading. She seldom describes anything, and is not felicitous when she attempts it. But instead of *description*, the common and easy resource of novelists, she has the rare and difficult art of *dramatic presentation*: instead of telling us what her characters are, and what they feel, she presents the people, and they reveal themselves. In this she has never perhaps been surpassed, not even by Shakespeare himself. If ever living beings can be said to have moved across the page of fiction, as they lived, speaking as they spoke, and feeling as they felt, they do so in *Pride and Prejudice*, *Emma*, and *Mansfield Park*. What incomparable noodles[2] she exhibits for our astonishment and laughter! What silly, good-natured women! What softly-selfish men! What lively, amiable, honest men and women, whom one would rejoice to have known!

† From *Blackwell's Edinburgh Magazine* (1859): 99–113.
1. Lockhart, *Life of Scott*, viii, 292.
2. Silly persons [*Editor*].

But all her power is dramatic power; she loses her hold on us directly she ceases to speak through the *personae*; she is then like a great actor *off* the stage. When she is making men and women her mouthpieces, she is exquisitely and inexhaustibly humorous; but when she speaks in her own person, she is apt to be commonplace, and even prosing. Her dramatic ventriloquism is such that, amid our tears of laughter and sympathetic exasperation at folly, we feel it almost impossible that she did not hear those very people utter those very words. * * * If the reader fails to perceive the extraordinary merit of Miss Austen's representation of character, let him try himself to paint a portrait which shall be at once many-sided and interesting, without employing any but the commonest colours, without calling in the aid of eccentricity, exaggeration, or literary "effects."

*   *   *

Mrs Elton, in *Emma*, is the very best portrait of a vulgar woman we ever saw: she is vulgar in soul, and the vulgarity is indicated by subtle yet unmistakeable touches, never by coarse language, or by caricature of any kind.[3] * * * [T]he characters reveal themselves; and in general reveal themselves only in the course of several scenes, so that extracts would give no idea of them.

We have endeavoured to express the delight which Miss Austen's works have always given us, and to explain the sources of her success by indicating the qualities which make her a model worthy of the study of all who desire to understand the art of the novelist. But we have also indicated what seem to be the limitations of her genius, and to explain why it is that this genius, moving only amid the quiet scenes of every-day life, with no power over the more stormy and energetic activities which find vent even in every-day life, can never give her a high rank among great artists. Her place is among great artists, but it is not high among them. She sits in the House of Peers, but it is as a simple Baron.[4] The delight derived from her pictures arises from our sympathy with ordinary characters, our relish of humour, and our intellectual pleasure in art for art's sake. But when it is admitted that she never stirs the deeper emotions, that she never fills the soul with a noble aspiration, or brightens it with a fine idea, but, at the utmost, only teaches us charity for the ordinary failings of ordinary people, and sympathy with their goodness, we have admitted an objection which lowers her claims to rank among the great benefactors of the race; and this sufficiently explains why, with all her excellence, her name has not become a household word. Her

---

3. Lewes then quotes many passages including Mrs. Elton [*Editor*].
4. The House of Peers (Lords) is the branch of the British Parliament designated for the aristocracy and the gentry with inherited titles, among the latter of which Lewes metaphorically places Austen [*Editor*].

fame, we think, must endure. Such art as hers can never grow old, never be superseded. But, after all, miniatures are not frescoes, and her works are miniatures. Her place is among the Immortals; but the pedestal is erected in a quiet niche of the great temple.

JULIET POLLOCK

Jane Austen[†]

*   *   *

It is a common fault with Miss Austen's young women that they are remarkably addicted to the contemplation of themselves and their own qualities with special reference to the effect they produce upon men. It is the first aim to be the object of a man's attention,—this desire not springing from a strong preference for some particular man, but from the general ambition of distinction in this kind. Emma wonders whether Frank Churchill will distinguish her before she has seen him. * * *

At the present day it is inconceivable that a clever girl, with a fine disposition, such as Miss Austen intends to represent in Emma, should go through such a course of meanness as her friendship with the weak-minded Harriet Smith exhibits, or should be guilty of such evil-thinking and evil-speaking as her jealousy of Jane Fairfax calls forth. * * *

In Miss Austen's fictions it is not the image of sorrow, of suffering, or want, which induces commiseration in the reader; but the exhibition of petty aims, vain strivings, low intellects, and mean jealousies, which excites pain, as it augments our appreciation of the weakness of human nature and the narrowness of life and thoughts when contracted to certain conditions. There is, however, much less of this small village, or watering-place, or country neighborhood kind of existence to be found in England now than there was in Miss Austen's days.

Railways have made movement general, if not universal. Few people remain rooted to any one spot. London is no longer unknown to the country. Travelling made easy to all classes has enlarged the circle of every individual experience. All the means of intercourse between man and man have increased and are increasing rapidly; ideas are in constant circulation; postage is cheap. No place is too isolated for the reach of magazines; no town, no country house is condemned solely to the interests of its own limits in space. * * *

†   From *St. Paul's Magazine* 5 (1870): 631–43.

Jane Austen's works,—though not devoured by young ladies of our
period with the same greediness as the new stories just come from
Mudie's,[1]—are still taken down by "the girls" from the maternal shelf,
when there is nothing else to be had, and are read,—by them,—with
tranquil interest. But they are pondered over with most attention and
most appreciation by men of thought and literary education.

ANNE RITCHIE

Jane Austen[†]

These people belong to a whole world of familiar acquaintances,
who are, notwithstanding their old-fashioned dresses and quaint
expressions, more alive to us than a great many of the people
among whom we live. * * * Dear books! bright, sparkling with wit
and animation, in which the homely heroines charm, the dull,
hours fly, and the very bores are enchanting. * * *
    [Austen] has a gift for telling a story in a way that has never been
surpassed. She rules her places, times, characters, and marshals
them with unerring precision. Her machinery is simple but complete; events group themselves so vividly and naturally in her mind
that, in describing imaginary scenes, we seem not only to read
them, but to live them, to see the people coming and going: the
gentlemen courteous and in top-boots, the ladies demure and
piquant; we can almost hear them talking to one another. No retro-
spects; no abrupt flights, as in real life: days and events follow one
another. * * * With Miss Austen days, hours, minutes succeed each
other like clock-work, one central figure is always present on the
scene, that figure is always prepared for company. * * *
    It is difficult, reading the novels of succeeding generations, to
determine how much of each book reflects of the time in which it
was written; how much of its character depends on the mind and the
mood of the writer. The greatest minds, the most original, have the
least stamp of the age, the most of that dominant natural reality
which belongs to all great minds. We know how a landscape changes
as the day goes on, and how the scene brightens and gains in beauty
as the shadows begin to lengthen. The clearest eyes must see by the
light of their own hour. Jane Austen's hour must have been a midday
hour: bright, unsuggestive, with objects standing clear, without relief
or shadow. She did not write of herself, but of the manners of her
age. This age is essentially an age of men and women of strained

---

1. London Lending Library owned and operated for profit by Charles Mudie (1818–1890).
   Mudie's was a critically important mechanism for distributing fiction to readers who
   could not afford to buy individual copies of novels.
† From *Cornhill Magazine* 24 (1871): 158–74.

emotion, little remains of starch, or powder, or courtly reserve. What we have lost in calm, in happiness, in tranquillity, we have gained in intensity. Our danger is now, not of expressing and feeling too little, but of expressing more than we feel. * * *

The living writers of to-day lead us into distant realms and worlds undreamt of in the placid and easily contented gigot[1] age. People are gifted with wider experiences, with aspirations and emotions that were never more sincerely spoken than they are now; but, for actual study of character, there seems but little taste. A phase, a mood of mind, a sympathy, is what we look for, and what we chiefly find among the present novelists. * * * One reason may be, perhaps, that characters in novels are certainly more intimate with us and on less ceremonious terms than in Miss Austen's days. Her heroines have a stamp of their own. They have a certain gentle self-respect and humour and hardness of heart in which modern heroines are a little wanting. Whatever happens they can for the most part speak of gaily and without bitterness. Love with them does not mean a passion so much as an interest—deep, silent; not quite incompatible with a secondary flirtation. * * * It was the spirit of the age, and, perhaps, one not to be unenvied.

HENRY JAMES

The Lesson of Balzac[†]

* * * Jane Austen, with all her light felicity, leaves us hardly more curious of her process, or of the experience in her that fed it, than the brown thrush who tells his story from the garden bough; and this, I freely confess, in spite of her being one of those of the shelved and safe, for all time, of whom I should have liked to begin by talking; one of those in whose favor discrimination has long since practically operated. She is in fact a signal instance of the way it does, with all its embarrassments, at last infallibly operate. A sharp short cut, one of the sharpest and shortest achieved, in this field, by the general judgment, came out, betimes, straight at her feet. Practically overlooked for thirty or forty years after her death, she perhaps really stands there for us as the prettiest possible example of that rectification of estimate, brought about by some slow clearance of stupidity, the half-century or so is capable of working round to. This tide has risen high on the opposite shore, the shore of appreciation—risen rather higher, I think, than the high-water mark, the highest, of her intrinsic merit and interest; though I grant indeed—as a point to be

---

1. Type of sleeve puffed and gathered from the shoulder to the elbow and narrow from the elbow to the wrist; *gigot* (French): leg of mutton, another term for this style of sleeve.
† From the *Atlantic Monthly* 96 (July 1905): 166–80.

made—that we are dealing here in some degree with the tides so
freely driven up, beyond their mere logical reach, by the stiff breeze
of the commercial, in other words of the special bookselling spirit;
an eager, active, interfering force which has a great many confusions
of apparent value, a great many wild and wandering estimates, to
answer for. For these distinctively mechanical and overdone reactions, of course, the critical spirit, even in its most relaxed mood, is
not responsible. Responsible, rather, is the body of publishers, editors, illustrators, producers of the pleasant twaddle of magazines;
who have found their "dear," our dear, everybody's dear, Jane so
infinitely to their material purpose, so amenable to pretty reproduc-
tion in every variety of what is called tasteful, and in what seemingly
proves to be saleable, form.

I do not, naturally, mean that she would be saleable if we had not
more or less—beginning with Macaulay, her first slightly ponderous
amoroso—lost our hearts to her; but I cannot help seeing her, a good
deal, as in the same lucky box as the Brontés—lucky for the ultimate
guerdon; a case of popularity (that in especial of the Yorkshire sisters), a beguiled infatuation, a sentimentalized vision, determined
largely by the accidents and circumstances originally surrounding
the manifestation of the genius—only with the reasons for the sentiment, in this latter connection, turned the other way. The key to Jane
Austen's fortune with posterity has been in part the extraordinary
grace of her facility, in fact of her unconsciousness: as if, at the most,
for difficulty, for embarrassment, she sometimes, over her workbasket, her tapestry flowers, in the spare, cool drawing-room of other
days, fell a-musing, lapsed too metaphorically, as one may say, into
wool-gathering, and her dropped stitches, of these pardonable, of
these precious moments, were afterwards picked up as little touches
of human truth, little glimpses of steady vision, little master-strokes
of imagination. * * *

* * *

REGINALD FARRER

Jane Austen, *ob.* July 18, 1917[†]

* * * Take it all in all, 'Emma' is the very climax of Jane Austen's
work; and a real appreciation of 'Emma' is the final test of citizenship
in her kingdom. For this is not an easy book to read; it should never
be the beginner's primer, nor be published without a prefatory synop-

† From the *Quarterly Review* 228 (July 1917): 23–25. Reprinted by permission of John
Murray (Publishers) Ltd.

sis. Only when the story has been thoroughly assimilated, can the infinite delights and subtleties of its workmanship begin to be appreciated, as you realise the manifold complexity of the book's web, and find that every sentence, almost every epithet, has its definite reference to equally unemphasised points before and after in the development of the plot. This it is that, while twelve readings of 'Pride and Prejudice' give you twelve periods of pleasure repeated, as many readings of 'Emma' give you that pleasure, not repeated only, but squared and squared again with each perusal, till at every fresh reading you feel anew that you never understood anything like the widening sum of its delights. But, until you know the story, you are apt to find its movement dense and slow and obscure, difficult to follow, and not very obviously worth the following.

For this is *the* novel of character, and of character alone, and of one dominating character in particular. And many a rash reader, and some who are not rash, have been shut out on the threshold of Emma's Comedy by a dislike of Emma herself. Well did Jane Austen know what she was about, when she said, 'I am going to take a heroine whom nobody but myself will much like.' And, in so far as she fails to make people like Emma, so far would her whole attempt have to be judged a failure, were it not that really the failure, like the loss, is theirs who have not taken the trouble to understand what is being attempted. Jane Austen loved tackling problems; her hardest of all, her most deliberate, and her most triumphantly solved, is Emma.

What is that problem? No one who carefully reads the first three opening paragraphs of the book can entertain a doubt, or need any prefatory synopsis; for in these the author gives us quite clear warning of what we are to see. We are to see the gradual humiliation of self-conceit, through a long self-wrought succession of disasters, serious in effect, but keyed in Comedy throughout. Emma herself, in fact, *is never to be taken seriously.* And it is only those who have not realised this who will be 'put off' by her absurdities, her snobberies, her misdirected mischievous ingenuities. Emma is simply a figure of fun. To conciliate affection for a character, not because of its charms, but in defiance of its defects, is the loftiest aim of the comic spirit: Shakespeare achieved it with his besotted old rogue of a Falstaff, and Molière with Celimène.[1] It is with these, not with 'sympathetic' heroines, that Emma takes rank, as the culminating figure of English high-comedy. And to attain success in creating a being whom you both love and laugh at, the author must attempt a task of complicated difficulty. He must both run with the hare and hunt with the hounds, treat his creation at once objectively and subjectively, get inside it to inspire it with sympathy, and yet stay outside it to direct laughter on

1. Abrasive flirt in *The Misanthrope* [Editor].

its comic aspects. And this is what Jane Austen does for Emma, with a consistent sublimity so demure that indeed a reader accustomed only to crude work might be pardoned for missing the point of her innumerable hints, and actually taking seriously, for example, the irony with which Emma's attitude about the Coles' dinner-party is treated, or the even more convulsing comedy of Emma's reflexions after it. But only Jane Austen is capable of such oblique glints of humour; and only in 'Emma' does she weave them so densely into her kaleidoscope that the reader must be perpetually on his guard lest some specially delicious flash escape his notice, or some touch of dialogue be taken for the author's own intention.

Yet, as Emma really does behave extremely ill by Jane Fairfax, and even worse by Robert Martin, merely to laugh would not be enough, and every disapproval would justly be deepened to dislike. But, when we release that each machination of Emma's, each imagined piece of penetration, is to be a thread in the snare woven unconsciously by herself for her own enmeshing in disaster, then the balance is recti-fied again, and disapproval can lighten to laughter once more. For this is another of Jane Austen's triumphs here—the way in which she keeps our sympathies poised about Emma. Always some charm of hers is brought out, to compensate some specially silly and ambitious naughtiness; and even these are but perfectly natural, in a strong-willed, strong-minded girl of only twenty-one, who has been for some four years unquestioned mistress of Hartfield, unquestioned Queen of Highbury. Accordingly, at every turn we are kept so dancing up and down with alternate rage and delight at Emma that finally, when we see her self-esteem hammered bit by bit into collapse, the nemesis would be too severe, were she to be left in the depths. By the merci-ful intention of the book, however, she is saved in the very nick of time, by what seems like a happy accident, but is really the outcome of her own unsuspected good qualities, just as much as her disas-ters had been the outcome of her own most cherished follies.

*   *   *

VIRGINIA WOOLF

[Wit, Taste, and Trivialities]†

The wit of Jane Austen has for partner the perfection of her taste. Her fool is a fool, her snob is a snob, because he departs from the model of sanity and sense which she has in mind, and conveys to us

† Excerpts from *The Common Reader*, by Virginia Woolf, copyright 1925 by Houghton Mifflin Harcourt Publishing Company and renewed 1953 by Leonard Woolf; reprinted by permission of the publisher.

unmistakably even while she makes us laugh. Never did any novelist make more use of an impeccable sense of human values. It is against the disc of an unerring heart, an unfailing good taste, an almost stern morality, that she shows up those deviations from kindness, truth, and sincerity which are among the most delightful things in English literature. * * *

What more natural, then, with this insight into their profundity, than that Jane Austen should have chosen to write of the trivialities of day-to-day existence, of parties, picnics, and country dances? No "suggestions to alter her style of writing" from the Prince Regent or Mr. Clarke could tempt her; no romance, no adventure, no politics or intrigue could hold a candle to life on a country-house staircase as she saw it. Indeed, the Prince Regent and his librarian had run their heads against a very formidable obstacle; they were trying to tamper with an incorruptible conscience, to disturb an infallible discretion. The child who formed her sentences so finely when she was fifteen never ceased to form them, and never wrote for the Prince Regent or his Librarian, but for the world at large. She knew exactly what her powers were, and what material they were fitted to deal with as material should be dealt with by a writer whose standard of finality was high. There were impressions that lay outside her province; emotions that by no stretch or artifice could be properly coated and covered by her own resources. For example, she could not make a girl talk enthusiastically of banners and chapels. She could not throw herself whole-heartedly into a romantic moment. She had all sorts of devices for evading scenes of passion. Nature and its beauties she approached in a sidelong way of her own. She describes a beautiful night without once mentioning the moon. Nevertheless, as we read the few formal phrases about "the brilliancy of an unclouded night and the contrast of the deep shade of the woods", the night is at once as "solemn, and soothing, and lovely" as she tells us, quite simply, that it was.

The balance of her gifts was singularly perfect. Among her finished novels there are no failures, and among her many chapters few that sink markedly below the level of the others. But, after all, she died at the age of forty-two. She died at the height of her powers. She was still subject to those changes which often make the final period of a writer's career the most interesting of all. Vivacious, irrepressible, gifted with an invention of great vitality, there can be no doubt that she would have written more, had she lived, and it is tempting to consider whether she would not have written differently. The boundaries were marked; moons, mountains, and castles lay on the other side. But was she not sometimes tempted to trespass for a minute? Was she not beginning, in her own gay and brilliant manner, to contemplate a little voyage of discovery? * * *

Vain are these speculations: the most perfect artist among women, the writer whose books are immortal, died "just as she was beginning to feel confidence in her own success."

E. M. FORSTER

Jane Austen[†]

*   *   *

I am a Jane Austenite, and therefore slightly imbecile about Jane Austen. My fatuous expression and airs of personal immunity—how ill they set on the face, say, of a Stevensonian![1] But Jane Austen is so different. She is my favourite author! I read and re-read, the mouth open and the mind closed. Shut up in measureless content, I greet her by the name of most kind hostess, while criticism slumbers. The Jane Austenite possesses little of the brightness he ascribes so freely to his idol. Like all regular churchgoers, he scarcely notices what is being said. For instance, the grammar of the following sentence from *Mansfield Park* does not cause him the least uneasiness:

> "And, alas! how always known no principle to supply as a duty what the heart was deficient in."

Nor does he notice any flatness in this dialogue from *Pride and Prejudice*:

> "'Kitty has no discretion in her coughs,' said her father; 'she times them ill.'
> "'I do not cough for my own amusement,' replied Kitty fretfully. 'When is your next ball to be, Lizzy?'"

Why should Kitty ask what she must have known? And why does she say "your" ball when she was going to it herself? Fretfulness would never carry her to such lengths. No, something is amiss in the text; but the loyal adorer will never suspect it. He reads and rereads. And Mr. R. W. Chapman's fine new edition has, among its other merits, the advantage of waking the Jane Austenite up. After reading its notes and appendixes, after a single glance at its illustrations, he will never relapse again into the primal stupor. Without violence, the spell has been broken. The six princesses remain on their sofas, but

† From *Abinger Harvest* copyright 1936 and renewed 1964 by Edward M. Forster, reprinted by permission of Houghton Mifflin Harcourt Publishing Company and the Provost and Scholars of King's College, Cambridge and The Society of Authors as the Literary Representatives of the E. M. Forster Estate. This essay is made up of three reviews of R. W. Chapman's work: "1. The Six Novels" (1924), "2. Sanditon" (1925), and "3. The Letters" (1932).

1. That is, an admirer of Robert Louis Stevenson [*Editor*].

their eyelids quiver and they move their hands. Their twelve suitors do likewise, and their subordinates stir on the perches to which humour or propriety assigned them. The novels continue to live their own wonderful internal life, but it has been freshened and enriched by contact with the life of facts. To promote this contact is the chief function of an editor, and Mr. Chapman fulfils it. All his erudition and taste contribute to this end—his extracts from Mrs. Radcliffe and Mrs. Inchbald, his disquisitions on punctuation and travel, his indexes. Even his textual criticism helps. Observe his brilliant solution of the second of the two difficulties quoted above. He has noticed that in the original edition of *Pride and Prejudice* the words "When is your next ball to be, Lizzy?" began a line, and he suggests that the printer failed to indent them, and, in consequence, they are not Kitty's words at all, but her father's. It is a tiny point, yet how it stirs the pools of complacency! Mr. Bennet, not Kitty, is speaking, and all these years one had never known! The dialogue lights up and sends a little spark of fire into the main mass of the novel. * * *

* * * How shall we drag these shy, proud books into the centre of our minds? To be one with Jane Austen! It is a contradiction in terms, yet every Jane Austenite has made the attempt. When the humour has been absorbed and the cynicism and moral earnestness both discounted, something remains which is easily called Life, but does not thus become more approachable. It is the books rather than the author that seem to reject us—natural enough, since the books are literature and the author an aunt. As Miss Bates remarked, "Dear Jane, how shall we ever recollect half the dishes!"—for though the banquet was not long, it has never been assimilated to our minds. Miss Bates received no answer to her most apposite question; her dear Jane was thinking of something else. The dishes were carried back into the kitchen of the Crown before she could memorize them, and Heaven knows now what they contained!—strawberries from Donwell, perhaps, or apricots from Mansfield Rectory, or sugar-plums from Barton, or hothouse grapes from Pemberley, or melted butter from Woodston, or the hazel nut that Captain Wentworth once picked for Louisa Musgrove in a double hedgerow near Upper-cross. Something has flashed past the faces of the guests and brushed their hearts—something as impalpable as stardust, yet it is part of the soil of England. * * *

* * *

378

D. W. HARDING

Regulated Hatred:
An Aspect of the Work of Jane Austen[†]

The impression of Jane Austen which has filtered through to the reading public, down from the first-hand critics, through histories of literature, university courses, literary journalism and polite allusion, deters many who might be her best readers from bothering with her at all. How can this popular impression be described? In my experience, the first idea to be absorbed from the atmosphere surrounding her work was that she offered exceptionally favourable openings to the exponents of urbanity. Gentlemen of an older generation than mine spoke of their intention of re-reading her on their deathbeds; Eric Linklater's cultured Prime Minister in *The Impregnable Women* passes from surreptitious to abandoned reading of her novels as a national crisis deepens. With this there also came the impression that she provided a refuge for the sensitive when the contemporary world grew too much for them. So Beatrice Kean Seymour writes (*Jane Austen*): "In a society which has enthroned the machine-gun and carried it aloft even into the quiet heavens, there will always be men and women—Escapist or not, as you please—who will turn to her novels with an unending sense of relief and thankfulness."

I was given to understand that her scope was of course extremely restricted, but that within her limits she succeeded admirably in expressing the gentler virtues of a civilized social order. She could do this because she lived at a time when, as a sensitive person of culture, she could still feel that she had a place in society and could address the reading public as sympathetic equals; she might introduce unpleasant people into her stories but she could confidently expose them to a public opinion that condemned them. Chiefly, so I gathered, she was a delicate satirist, revealing with inimitable lightness of touch the comic foibles and amiable weaknesses of the people whom she lived amongst and liked.

All this was enough to make me quite certain I didn't want to read her. And it is, I believe, a seriously misleading impression. Fragments of the truth have been incorporated in it but they are fitted into a pattern whose total effect is false. And yet the wide currency of this false impression is an indication of Jane Austen's success in an essential part of her complex intention as a writer: her books are, as she

[†] A paper read before the Literary Society of Manchester University in March 1939. Published in *Scrutiny* VIII (1940): 346–62, reprinted in *Regulated Hatred and Other Essays on Jane Austen*, ed. Monica Lawlor, (London: Athlone Press, 1998) 5–26. Reprinted by kind permission of Continuum International Publishing Group.

meant them to be, read and enjoyed by precisely the sort of people whom she disliked; she is a literary classic of the society which attitudes like hers, held widely enough, would undermine. * * *

In *Emma* [Austen's satire directs itself against the public]. Again Jane Austen seems to be on perfectly good terms with the public she is addressing and to have no reserve in offering the funniness and virtues of Mr Woodhouse and Miss Bates to be judged by the accepted standards of the public. She invites her readers to be just their natural patronizing selves. But this public that Jane Austen seems on such good terms with has some curious things said about it, not criticisms, but small notes of fact that are usually not made. They almost certainly go unnoticed by many readers, for they involve only the faintest change of tone from something much more usual and acceptable.

When she says that Miss Bates 'enjoyed a most uncommon degree of popularity for a woman neither young, handsome, rich, nor married', this is fairly conventional satire that any reading public would cheerfully admit in its satirist and chuckle over. But the next sentence must have to be mentally re-written by the greater number of Jane Austen's readers. For them it probably runs, 'Miss Bates stood in the very worst predicament in the world for having much of the public favour; and she had no intellectual superiority to make atonement for herself, or compel an outward respect from those who might despise her.' This, I suggest, is how most readers, lulled and disarmed by the amiable context, will soften what in fact reads, 'and she had no intellectual superiority to make atonement to herself, or frighten those who might hate her into outward respect'. Jane Austen was herself at this time 'neither young, handsome, rich, nor married', and the passage perhaps hints at the functions which her unquestioned intellectual superiority may have had for her.

This eruption of fear and hatred into the relationships of everyday social life is something that the urbane admirer of Jane Austen finds distasteful; it is not the satire of one who writes securely for the entertainment of her civilized acquaintances. And it has the effect, for the attentive reader, of changing the flavour of the more ordinary satire amongst which it is embedded.

Emma is especially interesting from this point of view. What is sometimes called its greater 'mellowness' largely consists in saying quietly and undisguisedly things which in the earlier books were put more loudly but in the innocuous form of caricature. Take conversation for instance. Its importance and its high (though by no means supreme) social value are of course implicit in Jane Austen's writings. But one should be aware of supposing that a mind like hers therefore found the ordinary social intercourse of the period congenial and satisfying. * * * But in *Emma* the style changes: the talk at the Cole's dinner party, a pleasant dinner party which the heroine enjoyed, is described as 'the usual rate of conversation; a few clever things said, a few downright silly, but by much the larger proportion neither the one nor the other—nothing worse than everyday remarks, dull repetitions, old news, and heavy jokes'. 'Nothing worse'!—that phrase is typical. It is not mere sarcasm by any means. Jane Austen genuinely valued the achievements of the civilization she lived within and never lost sight of the fact that there might be something vastly worse than the conversation she referred to. 'Nothing worse' is a positive tribute to the decency, the superficial friendliness, the absence of the grosser forms of insolence and self-display at the dinner party. At least Mrs Elton wasn't there. And yet the effect of the comment, if her readers took it seriously would be that of a disintegrating attack upon the sort of social intercourse they have established for themselves. It is not the comment of one who would have helped to make her society what it was, or ours what it is.

To speak of this aspect of her work as 'satire' is perhaps misleading. She has none of the underlying didactic intention ordinarily attributed to the satirist. Her object is not missionary; it is the more desperate one of merely finding some mode of existence for her critical attitudes. * * *

Hence one of Jane Austen's most successful methods is to offer her readers every excuse for regarding as rather exaggerated figures of fun people whom she herself detests and fears. * * *

[In *Emma*] she faces the far bolder conclusion that even a heroine is likely to have assimilated many of the more unpleasant possibilities of the human being in society. And it is not that society has spoilt an originally perfect girl who now has to recover her pristine good sense, * * * but that the heroine has not yet achieved anything like perfection and is actually going to learn a number of serious lessons from some of the people she lives with.

* * * [T]he story no longer progresses toward her vindication or consolation; it consists in her gradual, humbling self-enlightenment. Emma's personality includes some of the tendencies and qualities that Jane Austen most disliked—self-complacency, for instance, malicious enjoyment in prying into embarrassing private affairs, snobbery, and a weakness for meddling in other people's lives. But now, instead of being attributed in exaggerated form of a character distanced into caricature, they occur in the subtle form given them by someone who in many ways had admirably fine standards. * * *

This attempt to suggest a slightly different emphasis in the reading of Jane Austen is not offered as a balanced appraisal of her work. It is deliberately lop-sided, neglecting the many points at which the established view seems adequate. I have tried to underline one or two features of her work that claim the sort of readers who sometimes miss her—those who would turn to her not for relief and escape but as a formidable ally against things and people which were to her, and still are, hateful.

EDMUND WILSON

A Long Talk about Jane Austen[†]

There have been several revolutions of taste during the last century and a quarter of English literature, and through them all perhaps only two reputations have never been affected by the shifts of fashion: Shakespeare's and Jane Austen's. * * * [Austen] has compelled the amazed admiration of writers of the most diverse kinds, and I should say that Jane Austen and Dickens rather queerly present themselves today as the only two English novelists (though not quite the only novelists in English) who belong in the very top rank with the great fiction writers of Russia and France. * * *

Emma * * * is with Jane Austen what Hamlet is with Shakespeare. It is the book of hers about which her readers are likely to disagree most; they tend either to praise it extravagantly or to find it dull, formless, and puzzling. The reason for this, I believe, is that, just as in the case of Hamlet, there is something outside the picture which is never made explicit in the story but which has to be recognized by the reader before it is possible for him to appreciate the book. Many women readers feel instinctively the psychological rightness of the behavior attributed to Emma, and they are the ones who admire the novel. Some male readers, like Justice Holmes,[1] who was certainly a connoisseur of fiction yet who wrote * * * that, "bar Miss Bates," he was "bored by Emma," never succeed in getting into the story because they cannot see what it is all about. Why does Emma take up her two protégées? Why does she become so much obsessed by her plans for them? Why does she mistake the realities so and go so ludicrously wrong about them? Why does it take her so unconscionably long to reach the obvious rapprochement with Knightley?

The answer is that Emma is not interested in men except in the paternal relation. Her actual father is a silly old woman: in their household it is Emma herself who, motherless as she is, assumes the functions of head of the family; it is she who takes the place of the parent and Mr. Woodhouse who becomes the child. It is Knightley who has checked and rebuked her, who has presided over her social development, and she accepts him as a substitute father; she

† From Classics and Commercials (New York: Farrar, Straus and Giroux, 1950) 196–203. Reprinted by permission.
1. Oliver Wendell Holmes (1841–1935), distinguished Supreme Court Justice [Editor].

finally marries him and brings him into her own household, where his role is to reinforce Mr. Woodhouse. * * * Emma, who was relatively indifferent to men, was inclined to infatuations with women; and what reason is there to believe that her marriage with Knightley would prevent her from going on as she had done before: from discovering a new young lady as appealing as Harriet Smith, dominating her personality and situating her in a dream-world of Emma's own in which Emma would be able to confer on her all kinds of imaginary benefits but which would have no connection whatever with her condition or her real possibilities? This would worry and exasperate Knightley and be hard for him to do anything about. He would be lucky if he did not find himself saddled, along with the other awkward features of the arrangement, with one of Emma's young protégées as an actual member of the household.

I do not mean to suggest for *Emma* any specific Freudian formula, but I feel sure that it is one of her novels in which the author's own peculiar "conditioning" is most curiously and clearly seen. Jane Austen spent all her life with persons related to her by blood—her parents, her five brothers, her single unmarried sister—and the experience behind the relationships imagined by her in her novels is always an experience of relationships of blood, of which that between sisters is certainly the most deeply felt. * * * For, though Miss Austen's intelligence was free to follow and understand other women when they were flirting or comfortably married, hunting husbands or breaking their hearts, she seems always to have been held suspended by the web of her original family ties. To some special equilibrium of the kind, which she never felt the necessity of upsetting, she must partly have owed the coolness, the patience, the leisure of mind to work at writing for its own sake, that made it possible for her to become a great artist. * * *

CRITICISM

MARILYN BUTLER

"Emma"†

* * * *Emma* is the greatest novel of the period because it puts to
fullest use the period's interest in articulate, sophisticated characters, whose every movement of thought finds its verbal equivalent
in a nuance of speech. The language of *Emma* is functional and
related to the form, to a degree not found elsewhere even in Jane
Austen.

The plot to which the language harmoniously relates is the classic
plot of the conservative novel. Essentially, a young protagonist is
poised at the outset of life, with two missions to perform: to survey
society, distinguishing the true values from the false; and, in the
light of this new knowledge of 'reality', to school what is selfish,
immature, or fallible in herself. Where a heroine is concerned rather
than a hero, the social range is inevitably narrower, though often the
personal moral lessons appear compensatingly more acute. Nevertheless the heroine's classic task, of choosing a husband, takes her
out of any unduly narrow or solipsistic concern with her own happiness. What she is about includes a criticism of what values her class
is to live by, the men as well as the women.

The novel with a fallible heroine by its nature places more
emphasis on the action than the novel with an exemplary heroine.
But *Emma* is an exceptionally active novel. The point is established
first of all in the character of the heroine: Emma is healthy, vigorous, almost aggressive. She is the real ruler of the household at
Hartfield—in her domestic ascendancy she is unique among Jane
Austen's heroines. She is also the only one who is the natural feminine leader of her whole community. Every other Austen leading
lady is socially neglected or discounted. * * * It is a misreading of
Emma's character to say that she grasps at power, for she neglects
rather than exploits her opportunities at Highbury. Jane Austen's
purpose in giving her an exceptionally unfettered social position is
rather to leave her free to act out her willful errors, for which she
must take entire moral responsibility. The masterstroke is to make
the apparent spring of the action not Emma's quest for a husband,
but Harriet's. Social taboos would have prevented any young woman
from taking so commanding a role in pursuing a man for herself.
But Emma is unhampered by propriety when she takes the initia-
tive in choosing a husband for Harriet.

† From Marilyn Butler, *Jane Austen and the War of Ideas* (Oxford: Clarendon, 1975) 250–
74. © Oxford University Press 1975. Reprinted by permission of Oxford University Press.
Footnotes are the author's except where followed by [*Editor*].

So energetic a program of action demands steady judgement in an inexperienced girl if it is not to lead to disaster. As a sober critic of events Emma is off to a bad start, largely because of her attitude to her mentors. * * * Her governess Miss Taylor is being translated into Mrs. Weston; and Miss Taylor, it seems, has always supplied the soft kind of friendship that is founded on sympathy, rather than the more strenuous and critical guidance that fosters the judgement:

> It had been a friend and companion such as few possessed, intelligent, well-informed, useful, gentle . . . and peculiarly interested, in herself, in every pleasure, every scheme of her's [sic];—one to whom she could speak every thought as it arose, and who had such an affection for her as could never find fault.

The replacement of Miss Taylor's companionship by Harriet Smith's is a step further in the wrong direction: 'she is a flatterer in all her ways.' Small wonder then that Emma, although happy to plan marriage for another, does not yet contemplate it for herself. At the personal level marriage would mean submitting to continued moral assessment by a mature man, who would fortify the stronger, more rational, objective, and stringent side of Emma's mind. She is much more attracted to her self-indulgent spinsterhood, which renders her unchallengeable because her supposed mentor, her father, submits to her as readily as Harriet does:

> 'I have none of the usual inducements of women to marry. . . . Fortune I do not want; employment I do not want; consequence I do not want; I believe few married women are half as much mistress of their husband's house, as I am of Hartfield; and never, never could I expect to be so truly beloved and important; so always first and always right in any man's eyes as I am in my father's.'

Emma's presumption in thinking to direct Mr. Elton and Harriet into matrimony * * * does considerable damage to herself and to society. It is also a rehearsal for the more serious main action to come.

In the second and longer part of the novel, Emma casts herself with her usual confidence in the role of judge; and Jane Austen underwrites that part, in the sense that she takes very seriously the correctness, or otherwise, of Emma's observations. It is her duty to assess the two strangers, or virtual strangers, who have just entered the Highbury circle, Frank Churchill and Jane Fairfax. Clear knowledge of proffered friends, and clear knowledge of the self, are, as always in Jane Austen's world, interdependent.

Emma's judicial role is carefully established by flanking her with two other characters who aspire to the judgement-seat. The deliberations of Mrs. Weston and Mr. Knightley are of special interest to the reader, since it is Emma herself whom they watch. Although they both love her and have known her since childhood, the tone of their observations about her is very different. Mr. Knightley is balanced, analytical. 'She will never submit to anything requiring industry and patience, and a subjection of the fancy to the understanding.' Mrs. Weston lets affection cancel out her memories of Emma's failings.

When, at the end of the first volume, Emma's serious test as a judge of events is about to begin, it is Mrs. Weston's indulgent example which influences her. The two of them are together reading the letter in which Frank Churchill announces his arrival, and apologizes for not coming sooner. Emma sees that his excuses are flimsy, while Mrs. Weston takes up the position of a moral relativist. 'One ought to use the same caution, perhaps, in judging of the conduct of any one individual of any one family; but Enscombe, I believe, certainly must not be judged by general rules.' Later, Emma, perversely taking up Mrs. Weston's arguments, puts the very same point to Mr. Knightley. 'Nobody, who has not been in the interior of a family, can say what the difficulties of any individual of that family may be. We ought to be acquainted with Enscombe, and with Mrs. Churchill's temper, before we can pretend to decide upon what her nephew can do.'

In the first part of *Mansfield Park*, Jane Austen had already tried out a heroine in the role of philosophic bystander. This time she uses the device very differently, for the 'philosopher's' pretensions are satirized, her very pose of detachment shown as a form of individualistic conceit. Emma adopts a position of compromise between the two other assessors, and, as so often with Jane Austen, the median position between the two poles of right and wrong is by no means the most morally admirable of the three. Emma's mind is potentially cool and tough, like Mr. Knightley's. For her to adopt the 'soft' position of the gentle Mrs. Weston is a sign of willful error.

Just as the reader has been watching Emma from the first, along with Mr. Knightley and Mrs. Weston, so he shares Emma's vigil in the second and third volumes over Frank and to a lesser extent Jane. Like Frank, Jane heralds her arrival with a letter, which Emma is invited to comment on; it is a sign of her unjudicial bias against Jane that she contrives to avoid reading it. Once the two characters have appeared Emma studies them, though her attitude to Jane remains careless and prejudiced. Because the reader shares Emma's consciousness, he too is placed in the position of observer, and his insights into the mysterious couple are fleeting and tenuous. The

narrative method of the second, longer part of *Emma* cleverly
emphasizes the heroine's distance from real understanding, for time
and again she misreads a puzzling detail in Frank's behaviour, or
overhears a fragment of conversation, or intercepts a glance that has
no real meaning for her. It is the motif of the second and third volumes that the two opaque new characters are submitted for inspection to the three 'wise' ones. But of the latter, both Mrs. Weston and
Emma are far too much influenced by their preconceptions for
steady judgement. Mrs. Weston hopes that Frank will marry Emma,
Emma believes that it is she who attracts him, and so both conceive
that Frank is walking to Hartfield when he is really engineering a
call on Jane. They are so blinded that they can watch Frank talking
to Jane, and discuss Mrs. Weston's speculation that there may be a
match between Jane and Mr. Knightley. Only Mr. Knightley himself
perceives that there is some prior understanding between the two
strangers. In the scene in which he watches Frank tease Jane by
making up the word 'Dixon', his careful, literal registering of each
piece of evidence compares with the many scenes in which Emma
has suppressed such facts, because they do not fit her favourite
schemes.[1]

From the beginning there is perversity and injustice in the manner in which Emma meets the challenge of Frank and Jane. Because
Emma fears critical, rational friendship, she tries to avoid evidence
that will be in Jane's favour, and substitutes instead her own more
hostile fantasies, notably the idea that Jane is in love with Mr.
Dixon. It is true that Jane gives real cause for affront by her seemingly excessive reserve when Emma questions her about Frank
Churchill, but Emma is far too eager to make that one instance a
reason for mutual antipathy—'Emma could not forgive her.' Her
over-reaction compares with Mr. Knightley's opinion of Jane. He
agrees that she is reserved, but makes a distinction between reserve
founded on diffidence, and reserve occasioned by discretion; and
he retains his faith throughout in Jane's fundamental integrity. He
proves justified at least in the sense that Jane's part in the decep-
tion practised on Highbury is less active than Frank's. She avoids
telling the full truth, but she does not tell lies, nor go out of her way
to mislead others.

Frank Churchill, much the more energetic sinner of the two
newcomers, is treated from the beginning by Emma with willful
indulgence. Although her previous, correct understanding was that
Frank should have come to Highbury when his father remarried,

---

1. This is the only moment of the novel in which the reader enters the consciousness of a
   character other than Emma. Jane Austen's purpose is clearly to offer Mr. Knightley's
   very different habits of assessment for comparison.

she is so interested in the idea of him that she readily shares the more justified partisanship of his stepmother. Before long, during his first visit, she is more than half in love with him. Her partiality persuades her to forgive his visit to London in order (as she thinks) to have his hair cut:

> 'I do not know whether it ought to be so, but certainly silly things do cease to be silly if they are done by sensible people in an impudent way. Wickedness is always wickedness, but folly is not always folly.—It depends upon the character of those who handle it. Mr. Knightley, he is *not* a trifling, silly young man.'

Emma notices that Frank is so determined to have the dance that he brushes aside the evidence of his tape-measure. It is the equivalent of her own kind of egotism, or self-will, or perverse subjectivity, and she easily forgives it. Her observations tell her that he is morally light, and her reason supports her observation. But the attention he pays her is flattering, and of course Emma all along has liked what is agreeable better than what is challenging. As time goes on, and she is more and more certain that she will refuse Frank, her flirtation with him takes on a worse moral colouring. Providing she is not in love with him, she sees that she preserves her autonomy, and perhaps the whip-hand over him as well. So, very gradually, she is led to the moral trap she falls into on Box Hill.

Here, as elsewhere in *Emma*, there is a discrepancy between words on the one hand, truth on the other, which affects not merely speech but also trains of thought. Emma's rudeness to Miss Bates follows a conversation in which she and Frank have flirted with outstanding insincerity:

> . . . Frank Churchill grew talkative and gay, making her his first object. Every distinguishing attention that could be paid, was paid to her. To amuse her, and be agreeable in her eyes, seemed all that he cared for—and Emma, glad to be enlivened, not sorry to be flattered, was gay and easy too, and gave him all the friendly encouragement, the admission to be gallant, which she had ever given in the first and most animating period of their acquaintance; but which now, in her own estimation, meant nothing, though in the judgment of most people looking on it must have had such an appearance as no English word but flirtation could very well describe. . . . Not that Emma was gay and thoughtless from any real felicity; it was rather because she felt less happy than she had expected. She laughed because she was disappointed; and though she liked him for his attentions, and thought them all, whether in friendship, admiration, or playfulness, extremely judicious, they were not winning back her heart. She still intended him for her friend.

It is clear to the reader—even the reader not yet in the secret of Frank's engagement to Jane—that he does not mean many of the compliments he pays to Emma. But her part in the flirtation is also a sham. She does not care for him, and is merely gratifying her vanity at a superficial level, using Frank to make herself the center of attention and to stimulate her vivacity and wit. Now, therefore, Emma is also lying. She has gradually laid by any claim to be a judicious bystander. But she cannot prevent others from playing the part. It is her turn again, as she becomes aware, to be the subject of critical assessment. ('"It is rather too much to be talking nonsense for the entertainment of seven silent people."' '"Is Miss Woodhouse sure she would like to hear what we are all thinking of?"') Her attempt at careless laughter shows that one part of her concedes that she is being false and self-indulgent. Nervous, uneasy, and yet intoxicated with vanity, she rides the inspiration of the moment and is clever at the expense of Miss Bates. 'Emma could not resist.'

Box Hill has also been Frank's moral nadir. At a first reading, when we do not know the full circumstances, we may find Frank guilty only of the same mild transgression as Emma—that of following his own gratification, amusing himself by pretending a depth of feeling for Emma which is not there. It emerges however that by flirting with Emma he has been inflicting intolerable pain upon Jane Fairfax, whom he really loves. On further examination Emma's fault also takes on another dimension. She is less guilty than Frank in relation to Jane, because, though she sees afterwards that she must have 'stabbed Jane Fairfax's peace in a thousand instances', at the time she is not aware of it. Yet Emma *does* believe Harriet to be in love with the man she is flirting with, and Harriet, no less than Jane, is one of the affronted bystanders. The hurt to Miss Bates is not therefore a single instance, for there is a pattern in the novel of vulnerable single women, whom it is the social duty of the strong and rich to protect. There is accordingly a continuous link between Emma's errors and Frank's, because both arise out of related attitudes to the self and to others. Afterwards Emma discerns that Frank complicated the machinery of his plot unnecessarily, and gave Jane additional pain, because he enjoyed his own cleverness while he was deceiving people. His plot became an elaborate, indulged fantasy. He denies Emma's shrewd account, but because she knows herself better now, she knows him too. His actions have been uglier than hers, and yet there has been a significant symmetry between them. To a degree that became hurtful to their friends, both have been imaginists.

The aftermath of the crisis at Box Hill, Emma's discovery that Frank and Jane are engaged, and that she loves Mr. Knightley, brings her back to the directness and truth she is capable of when her judgement is clear. Once more, as when Frank first arrived, a key conversation occurs between the two would-be moral arbiters Emma and Mrs. Weston, with Frank as their subject. Mrs. Weston wants to postpone judgement until the arrival of Frank's letter. 'It may bring many extenuations. It may make many things intelligible and excusable which now are not to be understood.' But Emma's immediate response, as so often with her, is forceful and true:

> 'It has sunk him, I cannot say how it has sunk him in my opinion. So unlike what a man should be!—None of that upright integrity, that strict adherence to truth and principle, that disdain of trick and littleness, which a man should display in every transaction of his life.'

Above all she puts her finger on the social nature of the crime, the way it necessarily distorted Frank's relations with everyone at Highbury—'What has it been but a system of hypocrisy and deceit—espionage, and treachery?' All forms of inwardness and secrecy tend to be anti-social. There is a moral obligation to live outside the self, in honest communication with others.

The corollary of such clear judgements about others, one forced upon her above all by the discovery of how mistaken she has been over Harriet, is a new humility about herself. At last she accepts the need for self-criticism. 'To understand, thoroughly understand her own heart, was the first endeavour.' Such a recognition implies (for the first time in Emma's consciousness) total scepticism about herself, admission that her processes have been irrational, obscure, delusory. It implies the rejection, in fact, of subjective mental processes in favour of objective; rejection of individual 'lights' in favour of the more reliable guides of external evidence and impartial reasoning.

None of these discoveries means that Emma is necessarily more 'right' in any single instance at the end of the book than she was at the beginning. Even after she is humbled, she continues to make mistakes. She believes, for example, that she loves her father too much to marry Mr. Knightley, even if he should ask her. While Knightley is actually proposing, she continues to think him in love with Harriet. Afterwards, in talking over Frank with Knightley, she shows signs of straying into her earlier relativism—the second time that Emma and Knightley have sat in judgement over a letter of Frank's, and the second time that Emma slides back from an earlier, clearer moral perception. She even insists comically that Knightley must be mistaken when he tells her that Harriet is already engaged to Robert Martin: '"You were both talking of other things; of business, shows of cattle, or new drills—and might not you, in the confusion of so many subjects, mistake him?—It was not Harriet's hand that he was certain of—it was the dimensions of some famous ox."'

If it is not necessary for Emma to be right in every instance after she has seen the error of her ways, nor, in Jane Austen's moral universe, is it necessary for Mr. Knightley. He admits, for example, that because he was jealous of Frank, he was prejudiced against him—'I was not quite impartial in my judgment, Emma.' Some critics have concluded that because he is occasionally prejudiced or mistaken, or because he sees the truth simply, Jane Austen means to qualify what has hitherto seemed to be a clear moral tendency of the book.[2] This line of criticism seems to be based on a misconception about Jane Austen's view of character, which is no more static than it is ideal. * * * In one of the finest pieces of Victorian criticism of Jane Austen, Richard Simpson describes how for her characters the moral life is a continuous process:

> She contemplates virtues, not as fixed quantities, or as definable qualities, but as continual struggles and conquests, as progressive states of mind, advancing by repulsing their contraries, or losing ground by being overcome. . . . A character therefore unfolded itself to her . . . as a dramatic sketch, a living history, a composite force, which could only exhibit what it was by exhibiting what it did.[3]

By the end of the action, and throughout when she is with Mr. Knightley, Emma has that capacity for penetration to the truth which is the real hallmark of Jane Austen's admired characters. Instead of investing one character throughout with right opinions, as the lesser anti-jacobins do, Jane Austen depicts even the best minds as continually fallible, under the pressure of new evidence, and potentially undermined from within by selfishness. Her only constants are abstract qualities—directness, honesty, sincerity, humility—the characteristics striven for by people who care about truth. She sees perfectibility as a condition of human life, but not perfection. The continuous effort necessary in her moral world is one of the few points at which she seems almost Godwinian.[4]

* * *

2. E.g., F. W. Bradbrook, *Jane Austen: Emma* (E. Arnold's Studies in English Literature, no. 3) London, 1961, p. 50. ° ° ° The identity of Mr. Knightley's views with JA's is challenged radically in J. F. Burrows, *Jane Austen's Emma*, Sydney Studies in Literature, Sydney, 1968, pp. 9ff.
3. Anonymous article, 'Jane Austen', *North British Review*, April 1870; ed. B. C. Southam, *Jane Austen: The Critical Heritage*, London, 1968, pp. 249–50.
4. That is: to say, committed to the idea that human beings are perfectible if they simply act according to reason [*Editor*].

The fact that the story is to be worked out on a peculiarly verbal level is established in the comic prologue to the action, the Elton episode, where Emma allows herself to be deceived against her own better judgement by an assumed style. Mr. Elton's sycophantic manner always grates on her. She knows that he must be flattering her when he praises her drawing; and whoever it is meant for, the poem which ascribes 'soft eye' and 'ready wit' to the same person is something less than meaningful. But she deliberately suppresses the ideas of truth and accuracy which are natural to her. Mr. Elton's docility leads her by a natural association to think of him in conjunction with the humble Harriet. '"It will be an Exactly so, as he says himself"', she thinks, falling into his habit of inaccuracy as she apes his phrase. In fact Mr. Elton's soft manner is one of the falsehoods he assumes for the purpose of courting Emma. Mr. Knightley, who knows him in other contexts, sees through the speeches to the hard motive beneath. '"Elton may talk sentimentally, but he will act rationally."'

Emma lives with the flattery she receives from her preferred companions and from her own easy conscience. She and the reader hear a very different tone, one which jars indeed in its abrupt, unequivocal rhythms, when at intervals she encounters Mr. Knightley for one of the brief conversations that sound a counterpoint throughout the novel. Sometimes with his habitual brevity he offers her fundamental, unpalatable truths. '"You have been no friend to Harriet Smith."' Emma catches his tone when she talks to him, and their dialogues together are quick, direct, amused, concerned, decisive, the rhythms of two mature people who accept the otherness of other people and know how to communicate with them. An example is their brief exchange on the snowy night at the Westons, which contrasts pleasingly with Mr. Elton's blandness and Mr. John Knightley's brutality:

> 'Your father will not be easy; why do not you go?'
> 'I am ready, if the others are.'
> 'Shall I ring the bell?'
> 'Yes, do.'

Direct authorial interventions in the narrative are relatively rare in *Emma*. Yet the language is morally unambiguous: one style is very much to be preferred to all the others. Emma's dialogues with Mr. Knightley stand in the same relation to her own interior monologues as Robert Martin's prose does to Mr. Elton's poetry. One is manly and direct, the other over-elaborate, devious, and unreliable. Once we have heard Mr. Knightley, and heard Emma in conversation with him, we know how to assess the indirections, equivocations, and back-trackings of her train of thought. Her first, truthful responses include the admission that Robert Martin's letter is good, and that Harriet shows bad taste when she prefers Mr. Elton's poetry. In every case Emma's self-will suppresses the conclusion her reason has just reached on the basis of the evidence. And the reader always knows when she is wrong, because the novel's other style has given him the unmistakable note of simplicity and sincerity.

In order to understand Emma's role in the novel, we have to recognize her natural affinity with the truth. It is only a temporary perversity that leads her astray, a fact suggested by her firm, strong tone when she talks to her natural equal, Mr. Knightley. Not for her—or, at least, not then—the moral failings of the other female characters with whom she is compared: the soft palliations of Mrs. Weston, the constraint of Jane Fairfax, the mindless, characterless indecision of Harriet. Although Jane Austen called Emma 'a heroine whom no one but myself will much like',[5] many readers have found her attractive: as attractive, indeed, as any heroine in fiction. In discussing Emma's charm, Lionel Trilling quotes Cardinal Newman's observation, 'she makes me want to be kind to her', and adds on his own account that we exist in a peculiarly intimate relationship with her, as with the fallible side of ourselves.[6] It is an extension of this position, and lately a popular one, that Emma's mistakes themselves are what make her lovable; that they represent an inspired, intuitive grasping after a higher truth than Knightley's; that Jane Austen, recognizing this, thereby qualifies the rigidities of her own ethical position. This, surely, is a misconception. Emma makes mistakes in the first instance because, like all other human beings, she is fallible. She also makes more than she need, because for much of the novel she underrates the need for objective self-criticism, and positively shuns the best method of achieving it, which is the submission of oneself and one's actions to the honest, searching criticism of a friend. The fact remains that within the conservative ethic to which Jane Austen adheres, Emma's is a character of real moral superiority, and precisely because of its underlying truth.

* * *

On the one hand the novel has to do with prolific, fanciful thinkers and talkers, from Emma at her worst, and Frank Churchill habitually, down to the lesser figures. Some talk to be wrongly understood; some talk and are not listened to. Opposed to all these characters, who exist largely in a medium of words, is a firmly rendered notion of reality, linked in the novel to one laconic character. Highbury village and its main street; the rich surrounding farmland dominated by Donwell Abbey; in both these social worlds Mr. Knightley is ubiqui-

5. J. E. Austen-Leigh, *Memoir of Jane Austen*, ed. R. W. Chapman, Oxford, 1926, p. 157.
6. Lionel Trilling, 'Emma', *Encounter*, 49 (June 1957) 54–5.

tous, although he is seen in the novel much more continuously than he is heard. In the middle distance he is everywhere—conferring with Mr. Elton about parish affairs, or with Robert Martin about farming; detected sending apples to Miss Bates, or asking for her errands when he rides to Kingston. Highbury gatherings are not complete without him; unlike Emma, he is always present when the Coles or Eltons entertain. Compared with his active involvement in the community, Emma's conception of herself as first lady is a kind of figment of the mind. Although hers is an old and wealthy family, the Woodhouses' money has nothing to do with Highbury: they own very little land there. Emma may be mindful—at intervals, that is—of the duties of the rich towards the poor. She is also capable of flirting indiscriminatingly with the fashionable stranger, the innovator: Frank Churchill, individual, naturally motivated, and nevertheless the latest in the long anti-jacobin descent of charming, hypocritical seducers who enter a secluded community from a corrupt wider world. Emma is vulnerable, and one reason is that her stake in Highbury is not deep. Her very claim to social precedence is so precarious, while she remains a spinster, that she is superseded by Mrs. Elton. When she marries Mr. Knightley her rank will be secured, and she will become involved in the land by sharing in its ownership. The land, too, will have a wholeness it never had before, since Hartfield was 'but a sort of notch in the Donwell Abbey estate, to which all the rest of Highbury belonged'. At the end of the novel Emma is about to assume a clearly defined and permanent role in the community, and what is left outside has been touched with the insubstantiality which Burke gives to the people and ideas that will not belong.

There is thus a second element of contrast in the novel: not merely the difference between those who talk fallaciously, insincerely, or without communicating, and those who in Jane Austen's terms talk well; but between characters who merely talk, and the near-silent Mr. Knightley. It is even more than this, for Mr. Knightley has a wholly silent *alter ego*. The goal of all Emma's deluded endeavours, of so much self-deception, presumption, and specious inward argument—a husband for Harriet—is found at last in a character who is never heard to speak at all. Robert Martin acts, and simply is, with the solidity that comes from well-defined involvement with a physical world, and in the light of that reality the world of thought in the novel is as flimsy as Frank Churchill's pretended dream.

The final irony is that this most verbal of novels at last pronounces words themselves to be suspect. It has been called the first and one of the greatest of psychological novels. If so, it resembles no other, for its attitude to the workings of Emma's consciousness is steadily critical. Although so much of the action takes place in the inner life, the theme of the novel is scepticism about the qualities that make it up—intuition, imagination, original insight. * * * Emma matures by submitting her imaginings to common sense, and to the evidence. Her intelligence is certainly not seen as a fault, but her failure to question it is. The technical triumph is to employ the character-centred format, to place the action almost wholly within the hero-ine's consciousness, to enlist (as in the subjective tradition) the reader's sympathy; and at the same time, largely through the medium of language, to invoke the reader's active suspicion of unaided thought. Easily the most brilliant novel of the period, and one of the most brilliant of all English novels, it masters the subjective insights which help to make the nineteenth-century novel what it is, and denies them validity.

JAN S. FERGUS

Sex and Social Life in Jane Austen's Novels[†]

The definitive twentieth-century opinion of sexuality in Jane Aus-ten's novels was uttered at one of Gertrude Stein's parties in Mont-parnasse: '"You are talking of Jane Austen and sex, gentlemen?" said a tweedy Englishman with a long ginger moustache. "The subjects are mutually exclusive."'[1] The subjects exclude one another, how-ever, only when 'sex' is narrowly defined as explicit, exhaustive detail about what people do and feel in bed. Austen's own understanding of sexuality is much less narrow. She is interested in dramatising sex in everyday social life—in the drawing room rather than the bed-room. The courtship plots she creates allow her to explore the rela-tions between sex and moral judgement, sex and friendship, sex and knowledge—that is, between sex and character. In this sense, there is no escaping sexuality in Austen's novels. It is always present, treated with a variety and freedom that most modern readers over-look and that the novels of most of her contemporaries were unable, for various reasons, to achieve.

Austen's contemporaries were constrained both as readers and as writers of didactic domestic fiction by their own social context: by literary and social conventions that established very elaborate codes of behaviour for relations between the sexes. These conventions do not constrain Austen in the same way. Similarly, readers who share the tweedy Englishman's opinion are limited by a modern social

† From *Jane Austen in a Social Context*, ed. David Monaghan (Houndmills: Palgrave Macmillan, 1981), 66–85. © 1981 Palgrave Macmillan. Reprinted by permission.
1. John Glassco, *Memoirs of Montparnasse*, selections rpt *Gertrude Stein: A Composite Portrait*, ed. Linda Simon (New York: Avon, 1974), p. 174.

context: by conventions which define sex as sexual intercourse and dictate explicitness. These notions have prevailed long enough to provoke a reaction. Recent works by critics like Michel Foucault and George Steiner convey a sense of fatigue with sexual explicitness itself.[2] To different ends, both Foucault and Steiner are prepared to insist that sexuality may be more freely and powerfully expressed privately and tacitly than explicitly. Perhaps the shift in sensibility these writers may be anticipating, if it does occur, will make Austen's own broader vision of sexuality more accessible. But even Steiner, who identifies the 'sexual turbulence' Austen conveys below the surface of polite conversation, underestimates the extent and depth of her rendering of sexuality; he concludes that in Austen's novels sex is a 'limited terrain', confined by a 'necessarily public'[3] idiom. On the contrary: the very publicity of sex in Austen's novels—the constant awareness, the relentless dramatisation—is what makes her examination of it in social life so extensive and powerful.

A thorough study of Austen's treatment of sex in social life would have to address and answer several questions. What were some of the literary and social conventions governing sexuality during the time Austen composed her novels? What relations did these literary and social conventions have to one another and to documented sexual attitudes or sexual behaviour during this period? And finally, how does Austen render sexuality, and how does her treatment compare to the sexual conventions, attitudes and behaviour of her time. Although the first of these questions can be readily answered, the second is highly problematic. Human behaviour is, after all, frequently at odds with the codes or conventions that are supposed to govern it. Private sexual behaviour, and even private sexual attitudes, are notoriously likely to diverge from publicly proclaimed norms and are, for this reason, rarely documented and very hard to establish.[4] The best sources are private journals and letters, but even these are unsatisfactory: they are scarce and unrepresentative, for usually only those of aristocratic, political or literary figures

2. See Foucault, *The History of Sexuality*, Vol. 1, trans. Robert Hurley (New York: Pantheon, 1978), and Steiner, 'Eros and Idiom', in *On Difficulty and Other Essays* (New York: Oxford University Press, 1978), pp. 95–136.
3. Steiner, pp. 97, 131.
4. Lawrence Stone's *The Family, Sex, and Marriage in England 1500–1800* (New York: Harper and Row, 1977) is the most provocative recent work to document actual sexual behaviour during Austen's lifetime. But his work has only limited application to a study of sex in Austen's novels, for he does not really focus on courtship. The findings that do bear on courtship—e.g. that 'among the squirarchy, the median age at first marriage coincided with the median age at inheritance' (51)—cast only doubtful light on the novels. Do we conclude, for example, because the fathers of Austen's heroes have usually died, leaving Willoughby, Darcy, Bingley, Crawford, Mr Knightley and Captain Wentworth free to choose wives without parental opposition, that Austen has a sure grasp of the social world that Stone is describing or that she is merely attached to a convenient eighteenth-century plot convention?

survive; and these journals and letters are often uncandid or cen-
sored—by friends, by nineteenth-century editors, or by the author
himself. Sources which publicly proclaim ideal sexual conduct are,
on the other hand, endless, and the accepted norms themselves
remarkably stable, from the mid-eighteenth through the nineteenth
century. Courtship, however, because it is the one publicly approved
form of sexuality, is fully documented by both public and private
sources during this period. Courtship is also the focus of didactic
novelists and of Austen herself.

Publicity is not merely sanctioned in courtship but required. A
secret engagement like that between Frank Churchill and Jane Fairfax in *Emma* is felt to be reprehensible because it defies or mocks
'the world'; properly, Highbury should be aware of their relation
and Enscombe should endorse it. All available eighteenth-century
records—journals, letters, sermons, conduct books, essays and
novels—insist that every possible stage of courtship must be reached
in full view of the public eye. These stages—initial attraction, flirtation, infatuation and love—develop within a social world and are
subject to intense social scrutiny. Moreover, the public eye is readily
offended by any deviation from the various courtship conventions
which operate, to some extent, both in life and in literature; at least,
so we are told in conduct books written by a clergyman like Thomas
Gisborne or by moralists like Hester Chapone, Hannah More and
Jane West, in the didactic novels of writers like Samuel Richardson,
Fanny Burney, Maria Edgeworth and Elizabeth Inchbald, and even
in some contemporary journals and letters. Such moralists make it
their business to articulate the conduct appropriate to every stage of
courtship, often by taking a grim and detailed view of misconduct.
Only by contrast with their frequently absurd attitudes toward attraction, flirtation, infatuation and love can the freedom, wit and good
sense of Austen's treatment be fully appreciated.

Initial attraction between the sexes is a subject of many warnings,
for example, in conduct books addressed to young women. Love at
first sight is particularly reprobated. The likely consequence—a marriage based on 'mere personal liking, without the requisite foundation of esteem, without the sanction of parental approbation'—can
produce only 'misery and shame', as Mrs Chapone, among others,
affirms.[5] But oddly enough, despite the dazzling beauty enjoyed by
nearly all heroes and heroines, surprisingly little attention is paid in
didactic novels to the attractive power of good looks, upon women at

---

5. Hester Chapone, *Letters on the Improvement of the Mind* (1772; rpt with Dr John
    Gregory's *A Father's Legacy to his Daughters*, 1774 [London: Suttaby, Evance and Fox,
    1820]), *Letter* (5, p. 60). These two works were frequently reprinted together. Dr
    Gregory's section in this edition, pp. 141–80, will hereafter be cited as *Legacy*.

any rate. A reference to 'person' is conspicuously absent when a character in Edgeworth's *Patronage*, Rosamund Percy, praises Colonel Hungerford as having 'Temper, manners, talents, character, fortune, family, fame, every thing the heart of woman can desire.'[6] And indeed, most heroines scrupulously attribute their interest in a hero to his estimable qualities, not to his personal charms. Amusingly enough, male novelists are rather more prepared to permit their heroines, the 'angelic' Sophia Western and Clarissa Harlowe among them, to respond to male beauty—but never without the illusion, at least, that other virtues attend it. And although in all his novels Richardson attests the attractive power of 'person', he invariably regards it as inferior to the attractions of 'mind'. The moral turn typically given by Richardson and his contemporaries to the subject of initial attraction is especially emphatic in Anna Howe's lament to Clarissa that 'our likings and dislikings, as I have often thought, are seldom governed by prudence or with a view to happiness. The eye, my dear, the wicked eye has such a strict alliance with the heart, and both have such enmity to the understanding!'[7]

Although the conduct books only rarely warn young women against the seducing effects of good looks in men, such works continually put them on their guard against the seducing effect of their own charms on themselves, that is, against the 'consciousness of being distinguished by personal attractions'.[8] This consciousness makes women particularly susceptible to the elaborate compliments of flirtation, known also as gallantry, coquetry and polite raillery. Although women are adjured in the strongest terms not to coquet, much more frequent are exhortations to close their ears to compliments. Gisborne, for example, blames them for encouraging men to 'intoxicate the head, and beguile the heart, by every mode and every extravagance of compliment'.[9] A woman's vanity is always seen as her weakest, most vulnerable point. Hannah More, citing '*vanity, selfishness*, and *inconsideration*, that triple alliance in strict and constant league against female virtue', is severest against vanity. It is the most insidious and incurable of vices: it is 'diffused through the whole being, alive in every part, awakened and communicated by the slightest touch', and 'those persons know little of the conformation of the human, and especially of the female heart, who fancy that vanity is ever exhausted' by anything other than a

6. *Patronage*, 4 vols (London; J. Johnson, 1814), Vol. 11, p. 122.
7. *Clarissa or, the History of a Young Lady*, intro. John Butt, Everyman's Library, 4 vols (1932; rpt London: Dent, 1968), Vol. 11, pp. 116–17.
8. Thomas Gisborne, *An Enquiry into the Duties of the Female Sex* (London: T. Cadell, 1797), p. 36.
9. Gisborne, p. 102.

properly rigorous education.[1] In conduct books and novels, then, vanity is the likeliest source of a woman's misconduct or undoing; all Richardson's heroines are betrayed in some way by their vanity. This extreme vulnerability prompts Dr Gregory to conclude that 'Male coquetry is much more inexcusable than female, as well as more pernicious', but he adds with comfortable Podsnappery, 'it is rare in this country'.[2]

＊　＊　＊

In *Emma*, sex is less threatening but equally pervasive. The sexuality of Emma and particularly of Mr Knightley has often been denied. He is thought too stuffy, she too father-fond (to use Lovelace's term) for sexuality to flourish. But only wilful misreading can ignore the sheer vitality of both characters or can overlook passages like Mr Knightley's early description of Emma, full of open and unconscious sexual response: he praises Emma's looks, saying 'I have seldom seen a face or figure more pleasing to me than her's' and then, much more powerfully, 'I love to look at her'. Sexuality is as fluid in *Emma* as are Harriet's infatuations. An awareness of sexual energy is forced on the reader in nearly every page by Mr Knightley's jealousy, Emma's jealousy, Jane Fairfax's jealousy, Emma's delight in matching wills with Mr Knightley, her sexual game with Frank Churchill, and his with her and Jane. This sexual energy is channelled into social forms but not contained by them, and during the famous climactic scene at Box Hill all the teased, frustrated sexuality of the various characters explodes at last. Emma's much-cited insult to Miss Bates is buried in far more obviously ugly interaction, notably Frank Churchill's declaration to Emma that when he returns from abroad, 'I shall come to you for my wife'. This flirtatious remark is designed to torment Jane Fairfax, but torments Mr Knightley with equal success; both take it as serious courtship of Emma while Emma detects a 'commission' to groom Harriet for the post.

Hereafter, of course, the novel moves quickly from frustration and misjudgement to satisfaction in every sense. Every page of Austen's novels is charged with emotional, moral and social as well as sexual conflicts, and all are resolved in the end. What distinguishes Austen's treatment of sex in social life distinguishes all her concerns equally: she gives us resolutions in which sexuality is as tested and satisfied as is morality or any other aspect of character. Between major characters, the mentor relation, sexual antagonism,

1. *Strictures on the Modern System of Female Education* (1809), Ch. 2, rpt *The Works of Hannah More*, 2 vols (New York: Harper, 1835), Vol. 1, pp. 322, 323.
2. *Legacy*, p. 171.

flirtation and infatuation give way to or even lead to full knowledge and intimacy between equals. Though separate sexual roles are certainly adopted by Austen's married couples, her conclusions tend to disregard (without denying) the social conventions that make wives submissive to husbands. Instead, the endings celebrate an equality as complete as differences between the characters themselves allow. A witness to and model for this equality is the compromise that resolves *Emma*: out of respect for the conditions of Emma's life, Mr Knightley gives up his own home to live at Hartfield.

The social roles and activities Austen explores are the modes of sexuality in daily life, and they pervade the emotional, moral and intellectual lives of Austen's characters perhaps even more than they do our own; in this sense, her novels may have too much sex rather than too little. Austen's rendering of everyday sexuality takes for granted in ways unthinkable to her contemporaries and often ignored by moderns that every relationship can carry a sexual charge. Sexual response and excitement are, in Austen's novels, so much a part of ordinary social life that in significant ways social intercourse is sexual intercourse. By dramatising the interplay of character and sex in ordinary life, then, Austen gives us the unavoidable and complicated sex of our social lives, seen with a persuasiveness and wit that ought not to surprise us, knowing Austen, and with a relentlessness that does not surprise us, if we do know her.

MARY POOVEY

The True English Style[†]

In Jane Austen's society—and in her novels in a slightly different way—romantic love provided one of the very few opportunities for a woman to exercise fantasies of autonomy and power. In that brief interval between marriageability and marriage, a woman was empowered as never before; not only could she wield her mighty "negative" but she could also enjoy the attentions of a man—or men—intent upon impressing her. It is the unspoken "after" of this formula that made it a paradox and pushed it toward contradiction. For when a woman married, she was subsumed into the representative of her husband, losing her legal existence, her right to own property, even her responsibility for crime. This contradiction between imagined autonomy and legal negation is the contradiction that romantic love denies and the marriage plot suspends. And even

† From an address delivered to the Jane Austen Society in Philadelphia on October 8, 1983, printed in *Persuasions* 5 (16 December 1983): 48–51. Reprinted by permission.

though it does not appear in this precise form in *Emma*, I want to argue that this paradox—and the contradiction it foreshadows—constitutes the ideological tension the novel is trying to manage and the terms in which plot complications are engendered and resolved. Let me explain a little more fully what I mean.

Emma Woodhouse is sure from the very beginning of the novel that she will not marry, for she is perfectly aware that she does not lack the validation and power that other women seek through marriage. "I believe few married women are half as much mistress of their husband's houses as I am of Hartfield," she tells Harriet, "and never, never could I expect to be so truly beloved and important; so always first and always right in any man's eyes as I am in my father's." Emma sees with uncommon clarity the limitations marriage places upon women, and throughout the early part of the novel—even though she is obsessed with plotting romantic attachments for others—she is intent upon protecting herself from any emotional engagement that might lead to marriage vows. What Emma does not recognize is the extent to which she is already ensnared by the attractions of romantic love. Jane Austen uses this powerful attraction and Emma's blindness to entice her heroine to accept her "natural" place as a woman just like any other; she uses, in other words, the vanity associated with romantic love to distract Emma from the dependence that will come with marriage and that she is already defended against.

This ideological pattern is most sharply focused in the Box Hill episode, for in this scene Jane Austen separates vanity and dependence from the theme of love and marriage and then links them to each other as parts of a more general ethical pattern. Emma's vanity, of course, is immediately alluded to and soon gratified. Her initial disappointment with Frank—that he "listened without knowing what she said"—disappears when he begins to speak for the benefit of the assembled company. "Frank Churchill grew talkative and gay, making her his first object. Every distinguishing attention that could be paid, was paid to her." Neither Emma nor the reader is aware that Frank's behaviour is part of his troubled romance with Jane Fairfax. For Emma, this mock flirtation is explicitly *not* linked to romantic feelings: his attentions "were not winning back her heart." Because love seems safely distant, Emma is particularly unguarded. When Frank taunts the company, ostensibly on her behalf, to say whatever they are thinking, he is actually inviting his friends to indulge another version of the vanity permitted by romantic love. Only Emma is rash enough to take up his challenge. Even though he changes his command to a solicitation for "something very entertaining," Emma responds to his first invitation: her sharp jibe at Miss Bates expresses exactly what she thinks about the unfortunate old maid.

Emma's self-indulgence at this moment reproduces the indulgence she experienced as a child, when she enjoyed in Miss Taylor "one to whom she could speak every thought as it arose, and who had such an affection for her as could never find fault." The vanity Frank invites reawakens the "original narcissism" of his auditors, for implicit in his challenge is the opportunity to imagine, for just a moment, that every thought is as precious to one's listeners as to oneself, that one is, in short, the centre of a nonjudgmental little universe. Frank and his father continue to reinforce Emma's egotism when Mr. Weston makes a conundrum linking "perfection" to her name, and Frank asks her jokingly to find and form a wife for him. "And make her like myself," Emma complacently adds.

But the rest of Emma's companions are not so ready to accede to her "presiding," and when Mr. Knightley chides her for her "insolence," he makes explicit what is at stake in such indulgences of wit. Significantly, his argument turns on the issue of dependence and it appeals to the responsibilities that accrue to Emma's social position. "Were she your equal in situation," Mr. Knightley tells Emma, "I would not quarrel with you for any liberties of manner. . . . but, Emma, consider how far this is from being the case. She is poor; she has sunk from the comforts she was born to; and if she lives to old age must probably sink more. . . . You, who she had known from an infant, whom she had seen grow up from a period when her notice was an honour—to have you now, in thoughtless spirits, and the pride of the moment, laugh at her, humble her—and before her niece too—and before others, many of whom (certainly some) would be entirely guided by your treatment of her." Mr. Knightley reminds Emma not only of her current place in the social hierarchy but also of that moment when the notice of any adult—even Miss Bates—was an "honour" for a child. This reminder undercuts the egotism of the child's view of things, and in positioning Emma twice in relation to others—first as chronological inferior, then as social superior—Mr. Knightley points to the implicit connection between responsibility and dependence. Because some are dependent (whether as children or as the unprotected poor), others must assume responsibility; to assume responsibility is to voluntarily limit one's childlike desires, to think of others before or in relation to oneself.

We know Mr. Knightley is right. More important, Emma knows it. She is "forcibly struck" by his criticism, "agitated, mortified, grieved"—and, significantly, speechless. When Emma acknowledges that Mr. Knightley is right to identify her joke as vanity, and when she voluntarily accepts responsibility for someone else's dependence, she prepares herself to curb her egotism and to accept her dependence upon someone else. The way is then open for other revelations, which culminate in the exposure of her feelings about Mr. Knightley: "It darted through her, with the speed of an arrow, that Mr. Knightley must marry no one but herself!" The fact that accepting responsibility for a superior social position may not be exactly the same as accepting someone else's authority over you remains unexamined in this novel. Nor does it have to be examined, for Jane Austen still has in reserve the reward that makes dependence tolerable—the fulfilment promised by romantic love.

When Emma initially tells Harriet that she will not marry, she adds one important qualification. "Were I to fall in love," she says, "indeed, it would be a different thing." But, as we have seen, Emma has confidently believed herself immune to love. "I never have been in love," she says; "it is not my way, or my nature; and I do not think I ever shall." Love is always the unaccountable, indefinable, but undeniable qualification, theoretically capable of dismissing the "dangers of dependency" that Emma fears in marriage. But it is crucial for the preservation of this qualification—and the aesthetic resolution that it brings about—that genuine romantic love and all its complications remain offstage for most of the novel. This is true for at least two reasons. In the first place, the passion between Jane and Frank contains all the disruptive elements that Jane Austen is at pains to control. Their desire for each other defies class distinctions, social decorum, parental approval; it is an alliance formed in secret and operating subversively; it gives the lie to the illusion of class stability and the importance of thinking of others' comfort before one thinks of oneself. And in the second place, the romance between Frank and Jane reveals that, despite the promises of autonomy and power implicit in romantic love, it actually entails vulnerabilities as painful as any marriage may institutionalize. Given the strength of Jane's love for Frank and the weakness of her social position, she suffers more than we will ever know. The unspoken pain and desperation that just barely surface at Box Hill betray the genuine wounds that the "arrow" that gives Emma just a twinge can actually inflict.

To introduce these, complexities would imperil the resolution achieved by segmenting romantic love into its component issues. In *Emma*, Jane Austen simply does not focus on this mysterious and powerful desire. The wishes of Frank and Jane don't conflict with anyone else's desires, and because the novel's conclusion arranges the characters in their proper social places, there is no need to examine the way that personal desire can conflict with social order. Instead, romantic love remains unproblematic, uncompromised. Emma has remained blind to herself for so long that the recognition that she loves Mr. Knightley—accompanied, as it is, with the momentarily terrifying possibility that his affections might not be fixed—contains all the drama one could reasonably ask of love. Moreover, ending the novel, as Jane Austen does, with the wedding ceremony of Mr. Knightley and Emma suspends whatever questions we might have about Emma's ability to enjoy her new dependence. The last sentence of the novel has the effect of robbing the future of its potential for change, for its temporal stasis freezes the Knightleys' marriage in an eternal repetition of their current "perfect happiness." Here is the sentence: "In spite of these deficiencies, the wishes, the hopes, the confidence, the predictions of the small band of true friends who witnessed the ceremony, were fully answered in the perfect happiness of the union."

What I'm suggesting, then, is that *Emma* at least implicitly leaves more questions unanswered than we are accustomed to think it does. The problems about love and marriage, vanity and dependence, that inhere in the subplot and are raised in all kinds of peripheral ways are not really resolved. Given the contradictions implicit in the discrepancy between what the ideology of romantic love promised and the actual inequality marriage in this society entailed, resolution was in fact impossible. In order to preserve the ideology and the social order of which it is one anchor, Jane Austen displaces this unresolvable contradiction, separates and transforms its inherent issues, and resolves them for the purposes of her art within an ethical schema that we can all accept. This involves, of course, the substitution of an aesthetic resolution for a genuine social solution, but the fact that it both flatters our sense of our superior perception and gratifies our wish that no contradiction exists between love and marriage makes us as readers perfectly happy to overlook unanswered questions. We, like Emma, long to be "always first and always right." We, like Jane Austen, long for a world in which "perfect happiness" automatically aligns the personal desires of both men and women with society's moral imperatives.

Implicit in this reading of *Emma* is a theoretical model about the relationship of novels to the societies in which they are written, and perhaps if I make my assumptions clearer you'll be more inclined to grant that issues that are not explicitly dramatized can nevertheless be important to the dynamics of narrative. I am suggesting that narratives, like myths, are attempts to manage tensions and contradictions that are a part of the author's lived experience in society. Narratives, in other words, are symbolic actions. In the sense that they are only symbolic, they cannot really change social institutions; but in the sense that they are actions they can comment on society and on the desires that underwrite our willingness to accept even imperfect solutions. In the subtle aesthetic maneuvers necessary to transform and resolve actual social contradictions we as readers can identify the magnitude of the problems that continue to haunt our world. In our utopian desire for resolution we can feel both the force that can be harnessed for change and the powerful inertia we must overcome in order to change. My comment that Jane Austen does not resolve the contradiction between the promises of romance and the realities of marriage is not a criticism of her insight or her narrative skill. It is an observation about the way things were in her society for women and about how one crucial contradiction provided both vital complications for fictional plots and debilitating complications for actual women.

PATRICIA MEYER SPACKS

The Talent of Ready Utterance[†]

*   *   *

Jane Austen's *Emma*, dealing with village existence, evokes a society without a "world." The people who talk about one another in Highbury all have faces; reactions from neighbors and friends respond promptly to social deviation. The knowing narrator of the novel, who understands the kinds of restriction implicit in a tiny, intimate society, helps to locate the missing term in her heroine's experience, calling attention to the limitations of Emma's consciousness as well as of her society.

The relation between gossip as social prohibition and as narrative resource becomes explicit here: *Emma* articulates a grammar of gossip. Slightly past the mid-point of the novel, Mr. Knightley explains an important truth to Emma and Mrs. Weston. "Another thing must be taken into consideration too," he observes—"Mrs. Elton does not talk *to* Miss Fairfax as she speaks *of* her. We all know the difference between the pronouns he or she and thou, the plainest-spoken amongst us."[1] The entire novel glosses that difference, and elucidates the further distinction of the first-person pronoun from the others. When Emma violates decorum by talking *to* Miss Bates as she might have spoken *of* her—as a dullard—she prepares the way for a sequence of insights which ends by establishing her in a new relation to the first-person pronoun.

People talk a great deal about other people during *Emma*, for one main reason: to alleviate or forestall boredom. The lack of occupation to which some moralists had attributed the female propensity to gossip afflicts male and female characters alike. Only the male Knightleys partially escape, John working as a lawyer in London

---

† From *Gossip* by Patricia Meyer Spacks, copyright © 1985 by Patricia Meyer Spacks. Used by permission of Alfred A. Knopf, a division of Random House, Inc. and the author.
1. *Emma, The Novels of Jane Austen*, ed. R. W. Chapman, 3rd ed. (Oxford: Oxford University Press, 1933), 4.286.

and unable to comprehend the Highbury delight in trivial conversation, and George busy about his estate, willing to gossip with the others but less dependent on gossip as a resource. Unlike Austen's other novels, this one dwells on its own sense of confinement. "Imaginist" though she is, Emma faces a real, not an imaginary, problem in the lack of possibility her community affords. No new people: hence the sensational impact of Frank Churchill. No new things to do or see: hence the momentousness of an expedition to Box Hill or even to Donwell. Emma can play backgammon with her father, she can visit the few familiar people who surround her, she can shop for gloves or ribbons, do needlework or read or practice her music. Repeatedly the text emphasizes Highbury's limitations. At the very beginning, we learn that Emma, "with all her advantages, natural and domestic, . . . was now in great danger of suffering from intellectual solitude." Like everyone around her, she yearns for "news." "Oh! yes, I always like news." The only news available, the only kind relevant to her concerns, involves people she knows or those associated with them. Her impoverished world supplies little else in the way of delight. Walking to the door of a shop while Harriet vacillates over muslins, she seeks

> amusement.—Much could not be hoped from the traffic of even the busiest part of Highbury;—Mr Perry walking hastily by, Mr William Cox letting himself in at the office door, Mr Cole's carriage horses returning from exercise, or a stray letterboy on an obstinate mule, were the liveliest objects she could presume to expect; and when her eyes fell only on the butcher with his tray, a tidy old woman travelling homewards from shop with her full basket, two curs quarrelling over a dirty bone, and a string of dawdling children round the baker's little bow-window eyeing the gingerbread, she knew she had no reason to complain, and was amused enough; quite enough still to stand at the door. A mind lively and at ease can do with seeing nothing, and can see nothing that does not answer.

"A mind lively and at ease." The phrase appears to come from Emma's consciousness; her self-congratulation may recall dreadful Mrs. Elton's talk of her "resources." The liveliness and ease of Emma's mind get her into trouble, as her imagination goes to work on limited raw materials to create gossip which produces false expectations and pain for others. The "he" and "she" who inhabit Emma's imagination belong to the realm of fiction. She constructs shapely plots, domestic romances, about the unmarried; and when she figures as an actress in her own fictions, one begins to understand her difficulty with the first-person pronoun.

From some points of view, Emma seems all too completely at ease with what Virginia Woolf calls the vertical pronoun. Accustomed to rule in her small domain, suffering only the "real evils" of possessing "the power of having rather too much her own way, and a disposition to think a little too well of herself," unchastened by fears of the world, Emma functions insistently as an "I." Yet her version of "I" bears a troubling similarity to her notion of "he" and "she." She sees herself too, repeatedly, as a fictional character, imagining the audience that the village cannot adequately supply. Her entire relationship with Frank Churchill derives from and depends on her capacity to perceive herself from the point of view of admiring spectator. When she and Frank first dance together, "she found herself well-matched in a partner. They were a couple worth looking at." Dwelling as she does on the idea of being looked at, she neglects to recognize what she feels, thinking, rather, of what she might, or should, feel. When Frank reappears, after an absence from Highbury, she concludes that she has not, after all, really fallen in love with him. She gives him, however, "friendly encouragement, . . . which now, in her own estimation, meant nothing, though in the judgment of most people looking on it must have had such an appearance as no English word but flirtation could very well describe. 'Mr Frank Churchill and Miss Woodhouse flirted together excessively.' They were laying themselves open to that very phrase—and to having it sent off in a letter to Maple Grove by one lady, to Ireland by another." This preoccupation with what might be said about her, with, in fact, the gossip she may generate by her self-presentation as well as by her imagination—this preoccupation helps to make possible her thoughtless insult of Miss Bates. She has become so involved in her immediate social role, in her fantasy of being perceived as powerful, witty, and attractive, that she has lost awareness of others' feelings.

Harriet Smith, for all her stupidity and indecisiveness, parodies Emma. She too keeps constructing fictions round herself, less imaginative fictions than Emma specializes in, but constructions in the same genre. She too has trouble knowing her own emotions and accurately assessing other people's. Her failure to function as a full center of consciousness stems from intellectual inadequacy, Emma's, from more complicated sources; but both alike fall into gossip's trap of objectification. Gossip deprives other people of reality; it ends, the novel implies, by doing the same to the self.

Harriet's fictions, of course, in the neat structure of *Austen's* fiction, bring an end to Emma's. When it darts through Emma with the speed of an arrow that Mr. Knightley must marry no one but herself, she moves rapidly from self-dramatization to self-knowledge, toward the marriage that will chasten the excesses of her imagination. She starts now to concentrate on her feelings rather than her performance: to know herself as "I" rather than "she."

Gossip has provided not only an obstacle to the happy ending but a means toward fruition. In the penultimate chapter, Knightley offers Emma a brief account of how the engagement between Harriet Smith and Robert Martin finally came to pass. "This is all that I can relate," he concludes, "of the how, where, and when. Your friend Harriet will make a much longer history when you see her.—She will give you all the minute particulars, which only woman's language can make interesting.—In our communications we deal only in the great." Despite the ironic overtones of Knightley's commentary, he speaks literal truth: woman's language *can* make the trivial and mundane interesting, it can create histories of its own, and it differs from man's language, although men may also employ it. The history Austen has spun out of the daily experience of Highbury precisely demonstrates the point.

Homer Brown has observed, "Traditionally, two of the ways the novel has had of at once disguising and validating itself have been as letters and as gossip. . . . It is probable that part of the pleasure we derive from the classic novel is a pleasure similar to that derived from gossip."[2] Gossip's hermeneutic power generates the internal dynamic of *Emma*: we see its heroine interpreting minute particulars of her own and other people's experience; her acts of interpretation create the plot. Emma exists so completely as an "insider" that "outside" has virtually no existence for her. Her tiny society enables her to function with utter authority; no amount of experience convinces her of her final incapacity to know the meanings of other people's actions within that confined setting. Knightley's condemnation of her rudeness to Miss Bates also derives from the insider's position. In Highbury, one cannot judge people—as, elsewhere, the world does—on the basis of their social performances: one knows too much. Emma should have remembered Miss Bates's history, her personality, her emotional and economic situation. To operate always from inside carries its own penalties—not least of them Emma's inability to distinguish among the pronouns. Her self-objectification declares her yearning for an audience that *will* assess her performance, instead of one for which her performance merges with her history. She yearns, in other words, for a version of that world so threatening to Evelina and other novelistic heroines: the world that would, paradoxically, make her feel more real by fictionizing her.

Gossip carries particularly complex meanings in *Emma* because of the reader's implication in its patterns. The novel consistently invites us too to participate in acts of interpretation. Revealing again and again Emma's interpretive mistakes, giving us the grounds to judge them and her, it may lure us into believing ourselves more competent

2. Homer Brown, "The Errant Letter and the Whispering Gallery," *Genre* 10 (1997): 574–75.

than she to understand particularities. Guided by the knowing narrator, we can feel ourselves *super*-insiders. The text offers many particularities to understand. When Emma calls on Jane Fairfax shortly after the delivery of her new pianoforte, a gift which, Emma has decided, must come from Mr. Dixon, Jane does not at once sit down at the instrument. "That she was not immediately ready, Emma did suspect to arise from the state of her nerves"; and Emma of course believes herself to understand the proximate cause of nervous tension. The reader possesses the same data as Emma. If we have become, by this point in the novel, wary of Emma's hasty explanations, we face the problem of providing our own. Like a detective novel, the book keeps offering raw material for interpretation, the raw material of gossip, and requiring us to do something with it. The "correct" interpretation for many previous events emerges finally, in the revelation of the secret engagement between Frank and Jane. At this point, we must assess the quality of our own interpretations, realize the degree to which we, as readers, have participated in the making of the fiction—and realize, perhaps, that such participation belongs to a continuum with Highbury's endless speculation. Instead of the pleasure of reading other people's letters, we have been offered the gratifications of complicity—only to have our satisfaction in it repeatedly undermined. Women or not, we have been lured into acting like the women of moralistic stereotypes: lured into rewards and betrayals of speculative gossip. We do not talk out loud, of course; but our inner voices ask gossip's questions, make its judgments.

As usual, Austen provides a conservative text and a challenging sub-text. Emma will presumably settle down and behave herself and stop interpreting so wildly; Harriet will stop interpreting at all. The "longer history" of her engagement that Harriet might provide would surely prove tedious in the extreme. Highbury's gossip substitutes for meaningful life; the village's confinement limits growth and pleasure. Although Knightley jokes when he asserts that men "deal only in the great," his superiority to those around him indeed derives partly from his consistent stress on moral rather than merely social judgment. All these facts argue for a view of the novel as supporting values embodied in the moral commentary cited earlier: trivial and malicious talk reflects impoverished minds as well as experience, male talk about ideas communicates more meaning and value than female talk about people; by extension, the male realm provides the standard by which females can judge themselves and know themselves wanting. On the other hand, the vitality of *Emma* as a fiction, like that of Emma as a character, depends on insatiable interest in personality and its individual manifestations. The reader who has found herself or himself amused, entertained, and impressed by the vagaries of Emma's imagination, by her will to make interest where little obvious stuff of interest exists—such a reader must feel the loss involved in Emma's settling down under Mr. Knightley's exemplary tutelage. Emma has kept herself alive while all around decayed, kept herself alive with the energies of gossip. The novel has lured the reader into direct knowledge of the same energies. Talking of "he" and "she" must not substitute for knowing the self as "I" or for valuing the sensibilities of others as "you." On the other hand, the exercise of imagining "he" and "she" and dwelling on the possibilities of their experience enlivens the mind. And recognition of that fact implies at least temporary acceptance of a set of values and assumptions associated with the female and opposed to the usefulness of dealing only in the great. Fully accepting the standards of "society," *Emma* yet declares the need to evade them.

In both *Evelina* and *Emma*, female gossip—literal gossip in the later novel, its written counterpart in the earlier one—functions as a language of feeling, as a mode of personal development, as an evasion of external restriction. Indeed, it becomes a means of discovering selfhood, of declaring the self an expressive, judging consciousness. As a sub-text for the major line of narrative, it supports the imaginative and improvisational, valuing the private, implying the saving energies of female curiosity and female volubility, celebrating the possibility and the importance of a narrative of trivia. It exemplifies the subversive resources of the novel as genre. The official criticism of gossip derives from and depends on a realm of public value; it assumes the dominance of "society" as standard and sanction. Novels too declare the importance of society, but they value the individual. Inasmuch as eighteenth-century fiction delineated and defended the private, it often implicitly defended also what public moralists attacked. In fiction if not in didactic texts, the "talent of ready utterance" found its supporters: supporters who managed successfully to uphold the values of a women's sub-society even while articulating those of traditional social conformity. Fiction reveals more clearly what didactic texts only hint: that gossip, "female talk," provides a mode of power, of undermining public rigidities and asserting private integrity, of discovering means of agency for women, those private citizens deprived of public function. It provides also often the substance and the means of narrative.

412

TONY TANNER

The Match-Maker[†]

* * *

What is a girl with all the spirit, energy and wit—not to mention the privileges—of an Emma actually to do? Mr Knightley's sombre, juridical voice makes the point which poses the problem: 'She will never submit to any thing requiring industry and patience, and a subjection of the fancy to the understanding.' Emma is a clever but 'spoiled' girl and, having lacked external authority (both from her father and from her governess) when she was young, she has not internalised any authority which can direct and control her as she grows into a young woman. She says rightly—if 'playfully'—that she is a 'fanciful, troublesome creature'. She also regards herself as a very 'independent' person, though, as Mr Knightley says with uncharacteristic cryptic incompleteness but a very English use of aposiopesis, 'when it comes to the question of dependence or independence!' Emma will have both to complete that 'question' and answer it, but it will take her a long time. Marriage would seem to be the obvious answer to this problem of occupation, but for a long time she rejects that as a possibility. There is nobody suitable for her, as is pointed out by the one man whom *we* can see is the only possibility for her, but whom Emma misreads as she misreads practically everyone and everything else—particularly herself: 'there is nobody hereabouts to attach her; and she goes so seldom from home'. (Not only has she never seen the sea, she has not even seen the nearby Box Hill—we must realise that, with all her powers and privileges, Emma moves in a very constricted circle.) We are told that 'she had always wanted to do everything'— but in truth it must be recognised that by certain standards of achievement she can in fact do almost nothing. It is Harriet who, in all innocence and guileless directness, raises the problem when Emma has once again told her of her intention never to marry.

> 'Dear me! but what shall you do? how shall you employ yourself when you grow old?'
> 'If I know myself, Harriet, mine is an active, busy mind, with a great many independent resources; and I do not perceive why I should be more in want of employment at forty or fifty than one-and-twenty. Woman's usual occupations of eye and hand and mind will be as open to me then as they are now; or with

† From "The Match-Maker," in *Jane Austen* by Tony Tanner, pp. 186–89, Cambridge, Mass.: Harvard University Press, copyright © 1986 by Tony Tanner. Reprinted by permission of Harvard University Press and Palgrave Macmillan.

no important variation. If I draw less, I shall read more; if I give up music, I shall take to carpet-work.'

We have a fairly clear idea by now just how much reading, or carpet-work, Emma will do—at any age—and Harriet's crucial question remains totally evaded, if covered with a litany of confident but empty protestations. How will she employ herself—not only when she grows old, but tomorrow and tomorrow and tomorrow? John Knightley asks the question of the novel when he says, 'I wonder what will become of her.'

If Emma's occupation is not with books and carpets—not to mention those people in the classes below her—what is it? In a word it is in her imagination, or, rather, her imagination *is* her occupation. ('Fancy' and 'imagination' are here used fairly interchangeably and I cannot see that any Coleridgean distinction is intended.) A comment made by Emma as she—as usual, quite wrongly—imagines what Mr Elton is doing with her (characteristically) distorted portrait of Harriet, passing it round his family and planning a future with Harriet (how such an idea is to annoy Mr Elton!), applies more pertinently to herself: 'How cheerful, how animated, how suspicious, how busy their imaginations all are!' The main, and one might say generating, animated, suspicious busy imagination in the book is Emma's. Emma often makes a resolve to herself to 'repress imagination', but, as with her resolutions to give up match-making, the resolve is usually no sooner made than it is broken. You do not make the imagination unemployed as easily as she might think. She has, for instance, only to hear the barest fragments of information concerning the relationships obtaining between Jane Fairfax, the Campbells and the Dixons to put together in her mind the outlines of some slightly, but significantly, erotic—indeed adulterous—plot: 'At this moment, an ingenious and animating suspicion entering Emma's brain. . . .' Similar statements occur throughout the novel, and in this case we may note that the important word is 'animating'. Because what on earth—or, rather, what in Hartfield and Highbury—is going to 'animate' Emma, with her constantly brimming high spirits, if not the scenarios, indeed the fantasies, of her own brain? We can see her tolerably egoistical imagination at work in her relationship with Frank Churchill; we are told of 'the distinguished honour which her imagination had given him: the honour, if not of being really in love with her, of being at least very near it, and saved only by her own indifference'. This, we say at least, is not the description of a young lady in love—in any kind of love, unless it is with herself and her imagination. If we take a short sentence such as the following from chapter 46—'Her fancy was very active'—we can realise just where, for Emma, the action *is*. And it is not in Hartfield. Her playing, plying, ploying with the nobody—nothing, Harriet Smith, is just exactly a projection of her active 'fancy', her busy 'imagination'. Her occupation is principally concerned with tending a father who is the negative of a proper father, and tending her fantasies, which, because she is so curiously lonely (Highbury and Hartfield 'afforded her no equals'), encounter more collusions than obstacles. There is very little either in her upbringing or in her environment (apart from the solemn sageness of Mr Knightley) to prepare Emma for an unavoidable and significant encounter with the reality principle—or, things as they *are*.

Emma is 'perfection', 'faultless in spite of her faults', and many more enchanting things besides. But she is also, underneath the rank and money, a curiously displaced person, a centre without a circle, a figure-force of perpetual restlessness. In fact, although Emma is the centre of the novel, neither Hartfield nor she are actually at the centre of Highbury: 'Highbury the large and populous village almost amounting to a town, to which Hartfield, in spite of its separate lawn and shrubberies and name, did really belong, afforded her no equal. The Woodhouses were first in consequence there.' As Hartfield is slightly off-centre and separate topographically (and nominally)—literally just detectably ec-centric—so Emma is both 'first in consequence' and oddly out of social 'sequence'. She knows what is fitting but she herself doesn't quite 'fit'. She is at once an outsider and insider when it comes to Highbury (which means 'society' in this novel). And in fact, whereas in previous novels the potential threat to the given social order tends to come from outside (though not beneath, in class terms), it is in fact Emma herself, the central ec-centric, who is the potentially most disruptive figure in the society of this novel. She is the danger from within—if, that is, society itself is not beginning to seem like the danger from without. Perhaps the centre cannot hold because it is no longer worth holding. Certainly, things as they are being so unstimulating, narrow, repetitious, insufferably boring (evenings with her father, mornings with Miss Bates), Emma is a very active fantasist. From this fact springs many of the problems and fluttering (or boorish) misunderstandings in the novel. But from this fact also springs the novel itself.

*   *   *

CLAUDIA L. JOHNSON

Emma: "Woman, lovely woman reigns alone"[†]

There was a time, and not too long ago, when Austen was considered to be above—or was it really below?—the anxieties of authorship. For Richard Simpson, as for many of Austen's Victorian admirers, it was necessary to presume an "unconsciousness of [Austen's] artistic merits" in order to regard her, in his own words, as "dear Aunt Jane," a kindly spinster who never minded being interrupted while at work because her "powers were a secret to herself," and who was gratefully surprised to earn even the little money she did because she rated her own abilities too low to expect acknowledgment.[1] Encouraged by members of Austen's own family, who in the "Biographical Notice" and the *Memoir* protest with obtrusive defensiveness that Austen put her family before her art, such views have survived well into our own century. Taking particular care to "redeem" Austen from "any possible suspicion of superiority or conceit," R. Brimley Johnson asserts that Austen's "taste was strong against any parade of authorship, and her affection would have accused herself of both conceit and selfishness, had she required privacy for work, or allowed herself to be so absorbed as to neglect any social or domestic duty." R. W. Chapman later affirmed that "the sweetest reward of her labours" was nothing more ambitions or independent than "to have pleased her family." And as late as 1957, in the biographical sketch prefixed to his widely available edition of *Emma,* Trilling's stress on Austen's commitment to a charmed family circle assures us that Austen never upset the parlor or the dining room with overweening authorial preoccupations as unladylike as they are egotistical.[2]

For our current recognition of Austen's artistic self-consciousness we have to thank, not the discovery of any new information, but rather a disposition to pay attention to what has always been before us. Austen's account of the profits generated by her novels, for example, is now acknowledged to indicate an interest in matters as vulgar as commercial success. Her somewhat testy preface to *Northanger Abbey* is now permitted to betray lingering mortification at the refusal of Crosby & Co. to print this, her first formally submitted novel, and to convey a wish that readers properly consider

† From *Jane Austen: Women, Politics, and the Novel* (Chicago: U of Chicago P, 1988) 121–43. Reprinted by permission of the University of Chicago Press.
1. In B. C. Southam, *Jane Austen: The Critical Heritage* (London: Routledge and Kegan Paul, 1968), pp. 263, 265.
2. R. Brimley Johnson, *Jane Austen* (London: Sheed and Ward, 1927), p. 74.

the historical provenance of her work. And of course the remarks scattered throughout the letters and her collection of opinions about *Mansfield Park* and *Emma* plainly attest to an intense curiosity about responses to her novels outside the family circle. To all appearances, she deemed no opinion about her novels too stupid or malapropos to copy out and preserve for future reference.

Austen's concern about the fate of her novels with the public was deeply felt and often manifested itself in decidedly personal attitudes towards her heroines, about whose popularity with the public she was a good judge. Elizabeth Bennet, she was certain, was so delightful a creature that if readers did not like her, it was no fault of her own. But with Emma, Austen knew she was taking a risk. Authorial solicitude on her behalf, however, has proved a mixed blessing. Her statement "I am going to take a heroine whom no-one but myself will much like" has been treated more as an invitation to search out what is objectionable about Emma than as a calculated challenge to the judgments of her audience, for the criticism of Emma is freighted with alarming animosities.[3] Concerning this Austenian heroine, more than any other, commentary conspicuously gives the lie to the naive assumption that literary criticism is the business of disinterested professionals whose discussions evolve from ideologically neutral historical, aesthetic, or merely commonsensical criteria. If Austen enters the canon because she seemed to deny or devalue her authority, Emma has been the heroine critics have loved to scold precisely because it never occurs to her to apologize for the control she takes over the destinies of others. Because Emma is often charged with the same transgressions—being "arrogant, self-important, and controlling" or "narcissistic and perfectionist"—from which critics diligently attempted to exempt Austen, it is worth considering them at some length.[4] The absolution of one and the arraignment—sometimes indulgent and sometimes not—of the other alike derive from a profound discomfort with female authority, and female authority itself is the subject of *Emma*.

Determining the common denominator in much *Emma* criticism requires no particular cleverness. Emma offends the sexual sensibilities of many of her critics. Transparently misogynist, sometimes even homophobic, subtexts often bob to the surface of the criticism about her. Even those critics who do not specifically address the subject of gender employ loaded oppositions about moral and social values, supposedly endorsed by the author herself, which imply a sexual hierarchy reified in marriage. For example, A. Duckworth's conten-

3. J. E. Austen-Leigh, *A Memoir of Jane Austen* (London, 1870), p. 157.
4. Bernard Paris, *Character and Conflict in Jane Austen's Novels: A Psychological Approach* (Detroit: Wayne State University Press, 1978), pp. 69, 73.

tion that "Emma in the end chooses society rather than self, an inherited order rather than a spontaneous and improvised existence," implicitly opposes and prefers the orderly, patriarchal, rational, masculine, and, above all, right to the disorderly, subjectivist, imaginative, feminine, and self-evidently wrong.[5] In much *Emma* criticism, however, psychosexual concepts are not merely implicit. To many of this novel's most distinguished critics, Emma's want of feminine softness and compliancy is her most salient and most grievous shortcoming. Mudrick's assertion that Emma is a "confirmed exploiter" is an erotic complaint disguised as a moral one. His "Emma has no tenderness" really means that she is not sexually submissive to and contingent upon men: hers is "a dominating and uncommitting personality." Curiously enough, though, because he does not notice his own assumption of a masculine monopoly on desirable qualities, Mudrick inadvertently justifies Emma's dereliction from "femininity." If Mr. Woodhouse "is really" that most contemptible of creatures, "an old woman," we can hardly wonder that his daughter opts for the emotional detachment and the penchant for managing that could place her beyond such scorn. But though Mudrick complains that Emma "plays God," what he really means is that she plays man, and he, as well as others, will not permit her thus to elude the contempt that is woman's portion, do what she may. Wilson, who alludes ominously to Emma's "infatuations with women," and Mudrick himself, who darkly hints about her preference of "the company of women" whom "she can master and direct," treat Emma's "coldness" as though it were a culpably perverse refusal of their own sexual advances. To critics at a loss to account for how Emma could like Harriet more than she likes Mr. Elton, what other than an unacceptable attachment to women could possibly account for a failure to be impressed with and "humanly" committed to men.[6]

Readers who have not cared to ponder Emma's sexuality have still entangled her in unexamined and curiously revealing attitudes which are, if anything, more pernicious in their linkage of sex and politics. Blowing the whistle on readers who doubt that marriage will cure Emma, Wayne Booth, for example, declares with the preemptive dogmatism peculiar to outraged decency, "Marriage to an intelligent, amiable, good, and attractive man is the best thing that can happen to this heroine, and the readers who do not experience it as such are, I am convinced, far from knowing what Jane Austen

5. Alistair Duckworth, *Improvement of the Estate* (Baltimore: The Johns Hopkins Univ. Press, 1971), p. 148.
6. Marvin Mudrick, *Jane Austen: Irony as Defense and Discovery* (Princeton: Princeton University Press, 1952), pp. 181–206; Edmund Wilson, "A Long Talk About Jane Austen," *New Yorker* 20 (24 June 1944), p. 69.

is about."[7] Never implying that this highstrung young lady really needs a good man, Trilling argues that Emma's objectionable behavior derives from a sexual peculiarity more subversive than a mere passing disinterest in marriage: "The extraordinary thing about Emma," he claims, "is that she has a moral life as a man has a moral life." Emma's anomalous status as a moral agent is owing entirely to her self-love, a sentiment which in turn derives from "the first of virtues, the most basic and biological of the virtues, that of self-preservation." Untroubled by the Darwinian premise that nature, in the guise of biology, has in depriving women of the survival instinct, de facto barred them from the moral life, Trilling, it is true, does not chide Emma for her manly trespasses. But this is only because they are so reassuringly uncalculated and exceptional as to deserve his curiosity and his indulgence. Trilling also appeals to "the biological nature of moral fact" in his essay on *The Bostonians*, after all, and in that novel challenges to male hegemony that are based on *principle* meet with a very different response.[8]

In the animadversions of even the most sympathetic of Emma's critics, then, the political import of sexual difference is clearly exposed, for what they present as pertaining to female nature really pertains to female rule. Emma assumes her own entitlement to independence and power—power not only over her own destiny, but, what is harder to tolerate, power over the destinies of others—and in so doing she poaches on what is felt to be male turf. The royal dedication of *Emma* is often cited to account for the patriotism of its outbursts about English verdure, English reticence, and English social structure. But if it is appropriate to speak of *Emma* as a patriotic novel—and I believe it is—then it must be acknowledged that its patriotism is of a very unusual sort. Austen privately expressed hesitations about the Prince Regent in strong terms, and she inscribed the dedication to him only after realizing she had no choice.[9] When we recall further that Austen disapproved of His Royal Highness specifically because of his notorious infidelity to his wife, the inscription of a novel predominated by female power can conceivably look more like an act of quiet cheek than of humble submission. In stunning contrast with *Mansfield Park*, where husbands dominate their

7. Wayne C. Booth, *The Rhetoric of Fiction* (Chicago: University of Chicago Press, 1961), p. 260.
8. Lionel Trilling, "Introduction" to *Emma* (Boston: Houghton Mifflin, 1957), p. x; *The Opposing Self* (New York: Viking, 1955), p. 116. Such attitudes cannot be dismissed as the crudeness of a bygone era, for a tacit belief that for women, at least, biology is destiny still underpins recent criticism about *Emma*. P. J. M. Scott, for example, insists that "Miss Woodhouse"—as she is repeatedly called—is "frightened of the wedded state": see Scott, *Jane Austen: A Reassessment* (New York: Barnes and Noble, 1982), p. 64.
9. *Jane Austen's Letters to Her Sister Cassandra and Others*, ed. R. W. Chapman (London: 2nd ed., 1952), p. 504 (16 February 1813); F. B. Pinion, *A Jane Austen Companion* (New York: St. Martin's Press, rev. ed. 1976), p. 21.

households with as little judiciousness as decency, in *Emma* woman *does* reign alone. Indeed, with the exception of Knightley, all of the people in control are women: Mrs. Churchill's whims as well as her aches and pains are felt, discussed, and respected miles away from her sofa; at least some, if not all, people in the neighborhood accept Mrs. Elton's ministrations as "Lady Patroness"; and Emma's consciousness that she is considered "first" in consequence at Highbury may peeve her critics, but it does not faze her neighbors, and no one—least of all Mr. Knightley—questions her right to preeminence.

In its willingness to explore positive versions of female power, *Emma* itself is an experimental production of authorial independence unlike any of Austen's other novels. * * * The texture of *Emma* is remarkably spare. There is a hue and cry about an "infamous fraud upon the rights of men and women". But the crime in question is a conspiracy to deprive them of their dinner, not their dignity as autonomous agents. Austen does not allude to the tradition of political fiction as regularly in *Emma* as she does elsewhere, but such relative silence does not signify an abandonment of the political tradition. In fact, the case is quite the opposite. At the height of her powers, Austen steps into her own authority in *Emma*, and she participates in the political tradition of fiction, not by qualifying or critiquing it from within, but rather by trying to write from its outsides. *Emma* is assuredly unlike the anarchistic and egalitarian novels of Godwin, Holcroft, and Wollstonecraft in fundamentally accepting English class structure, and in being able to discriminate positive authority figures. Emma is frequently brought to task for her "snobbism." But if she offends democratic sympathies when she declares that "a farmer can need none of my help, and is therefore in one sense as much above my notice as in every other he is below it", she is merely describing with unwonted bluntness a mode of social organization which the most attractive of Austen's heroes—Darcy, for one—thrive on and honor without raising our dander. Knightley himself opposes Emma's plans to match Harriet with Mr. Elton, certainly not because Harriet should make up her own mind, but rather because, though "men of sense" and "men of family" will rightly scorn to marry her, she is good enough for a farmer such as Robert Martin.

But at the same time, *Emma* is a world apart from conservative fiction in accepting a hierarchical social structure not because it is a sacred dictate of patriarchy—*Mansfield Park* had spoiled this— but rather because within its parameters class can actually supersede sex. Thus *Emma* recuperates a world Austen savages in novels such as *Mansfield Park* and *Northanger Abbey*, in order to explore what was precluded in those novels, the place such a world can afford to women with authority. Though it may favor male rule, the social system sustained in *Emma* recognizes the propriety of female rule as well, and it is to this system that Emma, in the absence of any social superiors, owes her preeminence. * * *

Emma's self-assurance—"I always deserve the best treatment, because I never put up with any other"—is thus doubly unnerving because it exceeds the purely personal and is reinforced by a social privilege which commands a respect easier to extend to a man of Sir Thomas's stature than to a woman of Lady Catherine's, let alone Emma's. Furthermore, because we tend to read Austen's novels much as Mary Bennet would, as dramas of moral correction— where Marianne is properly punished for impetuosity, Elizabeth for her prejudice (and so on)—Emma's power is generally presented as the problem she must overcome. In no novel are Austen's methods particularly instructional, but *Emma* most conspicuously lacks the clarity of emphasis and the conclusory arguments that mark didactic fiction, omissions that have in fact disturbed many readers. One recent critic has vigorously complained that Emma's humiliation is too brief and too private, and that she is never vigorously "punished" for her wrongdoing; and many readers have been troubled that Emma shows no sign of "reform" by the end of the novel. The leisurely eddying of *Emma*'s pace, combined with the insistent ordinariness—not to say vapidity—of so much of its material, makes strident moralizing sound a bit strained.[1] As a result, the identification and assessment of the faults which are supposed to make humiliation and reform necessary have a hyperbolic ring to them. When one critic lists among Emma's reprehensible "mortifications" of others' feelings her curt refusal of Mr. Elton's inebriated proposal, one feels this is scraping the bottom of the barrel indeed.[2] Since the steady absorption of feminist perspectives into the corpus of Austenian criticism, the incommensurateness of action and reaction has been noted, and some readers, who presumably cannot understand why Mr. Elton's feelings are deemed worthier of indulgence than Emma's—have ventured to confess that they could never figure out exactly what Emma did to merit so much indignation in the first place.

What indeed? Austen anticipates the question as early as the fifth chapter, when Knightley and Mrs. Weston debate the wisdom of Emma's rule with the maturity and candor of opposition that mark so many of the disagreements in this novel. Emma has long been the subject of their quarrels, and Knightley has long been accustomed to monitor Emma with ready reproof. True to form, he warns that Emma's association with Harriet is "a bad thing". But

---

1. Scott, *Reassessment*, pp. 67–68.
2. Stuart M. Tave, *Some Words of Jane Austen* (Chicago: University of Chicago Press 1973), p. 246. I am much indebted to Tave's now classic study which so illuminates the distinctive features of Austen's language.

though they proceed from an anxiety for improvement that we can appreciate only later, even the very worst of Knightley's criticisms turn out to be fretfully minute: Emma, he complains, has never finished her reading lists; she has not applied her talents steadily; no one has ever gotten the better of her precocity; her new young friend will harm Emma by flattering her vanity, and Emma in turn will harm her by swelling her silly head. Mrs. Weston does not share Knightley's dire predictions about Emma's projects, because she considers her judgment worth relying on: "where Emma errs once, she is in the right a hundred times". Here is no blind dependence on the infallibility of Emma's authority, but instead a confidence in its basic soundness: "She has qualities which may be trusted; she will never lead any one really wrong; she will make no lasting blunder."

Emma amply corroborates Mrs. Weston's faith in the fitness of Emma's rule, but often so tactfully as to be almost imperceptible. This tact, however, is necessary first of all because Emma's best actions are of the sort which she, unlike Mrs. Elton, disdains to trumpet. A few strokes of the pen, for example, show that in her attentions to the poor and afflicted of her parish, Emma is intelligent, generous, compassionate, and—whatever she is in her studies—steady. Further, although Knightley thinks her "rather negligent" in contributing to the "stock" of Miss Bates's "scanty comforts", Emma's "own heart" ranks visits there an obligation. She is not shown to fuss over sending that hind-quarter of pork to the Bateses—though her father would mull and send less—and when she does explain to Knightley that respect for her father's peace prevents her from making her carriage of use to her neighbors, he smiles with conviction. Because she nowhere styles herself "Lady Patroness," we can only assume that Emma considers the performance of untold acts of kindness a duty attached to her social position requiring no announcement or praise.

Considering the contrast between Emma and Mrs. Elton can enable us to distinguish the use of social position from the abuse of it, a proper sense of office from a repulsive officiousness; and in the process it offers a glimpse of the conservative model of social control working well. The principle of difference between the two women and their rules is not finally reducible to class. What makes Mrs. Elton intolerable is not that she is new money and Emma is old, and that Mrs. Elton thus only pretends to prerogatives of status Emma comes by honestly. Mrs. Elton's exertions of leadership set our teeth on edge because of their insistent publicity, not because of their intrinsic fraudulence. Emma may be convinced that in attending their party she "must have delighted the Coles—worthy people, who deserved to be made happy!" but she keeps the satisfactions of condescension to herself. But by tirelessly asserting her centrality in the minds of others, Mrs. Elton bullies her auditors into frustrated acquiescence: "Nobody can think less of dress in general than I do—but upon such an occasion as this, when everybody's eyes are so much upon me, and in compliment to the Westons—who I have no doubt are giving this ball chiefly to do me honour—I would not wish to be inferior to others." Determined to advertise her sagacity, Mrs. Elton furthermore has a vested interest in airing what places others at a disadvantage, uncannily seizing on painful features of others' lives, and forcing them to the center of attention: "I perfectly understand your situation, however, Miss Woodhouse— (looking towards Mr. Woodhouse)—Your father's state of health must be a great drawback." But Emma has ready stores of "politeness" which enable her to respect what is delicate by leaving it unsaid. She feels gratified when Jane Fairfax divulges the hardships of living at home; but she exclaims "Such a home, indeed! such an aunt!" only to herself.

More than nicety is at issue here. Just as the impoliteness Lady Catherine and Darcy evinced towards others in persistently apprising them of their inferiority constituted a socially significant wrong, a theft of the self-satisfaction to which all are entitled, so do Mrs. Elton's bruited exertions of authority triumph improperly in the dejection of others—as when she, intervening as friend as well as patron, hastens Jane's assignment as a governess, or just as bad, when she colludes with her husband to humiliate Harriet publicly for her upstart pretensions. At her worst, Emma transgresses in much the same way when she mocks Miss Bates at Box Hill, or when she discloses her suspicions about Jane Fairfax to Frank Churchill. Shameful though these infractions are, they stand out precisely because they are so infrequent, and if Mrs. Elton's presence on the scene helps us to identify and to deplore them, it also helps appreciate how much better Emma handles herself by comparison. Generally Emma is, if anything, admirably forbearing: she endures page after page of "quiet prosings" and often vexing developments without letting slip the slightest impatience, and she brooks Mrs. Elton's presumption without so much as a sarcasm or protest. Unlike Mrs. Elton, Emma has a proper regard for public opinion that—with a few very important exceptions—restrains her impulse to abuse. Feelings of "pride or propriety" make Emma "resolve on not being the last to pay her respects" to the new bride, and when her neighbors celebrate Mrs. Elton's attractions, Emma lets the praise pass "from one mouth to another as it ought to do, unimpeded" by her own dissent. Because Emma does not wish to be "exposed to odious suspicions, and imagined capable of pitiful resentment," she behaves even more politely than she is inclined, while Mrs. Elton degenerates into the blatancy of incivility. The neighborhood that did not exist in *Mansfield Park* is everywhere in *Emma*. Emma herself defers to its civilizing restraints and in the process shows conservative ideology working at its best. * * * But Emma is an authority figure responsive to the morally corrective influence of public opinion. This is what makes her feel the truth of Knightley's reproach at Box Hill, and this is what makes her resolute, swift, and feeling in her amends.[3]

Emma is so remarkable a novel at least in part for its ability to include what is politely left unsaid. The excellence of Emma's rule is often disclosed tactfully, because if it were vaunted brusquely à la Mrs. Elton, it would show her father at too great a disadvantage. Mr. Woodhouse's two-fold hostility to disruption and indigestion so unfits him for the duties incumbent upon the head of a respected household that Emma is often obliged to ignore or to oppose him quietly for decency's sake, and in the process she displays powers of delicacy and forbearance which are the more impressive given the vivacity of her own temper and the incisiveness of her wit. When a most unpatricianlike selfishness on Mr. Woodhouse's part would exclude even as old and indispensable a friend as Mr. Knightley from dinner, Emma's "sense of right" interferes to procure him the proper invitation. Similarly, while Mr. Woodhouse's anxiety for the health of others compels him to take food away from the guests at his table, Emma takes the duties of "patriarchal hospitality" upon her own shoulders without stinting: she "allowed her father to talk—but supplied her visitors in a much more satisfactory style." Thus the narrative style of *Emma* shows, but does not call attention to, the courtesy with which Emma manages the household around her. Her diplomacy is characteristically inobtrusive, as when she steers hypochondrical companions away from topics, such as the insalubriousness of sea air, likely to occasion disputes not the less rancorous for their manifest pettiness; or when she intercedes to separate warring conversants, as when John Knightley indulges in one of his many eruptions of peevishness against Mr. Woodhouse himself.

This kind of superintendence is one of the prerogatives of rule, and it comes . . . spontaneously to Emma. * * * Progressives and reactionaries fought their ideological battles in the arenas of family and neighborhood, and the whos, whys, and why-nots of matchmaking were not the idle concerns of meddlesome women with nothing better to do. In Austen's fiction the making and prohibiting of matches preoccupies country squires * * * as much as it does well-meaning gossips * * *; and in this context, Mr. Woodhouse's opposition to marriage—"he lamented that young people would be in such

---

3. For a complementary discussion of the ethical importance of the community, see Julia Prewitt Brown, *Jane Austen's Novels: Social Change and Literary Form* (Cambridge: Harvard University Press, 1979).

a hurry to marry—and to marry strangers too"—is particularly comical. And even though, of all Austen's positive male authority figures, Mr. Knightley is remarkably the least officious and encroaching in this respect, as in all others, his recommendation that Emma mind her own business—"Leave him [Elton] to chuse his own wife. Depend upon it, a man or six or seven-and-twenty can take care of himself"—is slightly disingenuous, and he later retracts it. Far from being above applying his own understanding to other people's business, he oversees the personal affairs of his neighbors more closely than Emma does, and his indignation over Emma's "interference" with Harriet Smith is due in part to the embarrassment he feels for his own, now futile, interference with Robert Martin.

Emma is always taken to task for her scheme to improve Harriet, and this disapproval exposes the importance we ascribe to the sex differential in matters pertaining to authority. * * * Emma, with the "real good-will of a mind delighted with its own ideas" contemplates the patron-ward relationship with the same sense of personal gratification: "She would notice her; she would improve her; she would detach her from her bad acquaintance, and introduce her into good society; she would form her opinions and her manners." * * * But Emma realizes that bringing Harriet to Hartfield accords her a status which Emma herself is now obligated to respect. Accordingly, when Harriet just as inevitably turns on Emma and threatens to supplant her in Knightley's affections, Emma's own "strong sense of justice by Harriet" prompts her to admit that Harriet "had done nothing to forfeit the regard and interest which had been so voluntarily formed and maintained", and acknowledging her own responsibility for Harriet's aspirations, Emma declines to oppose, however heartily she may lament them.

* * *

If *Emma* begins with the assumption of a broad arena for legitimate and useful female rule independent from masculine supervision, then, it does not end with the assertion of its sufficiency. By the conclusion of her story, Emma is brought low, and marriage saves her. To scholars who see Austen as a political conservative this upshot is particularly grateful because it appears to rein her in. Indeed, Mr. Knightley does look like the benevolent, all-seeing monitor crucial to the conservative fiction of Austen's day. Hovering like a chaperon around the edges of every major scene—the portrait party at Hartfield, the dinner at the Coles, the word game at the Abbey, the outing at Box Hill—he is always on the lookout for wrongdoing and nonsense, always alert in his benefactions for the poor and innocent. Knightley himself confesses that with Emma his role as moral censor has been particularly obnoxious: "I have blamed you, and lectured you, and you have borne it as no other woman in England would have borne it," and he is probably right. Alternately beaming with heartfelt approval when Emma acquits herself properly, and frowning with pain whenever she misbehaves, he has been half paternal and half pedagogical in his watchfulness.

But this story is no less a "human disclosure" than any of the other stories in *Emma*. Accordingly, it does not tell all either; something is "a little disguised, or a little mistaken." Knightley is not, first of all, above imaginistic misreadings of his own, nor can he be. As his readiness to denounce Frank Churchill as an "Abominable scoundrel" attests, Mr. Knightley is just as apt as Emma to misconstrue where his interest is at stake, investing his upstart rival with the extremely literary character of the heartless cad. But Frank goes from "villain" to "not desperate" to a "very good sort of fellow" in a matter of moments as soon as Knightley learns that Emma never loved him. Furthermore, Knightley is not nearly so wise and all seeing as he appears to think. He extols "the beauty of truth and sincerity in all our dealings with each other," but many things—fortunately—have escaped his monitorship, Emma's worst faults among them. Knightley never learns, for example, that Emma did not stop with Mr. Elton, but proceeded to match Harriet and Frank; nor does he learn that Harriet, for her part, learned enough about gentility to disdain the very idea, and to prefer him instead, which is, after all, more than Emma had the wisdom to do. Emma, of course, must keep at least some of these humiliating little secrets to herself. To do any less would be an Eltonian trespass on Harriet's feelings. But even after Harriet's marriage takes the pressure off, Emma is still disingenuous about the "full and perfect confidence" she can now look forward to practicing as a conjugal "duty." She has had more to "blush" about than Harriet all along, and only moments later, Emma is blushing again, this time at the name of Dixon: "'I can never think of it,' she cried, 'without extreme shame.'" One wonders how Mr. Knightley would judge Emma's readiness not only to form scandalous thoughts about his favorite, but exultantly to impart them as well. But Emma's part in Jane's story is never disclosed, and Emma herself gets by with no more than some private embarrassment whenever she receives "a little more praise than she deserved." Austen's refusal to expose and to arraign a heroine reprehensible by conventional standards shows how she parts company with conservative counterparts, and given the morally privileged position monitor figures of Knightley's ilk enjoy in their fiction, Austen's determination to establish a discrepancy between what he knows and what we know about Emma is daring.

But Knightley is a far more extraordinary character than a monitor manqué. He himself does not set much store by his monitorship, and even though he always does lecture and blame, nothing ever comes of it. Monitors like Edgar Mandlebert[4] in *Camilla* and Edmund in *Mansfield Park* enforce their advice by threatening to withdraw affection and approval if they are not immediately obeyed—"advice" being for them, as we have seen in *Mansfield Park*, merely a decent term for "command." They stand as fair-weather friends who may turn on naughty charges at any minute. But Knightley and Emma stand on an equal footing, and this necessarily modifies the dynamic of advice giving, endowing it with more of the friendly directness that marks the advice scenes between Mrs. Gardiner and Elizabeth. For Knightley, advice is not a function of power. He does not assume that the parental liberty he takes in reproaching due him—indeed it is a "privilege rather endured than allowed." Being who and what she is, Emma dishes out almost as much as she gets, and when she does not follow his advice—which is almost always—he does not turn away.

Knightley, * * * is thus a fantastically wishful creation of benign authority, in whom the benefits and attractions of power are preserved and the abuses and encroachments expelled. As such he is the very reverse of Coelebs in More's *Coelebs in Search of a Wife*. To the extent that *Coelebs* tells young ladies to comport themselves modestly like sweet helpmates if they want to catch a husband, it holds forth the promise to girls across the kingdom that their skill at housewifery and their strenuous exertions of self-subordination will all pay off in the end, making them more desirable to the best sort of men than lively women, wits, and flirts. But *Emma* does the opposite. Here choosy men prefer saucy women—not women who place themselves at the margins, letting themselves be noticed only so they may show that they are not so vain as to crave attention, but women who love even the unflattering limelight, and who do not hesitate to pen themselves the subject of other people's news to Maple Grove and Ireland: "Mr. Frank Churchill and Miss Woodhouse flirted together excessively." In the character of Isabella, Austen shows that the good little wife cannot hold a candle to Emma: ". . . poor Isabella, passing her life with those she doated on, full of their merits, blind to their faults, and always innocently busy, might have been a model of right feminine happiness." The "might" here does more than underscore the difference between how Mr. Woodhouse deplores the destiny of "poor Isabella" and how more conventional people would envy it. It also places the statement outside narrative endorsement. Chattering vacuously, oblivious to how

---

4. Camilla's suitor in Frances Burney's novel *Camilla, or a Picture of Youth* (1796) [*Editor*].

she and her children endure the same curse of "living with an ill-tempered person" which she complacently pities in Mr. Churchill, Isabella has probably fewer claims to ready wit than Harriet herself. And to a man as discriminating as Knightley she presents "striking inferiorities" which serve only to throw Emma's "brilliancy" into higher relief. Wifely virtues are not meet for Emma; her hand, as he says somewhat proudly, "is the strongest," and he likes it that way.

The conclusion of *Emma* shares the polyvalence characteristic of the endings in Austen's later novels. The tenderness of Emma's filial piety—strong enough to make her hesitate to marry at all—proves her to be reassuringly devoted to precisely those relationships which political conservatives wanted to protect. Moreover, Emma's devolution to marriage with a man seventeen years her senior puts an end to her "reign alone," and brings her back within the confines of that relationship which she had offended so many readers by slighting. But problems still remain. Because Emma and Knightley are social equals, marriage itself does not present the same difficulty it had in *Pride and Prejudice*. * * * In order to secure Emma's prestige and the prerogative that comes with it, the ending of *Emma* turns back on the very outlines it seems to confirm. Mr. Knightley himself avers, "A man would always wish to give a woman a better home than the one he takes her from", and Mrs. Weston's feelings show that such generosity, far from being sublimely disinterested, confers an obligation which later affords "a man" the sweet pleasure of his wife's gratitude. But while Donwell Abbey is surely "a better home" than Hartfield, *Emma* closes by deferring Knightley's wish indefinitely to a time none wish to hasten—that is to say, until Mr. Woodhouse's death. As Emma well knows, Knightley's move into Hartfield is extraordinary considering his own power and independence: "How very few of those men in a rank of life to address Emma would have renounced their own home for Hartfield!" The conclusion which seemed tamely and placidly conservative thus takes an unexpected turn, as the guarantor of order himself cedes a considerable portion of the power which custom has allowed him to expect. In moving to Hartfield, Knightley is sharing *her* home, and in placing himself within her domain, Knightley gives his blessing to her rule.

* * *

428

MAAJA A. STEWART

The Heiress, Spinsters, and Gypsies†

∗　∗　∗

In Jane Austen's *Emma*, similar notations of poverty appear, but only in the margins of the dominant pattern of plenty that always avoids any suggestion of a causal relationship between the self-sufficient plenty and the brief visions of desperate poverty. These margins, however, conjoin the poverty of women with the poverty of the underclass in ways that could potentially disturb the novel's dominant celebration of complacent settlement. In the first book Emma translates her visit to the poor into a moral exercise: "These are the sights, Harriet, to do one good. How trifling they make every thing else appear!—I feel now as if I could think of nothing but these poor creatures all the rest of the day." Book 2 begins with Emma "speaking some time of what the poor must suffer in winter." Both of these brief glances at destitution lead seamlessly into discussions of Miss Bates, the former vicar's daughter, who now "has barely enough to live on." Similarly, in book 3 the marginal appearance in one of Miss Bates's monologues of the poverty of a common laborer leads to Emma's contemplation of Jane Fairfax and her poverty. The stories of the ostler who cannot support his aged and sick father without help from the parish and of the father who is pauperized in spite of his working twenty-seven years as a clerk to the former vicar give us brief glimpses of the kind of country life recorded by William Cobbett. Workers, not only vagrants, have been pauperized by a system no one quite understands.

Without drawing a parallel with the former vicar's clerk, Emma reflects a few paragraphs later on the unequal distribution of wealth as it affects women: "The contrast between Mrs. Churchill's importance in the world, and Jane Fairfax's, struck her; one was every thing, the other nothing—and she sat musing on the difference of woman's destiny, and quite unconscious on what her eyes were fixed, till roused by Miss Bates." Finally, Emma, in an unconsciously revolutionary burst of feeling, excuses Jane's lapse from morally prescribed behavior: "If a woman can ever be excused for thinking only of herself, it is in a situation like Jane Fairfax's.—Of such, one may almost say, that 'the world is not their's, nor the world's law.'" Jane, who has been educated above her station and therefore is absolved

† From *Domestic Realities and Imperial Fictions: Jane Austen's Novels in Eighteenth-Century Contexts* by Maaja A. Stewart (Athens: University of Georgia Press, 1993) 138–41. Reprinted by permission.

from normal moral judgment, bears a curious resemblance and contrast to the poor in book 1: Emma has "no romantic expectations of extraordinary virtue from those, for whom education had done so little." Although both Jane and the cottage poor are thus excused for their lapses from "normal" behavior, Emma's rhetoric notably effaces Jane's material conditions by placing her into an abstract and essentialized relationship with "the world." Whereas Emma has "no romantic expectations" about the poor, she invariably romanticizes the poverty of women such as Jane who inhabit the margins of her own class.

This kind of erasure from the text of the material conditions that determine women's lives appears especially clearly in Emma's elaborations of the two scenes of rural poverty. Effortlessly, she appropriates the reality of the poor into the dominant narratives of the gentry. In both scenes the poor are not directly represented: they become a topic of conversations in which the women of the gentry fictionalize their own experience. The first scene in book 1 encases the poor safely indoors, where they are immobilized further by sickness. Emma ministers to them with advice and broth from Hartfield. These poor belong to a social system envisioned as static and unchanging. The response of patrician charity is the only adequate response to the "scenes of distress" Harriet and Emma witness in the cottage: "If compassion has produced exertion and relief to the sufferers, it has done all that is truly important. If we feel for the wretched, enough to do all we can for them, the rest is empty sympathy, only distressing to ourselves." Emma does not allow the excess of feeling brought on by scenes of misery to work itself out in a reassessment of economic realities. Instead, she appropriates the feelings for the romantic courtship plot as the two women meet Mr. Elton: "'To fall in with each other on such an errand as this,' thought Emma; 'to meet in a charitable scheme; this will bring a great increase of love on each side.'"

Emma attempts a second, more significant, appropriation of the poor into the courtship plot in book 3, when Harriet is rescued from a group of "gipsies" by Frank Churchill. This rescue in Emma's mind will clearly fix the gender roles of the two into a romance: "Such an adventure as this,—a fine young man and a lovely young woman thrown together in such a way, could hardly fail of suggesting certain ideas to the coldest heart." In fictions such as Henry Fielding's *Joseph Andrews,* gypsies function the way Emma attempts to make them function in Harriet's story: by their unconventional and unlicensed activities, these nomadic people create temporary gaps in the rigid class boundaries of the dominant society, thus introducing mobility into the static system. They first give Joseph Andrews a working-class identity and then, when it is most needed to resolve the plot, an identity as a gentleman. It is significant that in spite of Emma's attempts, the gypsies in Austen's novel cannot be made to aid the resolution of the plot. A group consisting of a "stout woman" and children, who terrorize Harriet with their "clamorous, and impertinent" begging, the gypsies are re-formed by the text into a "gang, demanding more." They disappear from the text before the law can be activated against them, and their presence has no other effect than to mislead Emma in her interpretation of Harriet's affairs. Unlike the gypsies and peddlers in Fielding's fiction, Austen's gypsies resist incorporation into the narrative of the gentry. They are effaced from the text as they are from the dominant society.

The failure of the gypsies in *Emma* to act according to the narrative conventions that bring closure to traditional comic plots signals a similar failure of numerous other fictions by which the titular character attempts to adjust the poverty and social vulnerability of women. Her failure in this endeavor is inevitable: women's relationships to each other remain out of focus because the unacknowledged economic dimensions of their lives will frustrate any attempts to understand these lives as they intersect or to forge a community of women. The economically threatened women in the novel are, however, easily incorporated by Austen into the service of a conventional comic ending even as they resist Emma's attempts to confer power on them directly. Austen's use of women like Miss Bates, Harriet Smith, Miss Taylor–Mrs. Weston, and Jane Fairfax to support the celebration of "plenty" in the end is a clear example of a fictional closure that offers imaginary solutions to real problems.

Immobilized by the large economic forces that created the unprecedented possibilities of upward mobility for men, the poor thus reflect woman's reality in the novel. Emma's failure to draw this connection is central to Austen's construction of this heroine as she "dwindles into a wife" in spite of her emotional and economic independence. She cannot confer status on economically needy women like Harriet Smith. Austen, however, reduces Emma herself to the level of the weakest of them all—Miss Bates. The plot reinforces Emma's failure by spiritualizing poverty and weakness of women of the gentry as it constructs the heiress into a changing heroine. Her change, like Elizabeth Bennet's, is marked by a loss of wit and autonomy as she is disciplined to accept the male gaze. Reality, in the form of Austen's inscriptions of patriarchy in the novel, refuses to yield to Emma's desires as it educates and immobilizes this most independent of heroines firmly in the marriage plot.

D. A. MILLER

Broken Art[†]

Picture, if you can, a past moment of literary criticism when, institutionally empowered and rewarded, close reading was the critic's chief tool of professional advancement; his command of a *text*, his capacity to tease from it a previously invisible *nuance*, or illuminate it under a fresh *insight*, would as good as light the pipe in his mouth and sew elbow patches on his jacket, so unfailingly did he thus distinguish himself as the compleat, the full professor of English Literature. Now picture, if you need to, a future moment of literary criticism in which the same practice has fallen into total dereliction, and the *esprit de finesse* has ceded all its previous authority and prestige to the *esprit de géométrie*, more familiarly known as "theory." Even more efficiently than it once promoted its practitioner through the ranks of the professoriat, close reading now transforms him into an emeritus, antiquated and rambling, but not—alas for his pride!—too deaf to hear the resounding impatience of his audience that he get to the point, to the paradigm, which has become the only object of their peremptory, poverty-stricken desire. I don't mean to suggest by either exercise that, whether or not we ever lived in such a past, we should contemplate returning to it, or that, if such a future is indeed at hand, we should do our best to resist it. On the contrary, it is close reading in its humbled, futile, "minoritized" state that would win my preference in any contest. For only when close reading has lost its respectability, has ceased to be the slave of mere convenience, can it come out as a thing that, even under the high-minded (but now somewhat kitschy-sounding) rationales of its former mission, it had always been: an almost infantile desire to be *close*, period, as close as one can get, without literal plagiarism, to merging with the mother-text. (In an essay once, citing the first sentence of *Pride and Prejudice*, I left out the quotation marks.) But the point of picturing these two extreme conditions is not to get us to choose sides, but to recognize that, if we retain any vital relation to close reading whatsoever, as we all do, we must always be on both. For the practice of close reading has always been radically cloven: here, on one side, my ambition to master a text, to write *over* its language and refashion it to the cut of my argument, to which it is utterly indifferent; there, on the other, my longing to write *in* this language, to identify and combine with it. The adept in close reading must assert an autonomy of which he must also continually betray the weak and easily overwhelmed defenses.

† From *Jane Austen, or The Secret of Style* by D. A. Miller. © 2003 by Princeton University Press. Reprinted by permission of Princeton University Press.

These remarks on close reading may provide a metaphor, drawn from the homely lives of literary critics who don't write novels, for the fantasmatics of that technique of *close writing* that Austen more or less invented for the English novel, and which is *le style indirect libre,* or free indirect style. Ferguson has regretted the suggestive terminological affinity between free indirect style and style *tout court,* as leading us to link the device "with the unanalyzable notion of style rather than with the more substantial notion of representable form."[1] But of all traditional English novelists, Austen has long served us as the most striking example of both notions: of that self-evident secret which is Style, and that widely diffused representational technology known as the Novel. And the present essay has above all attempted to argue the inter-implication of the formal accomplishment of the Austen Novel, which matches uniquely impersonal narration to equally unprecedentedly rounded characters, and the fantasmatic achievement of Austen Style, as it bursts upon us (no matter how often or extensively we encounter it) in all the archaic authority of personal sourcelessness. We last left the secret of Style at this: that the stylothete harbors a hidden wish—of whose impossible fulfillment she has made an absolute refusal—to renounce the renunciation that makes her one. Let us now add the specification that it is above all in free indirect style, where the wish and refusal are most nearly joined, that this secret is kept and told.

The significance of free indirect style for Austen Style is not that it attenuates the stark opposition between character and narration, much less abandons it, but that it performs this opposition *at ostentatiously close quarters.* In free indirect style, the two antithetical terms stand, so to speak, as close as possible to the bar (the virgule, the disciplinary rod) that separates them. Narration comes as near to a character's psychic and linguistic reality as it can get without collapsing into it, and the character does as much of the work of narration as she may without acquiring its authority. Though free indirect style plainly offers *a third term* between character and narration, it is, or means to be, a nondialectical one: a kind of turnstile that helps organize the boundary, and recycle the binary, of an antithesis. Organize? Say rather flaunt: free indirect style gives a virtuoso performance, against all odds, of the narration's persistence in detachment from character, no matter how intimate the one becomes with the other. And its most daredevil feats do not occur where the narration is representing the consciousness of a fool like Sir Walter Elliot, or a cheapskate like John Dashwood, instances where the difference between narration and character is manifest at too many levels to be jeopardized even if both came to acquire the same ontological status. No, such feats occur when, in the course of vainly aspiring to narra-

1. Frances Ferguson, "*Emma* and the Impact of Form," *MLQ* (March 2000): 159.

tion, a character in turn inspires it with an equally impossible desire to renounce its condition for her own, as a fully representable person; in other words, in a case where it seems that if the structural bar of antithesis ever slipped away—which it never does—its place would be immediately taken by a mirror. For, no less than close reading, the close writing that is free indirect style is also given over to broaching an impossible identification. In the paradoxical form of an impersonal intimacy, it grants us at one and the same time the experience of a character's inner life as she herself lives it, and an experience of the same inner life as she never could. Though the irony that thus always accompanies free indirect style necessarily severs the identification with character, it nonetheless still presupposes it as one of its terms. Indeed, only in being severed, "lost," does this identification acquire fantasmatic force; only at the point of no return does it come back as a haunting apparition.

There is, of course, only one such case; her name is Emma Woodhouse. That some singularly intense authorial cathexis lodges in this character, Jane Austen has informed us herself: "I am going to take a heroine whom no one but myself will much like." By which, Austen does not mean to say that Emma is unlikable—an opinion from which countless generations of readers have dissented, just as they were supposed to. She is simply putting us on notice that no one can ever like Emma so well as her author. The name itself goes a long way to measuring just how well; even before it christened Miss Woodhouse, it had already enjoyed the privilege of being the name Austen most frequently chose for her heroines. In the juvenilia, as her biographer Park Honan has noted, Austen used the name Emma "with such affection that her parents might have wondered why they ever called her Jane."[2] To his list of examples—Emma Marlowe in "Leslie Castle"; Emma Marlow in "Edgar and Emma"; Emma Harley in "The Adventures of Mr. Harley"; Emma Stanhope in "Sir William Mountague"—we may add Emma Watson in "The Watsons" and the jokey stipulation in Austen's late "Plan of a Novel" that "the name of the work *not* . . . be *Emma*." For reasons of state—of Style, that is—Austen normally gives scant license to "the play of the signifier" in her novels, but the name Emma stands out as an exception. "What two letters of the alphabet are there, that express perfection?" Mr. Weston propounds. "M. and A.—Em—ma.—Do you understand?"[3] We understand even more, as we see the name—*aimé* indeed—reforming itself all over the text: not just *abbreviated* (as M.A.), but

2. Park Honan, *Jane Austen: Her Life* (New York: Faucett Columbine, 1987), p. 72.

3. Honan points out that "Mr. Weston's joking allusion is to the eighteenth-century philosopher of happiness, Francis Hutcheson, who in his *Beauty and Virtue* had worked out a small, bizarre formula with M and A as its keys: 'Since then *Benevolence*, or *Virtue* in any *Agent*,' he had written with some mathematics to help him, 'is as M/A, or M + 1/A, and no *Being* can act above his *natural Ability*; that must be the Perfection of Virtue where M = A, or when the *Being* acts to the utmost of his power for the *publick Good*'" (p. 356).

also *replicated* (in "little Emma," Emma's niece); *inverted* (into "Anne," Mrs. Weston's first name); *crossed* (with "Anne" to yield "Anna," the child that Mrs. Weston thus seems to have had by Emma rather than Mr. Weston); and *extended* (into "my Emma," which, as a mode of one character's addressing another, is unparalleled in Austen's novels, and even here is employed only by Mrs. Weston at her most maternal and Mr. Knightley after having become Emma's betrothed).[4] And, of course, Mr. Weston's literalization of the name, harking back to the game of anagrams played earlier in the novel, invites us to search out words in all four of its letters. Whether we simply reverse the order of these, and find Flaubert before the fact ("Emma, c'est moi"), or variously draw out of them the twinned themes of narcissism and maternity (me, ma, me-ma, ma-me, mame), the name already broaches the open secret of an impossible identification between the No One who is narrating and the most fully characterized Person in all Austen.

Free indirect style in *Emma* having been the subject of countless discussions, I confine my own to a single extraordinary moment in the novel: the passage that straddles the end of book II, chapter 2, and the beginning of book II, chapter 3. In II, 2, on meeting Jane Fairfax after a long absence, Emma recognizes, as though for the first time, her extraordinary beauty: "her face—her features—there was more beauty in them all together than she had remembered." And this beauty, so much the more forceful in its impression on Emma for having rectified her earlier mistake, and awakened her from previous oblivion, prompts her to feel that she has "injured" Jane by her "past prejudices and errors." "In short, she sat, during the first visit, looking at Jane Fairfax with twofold complacency; the sense of pleasure and the sense of rendering justice, and was determining that she would dislike her no longer." It is quite as though the text were exemplifying Elaine Scarry's contention that an encounter with beauty—most powerfully when it catches us by surprise—disposes us toward being just.[5] But beauty in Jane Austen, like the beauty *of* Jane Austen, does not embody the plenitude and inclusiveness either of Scarry's ideal or of Scarry's own enchanting style of argumentation. On the contrary, as I've already suggested, the aching beauty of Austen Style has everything to do with the fact that it invites and sustains in whoever encounters it an invidious fantasy of plenitude and *ex*clusiveness. So, unsurprisingly, on a second meeting, Emma finds that "these were charming feelings—but not lasting," as Jane's former provocations, all amounting to forms and instances of *reserve*, have reappeared. Jane is disgustingly, is suspi-

4. Of course, the narrator of *Mansfield Park*—on one of those rare moments when the narration becomes a narrator—may speak of "my Fanny," as does Jane Austen of "my Emma," when referring either to the novel or the character in her correspondence.
5. Elaine Scarry, *On Beauty and Being Just* (Princeton: Princeton University Press, 1999).

ciously reserved, Emma decides; and if anything can be more, where all is most, she is more reserved on the subject of Weymouth and the Dixons than anything. The chapter ends thus:

> The like reserve prevailed on other topics. She and Mr. Frank Churchill had been at Weymouth at the same time. It was known that they were a little acquainted; but not a syllable of real information could Emma procure as to what he truly was. "Was he handsome?"—"She believed he was reckoned a very fine man." "Was he agreeable?"—"He was generally thought so." "Did he appear a sensible young man; a young man of information?"—"At a watering place, or in a common London acquaintance, it was difficult to decide on such points. Manners were all that could be safely judged of, under a much longer acquaintance than they had yet had of Mr. Churchill. She believed every body found his manners pleasing." Emma could not forgive her.

And here is how the following chapter begins:

> Emma could not forgive her;—but as neither provocation nor resentment were discerned by Mr. Knightley, who had been of the party, and had seen only proper attention and pleasing behaviour on each side, he was expressing the next morning, being at Hartfield again on business with Mr. Wood-house, his approbation of the whole; not so openly as he might have done had her father been out of the room, but speaking plain enough to be very intelligible to Emma. He had been used to think her unjust to Jane, and had now great pleasure in marking an improvement.

You will have observed the strangeness of the same phrase being used both at the end of one chapter and at the beginning of the next, as though just for a moment, this impeccable Style, like an old-fashioned phonograph stylus, had got stuck in a groove, or as though the narrative machinery were experiencing a brief, but unprece-dented technical malfunction in shifting gears. But the minor panic this moment provokes in us—what are we to make of it? how are we to read it?—lasts only until we understand we will never be asked to make anything of it, or to read it at all. It is, if anything, a stylistic mishap, irrelevant to the story that now proceeds in a soothing and total indifference to it. The inconsequence of this odd little repeti-tion makes us overlook its startling weirdness, or more accurately, prevents us from retaining our sense of this weirdness. No wonder that, in a novel saturated in commentary—a commentary, moreover, by no means inhibited by a fear of the trivial or obvious—this strange feature has always passed with no more remark than Robert Fer-rars's toothpick case; there seems to be nothing in it.

By way of breaking the silence, let me harp on the oddity of the moment. To my knowledge, it has no parallel in nineteenth-century fiction, but even if it did, it would still seem curiously out of place in Austen, where the usual justifications for a rhetoric of repetition—emphasis, clarity, the exigencies of transition—don't quite apply. After all, this is a world where it is only the stupid and the chattering who lack the sense not to repeat themselves; and this is a work in which a stern principle of concision shows no mercy in throwing overboard the redundancies elsewhere supposed to give narration needed ballast. Even supposing a legato effect were intended, it would invariably be spoiled on being obliged to leap the hurdle of a chapter break, which, like a fade-to-black in film, executes as strong an internal disconnect as the Novel has at its disposal. In an artist whose sentences frame everything with elegant edges, there is something unseemly, or clumsily seamed, about these borders.

This is, at any rate, one way of looking at it. But here is another. Once we examine each of the two identical sentences in the context of its respective paragraph, it becomes clear that a shift, a change, has occured in the time or space between them. During the chapter break, what had been the indirect and impersonal *performance* of Emma's consciousness has become the mere matter-of-fact *notation* of that thought. On its first occurrence, "Emma could not forgive her" mimics Emma's conscious if unreflective mood. By the time of the second, without a word being altered, the sentence has been distilled into what Ann Banfield calls a "fact of the fiction"; a kind of stone on which Mr. Knightley is already stumbling in the scene that emerges.[6] What generates the first "Emma could not forgive her" is Emma's own affective consciousness, intimately accessed and ironically inflected by its free indirect narrative performance. What generates the second "Emma could not forgive her" is pure narration, a detached consciousness to which Emma's own has ceased to contribute, having been reduced to a little bit of information useful to the plot. By virtue of repeating the same formula (truly magical), we move from free indirect style—for all its irony, always grounded in an intimate identificatory relation to the image of a person—to mere omniscient narration, more remote in its detachment, and less engagé in its impersonality. What makes this shift worth our attention is neither that it *is* a shift, for such movements in and out of free indirect style happen all over *Emma*; nor that it is "undecidable," for I take it we all agree that we are further inside Emma on one side of the break and further removed from her on the other. It is the form

6. Ann Banfield, *Unspeakable Sentences: Narration and Representation in the Language of Fiction* (Boston: Routledge and Kegan Paul, 1982), p. 217. My understanding of the two Emma-could-not-forgive-hers follows on Banfield's distinction between "pure narration" and "represented consciousness."

that the shift takes here—a repetition across a chapter break—that makes it unique. For if we even recognize the difference in the repetition, we do so only belatedly, on looking back at it from the context that comes to be built around it. And this belatedness of perception only underscores the shift more heavily, as though, without being thus retrospectively startled by it, we might have overlooked it—as in fact, of course, at the actual moment it seems to have taken place (on the second occurrence of "Emma could not forgive her"), we already *must* have done.

Far from evincing a lapse in Austen's celebrated economy, the repetitive transition ends up being an awesome illustration of it: finally perceived, her adroit arrangement surprises us into discovering the difference between two narrative modes across one and the same phrase. Yet neither can this transition be reduced to the declaration of a purely formal mastery; the toothpick case, we know, is never entirely empty. Besides the stylistic fluency, then, we need to recognize the retardation, the hesitation, the reluctance, I should finally say the impossibility, so insistently dramatized in the transition. It is as though the narration were trying, and failing, to pull away from the attraction of free indirect style—from that identification with an image of the Person which is the only thing that distinguishes it, fantasmatically speaking, from its usual "omniscient" mode. But in the course of shaking off its secret, severed identification with Emma, it has produced a cloud of dust that only resettles on it, as the telltale residue of that same identification. It seems as hard for Jane Austen to relinquish her identificatory cathexis on Emma, or to cool it down into an even more detached form, as it is for Emma to relinquish her grudge against Jane Fairfax. In a way, of course, this cathexis is not simply *like* a grudge; it is itself a grudge, against the possibility that the stylothete is denied.

Why at bottom does Emma resent Jane Fairfax? "Mr. Knightley had once told her it was because she saw in her the really accomplished young woman, which she wanted to be thought herself." "Emma could not forgive her/Emma could not forgive her": so Style flaunts its mastery, its ability to enter and then exit a character's state of mind at will, while always retaining, at whatever level of intimacy, the immunity of its impersonality. But so also Style avows how deeply, in a former life, it might have desired the identification with that full social being who, for all her faults, is faultless in the complete acceptability of her social representation: handsome, clever, rich, and, as everybody already knows, destined to be coupled too. It gazes in fascination on that identification from which, already discernibly detached, it must now pull back even further. "Emma could not forgive her/Emma could not forgive her": that is finally to say, Emma can never be *forgotten* by her, who is not Jane Fairfax but Jane

Austen. After all, it is this Jane who, far more consistently than her namesake in the novel, exhibits "such coldness and reserve—such apparent indifference whether she pleased or not"; and who thus may be seen to acknowledge here the incontrovertible truth of what, under the *nom de guerre* of Fairfax, Emma can't bear in her. The melancholy of Austen Style lies not in the fact that its renunciation of the world—the renunciation that has allowed it to make a world—is never complete, but in the fact that its renunciation of the world may never be *in*complete, may never be modified or muted. What most argues the melancholy of the passage at hand is not the reluctance of the withdrawal, so much as the dry, wittily mechanical necessity of it. To a large extent, as I suggested in the first chapter, Austen's persistent moral condemnation of style—as by turns trivial, factitious, misleading, dangerous, evil—is a strategy of camouflage: shameful sign of the Woman, style must always be "over there," in Robert Ferrars's empty toothpick case. But surely what also motivates this condemnation is Style's own sense of the untruth in its exclusive self-sufficiency: the knowledge that with its constant and rigorous self-denial it does not simply counter a fear of reverting to the abject subject who would no longer have even the dubious protection of style; it also seeks to advance a dream that it might correspond to the plenitude of a Person. The beauty of Style, I have claimed, lies in the way it shuts out the world that would otherwise shut out the stylothete. This beauty, though, is also the melancholy of Style; its exclusive plenitude obliges Style always to harbor a dialectical reminder not just of that excluded self it had to give up, but also of that included self it never had, and so never *will* give up, for it is what we might properly call its ego ideal. Ultimately, then, Austen's God is not Schelling's, with the perverse need of perfection for imperfection; on the contrary, her deity presents one kind of perfection melancholically longing to be coupled with another. That is why, to anyone with the smallest sense of style, of Austen Style at any rate, *Emma* must be considered both the most perfect *and* the most melancholy of her novels, because here the perfection of Style, of No One, opens the secret of its impossible desire to possess the perfection of a Person who has, who is, everything. "Harriet was nothing . . . [Emma] was every thing herself." Though Austen could not have known the Germanic origin of the name, the stylothete is full of appreciation—full of nothing, finally, but appreciation—for the fact that "Emma" means *whole*.

＊　＊　＊

EMILY AUERBACH

An Imaginist Like Herself[†]

* * *

Emma asks readers * * * to open their minds to new ideas about what a marriage should be. The novel opens and ends with wedding days and presents various forms of union. Mr. Knightley calls Miss Taylor "very fit for a wife" for Mr. Weston because she has learned "the very material matrimonial point of submitting [her] own will, and doing as [she is] bid." Mrs. Weston seems not to mind that her husband opens her mail. Although Austen has her hero praise such traditional subjection, she presents him as one who in actuality prefers a strong-willed woman, a counterpart. When Emma quips that "such a girl as Harriet is what every man delights in" rather than women with "well informed minds," Mr. Knightley retorts, "Men of sense . . . do not want silly wives." He wants equality with Emma ("Cannot you call me George?") and romance ("Brother and sister! no indeed"), not a continuation of the teacherly role he has played in the past. Unlike his brother John, George Knightley does not seek a wife who will merely murmur "Very true, my love" with uncritical devotion.

As in *Pride and Prejudice*, Austen contrasts traditional notions of romantic courtship with a slowly developing relationship. Mr. Knightley and Emma take their time on the way to the altar. As in *Mansfield Park*, semifraternal ties evolve into a conjugal union. Early on in *Emma*, Mr. Knightley admits that Emma seems as much his sister as does his sister-in-law, Isabella. He teases Emma with the air of a fond, rather patronizing older brother. Emma never even thinks of Mr. Knightley as a prospective husband until near the end, though her distress at his lack of dancing suggests she does not wish him relegated to the fuddy-duddy corner. Emma says to Mr. Knightley of the feasibility of their dancing together, "You know we are not really so much brother and sister as to make it at all improper."

In a sense, Mr. Knightley and Emma have been behaving like a husband and wife for quite some time. From the beginning of the novel, Austen makes a point of showing Mr. Knightley and Emma functioning at dinner parties like a married couple skillfully maneuvering conversation to keep from distressing their guests. They share in their love of nieces and nephews and already seem to have created a cozy feeling of "home." Each is acutely aware of the other one's

† From *Searching for Jane Austen* by Emily Auerbach. © 2004 by the Board of Regents of the University of Wisconsin System. Reprinted by permission of the University of Wisconsin Press.

440 EMILY AUERBACH

comings and goings. They talk with openness and equality: "We always say what we like to one another." With years of friendship "all right, all open, all equal," it is not surprising that their eventual marriage can possess "something so like perfect happiness."

As in the case of the animated Elizabeth Bennet and reserved Mr. Darcy in *Pride and Prejudice*, Austen presents her happiest marriages in *Emma* as those where the union benefits both partners, like a completion of self. Presumably Emma, Harriet Smith, and Frank Churchill will acquire discipline and rationality; in turn, Mr. Knightley, Robert Martin, and Jane Fairfax may gain imagination and playfulness. As Mr. Knightley observes of the marriage between Frank and Jane, "I am very ready to believe his character will improve, and acquire from her's the steadiness and delicacy of principle that it wants . . . with such a woman he has a chance." Frank and Emma realize in their final conversations that they would have been far too alike—both of them too fanciful, manipulative, and willful—to complement each other well as husband and wife. As Austen wrote in a letter, "Marriage is a great Improver" (20 November 1808).

But marriage can also be a great De-prover if partners bring out the worst in each other. The rejected Mr. Elton acquires a Mrs. Elton with "delightful rapidity" and soon becomes nearly as "hardened as his wife . . . growing like her." The only "finery" in their marriage is on the outside of their bodies. Every thing about this marriage is artificial, including Mrs. Elton's affected use of *caro sposo* to refer to her husband and her pretense that he is her "lord and master" when in fact she has the upper hand. Mrs. Elton gets the final spoken words in *Emma*—a condemnation of Emma and Mr. Knightley's wedding as a pitiful and shabby business because it lacks lace. One suspects that far too many modern-day Mrs. Eltons focus on display rather than substance, valuing the wedding day more than the perfect happiness of the union.

Austen adds a feminist twist to the ending of *Emma* by implying that her bossy, competitive heroine may still be scheming to stay more in control of her life than most married women. In a letter, Austen had discussed "pitying a young woman . . . because she cannot live in two places at the same time, & at once enjoy the comforts of being married & single" (8 February 1807). Emma comes the closest of any Austen heroine to proving a young woman *can* do just that. Emma will marry yet stay at home, remaining "always first and always right" to her father. Emma still thinks in competitive, egotistical terms, counting "on being *first* with Mr. Knightley."

Like all other Austen heroines, Emma marries and supposedly lives happily ever after. Yet readers never forget the astonishing conversation Austen offers on celibacy between Emma and Harriet. Emma begins,

"My being charming, Harriet, is not quite enough to induce me to marry; I must find other people charming—one other person at least. And I am not only, not going to be married, at present, but have very little intention of ever marrying at all. . . . I must see somebody very superior. . . . I cannot really change for the better. If I were to marry I must expect to repent it."

"Dear me!—it is so odd to hear a woman talk so!"

"I have none of the usual inducements of women to marry. . . . I believe few married women are half as much mistress of their husband's house, as I am of Hartfield; and never, never could I expect to be so truly beloved and important; so always first and always right in any man's eyes as I am in my father's." . . .

"But still, you will be an old maid! and that's so dreadful!"

"Never mind, Harriet, I shall not be a poor old maid; and it is poverty only which makes celibacy contemptible to a generous public! . . . [A] single woman, of good fortune, is always respectable, and may be as sensible and pleasant as anybody else."

It is indeed, as Harriet Smith says, "so odd to hear a woman talk so." *Emma* contains some of the most direct discussions of women's hampered existences and threatened destinies in all of Austen. Emma speaks in the same bold voice Austen adopts herself in a letter to her niece: "Single Women have a dreadful propensity for being poor—which is one very strong argument in favour of Matrimony" (13 March 1817). Remove poverty as a factor and women acquire the freedom to say no.

*   *   *

GABRIELLE D. V. WHITE

[*Emma* as Subversive of the Slave Trade][†]

*   *   *

Jane Austen takes for granted the guilt of the slave trade. The impression can be given that because she takes for granted agreement on the slave trade she focuses on governesses. But authorial focus is not so likely to be on the job of a governess if it was not after all the focus for her character Jane Fairfax. The author does not herself in the narrative seem to focus on protest at the job of a governess. In any case, where governesses are concerned the description

† From Gabrielle D. V. White, *Jane Austen in the Context of Abolition* (Houndmills: Palgrave Macmillan, 2006), 70–72. © 2006 Palgrave Macmillan. Reprinted by permission.

targets not doing the job but the experience at the hands of governess-trade at 'advertising offices'. To be traded is to be treated as a commodity. To change that in the case of victims of the slave trade would be to cease having slaves as property.

I draw the conclusion that in comparing the victims of the slave trade to those of governess-trade the author's concern is for the victims of the prohibited slave trade who remain enslaved. The need later in the narrative to reassess one's ideas about the secretly engaged Jane Fairfax provides a way of emphasizing this issue of the slave trade, by inviting a second look at what has been said and done earlier, including what was actually said in the dialogue. The need to reassess indicates there could be a need to change one's mind about what may at first have been taken to be the case in the dialogue.

Jane Fairfax's influence in the wider world is represented as something to be relied on. In chapter 51, speaking of her and her fiancée, Mr Knightley says:

> I am very ready to believe his character will improve, and acquire from her's the steadiness and delicacy of principle that it wants.

For a contemporary reader in Britain, prior to Emancipation, he or just as importantly she is part of a reader audience for whom the need to reassess what has been said and done earlier in the novel could mean being prompted to think further about the continuing slavery of the victims of the slave trade.

The concern about abolition raised in the dialogue is carried through the entire narrative because of the link with Maple Grove. Another effect of seeing so much in the narrative through Emma's consciousness is that we are grounded with her in Highbury so that what is kept distant, keeps itself distant or is excluded, becomes alien and its ideas not those we wish to identify with. Looking back, this is effective from the first chapter, when the topic is raised of a marriage for Mr Elton, who will use casual imagery of slavery in his Charade and again at the end of Volume One, through Volume Two from the introduction of Mrs Elton, whose first topic of conversation when returning Emma's call is Maple Grove and its promise to visit in the spring or summer at the latest, to the climax of Volume Two incorporating the dialogue referring to the slave trade, and is then consolidated in the final Third Volume by the discrediting of Mrs Elton as not welcoming a happy outcome of Jane Fairfax's secret engagement, calling into question thereby Mrs Elton's credentials for judging friendship in her earlier description that 'Mr Suckling was always rather a friend to the abolition', the narrative culminating in the resolution of all difficulties at the finish, bar those perceived by the excluded and rejected, satirized world of Maple Grove. The world of Maple Grove has effectively been marginalized.

This is subversive of the status quo, in presenting a world that readers would not want to identify with but from which they would prefer to disassociate themselves. Maple Grove has broken its promise to visit the newly married Eltons, and Mrs Elton, in trying to cling on to the wealthy connection, involves herself in hypocrisy for the comedy of the concluding paragraph. Having earlier expressed a horror of finery shortly after her outburst on the slave trade, she now declares that, from the particulars given her by Mr Elton, the lack of finery at Emma's wedding makes for so shabby an affair that when she heard of it Selina would stare. Such a light touch can nevertheless succeed in planting the idea that, over against Mr Knightley's stewardship of resources and the relative modesty of expenditure in Highbury, excessive consumption at Maple Grove is unwarranted. In viewing Maple Grove from this perspective there would be no succour out in the external world for any idea of supporters of the status quo that emancipation would wrongly injure vested interests. To be so suggestive, of there being no good future for Maple Grove values, is in itself subversive.

Thus I conclude Jane Austen sought to undermine the views of those still supporting the status quo of chattel slavery. This would be a quiet revolution in the sense that opposition is not forced upon the reader but clearly suggested. Earlier, before 1807, abolitionist emphasis had been on abolition of the slave trade itself. To work now for abolition of slavery in the face of offers of amelioration of conditions for an institution that, it could always be said, went back to time immemorial would be tougher going. The subtlety of Jane Austen's approach was particularly called for in order that what she said in speaking of the guilt of the slave trade and the misery of its victims could not be used counter-productively.

RICHARD JENKYNS

[Mr. Woodhouse]†

* * *

Mr Woodhouse is one of Jane Austen's finest achievements. Of course, he has always been enjoyed—quite rightly—as one of her best comic creations, a lovable old silly, but her cleverness lies in making him at the same time a monster, the villain of the piece. I

† Reprinted by permission of Oxford University Press.

noted before that the first speaker in *Mansfield Park* is Mrs Norris. In *Emma* the first words of dialogue are given to Mr Woodhouse. And indeed there is an odd parallelism between these two so different figures: Mr Woodhouse too is the 'bad fairy' who has to be defeated if the heroine is to be happy. In his lack of vitality or zest for life the character in *Mansfield Park* whom Mr Woodhouse most resembles is Lady Bertram. But he comes nearest to Mrs Norris as an enemy of life and an enemy of other people's enjoyment.

It is illuminating to consider Mr Woodhouse in terms of the novel's structure. As we have seen, Jane Austen's plots in some formal respects show rather little variety. And just as each of the novels follows the basic pattern 'girl meets boy, girl marries boy', so each of them is supplied with a villain, whose machinations threaten the heroine's happiness: General Tilney, Lucy Steele, Wickham, Mrs Norris, William Walter Elliot, and in *Sanditon* Sir Edward Denham. Willoughby, though a more ambiguous case, might be added to the list, thus providing two villains for the novel with two heroines, though perhaps he should be rather be placed in the category most ripely realized in Henry Crawford: the moral agent who faces the choice of Hercules, between virtue and vice, and takes the wrong turning. The one apparent exception to this otherwise inexorable pattern is *Emma*. Here the two obviously nasty characters, Mrs Elton and her husband (the latter corrupted in the course of the narrative, but once corrupted, fixedly mean), do not count as villains in terms of the plot or story pattern, because they have no power over the heroine's life. Nonetheless, *Emma* is indeed no exception, because it does after all have a villain; and among Jane Austen's villains, Mr Woodhouse enjoys perhaps the longest and most continuous success of all.

He is also the stealthiest of the villains, so much so that many readers have not seen through him. In the film *Emma* he was portrayed as a rosy old buffer; I do not know how widespread that view of him remains. His monstrousness has been underestimated perhaps because the author is herself so stealthy, allowing into the text very few words overtly critical of him ('gentle selfishness', 'mild inexorability'), and even these tempered. A great deal of *Emma*, especially its later parts, is written in the form of interior monologue—another example of Jane Austen's originality and openness to experiments in technique. But with Mr Woodhouse she uses the theatrical method: his nature is revealed almost entirely through his own words and actions.

He is an adept at false solicitude. The first thing that we see him doing is stopping his daughter going to see her best friend: he inhibits Emma from visiting Mrs Weston at Randalls, and claims that it is out of consideration for his servant James. A couple of chapters later we learn the fraudulence of this: three of the local ladies 'were fetched and carried home so often that Mr Woodhouse thought it no hardship for either James or the horses'.[1] He tries to get Mr Weston and Miss Taylor to postpone their wedding—solicitude again—because of the rain.[2] (This introduces another facet of his character, an impertinent officiousness which interferes in matters that are none of his business.) He tries to stop them having a wedding cake, and then to stop anyone eating it, supposedly from a tender concern for their digestion. The truth is that he is a solipsist, who 'could never believe other people to be different from himself. What was unwholesome to him, he regarded as unfit for any body . . .' The prospect of anyone eating cake disturbs his 'benevolent nerves', a nice phrase.[3]

He instinctively thinks of agreeable people as objects pleasant to himself. Jane Fairfax is 'a very pretty sort of young lady, a very pretty and a very well-behaved young lady indeed'. Tellingly, these are much the terms in which he has earlier described the housemaid: 'she is a civil, pretty-spoken girl . . . Whenever I see her, she always curtseys and asks me how I do, in a very pretty manner.'[4] But indeed, people only exist to serve his comfort, the gentlefolk no less than the servants. When Elton sends a 'long, civil, ceremonious note' to him, pointedly excluding Emma, she thinks that he is bound to notice the insult to his daughter; but he does not.[5] Though he is against matrimony, he never sees a marriage coming;[6] how could he, when he is interested in no person but himself? That incuriosity about anyone else makes him flatten out some very different characters into uniformity: he describes even Mrs Elton in the same terms as Jane Fairfax and the housemaid: 'considering we never saw her before, she seems a very pretty sort of young lady . . . She speaks a little too quick . . . However, she seems a very obliging, pretty-behaved young lady . . .'[7] There is in this a mixture of imperceptiveness and solipsism ('considering we never saw her before'—a person has no characteristics until she is before Mr Woodhouse's eyes).

'Every friend of Miss Taylor,' says Knightley, 'must be glad to have her so happily married.'[8] That lets the cat out of the bag. Mr Woodhouse is no friend to her, but indeed her most implacable enemy, who would ruthlessly have destroyed her hope of happiness, given the chance. Moreover, his attitude towards her reveals another of his

1. *Emma* vol. i, chs. 1 and 3.
2. *Emma* vol. i, ch. 1.
3. *Emma* vol. i, ch. 2.
4. *Emma* vol. ii, ch. 3; vol. i, ch. 1.
5. *Emma* vol. i, ch. 17.
6. *Emma* vol. ii, ch. 5.
7. *Emma* vol. ii, ch. 14.
8. *Emma* vol. i, ch. 1.

characteristics: his inexorability. Like the Japanese soldier in the jungle refusing to believe in his country's surrender, he declines to accept that she is married: Miss Taylor she remains—indeed 'poor Miss Taylor', for his colossal egoism will not accept that anyone can be happy who has separated herself from his society. He is against life: thus he is depressed by his elder daughter Isabella's attachment to her husband—sex is another of the things he is against—and instead of delighting in the ordinary, boisterous pleasures of his grandchildren, he frets about them.[9] And if one thinks about it, his opposition to all marriage is a brutal insult to the memory of his wife. Indeed, it implies something about the nature of his marriage. No word is said about that, but we do learn from Mr Knightley's mouth that his wife was talented; this is where Emma has got her quickness and cleverness from.[1] We might reflect on what the character of her life is likely to have been, once she realized what sort of man she had married. In *Persuasion* we are told explicitly that the heroine's late mother strove to do the best she could with the desolating discovery that her husband was vacuous;[2] in *Emma* we are left to infer it.

Mr Woodhouse is against life's homelier pleasures too. He 'would have made a difficulty if he could', we are told at one point, about some simple arrangement.[3] Recurrently he stops people eating.[4] Miss Bates describes one such occasion:[5]

> There was a little disappointment.—The baked apples and biscuits, excellent in their way, you know; but there was a delicate fricassee of sweetbread and some asparagus brought in at first, and good Mr. Woodhouse, not thinking the asparagus quite boiled enough, sent it all out again. Now there is nothing grandmamma loves better than sweetbread and asparagus—so she was rather disappointed, but we agreed we would not speak of it to anybody . . .

That was a good evening's work for Mr Woodhouse—depriving a poor old woman of one of her few enjoyments. It is also significant that he has fooled Miss Bates ('*good* Mr. Woodhouse') into a belief in his beneficence: he is not only a fraud but a successful fraud. Jane Austen knows, however, that his obsession over food is not only valetudinarianism but *gourmandise*, the fussiness of a perverted epicureanism. He insists that apples must be baked: it is the only way that he thinks the fruit thoroughly wholesome.[6] C. S. Lewis's Screwtape

---

9. *Emma* vol. i, ch. 9.
1. *Emma* vol. i, ch. 5.
2. *Pers.* vol. i, ch. 1.
3. *Emma* vol. i, ch. 13.
4. *Emma*, e.g. vol. ii, ch. 8.
5. *Emma* vol. iii, ch. 2.
6. *Emma* vol. ii, ch. 9.

notes that there is a gluttony of delicacy as well as a gluttony of excess; Mr Woodhouse is a glutton of delicacy.

We are assured that he is 'everywhere beloved for the friendliness of his heart and his amiable temper'. His 'good nature' is listed, along with his money and the appeal of his daughter, as one of the causes why he can draw others to himself.[7] But there are indications that others' view of him is not quite so uniformly favourable. Thus it is made evident that John Knightley, despite his 'great regard for his father-in-law, and generally a strong sense of what was due to him', finds him extremely irritating; and on one blessed occasion he exploits Mr Woodhouse's nervousness to bully him, 'pursuing his triumph rather unfeelingly'.[8] Some phrases are ambiguous: 'Papa is only speaking his own regret,' Emma explains, after Mr Woodhouse has implied that Mrs Weston is none too well. Perhaps she says more than she intends.[9] 'You quite forget Mr. Weston,' she adds a little later, after her father has complained that though Mrs Weston comes to see him often, she is always obliged to go away again. Indeed: he 'forgets' the interests of anyone other than himself. Mrs Weston's own true feelings also break out toward the end of the book: no one but Mr Knightley, she reflects, could 'know and bear with Mr. Woodhouse'.[1] We might reflect, in turn, that before her marriage she had been compelled to know and bear with Mr Woodhouse for many years: 'poor Miss Taylor', after all. At the end of the book, part of Emma's liberation is that she can now see through her father. Before, we have overheard her telling herself that her father's tenderness of nature is what has made him generally loved. Now she can mimic his silliness (with affection to be sure) as she has mimicked others in her world: 'I wish I may not sink into "poor Emma" with him at once.— His tender compassion towards oppressed worth can go no farther.'[2] There is some ambiguity about that last sentence, but it sounds as though Emma has at last begun to recognize how limited and superficial is his supposed kindliness.

He is an octopus whose tentacles draw others towards himself. His rank and wealth enable him to 'command the visits of his own little circle'.[3] He has succeeded in making the world revolve around his person: everyone must spend time and trouble thinking about him. When the Westons, for example, want to give a dinner party, it is he who determines that the hours must be early and the numbers few, his 'habits and inclination being consulted in every thing'.[4] It is not

7. *Emma* vol. i, chs. 1 and 2.
8. *Emma* vol. i, chs. 11 and 15.
9. *Emma* vol. i, ch. 11.
1. *Emma* vol. iii, ch. 17.
2. *Emma* vol. ii, ch. 13; vol. iii, ch. 17.
3. *Emma* vol. i, ch. 3.
4. *Emma* vol. i, ch. 13.

enough for him to have his own comforts satisfied: his employment is to destroy the pleasures of others. In his own words, 'the sooner every party breaks up, the better.'[5] At the Donwell strawberry party, he is supplied with a comfortable room set up for his convenience, 'Books of engravings, drawers of medals, cameos, corals, shells' and other curios are produced to entertain him, but it is not enough: to complete his pleasure he must damage that of others. Mrs Weston must sit with him, deprived of the enjoyment of the sunny summer gardens, until Emma (a sign, incidentally, of her unobtrusive kindness) comes to relieve her.[6]

Is this account of Mr Woodhouse too hard on him? It might be objected that he is too passive a personality to be the active force of malignancy that I have represented. It might be objected too that if he is as malignant as I have said, why is he so well beloved? But it is in these very paradoxes that Jane Austen's brilliance lies. At first sight Mr Woodhouse may seem to be a first-rate comic cut, very amusing but no more. But Jane Austen's wit, and her psychological penetration, show that his passivity is aggressive and rapacious. There are, as we have seen, some hints that Mr Woodhouse may not be altogether as well beloved as Emma supposes, but certainly he commands a fair bit of affection. And indeed there is something charming and lovable about the old boy. So amiable and yet a monster—the genius of the portrayal lies in just this, that both things are true. There is both likeness and unlikeness to the way in which Jane Austen has handled Fanny Price. This most passive of heroines turns into a 'daemon'. That, of course, is Mrs Norris's view, and Fanny is genuinely good; the portrait of Mr Woodhouse examines in a different way the idea first discovered and explored in *Mansfield Park,* of how passivity may become power. Mr Woodhouse is also remarkably in advance of his time as a study of subconscious motivation. I have described him as a villain and a destroyer, but we are not to imagine, of course, that he has clearly articulated his motives to himself. Nor is his amiability feigned. The interplay of conscious and unconscious motives is very finely observed; that is why he can be both so ineffectual and so dangerous, such a menace and such a dear.

But he remains a bloodsucker, fastened upon his daughter's flesh. In *Clueless* (the film comedy which transfers the *Emma* story to modern Los Angeles) the father is made into a successful, driven lawyer, very unlike the idle potterer in the book; but this film does seem to understand, as the other film versions of *Emma* do not, both that the father is needed by his daughter, as the object on

5. *Emma* vol. ii, ch. 7.
6. *Emma* vol. iii, ch. 6.

which a warm heart can expend its natural affection, and that he is an incubus. Mr Woodhouse's crime is to use his daughter's love for himself in a plot to blight her life, if he can. We know that he is hostile to all matrimony, and we can see how near he comes to succeeding with Emma when she explains to Harriet why she means never to marry:[7]

> Fortune I do not want; employment I do not want; consequence I do not want; I believe few married women are half as much mistress of their husband's house, as I am of Hartfield; and never, never could I expect to be so truly beloved and important; so always first and always right in any man's eyes as I am in my father's.

Mr Woodhouse, that is to say, has been wrapping Emma in flattery as a spider wraps a fly. Harriet's response—that Emma will turn into an old maid—may seem merely conventional, but ironically she is the one showing sense this time.

Mr Woodhouse fails to prevent Emma's engagement, but he fights on to prevent her happiness to the last, and he is defeated, thanks to the incident in the poultry-yard, only on the very last page. Even then, the victory is not complete, for though he has finally allowed Emma to marry her lover, he has required them to live in his house. Knightley must quit his beloved Donwell, and Emma must still live with the man who has shackled her. (It is amusing to find that Jane Austen is reported, in private conversation, to have taken pity on them and killed Mr Woodhouse off after a couple of years; but that lies outside the novel.[8])

* * *

DAVID MONAGHAN

Emma and the Art of Adaptation[†]

Prior to the Jane Austen boom of the 1990s, almost all film versions of her novels were made for television and conformed to the conventions of the BBC classic drama house style. * * * They are thus characterized by textual fidelity, solid acting, and use of historically accurate settings and costumes. However, this carefully cultivated "verisimilitude" is usually "superficial."[1] * * * Pre-1990

---

7. *Emma* vol. i, ch. 10.
8. *Memoir*, 119 (140).
† From *Jane Austen on Screen*, ed. Gina Macdonald and Andrew F. Macdonald, copyright © 2003 Cambridge University Press. Reprinted with permission.
1. Robert Giddings et al., *Screening the Novel* (New York: Macmillan, 1990,) 166.

adaptations also tend to make use of unobtrusive and conservative camera and editing techniques that reflect their creators' unwillingness to rethink Austen's novels in visual terms.

*   *   *

Some of the various ways in which more recent filmmakers have been ready to deviate from this model are well illustrated by a consideration of the four adaptations of *Emma* made for film and television during the last twenty years. The most substantial are two feature-length films that relate in very different ways to their common source text. The ITV/A&E co-production, *Emma* (1996), written by Andrew Davies and directed by Diarmuid Lawrence, will be explored at length in the main body of this paper. * * *

Amy Heckerling's *Clueless*, made for Paramount Pictures in 1995, is very different from the ITV/A&E *Emma*, not just because it is a product of the Hollywood studio system rather than of British television but because it much more completely flouts the principle of fidelity by relocating Jane Austen in late twentieth-century Beverly Hills. * * * Heckerling is clearly aware of the intertextual possibilities inherent in her double time frame and her examination in *Clueless* of female maturation in contemporary American society acquires a depth generally lacking in the teen movie genre. She is able to play off the problems facing a young woman seeking a firm foothold on the ever-shifting sands of a postmodern cultural landscape against those of heroine who is faced with what seems at times an all-too-stable world of moral absolutes and established ways of behaving.

Although their origins are quite different, *Emma* (1996), written and directed by Douglas McGrath for Miramax and starring Gwyneth Paltrow, and the 2009 BBC serialization of *Emma* have a good deal in common in that they are both curious hybrids that display characteristics of the BBC classic drama and the Hollywood film. Both stay close to Austen in terms of incident, plot and characters. However, neither engages very intelligently with its source text. McGrath substitutes a superficial and silly heroine for the complex Emma created by Austen and cultivates an elegant and vital visual surface rather than thematic complexity. The Emma created by writer Sandy Welch and director Jim O'Hanlon is less consistently silly but, particularly in her encounters with Harriet Smith and Mrs. Weston, Romola Garai seems to have modeled her Emma on Gwyneth Paltrow's. While often visually impressive, the Welch/O'Hanlon version of *Emma* lacks thematic coherence. The film's bold opening which goes back into Emma's childhood to create a contrast between Emma's secure situation at Hartfield and the condition of exile into which Jane Fairfax and Frank Churchill are cast finally acquires significance in Welch and O'Hanlon's late exploration of Emma's close bonds with her father and in their presentation of Frank and Jane as two orphans clinging together like precursors of Dickens's wards in Chancery. However, the main body of the Welch/O'Hanlon *Emma* fails to develop the thematic potential of its intriguing beginning; instead, very much in the manner of its pre-1990 predecessors, the 2009 serial is content to simply lead the viewer through all of the main scenes from *Emma*. Like these earlier adaptations, it functions more as an illustrated supplement to its source text than as an independent work of art.

*　*　*

Scriptwriter Andrew Davies and director Diarmuid Lawrence shape the surface of the ITV/A&E *Emma* in accordance with a set of conventions familiar to fans of classic television drama. Davies' script is faithful to the main trajectories of the plot of the original novel and he puts a great deal of trust in the dramatic possibilities of Austen's diction and sentence structures. *　*　* Similarly, the ITV/A&E *Emma* often has the look of the BBC classic serial in that Lawrence's direction, particularly early in the film, frequently involves nothing more adventurous than establishing shots followed by cutting from speaker to speaker, usually in close up or mid-shot.

The first obvious indication that the ITV/A&E *Emma* is, on the whole, a much more serious and innovative piece of work than the general run of television adaptations is provided by the film's script. Whereas most televised versions of Austen are content to subordinate character and theme to the ready appeal of the romance plots around which her novels are structured, Davies creates complex characters and points up what he considers to be some of *Emma*'s major themes. The specific set of circumstances that are in large part responsible for Emma's meddlesome behavior and for her excursions into fantasy are, for example, sketched out in the course of several conversations that reveal not only Highbury's leading citizens, but also the much younger Emma, as almost pathological enemies of change. Having rejected courtship and marriage for herself, Emma seeks alternative outlets for her youthful energies and inquiring mind in fantasy and matchmaking. Without this kind of explanatory framework, it is almost impossible to judge the Emma who interferes in the lives of others as anything but a spoilt and silly young woman of the type that Gwyneth Paltrow plays in McGrath's version of *Emma*. *　*　*

Not only does Davies create a much more complex heroine than is typically to be found in televisual adaptations of classic novels, but he and Lawrence also tease out the broader social implications of Emma's personal situation. The filmmakers' decision to flesh out Austen's fictional world, which deals almost exclusively with the leisured and professional classes, by introducing some of the many servants and laborers upon whom the personal and economic well-being of the landed gentry depended provides the most obvious visual clue to their interest in the historical context within which the action of *Emma* is located. * * * The presence of liveried footmen charged with moving the brocaded kneeling cushions of Mr. Knightley's strawberry-picking guests is particularly pointed because it momentarily transforms Donwell Abbey into something like Versailles in the days preceding the French Revolution. * * *

Taken in the context of the whole film, however, scenes such as the Donwell visit serve more to flesh out Austen's own sometimes critical portrayal of the gentry rather than to sustain the notion that Davies and Lawrence are, except incidentally, intent on viewing a novel written in 1816 through the lens of late twentieth-century egalitarian social values. * * *

Indeed, the creators of the ITV/A&E *Emma* are even more emphatic than Austen about the challenges facing the ruling classes in early nineteenth-century England, because they want to make sure that a modern audience recognizes the larger drama that lies beneath the surface of Austen's comic exploration of the manners and morals of the gentry. * * *

Davies and Lawrence's understanding of Austen very much resembles that of critics who read her as ideologically aligned with early nineteenth-century England's ruling classes, particularly with the gentry, * * * a group that cultivated ideals of duty and concern for others.[2]

Davies' script skillfully encompasses the major thematic threads outlined above. A film, though, is more than a script and any analysis of the ITV/A&E *Emma* that fails to take into account the contribution make by Diarmuid Lawrence's acute visual imagination can hardly hope to do full justice to this remarkable adaptation of Austen's novel. * * *

The ITV/A&E *Emma* opens with a sequence of four scenes, three of them invented by Davies, that introduce the film's most important personal and social conflicts and that establish a vital link between visual style and the issue of social vitality. In the first of these scenes, Davies and Lawrence replace the leisurely passages of narrative commentary that get the novel underway with a dramatic raid on the Woodhouse's chicken house. * * * In combination, the scene's visual and aural devices generate intense energy and a sense of danger. * * * The atmosphere of the similarly invented wedding scene that follows is quite different. Dark night gives way to sunny

---

2. See, for example, the essay by Marilyn Butler in this Norton Critical Edition [*Editor*].

day and perilous improvisation is replaced by predictable ritual. Yet this second episode, with its pre-wedding bustle, sudden cut away from the church in mid-ceremony, and final crane shot of the Westons' carriage speeding down Highbury's main street accompanied by jaunty music, is no less energetic than the first.

The only breaks in the rapid flow of these two scenes are created by the introduction of the static figures of Emma and her father. * * * The loss of energy that is associated with the appearances of the Woodhouses is even more pronounced in the dining-room scene that comes next in the sequence. The slow-paced and fairly routine editing, dim lighting and deliberate and mournful music that characterizes this episode prefigures the style of much of the first half of the film.

The style of this part of the ITV/A&E *Emma* is thus very much that of the standard television adaptation. However, we have already seen that director Lawrence is not wedded to televisual conventions. * * * Instead, he is seeking to develop a complex visual style capable of communicating the film's main themes. Far from being merely conventional, the Hartfield dinner scene is filmed in a manner that dramatizes the moribund character of the gentry. The very different techniques employed in the scenes that precede it suggest that the void that is opening up in Highbury society can be filled in one of two ways.

The dark energy of the chicken house raid creates the strong impression that loss of authority at the top might encourage the lower orders to follow the lead of the French by giving violent physical expression to their discontents. * * * The connection established here between energy and social upheaval is reinforced later in the film when Lawrence employs a combination of low-and high-angle tracking shots and an upbeat musical score to film the arrival of the vulgar and social-climbing, but crudely vital bourgeoise, Mrs. Elton. * * *

There is, however, an alternative to social upheaval, either of a revolutionary or economic/ideological kind. It is introduced into the ITV/A&E *Emma* by the energetic manner in which Lawrence films the Westons' wedding and, in particular, their exit from the village, which matches the sprightliness of Mrs. Elton's arrival. What this montage suggests is that the gentry can survive so long as it grasps the principle that change has an essential part to play in ensuring a society's long-term stability. Highbury * * * will wither and die unless a new generation accepts responsibility for revitalizing the community. * * * The main burden of change in the ITV/A&E *Emma*, as in the novel, falls on Emma Woodhouse who, at almost twenty-one years of age, is more than old enough to make the difficult transition from adolescence to adulthood. * * *

However, as the next scene—another invented episode in the village church—demonstrates, once again in entirely cinematic terms, Emma is not yet ready to become involved in socially productive behavior and redirects her creative energies into fantasy and meddling. * * * The stimulating effect on Emma's view of the world of the romantic connection that she quickly begins to forge between Harriet and Elton * * * is expressed by a low angle mid-shot that transforms Elton into a towering black cassocked figure aloft in his pulpit and by a tilt down from a suddenly illuminated window to Harriet transformed into an angel by the shimmering golden light in which she is now bathed. * * *

The scene in the church is significant not just because it gives visual expression to the seductive effect of fantasy on Emma but also because it immediately points up the negative impact that Emma's behavior can have on the established order.

Following this four-scene overture, the main action of the ITV/ A&E *Emma* charts a course close to that of its source text. Regardless of the reactionary forces at work in Highbury, new social influences gradually begin to make themselves felt. The spirit of change introduced by Miss Taylor's marriage intensifies with the arrival in the village of a stream of newcomers who simultaneously stimulate and threaten the Highbury community. * * * In order to find cinematic analogies for the process by means of which Highbury * * * changes in order to become itself once again, Davies and Lawrence * * * structure their film around the cycle of the seasons, nature's prime example of the classical conservative concept, best expressed in the writings of Edmund Burke, of continuity achieved through constant flux.

In the first part of the film, covering the late autumn and winter months, static camera work, dark lighting, and drably colored landscapes and costumes combine to create a lifeless *mise en scène* that is the perfect objective correlative for a Highbury community which has not yet begun to shake off its contented lethargy.

As winter turns into spring, however, the revitalization of Highbury begins with the arrival of two newcomers, Jane Fairfax and Frank Churchill. * * * In the scenes that follow, during which Mrs. Elton makes her first appearance, the action moves between sunny, colorful exteriors and interiors now frequently lit by natural light pouring through large windows rather than by dim candles and flickering fires. Emma is now frequently seen wearing white dresses made of light fabrics. At the same time, a new fluidity marks Lawrence's directorial style. * * *

It is not until the Crown Ball, however, that the vitality of the spring-summer *mise en scène* is fully matched by the film's camerawork, * * * which serves to capture the complex dynamics at work, not just in the dance, but between the evening's main participants.

The overt ritualism of the Crown Ball scene prepares the way for a transformation in the way that landscape functions in the ITV/A&E *Emma*. Up to this point in the film, Lawrence, as is the case with Austen in her novel, has been content to establish a predominantly metonymic relationship between the transition from winter to spring to summer and the opening up and energizing of Highbury society. However, beginning with the visit to Donwell Abbey, landscape takes on a much more overtly symbolic role. Thus, the view that Lawrence provides of Donwell's honey-coloured stone exterior glowing amidst the brilliant green summer landscape is, as Davies requested in his script, "pretty breathtaking."[3] The following scene, in which the camera tracks gracefully around the Abbey ruins with their colorful flower beds and emerald green lawns, has a lyrical quality that confirms a change in the film's approach to landscape.

* * * Davies and Lawrence are here * * * proposing that the resolution of their film's conflicts will involve the creation of an accord between individual, social group and nature. The ITV/A&E *Emma* is thus becoming, in a much more overt way than is ever the case in Austen's novel, as much Burkeian[4] allegory and fertility ritual as comedy of manners.

However, while the natural world is held up as an ideal in both the Donwell episode and the visit to Box Hill that follows, the inhabitants of Highbury are not yet ready to become one with nature. Thus, images of harmony between the human and the natural during the Donwell and Box Hill scenes are always ironic. At Box Hill, for example, a large tree spreads its branches protectively over six members of the Highbury touring party. However, the apparent unity between the human and the natural suggested by this image is undercut by the way in which the tree trunk separates the Eltons from the rest of the party. * * *

* * * Idealized natural settings cannot * * * be free of irony until Emma has come to a better understanding of her own personal desires and social obligations. The first and most crucial of such scenes occurs in the garden at Hartfield. * * * The scene begins with Emma in despair at the prospect of losing Knightley to Harriet but ends with a condition of harmony not only between the lovers and within a community that will undoubtedly benefit from the impending transfer of power from Mr. Woodhouse to a younger, more vital generation, but also, as earlier apparently ironic images of a despairing Emma's hand brushing a bed of lavender and of her reflection in

3. Sue Birtwistle and Susie Conklin, *The Making of Jane Austen's "Emma"* (London: Penguin, 1998) 129.

4. A representation in fictional form of the idealized notion of the progress of British culture and history put forward by the parliamentarian and writer Edmund Burke (1729/30–1797) in his influential *Reflections on the Revolution in France* (1790) and other political writings. [Editor].

the pond have in fact accurately predicted, between the human and the natural. * * *

The mythic dimensions of the Burkeian integration of personal, social, and natural achieved in the garden at Hartfield are reinforced by the two invented episodes with which the main action of the ITV/A&E *Emma* concludes. The first is a harvesting scene in the fields above Donwell Abbey which is made mythic by the use of golden filters. In such a context there is a certain inevitability about the way in which the threat of class conflict that loomed earlier in the film is finally dissipated as laborers in the fields, the yeoman Robert Martin passing by on a haycart, and the gentleman, Mr. Knightley, seated on his horse, are united by a common economic activity and a shared closeness to nature. The next scene, a harvest supper organized by Mr. Knightley for the entire community, includes a number of images of class harmony. * * * However, in this instance, the film's mythic and socially specific dimensions are more equally balanced than was previously the case. Lawrence's continued use of golden filters gives a timeless feel to the harvest festival while a very specific ideological and historical context is created by Davies' invention of Burkeian speech in which Mr. Knightley discourses about the duties of landlord and tenant and the need to balance "stability" and "change."[5]

* * *

However, while there is something intensely satisfying about the image of social harmony embodied in the great communal dance that concludes the harvest supper, it would be a betrayal of Austen and of the Burkeian ideology around which, in Davies and Lawrence's view, she shapes her novel to end at a moment of frozen perfection. Therefore, Davies and Lawrence add a coda to the ITV/A&E *Emma* by cutting away from the dance to another dark nighttime chicken-house raid. The effect of this repetition of the event with which they began their narrative is not only to put the world of the film back into motion but to give it the circular shape needed to remind viewers that, according to classical conservative ideology, the wheel is always turning because the process of social correction and conservation is never completed. By marrying Mr. Knightley Emma has achieved an ending but she has also made a beginning. * * * The ITV/A&E *Emma* retains a close relationship with its source text, and, indeed, offers a subtle and complex reading of Austen's great novel. However, it ultimately deserves to be viewed as a distinct work of art that functions effectively according to the conventions of a very different medium from the one in which Austen is working.

5. Birtwhistle and Conklin, 151.

Jane Austen: A Chronology

1775   Jane Austen born, December 16, at Steventon, Hampshire, the seventh of eight children of the Rev. George Austen. George III is on the throne of England.

1784   Formal education ends at age 9, at school in Reading.

1789–91   Between the ages of 14 and 16, she writes a novel called "Love and Freindship," a "History of England," and stories called "Lesley Castle" and "A Collection of Letters."

1793–96   Writes "Lady Susan" and "Elinor and Marianne," the earliest version of *Sense and Sensibility*.

1797   Writes "First Impressions," the earliest version of *Pride and Prejudice*.

1797–98   Rewrites "Elinor and Marianne" as *Sense and Sensibility* (which remains unpublished until 1811).

1798–99   Writes *Susan*, an early version of *Northanger Abbey* (published posthumously in 1818).

1801   Austen family moves to Bath.

1804–5   Writes "The Watsons," possibly an early version of *Emma*.

1805   Her father dies, and the following year the family moves to Southampton.

1809   They move to Chawton, in Hampshire, where after an interval of several years her major works were composed.

1810–11   Rewrites "First Impressions" as *Pride and Prejudice* and revises *Sense and Sensibility* for publication.

1811–20   The Regency: George, Prince of Wales, takes over the powers of George III, who lives on until 1820.

1811   *Sense and Sensibility* published at last, anonymously— like all her other works; writes *Mansfield Park*.

1813   *Pride and Prejudice* published.

1814   Writes *Emma* and publishes *Mansfield Park*.

1815   Writes *Persuasion*.

1816   *Emma* published, dedicated to the Prince Regent.

1817   Jane Austen dies at the age of 42 in Winchester, of Addison's disease, leaving "Sanditon," an unfinished novel.

1818   *Northanger Abbey* and *Persuasion* published, again anonymously.

Selected Bibliography

• indicates works included or excerpted in this Norton Critical Edition.

Jane Austen's Writings

Austen, Jane. *The Cambridge Edition of the Works of Jane Austen*. Ed. Janet Todd, et al. Cambridge: Cambridge UP, 2005–08.
• ———. *The Novels of Jane Austen*. Ed. R. W. Chapman. 5 vols. 3rd ed. London: Oxford UP, 1954.
• ———. *Jane Austen's Letters*. Ed. Deirdre Le Faye. 3rd ed. New York: Oxford UP, 1995.

Illustrated Background Studies

Austen-Leigh, J. E. *Memoir of Jane Austen*. 2nd ed (1871). Ed. R. W. Chapman. Oxford: Clarendon, 1926.
Brown, Ivor, and C. V. Wedgwood. *Jane Austen and Her World*. London: Lutterworth, 1966.
Lane, Maggie. *Jane Austen's England*. New York: Robert Hale, 1986.
Laski, Marghanita. *Jane Austen and Her World*. New York: Viking, 1969.
Le Faye, Deirdre. *Jane Austen: The World of Her Novels*. New York: Abrams, 2002.
Nicolson, Nigel. *The World of Jane Austen*. London: Phoenix Illustrated, 1991.
Todd, Janet, ed. *Jane Austen in Context*. Cambridge: Cambridge UP, 2005.
Watkins, Susan. *Jane Austen's Town and Country Style*. New York: Rizzoli, 1990.

Biographical and Critical Studies

Armstrong, Nancy. *Desire and Domestic Fiction*. New York: Oxford UP, 1987.
• Auerbach, Emily. *Searching for Jane Austen*. Madison: U of Wisconsin P, 2004.
Bloom, Harold, ed. *Modern Critical Interpretations: Jane Austen's* Emma. New Haven: Chelsea House, 1987.
Booth, Wayne. *The Rhetoric of Fiction*. Chicago: U of Chicago P, 1961.
Brown, Julia Prewitt. *Jane Austen's Novels: Social Change and Literary Form*. Cambridge: Harvard UP, 1979.
• Butler, Marilyn. *Jane Austen and the War of Ideas*. Oxford: Clarendon, 1975.
Copeland, Edward, and Juliet McMaster, eds. *The Cambridge Companion to Jane Austen*. Cambridge: Cambridge UP, 1997.
Duckworth, Alistair. *The Improvement of the Estate: A Study of Jane Austen's Novels*. Baltimore: Johns Hopkins UP, 1971.
Dussinger, John. *In the Pride of the Moment: Encounters in Jane Austen's World*. Columbus: Ohio State UP, 1990.
• Farrer, Reginald. "Jane Austen, *ob.* July 18, 1917." *Quarterly Review* 228, (July 1917): 23–25.

Fergus, Jan. *Jane Austen: A Literary Life*. New York: St. Martin's, 1991.

• ———. "Sex and Social Life in Jane Austen's Novels." In *Jane Austen in a Social Context*, ed. David Monaghan. Totowa, NJ: Barnes & Noble, 1981. 66–85.

• Forster, E. M. *Abinger Harvest*. New York: Harcourt, 1936.

Galperin, William H. *The Historical Austen*. Philadelphia: U of Pennsylvania P, 2003.

Gard, Roger. *Jane Austen's Novels: The Art of Clarity*. New Haven: Yale UP, 1992.

Gay, Penny. *Jane Austen and the Theatre*. Cambridge: Cambridge UP, 2002.

Giffin, Michael. *Jane Austen and Religion: Salvation and Society in Georgian England*. Basingstoke: Palgrave Macmillan, 2002.

Halperin, John. *The Life of Jane Austen*. Baltimore: Johns Hopkins UP, 1984.

• Harding, D. W. *Regulated Hatred and Other Essays on Jane Austen*, ed. Monica Lawlor. London: Athlone Press, 1998.

Harris, Jocelyn. *Jane Austen's Art of Memory*. Cambridge: Cambridge UP, 1989.

Heydt-Stevenson, Jillian. *Austen's Unbecoming Conjunctions: Subversive Laughter, Embodied History*. Basingstoke: Palgrave Macmillan, 2005.

Honan, Park. *Jane Austen: Her Life*. London: Weidenfeld and Nicholson, 1987.

• James, Henry. "The Lesson of Balzac." *Atlantic Monthly* 96 (July 1905): 166–80.

• Jenkyns, Richard. *A Fine Brush on Ivory: An Appreciation of Jane Austen*. New York: Oxford UP, 2004.

• Johnson, Claudia L. *Jane Austen: Women, Politics, and the Novel*. Chicago: U of Chicago P, 1988.

———. *Equivocal Beings: Politics, Gender, and Sentimentality in the 1790s*. Chicago: U of Chicago P, 1995.

Johnson, Claudia L., and Clara Tuite, eds. *A Companion to Jane Austen*. Chichester: Wiley-Blackwell, 2009.

Kirkham, Margaret. *Jane Austen, Feminism and Fiction*. Totowa, NJ: Barnes & Noble, 1983.

• Lane, Maggie. *Jane Austen's World*. London: Carlton, 1996.

Lascelles, Mary. *Jane Austen and Her Art*. Oxford: Oxford UP, 1939.

Le Faye, Deirdre. *Jane Austen*. Oxford: Oxford UP, 1998.

———. ed. *Jane Austen: A Family Record*. Boston: G. K. Hall, 1989.

• Lewes, G. H. "The Novels of Jane Austen." *Blackwell's Edinburgh Magazine* (July 1859): 99–113.

Litvak, Joseph. "Reading Characters: Self, Society, and Text in *Emma*." *PMLA* 100 (1985): 763–73.

Looser, Devoney, ed. *Jane Austen and Discourses of Feminism*. New York: St. Martin's, 1995.

———. "'The Duty of Woman By Woman': Reforming Feminism in *Emma*." In *Jane Austen's* Emma, ed. Alistair Duckworth. New York: Bedford/St. Martin's, 2002. 577–93.

Litz, A. Walton. *Jane Austen: A Study of Her Artistic Development*. New York: Oxford UP, 1965.

Lynch, Deidre, ed. *Janeites: Austen's Disciples and Devotees*. Princeton: Princeton UP, 2000.

• Macaulay, Thomas Babington. "Review of Madame D'Arblay's Diaries and Letters." *Edinburgh Review* 76 (1843): 561–62.

• Macdonald, Gina, and Andrew F. Macdonald, eds. *Jane Austen on Screen*. Cambridge: Cambridge UP, 2003.

Mandal, Anthony. *Jane Austen and the Popular Novel: The Determined Author*. Basingstoke: Palgrave Macmillan, 2007.

McMaster, Juliet. *Jane Austen the Novelist*. New York: St. Martin's, 1995.

McMaster, Juliet, and Bruce Stovel, eds. *Jane Austen's Business: Her World and Her Profession*. New York: St. Martin's, 1996.

Michaelson, Patricia Howell. *Speaking Volumes: Women, Reading, and Speech in the Age of Jane Austen*. Stanford: Stanford UP, 2002.
• Miller, D. A. *Jane Austen, Or the Secret of Style*. Princeton: Princeton UP, 2003.
Mudrick, Marvin. *Jane Austen: Irony as Defense and Discovery*. Princeton: Princeton UP, 1967.
Myer, Valerie Grosvenor. *Jane Austen: Obstinate Heart*. New York: Arcade, 1997.
Nokes, David. *Jane Austen: A Life*. New York: Farrar, Straus, 1997.
• Pollock, Juliet. "Jane Austen." *St. Paul's Magazine* 5 (1870): 631–43.
• Poovey, Mary. *The Proper Lady and the Woman Writer: Ideology as Style in the Works of Mary Wollstonecraft, Mary Shelley, and Jane Austen*. Chicago: U of Chicago P, 1984.
• Ritchie, Anne. "Jane Austen." *Cornhill Magazine* 24 (August 1871): 158–74.
Shields, Carol. *Jane Austen*. New York: Viking, 2001.
• Scott, Sir Walter. "Review of *Emma*." *Quarterly Review* 14 (1815): 188–201.
Southam, B. C. *Jane Austen's Literary Manuscripts*. Oxford: Oxford UP, 1964.
———, ed. *Critical Essays on Jane Austen*. Vol. 1. London: Routledge, 1968.
———, ed. *Jane Austen: The Critical Heritage*. London: Routledge, 1968.
———, ed. *Jane Austen: The Critical Heritage: 1870–1940*. Vol. 2, London: Routledge, 1987.
• Spacks, Patricia Meyer. *Gossip*. New York: Knopf, 1985.
Spence, Jon. *Becoming Jane Austen*. London: Hambledon and London, 2003.
• Stewart, Maaja A. *Domestic Realities and Imperial Fictions: Jane Austen's Novels in Eighteenth-Century Contexts*. Athens: U of Georgia P, 1993.
Stovel, Bruce, and Lynn Weinlos Gregg, eds. *The Talk in Jane Austen*. Edmonton: U of Alberta P, 2002.
Sulloway, Alison G. *Jane Austen and the Province of Womanhood*. Philadelphia: U of Pennsylvania P, 1989.
• Tanner, Tony. *Jane Austen*. Cambridge: Harvard UP, 1986.
Tomalin, Claire. *Jane Austen: A Life*. London: Penguin, 1997.
Trilling, Lionel. "*Emma* and the Legend of Jane Austen." *Beyond Culture: Essays on Literature and Learning*. London: Seeker & Warburg, 1966. 31–55.
Troost, Linda, and Sayre Greenfield, eds. *Jane Austen in Hollywood*. Lexington: UP of Kentucky, 1998.
Tuite, Clara. *Romantic Austen*. Cambridge: Cambridge UP, 2002.
Waldron, Mary. *Jane Austen and the Fiction of Her Time*. Cambridge: Cambridge UP, 1999.
Watt, Ian. "Jane Austen and the Traditions of Comic Aggression." *Persuasions* 3 (16 Dec. 1981): 14–15, 24–28.
• White, Gabrielle D. V. *Jane Austen in the Context of Abolition: A Fling at the Slave Trade*. Basingstoke: Palgrave Macmillan, 2006.
• Wilson, Edmund. "A Long Talk about Jane Austen." *Classics and Commercials*, 196–203. New York: Farrar, Straus, 1950.
Wiltshire, John. *Jane Austen: Introductions and Interventions*. Basingstoke: Palgrave Macmillan, 2006.
• Wise, Thomas James, and J. Alexander Symington, eds. *The Brontës, Their Lives, Friendships, and Correspondence*. Vol. 3. Boston: Houghton Mifflin, 1933.
* Woolf, Virginia. "Jane Austen" in *The Common Reader*. New York: Harcourt, Brace, and World, 137–49.

Film/Television Adaptations of Emma

Emma. Writer Judy Campbell. Director Michael Barry, BBC, 1948.
Emma. Writers Martine Bartlett and Peter Donat. NBC, 1954.
Emma. Writer Vincent Tilsley. Director Campbell Logan. BBC, 1960.
Emma. Writer Clair Roskam. Director John Desmond. CBS, 1960.
Emma. Writer Denis Constanduros. Director John Glenister. BBC, 1972.

Clueless. Writer and director Amy Heckerling. Paramount, 1995.

Emma. Writer and director Douglas McGrath. Miramax, 1996.

Jane Austen's Emma. Writer Andrew Davies. Director Diarmuid Lawrence. ITV/A&E, 1996.

Emma. Writer Sandy Welch. Director Jim O'Hanlon. BBC, 2009.

Secondary Readings on Film Adaptation

Bluestone, George. *Novels into Films.* Berkeley: U of California P, 1957.

Chatman, Seymour. *Coming to Terms: The Rhetoric of Narrative in Fiction and Film.* Ithaca, NY: Cornell UP, 1990.

———. "What Novels Can Do That Films Can't (and Vice Versa). *Critical Inquiry* 7.1 (1980): 121–40.

Cohen, Keith. *Film and Fiction.* New Haven: Yale UP, 1979.

Eisenstein, Sergei. "Dickens, Griffith, and the Film Today." *Film Form: Essays in Film Theory*, ed. and trans. Jay Leyda. New York: Harcourt Brace Jovanovich, 1949. 195–255.

Elliott, Kamilla. *Rethinking the Novel/Film Debate.* Cambridge: Cambridge UP, 2003.

Leitch, Thomas. "Twelve Fallacies in Contemporary Adaptation Theory." *Criticism* 45.2 (2003): 149–72.

• McDonald, Gina, and Andrew F. McDonald. *Jane Austen on Screen.* Cambridge: Cambridge UP, 2003.

McFarlane, Brian. *Novel to Film: An Introduction to the Theory of Adaptation.* Oxford: Clarendon, 1996.

Stam, Robert. "Introduction: The Theory and Practice of Adaptation." *Literature and Film: A Guide to the Theory and Practice of Film Adaptation*, ed. Robert Stam. Oxford: Blackwell, 2005. 1–52.